Palgrave Politics of Identity and Citizenship Series

Series Editors
Varun Uberoi
Brunel University London
London, UK

Nasar Meer
University of Edinburgh
Edinburgh, UK

Tariq Modood
University of Bristol
Bristol, UK

The politics of identity and citizenship has assumed increasing importance as our polities have become significantly more culturally, ethnically and religiously diverse. Different types of scholars, including philosophers, sociologists, political scientists and historians make contributions to this field and this series showcases a variety of innovative contributions to it. Focusing on a range of different countries, and utilizing the insights of different disciplines, the series helps to illuminate an increasingly controversial area of research and titles in it will be of interest to a number of audiences including scholars, students and other interested individuals.

More information about this series at
http://www.palgrave.com/gp/series/14670

Tamás Kiss · István Gergő Székely
Tibor Toró · Nándor Bárdi
István Horváth
Editors

Unequal Accommodation of Minority Rights

Hungarians in Transylvania

palgrave
macmillan

Editors
Tamás Kiss
Romanian Institute for Research
on National Minorities
Cluj-Napoca, Romania

István Gergő Székely
Romanian Institute for Research
on National Minorities
Cluj-Napoca, Romania

Tibor Toró
International Relations and European
Studies Department
Sapientia Hungarian University
of Transylvania
Cluj-Napoca, Romania

Nándor Bárdi
Institute for Minority Studies
Hungarian Academy of Sciences, Centre
for Social Sciences
Budapest, Hungary

István Horváth
Romanian Institute for Research
on National Minorities
Cluj-Napoca, Romania

Palgrave Politics of Identity and Citizenship Series
ISBN 978-3-030-07673-3   ISBN 978-3-319-78893-7 (eBook)
https://doi.org/10.1007/978-3-319-78893-7

Cover credit: Istvan Kadar Photography/Getty Images

Printed on acid-free paper

This Palgrave Macmillan imprint is published by the registered company Springer International Publishing AG part of Springer Nature
The registered company address is: Gewerbestrasse 11, 6330 Cham, Switzerland

Contents

List of Figures

List of Tables

1

Introduction: Unequal Accommodation, Ethnic Parallelism, and Increasing Marginality

Tamás Kiss

Our volume offers an in-depth, multidisciplinary analysis of the major social and political processes affecting Hungarians in Romania after the regime change in 1989. Its thematic chapters combine primarily the perspectives of political science and the sociology of ethnic relations and reflect the findings of a broad array of empirical investigations carried out in Transylvania, mainly within the Romanian Institute for Research on National Minorities.

Central to the topic of our volume is the so-called *Romanian model of ethnic relations*. This expression emerged around the turn of the millennium, being used extensively by the Romanian diplomacy in the context of Euro-Atlantic integration to highlight how ethnic coexistence in Romania has been relatively peaceful compared to other states of Southeastern Europe, thus providing an example for how ethnic tensions might be diffused (Nastasă and Salat 2000). Social scientists

T. Kiss (✉)
Romanian Institute for Research on National Minorities,
Cluj-Napoca, Romania

T. Kiss et al. (eds.), *Unequal Accommodation of Minority Rights*,
Palgrave Politics of Identity and Citizenship Series,
https://doi.org/10.1007/978-3-319-78893-7_1

were also quite optimistic about the capacity of Romania's young democracy to accommodate Hungarian minority claims (Csergő 2002, 2007; Mihailescu 2008; Saideman and Ayres 2008; Stroschein 2012). The main reasons for this optimism were that throughout most of the 1996–2012 period, the dominant ethnic party representing the Hungarian community participated in a number of coalition governments and that quasi-institutionalized bargaining mechanisms have taken shape between Romanian and Hungarian political actors. Some analysts even envisioned that Romania was moving toward some sort of consociational democracy (Mungiu-Pippidi 1999; Andreescu 2000; Brusis 2015). Other scholars were more cautious, arguing that the major elements of the Romanian way of conflict resolution have been based on political bargaining between minority and majority elites (Csergő 2007; Stroschein 2012), and have led to the cooptation of the Hungarians into executive power (Medianu 2002; Horváth 2002; Saideman and Ayres 2008) and a shift toward a more pluralistic approach in minority policies (Horváth and Scacco 2001; Ram 2003; Dobre 2003). This pluralistic shift has meant primarily the recognition of the organizations of the minorities (formed on the ethnic principle) as legitimate representatives of their communities (Bíró and Pallai 2011; Horváth 2013) and some important concessions in minority language use and education (Csergő 2007; Stroschein 2012; Horváth 2013).

Given these attributes, Romania was and is still often invoked as an example of successful conflict resolution and minority accommodation. However, we argue that such an assessment is rushed, and there is a dearth of literature that considers indeed realistically the actual working of the "Romanian model".[1] With this volume, we wish to contribute to fill this gap. Using an analysis of the most important processes affecting Transylvanian Hungarians, we aim to provide an assessment of the major features, functioning and consequences of the Romanian model of ethnic relations.

The book is structured in three parts and focuses on five broad and interlinked topics: (1) the Romanian regime of minority policies;

[1]Medianu (2002) and Horváth (2002) are obviously such examples.

(2) the political agency exercised by Transylvanian Hungarian elites; (3) the meso-level institutional structures sustaining ethnic parallelism; (4) the social and demographic consequences of the institutional and discursive order of ethnic relations in Romania; and (5) the strategies of boundary reinforcement employed by the Hungarian elites. Each of these topics implies a different level of analysis, and our objective is also to provide empirically grounded hypotheses concerning the interrelation between these levels, which could be tested in the future also in the case of other ethnic or national minorities.

This introductory chapter has three parts. In the first section, we present our basic assumptions and sketch our conceptual-theoretical framework, which are rooted in the traditions of historical institutionalism and social constructivism. The second section outlines the structure of the volume and highlights the most important arguments addressed in each chapter. We conclude by summarizing some basic information regarding Transylvania and its Hungarian community.

1 Conceptual Tools

The chapters of the volume combine multiple disciplinary perspectives, including demography, political and social history, the sociology of economics and religion, and legal studies, with a particular emphasis on political science and the sociology of ethnic relations. The conceptual frameworks used by the authors of each chapter also vary, but are rooted in two broad theoretical approaches: historical institutionalism (Hall and Taylor 1996; Thelen 1999; Pierson 2000; Gorenburg 2003; Stroschein 2012) and social constructivism and the boundary-making approach (Barth 1969; Lamont and Molnár 2002; Alba and Nee 2003; Alba 2005; Wimmer 2013; Lamont et al. 2016). Historical institutionalism is the primary analytical framework in the first two parts of the book (dedicated to political and institutional processes), while social constructivism plays a pivotal role especially in the third part (focusing on processes of ethnic classification and boundary maintenance). The volume is also united by six underlying assumptions that govern the analyses throughout the book. These are:

1. *Institutional orders generally produce asymmetrical opportunities for the various actors involved in political processes.* Historical institutionalists argue that contention and conflict between different groups play an important role in political processes. The outcome of these battles, however, is conditioned by the institutional order of the state, which is not a neutral broker of the relations between different societal actors. On the contrary, historical institutionalists view the state as an institutional complex that produces profound asymmetries between different actors (Hall and Taylor 1996). The focus on the nationalizing state in the study of ethnic politics (Brubaker 1996, 2011) is connected to this institutional perspective, well suited for investigating the power asymmetries immanent in the institutional structure.

2. *Both formal and informal rules matter.* Historical institutionalists define institutions as "*formal or informal procedures, routines, norms and conventions embedded in the organizational structure of the polity*" (Hall and Taylor 1996, p. 398). The distinction between formal and informal institutions is crucial to assessing the Romanian minority policy regime. Drawing on the definition provided by Rechel (2009a), under the term *minority policy regime* we understand the totality of legal and informal rules governing ethnic relations and minority accommodation. While the majority of existing comparative research—especially studies comparing a large number of cases—focuses only on the legal framework of minority protection and minority policy (Rechel 2009b; Székely and Horváth 2014), we believe that informal rules are at least as important as formal ones and that in the "Romanian model of ethnic relations" the level of informality is rather high.[2]

3. *Institutions shape the behavior of the political actors.* As Hall and Taylor (1996) and Thelen (1999) emphasize, there are three distinguishable perspectives within the theories of "new institutionalism": historical, sociological, and rational choice institutionalism. Historical and sociological institutionalisms rely on culturalist explanations of human agency, which argue that institutions shape the worldview of

[2]On the significance of informal institutions in historical institutionalism, see Tsai (2014). Stroschein (2012) also emphasized the role of informality in ethnic politics in Romania.

actors and, as frameworks of socialization, are conducive to certain habits and routines of problem solving. Rational choice institutionalism, on the other hand, perceives human behavior as instrumentally rational. According to this perspective, institutions play a pivotal role in the coordination of collective action by providing information concerning the behavior of other actors and by establishing mechanisms to enforce agreements and penalties for those who break the rules (Hall and Taylor 1996, p. 939). While some of the chapters of this volume rely on rational choice argumentation,[3] we assume that the political agency of minority actors is not completely strategic. Institutions play a key role in historically conditioned processes of socialization and are conducive to certain habituses and self-perceptions. Additionally, the political agency of the Hungarian elites of Transylvania has a strong value-rational component (Csergő and Regelmann 2017; Varshney 2003), and minority institutions play a pivotal role in sustaining a collectivist ethic prevalent among Hungarian elites (Bárdi et al. 2014).

4. *The concept of path dependence used by historical institutionalists plays a key role in our analysis.* Pierson (2000) distinguished between a broader and a narrower definition of path dependence. In a broad sense, it refers to the importance of the historical sequence of events, and as Pierson argues, it merely means that "history matters". The narrower definition is connected to the model of increasing returns and emphasizes how "*previous steps in a particular direction induce further movement in the same direction*" because "*the relative benefits of the current activity compared with other possible options increase over time*" (Pierson 2000, p. 152). The historical perspective is important throughout our analysis, and in this sense, we rely on the broader (and more blurred) definition of path dependence. However, in certain parts of our argument, we employ the concept of path dependence more systematically and thus more narrowly. In the chapters dedicated to political processes, we outline the major historical junctures that brought about a reorganization of the institutional settings and thus inaugurated new phases of institutional and political processes. These junctures include the regime change

[3]Chapter 9 authored by Zsombor Csata is the most systematic in this respect.

of 1989/1990, which led to the crystallization of the institutional framework that shapes minority policy agency today. We also employ the concept of path dependence at the micro-level, for instance, when arguing that the biographies of ethnically mixed families are also path dependent (in the narrower sense suggested by Pierson).

5. The idea that *institutions shape not only the preferences and possibilities of the actors but also their identities* provides an important link between social constructivism and institutionalism (Laitin 1998; Gorenburg 2003). As Gorenburg argues, institutionalists assume that ethnic identities are constructed and mutable but do not accept that "ethnic entrepreneurs" (or political actors in general) can easily manipulate them (2003, p. 4). This is not to say that political intentions and political battles do not play a pivotal role in identity formation, but that their impact is mediated by institutions. Acknowledging that the impact of political intentions on identity formation is mediated by institutions leads us to the so-called constructivist compromise proposed by several scholars, including Smith (1995), Chandra (2006), and Wimmer (2013). These scholars recognize the key role of elite discourses and institutions in the formation of group identities, but they also emphasize the limits of elite capacities to alter (or manipulate) the content of identities. It is in this sense that Chandra writes about the "constrained change" (or from another perspective: the relative inertia) of ethnic identities (2006, pp. 414–416).

6. *Minority institutions may provide a framework for the reproduction of groupness and play a crucial role in boundary maintenance.* As Wimmer argues, social sciences were long dominated by the Herderian paradigm, which asserts that ethnic groups should be perceived as well-bounded entities, characterized by a specific cultural heritage, shared sense of solidarity and common identity (2013, pp. 17–21). Following the constructivist turn, students of ethnic relations radically questioned this Herderian perspective (Jenkins 2008, pp. 10–16; Wimmer 2013, pp. 22–31), and their attention shifted "*from groups to groupness as variable and contingent rather than fixed and given*" (Brubaker 2004, p. 12). Groupness (in the sense of shared identity and group solidarity) has become an important concept in the sociology of ethnic relations. However, this concept is used with different meanings. According

to Brubaker, groupness is an *event* that may (or may not) occur (2004, p. 12). Consequently, Brubaker et al. (2006) investigate groupness at the level of everyday interactions and ask whether people in spontaneous and rather informal settings used (or did not use) ethnicity as an interpretative scheme. They argue that in situations where people did not use "ethnic lenses", groupness did not occur and the group-making efforts of ethnic entrepreneurs (engaged in "nationalist politics") had failed. But while Brubaker et al. view groupness (at the micro-level) as an ephemeral phenomenon, other scholars perceive groupness to be a more enduring characteristic of intergroup relations. Wimmer (2013) also defines groupness at the micro-level, describing it as a characteristic of personal networks, namely as a high proportion of in-group relations at the expense of intergroup relations. He conceptualizes (the degree of) groupness as one of four characteristics of ethnic boundaries, the others being political salience, cultural differentiation, and persistence. Furthermore, Wimmer distinguishes between *groupness* and *closure*. Both groupness and closure may lead to a low frequency of intergroup relations and high frequency of in-group relations. However, in the case of closure, this is a consequence of the rejection, discrimination, and exclusion exercised by members of the dominant group, whereas in the case of groupness, it is the consequence of internal identity processes or self-isolation.

Lamont et al. take a different approach to groupness, treating it as a meso-level phenomenon that has a very important impact on the micro-level because it shapes individual actions and self-perceptions (2016, pp. 22–27). The authors also distinguish between two dimensions of groupness, namely self-identification and group boundaries.

We argue that minority institutions play a crucial role in both of these dimensions of groupness, which could also be interpreted as the psychological and social dimensions of group belonging. In capturing the *psychological aspects* of groupness, the approach taken by Fenton (2003, p. 88) and Jenkins (2008, p. 48) is very useful. According to these scholars, during childhood, ethnic group members may deeply internalize ethnic belonging as personal feelings and experiences. This happens in circumstances where ethnic cleavages appear in well-defined forms even in everyday life. The internalization of ethnic belonging goes hand in hand with the internalization of its markers, such as language and religion. In this process, ethnic belonging is inscribed in the deepest layers of personal identity, similarly to gender, for example, and thus, ethnic identification is not independent from psychological, emotional, and cognitive personality constructs, or from personal integrity, security, and safety. One could argue that a dense network of ethnic institutions (family, educational system in the minority language, etc.) provides a framework for such types of ethnic socialization and is conducive to a high level of consciousness and relatively rigid patterns of self-identification. In understanding the social aspects of groupness, the framework of boundary maintenance proposed by Wimmer (2013), Lamont and Molnár (2002), and Lamont et al. (2016) is useful in demonstrating how ethnic institutions increase the probability of homophily in the various social relations.

2 Main Arguments and the Structure of the Volume

This volume consists of three parts and targets five different topics, at different levels of analysis. Table 1 provides an overview of these topics, lists the key concepts used in the analysis, and briefly summarizes the major arguments of the book.

The first part of the book provides a macro-level institutional analysis focused on two interrelated aspects of ethnic politics, namely Romania's minority policy regime and the ethnic claims-making strategies of the Hungarian minority elites. Our first major argument refers to the Romanian minority policy regime: We argue that despite the above-mentioned optimistic outlook characteristic around the turn of the millennium, Romania's political system and minority rights regime have consolidated in a form that perpetuates the power asymmetry between the titular Romanian majority and the Hungarian minority. Also, as an unintended consequence of the conflict resolution strategies of international actors, the model has also led to high levels of informality and political patronage. Our second argument is also closely linked

Table 1 The structure, the levels of analysis and the main arguments of the volume

	Part	Level of analysis	Key concepts	Main arguments
1	The minority rights regime and political strategies	The minority rights regime (macro-institutional)	Nationalizing state; minority policy regime; unequal accommodation	The Romanian model of ethnic relations can be described as unequal accommodation. It maintains the asymmetries between minority and majority categories, while its unintended consequences include high levels of informality and political particularism
		Political claims-making strategies of minority actors (macro-institutional)	Minority political agency; strategies of claims-making	The claims-making of the minority also relies on particularism and highly informal bargaining with majority actors
2	Ethnic parallelism: political program and social reality	Institutions and social domains (meso-institutional)	Ethnic parallelism	Minority political agency has two complementary aspects: claims-making (bargaining with majority elites) and community organizing (ethnic institution building)
				Community organizing leads to a high level of ethnic parallelism

(continued)

Table 1 (continued)

	Part	Level of analysis	Key concepts	Main arguments
3	Socio-demographic processes and ethnic boundary maintenance	Demographic processes, systems of ethnic classification and stratification (macro-social and macro-demographic)	The consequences of asymmetries	The power asymmetries produced by the institutional order of the nation-state contribute to the demographic erosion and social marginalization of the minority community
		Assimilation and boundary reinforcement (macro- and micro-social)	Groupness vs. closure; boundary policing	The discursive and institutional order prevalent in Romania does not support boundary blurring; boundary policing is also conducive to bright boundaries

to the characteristics of the minority policy regime, but refers to the strategies of minority claims-making. We argue that because the institutional environment of minority policy is characterized by informality and patronage, the problem-solving strategies of the Hungarian minority elites have also conformed to this opportunity structure. This has led Hungarian elites to focus more on resource allocation and less on agency related to minority rights in the past two decades.

The second part of the volume deals with meso-level institutional processes and, in particular, the functioning of the ethnically separate organizational structures operated by the ethnic Hungarians in different social domains. We argue that minority political agency has *per definitionem* two complementary dimensions, namely *claims-making* and bargaining, respectively *community organizing*. With regard to the latter aspect, the idea of ethnic parallelism is of key importance at both the programmatic (discursive) and the institutional level. The Hungarian elites of Transylvania have responded to the asymmetric institutional setting in which they had found themselves by pursuing a program of ethnic parallelism. The chapters in this second part of the volume discuss this ethnic parallelism, defining it as a political project and assessing the degree to which it has actually been accomplished. This analysis shows that the situation can best be described as a duality of ethnically separated and non-separated social fields, where some social fields are ethnically separated, even if only partially, while others are not separated by ethnicity at all. Another key conclusion of this second part is that the incompleteness of the ethnic institutional structures erodes the reproductive capacity of the community, but at the same time encapsulation into these structures can be regarded as a factor conducive to social marginalization. Thus, our analysis tries to capture a major dilemma facing minority elites: how to maintain the ethnic boundaries (without which ethno-cultural reproduction is jeopardized), while also preventing perpetual marginalization in a centralized majoritarian, nationalizing state.

The final part of this volume presents empirical evidence to support these conclusions of the second section. To this purpose, the final chapters consider how power asymmetries produced by the institutional order of the nation-state are shaping macro-level demographics and societal processes. Macro-processes are obviously not independent from the political-institutional structures framing the everyday life of the minority community; thus, of central importance here is the argument that in modern nation-states there is an all-embracing power asymmetry between minority and majority categories. The consequences of these power asymmetries are discussed in detail in the last three chapters, namely: (a) the demographic processes leading to the decline of the Hungarian population in Romania; (b) the processes of official and everyday classification; (c) the changes in the system of ethnic stratification; and (d) the processes of identity change and assimilation to the majority ethnic group. Here, we also focus on the policies of boundary maintenance and reinforcement practiced by the Hungarian elites, which (besides the network of minority institutions) have a pivotal role in preventing the blurring of ethnic boundaries.

2.1 The Minority Rights Regime and Political Strategies

The first part of our volume focuses on the relationship between the Romanian minority policy regime and minority claims-making. This part is composed of three chapters. In Chapter 2, Nándor Bárdi and Tamás Kiss offer a historical introduction to the political processes affecting Transylvanian Hungarians that followed the regime change in 1989/1990. The authors review the century-long political history of the Hungarians in Transylvania since the province became part of Romania to identify the turning points that had a significant impact on the opportunity structures for claims-making. They also devise a periodization based on three aspects, namely the general features of the political regime in Romania, the changes in the strategies of minority claims-making, and the characteristics of the minority institutional field. In Chapter 3, Tamás Kiss, Tibor Toró, and István Gergő Székely focus on the Romanian minority policy regime and identify strategies of minority claims-making after the fall of the Communist regime. They provide a detailed timeline and a historical narrative of the processes affecting the Transylvanian Hungarian minority field. The authors also use a modified version of Brubaker's (1996) triadic nexus model to emphasize the asymmetric interrelations between the minority field, the Romanian minority policy regime, and Hungary's kin-state activities. The authors of Chapter 4, István Horváth and Tibor Toró, analyze Romania's linguistic policies, the existing minority language rights, and how they have been implemented, as well as the patterns of language use among Transylvanian Hungarians.

At the core of the first part of the volume is the notion that *unequal accommodation* defines the Romanian model of ethnic relations. It should be noted that this concept of unequal accommodation has a paradoxical status in the literature of diversity management. On the one hand, it is legitimate to argue that some elements of the model are identical or similar to those found in resolution strategies of (soft or nonviolent) ethnic conflicts put forward by international actors.[4] On the other hand, unequal accommodation is rarely considered as a *sui generis* model of diversity management in the literature,[5] and case studies focusing on the (intended or unintended) consequences of the model are virtually absent, despite the fact that the model can be considered quite widespread throughout Central and Eastern Europe.

Minority policy paradigms (and conflict resolution strategies) are often classified as either *integrationist* or *accommodationist* (McGarry et al. 2008). The former approach advocates a common, trans-ethnic identity and political culture and tries to "integrate" minorities through a universalist institutional and political framework. The latter allows for substate political loyalties and institutions through which minorities are able to reproduce themselves as (quasi)political communities.

Another useful concept in understanding the idea of unequal accommodation is that of *ethnic democracy*, a term coined by Smooha (2001). In ethnic democracies, the titular group exercises hegemonic control over the institutional structure of the state. Such arrangements can be contrasted with more pluralistic approaches of popular sovereignty,

---

[4]In case of violent ethnic conflicts, institutional actors often propose consociational arrangements and segmental autonomies. See Kymlicka (2007, 2011).

[5]Bíró and Pallai (2011) constitute an exception. They argue that "political accommodation" (with Romania as its paradigmatic case) constitutes a distinct paradigm of minority policies and define it similarly to what we call unequal accommodation.

where non-titular groups also have adequate access to state institutions. From the perspective of the integrationist–accommodationist continuum, one may argue that unequal accommodation grants minority elites more power than integration but less than (constitutional) accommodation. In this framework, minority organizations are recognized as the legitimate representatives of the concerned groups and minority elites are co-opted into executive power structures. However, this happens without the full constitutional recognition of ethno-cultural diversity and without institutional guarantees of power-sharing among ethnic groups. From the perspective of the ethnic democracy framework, it could be argued that unequal accommodation entails a renunciation by majority actors to the hegemonic control of the state institutions, as representatives of the minority are also included into executive power. However, we believe that much more important than the fact of inclusion is its lack of institutionalization. Consequently, the governmental participation and the bargaining power of the minority elites depend on the political constellations of the day and are often of an ad hoc nature, as there are no constitutional or legal guarantees for this.

Though further research would be needed to establish this with certainty, it appears that this model of managing ethno-cultural differences is quite pervasive throughout Central and Eastern Europe and its proliferation was arguably facilitated by transnational actors during the Euro-Atlantic pre-accession period (Horváth 2002).[6]

Despite its empirical relevance, the model of unequal accommodation remains severely undertheorized in the literature, and comparative investigations and case studies about it are scarce (e.g., see Medianu 2002; Pettai and Hallik 2002; Kiss and Székely 2016). This shortcoming is even more striking when taking into account the abundance of studies on the consociational arrangements in Bosnia and Herzegovina (e.g., Belloni 2004; Kasapović 2005; Balić and Izmirlija 2013; Hodžić

[6]For instance, the Lund Recommendations on the Effective Participation of National Minorities in Public Life (OSCE-HCNM 1999) explicitly call for the inclusion of minority representatives into executive power (but without urging institutionalized power-sharing).

and Mraović 2015; Orlović 2015) or even the burgeoning comparative research of autonomy arrangements in Eastern Europe (Smith and Cordell 2007; Smith 2013; Salat et al. 2014; Malloy et al. 2015). We hope that our volume will constitute a step forward toward the comparative research of minority policy regimes of this middle-ground type, which are not based on consociational arrangements or segmental autonomies but do not reflect fully integrationist or assimilationist philosophies either. It is with this objective in mind that we formulate some hypotheses in this book, the testing of which calls for further research in the countries of the Central and Eastern European region.

We put forward two main arguments about the characteristics of the Romanian minority policy regime. The first is that it maintains asymmetries between majority and minority categories, and the second is that it relies on informal bargaining and political particularism. This second characteristic may be perceived as an unintended consequence of the security-oriented conflict resolution strategy advocated by international actors in the 1990s. International actors pushed for elite-level bargaining between minority and majority actors but did so without calling for legal institutional guarantees of power-sharing. We argue that political particularism was an unintended but inevitable consequence of this framework.

While we consider the Romanian minority policy regime to be the most important factor shaping the ethno-political processes in the country, the phenomenon that we are most interested in is the political strategies employed by the Hungarian elites. This latter phenomenon has been extensively researched in the past two decades. Scholars have focused, among others, on contention and deliberation related to ethno-linguistic issues (Csergő 2007; Stroschein 2012) and on the relationship between nationalist mobilization and everyday practices of ethnic classification (Brubaker et al. 2006). Several studies have emphasized that Transylvanian Hungarians have been successful in sustaining peaceful ethnic mobilization (Stroschein 2001; Csergő 2007; Gherghina and Jiglau 2011; Stroschein 2012; Kiss and Székely 2016; Kiss 2017) and multilevel political agency (Csergő and Regelmann 2017; Waterbury 2017). The Transylvanian Hungarian case is also a typical example of ethnic block voting, given that since 1990, the overwhelming majority of ethnic Hungarians who participated in Romanian elections have supported a single robust ethnic party, RMDSZ.[7]

In this volume, we do not engage into the micro-level analysis of the voting behavior of Transylvanian Hungarians,[8] but we focus on the political strategies of the Hungarian elites. It should be noted that ethnic minority elites do not necessarily act through ethnic parties and minority voters do not inevitably support parties organized around their ethnic identity. The distinction between ethnic, multiethnic, and non-ethnic (or mainstream) parties employed by Horowitz (1985) and Chandra (2011) is a useful starting point in this respect. Transylvanian Hungarians are quite different from other ethno-national minorities of Central and Eastern Europe with regard to their claims-making and mobilization patterns.[9] For instance, the Russian speakers of Estonia and Latvia have supported mostly non-ethnic (or mainstream) parties since their host countries declared their independence from the Soviet Union (Csergő and Regelmann 2017, pp. 6–10). In 2009 in Slovakia, after a one-decade period of claims-making through a single ethnic party, Hungarians have become divided fairly equally between an ethnic party (Party of the Hungarian Community) and a multiethnic party (Most–Híd) (Bochsler and Szöcsik 2013). This variation in the behavior of minority elites and voters underscores the fact that neither the persistence and political salience of group boundaries nor the gradual loss of their political significance can be taken for granted. Instead, minority mobilization and political participation need to be addressed through empirical research to identify the factors conducive to one pattern of behavior or another.

Furthermore, in our analysis of ethno-political processes in Romania, the concept of *minority political agency* is of primary importance. We use this concept in the sense developed by Csergő and Regelmann

---

[7]In Hungarian: Romániai Magyar Demokrata Szövetség; in Romanian: Uniunea Democrată Maghiară din România (UDMR), in English Democratic Alliance of Hungarians in Romania (DAHR). In the case of Hungarian organizations, we will use the Hungarian acronyms throughout the book.

[8]For studies about his topic, see Kiss et al. (2017) and Kiss (2017).

[9]For a typology of minority voting in Eastern Europe, see Csergő and Regelmann (2017).

(2017), to denote the ability of minority groups (or minority elites) to influence political processes and minority policies. It is also important that the authors' call to focus on minority agency goes counter to the approach widely held in the literature, which treats minority groups as mere recipients or targets of the policies designed by other political actors (most importantly, by the state).

2.2 Ethnic Parallelism: Political Program and Social Reality

The political agency of minority actors has two interconnected dimensions. The first is ethnic claims-making and bargaining with majority political actors. The second refers to community organizing, performed through the establishment and maintenance of an institutional framework that underpins the ethno-cultural reproduction of the minority group. These two dimensions are evidently interlinked, but it is worth separating them analytically.

Several scholars emphasize the centrality of ethnic reproduction in the political agency exercised by the Hungarian elites. Csergő (2007) highlights the salience of the issue of Hungarian-language use, while Stroschein (2012) focuses on the prominence of education in the vernacular in the political claims-making of the Hungarians. Both aspects are intimately linked to the issue of ethno-national reproduction. Brubaker et al. (2006) and Brubaker (2009) emphasize that in Transylvania (at least in areas where Hungarians do not constitute a majority), ethnicity has less territorial and more institutional bases. The extended network of Hungarian institutions, ranging from a Hungarian-language educational system, to Hungarian churches, NGOs, media, and workplaces, plays a key role in the ethno-cultural reproduction of the community. Inside these institutions, Hungarians may act as, and are socialized as, Hungarians. Consequently, this "institutionally sustained Hungarian world" is crucial in the long-term ethno-cultural reproduction of the community (Brubaker 2009, p. 210). Other scholars also emphasize that the establishment and maintenance of this institutionally sustained Hungarian world could be considered to be the hidden agenda of all Transylvanian Hungarian political programs elaborated since the Treaty of Trianon (Biró 1998a; Kántor 2000; Bakk 2000b; Kántor and Bárdi 2002; Lőrincz 2008).

Building on this dual nature of minority political agency, our volume also explores how these two dimensions embody rather different tasks and how they should be performed in different arenas. An interesting conceptualization for this can be borrowed from Tsebelis (1990), who reinterprets Lijphart's (1969, 1977, 2004) model of consociational democracy in terms of nested games. According to Tsebelis, elites of the different societal segments have to act simultaneously in two arenas: in the parliamentary arena (where they have to deal with elites of other segments) and in the electoral arena (where they have to maintain the support of their own constituency). Bargaining across the social segments in the parliamentary arena requires more consensus-oriented behavior, while electoral mobilization is best served by appealing to intra-group solidarity and often requires less consensus-oriented messages.

We have to stress that Tsebelis discusses consociationalism as a legally/constitutionally designed framework of politics, where the formal rules of the political game make voting across segments highly improbable. According to Lijphart (1977), consociational democracies have four constitutive elements: mutual veto, grand coalition, proportionality, and segmental autonomy, each of which should be constitutionally specified. Compared to this model, Romania certainly does not constitute a consociational democracy (Székely 2011).

While Romania may not fit into a consociational model, it does contain what Lijphart calls a "social pillars" or "pillarization". These are characteristics of deeply divided societies, where (ideological, religious, or ethnic) cleavages take an institutional form. Pillars are actually dense institutional nets covering many social domains (ranging from education to mass media, recreation, social, and health care) and organized in separate structures that stand in contrast to the mainstream societal culture (if such a mainstream exists). In Romania, Transylvanian Hungarians could be considered a genuine social *pillar*, while Romanians cannot, as due to their overwhelming demographic dominance their societal culture can be considered the mainstream, and pillar-like social organization loses its point. The existence of these dense institutional pillars makes it possible for members of minority (religious, ideological, or ethnic) segments of a society to live their life among their own, encapsulated in their institutionally sustained world. Transylvanian Hungarian elites are interested in the maintenance of this pillarized structure of the Hungarian community. Thus, in the case of Hungarians in Romania, Tsebelis' nested game should be restated in the following way: The Transylvanian Hungarian political class must engage in bargaining with majority political actors, while at the same time they also have to deal with organizing the institutional network underpinning the pillarized character of the community, or, as we will call it throughout the volume, ethnic parallelism.

The idea of a pillar consisting of a dense institutional network has been central to Transylvanian Hungarian political thinking since the interwar period. In the political rhetoric and self-representation of the Hungarian elites, the idea of the pillar (and institutionalized ethnic parallelism) emerged under the notion of the "Minority Society" (*Kisebbségi Társadalom*). Transylvanian Hungarian political thinkers envisaged this Minority Society as an ethnically integrated institutional structure that would enable the members of the community to live their lives inside a "Hungarian world" (without having to consider that they live physically within the borders of Romania). This institutional structure, or parallel Hungarian world, is also of central importance for the ethno-cultural reproduction of the Hungarian community. However, as an analytical tool, the metaphor of "Minority Society" only partially describes the social organization of the Transylvanian Hungarian community. It is true that in certain contexts, the existence of a well-structured and ethnically integrated institutional system suggests that Transylvanian Hungarians can be perceived as a distinct social segment or social pillar. However, the lack of certain institutional structures in certain domains and the fact that the institutional network does not encompass the entire community suggest that the Transylvanian Hungarian community cannot be regarded as a stand-alone societal segment or pillar.

The second part of this volume focuses precisely on this phenomenon of ethnic parallelism in the case of Transylvanian Hungarians. It explores the meso-level institutional processes characteristic of different social domains, which exert a strong influence on groupness and ethnic boundary maintenance. The introductory chapter of this part, authored by Tamás Kiss and Dénes Kiss, focuses on the dual character of ethnic parallelism as program and social reality. The scholars provide both a historical outline of the programmatic idea of the Minority Society and a model through which existing ethnic parallelism can be empirically captured.

In the remaining chapters of the second part, authors discuss the institutional structures sustaining the Hungarian community as a separate societal segment. In Chapter 6, Attila Z. Papp, János Márton, István-Gergő Székely, and Gergő Barna explain how the Hungarian-language educational system is of central importance not only for the ethno-cultural reproduction of the Hungarian community, but also for the institutional system underpinning ethnic parallelism. The current structures of Hungarian-language education were established during the early 1990s when a substantial expansion of Hungarian secondary-level education occurred (as compared to the situation characteristic in the 1980s). This publicly financed Hungarian-language educational system is actually one of the most important pluralistic elements of the Romanian minority policy regime. Yet, no forms of educational autonomy exist, and it is doubtful whether the totality of educational institutions that teach (also) in Hungarian can be considered a specific subsystem within Romania's broader educational system. Still, the importance of the Hungarian educational network from the perspective of the minority institutional system is undeniable, as approximately ten thousand teachers work in it. This group of teachers represents 4.9% of the total number of teachers in Romania and, according to the 2002 census, represents 6.6% of the Hungarian non-agricultural working force.

Churches, analyzed by Dénes Kiss in Chapter 7, are another important segment of the Hungarian institutional network. In Romania, ecclesiastical religiosity is very high compared to other countries in Europe, and churches play a relatively important role in society. In Transylvania, contrary to some other regions of the Carpathian Basin, the religious and ethnic cleavages reinforce each other. Romanians are overwhelmingly Eastern Orthodox, and the Romanian Greek Catholic Church represents the other historical Romanian confession. Conversely, 94% of Hungarians belong to one of the "Hungarian religious denominations", with 46% belonging to the Calvinist Reformed Church, 41% to the Roman Catholic Church, 5% to the Transylvanian Unitarian Church, and 1% each to the Lutheran and the Hungarian Greek Catholic Church. Taken together, these can be considered the (more or less) "Hungarian national churches", although neo-protestants also have separate Hungarian congregations (comprising 2.5% of the Hungarian population).

The third institutional structure sustaining the parallel Minority Society is the Hungarian-language media, analyzed in Chapter 8 by Tamás Kiss. The media consumption of Transylvanian Hungarians is characterized by the dominance of the Hungarian language. However, there is no unitary media structure controlled by the Transylvanian Hungarian elites. Kiss explains that when it comes to television, Transylvanian Hungarians are increasingly integrated into a Hungary-centric "mediascape". Of the nearly three hours a day spent watching television, approximately two are spent watching (public and private) television channels broadcasted from Hungary. As for radio stations and printed media, Hungarian-language media outlets from Transylvania dominate the consumption of Transylvanian Hungarians. However, there are no radio stations and newspapers covering the entire territory of Transylvania; instead, county-level newspapers and local radio stations remain the primary source of information. Additionally, while approximately one quarter of Transylvania's Hungarians consume primarily Romanian-language media, this pattern of media consumption is limited mostly to the dispersed Hungarian communities of Transylvania and Banat.[10]

[10]The institutional pillar underpinning the separate social organization of the Hungarian community also includes the Hungarian cultural institutions, the Hungarian dominated local governments, and the habitus of political participation though ethnic parties. However, except for the organization of politics along ethnic lines, which is discussed in Chapter 3, these institutional elements are only touched upon briefly in various chapters of the book.

There are also several social fields where ethnic parallelism and separation are not characteristic or do not work. This incomplete character of institutionalized ethnic parallelism is important for two reasons. First, the separateness of ethnic segments and their institutional completeness constitute the basis of all accommodationist and autonomist political projects. Second, institutional completeness is a major condition for the successful control of social mobility channels by the ethnic minority elites and for keeping the socially mobile members of the ethnic group within the community. In short, the institutional parallelism of the Hungarian community is far from being complete. For example, health and social care or trade unions are not ethnically organized at all. Additionally, the ethnic determinants of economic activity are also systematically underestimated by the Transylvanian Hungarian elites. As Zsombor Csata discusses it in Chapter 9, the economic sector is not perceived as being ethnically divided, despite the fact that there are initiatives that might point toward an ethnically coordinated economic sector.

2.3 Socio-demographic Processes and Ethnic Boundary Maintenance: The Consequences of Power Asymmetries

The last important task of our volume is to capture the consequences of the power asymmetries that characterize the institutional and discursive order shaping ethnic relations in Romania. This focus on asymmetries is present throughout all chapters of the volume. The very notion of unequal accommodation suggests that there is a basic asymmetry between majority and minority categories. The primary reason this asymmetry exists is because Romania has maintained its nationalizing state character (Brubaker 1996, 2009, 2011), despite a cautious shift toward a more pluralistic minority policy regime. The macro-social and demographic consequences of these asymmetries are touched on throughout the book (in the political order, in language economy, the design of certain social fields, etc.), but analyzed in detail in the third part of the volume, authored by Tamás Kiss.

Chapter 10 in the final part of the volume consists of two main sections related to power asymmetries. The first discusses the demographic trends affecting Transylvanian Hungarians in the last century, focusing primarily on the post-Communist period, while the second addresses the processes of ethnic classification. Demographic erosion is obviously one important consequence of the nationalizing policies. Assimilation is one important demographic consequence of these power asymmetries. In Transylvania, ethnic exogamy and mixed marriages play a central role in the process of assimilation. Children growing up in mixed families go through an imbalanced process of ethnic socialization. As a consequence, the acquisition of the majority Romanian language and culture, which define membership in the majority ethnic category, is taken for granted, while the acquisition of competences necessary to be recognized as Hungarian is exceptional. Another demographic trend affected by power asymmetries refers to the migratory processes of ethnic un-mixing (Brubaker 1998), which have further contributed to the homogenization of the ethnic landscape in Transylvania. Ethnically selective processes of internal migration played a crucial role in the fact that the major urban centers of Transylvania lost their "minority majority". The chapter also argues that different "regimes of counting" (e.g., official classification) are also conducive to asymmetries, in this case on the discursive level.

Chapter 11 focuses on the system of ethnic stratification. It begins by outlining the historical changes that occurred in the positions in society of Transylvanian Hungarians, who used to dominate urban centers, the administration, and the emerging system of capitalist industrial production before 1918. During the interwar period, a dual system was characteristic, in which Romanians dominated the state and the administrative structures but not the economy and urban societies. The changes that occurred during state socialism were the most consequential, accounting for the current characteristics of the system of ethnic stratification. The chapter goes on to outline the presently existing ethnic inequalities and emphasizes several processes that contribute to the increasing marginalization of the Transylvanian Hungarians.

The last chapter of the book analyzes the relationship of ethnicity and marriage (ethnic endogamy and exogamy). Mixed marriages and the re-classification of children born in mixed families are considered channels of identity change. The chapter relies on the typologies of Wimmer regarding positional moves vis-á-vis existing boundaries (2013, pp. 44–79) and argues that relatively high levels of ethnic mixing are not conducive to the blurring of ethnic boundaries between Hungarians and Romanians. This apparently puzzling phenomenon is a consequence of the meso-level institutional strategies and boundary policing of the Hungarian elites.

3 Transylvania and Its Hungarian Community

The last task of this introduction is to provide some general information concerning Transylvania and its Hungarian community. We use Transylvania in a broader sense, to include not only the territory of the historical Transylvania, but also the Banat region and the area next to the Hungarian border called Crişana by Romanian and Partium by Hungarian geo-historiographers. This actually means all the territories that used to belong to the Hungarian part of the Hapsburg Monarchy until the end of World War I, but which were transferred to Romania through the Treaty of Trianon, making up an extensive area of 107 thousand square kilometers. According to the 2011 census, more than 1.2 million people declared themselves to be of Hungarian ethnicity in Romania, with 99.1% of them living in Transylvania. This volume focuses predominantly on the territory of Transylvania, while only discussing tangentially the ethnic Hungarians living in other parts of Romania, such as the Csángós of Moldavia (*Moldova* in Romanian).

The Hungarians of Transylvania are Romania's most numerous minority communities and are one of the largest and most politically mobilized minorities in Europe. Overall, Hungarians represent approximately 19% of Transylvania's population and 6.5% of Romania's population. Transylvania has been divided into 16 counties since 1968, and significant Hungarian communities live in almost all of these counties. However, Transylvania is highly diverse, and its ethno-demographic characteristics vary from region to region. To accommodate for this, we divide Transylvania into four regions based on the distribution and

Fig. 1 Hungarians in Transylvania (*Source* Map created by Samu Márton Balogh based on census data)

weight of the Hungarian population. Figure 1 shows the spatial distribution of the Transylvanian Hungarians, along with the four regions outlined below and the major urban centers.

The first of the four regions is the Székely Land (also called Szeklerland), which is a well-defined historical region. Its inhabitants, the Székelys (or Szeklers) share a distinctive ethno-regional identity, despite the fact that they have been a part of the modern Hungarian nation since the 1848 revolution (Hermann 2003). Central to the Székely ethno-regional identity is the region's relatively compact Hungarian character and the memory of its autonomous status, which was held until 1876. The Székely Land is the largest Hungarian ethnic block outside of Hungary and includes the counties of Covasna/Kovászna, Harghita/Hargita, and the eastern and central part of Mureş/Maros county.[11]

[11]We should also note that Székely Land has no legally codified borders and, as a consequence, different actors use different spatial definitions of it.

The proportion of Hungarians is approximately 80% (depending on how the region is defined). The number of Hungarians living in this area is approximately 475,000, making up 38% of the total Transylvanian Hungarian population.

The Székely Land region is dominated by rural settlements and small towns. The most important (small or middle sized) towns are Sfântu Gheorghe/Sepsiszentgyörgy, Miercurea Ciuc/Csíkszereda, and Odorheiu Secuiesc/Székelyudvarhely. All three have a Hungarian demographic majority: The first has approximately 55,000 inhabitants, and the latter two have populations below 40,000. The largest urban settlement of the Székely Land is Târgu Mureș/Marosvásárhely (with a population of about 135,000), which also used to be the seat of the Magyar Autonomous Region (which contained most of the Székely Land) between 1952 and 1968.[12] However, the city lost its Hungarian demographic majority during the 1990s. As a consequence, local institutions and local politics are no longer dominated by Hungarians elites, contrarily to other parts of the Székely Land. This is the reason why we do not treat the city together with the rest of the Székely Land, but include it into the second region, discussed below.

Our second region is Central Transylvania, comprising Cluj/Kolozs county and the Western parts of Mureș/Maros county. While the center of the former county, Cluj/Kolozsvár, clearly belongs to this region, we also include Târgu Mureș/Marosvásárhely here, due to its increasing detachment from the other parts of the historical Székely Land. These two cities are the most important urban centers of Transylvania's Hungarian community, and home to the two numerically largest Hungarian communities in Transylvania. Before the onset of state-socialist modernization, both had a Hungarian demographic majority. However, in Cluj/Kolozsvár the proportion of Hungarians fell to 23% in 1992 and to 16% in 2011. In Târgu Mureș/Marosvásárhely, Hungarians made up 52% of the population in 1992 and 45% in

[12] The Magyar Autonomous Region was restructured in 1962. The territories of the present-day Covasna county were attached to Brașov/Brassó Region, while some Romanian majority territories West of Târgu Mureș/Marosvásárhely were attached to the region, which was also renamed Mureș-Magyar Autonomous Region.

2011. Both towns were sites of ethno-political tensions and Romanian–Hungarian rivalry. During communism, it was an explicit policy objective of the regime to alter the ethnic makeup of these towns. In Târgu Mureș/Marosvásárhely, the increase of the Romanian population occurred mostly during the 1980s, and interethnic tensions culminated in violent ethnic clashes in March 1990 (László and Novák 2012, pp. 15–18, 206–228). In Cluj/Kolozsvár, no similar clashes have occurred; however, symbolic ethnic rivalry led to some political tensions, especially during the tenure of the ultra-nationalistic mayor Gheorghe Funar.[13] As for the entire region of Central Transylvania, the proportion of Hungarians was 22% in 2011, and 20% of all Transylvanian Hungarians live in this area.

The third region we identify is called Partium by Hungarians and Crișana by Romanians. It comprises the northwestern counties of Bihor/Bihar and Satu Mare/Szatmár situated next to the Hungarian border, as well as Sălaj/Szilágy county. Overall, Hungarians make up 23–35% of the total population of these counties. However, if we narrow the focus to the ethnically mixed parts of these counties (leaving aside areas inhabited by Romanians as a block), Hungarians comprise a slight majority. The most important urban centers in this region are Oradea/Nagyvárad and Satu Mare/Szatmárnémeti, of which both have a Romanian majority but with important Hungarian communities.

Finally, significant Hungarian communities also live in the northern parts of Transylvania (Maramureș/Máramaros and Bistrița-Năsăud/Beszterce-Naszód counties), as well as in its southern counties (Brașov/Brassó, Alba/Fehér, Sibiu/Szeben, and Hunedoara/Hunyad), and in the Banat (Arad, Caraș-Severin/Krassó-Szörény, and Timiș/Temes counties). However, most Hungarians living in these counties live dispersed among a large Romanian majority. Additionally, in none of the above counties or in their major urban centers does the proportion of Hungarians exceed 10% (Brașov/Brassó, Timișoara/Temesvár, Arad, Baia Mare/Nagybánya). However, approximately 216,000 ethnic Hungarians live in these areas, making up 17% of Transylvania's total Hungarian population.

---

[13]Brubaker et al. (2006) have argued that ethnic tensions did not characterize everyday interethnic relations in the town.

References

Alba, R. (2005). Bright vs. blurred boundaries: Second-generation assimilation and exclusion in France, Germany, and the United States. *Ethnic and Racial Studies, 28*(1), 20–49.

Alba, R., & Nee, V. (2003). *Remaking the American mainstream: Assimilation and contemporary immigration*. Cambridge, MA: Harvard University Press.

Andreescu, G. (2000). Continuarea participării UDMR la guvernare – prima fază a democrației consensualiste românești? *Provincia, 1*(7), 2–3.

Bakk, M. (2000). Modellviták – rejtett stratégiák. *Magyar Kisebbség, 6*(1), 8–12.

Balić, L., & Izmirlija, M. (2013). Consociation in Bosnia and Herzegovina: Practical implementation of the theoretical principles. *South-East European Journal of Political Science, 1*(3), 121–134.

Bárdi, N., Gidó, A., & Novák, C. Z. (2014). *Együtt és külön: az erdélyi magyarok önszerveződése (1989–1990)*. Kolozsvár: Nemzeti Kisebbségkutató Intézet.

Barth, F. (1969). *Ethnic groups and boundaries: The social organization of culture difference. Scandinavian University books*. Bergen: Universitetsforlaget; London: Allen & Unwin.

Belloni, R. (2004). Peacebuilding and consociational electoral engineering in Bosnia and Herzegovina. *International Peacekeeping, 11*(2), 334–353.

Bíró, A., & Pallai, K. (2011). *Public financing of national minority organisations: Policy paradigms, policy regimes and good practice*. Study prepared for the committee of experts on issues relating to the protection of national minorities. Strasbourg: Council of Europe.

Biró, Z. A. (1998). Intézményesedési folyamatok a romániai magyarság körében. In Z. A. Biró (Ed.), *Stratégia vagy kényszerpályák? Tanulmányok a romániai magyar társadalomról* (pp. 16–47). Csíkszereda: Pro-Print.

Bochsler, D., & Szöcsik, E. (2013). Building inter-ethnic bridges or promoting ethno-territorial demarcation lines? Hungarian minority parties in competition. *Nationalities Papers, 41*(5), 761–779.

Brubaker, R. (1996). *Nationalism reframed nationhood and the national question in the New Europe*. Cambridge and New York: Cambridge University Press.

Brubaker, R. (1998). Migrations of ethnic unmixing in the "New Europe". *International Migration Review, 32*(4), 1047.

Brubaker, R. (2004). *Ethnicity without groups*. Cambridge, MA: Harvard University Press.

Brubaker, R. (2009). National homogenization and ethnic reproduction on the European periphery. In M. Barbagli & H. Ferguson (Eds.), *La teoria sociologica e lo stato moderno: saggi in onore di Gianfranco Poggi* (pp. 201–221). Bologna: Il mulino.

Brubaker, R. (2011). Nationalizing states revisited: Projects and processes of nationalization in post-Soviet states. *Ethnic and Racial Studies, 34*(11), 1785–1814.

Brubaker, R., Feischmidt, M., Fox, J., & Grancea, L. (2006). *Nationalist politics and everyday ethnicity in a Transylvanian town*. Princeton: Princeton University Press.

Brusis, M. (2015). The European Union and interethnic power-sharing arrangements in accession countries. *Journal on Ethnopolitics and Minority Issues in Europe, 14*(4), 60–78.

Chandra, K. (2006). What is ethnic identity and does it matter? *Annual Review of Political Science, 9*(1), 397–424.

Chandra, K. (2011). What is an ethnic party? *Party Politics, 17*(2), 151–169.

Csergő, Z. (2002). Beyond ethnic division: Majority-minority debate about the postcommunist state in Romania and Slovakia. *East European Politics & Societies, 16*(1), 1–29.

Csergő, Z. (2007). *Talk of the nation: Language and conflict in Romania and Slovakia*. Ithaca: Cornell University Press.

Csergő, Z., & Regelmann, A.-C. (2017). Europeanization and collective rationality in minority voting. *Problems of Post-Communism, 64*(5), 291–310.

Dobre, A. M. (2003). EU conditionality building and Romanian minority rights policy: Towards the Europeanisation of the candidate countries. *Perspectives on European Politics and Society, 4*(1), 55–83.

Fenton, S. (2003). *Ethnicity. Key concepts*. Cambridge and Malden, MA: Polity Press.

Gherghina, S., & Jiglau, G. (2011). Explaining ethnic mobilisation in post-communist countries. *Europe-Asia Studies, 63*(1), 49–76.

Gorenburg, D. P. (2003). *Minority ethnic mobilization in the Russian Federation*. Cambridge and New York: Cambridge University Press.

Hall, P. A., & Taylor, R. C. R. (1996). Political science and the three new institutionalisms. *Political Studies, 44*(5), 936–957.

Hermann, G. (2003). *Náció és nemzet: székely rendi nacionalizmus és magyar nemzettudat 1848-ig*. Csíkszereda: Pro-Print.

Hodžić, E., & Mraović, B. (2015). Political representation of minorities in Bosnia and Herzegovina: How reserved seats affect minority representatives' influence on decision-making and perceived substantive representation. *Ethnopolitics, 14*(4), 418–434.

Horowitz, D. L. (1985). *Ethnic groups in conflict.* Berkeley: University of California Press.

Horváth, I. (2002). *Facilitating conflict transformation: Implementation of the recommendations of the OSCE High Commissioner on National Minorities to Romania, 1993–2001* (Working Paper). Hamburg: CORE.

Horváth, I. (2013). The Romanian Roma: The dilemma of integration. In E. Dácz (Ed.), *Minderheitenfragen in Ungarn und in den Nachbarländern im 20. und 21.* Jahrhundert (pp. 305–325). Baden-Baden: Nomos.

Horváth, I., & Scacco, A. (2001). From the unitary to the pluralistic: Fine-tuning minority policy in Romania. In A. Bíró & P. Kovács (Eds.), *Diversity in action: Local public management of multiethnic communities in central and eastern Europe* (pp. 243–271). Budapest: OSI.

Jenkins, R. (2008). *Rethinking ethnicity* (2nd ed.). Thousand Oaks, CA: Sage.

Kántor, Z. (2000). Kisebbségi nemzetépítés. A romániai magyarság mint nemzetépítő kisebbség. *Regio, 11*(3), 219–241.

Kántor, Z., & Bárdi, N. (2002). The democratic alliance of Hungarians in Romania (DAHR) in the government of Romania from 1996 to 2000. *Regio. Minorities, Politics, Society, 2*(1), 188–226.

Kasapović, M. (2005). Bosnia and Herzegovina: Consociational or liberal democracy? *Politička misao, 17*(5), 3–30.

Kiss, T. (2017). Beyond the ethnic vote: Shifting determinants of the electoral behavior of Transylvanian Hungarians. *Problems of Post-Communism*, 1–17. https://doi.org/10.1080/10758216.2017.1336422.

Kiss, T., & Székely, I. G. (2016). Shifting linkages in ethnic mobilization: The case of RMDSZ and the Hungarians in Transylvania. *Nationalities Papers, 44*(4), 591–610.

Kiss, T., Székely, I. G., & Barna, G. (2017). Factors affecting turnout among ethnic minority voters: The case of Hungarians in Transylvania. *Intersections. EEJSP, 3*(4), 87–119.

Kymlicka, W. (2007). *Multicultural odysseys: Navigating the new international politics of diversity.* Oxford and New York: Oxford University Press.

Kymlicka, W. (2011). Beyond the indigenous/minority dichotomy? In S. Allen & A. Xanthaki (Eds.), *Reflections on the UN declaration on the rights of indigenous peoples* (pp. 183–208). Oxford and Portland, OR: Hart Publishing.

Laitin, D. D. (1998). *Identity in formation: The Russian-speaking populations in the near abroad.* The Wilder House series in politics, history, and culture. Ithaca: Cornell University Press.

Lamont, M., & Molnár, V. (2002). The study of boundaries in the social sciences. *Annual Review of Sociology, 28*(1), 167–195.
Lamont, M., Silva, G. M., Welburn, J. S., Guetzkow, J., Mizrachi, N., Herzog, H., & Reis, E. (2016). *Getting respect: Responding to stigma and discrimination in the United States, Brazil, and Israel.* Princeton, NJ: Princeton University Press.
László, M., & Novák, C. Z. (2012). *A szabadság terhe. Marosvásárhely, 1990. március 16–21.* Csíkszereda: Pro-Print.
Lijphart, A. (1969). Consociational democracy. *World Politics, 21*(2), 207–225.
Lijphart, A. (1977). *Democracy in plural societies: A comparative exploration.* New Haven: Yale University Press.
Lijphart, A. (2004). Constitutional design for divided societies. *Journal of Democracy, 15*(2), 96–109.
Lőrincz, D. J. (2008). A kolozsvári magyarok társadalma. *Regio, 19*(2), 240–256.
Malloy, T. H., Osipov, A., & Vizi, B. (Eds.). (2015). *Managing diversity through non-territorial autonomy: Assessing advantages, deficiencies, and risks.* Oxford: Oxford University Press.
McGarry, J., O'Leary, B., & Simeon, R. (2008). Integration or accommodation? In S. Choudhry (Ed.), *Constitutional design for divided societies: Integration or accommodation?* (pp. 41–88). Oxford and New York: Oxford University Press.
Medianu, N. (2002). Analysing political exchanges between minority and majority leaders in Romania. *Global Review of Ethnopolitics, 1*(4), 28–41.
Mihailescu, M. (2008). The politics of minimal "consensus": Interethnic opposition coalitions in post-communist Romania (1990–96) and Slovakia (1990–98). *East European Politics & Societies, 22*(3), 553–594.
Mungiu-Pippidi, A. (1999). *Transilvania subiectivă.* București: Humanitas.
Nastasă, L., & Salat, L. (Eds.). (2000). *Relații interetnice în România postcomunistă.* Cluj: Fundația CRDE.
Orlović, S. (2015). Consociational experiments in the western Balkans: Bosnia and Herzegovina and Macedonia. *New Balkan Politics, 17,* 29–50.
OSCE-HCNM. (1999). *The Lund Recommendations on the effective participation of national minorities in public life & explanatory note.* OSCE High Commissioner on National Minorities.
Pettai, V., & Hallik, K. (2002). Understanding processes of ethnic control: Segmentation, dependency and co-optation in post-communist Estonia. *Nations and Nationalism, 8*(4), 505–529.

Pierson, P. (2000). Increasing returns, path dependence, and the study of politics. *American Political Science Review, 94*(2), 251–267.
Ram, M. H. (2003). Democratization through European integration: The case of minority rights in the Czech Republic and Romania. *Studies in Comparative International Development, 38*(2), 28–56.
Rechel, B. (2009a). Introduction. In B. Rechel (Ed.), *Minority rights in central and eastern Europe* (pp. 3–16). London and New York: Routledge.
Rechel, B. (Ed.). (2009b). *Minority rights in central and eastern Europe*. London and New York: Routledge.
Saideman, S. M., & Ayres, R. W. (2008). *For kin or country: Xenophobia, nationalism, and war*. New York: Columbia University Press.
Salat, L., Constantin, S., Osipov, A. G., & Székely, I. G. (2014). *Autonomy arrangements around the world: A collection of well and lesser known cases*. Cluj-Napoca: Institutul pentru Studierea Problemelor Minorităților Naționale.
Smith, A. D. (1995). Gastronomy or geology? The role of nationalism in the reconstruction of nations. *Nations and Nationalism, 1*(1), 3–23.
Smith, D. J. (2013). Non-territorial autonomy and political community in contemporary central and eastern Europe. *Journal on Ethnopolitics and Minority Issues in Europe, 12*(1), 27–55.
Smith, D. J., & Cordell, K. (Eds.). (2007). *Cultural autonomy in contemporary Europe*. London and New York: Routledge.
Smooha, S. (2001). *The model of ethnic democracy* (ECMI Working Paper 13).
Stroschein, S. (2001). Measuring ethnic party success in Romania, Slovakia, and Ukraine. *Problems of Post-Communism, 48*(4), 59–69.
Stroschein, S. (2012). *Ethnic struggle, coexistence, and democratization in eastern Europe. Cambridge studies in contentious politics*. Cambridge and New York: Cambridge University Press.
Székely, I. G. (2011). *Democrație consociaționistă sau împărțirea puterii în societăți multietnice. Cadru teoretic și patru studii de caz*. Cluj: Institutul pentru Studierea Problemelor Minorităților Naționale—Kriterion.
Székely, I. G., & Horváth, I. (2014). Diversity recognition and minority representation in central and southeast Europe: A comparative analysis. *Nationalities Papers, 42*(3), 426–448.
Thelen, K. (1999). Historical institutionalism in comparative politics. *Annual Review of Political Science, 2*(1), 369–404.
Tsai, K. S. (2014). *Informal institutions and historical institutionalism*. APSA 2014 annual meeting. 14 August 2014. Available at SSRN: https://ssrn.com/abstract=2454845.

Tsebelis, G. (1990). *Nested games: Rational choice in comparative politics. California series on social choice and political economy*. Berkeley: University of California Press.

Varshney, A. (2003). Nationalism, ethnic conflict, and rationality. *Perspective on Politics, 1*(1), 85–99.

Waterbury, M. A. (2017). National minorities in an era of externalization. *Problems of Post-Communism, 64*(5), 228–241.

Wimmer, A. (2013). *Ethnic boundary making: Institutions, power, networks. Oxford studies in culture and politics*. New York: Oxford University Press.

Part I

The Minority Rights Regime and Political Strategies

2

Minority Political Agency in Historical Perspective: Periodization and Key Problems

Nándor Bárdi and Tamás Kiss

Our volume focuses on the political, institutional, and macro-social processes concerning Transylvanian Hungarians following the regime change of 1989. This chapter should be regarded as an introduction to the first part of the book, focusing on the political processes. As such, the analysis presented here has a larger time horizon and tries to outline the major turning points of the century-long political history of the minority community under investigation. We start from

N. Bárdi (✉)
Institute for Minority Studies, Hungarian Academy of Sciences, Centre for Social Sciences, Budapest, Hungary

T. Kiss
Romanian Institute for Research on National Minorities, Cluj-Napoca, Romania

T. Kiss et al. (eds.), *Unequal Accommodation of Minority Rights*, Palgrave Politics of Identity and Citizenship Series, https://doi.org/10.1007/978-3-319-78893-7_2

the inauguration of Romanian authority in Transylvania[1] and trace the most important historical events and processes until the post-Communist period.

Our historical overview focuses on the changing forms of *minority political agency*. We wish to emphasize from the very beginning that we do not perceive the minority community as passively bearing or suffering the consequences of the historical events. In the focus of our attention are the strategies employed by the minority elites through which they tried to adapt to the changing minority policy regimes of Romania, to Hungarian–Romanian interstate relations and the international environment. These adaptive strategies can be interpreted as responses to the frequent and often radical changes of power structures.

When we speak about *minority political agency*, we draw heavily on the ideas of Csergő and Regelmann (2017). As they emphasized, the majority of students of ethnic politics perceive minority groups as mere recipients of the policies designed by other political actors (most importantly, by the state). Minority political agency denotes the ability of the minority groups (or minority elites) to influence political processes and minority policies. The term also refers to (formally and informally) institutionalized means of ethnic claim-making, including language use, minority and human rights, socioeconomic equality, minority empowerment, and self-government. Several aspects of our approach concerning minority political agency should be highlighted:

1. In our understanding, minority political agency has *two complementary dimensions*, namely political claim-making and institution building. Electoral politics, parliamentary representation, and the activity of minority rights organizations (in both domestic and international fora) are forms and tools of political claim-making. The political

[1]The historical representation of this event is in sharply contrast in the Hungarian and Romanian historiographies and public spheres. In 2018, Romania celebrates the 100th anniversary of the 1918 National Assembly at Alba Iulia/Gyulafehérvár. According to the Romanian historical representation, Transylvania belongs to Romania due to the proclamation of the "Great Union". According to the Hungarian public representations, Transylvania was lost due to the Treaty of Trianon in 1920, which is represented as the major national tragedy of the Hungarians.

class (gelled together in ethnic parties) and minority rights activists are the major agents of this process. The second component of minority political agency is institution building and community organizing. As we will see Chapter 5, the notion of the Minority Society (*Kisebbségi Társadalom*) has a central place in the political imagination of the Transylvanian Hungarian elites. This involves a dense institutional net of Hungarian institutions which underpin the ethno-cultural reproduction of the Transylvanian Hungarian community. The chapters of this book argue that instead of a loose category of Hungarian speakers, one can legitimately speak of a Transylvanian Hungarian community, able to imagine itself as a Minority Society. However, this cannot be taken for granted but is a consequence of the community organizing capacities of the elites on the one hand, and of the institutional structures underpinning cultural and identity reproduction on the other.

2. Minority political agency (in both its dimensions) is *constrained* by the institutional order of the nation-state. Minority political actors are by definition in asymmetrical positions vis-á-vis majority actors. However, the degree of constraints may vary greatly across periods and political regimes. As for our historical overview, the distinction between democratic and authoritarian/totalitarian regimes is of central importance. These are ideal types, and the empirical cases can be placed on a continuum between them. For instance, the Romanian political regime of the interwar era belongs to the gray zone of hybrid regimes (Diamond 2002), combining democratic traits (most importantly, regular elections) with political repression. State socialism can be characterized as a totalitarian regime with some periods of liberalization. During this period, political organizations could not act independently of the party state and, consequently, no institutionalized and formalized claim-making was possible. The minority policy regime is also of central importance.[2] Consociation would mean institutional and legal guarantees for sustainable minority political agency and minority

[2]By minority rights regime, we understand the totality of policies in a specific country that "accommodate diversity and grant members of minorities certain rights" (Rechel 2009, p. 8).

empowerment (Lijphart 2004; Taylor 2009). However, such an arrangement has never been achieved by the Transylvanian Hungarian elites.

3. We perceive minority political agency, and thus the political history of the Transylvanian Hungarians, as a sequence of *reactive strategies*. Minority elites in fact have aimed to counterbalance the nationalizing attempts of the state owned by the titular group[3] and to organize an institutional system that underpins the ethno-cultural reproduction of the Hungarian community.

4. In our concept of agency of the minority elites, the historically conditioned processes of socialization (or one might say, *habitualization*) are of central importance. We are convinced that models that take into account only synchronic relations fail to capture the functioning of the minority political field and to understand minority political agency.[4] In the socialization of the minority elites, the existing frameworks of minority institutions are of central importance. In the section concerning the institutional processes, we will see that Hungarian elites perceive the dense net of minority institutions as one underpinning the ethno-cultural reproduction of the community. We argue that the same institutional system is also of central importance in the elites' own socialization. As this chapter will outline, the net of minority institutions that provide a framework for the socialization of the Transylvanian Hungarian elites has varied considerably. In some periods, the minority institutions acted relatively independently, while in other periods they were under tight state control. Consequently, the different generational groups of Transylvanian Hungarian elites have acquired different habituses.[5] The habitual differences among generational groups (socialized, for instance, in interwar, state-socialist, or post-Communist periods)

---

[3]On the nationalizing state, see Brubaker (1996, 2011). For the ethnic ownership of state structures, see Wimmer (2002).

[4]See, for instance, the triadic model of Brubaker (1996), which analyzes the interactions between the minority field, the nationalizing state, and the kin-state.

[5]Here, we use the concept of habitus of Bourdieu (1985), meaning the "enduring dispositions" that shape the "base-lines" of human action.

could be quite significant, and these differences have shaped profoundly the tactical elements and the content of minority political agency. The larger ideological influences ("Zeitgeist") were also constitutive. The policies envisaged by the minority elites were different in eras when corporative fascism or leftist egalitarianism was hegemonic, compared to periods when (neo)liberalism was in a dominant position.

5. Next to the habitual elements that vary across generations, the minority political agency of the Hungarian elites has a strong value-rational component. This is also historically conditioned and connected to the feeling of national belonging on the one hand, and to a collectivist ethic[6] on the other. During the nineteenth century, the political class of Hungary was unable to incorporate its nationalities into the process of Hungarian nation building. Nevertheless, Transylvanian Hungarians took part in this process, and consequently, a strong sense of belonging to the Hungarian nation took shape among them. After 1918, they found themselves in a rather different institutional context, characterized by the dominance of the titular majority. One could say that they were caught between the constitutive memory of the Hungarian nation building on the one hand and the actual nation-building processes of the titular elites on the other. As a reaction, minority elites have engaged in a process of minority nation building (Csergő 2007; Kántor 2001) and tried to create the institutions of an ethno-nationally integrated parallel society. Consequently, Transylvanian Hungarians have become part of the political, social, and economic system of the newly formed states, but it is doubtful whether they have become members of the Romanian political community (Salat 2008). The integration of the Hungarians into a new political community was also hindered by the fact that Romanian nation building had been designed exactly to question their social positions and limit their influence (Livezeanu 1995).

[6]In this collectivist ethic, the ideal of "serving the people" was of central importance. See Bárdi et al. (2015).

This chapter is composed of three main parts. First, we briefly summarize the historical evolution of the definitions of the Transylvanian Hungarians employed by different actors engaged in ethnic politics. Second, we outline a periodization based on the changes in the two major types of political agency, namely forms of ethnic claim-making and opportunities for maintaining a system of minority institutions. Third, we summarize our arguments and make some concluding remarks.

1 Competing Definitions of the Hungarians in Transylvania

Before outlining a periodization, it is worth highlighting that the definition of the Hungarian community in Transylvania/Romania has also changed according to the political aims of the power centers which tried to extend their influence over it.

First, from the perspective of the minority elites, a distinction should be made between a *community of constraint* and both the ethnically and regionally defined *minority community*. The term community of constraint is related to that of "accidental diaspora" used by Brubaker (2000). Generally speaking, "diaspora constellations" have three main characteristics, namely (1) spatial dispersion, (2) homeland orientation, and (3) boundary maintenance vis-á-vis the national majority (Safran 1991). Accidental diasporas (as communities of constraint) are different, as they do not emerge due to the "movement of people across the borders" but due to the "movement of borders across people" (Brubaker 2000, pp. 2–3). Nevertheless, orientation toward the external homeland and boundary maintenance vis-á-vis the majority are constitutive in the case of accidental diaspora too. In our case, this means a Hungary-centered identity construction which might also induce a desire to "return", either in the form of territorial revision or repatriation. Obviously, the Treaty of Trianon produced a community of constraint (or accidental diaspora), as it abruptly separated Transylvanian Hungarians from the rest of the Hungarian nation. Initially,

Transylvanian Hungarian political elites tried to remain loyal to the Hungarian government and state administration. The most important conflict connected to the change of state sovereignty involved the oaths of loyalty toward the Romanian king which administrative staff had to take in order to maintain their position and escape being expelled.[7] Hungarian elites have gradually adapted to the changed institutional realities; however, territorial revision remained their most important future expectation during the interwar period.

Nevertheless, identity constructions have gradually changed. An accidental diaspora (i.e., a collective identity focused on Hungary as an external homeland) has been transformed into a *minority community* glued together by common experiences and a sense of common historical destiny. In this new identity construction, both ethnic and regional elements became constitutive. Most importantly, the representation of the homeland of Transylvanian Hungarians has changed profoundly. Today, very few of them would claim that Hungary (either in its actual or in its historical form) is their homeland. The notion of homeland actually refers to Transylvania, or to even smaller regional units, such as Székely Land, Banat, or Partium (Veres 2014; Papp 2014). Under these circumstances, the main question is whether they are able to create a sense of homeliness in the territories they inhabit. In the new institutional context, the term *autochthonous minority community* has also become central in the self-representation of the Hungarian elites.

During the interwar period, minority elites emphasized their opposition to Romanian nationalizing efforts and defined their community as a *national minority*, meaning a part of the Hungarian nation which lives under the sovereignty of another nation-state. Another constitutive element of their self-definition was that of a self-supporting political community which should have been integrated into Romania's polity in communitarian terms through segmental autonomy. These definitions continue to maintain their relevance also today.

Second, the self-representation of the Hungarians has constantly been in contrast to their representation by the titular elites. During

[7]See in detail Mikó (1941, pp. 16–17) and Bárdi (2013, pp. 121–131).

the interwar period, Romanian elites considered Hungarians as an *imperial minority*, remnants of the historical "Hungarian Empire". As emphasized, the Romanian elites perceived the Hungarian population, especially that of the urban centers (where they constituted the dominant element), as alien enclaves and as a factor hindering the integration of the newly gained territories into the Romanian nation-state (Livezeanu 1995). Additionally, the self-organization and self-defense of the Hungarians and especially their loyalty toward Hungary were perceived as a major security threat. After World War II, there was no major change in these perceptions of the Hungarian minority as a security threat. This feeling strengthened following the anti-Communist uprising in Hungary in 1956 and developed into outright paranoia during the Ceaușescu period. Meanwhile, the social and demographic positions of the Hungarians weakened considerably, while Hungary lost its ability and willingness to claim for a territorial revision. Following the regime change, the Hungarian "threat" was repeatedly discussed in the Romanian mass media and public sphere, especially during the early 1990s. The spectacular self-organization of the Hungarian community and the continuous presence of RMDSZ in the Romanian political field are subjects of reproach for many Romanians. Political actors routinely appeal to these feelings to gain electoral ground. However, the "Hungarian question" has lost its gravity. The perception that the "problem" will be solved by the demographic decline and emigration of the community has gained ground among Romanian elites (Boia 2015; Dumbrava 2016).

Official designations have also changed. During the interwar period, the term "national minority" (*minoritate națională*) was prevalent.[8] After 1944, the term "nationality" (*naționalitate*) or "cohabiting nationality" (*naționalități conlocuitoare*) was used.[9] Following 1984, the terms "workers of Hungarian nationality" (*oamenii muncii*

---

[8]The 1923 Constitution recognized only religious minorities, while the 1938 Constitution introduced the term "race"; however, the phrase "national minority" (*minorităti naționale*) has maintained its prominence during this period. See Scurtu and Boar (1995, p. 783) and Scurtu (1999, p. 515).

[9]This was due primarily to Soviet terminological influence (*narodnost*).

de naționalitate maghiară) and "Romanians of Hungarian nationality" (*români de naționalitate maghiară*) were used. These terminological changes marked changes in the focus of nationality policies. "National minority" denoted a part of another nation living under Romanian sovereignty. "Nationality" denoted a separate entity from both the national majority and the external homeland, while the paradoxical expression "Romanian of Hungarian nationality" was indicative of the assimilatory intentions of the national-Communist regime. After the change of regime in 1989, the official designations oscillated between "national minority" and "ethnic group".[10]

Third, from a kin-state perspective the increasing regionalization of identity structures and the changes in the concept of homeland can be interpreted as a divergence in the evolution of a formerly unitary Hungarian national identity[11] (Szarka 2002, 2010). During the interwar period, territorial revision was perceived as the solution to "counter-balance" these tendencies. In the state-socialist period, Hungarian authorities not only renounced territorial claims but also fostered a redefinition of the Hungarian nation which would include only the resident population of the country (Ludanyi 1995). This concept lost its legitimacy during the 1980s when several groups of dissidents used the issue of Hungarian minority communities to confront the regime of János Kádár, and some prominent members of the Hungarian Socialist Workers Party (MSZMP), like Mátyás Szűrös and Irme Pozsgai, also tried to increase their legitimacy through referring to the broader culturally defined national community. After the regime change, a program of "virtual" national reunification (Csergő and Goldgeier 2004) was launched, culminating in the modification of citizenship legislation in May 2010. The new law made it possible for members of the minority Hungarian communities to acquire Hungarian citizenship without residing in Hungary. This, together with other elements (such as the inclusion of the Transylvanian Hungarians into a Budapest-centered

[10]The official classification is discussed in detail in Chapter 10.

[11]One should note that in Transylvania a regionally specific (Transylvanian) Hungarian identity was more historically grounded than in other territories lost by the Hungarian state.

mediascape and increasing the volume of financial support channeled across the borders), led to a new shift toward the "diaspora constellation" and might put an end to the project of the minority community (Salat 2011, pp. 186–190). The official designations employed in Hungary to refer to the minority communities also mirror this tendency or policy intent. Until the second Orbán government took office, the terms "trans-border Hungarians" or "Hungarians beyond the borders" (*határon túli magyarok*) had been used; since then, "Hungarians living in external homelands" (*külhoni magyarság*) is the official designation. This expression implies a demand for the (evidently virtual) reunification of the previously diverging concepts of homeland across the Carpathian Basin.

2 Periods in the Political History of Transylvanian Hungarians

In what follows, we distinguish four major periods, while some of these can be divided into further subperiods. The first period started with the inauguration of Romanian authority in 1918 and ended with the return of Northern Transylvania to Hungary in 1940. During this period, Transylvanian Hungarians lived under a constitutional monarchy, except for the period between 1938 and 1940 when the short-lived royal dictatorship of King Carol II functioned. The second period lasted from 1940 to 1944, when the northern and eastern parts of Transylvania belonged to Hungary, while Hungarians in Southern Transylvania and Banat lived under the dictatorship of Ion Antonescu. The third period lasts from 1945 to 1989, and the largest part of this era (apart from the first few years) passed under state socialism, when both Romania and Hungary were part of the Soviet Bloc in a bipolar system of world politics. The essential characteristics of the Romanian Communist regime were its centrally planned economy and the fusion of the state administration with the Communist party. The last period is that following 1989, when the transition toward a democratic system and market economy began.

The forms of political agency that Transylvanian Hungarian elites have engaged in have varied across the periods. During the interwar period, Transylvanian Hungarians had to face the nationalizing policies of the Romanian state; however, these policies were limited by a (more or less) functioning constitutional system and (a constrained) rule of law. In the framework of the Romanian Kingdom, Hungarians were able to operate a well-developed institutional system and made claims through their own ethnic parties (Hungarian Union, Magyar Party). This became possible again only after the regime change of 1989, but the two periods are far from being similar, because in the meanwhile a radical alteration of the system of ethnic stratification had taken place.[12] Segmental and territorial autonomy were at the forefront of the Hungarians' programmatic goals in both the interwar and post-Communist period, but paradoxically, the only arrangement bearing some features of an autonomy functioned in the 1950s, in the framework of a totalitarian regime. The Magyar Autonomous Region (in place between 1952 and 1960, and in a more diluted form further until 1968) is perhaps best interpreted as an arrangement providing territorialized minority (language) rights, following the Soviet model (Gorenburg 2003); however, it may hardly be considered a form of social or political pluralism (Table 1).

From the perspective of our arguments, the Communist takeover beginning in 1944 is the most important turning point between 1918 and 1990, because the state-socialist regime completely altered the forms of minority political agency. First, the Hungarian minority parties of the interwar period won their legitimacy in parliamentary and local elections and formulated their ethno-political claims based on this legitimacy. The Communist takeover put an end to the (limitedly) democratic institutional system that functioned during the constitutional monarchy. During state socialism, the articulation of "Hungarian interests" was possible only in the framework of organizations established from above by the Communist authorities. The Hungarian People's Union functioned between 1944 and 1953; the Council of Workers

[12]See Chapter 11 for details.

Table 1 Minority political agency and the institutional network of the Transylvanian Hungarians in a historical perspective

Major period	Subperiods (according to the possibilities and strategies of claim-making)	General political regime	Minority political agents	Institutional framework
Interwar period (1918–1940)	Inauguration of Romanian authority (1918–1920)	Constitutional monarchy; hybrid regime (with partially fair elections and constrained rule of law)	Passive resistance	Strong net of minority institutions, including cultural, educational and economic institutions operated by the Hungarian Churches, community associations and private persons
	Beginnings of self-organization (1920–1922)		Hungarian Union[a]	
	Period of political pacts (1923–1927)		Magyar Party (OMP)[b] acting in coalition with majority and German political actors	
	Period of independent political agency (1923–1937)		Magyar Party (OMP) acting independently	
	Self-organization in a corporatist framework (1938–1940)	Royal dictatorship	Hungarian People's Community[c] inside the National Renaissance Front	
World War II (1940–1944)	"Short Hungarian world" Hungarian authority in Northern Transylvania	Hybrid regime to fascist dictatorship (Hungary)	Transylvanian Party[d] (in Northern Transylvania);	
	Antonescu period in Southern Transylvania	Fascist dictatorship (Romania)	Hungarian People's Community	

(continued)

Table 1 (continued)

Major period	Subperiods (according to the possibilities and strategies of claim-making)	General political regime	Minority political agents	Institutional framework
state-socialist period (1945–1989)	Establishment of state-socialist framework (1945–1952)	"People's democracy" with elections but growing control of the Communist Party over the political system	Hungarian People's Union[e] allied with the Romanian Communist Party	Nationalization of church, community and private properties, meaning the end of the self-sustained institutional system
	Gheorghiu-Dej period (1953–1964) Ceaușescu era (1965–1989)	Totalitarian regime (with short periods of liberalization in 1956/57 and 1968/71)	No minority political organization Hungarian Workers' Union[f] as puppet organization	Minority institutional system controlled entirely by the party state. "institutional booms" and cyclical narrowing during both the Gheorghiu-Dej and Ceaușescu period; Magyar Autonomous Region (until 1968) Bolyai University (until 1959)

(continued)

Table 1 (continued)

Major period	Subperiods (according to the possibilities and strategies of claim-making)	General political regime	Minority political agents	Institutional framework
Post-socialist period (after 1990)	Establishing the organizational structures of ethnic politics (1990–1993) Elaborating the model of self-determination (1993–1996) Governmental (1996–2004)	Democratic regime	Democratic Alliance of Hungarians in Romania (RMDSZ) in opposition (1990–1996) and as part of the executive power (1996–2004)	Institutionalization of asymmetric ethnic parallelism partially in the form of NGOs and for-profit organizations, partially in the form of publicly financed institutions
	Intra-ethnic competition (2004–2014) Erosion of the unequal accommodation model		RMDSZ, Hungarian Civic Party (MPP), Hungarian People's Party of Transylvania (EMNP)	

[a]In Hungarian: Magyar Szövetség; in Romanian: *Uniunea Maghiară*
[b]In Hungarian: *Országos Magyar Párt*; in Romanian: *Partidul Maghiar* or *Partidul Național Maghiar*
[c]In Hungarian: *Magyar Népközösség*; in Romanian: *Comunitatea Populară Maghiară* din România
[d]In Hungarian: *Erdélyi Párt*
[e]In Hungarian: *Magyar Népi Szövetség*; in Romanian: *Uniunea Populară Maghiară*
[f]In Hungarian: Magyar Dolgozók Országos Szövetsége; in Romanian: *Uniunea Oamenilor Muncii de Naționalite Maghiară din România*

of Hungarian Nationality was established in 1968. However, the former lost its organizational autonomy by 1948, while the latter can be perceived as a puppet organization of the party state. Several groups of intellectuals and officials within the ranks of the party state also claimed that they represented the interests of the Hungarian community; however, they were neither elected nor accountable.

Second, nationalization and collectivization meant not only that the middle classes lost their material foundation, but also that Hungarian church and community properties were confiscated. As a consequence of these processes, the maintenance of the autonomous structure of minority institutions became impossible. The system of ethnic stratification was also altered during the state-socialist period. Many urban centers had been dominated by the Hungarians during the interwar period, and their dominance increased in Northern Transylvania during 1940 and 1944. State socialism put an end to this dominance. The strata of Hungarian aristocrats, land owners, traders, entrepreneurs, and bourgeoisie disappeared. The urban middle classes and the strata of artisans radically weakened. This was conducive to further degradation of the institutional system.

Third, the 1947 peace treaties put an end to the international political agency exercised by the Transylvanian Hungarian political elites. The framework of this agency was the League of Nation's system of minority protection that operated during the interwar period. Transylvanian Hungarians repeatedly put on the agenda of the Council of the League the violations of minority rights in Romania (Zeidler 2003). After World War II, no such possibility existed.

2.1 Periodization Based on the Strategies and Possibilities of Claim-Making

Obviously, we do not consider Hungarian political elites a homogeneous and monolithic entity. There were numerous debates and conflicts within the community, and some of them crystallized as enduring internal cleavages. We have already mentioned that the differences in the conceptions about minority policy and the tactics of ethnic claim-making can be correlated with the various generational groups that succeeded each other. Regional interests and identities (Székely Land, Cluj/Kolozsvár, Partium) and class positions (Bárdi 2000, 2005) brought about additional differences. The turning points in the strategies and tactics of claim-making were obviously connected to the changes in the general political context. However, they can also be interpreted (at least partially) as the consequence of changes in the internal power relations of the Transylvanian Hungarian elites (along the above-mentioned dimensions).

2.1.1 The Interwar Period

During the interwar period, the system of ethnic stratification in Transylvania can be characterized a dual structure: On the one hand, the Romanian majority held political and administrative power; however, on the other hand minorities (Hungarians, Germans, and mostly Hungarian-speaking Jews) dominated the economic sector and urban societies. Consequently, autochthonous Transylvanian Romanian elites found themselves in a disadvantaged position vis-á-vis the Bucharest elites concentrated in the National Liberal Party.[13] They lacked sufficient capital, and if they wanted to take advantage of regional ethnic competition, they needed to turn to Bucharest for help. Their party, the Romanian National Party[14] led by Iuliu Maniu, had to merge with the Peasant Party[15] based in Bessarabia to gain statewide influence. The Hungarian political elites found themselves trapped between the interests of the Transylvanian Romanians and the Bucharest elites. Under these circumstances, they tried to bargain with different political actors and adopted a rather defensive standpoint (in order to maintain the social positions of the Hungarian community). At the level of political

[13]In Romanian: *Partidul Național Liberal.*

[14]In Romanian: *Partidul Național Român.*

[15]In Romanian: *Partidul Țărănesc.*

programs, collective autonomy was of central importance. However, at a more practical level, the monitoring of and the struggle against the violation of the minority and human rights of Hungarians were at the center of political agency.

The interwar era can be divided into five periods.

1. Between December 1918 (when the Assembly of Alba Iulia/Gyulafehérvár declared the union of Transylvania with Romania) and November 1920 (the ratification of the Treaty of Trianon), changes in state structure and sovereignty took place. As already mentioned, the Hungarian elites tried to maintain their institutionalized relations with the Hungarian government and hesitated to cooperate with the Romanian authorities.

2. Many historiographers label the whole period between 1918 and 1922 as one of political passivity. However, it would be more appropriate to regard the period between November 1920 and December 1922 as the one when self-organization began. Most importantly, the Hungarian Union was established during this period. It entered electoral competition in 1922 with moderate success due to the fact that quite many Hungarians were left off the electoral lists and coercion was extensively employed during the elections (Mikó 1941, pp. 26–28).

3. The Magyar Party (OMP) was established on December 28, 1922. This was one of the most important moments of the political self-organization of the Transylvanian Hungarian community (Mikó 1941; Horváth 2007; György 2003). Subsequent periods may be delimited according to the changes in the strategy of claim-making of the Hungarian party. The period between 1922 and 1926 might be called one of political pacts. The leadership of OMP tried to integrate into the Romanian polity (and to improve the fairness of the organization of parliamentary and local elections) through electoral agreements made with Romanian political parties. The famous "pact of Ciucea/Csucsa" (*csucsai paktum*) was agreed on November 25, 1923, between the leadership of OMP and that of the People's Party led by Alexandru Averescu. Although heavily contested within the party leadership, the pact helped OMP to break out from isolation and ran in

Table 2 Parliamentary electoral results of Hungarian political organizations between 1922 and 1948

Year	Electoral formation	Electoral results		Seats won by Hungarian organizations	
		Votes	%	Parliament	Senate
1922	Hungarian Union	n.d.	n.d.	3	3
1926	MP from the People's Party-led electoral alliance	1,366,160	52.0	15	12
1927	MP from Hungarian-German Bloc	173,517	6.28	8	1
1928	Magyar Party	172,699	6.08	16	6
1931	Magyar Party	139,003	4.75	10	2
1932	Magyar Party	141,894	4.75	14	3
1933	Magyar Party	119,562	4.01	8	3
1937	Magyar Party	136,139	4.43	19	3
1939	Hungarian People's Community inside National Renaissance Front	1,587,514	100	9	6
1946	Hungarian People's Union	568,862	8.3	29	
1948	Hungarian People's Union in People's Democratic Front	6,959,936	93.2	30	

Source Mikó (1941, pp. 60, 73, 235) and Nohlen and Stöver (2010)

the parliamentary elections in 1926 within an electoral alliance with the People's Party. As for the 1927 elections, the Hungarians allied with the German Party and created the so-called Hungarian-German Bloc. However, this formation proved to be inconvenient for the German elites, as the Hungarians were considered irredentists by the Romanian political actors. Nor did the Hungarian elites insist on maintaining the Minority Bloc, as they would have had to renounce several parliamentary seats for the benefit of the Germans (Table 2).

4. Between 1928 and 1937, OMP contested the elections on its own. This later period can be labeled one of independent claim-making and political agency. OMP not only ran independently in the elections but also became increasingly active on the international political scene, filing a series of complaints at the League of Nations with regard to a sequence of cases affecting the minority and human rights of the Transylvanian Hungarians. As another indicator of its independence, the Magyar Party demarcated itself from both the anti-revisionist movement in Romania and revisionist propaganda in Hungary.

5. The last period of the interwar era, that of royal dictatorship or absolute monarchy, lasted from 1938 to 1940. The royal dictatorship

began with the abolishing of the parliament and a ban on political parties. During this period, only parties and candidates authorized by the government were allowed to run in elections. Political representation was also reorganized on corporatist grounds, whereby different occupational groups elected their representatives. The Hungarian People's Community (*Magyar Népközösség*) operated in the framework of the National Renaissance Front (*Frontul Renașterii Naționale*). The establishment of the corporative frameworks also meant a generational change in the political leadership of the Hungarian community. The younger generation proved to be more active at social organization and succeeded in doing what the older generation of politicians had failed to do, namely to incorporate the Hungarian working class into the minority political organization. However, during this period the Hungarian elites did not have the possibility to elect the leadership of their political organization. Following a process of bargaining with the Romanian government, Miklós Bánffy (former minister of foreign affairs of Hungary and a familiar of the Romanian royal court) became the leader of the Hungarian People's Community for the entire period of the royal dictatorship (Horváth 2007, pp. 219–237).

2.1.2 During World War II

Following the Second Vienna Award, a dual periodization is needed. In this period, Hungarians who remained in Southern Transylvania and Banat had to face increasing oppression in the framework of the Antonescu regime. One could argue that they became a kind of "second class minority" compared to the Germans, who had been endowed with special collective rights in the context of Romania's alliance with Nazi Germany. Nevertheless, the situation of the Romanian Roma and Jews was even worse. Hungarians in Southern Transylvania (similar to Romanians in Northern Transylvania) found themselves in the situation of hostages. Their situation was determined by the principle of the so-called reciprocity between Hungary and Romania, meaning that the violation of human rights of one of the minority groups implied similar abuses on the other. Due to the intensive process of emigration, the number of Hungarians in Banat and Southern Transylvania decreased by 40% (Balogh 1999, 2004). The People's Community in Romania remained the political organization that represented the Hungarians.

The political elites of Northern Transylvania tried to proceed with multiple parallel tasks. They wanted to integrate as an independent and unitary (Transylvanian) block into the Hungarian political system, but they also tried to obtain funds for regional development. Meanwhile, they succeeded in maintaining the autonomous structure of the Transylvanian Hungarian institutional web developed during the interwar period. They used the rhetoric of Hungarian regional supremacy (presented as the interest of the Hungarian nation as a whole) to perform all these tasks simultaneously (Egry 2008). The (non-elected) representatives of Transylvania were inaugurated in the Hungarian Parliament in October 1940. The next six months (until May 1941) involved a period of organizing the structure of the Transylvanian Party (*Erdélyi Párt*). The newly organized party had made an attempt to represent regional interests independently; however, it was forced to make an agreement with the government led by László Bárdossy. According to the terms of the deal, the Transylvanian Hungarian elites accepted the prime minister as their party leader, meaning an alliance with and integration into the governing Party of the Hungarian Life (*Magyar Élet Pártja*). In exchange, the governing party did not establish its own organizational structures in Transylvania. Following the fall of 1943, the leadership of the Transylvanian Party was already focusing on the post-war period and trying to build alliances with leftist political actors. The German occupation of Hungary (19 March 1944) led to a schism in the Transylvanian Party. Some of its leaders persisted in the German alliance, while others established relations with the anti-Nazi forces. This latter group established the Hungarian Council in Cluj/Kolozsvár after Romania switched sides from the Axis to the Allies. However, the association proved to be unsuccessful in convincing the Hungarian government to try to negotiate a cease-fire.

2.1.3 Hungarians During State Socialism

The state-socialist era can be divided into three main periods, namely 1944–1952 (when the state-socialist frameworks of minority policy were established), 1953–1964 (marked by Gheorghe Gheorghiu-Dej as first secretary of the Romanian Communist Party), and 1965–1989 (dominated by Nicolae Ceauşescu) (Vincze 2003a, p. xv).

1. After the end of World War II, the major question referred to the political relations between the Hungarian community and state socialism. The period was characterized by the relatively strong influence of the Hungarians in the emerging power structures of the "people's democracy". After 1944, leftist groups and organizations took a leading role among Hungarian elites. The (leftist) Hungarian elites did not have many political alternatives. The historical (non-Communist) Romanian parties considered Transylvanian Hungarians to be collectively responsible for the transfer of Northern Transylvania to Hungary. They were also inspired by the Beneš decrees in Czechoslovakia and urged a "population exchange", which practically would have meant the forced migration of the Transylvanian Hungarians (Achim 2007; Balogh and Olti 2006). Under these circumstances, an alliance with the Communists seemed to be an obvious option. Otherwise, Hungarians were highly overrepresented in all leftist movements (including the Communist Party) in Transylvania.

The Romanian administration was reinstalled in Northern Transylvania in 1944 (August–November); however, following atrocities committed against Hungarian civilians, the Soviet military leadership expelled it temporarily (November 1944–March 1945). Hungarians gained a prominent role in the intermittent power structures. The Hungarian People's Union was established on October 16, 1944, on the basis of the Hungarian Workers Union in Romania,[16] a leftist organization with roots in the interwar period. The Union was an ally of the National Democratic Front, led by the Communist Party,

[16]In Hungarian: *Magyar Dolgozók Országos Szövetsége* (MADOSZ); in Romanian: *Uniunea Oamenilor Muncii Maghiari din România.*

while the Hungarian community was perceived by the larger public as supporting social and political transformations toward a Soviet-type regime (Lőnhárt 2008; Nagy and Olti 2009). In the 1946 elections, the Hungarian People's Union ran independently and won 8.3% of the votes. The Union was actively involved in minority rights protection. It objected, for instance, in the so-called CASBI case (which could be interpreted as the hidden nationalization of Hungarian proprieties) and in the case of the nationalization of Hungarian church and community proprieties. However, in 1948 the Union joined the electoral alliance of the National Democratic Front and practically ceased to exist as an independent political agent. The organization was officially abolished in 1953.

2. Another question relevant to the whole state-socialist period is whether it is meaningful speak about minority political agency at all in a period that lacked institutionalized forms of political pluralism. This also meant that Hungarian elites lacked formal structures through which they could formulate their political options and claims. Consequently, a rather specific form of representation emerged, based on informal channels, personal relations, and positions in the power structure of the party state. The Hungarian cultural elites and the party cadres of Hungarian origin had to operate in this framework, characterized by high levels of informality and a lack of explicit and public claim-making. The content of "Hungarian interests" also became rather obscure due to the lack of public debate concerning different policy alternatives. However, in many cases it seemed obvious to the elites what Hungarian interests were, and they associated them with the maintenance of the Hungarian institutional system. Hungarian cultural elites (and many Hungarian cadres from the party state) represented themselves as serving the Hungarian community and pushing for Hungarian interests. However, this might also be regarded as a mere legitimizing discourse.[17]

The second period is marked by the consolidation of the leadership of Gheorghe Gheorghiu-Dej. Between 1953 and 1956, a dual process

[17]On this ambivalent situation, see Lőrincz (2004).

took place. In the Magyar Autonomous Region, state-socialist modernization was carried out in a dominantly Hungarian-speaking institutional framework. However, outside this entity opportunities for using the Hungarian language considerably narrowed and the unmaking of the Hungarian institutional system began.[18] The year 1956, with the anti-Communist uprising in Hungary, was obviously an important turning point. Initially (in 1956/1957), a process of de-Stalinization also began in Romania. However, the suppression of the Hungarian uprising and the subsequent withdrawal of Soviet forces from Romania led to a (renewed) consolidation of the power of Gheorghiu-Dej. After this event, a new framework for minority policies was established. The fight against "revisionist" tendencies (referring to both de-Stalinization and Hungarian claims) became a prominent slogan. The period between 1957 and 1961 was marked by several waves of repression during which many Hungarians were sentenced and imprisoned. The overall consequence was the loss of influence of Hungarians leftists.

3. The time of the Ceauşescu regime can be divided into four shorter periods. Between 1965 and 1968 multiple changes occurred. This was a period in which the politics of intra-Bloc national sovereignty was announced, but trends toward liberalization were also remarkable. The next 4–6 years were characterized by a sort of compromise between the Hungarian elites and the regime. This was a period of "taking a breath", as many Hungarian intellectuals have emphasized (Novák 2011, 2017). The Hungarian Workers' Union was established in this context in 1968. After 1973, the consequences of the so-called mini cultural revolution[19] were also made felt in the domain of minority policies. The degradation of the minority institutional system began, while nationalist tendencies and conflicts with Hungary's Communist leadership became

[18]See the report of Iván Kálló, the Hungarian ambassador in Bucharest (21 September 1950), or the reports of the Party Committee of the Bolyai University on educational issues (December 1954–March 1955), published in Vincze (2003b, pp. 137–139, 179–190).

[19]The notion of a "mini cultural revolution" is anecdotal. Nicolae Ceauşescu, following his official visit to China in 1971, announced that a period of ideological restrictions would follow. This meant an end to liberalization and the policy measures targeted at winning over the support of different social groups. Adepts of economic reform and rationalization were also marginalized until 1974.

aggravated.[20] In the second half of the 1980s (following protests related to the Lăncrănjan case[21]) party cadres of Hungarian origin were increasingly perceived as unreliable.

After the changes of the late 1970s, the new generation of intellectuals could not completely integrate into the incomplete system of Hungarian institutions. As compared to the earlier generation, they stood markedly outside the party rhetoric and the bargaining mechanisms of minority politics. They tried to create their own system of expression (public discourse and public sphere). They also formed cultural organizations that could not be integrated into the institutional frameworks of the time. Active resistance began with the 1982 issue of the *Ellenpontok* (counterpoints) samizdat journal. The only Hungarian institution that maintained its integrity was the Roman Catholic Church (which had rejected state control after 1948). The Reformed Church had already been nationalized, and from its conflict-loaded institutional environment László Tőkés, the pastor of the Temesvár/Timișoara parish came to the fore; when he was facing forced evacuation, the ensuing protest against this marked the beginning of the Romanian anti-Communist uprising in December 1989.

Immediately after the regime change, the army assumed executive power in Romania. The Hungarian-dominated small- and middle-sized towns constituted an exception. There, local governments were run by

[20]1977: the Oradea/Nagyvárad–Debrecen meeting. János Kádár (the first secretary of the Hungarian Socialist Worker's Party) succeeded in passing the initiative of opening consulates in Cluj/Kolozsvár and Szeged. However, neither the bilateral relations nor the situation of the Hungarian minority improved considerably. 1982–1983: several openly anti-Hungarian documents were published. 1986–1987: a campaign was run against the volume History of Transylvania (*Erdély Története*), published in Hungary. 1988: a meeting was held in Budapest against the territorial systematization in Romania that endangered several hundreds of Hungarian villages. In reaction, the Hungarian consulate of Cluj/Kolozsvár was closed down by the Romanian authorities.

[21]Ion Lăncrănjan's book, entitled "A few words about Transylvania" (*Cuvânt despre Transilvania*), was published in 1982. The author, who was associated with the official propaganda of the regime, criticized the minority policy of the Romanian Communist Party due to its "softness", accused János Kádár and Hungary's Communist leadership of irredentism, and formulated similar charges against the Hungarian minority of Transylvania. See Vincze (2006).

self-organizing groups who (in the majority of cases) helped into power groups of Hungarian economic and technocrat elites that had been marginalized during the early 1980s (Bárdi et al. 2014).

2.1.4 Changing Strategies of Ethnic Claim-Making After 1989

A detailed analysis of the changing claim-making strategies of the post-Communist period is provided in the next chapter of this section. Here, we outline only briefly a fivefold periodization. We distinguish the periods primarily according to the changes in the strategies employed by the most important ethnic party and an umbrella organization of the Transylvanian Hungarians, established soon after the regime change: the Democratic Alliance of Hungarians in Romania (RMDSZ).

1. The first period (1990–1993) was characterized by intensive institution building. The organizational framework of RMDSZ was also established during this period. In the structure of RMDSZ, the territorial branches have played a crucial role from the very beginning, enjoying a large degree of organizational autonomy. Next to them, the so-called platforms were also created, representing certain ideological orientations. However, the significance of these platforms has gradually decreased during the last two decades. After the 1990 and 1992 parliamentary elections, it became evident that the overwhelming majority of Transylvanian Hungarians supported the political alternative offered by the newly established organization. Consequently, RMDSZ was able to obtain parliamentary representation proportional to the share of the Hungarians in Romania's population.

2. On its 1993 congress, RMDSZ included autonomy and collective rights into its program. A new organizational structure was also adopted, with an internal "mini-parliament" (which was envisaged to be directly elected, in theory by all ethnic Hungarians living in Romania) designed to serve as the basis of a future self-government. These were the basic elements of the model of the so-called auto-determination, or self-government. However, internal elections were never held, nor was a register of the Hungarians in Transylvania ever completed. Since 1995,

RMDSZ has become a more party-like organization, and political decision-making has become increasingly centralized.

3. In 1996, RMDSZ became a member of the governing coalition led by the center-right Romanian Democratic Convention (CDR, *Convenția Democrată Română*). Between 2000 and 2004, RMDSZ provided parliamentary support to the government of the Social Democratic Party (PSD, *Partidul Social Democrat*). County-level political bargaining with Romanian political actors was also an important tool of the vindication of minority interests. During this period, a model that can be called unequal accommodation (or asymmetric bargaining) took shape. This involved inclusion in the executive power of the Hungarian elites but without institutional guarantees of ethnic power-sharing.

4. The radical wing of RMDSZ led by László Tőkés left the organization in 2003. This could be considered the beginning of a new period—one of intra-ethnic political competition. Over the next few years, two other Hungarian political parties have been established: the Hungarian Civic Party was registered in 2008 and the Hungarian People's Party of Transylvania in 2011. In spite of intra-ethnic electoral competition, RMDSZ has maintained its dominance inside the community. The authors of the following chapter argue that this was due primarily to its monopoly on resource allocation.

5. Following 2014, there were signs of the erosion of the model called unequal accommodation throughout the volume. The period was also marked by an increasing influence of Hungary's kin-state policy.

2.2 Institutional Dynamics

As already mentioned, there is another dimension of minority political agency, namely institution building and community organizing. In this respect, the concept of the *Minority Society* is of central importance. The Minority Society was a programmatic idea elaborated during the interwar period. Political thinkers such as István Sulyok (1931) envisaged a dense net of institutions organized on ethnic basis, ranging from an educational system, publishing houses, and cultural and religious institutions to economic organizations. The concept of the Minority Society and the institutional net that sustains ethnic parallelism are discussed in Chapter 6. Here, we outline only the major changes that occurred in the Hungarian institutional system.

During the interwar period, a rather strong network of minority institutions was formed, including a Hungarian-language educational system. One should emphasize that this institutional net was organized in the form of an "ethno-civil society" as the Romanian state did not finance the functioning of Hungarian institutions. The Hungarian churches played a central role in sustaining the Minority Society. The Hungarian-language educational system consisted of private denominational schools and the churches also operated a wide range of other institutions (hospitals, publishing houses, etc.). Private funds and private associations also played a crucial role, and several institutions were in the hands of local ethnic communities. Due to this financial autonomy, the Romanian state was not able to control these institutions, while Hungarian elites exercised direct control over them.[22] After Northern Transylvania became again part of Hungary in 1940, this "minority institutional field" maintained some degree of autonomy vis-á-vis Budapest. Transylvanian Hungarian elites argued that this institutional structure was needed to represent Hungarian interests in the context of ethnic competition (Egry 2008).

As already mentioned, after 1944 the leftist elites and the Hungarian People's Union took the lead. There was a sharp debate inside the Union regarding whether the minority institutional system should be maintained, or whether it had become redundant in a context of Leninist minority policies (Vincze 1999). In 1948, the process of nationalization put an end to this debate, and ultimately, the Hungarian People's Union (then functioning as an organ of integration into or transmission for the Communist Party) was also suspended.

[22]This institutional system was described in the so-called Hungarian Yearbooks of Transylvania, published first in 1930 and then again in 1937 with the intention to provide synthetic representations of all aspects of the life of Transylvanian Hungarians (Sulyok and Fritz 1930; Kacsó 1937).

During the state-socialist period, minority organizations were operated and controlled by the party state; this represented a totally new institutional constellation. In parallel, a new perspective gained ground in the 1950s, according to which minority policies should focus primarily on language use. However, the use of the Hungarian language was possible only in the framework of minority institutions. The activity of the Hungarian churches was strictly constrained to religious matters. Except for the Roman Catholic Church, the Hungarian denominations accepted the control of the party state over their activities. The Bolyai University in Cluj/Kolozsvár was established in 1945. During the late 1940s and 1950s, it functioned as a rather important medium of the socialization of the Hungarian elites. The Magyar Autonomous Region was established in 1952, designed on the Soviet model of territorialized minority rights (Bottoni 2018, pp. 51–93). Inside this region, comprising by and large the Székely Land, the Hungarian language was widely used as an official language, but outside it the use of Hungarian was considerably suppressed.

The year 1956 can be considered a turning point in the institutional processes too. After the anti-Communist uprising in Hungary, the leadership of Romania's party state considered the existence and operation of separate Hungarian institutions as a security threat. Alongside the (perceived) danger of Hungarian separatism, the major problem was that this institutional system produced cultural patterns and future perspectives that diverged from the official ones. The consequence was the restructuring of the institutional system. The Bolyai University was merged with the Romanian-language Babeş University in 1959. Many Hungarian high schools were also merged with Romanian ones. The Magyar Autonomous Region was restructured, too: The southern part of Székely Land (present-day Covasna/Kovászna county) was attached to the Region of Braşov/Brassó, while Romanian-majority territories were added to the autonomous province, which was also renamed to Mureş/Maros-Magyar Autonomous Region.

Following the rise to power of Ceauşescu, and especially after 1968, a sequence of new Hungarian cultural institutions and media outlets was established. It is also of central importance that after the territorial-administrative reorganization of 1968 two Hungarian-majority counties were created (Harghita/Hargita and Covasna/Kovászna). In these counties, the intuitional system operated largely in Hungarian during the 1970s. During the late 1970s and especially during the 1980s, the Hungarian institutional and educational system shrunk considerably, and a new wave of ethnic institution building only began after the regime change.

3 Concluding Remarks

In this chapter, we have focused on minority political agency (Csergő and Regelmann 2017) and argued that, in spite of the existing power asymmetries established by the institutional order of the nation-state, Transylvanian Hungarians cannot be perceived as simple recipients or objects of minority policies designed by the majority. During the past one hundred years, minority elites have been able to elaborate their own strategies and to sustain their own policy alternatives. Nevertheless, their political agency was constrained to varying degrees by the opportunity structures of the different political regimes; thus, we have conceptualized minority policy agency as a sequence of reactive strategies aimed at counterbalancing the nationalizing efforts of state power.

We have also argued for the necessity of a multidimensional model of political agency. An analytical distinction between political claim-making and ethnic institution building proved to be useful. Ethnic claim-making refers to the elaboration and representation of different policy alternatives concerning ethnicity and related issues. Political struggles aimed at altering the regulation of official language use, the use of national symbols, or the entire model of integration of the minority community come under this label, but ethnic claim-making may also target a more equal redistribution of state funds and investments. Institution building and community organizing constitute another dimension of the agency of ethnic minority elites. While obtaining political representation is the professed choice of a narrower political class, in the operation of ethnic institutions a broader stratum of community activists is involved.

The models of ethnic claim-making and the representation of minority interests depend on a more general political, legal, and institutional framework. In Romania, formal ethnic power-sharing has never been institutionalized. Consequently, Hungarian elites have tried to vindicate their political alternatives through more or less informal channels. During the interwar period and following the regime change of 1989, the bargaining process with majority political actors was of key importance. Through this bargaining, numerous benefits were obtained; however, the central programmatic goal of both interwar and post-Communist elites—namely the political integration of the Hungarian community through the form of segmental autonomy and power-sharing—was never achieved. During the state-socialist period, the representation of minority interests was even more informal and was performed through the personal relations of the cultural elites or ethnic Hungarian members of the administrative structure. As no open debate and explicit claim-making was allowed, even the very content of "minority interests" became rather obscure.

As for institutional processes, the concept of the Minority Society is of central importance. Hungarian elites perceived their community as a distinct societal entity and were engaged in a process of minority institution building. Creating institutional completeness was an explicit aim in both the interwar and the post-Communist periods. Inside these institutionally defined places, the Hungarian language was used and some analysts have argued that thus they could be interpreted as tools of minority nation building (Kántor 2001). The dense network of minority institutions and the organization of certain social fields along ethnic lines have led to a certain degree of ethnic parallelism. Conversely, during state socialism Hungarian institutions were operated and controlled by the party state, and cyclical changes involving periods of institutional booms and shrinking could be distinguished. The Magyar Autonomous Region, a result of the implementation of the Soviet model of territorialized minority rights, was perhaps the most important piece of the institutional system of the Hungarian minority community during this period.

Another important issue is the control of the minority elites over the institutional system. During the interwar period, this was mostly taken for granted as the state did not finance the system. During the state-socialist period, the party state had ultimate control. After 1989, this issue became rather complex as the system of the minority institutions are partially state-financed, and (due to the lack of segmental autonomy) Hungarian elites can exert only a restricted level of control over the institutional system. These complex relations will be discussed in greater detail in some of the chapters to follow.

References

Achim, V. (2007). A második világháború alatti román lakosságcseretervekről. *Múltunk, 52*(4), 4–17.

Balogh, L. B. (1999). *Dél-erdélyi magyarság 1940–1944*. Available at: http://balogh.adatbank.transindex.ro/. Accessed 10 March 2017.

Balogh, L. B. (2004). A dél-erdélyi magyar kisebbség helyzete (1940–1944). In Z. Körmendy (Ed.), *Korrajz 2003. A XX. Század Intézet Évkönyve* (pp. 39–53). Budapest: XX. Század Intézet.

Balogh, L. B., & Olti, A. G. (2006). A román-magyar lakosságcsere kérdése 1940–1947 között. *Kisebbségkutatás, 15*(4), 597–620.

Bárdi, N. (2000). Cleavages in cross-border magyar minority politics, 1989–1998. *Regio, 1*, 3–36.

Bárdi, N. (2005). Generation groups in the history of hungarian minority elites. *Regio, 1*, 109–124.

Bárdi, N. (2013). *Otthon és haza: tanulmányok a romániai magyar kisebbség történetérol* (p. 647). Csíkszereda: Pro-Print.

Bárdi, N., Filep, T. G., & Lőrincz, D. J. (2015). *Népszolgálat. A közösségi elkötelezettség alakváltozatai a magyar kisebbségek történetében*. Pozsony: Kalligram.

Bárdi, N., Gidó, A., & Novák, C. Z. (2014). *Együtt és külön: az erdélyi magyarok önszerveződése (1989–1990)*. Kolozsvár: Nemzeti Kisebbségkutató Intézet.

Boia, L. (2015). *Cum s-a românizat România?* (p. 144). București: Humanitas.

Bottoni, S. (2018). *Stalin's legacy in Romania: The Hungarian autonomos region, 1952–1960*. Lanham, MD: Lexington Books.

Bourdieu, P. (1985). The genesis of the concepts of habitus and field. *Sociocriticism, 2*(2), 11–24.

Brubaker, R. (1996). *Nationalism reframed nationhood and the national question in the New Europe*. Cambridge and New York: Cambridge University Press.
Brubaker, R. (2000). Accidental diasporas and external "homelands" in central and eastern Europe: Past and present. *IHS Political Science Series*, 71, 1–19.
Brubaker, R. (2011). Nationalizing states revisited: Projects and processes of nationalization in post-Soviet states. *Ethnic and Racial Studies, 34*(11), 1785–1814.
Csergő, Z. (2007). *Talk of the nation: Language and conflict in Romania and Slovakia*. Ithaca: Cornell University Press.
Csergő, Z., & Goldgeier, J. M. (2004). Nationalist strategies and European integration. *Perspectives on Politics, 2*(1), 21–37.
Csergő, Z., & Regelmann, A.-C. (2017). Europeanization and collective rationality in minority voting. *Problems of Post-Communism, 64*(5), 291–310.
Diamond, L. J. (2002). Thinking about hybrid regimes. *Journal of Democracy, 13*(2), 21–35.
Dumbrava, C. (2016). Reproducing the nation: Reproduction, citizenship and ethno-demographic survival in post-Communist Romania. *Journal of Ethnic and Migration Studies, 43*(9), 1490–1507.
Egry, G. (2008). *Az erdélyiség színeváltozása. Kísérlet az Erdélyi Párt ideológiájának és identitáspolitikájának elemzésére, 1940–1944*. Budapest: Napvilág.
Gorenburg, D. P. (2003). *Minority ethnic mobilization in the Russian Federation*. Cambridge, UK and New York: Cambridge University Press.
György, B. (Ed.). (2003). *Iratok a Romániai Országos Magyar Párt történetéhez*. Csíkszereda: Pro-Print; Kolozsvár: Erdélyi Múzeum Egyesület.
Horváth, S. F. (2007). *Elutasítás és alkalmazkodás között: a romániai magyar kisebbségi elit politikai stratégiái (1931–1940)*. Csíkszereda: Pro-Print.
Kacsó, S. (Ed.). (1937). *Erdélyi magyar évkönyv, 1937. A kisebbségi magyar polgár kézikönyve*. Brassó: Brassói Lapok.
Kántor, Z. (2001). Nationalizing minorities and homeland politics: The case of the Hungarians in Romania. In B. Trencsényi (Ed.), *Nation-building and contested identities: Romanian and Hungarian case studies* (pp. 249–274). Budapest: Regio Books; Iași: Polirom.
Lijphart, A. (2004). Constitutional design for divided societies. *Journal of Democracy, 15*(2), 96–109.
Livezeanu, I. (1995). *Cultural politics in greater Romania: Regionalism, nation building & ethnic struggle, 1918–1930*. Ithaca: Cornell University Press.

Lőnhárt, T. (2008). *Uniunea Populară Maghiară în perioada instaurării regimului comunist în România*. Cluj-Napoca: Argonaut.

Lőrincz, D. J. (2004). Ambivalent discourse in eastern Europe. *Regio: A Review of Studies on Minorities, Politics, and Societies, 7*, pp. 148–171.

Ludanyi, A. (1995). Programmed amnesia and rude awakening: Hungarian minorities in international politics, 1945–1989. In I. C. Romsics (Ed.), *20th century Hungary and the great powers* (p. vii, 391 pp.). Boulder, CO: Social Science Monographs; Highland Lakes, NJ: Atlantic Research and Publications, Inc.; and New York: Distributed by Columbia University Press.

Mikó, I. (1941). *Huszonkét év: az Erdélyi Magyarság politikai története 1918. December 1-től 1940. Augusztus 30-ig*. Budapest: Studium.

Nagy, M. Z., & Olti, A. G. (Eds.). (2009). *Érdekképviselet vagy pártpolitika?: iratok a Magyar Népi Szövetség történetéhez, 1944–1953*. Csíkszereda: Pro-Print.

Nohlen, D., & Stöver, P. (2010). *Elections in Europe: A data handbook* (1st ed.). Baden-Baden: Nomos.

Novák, C. Z. (Ed.). (2011). *Aranykorszak?: a Ceauşescu-rendszer magyarságpolitikája I. 1965–1974*. Csíkszereda: Pro-Print.

Novák, C. Z. (Ed.). (2017). *Holtvágányon: a Ceauşescu-rendszer magyarságpolitikája II. 1974–1989*. Csíkszereda: Pro-Print.

Papp, A. Z. (2014). Kisebbségi identitáskonstrukciók a kettős állampolgárság által. *Regio, 22*(1), 118–155.

Rechel, B. (2009). Introduction. In B. Rechel (Ed.), *Minority rights in central and eastern Europe* (pp. 3–16). London and New York: Routledge.

Safran, W. (1991). Diasporas in modern societies: Myths of homeland and return. *Diaspora: A Journal of Transnational Studies, 1*(1), 83–99.

Salat, L. (2008). Are members of the Hungarian minority in Romania part of the Romanian political community? *Studia Politica: Romanian Political Science Review, 8*(2), 337–366.

Salat, L. (2011). A politikai közösség kérdése a többség–kisebbség viszonyának a nézőpontjából. *Magyar Kisebbség, XVI*(3–4), 159–190.

Scurtu, I. (Ed.). (1999). *Minoritătile naţionale din România, 1931–1938. Documente*. Bucureşti: Arhivele Naţionale ale României.

Scurtu, I., & Boar, L. (Eds.). (1995). *Minorităţile naţionale din România, 1918–1925. Documente*. Bucureşti: Arhivele Statului din România.

Sulyok, I. (1931). A kisebbségi kérdés szociológiai oldal. *Erdélyi Múzeum, 36*(4–6), 170–181.

Sulyok, I., & Fritz, L. (Eds.). (1930). *Erdélyi Magyar Évkönyv 1918–1929*. Kolozsvár: Juventus.

Szarka, L. (2002). Kényszerközösségek és védtelen védhatalom. A trianoni békeszerződés és a kisebbségek. In F. Glatz (Ed.), *Magyarország és a magyar kisebbségek: történeti és mai tendenciák* (pp. 17–30). Budapest: Magyar Tudományos Akadémia.

Szarka, L. (2010). Egy évszázad kisebbségben. *Korunk, 21*(4), 59–76.

Taylor, R. (2009). *Consociational theory: McGarry and O'Leary and the Northern Ireland conflict*. London and New York: Routledge.

Veres, V. (2014). Identity discourses on national belonging: The Hungarian minority in Romania. *Romanian Journal of Political Science, 14*(1), 61–86.

Vincze, G. (1999). *Illúziók és csalódások. Fejezetek a romániai magyarság második világháború utáni történetéből*. Csíkszereda: Státus.

Vincze, G. (2003a). Bevezető. In G. Vincze (Ed.), *Történetei kényszerpályák – kisebbségi reálpolitikák II. Dokumentumok a romániai magyar kisebbség történetének tanulmányozásához 1944–1989* (pp. xv–xxviii). Csíkszereda: Pro-Print.

Vincze, G. (2003b). *Történetei kényszerpályák – kisebbségi reálpolitikák II. Dokumentumok a romániai magyar kisebbség történetének tanulmányozásához 1944–1989*. Csíkszereda: Pro-Print.

Vincze, G. (2006). Lăncrănjantól Lăncrănjanig. Fejezet a magyar–román kapcsolatok nyolcvanas évekbeli történetéből. *Magyar Kisebbség, 10*(3–4), 262–352.

Wimmer, A. (2002). *Nationalist exclusion and ethnic conflict: Shadows of modernity*. Cambridge, UK and New York, NY, USA: Cambridge University Press.

Zeidler, M. (2003). A Nemzetek Szövetsége és a magyar kisebbségi petíciók. In N. Bárdi & C. Fedinec (Eds.), *Etnopolitika: A közösségi, magán- és nemzetközi érdekek viszonyrendszere Közép-Európában* (pp. 59–83). Teleki László Alapítvány: Budapest.

3

Unequal Accommodation: An Institutionalist Analysis of Ethnic Claim-Making and Bargaining

Tamás Kiss, Tibor Toró and István Gergő Székely

In this chapter, we rely on the historical institutionalist framework[1] sketched in the introductory chapter, and continue to use a primarily agency-based approach. As already mentioned, it is our belief that minority political agency[2] has two complementary dimensions, namely political claim-making (including electoral politics, bargaining

[1]For methodological and theoretical details, see Hall and Taylor (1996), Thelen (1999), Pierson (2000), Gorenburg (2003), and Stroschein (2012).

[2]As used by Csergő and Regelmann (2017).

T. Kiss (✉) · I. G. Székely
Romanian Institute for Research on National Minorities, Cluj-Napoca, Romania

T. Toró
International Relations and European Studies Department, Sapientia Hungarian University of Transylvania, Cluj-Napoca, Romania

T. Kiss et al. (eds.), *Unequal Accommodation of Minority Rights*, Palgrave Politics of Identity and Citizenship Series,
https://doi.org/10.1007/978-3-319-78893-7_3

between political elites, and minority rights advocacy) and community organizing (building, maintaining, and operating a network of ethnic institutions). This chapter focuses on the political claim-making of Transylvanian Hungarians, pursued primarily through bargaining. However, the relation between the two aspects of minority political agency is also a central topic of the chapter. We argue that during the 1990s, these dimensions were not separated formally. The Democratic Alliance of Hungarians in Romania (RMDSZ)[3] established in January 1990, provided the framework for a wide-scale Hungarian national movement, and aimed to foster a significantly broader spectrum of political participation among Transylvanian Hungarians than mere electoral mobilization or political claim-making. This is why several authors have described RMDSZ as both a social movement and an ethnic party (Szilágyi 1991). Others have argued that one should go beyond the formal programmatic elements of the Transylvanian Hungarian political elites and emphasize that building and broadening an ethnically separate institutional field—crucial for ethnic boundary maintenance—was the most important implicit program of RMDSZ (Biró 1998b; Bakk 2000b; Kántor 2000; Brubaker et al. 2006).[4] As we will demonstrate, however, it was the outcome of a later institutional development that political claim-making and ethnic institution building became institutionalized in separate structures.

The core argument of this chapter is that for most of the post-Communist period, the approach of Romania toward the Hungarian community living on its territory is best described by a model that we call *unequal accommodation.* The following formal-institutional elements are of primary importance for this model: (1) minority organizations are recognized as legitimate representatives of their communities and, consequently, have a monopoly in terms of bargaining over issues that concern their community; (2) no institutional guarantees of power-sharing exist and, consequently, those elements of de facto power-sharing that exist

[3]In Hungarian, Romániai Magyar Demokrata Szövetség; in Romanian Uniunea Democrată Maghiară din România. We use the Hungarian abbreviation.

[4]See Brubaker (2009).

rest only on ad hoc political deals; and (3) at a general level, the state is defined and understood as the state of the titular group, even if ethnic diversity is recognized in various laws and policies.

However, neither the functioning of the Romanian model nor the claim-making strategies of Transylvanian Hungarian elites can be properly understood by only taking into account formal elements. This is why the historical institutionalists' understanding of political agency, as shaped by both formal and informal institutions, will be of central importance in this chapter. Unequal accommodation and asymmetric bargaining rely to a great extent on informal arrangements and deals that are made between the majority and minority elites. It is very telling of the level of informality that the minutes (or any written records) concerning the meetings and discussions between minority and majority elites are usually lacking.[5] As we will see, other constitutive elements shaping the political strategies of the Hungarian political class are the uncertainty of the legal environment and the high level of political particularism (political patronage, clientelism, and pork-barrel politics).

Brubaker's well-known triadic-nexus model (1995, 2000) which focuses on the interrelation between nationalizing states, minority elites, and external homelands is also central to our analysis, but with several restrictions. The above-mentioned entities are conceived by Brubaker as social fields in a Bourdieusian sense.[6] The author argues that their dynamics cannot be properly interpreted without taking into consideration their interrelations too. According to Brubaker's model, more than one power center attempts to exert influence on minority populations (in our case, Transylvanian Hungarians). The first is the nationalizing state. From a Romanian perspective, Transylvanian Hungarians

[5]In the majority of cases, internal RMDSZ meetings are not documented, which also indicates a strong inclination toward informality in the Transylvanian Hungarian political culture.

[6]Bourdieu defines fields as social domains with their own organizing rules. The actors in such fields share a common frame of reference and compete for resources and positions with each other. As for the (always relative) autonomy of different fields, Bourdieu used the metaphor of "prism" and "refraction" (Bourdieu 1993a, p. 164). The question is to what extent an institutional structure is able to transform external influences "*according the specific logic of the field*". See Chapter 5 for a more detailed discussion.

constitute a *national minority* or a *minority ethnic group*,[7] which should be integrated or accommodated. Of the factors shaping ethno-political processes, the Romanian minority policy regime (as institutionalized by the state) is certainly the most important. Minority elites (in our case the Transylvanian Hungarian political class) constitute the second significant power structure that tries to exert influence on the minority population. Contrary to our model of unequal accommodation, Brubaker draws neither an analytical nor a normative distinction between the position of minority elites and majority political actors, as both are characterized as trying to exert their influence on the minority population.[8] However, there is a clear asymmetry between the actors involved, majority actors having the state, with all its means and resources at their disposal, while the tool kit of the minority elites is considerably more limited. The last factor in Brubaker's model is the so-called external homeland, which regards the minority population as part of its politically divided nation, or even as an external diaspora. Brubaker emphasizes that the term diaspora (like the terms ethnic/national minority and self-sufficient political community) constitutes a political claim and a program. Diaspora implies that the primary reference point of the minority population should be its external homeland (Brubaker 2005). Brubaker's model has been revised

[7]In Romania, the terms ethnic group and national minority are used interchangeably in official contexts. For instance, until 2002 the census asked about individuals' "ethnicity", not their "nationality". Further, the Romanian Government has Department of *Interethnic* Relations. However, in parliament, there is a fraction of "*national minorities*". The Romanian Institute for Research on *National Minorities* was established as a governmental body in 2007. Also, several official documents use the term "national minority".

[8]The "ethnicity-without-groups" thesis is of central importance here (Brubaker 2004). Brubaker reinterprets the old distinction between category and group, which he traces back to Marx and Weber and which plays a central role in the sociology of Bourdieu (1991, pp. 229–252) and Jenkins (2008). Categories are created by (powerful) external observers, while members of categories do not necessarily share any sense of belonging to them. On the contrary, groups need an internally shared sense of belonging and solidarity. Brubaker took a rather radical step by suggesting to avoid considering ethnic categories to be groups at all. He argues that by considering ethnic categories groups, we reify the perspective of ethnic elites (ethnic entrepreneurs) who seek to (re)present these entities as mobilized, internally solidary, and ready to act collectively. Brubaker's analytical perspective obviously deconstructs and delegitimizes the position of ethnic elites and treats them (along the majority political actors) as external observers.

(Brubaker 2011) and criticized or further developed by several scholars (e.g., Smith 2002; Pettai 2007; Wolczuk 2010; Cercel 2017). From the perspective of this chapter, the most important addition to the original model is the argument of Smith (2002) that neither nation building nor minority claim-making can be properly understood without taking into account the infusion of transnational organizations and their norms concerning minority rights.

Two additional conditions relating to unequal accommodation can be outlined. First, unequal accommodation works primarily if the influence of kin-state actors on the minority political field is marginal compared to the influence of the minority policy regime of the "host" state and of the minority political actors. In a political regime that relies strongly on political patronage, this means that the resources that become available through bargaining with majority actors are incomparably more significant than the resources obtainable from the kin-state. Otherwise, minority elites would not be interested in adapting and moderating their claims (Jenne 2007). Our argument is that in the period between 1990 and 2014, this condition was fulfilled. However, after 2014, the capacity of RMDSZ to access funds from Romania's budget decreased, while kin-state support substantially increased, leading to a more accentuated influence of Hungary. This is one of the factors that might potentially erode the model of unequal accommodation.

A second important condition is the limited infusion of norms of transnational organizations (Risse 1999, p. 531). Here, the reference to the rule of law is of primary importance. In the framework of unequal accommodation, not only resource allocation but also the implementation of existing legislation becomes a matter of political bargaining. Consequently, increased references to the rule of law and the emergence of alternative techniques of minority rights advocacy (which may also have a transnational dimension) can also erode the model.

The chapter is structured as follows. First, we discuss Romania's minority rights regime, which delineates the room for maneuver of the Hungarian political elites. Furthermore, making use of survey data, we also touch upon the perceptions of the Romanian majority about how legitimate they regard Hungarian ethno-political demands.

The second part of the chapter is dedicated to the institutionally conditioned strategies of claim-making of the Transylvanian Hungarian political class. We argue that claim-making through asymmetric bargaining has become the dominant strategy since 1996, when RMDSZ was co-opted into executive power. We also discuss the relation of asymmetric bargaining to other strategies of claim-making. At the end of the section, we enumerate the factors conducive to the erosion of unequal accommodation and discuss the most important changes in Hungary's kin-state policy. In the third part of the chapter, we present two case studies, to further illustrate the characteristics and limits of unequal accommodation; the first about autonomy claims, and the second about minority language rights advocacy. The chapter ends with an assessment about the chances of the development of a large-scale civic minority rights advocacy movement, which could emerge as a serious alternative or complementary strategy to claim-making based exclusively on political bargaining.

1 The Main Features of the Romanian Minority Policy Regime

In the first part of this long chapter, we describe Romania's policies toward minorities and highlight the ambivalent nature of the system. On the one hand, the legal framework not only tolerates the political articulation of ethnicity, but in certain respects even encourages it; on the other hand, despite the presence of pluralistic elements, the Romanian political actors are rather consensual in their refusal to codify further formal guarantees for the Hungarians, thus interethnic cooperation is based instead on informal deals. We conceptualize this rather ambivalent approach as one of *unequal accommodation*. We further argue that one of the main factors that prevent a further move toward the institutionalization of pluralistic measures is the unfavorable attitudes of the majority population toward various minority rights, which we illustrate with survey data.

1.1 Minority Policy Paradigms Between Integration and Accommodation

One should distinguish between minority policy paradigms and minority policy regimes (Bíró and Pallai 2011, p. 3). On the one hand, *minority policy paradigms* are based on political philosophies that concern the management of ethnic and cultural diversity and might be perceived as coherent sets of principles and tools conducive toward a certain kind of minority policy. On the other hand, *minority policy regime* is a more descriptive term and refers to empirical cases. The latter can be defined as the totality of the legally codified elements and more or less formalized institutional norms concerning minority policy (Rechel 2009). While minority policy paradigms are normatively and logically coherent, minority policy regimes might be quite inconsistent, as they are the result of historical institutional processes shaped by the conflicting interests of the minority and majority elites and international pressure.

Students of ethno-politics often distinguish between accommodationism and integrationism (McGarry et al. 2008; Choudhry 2008). These are distinct (and in many respects, opposing) political philosophies concerning the management of ethnic and cultural diversity. However, as tools for empirical analysis, they can only be used as ideal types in a Weberian sense. This means that empirical cases (minority policy regimes) often combine integrationist and accommodationist elements and can actually be located somewhere between full-blown accommodation and pure integration. Consequently, it is better to conceive of accommodation and integration as a continuum between two ideal types rather than a dichotomy. According to accommodationist arguments, ethnic groups are well-bounded entities, and once ethnic cleavages gain political significance, the chance of the politically active nature of ethnic categories being perpetuated is high. Consequently, they promote institutional-political arrangements that provide opportunities for various groups to publicly express their identities, to protect themselves from the majority, and to be in charge as much as possible of the management of their own community issues.[9] Conversely, integrationists assume that ethnic identities are more flexible and group boundaries are more permeable. Given these circumstances, (politically) activated categories can easily lose their (political) significance, as Chandra aptly put it (2012, p. 12). Additionally, as McGarry et al. (2008) point it out, adherents of the integrationist line of thought regard it as a normative requirement that belonging to "particular" ethnic categories eventually dissolves into a "common" or "supra-ethnic" identity and political culture. Consequently, they argue for political, institutional, and constitutional arrangements that inhibit the political activation of ethnic identities. Furthermore, as they emphasized, integrationism is obviously the mainstream perspective, as supranational structures and international organizations such as the European Commission, the OSCE High Commissioner on National Minorities, the United Nations, the International Monetary Fund, and the World Bank favor integration over accommodation. Kymlicka (2007, 2011) has argued that international organizations in fact have an ambiguous and inconsistent position: they generally support integration, but in response to bloody conflicts usually propose accommodation.

It is not among the tasks of this chapter to provide a detailed historical analysis of the Romanian minority policy regime. Suffice to emphasize that, due to the bargaining process with the Transylvanian Hungarian elites and international pressure, there was a major shift during the late 1990s and early 2000s. The period between 1989 and 1993 can be described as that of the institutionalization of majority nationalism, or of the hegemonic control of the state (Horváth 2002). Romanian political elites were consensual that the state should be reconstructed on the basis of national sovereignty, whereby "the people", following whose will was the underlying principle of democratic legitimacy, should be defined in ethnic and cultural terms, as the Romanian people (Csergő 2007, p. 25; Stroschein 2012). According to this concept, the titular majority "owned" all state institutions

[9]Both of the arguably most influential authors in the field of institutional design for ethnoculturally divided societies, Arend Lijphart (1977) and Donald Horowitz (1991), represent this perspective, despite their diverging opinions about the way in which interethnic cooperation unfolds.

(Wimmer 2002), which were designed to reinforce national reproduction.[10] In this framework, the stress was on strong central governmental control, while regional and minority claims for self-government (or even administrative decentralization) were depicted as challenging state sovereignty (Csergő 2013). During this period, Hungarian elites also (re) defined their community in national terms and demanded institutions and minority rights that would guarantee cultural reproduction and the community's "share of popular sovereignty" (Csergő 2007, p. 25). An ultimate goal of the Hungarian minority elites, thus of RMDSZ, was autonomy or, in other words, recognition of the Hungarian population as a self-sustaining political community.

However, beginning in the 1990s, a process of reconciliation between the Hungarian and Romanian elites also started. The Romanian minority policy regime adopted some pluralistic characteristics, while the representatives of the Hungarian community were co-opted into executive power. Consequently, analysts often argue that Romania has shifted toward a pluralistic (Horváth and Scacco 2001) or accommodationist model (Bíró and Pallai 2011, p. 24). At the turn of the millennium, some analysts even suggested that this shift could be interpreted through the concept of consociational democracy, as proposed by Arend Lijphart,[11] or at least have argued that some form of institutionally defined power-sharing is a possible and desirable future for the Romanian political community.[12] However, the political participation (or the integration into Romanian polity) of Hungarians cannot be adequately interpreted in the framework of consociational democracy or institutionalized power-sharing (Medianu 2002; Székely 2011). The main reason for this is that in Romania the legal or institutional guarantees that are characteristic of consociationalist regimes are absent. Because of this, achievements in resource allocation or representation in

[10]See also the concept of the nationalizing state in Brubaker (1996, pp. 79–106; 2011).

[11]According to Lijphart (1977, p. 106), plural societies have two main distinct features. First, divided societies are organized in distinct segments or pillars (zuilen in Dutch). Second, despite these deep cleavages and the lack of a unitary political culture, political elites behave in an accommodative way.

[12]For a detailed account of this debate, see Székely (2011, pp. 157–168).

public institutions are not connected to legal codification. The inclusion of the Hungarians and the share of public resources they are able to obtain always depend on ad hoc, one-off bargaining (Salat 2003; Bakk et al. 2004; Toró 2013).

1.2 Formal and Informal Rules Governing Minority Policy

Székely and Horváth (2014) offer a comparative characterization of the minority policy regimes in Central and Southeastern Europe. In a similar manner, Horváth and Toró in Chapter 4 position the language policy of Romania in comparison with 16 Central and Eastern European states. The typology outlined by the authors reveals the dual character of Romanian institutional settings and shows that it is difficult to classify Romania's minority policy on the accommodationist–integrationist scale.

1. Relying on the constitutional definition of the Romanian political community (as the source of sovereignty) and the (lack of any) general recognition of cultural diversity, Romania can be characterized as applying a *mono-ethnic* definition of the state (Székely and Horváth 2014, p. 134). According to the Romanian constitution, the source of sovereignty is the Romanian people in an ethnic sense, and the state is designed to protect the culture and the interests of this people. As a consequence, the main characteristic of Romanian institutional order is asymmetry between the categories of minority and majority, which is obviously reproduced in various everyday settings.[13] It should be emphasized that the (quasi-)hegemonic control of the state by the dominant ethnic group is univocally supported by all relevant Romanian political actors. None of the political parties that have entered the Romanian parliament (except for RMDSZ) has ever criticized this setting.

---

[13]As we will see in the last section of this volume, institutional asymmetry has serious demographic consequences. It is the principal factor driving assimilatory processes, and it is among the key factors causing emigration. These institutionalized asymmetries also have a serious impact on the system of ethnic stratification.

2. The Romanian minority policy regime has some pluralistic characteristics, the most important of which concerns minority political representation. Generally speaking, the Romanian institutional and legal order not only tolerates but even facilitates the political representation of ethnic identities; moreover, it does this through the minorities' own ethnic parties. There are several (more or less explicit) provisions in Romanian electoral legislation that support this. The first (indirect) feature is that ethnic parties are not legally banned.[14] A second (also indirect) feature is that there are no provisions that create unfavorable conditions for ethnic parties (most importantly, for RMDSZ). From the perspective of the Hungarian community, the maintenance of the proportional character of the Romanian electoral system is of central importance.[15] The third (explicit) feature is that small-size minorities can obtain preferential seats under quite favorable conditions. This provision, however, is less relevant from the perspective of the nearly one-and-a-half million Transylvanian Hungarians. The fourth (quasi-explicit) favorable feature is the existence of alternative thresholds which were introduced into the electoral laws of 2008[16] and 2015.[17] Although these articles do not make explicit references to minorities, they were obviously designed to benefit RMDSZ (which is the only relatively small party with a territorially concentrated electorate). According to the 2008 Electoral Law, parties that simultaneously obtained a plurality in six constituencies for the Chamber of Deputies and three constituencies for the Senate entered parliament even if they did not meet the five percent national threshold. According to the 2015 Electoral Law, parties

---

[14]Bulgaria, Turkey and, until 2001, Albania are contrasting examples in this respect in the Southeastern European region.

[15]With a Westminster-type electoral system, the political representation of the Hungarian community could be reduced to the Székely Land (an area inhabited overwhelmingly by Hungarians but home only to slightly more than one-third of the Transylvanian Hungarian community).

[16]Law No. 35/2008.

[17]Law No. 208/2015.

obtaining more than 20% of the votes in at least four counties can enter parliament even without passing the five percent national threshold. As a fifth element, the borders of single-member districts in the 2008 and 2012 elections (the only elections during which SMDs existed) were drawn up in a manner that was favorable to RMDSZ: Hungarian speakers constituted a demographic majority in 15 constituencies for the Chamber of Deputies and seven constituencies for the Senate.

Political mobilization through ethnic parties is also sustained by non-legislative elements of the Romanian political system. Two intimately interlinked informal norms governing the political processes should be emphasized: First, Romanian political actors do not target Hungarian voters, and second, they regularly engage in bargaining with minority organizations. It is of central importance that the character of this bargaining is deeply asymmetrical. Majority political actors perceive the Hungarian electorate as a "disciplined" community, whose members follow faithfully the instructions of their political leaders. Under these circumstances, the dominant perception among mainstream parties is that targeting the Hungarian electorate does not pay off.[18] However, this perception is sustained by instrumental considerations too. During the last two decades, RMDSZ has been eager to enter into practically any coalition with majority actors both at national and local levels. The asymmetry of the bargaining process means that the costs of including RMDSZ into governing coalitions (either at the national or at the local level) are considerably lower than in the case of other (majority) political partners. At the national level, the relatively low cost of partnering with RMDSZ is a consequence of its regionally concentrated interests. For example, considering public office or public sector jobs, one can see that RMDSZ is by default directly interested (and able to deliver personnel) only in counties inhabited by Hungarians. Outside

[18]The sole notable exception was Traian Băsescu, president of Romania from 2004 to 2014, who tried to communicate directly with the Hungarian electorate during his campaigns. His attempts were rather successful as the majority of the Hungarians supported Băsescu in the 2009 presidential election and in the two referenda aimed at his dismissal (in 2007 and 2012).

Transylvania, RMDSZ cannot fill the available positions even at the top level (because Hungarian candidates are rarely willing to move to distant parts of the country to occupy such positions, and RMDSZ is unwilling to incorporate ethnic Romanians to overcome this problem). Theoretically, RMDSZ could be compensated with extra positions in counties with a significant share of Hungarians, where no (or less serious) staffing problems would arise. But this does not actually occur, because the asymmetric character of the Romanian political structure does not allow for the underrepresentation of ethnic Romanians in Transylvanian counties (while easily allowing for the underrepresentation of Hungarians both locally and nationwide). Thus, the theoretical maximum RMDSZ can achieve is the proportional representation of Hungarians in Transylvania. In this case, however, RMDSZ ends up (at best) with a share of public offices that mirrors the proportion of Hungarians in the country's population, but not the party's share in the winning coalition. Furthermore, RMDSZ has so far been unable to secure even the proportional representation of Hungarians in practice. This also means that "extra profit" is obtained by the majority participants of the winning coalitions. To conclude, majority parties tolerate the presence of Hungarians in the government or local executive power, but only to a level that is well below their proportion in the winning coalition. Mainstream political parties are not interested in the organizational incorporation of Hungarians either. In regions where Hungarians represent a significant proportion of the population, mainstream parties function mostly as *Romanian ethnic parties* (i.e., parties reserved for local ethnic Romanians). This is most evident in the two Hungarian-majority counties (Harghita/Hargita and Covasna/Kovászna), where in fact all mainstream parties perpetually act as the defenders of the "Romanian minority". In these counties with a Hungarian-majority population, monopolizing the local structures of the mainstream parties and confronting RMDSZ (instead of opening up the mainstream parties toward Hungarians) obviously pays off for the relatively small local Romanian elites. This strategy cannot lead to (local-level) electoral success due to the demographic dominance of Hungarians in these areas, but it secures more resources for the

Romanian elites, primarily through the deconcentrated institutions[19] "*that cannot be entirely handed over to Hungarians*". In the ethnically more balanced counties (like Mureș/Maros and Satu Mare/Szatmár), it is obviously the ethnic cleavage that represents the main organizing principle of local politics. Here, mainstream parties have a good chance of electoral success, yet the relatively high proportion of Hungarians (~38 and ~35%, respectively) remains a continuous threat to them. It is not at all accidental that before the local elections formal or informal negotiations between mainstream parties routinely take place in these counties, and "Romanian grand coalitions" are often formed against RMDSZ. This "Romanian unity" is of course a serious obstacle to opening up the mainstream parties toward Hungarians (Kiss and Székely 2016).

3. Language and educational policies also have some pluralistic characteristics in Romania. However, the asymmetries between the majority and minority categories are encoded in these legislative and policy domains too. Stroschein emphasizes that intensive Hungarian ethnic mobilization in the early 1990s focused in particular on language and educational policy, and, in the context of Euro-Atlantic integration, the Romanian state made important concessions to Hungarians on these issues (Stroschein 2012). With regard to language policies, one should first underscore that–in spite of these concessions—there remained a basic asymmetry in the public use of the Romanian and the minority languages. According to the constitution, Romanian is the sole official language of the country, and no other languages are mentioned as having any kind of special status. However, according to the 215/2001 Law on Local Administration, in local administrative units where a minority reaches proportions of 20%, persons belonging to the minority may use their mother tongue in oral and written communication with the local administration. According to Governmental Ordinance 1206/2001, in

[19]Deconcentrated institutions refer to the county-level offices of the institutions of the central (governmental) administration (as opposed to decentralized institutions, which are subordinated to local- or county-level administrations).

these administrative units, staff who are able to communicate in minority languages should be employed in jobs involving interaction with the public. Furthermore, Romania has ratified the European Charter for Regional or Minority Languages, which creates quite favorable conditions for the use of the Hungarian language in public. However, these legal provisions have been implemented only selectively and have failed to create meaningful and effective bilingualism in local administration. Neither have provisions prescribing the employment of officials competent in minority languages been systematically implemented, nor have any other preconditions of bilingualism (especially written bilingualism) been met (Toró 2017a). Consequently, one may legitimately use Csergő's characterization of the Romanian regime of language policy as language predominance (2007, p. 117).

As for education, Law 1/2011 on National Education is of primary importance. It contains quite favorable provisions concerning minority language education. These provisions, however, also have not been systematically implemented. For instance, in administrative units in which instruction in minority languages is provided in more than one school, at least one separate minority educational institution with an independent legal personality should be created.[20] However, this provision has not been systematically implemented. Another rather notorious example is that of the University of Medicine and Pharmacy of Târgu Mureș/Marosvásárhely, which has been designated a "multicultural and multilingual" university under the law, although Hungarian departments have not been created even seven years after the law entered into force. Chapter 6 on Hungarian-language education also highlights that the lack of decisional competences significantly hinders the abilities of Hungarian elites in educational planning.

The uncertainty of the legal environment should be stressed regarding both linguistic rights and education. Legal provisions that look very nice on paper are not implemented at all, or are only partially

[20]Law No. 1/2011, art. 45(5).

implemented, and this creates severe difficulties and unfavorable conditions for the enforcement of (theoretically existing) minority rights. As we will see, the implementation of legal provisions also becomes part of a process of political bargaining.

1.3 Majority Perceptions of Minority Rights and Claims

Besides the above-discussed ambivalence inherent to the minority policy regime, there is an additional factor hindering the implementation of existing legal provisions—namely, the fact that the vast majority of the Romanian public is unanimous with regard to the minority policy regime. Romanians overwhelmingly support and take for granted the characteristics of the institutional environment that affirm the mono-ethnic nature of the state (or at least the dominance of the titular nation), and reject most characteristics that tend toward ethnic pluralism. From the majoritarian perspective, the politically active nature of the Hungarian ethnic minority is an anomaly. We offer an overview of Romanian public perceptions of Hungarian claims by examining the perceived legitimacy of various types of minority rights/claims from the perspective of the majority, relying on ten surveys representative of the adult population of Romania carried out between 1995 and 2016.[21]

[21]In 1995 and 1996, one of the major polling companies in Romania, the Institute of Marketing and Polls (Institutul de Marketing şi Sondaje, IMAS; http://www.imas-inc.com), conducted quantitative studies concerning ethnic relations in Romania. In 1995, a total of 1376 subjects were interviewed, while in 1996, this number had increased to 1582. The number of ethnic Romanian respondents was 1032 and 1098, respectively (IMAS: Relaţii interetnice în România. Sondaje de opinie 1994–1996. Aprilie 1996). We did not succeed in acquiring the databases; only the research reports were accessible in the archive of the Ethno-cultural Diversity Resource Center (Centrul de Resurse pentru Diversitate Etnoculturală, CRDE, a Cluj-based NGO engaged in promoting inter-cultural peace and justice; http://www.edrc.ro/). The 2000, 2001, and 2002 surveys were part of the Etno barometer project run by CRDE. In 2000, the Research Centre on Interethnic Relations (Centrul de Cercetare a Relatiilor Interetnice or CCRIT, a Cluj-based research center run by the Sociology Department of Babeş-Bolyai University, http://www.ccrit.ro/) was in charge of the fieldwork, while in 2001 and 2002, Metro Media Transilvania (a major public opinion polling company based in Cluj; http://www.mmt.ro/) took over this role. In 2000, a total of 2051 people were interviewed, including 1253 ethnic Romanians. Different subgroups (ethnic

A standard question concerning general perceptions about minority rights in Romania was included in each of the ten surveys. Between 1995 and 2016, the proportion of respondents who felt that "*minorities have too many rights*" increased slightly, while the proportion of those who felt that more effective minority protection measures were needed decreased. A majority of respondents (50–61%) felt that minorities have "*just enough rights*" (Fig. 1).

The 1995, 1996, 2012, 2014, and 2016 surveys contained a similar block of questions regarding the acceptance of various minority rights and ethno-political claims (see Fig. 2). The questions referred specifically to the rights granted to the Hungarian community (and not in general to minority rights).

The majority of the enumerated items belong to the category of minority language rights. The questions referred to the acceptance of the following minority language rights: native-language primary and secondary education ("*Do you support allowing Hungarians to attend primary and secondary schools in which instruction is held in their mother tongue?*"), university education in the vernacular ("*Do you support allowing Hungarians to pursue studies at universities in their mother tongue?*"), separate educational institutions ("*Do you support allowing Hungarians to have separate schools and universities?*"), official use of the Hungarian language ("*Do you support allowing Hungarians to use their mother tongue in public institutions, such as bodies of local government and courts*

Hungarians, and ethnic Romanians living in Hungarian-majority counties) were represented by separate subsamples. In 2001 and 2002, the national representative sample was 800 respondents. Separate subsamples for Roma (600) and Hungarian (600) populations were created, and an additional 200 Transylvanian ethnic Romanians were interviewed. The 2006 survey was carried out by CCRIT and financed by the Department for Interethnic Relations of the Romanian Government. The survey was carried out using a sample representative for Romania of 1170 respondents. In 2008, 2012, 2014, and 2016, the Romanian Institute for Research on National Minorities (Institutul pentru Cercetarea Problemelor Minorităților Naționale, ISPMN, a Cluj-based research institute subsidized by the Romanian Government; www.ispmn.gov.ro) carried out empirical studies concerning the same issue. In 2008, the national sample consisted of 1189 respondents, and a sample of 537 Transylvanian Hungarians was added. In 2012, the size of the national sample was 1200. Transylvanian Hungarians were represented by a separate sample of 1991, and an additional 491 Transylvanian Romanians were interviewed. In 2014, there was a national sample of 1200 and a Transylvanian Hungarian sample of 668 respondents. In 2016, the national sample included 1138 respondents with interviews with an additional 1023 ethnic Hungarians.

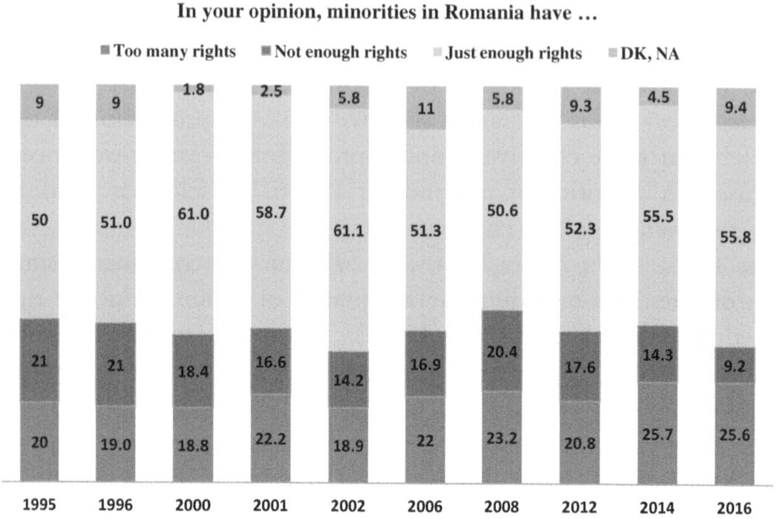

Fig. 1 Attitudes toward minority rights at national level (2000–2014) (*Source* Surveys by IMAS (1995, 1996), CCRIT (2000, 2006), MetroMedia Transilvania (Etno barometer 2001, 2002), and Romanian Institute for Research on National Minorties (2008, 2012, 2014, 2016))

of justice?"), and Hungarian-language TV programs on state-financed channels ("*Do you support allowing TV programs targeting Hungarians to be produced by state-financed channels?*"). As already mentioned, the law regulating the use of minority languages in local administration was passed in 2001, hence, in 1995 and 1996 the official use of Hungarian had not yet been legally codified, and, accordingly, only Romanian could be used in official settings. Another question referred to the acceptance of Hungarian claims for territorial autonomy ("*Would you support granting Hungarians autonomy in regions in which they constitute a majority?*"). This refers to more than minority language rights; it implies the recognition of the Hungarian community as a distinct and autonomous political entity, a situation rather distant from the present Romanian legal-institutional order.[22] This question was asked only in the 2014 and 2016 surveys. Another item of the 2012, 2014, and 2016

[22]For a useful typology of minority rights/claims, see Bauböck (2007).

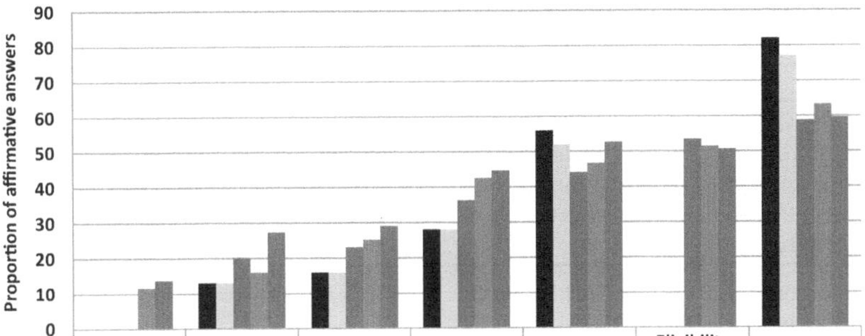

	Territorial autonomy	Official use of Hungarian	Separate schools	Native language university	Native language education	Eligibility for election to public office	H. public broadcastin g
1995		13	16	28	56		82
1996		13	16	28	52		77
2012		20	23	36	44	54	59
2014	12	16	25	43	47	52	63
2016	14	27	29	45	53	51	60

Fig. 2 Acceptance of granting various rights to Hungarians among ethnic Romanians (proportion of affirmative/positive answers) (*Source* Surveys by IMAS (1995, 1996) and Romanian Institute for Research on National Minorties (2012, 2014, 2016))

surveys concerned the eligibility of ethnic Hungarians for elected public offices ("*Do you agree that Hungarians should be eligible for elected public offices, such as mayor or deputy in the Romanian Parliament?*"). Responses to this question offer a way of gauging the general acceptance of the principle of equality among citizens. The acceptance of eligibility for elected public office could be considered an integrationist minimum and taken for granted as a foundational element of any democratic institutional order.[23]

There were also items referring to various minority rights/claims in 2000, 2001, 2002, and 2006 surveys. As seen in Table 1, questions concerning Hungarian-language education and autonomy are not directly comparable with the items discussed above; however, they

[23]In this sense, it is situated outside (or below) the typology of minority policy regimes elaborated by McGarry et al. (2008) or minority rights by Bauböck (2007).

Table 1 Acceptance of Hungarian-language education and territorial autonomy among ethnic Romanians (2000–2006)

	2000	2001	2002	2006
The Romanian state should provide Hungarian-language education at all levels	42.6	31.6	51.6[a]	47.3[a]
Hungarians should have a larger degree of autonomy in counties where they constitute a majority	–	20.4	19.1	18.6

Source Surveys by CCRIT (2000, 2006) and MetroMedia Transilvania Etnobarometer (2001, 2002)

[a]In 2002 and 2006, the wording of this item was different: "The Romanian state should provide native-language education for Hungarian children"

could be useful for indicating general trends regarding the acceptance of Hungarian minority claims.

The first obvious conclusion is that the degree of acceptance of the various existing rights and further claims is quite low. A vast majority of Romanians not only perceive autonomy as an illegitimate claim (in 2016, barely 14% accepted this claim), but also consider existing minority language rights to be illegitimate privileges. Around half of respondents believe that it is not appropriate that Hungarians are educated in their mother tongue. Only one-third of Romanians can accept Hungarian-language education at the tertiary level, and only 13–27% the use of Hungarian in official settings. The widespread rejection of minority language rights hinders considerably the implementation of legal provisions concerning this issue. Acceptance of public broadcasting in Hungarian is the highest (approximately two-thirds of ethnic Romanians agree with this). We should also add that nearly one-half of the Romanian respondents did not accept the eligibility of Hungarians for election as mayor or deputy, thereby highlighting the popular support for (a quite hegemonic version of) the dominant ethnic model of governance.

The second conclusion is that there is no linear trend concerning the acceptance of minority rights. In the case of Hungarian-language public broadcasting (i.e., minority language education), acceptance has decreased compared to the mid-1990s. In the case of Hungarian-language university education and separate schools, there has been an increase in the degree of acceptance. Acceptance of autonomist claims has also declined. One may highlight that the expectation was widespread that the repeated governmental participation of the Hungarian minority would increase the acceptance of minority rights/claims among the Romanian majority (Horváth and Lazăr 2001; Veres 2008; Salat 2011). Survey results, however, do not support this interpretation/narrative. Romanian public opinion has not become increasingly tolerant or moderate toward Hungarian ethno-political claims or minority language rights.

1.4 Placing Romania in Typologies of Minority Policies

The year 1989 represented a major juncture in the Romanian minority policy regime. Following the collapse of state socialism, spectacular mobilization and self-organization of the Hungarian community occurred and, importantly, the Romanian state and Romanian political actors recognized minority organizations as legitimate representatives of their communities. During the 1990s and 2000s, Romania moved toward a more pluralistic approach concerning language and educational policies. One should emphasize, however, that this shift can be perceived as a rather pragmatic response to minority demands coupled with external pressure in the context of the pursuit of Euro-Atlantic integration (Bíró and Pallai 2011, p. 25). Majority elites did not reconstruct their approach and philosophy toward the management of cultural differences and did not renounce their claims for exclusive ownership over the state structures. Neither a law granting decisional competences for minorities over their institutional system (cultural autonomy) nor any legally codified form of ethnic power-sharing was adopted by the parliament. Existing elements of de facto power-sharing and even the implementation of legislation in force is highly politicized and depends on ad hoc processes of bargaining.

Several authors have tried to place Romania's minority policies in existing typologies. The starting point of Bíró and Pallai was the accommodationist–integrationist scale (2011, pp. 24–26). They argued that Romania has moved toward the accommodation of minority rights, even if in a very cautious and inconclusive way. They concluded that in fact three minority policy paradigms could be distinguished (namely integration, constitutional accommodation, and political accommodation). The integrationist perspective has been characterized earlier. Constitutional accommodation is similar to consociationalism, where the segmental autonomy of the minority and ethnic power-sharing are legally codified. By political accommodation, the authors mean that some sort of de facto power-sharing is present, but without legal and institutional guarantees. Consequently, the accommodation of minority rights is not inherent in the institutional and legal structure but depends on the actual bargaining power of the minority organizations. The authors characterize Romania as a paradigmatic case of *political accommodation.*

Medianu (2002) and Horváth (2002) used as points of reference the theoretical models of hegemonic control on the one hand, and consociation or institutionalized power-sharing on the other. Hegemonic control is characteristic of the so-called ethnic democracies,[24] where the dominant group maintains exclusive control over the state. The authors argued that the "*Romanian model of inter-ethnic relations*"[25] is neither hegemonic control nor institutionalized power-sharing; instead, they propose calling it *control through co-optation.* Through this expression, the authors emphasize the central importance of the co-optation of the Hungarian elites into executive power. The notion implies that elements of de facto power-sharing are instituted for practical reasons, with the aim of neutralizing or at least moderating Hungarian ethno-political claims without having to compromise the national character of the state (i.e., without having to give up the basically exclusive control of ethnic Romanians over it).

In our opinion, both terms—political accommodation and control through co-optation—are appropriate. However, we use a third one,

---

[24]See Smooha (2001), who refers to Israel as a paradigmatic case of ethnic democracy. The Eastern European examples close to this ideal type are Estonia and Latvia (Järve 2000; Melvin 2000).

[25]The "Romanian model of inter-ethnic relations" was an expression prevalent at the turn of the millennium in Romanian public discourse. See, for example, Nastasă and Salat (2000), a volume sponsored by USAID about the "Romanian model" of interethnic peace and stability.

namely that of the *unequal accommodation* of minority rights. Through this, we would like to emphasize the asymmetric relations between the minority and majority. It is also worth highlighting the dual character of the Romanian minority rights regime: on the one hand, the privileges of the titular category are deeply anchored in the legal and institutional order, while on the other, this order expressly supports the political representation of ethnic identities and in practice allows for a high degree of ethnic parallelism. This duality also defines the conditions of the integration of Transylvanian Hungarians in Romanian polity. Due to characteristics favoring ethnic parties, RMDSZ has managed to maintain a monopoly over the resources set aside for the Hungarian community. However, in the absence of legally codified forms of ethnic power-sharing, the main Hungarian ethnic party functions in a deeply asymmetric relationship to majority political actors, and this institutional setting has also hampered the emergence of political pluralism inside the Hungarian community (see Székely 2014).

2 Strategies and Periods of Minority Political Claim-Making

In the previous section dedicated to the Romanian minority policy regime, we emphasized the significance of unequal accommodation, which emerged as a model of minority policy during the 1990s. Here, we deal with the other side of the coin and characterize unequal accommodation as a strategy deployed by the minority elites. Through a discussion of the history of RMDSZ, we show how this model gained prominence in the second half of the 1990s also in the political thinking of the Hungarian political class,[26] although alternative strategies have been present during the entire period under investigation (with varying significance). We describe how the interiorization

[26]By this term, we mean the professionalized part of the Hungarian political elite, which can be differentiated from the broader stratum of intellectuals and activists, who are busy mostly with operating and developing the Hungarian institutional network and to a lesser extent with political claim-making.

of this model by the top leadership of RMDSZ, which also implied increased reliance on resource-based legitimation (instead of policy or programmatic issues) exacerbated the tensions present from the very beginning within the Hungarian political movement, leading to the emergence of a series of alternative Hungarian political organizations backed by Hungary's right-wing Fidesz party. However, a number of more recent developments seem to signal that the model of unequal accommodation is crumbling. We also discuss these more recent tendencies, most importantly the reconfiguration of the relationship between the Hungarian political actors of Transylvania and those of Hungary (including the naturalization and enfranchisement of the Hungarian minorities) and the increasing marginalization of RMDSZ in the Romanian polity.

As one can see in Table 2, at the parliamentary elections held since the regime change of 1989–1990, the overwhelming majority of Hungarians

Table 2 Results of Hungarian political competitors at the elections for Romania's parliament, president and the European Parliament (1990–2016)

			Chamber of Deputies / European Parliament			**Senate**			**President (1st round)**		
Election	**Turn out**	**Electoral competitor**	**Votes**	**%**	**Seats**	**Votes**	**%**	**Seats**	**Candidate**	**votes**	**%**
1990 (May 20)	86,19 %	RMDSZ	991,583	7.23	29	1,004,353	7.2	12	No Hungarian candidate		
		Independent Hungarian Party	2,578	0.02	0						
1992 (September 27)	76,29 %	RMDSZ	811,290	7.46	27	831,469	7.58	12	No Hungarian candidate		
1996 (November 3)	76,01 %	RMDSZ	812,628	6.64	25	837,760	6.82	11	György Frunda	761,411	6.02
		Hungarian Free Democratic Party of Romania	14,333	0.12	0	12,103	0.10	0			
		Independent candidates	2,356	0.02	0						
		Forum of Székely Youth	2,142	0.02	0						
2000 (November 26)	65.31 %	RMDSZ	736,863	6.80	27	751,310	6.90	12	György Frunda	696,989	6.22
		Hungarian Free Democratic Party of Romania	3,510	0.03	0	498	<0.01	0			
2004 (November 28)	58.51 %	RMDSZ	628,125	6.17	22	637,109	6.23	10	Béla Markó	533,446	5.10
		MPSZ candidates on People's Action Party lists[a]	10,374	0.10	0	10,509	0.10	0			

Table 2 (continued)

			Chamber of Deputies / European Parliament			Senate			President (1st round)		
Election	Turn out	Electoral competitor	Votes	%	Seats	Votes	%	Seats	Candidate	votes	%
2007 (November 25)	29.47 %	RMDSZ	282,929	5.52	2						
		László Tőkés (independent)	176,533	3.44	1						
2008 (November 30)	39.20 %	RMDSZ	425,008	6.17	22	440,449	6.39	9			
		Independent candidates[b]	13,650	0.20	0	9,003	0.12	0			
		Candidates on Green Ecologist Party lists[c]				6,372	0.09	0			
2009 (June 7)	27.67 %	RMDSZ (with László Tőkés on the list)	431,739	8.92	3						
2009 (November 22)	54.37 %	RMDSZ							Hunor Kelemen	372,761	3.83
2012 (December 9)	41.76 %	RMDSZ	380,656	5.14	18	388,372	5.25	9			
		EMNP	47,955	0.67	0	58,754	0.79	0			
2014 (May 25)	32.44 %	RMDSZ	350,689	6.29	2						
2014 (November 2)	53.17 %	RMDSZ							Hunor Kelemen	329,727	3.47
		EMNP							Zsolt Szilágyi	53,146	0.56
2016 (December 11)	39.42 %	RMDSZ (with MPP candidates on the lists)	435,969	6.18	21	440,409	6.24	9			

[a]In several counties with a significant Hungarian population (Harghita, Covasna, Mureş, Satu Mare, Sălaj) the People's Action Party ceded its lists to candidates of the Hungarian Civic Alliance (Magyar Polgári Szövetség), as the latter failed to register as a political party
[b]Some of these candidates were endorsed by the Hungarian Civic Party (Magyar Polgári Párt), which did not field candidates of its own
[c]In Harghita county
Source Central Electoral Bureau

have supported an ethnic party, namely RMDSZ. Mainstream parties have never been able to successfully appeal to ethnic Hungarian voters, and despite the appearance of intra-ethnic challengers—some of them even relatively successful at second-order elections (local, for the European Parliament) in the late 2000s—RMDSZ was able to keep its quasi-hegemonic position within the Hungarian electorate. Although the absolute number of votes obtained by RMDSZ has decreased quite significantly over the years, this occurred in the context of a general decline of electoral turnout in Romania. Consequently, according to our estimates, the proportion of RMDSZ voters among ethnic Hungarians who have turned out to vote has never fallen below 80% at parliamentary elections.[27] Romanian political analysts and pundits also frequently emphasize that RMDSZ has been the most stable actor in the Romanian party system since 1989 (surpassing all mainstream parties in this respect). This stability of the electoral fortunes of RMDSZ is also the main reason why the periodization that will be presented below is framed with reference to the history of this political organization.

However, beyond this apparent stability, very significant changes occurred in the past two decades. A core aspect of these developments has been discussed by Kiss and Székely (2016), who argued that the nature of the linkages between RMDSZ and its voters has undergone a gradual, yet significant shift from programmatic toward clientelistic exchanges. Our goal in this chapter is to place these changes into a broader context.

In what follows, we present a periodization and a typology of the strategies of minority interest representation and claim-making employed by the Transylvanian Hungarian political class. These two dimensions are the major tools of our analysis. Table 3 summarizes our model.

Our periodization and typology were designed to facilitate the understanding of relations between these strategies which were shaped by the institutional context—most importantly by the Romanian minority policy regime, but also by Hungary's kin-state policy and the international regime of minority and human rights protection.

1. *The model of informal-individual bargaining* is a strategy inherited from the Communist period when formal channels of ethnic claim-making were absent. Under these circumstances, "Hungarian interests" could be vindicated only by making use of personal positions

[27]This is not true regarding local elections. In the ethnically compact Hungarian-majority Székely Land region, RMDSZ had to face much stronger intra-ethnic challenges from other Hungarian ethnic parties and independent (Hungarian) candidates. It not true with regard to elections to the European Parliament either, which we will discuss briefly in a subsequent section.

Table 3 Periods and strategies of Hungarian political claim-making after 1989

Periods		Strategies (institutionalized forms) of minority interest representation			
		Informal-individual bargaining	Constitutional accommodation	Unequal accommodation (asymmetric bargaining)	Minority rights advocacy
1990–1992	Establishment of organizational structures of ethnic politics	Significant, inherited by former regime	Implicit, then explicit claim	Absent	Present and significant
1993–1996	Elaboration of model of self-determination	Decreasing significance	Dominant claim at programmatic level, but no realistic strategy for achieving it; does not shape actual political processes	Emerging as a dominant framework	
1997–2003	Governmental participation	Sporadically present		Predominant	Practically absent
2004–2014	Intra-ethnic competition			Dominant	
2014–	Erosion of unequal accommodation model			Dominant but of reduced significance due to the lack of resource allocation capacities	Sporadically present

in the power structure and through the interpersonal networks of ethnic Hungarians who held important offices in the party state. However, the political habitus (used in the Bourdieusian sense)[28] developed in the institutional context of the former regime survived the regime change. RMDSZ leaders (especially those well-embedded in the former power structures of the party state) have frequently attempted to "solve" certain issues through their personal connections and networks and have claimed legitimacy through delivering these results to the community (Domokos 1996, pp. 149–150, 277–280). Obviously, this strategy is only able to work with regard to concrete goals and problems—e.g., the restitution of schools or real estate, the financing of organizations, the establishment of Hungarian-language schools, and so on.

2. The model of *constitutional accommodation* has been the most important goal of RMDSZ at the declarative/programmatic level throughout the entire period that has elapsed since the regime change. At the core of these claims is a pursuit of collective rights and political autonomy for the Hungarian community. During the 1990s, many proponents of this model believed that this objective could be attained through the "internationalization of the Hungarian problem"; that is, by petitioning the international community. Consequently, strong emphasis was put on international claim-making. As we will see, autonomy remained a central programmatic element throughout the entire period. However, constitutional accommodation has not been achieved and, as one of our case studies will illustrate, autonomy claims actually have become performative acts, with no real strategy to achieve them.

[28]Bourdieu conceptualized habitus as "a system of dispositions acquired by implicit or explicit learning which functions as a system of generative schemes, generates strategies which can be objectively consistent with the objective interests of their authors without having been expressly designed to that end" (1993b, p. 76). The habitus of the actors and their positions acquired in the political field are interrelated. On the one hand, some positions need a certain set of dispositions, on the other hand actors and their dispositions can be shaped by the positions they find themselves in. All in all, the relationship between the two—habitus and position—will shape the space of possibilities of each actor within the field (Bourdieu 1993a, pp. 63–64).

3. The model of *unequal accommodation* was discussed in detail in the previous section that dealt with the Romanian minority policy regime. The starting point of this strategy was that Romanian political actors recognized RMDSZ as the legitimate representative of "Hungarian interests". Consequently, within the Hungarian community RMDSZ (or more precisely, its top leadership) gained a monopoly in the process of bargaining with Romanian political actors. Compared to the model of individual-informal bargaining, this implied both centralization and formalization of the bargaining process. However, compared to constitutional accommodation, the lack of institutional guarantees of ethnic power-sharing is a defining feature. Governmental participation has become a central element of this a strategy, as this was perceived as the most effective tool of increasing the political bargaining power of the minority organization. In this sense, governmental participation was perceived and presented by RMDSZ leaders as a non-ideological means of claim-making, justified by the need to look for Romanian partners irrespective of their "ideological color" or membership in international party families. They also formulated the principle of "equal distance" toward Romanian political parties.[29] However, these features would only have been functional in a more formalized ethnic power-sharing setting, in which ethnic relations have a clear institutional framework and depend less on everyday political relations. Consequently, in the actual Romanian political context (where bargaining for minority claims in many cases implies supporting measures that have heavy partisan loading in the Romanian party system), "depolitization" and "equal distances" could not be developed into a coherent framework.

4. *Minority rights advocacy* is a strategy connected to the infusion of norms and techniques of human rights protection. In this framework, international human and minority rights treaties are used as a point of

[29]These ideas were most clearly emphasized by Béla Markó, president of RMDSZ between 1993 and 2011, in an article about the post-1996 period of Transylvanian Hungarian politics (Markó 2009).

reference. The Framework Convention for the Protection of National Minorities and the European Charter for Regional or Minority Languages should be mentioned here. These treaties were ratified by Romania in 1995 and 2007, respectively. Without entering into detail, their implementation is backed by a complex system of monitoring, and references to the treaties and connections to the monitoring system are central elements of minority rights advocacy. Norm infusion requires an adequate framing compatible with the language used by international NGOs (Keck and Sikkink 1999; Merry 2006), and those engaged in this strategy should be able to "talk the talk" of human rights protection. Assistance from kin-state actors can also significantly boost the efficacy of this strategy, and (especially after EU accession), minority advocacy actors received support from Hungary. Besides transnational connections, the existence of local-level ("grassroots") NGOs is crucial to this strategy, which should pressure authorities to change minority legislation or (even more importantly) to implement the existing legal framework.

The main reason for the waning of this strategy after 1996 was that it is actually at odds with the model of unequal accommodation. The opportunities for political actors involved in claim-making through bargaining to pursue this strategy are rather limited, because if they are part of the establishment (they participate in power), then advocating internationally against the policies of that establishment would not only amount to inconsistent behavior but would also decrease credibility. As we will see, more recently there has been some resurgence in minority rights advocacy, as a number of NGOs independent of RMDSZ have emerged, but the strategy is still present among Transylvanian Hungarians only sporadically.

2.1 Establishing the Organizational Structures of Ethnic Politics (1990–1992)

The political organization of the Transylvanian Hungarians began right after the regime change. Many observers perceived the organizational capacity of this minority as rather unexpected, given the assimilationist and nationalizing policies of the Ceaușescu period in the 1970s and 1980s. As discussed in Chapter 2, during state socialism Hungarian elites lacked the organizational structures through which explicit political claim-making could have been possible. Another important tendency was the shrinking of Hungarian institutional networks (schools, cultural institutions, and mass media) and of the possibilities for using the Hungarian language.

In this spectacular mobilization, both structures established by the elites and spontaneous actions of the masses played important roles. The organizational structures of ethnic politics have been established relatively early. During the first weeks following December 1989, the major question was whether Hungarians should organize themselves independently or if they should act within the framework of the National Salvation Front (*Frontul Salvării Naționale*). This was a kind of interim executive power structure with local branches throughout the country and even in larger factories and institutions with a large number of employees (such as hospitals and schools). Parallel to the FSN, Hungarian local initiative groups also formed in Transylvanian cities as early as December 1989, of which RMDSZ emerged officially on January 7, 1990, based on a manifesto issued by Hungarian intellectuals in Bucharest on December 25, 1989. It is important to emphasize that ordinary people played a crucial role in the mass mobilization of Hungarians in the early 1990s. Based on an event analysis of several protests in Cluj/Kolozsvár, Miercurea Ciuc/Csíkszereda and Târgu Mureș/Marosvásárhely (including the bloody interethnic clash in the latter town in March 16–21, 1990),[30] Sherrill Stroschein (2012) concluded that it was ordinary people (students and workers) and not political leaders who played a crucial role in these actions. They mobilized themselves primarily along issues of education in the vernacular and Hungarian-language use, which were significantly restricted during the 1970s and 1980s. The political elites were less active in terms of mass mobilization

[30]On this, see Stroschein (2012, pp. 94–121) and László and Novák (2012).

but played a significant role in the ultimate framing of the events and eventually also in the demobilization of the masses (Stroschein 2012, p. 24). Consequently, the process of mobilization of the early 1990s is best interpreted through a more balanced approach that takes into account the impact of both elite actors and the masses. These considerations seem to contrast sharply with the so-called instrumentalist arguments, according to which nationalist mobilization is elite driven.[31]

As is it characteristic of societies transitioning from authoritarianism to democracy, in the period following the regime change formal institutions of political interest formation were absent in Romania. However, in Romania, the lack of such institutionalized channels was striking even in an Eastern European comparison. In many Eastern European countries (Bulgaria, Czechoslovakia, Hungary, Eastern Germany, and Poland), this role was played by the so-called Round Table Talks between the regime and its opposition during the late 1980s (Bozóki 2002). Under such circumstances, it is less surprising that in Romania, the regime change and the period that followed it were characterized by mass mobilization, mass protests, and even violence. On the one hand, mass mobilization occurred along class lines; the social movement of the Jiu Valley miners led to one of the most virulent protests in post-Communist Eastern Europe (Vasi 2004). On the other hand, Stroschein has argued that due to the lack of formal channels of political claim-making, the ethnic separation of the polity also took place in a rather informal and spontaneous way (2012, pp. 4–15). In this process, extra-institutional means of political claim-making and mass protest played a pivotal role.

RMDSZ quickly institutionalized and developed organizationally in the first part of 1990. Its first congress was held in Oradea/Nagyvárad between April 21–23, 1990, where two main issues of general relevance and far-reaching consequences were debated. The first one was the location of the RMDSZ headquarters, which was connected to a more general debate concerning the positioning of RMDSZ in the Romanian political field. The first option was to locate the headquarters in Cluj/

[31]See Gorenburg (2003) and Vermeersch (2011) for a different approach to ethnic mobilization.

Kolozsvár, which would have meant a pronounced Transylvanian identity and emphasis on community organizing. The second option was Bucharest, which would have signaled the intention to integrate into the Romanian polity. The issue was solved through a compromise: the presidency of RMDSZ was established in Bucharest, but the secretariat general started its operations in Cluj/Kolozsvár. The second dilemma referred to the relation toward the Communist regime. The question was whether former cadres of the party state should be allowed to hold positions in RMDSZ. Generally speaking, cultural elites played a crucial role in the creation of RMDSZ. However, some of them participated in the shrinking organizational structures of the Hungarian minority during the former regime, while others tried to define themselves outside or even in opposition to these institutional structures. One should emphasize that the dissident movement was relatively weak among Transylvanian Hungarians (and in Romania in general), and activities outside of official organizational structures mainly involved only the maintenance of isolated informal networks (though some of these had connections to the dissident movements of Hungary). The opposition between former dissidents and former allies of the party state came to the fore with regard to the election of the president of RMDSZ, too. One of the main candidates, Géza Domokos, used to be a substitute member of the Central Committee of the Romanian Communist Party. Other personalities whose names were circulated for the presidency were the pastor László Tőkés, who became a symbol of the resistance during the events in Timișoara/Temesvár in December 1989, and the former dissident Géza Szőcs. Domokos commanded a relatively reliable network and his support was incontestable among the local cultural intellectuals, who represented the main body of the nascent RMDSZ. Consequently, he became the president of the organization, while Szőcs was elected as executive president and Tőkés become the honorary president of RMDSZ.

RMDSZ remained quite polarized during the whole period along both organizational and programmatic issues. The Cluj/Kolozsvár-based General Secretariat was dominated by Szőcs, while Domokos, who was based in Bucharest, could rely on the parliamentary group and was obviously far better embedded into the Romanian political class than any other actor from the minority political field. The related programmatic conflict can be summarized as follows: Szőcs advocated a politics of "passive resistance" which rejected bargaining with Romanian political actors and urged an internationalization of claim-making and minority rights advocacy. Domokos emphasized that there was no alternative to cooperation with Romanian political actors. He had close relations with the Democratic National Salvation Front (*Frontul Democrat al Salvării Naționale*), which splintered from the abovementioned National Salvation Front led by Ion Iliescu. The faction led by Domokos also argued that more "radical" ways of ethnic claim-making and minority rights advocacy could lead to bloody conflicts akin to those that erupted in the Western Balkans.[32]

The process of bargaining sustained by Domokos was not formalized and relied exclusively on the personal relations of Domokos and other leaders of RMDSZ. In the absence of formal political agreements between RMDSZ and the majority parties, Hungarian leaders who were in the position to do so engaged in "procurement" affairs, often without any authorization from the official leadership of RMDSZ. Based on these factors, we classify the period between 1990 and 1992 as being dominated by the conflict between a strategy of informal-individual bargaining and one based on internationalized minority rights advocacy.

2.2 The Model of "Self-determination" (1993–1996)

The period between 1993 and 1996 saw rather important but not necessarily unidirectional developments. Most importantly, the radicalizing explicit programmatic goals of RMDSZ (with autonomy and the model of "self-determination" at the forefront) and actual political strategies became increasingly detached from each other, marking the beginning of the model of unequal accommodation.

The third congress of RMDSZ, held on January 15–17, 1993, in Brașov/Brassó, was important not only because it elected Béla Markó as

[32]See Domokos (1991). The article sparked heavy debates among the Transylvanian Hungarian political elite and intelligentsia at the time.

president (who remained in this position for 18 years) but also because crucial programmatic and organizational changes were adopted. The election of Markó resolved the conflict between the Domokos and Szőcs wings, as both factions agreed on his presidency. At the programmatic level, the elaboration of the so-called model of "self-determination" was of central importance.[33] The model had two important pillars. The first one was the central place of autonomy and collective rights in the claims of RMDSZ. Earlier, the so-called autonomists (or "radicals", as they were called by the Romanian-language press) repeatedly criticized the Domokos-wing for their politics based on consensus-oriented bargaining with the majority actors. In 1991, as a result of their activity, RMDSZ formulated a document entitled the Cluj Declaration (*Kolozsvári Kiáltvány*), which specified autonomy and internal self-determination as the main objectives of the organization. The 1993 congress went even further and adopted a new autonomist program.

The second element was a new organizational structure, which has been described since then by analysts as the "state in the state" (Biró 1998a, pp. 44–49), "self-government" (Bakk 2000a, pp. 21–25; Tőkés 1999, p. 55), and "auto-determination" (Bakk et al. 2004) model. The designers of the model thought that RMDSZ should serve as the framework for self-determination until the Romanian state officially recognized the autonomy of the community. According to that concept, this organizational structure should have functioned simultaneously as a framework for Hungarian ethno-civil society and as a political party. The organizational bodies of RMDSZ deliberately imitated the structure of states, with a president, a specialized governing body (the Executive Presidency) and a parliament-like assembly (the Council of Deputies). Internal elections were at the very heart of the concept. The Council of Deputies should have been directly elected by all ethnic Hungarians in theory, and the so-called platforms (i. e., RMDSZ factions organized around political ideologies) should have run in the elections. The model was adopted by congress; however, it has never been fully implemented and internal elections have never been held.

[33]See, for a detailed presentation, Toró (2016, pp. 87–90).

The significance of the model of self-determination cannot be understood properly by taking into account only the programmatic issues and the moderate-radical debate. The first step toward a better understanding is to reiterate the central element of our concept of minority political agency, namely the duality of the objectives of community organizing (i.e., building and operating a system of ethnic institutions) and political claim-making. One of the major questions was how to deal organizationally with this duality. During the first years after 1989, RMDSZ was a movement-like organization: It actually provided the frame for the reaffirmation of Hungarian national identity and aimed to promote the significantly broader spectrum of political participation of the Transylvanian Hungarians than mere electoral mobilization or political claim-making. RMDSZ did not even define itself as a political party, and analysts also described RMDSZ as an organization fulfilling several functions or roles during the first half of the 1990s. For instance, Szilágyi (1991) discussed RMDSZ the *social movement* alongside RMDSZ the *political party*. Reference to the social movement implied community organizing and constructing the ethno-civil society. Reference to political party suggested politics in a narrower sense.

However, as already highlighted, the relation between these two dimensions was not devoid of tension between 1990 and 1993. We have already discussed these tensions in terms of programmatic disagreements: those who advocated negotiations with the majority political actors favored more moderate (and thus more attainable) policy targets, while those who prioritized the development of ethnic institutions (and implicitly, the central function of the latter; namely boundary maintenance[34]) supported a more intransigent position. But from an institutionalist perspective, these issues did not simply boil down to a matter of the program, because the actors coalescing in the two factions had to act in totally different institutional environments. Those interested in community organizing acted in local societies and were interested in the creation and maintenance of ethnically bounded institutions. Those representing the community in the Romanian polity acted in a different

[34]See the Introduction of the volume, Chapters 5 and 12.

institutional setting, dominated by majority actors. It is not accidental that these differences have led to different habituses, and different worldviews.[35]

These institutionally conditioned differences are quite relevant, and one might argue that such constellations are very likely to appear in *pillarized* societies.[36] Lijphart (1977) says little about the internal political organization and internal debates of the social pillars. However, the accommodative behavior and moderation of political elites are the major cornerstone of his theory of consociationalism. It also seems that the split between top leaders (engaged in bargaining with elites of other segments) and the subelite level of activists (engaged in organizing the institutional network that sustains the former pillar) is of central importance to him. Tsebelis (1990) has provided a more elaborate theory about this feature, conceptualizing the situation as a nested game in which the elites of societal segments must balance between two major principles. First, in the arena of interethnic bargaining, they have to maintain a cooperative relationship with the political leaders of the rival segments. Second, in the intra-ethnic electoral arena, they must retain the support of their *followers*, who (if the social segment they claim to represent is really encapsulated) may hold a more intransigent position. It is of primary importance what Lijphart writes about such "followers":

> The term 'follower' here does not refer primarily to the mass public, which tends to be rather passive and apolitical almost everywhere and therefore does not present a great danger to the possibilities of elite accommodation, but refers more specifically to the middle-level group that can be described as sub-elite political activists. (Lijphart 1977, p. 53)

In our reading, it is actually the changing relations between the wider stratum of "sub-elite activists" who were involved more directly in the building and maintenance of ethnic institutions on the one hand and political leadership on the other that is the most interesting feature of

[35]See Hall and Taylor (1996) and Thelen (1999) for accounts on the impact of the institutional environment on political agency.

[36]This problem is analyzed in Chapters 1 and 5.

the political history of Transylvanian Hungarians. The so-called model of "self-determination" was in fact an attempt to institutionalize this relation in a manner in which subelite activists (or representatives of ethno-civil society) would have exercised some kind of control over the political leadership.

Nevertheless, the model of unequal accommodation may also be traced back to this period. This was connected to the start of a more centralized and formalized process of bargaining between majority actors and RMDSZ leadership. Through this, Romanian political actors recognized RMDSZ leadership as the only legitimate representative of the minority community. Obviously, this process required moderation on both sides.

Several factors contributed to the initiation of such a bargaining process. Probably the most important was pressure exerted by international actors, which persuaded the Romanian political elite about the necessity of negotiating with RMDSZ. Given the context of the Yugoslav wars and the disintegration of the Soviet Union, the question of Transylvanian Hungarians seemed to be an issue of *security policy* for the international community. The first serious attempt to facilitate negotiations between the Romanian government and RMDSZ occurred in July 1993, in the context of Romania's accession to the Council of Europe (Horváth 2002, pp. 33–36). The negotiations were organized by an NGO specialized in elite-level interethnic dialogue, *Project on Ethnic Relations* (sponsored by the US government), while RMDSZ was represented by leaders belonging (by that time) to the second echelon. The event resulted in a jointly signed recommendation for improving interethnic relations in Romania, which, however, ultimately failed to be implemented. A direct consequence of this endeavor was the so-called Neptun-gate scandal (named after the seaside resort where the meetings took place), one of the most serious confrontations inside RMDSZ. The essence of the Neptun affair was this: after the fact of the negotiations became common knowledge, a large majority of RMDSZ deputies condemned the politicians who had participated in the meetings and issued a declaration which stated that the negotiators lacked a mandate to act in the name of the party.

It is important to note that the actual process of accommodation through bargaining took shape not only in the context of programmatic "radicalization", but also in the context of the attempts of community activists (at the time with a majority inside the organization) to establish institutionalized control over the top leadership. As discussed in the introductory chapter, the problem of minority accommodation was addressed almost exclusively through the security-driven understanding of transnational organizations, and this perspective dominated the scientific literature too (e.g., Chandra 2005; Birnir 2007; Alonso and Ruiz-Rufino 2007; Cederman et al. 2009). However, there is another important consideration, namely that of accountability. Although for space considerations, we are unable to deal with the electoral behavior of Transylvanian Hungarians in detail, the main feature of this remains a block vote for ethnic parties, primarily RMDSZ.[37] This is quite understandable, given that in the actual institutional environment minority voters cannot expect mainstream majority political parties to advocate minority interests. Consequently, they either vote for the dominant ethnic party or abstain from voting. If ethnic block voting were to become habitual (Kiss et al. 2017), it would be illusive (or hypocritical) to link accountability with the electoral process. Without proper institutionalized mechanisms of intra-organizational control, ethnic leaders gain strong entitlement to manage political processes without actually being accountable.[38]

2.3 Governmental Participation and Its Consequences (1997–2003)

The model of unequal accommodation was the dominant strategy of minority interest representation between 1997 and 2003. The most important moment occurred in 1996, when—following the electoral

[37]For explanatory accounts of the voting behavior of Transylvanian Hungarians, see Székely (2014), Kiss and Székely (2016), Kiss (2017a), and Kiss et al. (2017).

[38]Csigó (2016) argues that the lack of intra-party democracy and meso-level institutions for bridging the gap between civil society and politics are more general problems in Eastern Europe.

victory of the center-right opposition coalition—RMDSZ joined the new government. According to Horváth, the propensity of the center-right parties to coalesce with RMDSZ did not stem from a deliberate strategy to defuse interethnic tensions, but rather reflected tactical concerns (such as securing the support of Hungarian voters for the second round of the presidential elections) (2002, p. 45). Nonetheless, the desire to impress the international community was probably the decisive factor. International actors (primarily the OSCE High Commissioner on National Minorities) also played a key role in keeping RMDSZ within the governmental coalition between 1996 and 2000 (Horváth 2002, p. 47). After 2000, RMDSZ was almost continuously part of the governing coalitions or supported them in parliament,[39] in spite of the softening of international pressure on Romania.

From the perspective of our study, it is of primary importance that RMDSZ has undergone significant changes since it became a regular partner in governmental coalitions. The most obvious manifestation of this is the moderation of RMDSZ, or more precisely, its shift toward more *accommodative behavior* in relation to Romanian political actors. In what follows, we outline the major changes in RMDSZ's political agency and in the structure of the Transylvanian political field; changes which were connected to the institutionalization of the asymmetric bargaining model. Some of these processes should be considered the unintended consequences of RMDSZ's entering into government.

2.3.1 Programmatic Moderation and the Split Between "Radicals" and "Moderates"

The first consequence of the shift toward unequal accommodation was programmatic and rhetorical moderation. Demands for autonomy were pushed into the background, even if only temporarily. This became obvious as early as the 1996 electoral campaign when RMDSZ fielded a candidate of its own for Romania's presidency in the person of György

---

[39]RMDSZ provided parliamentary support to the government between 2000 and 2004 and was part of governing coalitions between 2004 and 2008, 2010 and 2012, and most of 2014.

Frunda. In the 2000 electoral program of RMDSZ, there were no references at all to autonomy. Content analysis of the parliamentary speeches of RMDSZ deputies highlighted that they used a wide array of discursive strategies to advance their claims, such as the de-ethnicization of issues, the argument of useful contribution to the general development of Romania, or that of referring to territorially rather than ethnically defined constituencies. It seems that the strategy of de-ethnicization in debates regarded as important to the Hungarian community was an important characteristic of the bargaining process, which was perceived to help representatives achieve their goals.[40]

This accommodative political strategy, and especially the explicit programmatic moderation pursued by the central leadership, deepened divisions within RMDSZ. The so-called moderates (who were busy with governmental and administrative work and controlled the resources that could be channeled to the community) succeeded in consolidating their majority within the organization. In the meantime, the "radicals" (who advocated a more intransigent position and wished to define clear conditions for the participation of RMDSZ in power) accused the former of excluding a considerable part of the organization from decision-making. However, RMDSZ remained intact between 1997 and 2003, and such debates remained inside its organizational framework.

2.3.2 The "Professionalization" of the Political Class: The Split Between the Party Leadership and Minority Activists

As a second consequence, the split between the two forms of minority political agency and the distance between the political leadership and community activists has deepened. From our institutionalist perspective, this split is far more important than that which occurred between "radicals" and "moderates". Throughout this volume, we perceive minority political agency as having two core components, namely political claim-making and community organizing. In the framework of

[40]See Toró (2017b) for a detailed analysis.

unequal bargaining, RMDSZ prioritized the *parliamentary arena* and the (often covert) negotiations with majority political actors. In this context, the main aim of RMDSZ became governmental participation, and the main legitimizing principle (toward the Hungarian community) was the allocation of public resources to Hungarian institutions and regions populated by Hungarians. This shift toward a strategy reliant on bargaining with majority political actors was legitimized by the arguments of RMDSZ president Markó, who stated that "*the problems of Hungarians in Romania can be solved only in Romania through governmental action*" (i.e., by means of law and state power, through political compromise with majority political actors). This shift in political strategy was interrelated with a gradual change of party elites. As shown by Biró (1998b), intellectuals who worked in cultural domains (some of whom had played a mediating role between the Hungarian community and the party-state structures during state socialism) occupied dominant positions in the first half of the 1990s. However, this group of intellectuals gradually lost ground to economic, entrepreneurial interest groups. Indirectly, the change of party elites further contributed to the erosion of a habitus consistent with community organizing and movement-type political action.

However, we would like to emphasize that the erosion of a habitus (and legitimizing principle) focused on community organizing and building/operating a parallel Minority Society did not mean that RMDSZ ceased to initiate programs aimed at improving or broadening the Hungarian institutional network. Our main argument is that an essential split occurred within the formally integrated Hungarian national movement between the emerging (or more euphemistically, "professionalizing") *political class* and the broader stratum of intellectuals and activists in charge of operating and developing the Hungarian institutional network. This split came about primarily because of the growing importance of the *parliamentary arena* and bargaining with Romanian political leaders. Negotiations between RMDSZ and Romanian parties routinely take place at the top level (several dozen politicians are involved at most) while the broader stratum of political and community activists is squeezed out of the ongoing political processes.

2.3.3 Political Patronage

The split between the political class and the subelite level of community activists was also connected to a change in the nature of linkages between the political class and its electorate. In this respect, it is of central importance that analysts like Aldrich (1995) and Kitschelt (2001) have stressed that parties not only elaborate political programs, but also establish an organizational infrastructure to mobilize voters. In modern electoral politics, these two aspects are of equal significance in establishing linkages between parties and their electorate. This approach redirects the focus of research onto political particularism; namely pork barrel, political patronage, and clientelistic exchanges between parties and their electorate (for a typology, see Kopecký and Scherlis 2008). The hypothesis in this literature that ethnic parties are inclined toward political particularism is well supported (Fearon 1999; Kitschelt 2001; Chandra 2004; Posner 2005; Laitin and Van der Veen 2012).

In the early 1990s the Hungarian national movement was organized primarily around programmatic or policy issues and less around resource-related considerations. One of the reasons for this was a climate generally hostile toward Hungarians, the Romanian governing parties being reluctant to allow Hungarians to access power and state resources for fear of losing votes. It seems that under the circumstances of unequal accommodation, material incentives became crucial in maintaining the stability of linkages between RMDSZ and its electorate. In fact, the most substantial element and legitimizing principle of the model of political representation implemented by RMDSZ has rested on the targeted allocation of public funds and public sector jobs. Given the geographical concentration of Hungarians, lobbying for better infrastructure in Hungarian-populated areas has also become a straightforward goal of RMDSZ.

We would like to note that we do not think that political patronage is an intrinsic characteristic of ethnic parties (or of certain parties); rather, we regard it as characteristic of the entire political regime (or of some segments of the political field). In this respect, Chandra's (2004) term "patronage democracy" is of central importance. According to this author, patronage democracies have several characteristics in common.

First, the state is the main formal employer (or one of the main employers), and there is interlocking between the political field and the economy (for instance, state institutions are important contractors for economic actors). Second, elected officials have significant space for maneuver in the implementation of policy decisions and the allocation of public funds. Under these circumstances, there is an increasing likelihood that political particularism and the desire to obtain direct material benefits will motivate voters in their electoral choices. In Chandra's formulation, benefits utilized both personally (jobs, social benefits, etc.) and collectively (roads, schools, sewerage, and other infrastructural investments)—obtained in exchange for electoral support—come under the label political patronage. According to Chandra, in patronage democracies voting behavior becomes more instrumental (expressive motivations lose ground), but voters are poorly informed regarding political programs and in fact find this type of information to be quite inutile. What is of key importance is policy implementation. The main questions are who implements the policy and whether the interests of particular groups will be hurt during the implementation. According to Chandra, under the circumstances of patronage democracy, people prefer candidates of their own ethnic background. However, not all ethnic parties succeed but only those that have the chance to gain office and to provide material benefits to their followers. Otherwise, such parties will fail, irrespective of their ethnic appeal. In other words, success depends on three factors: (1) ethnic demography; (2) the monopoly of the party concerning representation of the group under investigation; and (3) access to public funds. If the ethnically defined segment of the electorate is not large enough, or the candidate does not have access to state resources, voters will act strategically and support another candidate (even of another ethnic background) who is able to fulfill expectations concerning political patronage.

Two considerations are essential to understanding the significance of political patronage in the Romanian minority policy regime. The first is that in Romania political patronage is quite widespread (Volintiru 2012). The second is that political patronage networks in Transylvania are to a great extent ethnically segmented. The bargaining monopoly of RMDSZ also means that RMDSZ has a quasi-monopoly on the allocation of funds to Hungarian cultural institutions and Hungarian-inhabited settlements. In this respect, local administrations are of key importance. Romania moved toward a more decentralized administrative structure in the pre-accession period (1999–2007) and, according to analysts, this decentralization also reconfigured networks of political patronage. Mayors of major cities and county council presidents emerged as important actors as they have obtained a central role in coordinating local-level political actors; the latter are able to lobby for investments through county-level actors. We highlight that, under these circumstances, RMDSZ obtained broader opportunities in the Hungarian-majority area (in Harghita/Hargita and Covasna/Kovászna counties) where it dominated both the local administrations and the county councils. However, in the ethnically mixed counties (Mureș/Maros, Satu-Mare/Szatmár, Bihor/Bihar, Sălaj/Szilágy, and Cluj/Kolozs), the ethnic segmentation of patronage networks occurred, with Hungarian mayors and local elites lobbying through RMDSZ for public funds.

2.3.4 Lack of Minority Rights Advocacy

As a consequence of unequal accommodation, RMDSZ practically renounced alternative ways of claim-making, most importantly regarding minority rights advocacy in internal and international fora. Several main conclusions from the literature concerning the infusion of human rights norms should be discussed here in more detail. First, as many scholars have argued, effective policy change in human rights can be achieved only if the norm-violating state is simultaneously pressured from "above" and from "below": by international organizations and transnational advocacy networks on the one hand, and by local NGOs and domestic actors on the other (Risse-Kappen et al. 1999; Keck and Sikkink 1999). In other words, norm infusion depends on cooperation between networks of domestic and transnational actors which put the norm-violating state on the international agenda, adding to pressure for it to comply. This has been called the "boomerang effect" by some authors (Keck and Sikkink 1999), and the "spiral model" by others

(Risse 1999). By applying pressure on the state, transnational advocacy networks push the state toward accepting human rights. Domestic actors (with the ongoing help of the international community) also play a central role: They should be engaged in a deliberative process that pushes states to make policy changes first, and implement these later. An interconnected conclusion is related to "framing": In finding transnational partners, domestic civil actors need to articulate their causes in a language compatible with human rights which is understood and accepted by the international community (Keck and Sikkink 1999; Merry 2006). In other words, international organizations or members of the international community will become involved only if a certain kind of discourse is employed—that of the rule of law and human rights. The strategy outlined above is considered to be successful mostly because states (1) do not like to be in the spotlight of international criticism, (2) in many cases are vulnerable to international coercion, and (3) adopt the beliefs and behavioral patterns of the international organizations or treaties they are part of. Furthermore, many authors believe that even if state engagement is instrumental at first, by opening the door to human rights the former will ultimately change to respect them (Risse-Kappen et al. 1999; Goodman and Jinks 2004).

Unequal accommodation has clearly hindered the development of minority rights advocacy among Transylvanian Hungarians. At the internal level, few Hungarian NGOs are independent of RMDSZ. This is the result of the path-dependent evolution of the Hungarian institutional system on the one hand, and of the requirements of asymmetric bargaining on the other. As mentioned already, RMDSZ has become both the representative political organization of Hungarians and the organizer of a parallel "ethno-civil" society. From a practical standpoint, this means that in the early periods of institutionalization, a large number of NGOs were created by people linked to RMDSZ, with the objective of creating and strengthening the parallel Minority Society and maintaining the boundary between Hungarians and the national majority.[41] Of course, this did not mean that all NGOs were controlled

---

[41]See Chapter 5 for details.

by RMDSZ; there was often natural cooperation and symbiosis between the ethnic party and those organizations that were interested in minority rights and institution building.

Governmental participation even strengthened the control of RMDSZ over Hungarian NGOs. Through receiving state funds and controlling many financial resources,[42] RMDSZ started supporting NGOs, creating a relationship of dependency (or patronage) with them. Unequal bargaining also required unity, and RMDSZ ideology called upon Hungarian NGOs and civil organizations to rally around the flag. As Béla Markó pointed out, "*parliamentary politics can be successful only if we all say black or we all say white. By seeing one and a half million Hungarians behind us, Romanian political actors can be forced to solve our problems*" (Markó 2008). In other words, RMDSZ expected Hungarian organizations and institutions to support its endeavors and to refrain from focusing on issues that are politically salient, leaving them to negotiate resolutions. This type of attitude is particularly salient when advocacy NGOs criticize the politics of RMDSZ with regard to claim-making and policy resolution in the domain of language rights. For instance, in April 2017 at the initiation of RMDSZ, the law regulating the staffing of healthcare institutions was modified, binding hospitals and nursing homes to hire minority language-speaking staff (CD 2017). This was framed by the political elite as having solved the issue of language rights in the domain of health care. The Advocacy Group for Freedom of Identity (AGFI), an independent NGO consisting of lawyers, drew the attention of the public to the fact that the issue of minority language usage in hospitals is far from being resolved with the new legislation, as institutions can comply with the law by merely employing a single person who speaks some Hungarian (Szabó 2017). RMDSZ dismissed these "accusations" and called for "collaboration and unity", and for "helping each other with our initiatives" instead of "pointing a finger and setting back each other's

[42]RMDSZ regularly announces calls for grants for NGOs through the Communitas Foundation, but it can also control the flow of resources meant for NGOs from the Department of Interethnic Relations and many local councils.

actions" (RMDSZ 2017). To sum up, the relationship of RMDSZ with Hungarian NGOs is asymmetric. RMDSZ is interested in demobilizing NGO and civil activity to increase its bargaining power in coalition talks. This is achieved on the one hand by controlling these organizations through financial support or personal connections, while on the other hand, the few independent NGOs are pressured and marginalized through invocation of the importance of unity and collaboration.

The use of international human rights treaties, strategic litigation, and reference to rule of law which would guarantee "argumentative consistency" (Risse 1999) are almost completely absent from the claim-making repertoire of the Transylvanian Hungarians. As pointed out, most NGOs that could pursue legal action are linked to RMDSZ, which is not interested in the legal resolution of cases, or in shifting the discourse to an excessively technical level. This leads to discursive incompatibility with international advocacy networks and international treaty monitoring bodies. In many cases, the discursive action of RMDSZ is balanced between the language of human rights protection and its own legitimizing and mobilizing discourse. Thus, the more technical language of minority rights advocacy is matched with symbolic and political reasoning. This influences both the selection of cases and the rhetoric of the argumentation. The chosen cases are symbolically and politically saturated. For instance, in the past few years, a local Romanian NGO started to attack Hungarian-majority local governments in court, asking them to take down the Székely flag. Although the legal underpinning of these cases is not clear, and the problem is marginal in terms of advocacy (but central from a symbolic perspective), RMDSZ initiated extensive political maneuvers to "protect the flags", and even negotiated a law that would allow the flag to be flown. Another problem is that the objective of the chosen discourse is not primarily to efficiently find solutions but vote maximization and self-legitimation. Demonstrative of this perspective is the speech delivered by Erika Benkő, a future member of the Romanian parliament, at the 2016 UN Forum on Minority Issues, which happened to coincide with the parliamentary electoral campaign in Romania. The candidate for parliament argued that "the Hungarian community is constantly being attacked by the Romanian authorities" and "the commonalities of the community are nationalized, community leaders are persecuted because they use their national symbols, schools are closed down, school principals are investigated by the anti-corruption prosecutor's office just because they have re-established a historical high-school" (RMDSZ 2016). This rather apocalyptic speech was obviously out of place and dissonant at a forum dedicated to "Minorities in situations of humanitarian crisis". Compared to the countries that many of the minorities represented at the Forum came from, Romania clearly can be considered a working democracy with a strong human rights framework. We will return to the shortcomings resulting from the lack of minority rights advocacy and the limits of asymmetric bargaining through two parallel case studies in a separate subchapter.

2.4 Intra-ethnic Competition (2004–2014)

The period between 1997 and 2003 might be perceived as a "golden age" of unequal accommodation. After 2003, however, several factors considerably weakened the bargaining potential of RMDSZ. These tendencies will be discussed in the next section. Here, we address the most obvious factor with the potential to weaken the bargaining potential of any dominant ethnic party, namely intra-ethnic competition.

As already mentioned, "moderates" immersed in governmental administrative work have consolidated their position and gained a clear majority inside the organization, while "radicals" have become increasingly marginalized. The symbolic moment of the intra-ethnic split occurred on February 10, 2003, when László Tőkés and his allies—coalesced into the Reform Platform—left the Alliance. Tőkés was dismissed from the position of honorary president of RMDSZ, while he and his allies established the Hungarian National Council of Transylvania (EMNT[43]). The Székely National Council (SZNT), another autonomist organization, was also formed in 2003. According to their constitutive acts, EMNT and SZNT were not political parties but movements

[43]In Hungarian, Erdélyi Magyar Nemzeti Tanács; in Romanian, Consiliul Național Maghiar din Transilvania.

aimed at the realization of autonomy. However, the initiative clearly marked the beginning of intra-ethnic political competition. The second important moment was that of the 2007 European parliamentary elections, when Tőkés, once a charismatic leader and perceived as the hero of the Timișoara/Temesvár events of December 1989, ran as an independent candidate and won an EP seat with approximately 36% of the votes cast by Hungarians. Although RMDSZ also entered the EP and obtained two seats, the results shocked the leadership of RMDSZ, while Tőkés emerged as a strong challenger.

Subsequently, two intra-ethnic challenger parties were registered; namely the Hungarian Civic Party (MPP[44]) in 2008, and the Hungarian People's Party of Transylvania (EMNP[45]) in 2011. However, as one can see in Table 2, neither MPP nor EMNP was able to reproduce the results of Tőkés, which were evidently connected to his personal charisma.[46] MPP obtained relatively good results in the 2008 local elections in the Székely region; however, it did not succeed in winning the seats of the president of the councils of the two Hungarian-majority counties or the mayoral offices of the county seats. EMNP was the sole Hungarian party that ran in the parliamentary elections against RMDSZ. This happened in 2012, but without considerable success. RMDSZ entered parliament with 5.1% of valid votes, while EMNP received only 0.7%. EMNP also fielded a candidate in the 2014 presidential election who obtained 0.6% of all valid votes, while the RMDSZ candidate received 3.5%. Although MPP and EMNP are still active currently, we believe that intra-ethnic electoral competition was most salient between 2004 and 2014. However, RMDSZ maintained its dominance even during this period. After 2014, it is less meaningful to speak about internal political competition, since MPP reached an agreement with RMDSZ

[44]In Hungarian, Magyar Polgári Párt; in Romanian, Partidul Civic Maghiar.

[45]In Hungarian, Erdélyi Magyar Néppárt; in Romanian, Partidul Popular Maghiar din Transilvania.

[46]See Kiss et al. (2017) for a more detailed analysis of voter motivations and links between Hungarian elites and their constituency.

for the 2016 parliamentary elections and accepted several positions on RMDSZ's list, while EMNP did not field candidates.

The central question concerning intra-ethnic competition is how RMDSZ succeeded in maintaining its intra-ethnic dominance in spite of emerging competition. In this context, one cannot avoid addressing the ethnic outbidding model (Horowitz 1985; Rabushka and Shepsle 1972), which postulates that the presence of multiple ethnic parties is detrimental to stability, as it leads to a spiral of increasingly radical claims. At first glance, the Transylvanian Hungarian political arena seems to be an ideal setting for ethnic outbidding. RMDSZ moderated its claims and this resulted in an intra-ethnic political split. The challenger groups tried to position themselves as the authentic representatives of the initial autonomist program of the Transylvanian Hungarian national movement.

Analysts have outlined several explanations of why outbidding was not successful. First, Stroschein argued that in the case of the Hungarians of Romania, "outbidding is more likely to be a luxury of enclave regions" (2011, p. 189). Ethnic outbidding and the competitor parties were more successful at the local level, in municipalities where due to their high proportions, Hungarians were not constrained to act unitarily. At the national level, it would be too hazardous for Transylvanian Hungarians to vote for organizations other than the dominant ethnic party. It should be noted that Stroschein speaks about "outbidding", but in fact her dependent variable only captures the success of a challenger ethnic party (regardless of the intensity of its claims), not the success of an outbidding challenger, as her study does not contain arguments about why a challenger may succeed on a more radical platform—it only concludes that intra-ethnic competition is more likely to occur in areas where it does not endanger the representation of the minority.

Second, one should emphasize that RMDSZ adopted quite different strategies to communicate its programmatic moderation between 1996 and 2003 (when there was no intra-ethnic competition) and after 2004 (when intra-ethnic competition appeared) (Kiss 2015). During the first period, the dominant coping strategy was the formal adaptation of ethnic claims to political "realities". Later (around 2004), under the circumstances of emerging intra-ethnic competition, an alternative strategy based on dual discourse emerged. In other words, a split occurred between formal programmatic elements and the actual agenda of political negotiations with Romanian political partners. This means that while autonomy was reinserted as a central element of the political program and the internal political rhetoric of RMDSZ, no real strategy was associated with it concerning implementation. Formal programmatic elements, however, have little relevance in shaping the political strategy of RMDSZ. This situation raises also relevant theoretical questions. The shift from the formal programmatic moderation of ethnic claims to a dual rhetoric was caused by the emergence of intra-ethnic competition, and the situation is rather similar to that described by Mitchell et al. (2009) in Northern Ireland when Sinn Féin and the Democratic Unionist Party engaged in pragmatic bargaining, while still delivering intransigent messages toward their own electorate. They labeled this behavior—consisting of a dual strategy of radicalizing electoral messages and a rather pragmatic stance toward external political partners—*ethnic tribune politics*. We discuss the claims and "struggle" for autonomy of Transylvanian Hungarians as a case study in the next subchapter.

Third, accounting for shifts toward more radical or moderate programmatic goals is not always sufficient for understanding changes in intra-ethnic political dynamics (Kiss and Székely 2016; Kiss 2017a). A more complex model is needed, where next to the ethno-political programs (offered to identity voters), clientelistic exchanges and pork barrel politics are also taken into account. It is evident that this is the domain in which RMDSZ has clearly surpassed its intra-ethnic competitors (EMNP and MPP). Transylvanian Hungarians believed that RMDSZ was able to bargain with Romanian politicians and to attract state funds for Hungarian-inhabited regions, while few of them attributed the same ability to MPP or EMNP. Otherwise, in the eyes of Hungarian voters, ethnic bargaining is not necessarily at odds with an intransigent position regarding the "interests of the Hungarian community". This is well illustrated by the fact that in spite of the importance of pork barrel politics, voters appreciate representatives who "*represent the interests of the Hungarian community firmly, without compromise*" or who "*are concerned primarily with the problems of the Hungarian community*". It is important that MPP and EMNP did not succeed in surpassing RMDSZ in this dimension either.

Fourth, Székely (2014) proposed the use of the model of nested games provided by Tsebelis (1990). Tsebelis argued that elites in consociational models (or more precisely, in pillarized societies)[47] are simultaneously engaged in games in two different arenas: in the parliamentary (and governmental) arena, and in the electoral arena. The payoff for the elites in the nested game is a combination of the payoffs from the two arenas. The parliamentary game is nested within the electoral game; that is, what happens inside the latter segment has a more significant impact on how the elites behave in bargaining than the other way around. Inversely, capacities to mobilize voters may depend on the results of games within the parliamentary arena. In the case of Transylvanian Hungarian elites, three nested games should be analyzed simultaneously. The first is the parliamentary arena in Bucharest, the second the electoral battles, and the third the kin-state policy enacted by Hungary. From this perspective, what is crucial is that the two smaller parties were only very loosely integrated into the Romanian political field. They practically lacked Romanian political contacts and, consequently, were not perceived by the Hungarian electorate as having serious bargaining power. They could rely only on resources provided by political actors from Hungary, as they were also unable to obtain control of a significant number of local governments. However, their position also used to be ambivalent in this dimension. They were favored (and in certain respect, created) by Viktor Orbán's Fidesz. However, Orbán and his right-wing party did not have a stable and well-defined strategy of favoring certain actors. Various factions within Fidesz acted as patrons for both MPP and EMNP.[48] Additionally, in 2013 a process of rapprochement began between Fidesz and RMDSZ.

[47] In the model, it is not the consociational arrangement per se that is important, but the fact that ethnic boundaries are relatively rigid and politically salient and, consequently, voting across ethnic lines is absent (or not significant).

[48] MPP was supported by László Kövér, EMNP by Zsolt Németh.

2.5 The Erosion of Unequal Accommodation? (2014–)

In the introduction to this chapter, we listed several factors that might be conducive to the erosion of the asymmetric accommodation model. Some of these factors were present during the previous periods as well. However, some of them reached a critical level after 2014; consequently, we believe that an erosion of the model of unequal accommodation is likely (although not certain).

The first important factor is the changes in the international political environment. The transnational institutional and political context of Europeanization has favored unequal accommodation. The Lund Recommendations on the Effective Participation of National Minorities in Public Life (OSCE-HCNM 1999) explicitly called for the inclusion of minority representatives into the executive power (but without urging institutionalized power-sharing). As already mentioned, transnational actors played a crucial role in initiating a process of bargaining between RMDSZ and Romanian political actors in the early 1990s, as well as in keeping RMDSZ within the governmental coalition between 1996 and 2000. However, the pressure of transnational actors on national governments in Eastern Europe to bargain with minority organizations or to include them into executive power decreased during the 2000s. This was connected to a general shift toward a more integrationist approach and discourses stressing the norms of non-discrimination and individual rights, while emphasizing the dangers of empowering minority groups and that such empowerment strengthens ethnic boundaries and leads to permanent institutional segregation (see OSCE-HCNM 2012; or Csergő and Regelmann 2017 on this matter). Issues that cannot be communicated in the language of individual rights cannot be successfully put on the agenda of transnational organizations. As discussed earlier, Hungarian political actors did not succeed in properly framing their claims in the terminology of international actors and putting them into the international arena. From this perspective, one might argue that the Hungarian elites immersed in asymmetric bargaining have undermined their own capacities for claim-making.

Second, the whole model of asymmetric bargaining relies strongly on a combination of the high level of political particularism and an uncertain legal environment. We have already emphasized both the prominent role of pork barrel politics and political patronage in the functioning of such informal and ad hoc arrangements of ethnic power-sharing, and the fact that the implementation of existing legal provisions can also be conditional on political bargaining. Moreover, the Hungarian political class was socialized to attain legal implementation through particularistic arrangements. The case studies included in the following subchapter will discuss two cases connected to the implementation of legislation on language use. However, the process of property restitution might also be mentioned. The case of Székely Mikó High School (Székely Mikó Kollégium) in Sfântu Gheorghe/Sepsiszentgyörgy is relatively well-known to those familiar with the Transylvanian Hungarian case or politics in Romania. The building hosting the school was returned to the Reformed Church in 2002. In October 2012, two of the three members of the Restitution Committee (Attila Markó and Tamás Marosán) were sentenced to three years in prison, while the third member (Silviu Clim) received a suspended sentence of three years. Subsequently, RMDSZ ran a communication campaign conveying the message that the National Anticorruption Directorate (DNA) and the court of justice were politically motivated and were planning to stop or reverse the process of restitution of church properties. This may be true. More important than this from our perspective, however, the case is illustrative of the fact that in a political context increasingly dominated by the fight against corruption, the "usual" tools of asymmetric bargaining (pork barrel politics and particularistic deals concerning legal implementation) are no longer available. DNA and anti-corruption rhetoric have criminalized the particularistic functioning of the Romanian political system and it is not clear yet whether Romania will continue to be a patronage democracy or not. In this framework, the model of the unequal accommodation of minority claims might prove to be the "collateral damage" of the anti-corruption campaign.

Third, as already mentioned, an important precondition of the functioning of asymmetric bargaining is the relatively marginal influence on kin-state actors in the minority political field. In a system strongly based on political patronage, this requires that the funds available through bargaining with majority political actors surpass those offered by the kin-state. Between 1990 and 2014, this was arguably the case. However, more recently several factors have increased the power of kin-state actors to influence the political process among Transylvanian Hungarians. It is these factors to which we turn in the next section.

2.6 Hungary's Kin-State Influence and the Model of Unequal Accommodation

Hungary's kin-state behavior is particularly extensively researched (Csergő and Goldgeier 2006; Kántor 2014; Pogonyi 2017; Waterbury 2010); consequently, it is beyond the scope of this chapter and of our volume to provide a detailed analysis of Hungarian kin-state policies.

Naturally, kin-state policies and their influence on the ethnic kin can be approached from numerous theoretical perspectives and at several levels. Here, we are not interested in the security dimension, which is one of the most often employed theoretical frameworks and in which too assertive kin-states are mostly viewed with suspicion, as destabilizing actors (Jenne 2007; Saideman and Ayres 2008). Our main interest lies in the relation of the kin-state actors to the model of unequal accommodation and on their strategies for influencing the political processes within the Transylvanian Hungarian political field. To this purpose, we will carry out a comparative assessment of the alternative patronage networks available in the host- and the kin-state.

Of the interrelated, yet analytically distinguishable aspects of Hungary's kin-state policies the first concerns leverage over the minority political field and the interethnic political processes in the neighboring countries. The second aspect entails the financial support provided for the institutional system of ethnic kin communities. The third dimension is the extension of the political community of the kin-state toward ethnic kin living beyond the borders through citizenship and enfranchisement policies, which are equivalent to "virtual" national reunification (Csergő and Goldgeier 2004).

With regard to the impact of kin-state behavior on the bargaining between minority actors and their host states' governments, Jenne has argued that the former will radicalize their claims when they perceive firm support from the kin-state, and this may bring about repression from the host state's government, leading to a state of conflict; conversely, if the minority knows that it lacks external support, it is likely to accommodate to the majority, even if the majority is repressive (2007, pp. 38–49). This is to some extent similar to our argument, as we will show that strong kin-state involvement is incompatible with the model of unequal accommodation. However, according to our account, more assertive kin-state behavior is not necessarily coupled with more radical minority claims, and as yet, it has not led to repression by the Romanian state either. While such an outcome cannot be excluded, we believe that alternative scenarios are also plausible, for instance, a gradual detachment of the Hungarian community from the Romanian polity and an implicit "meeting" of the interest of the two states with regard to the situation of the Hungarian community. While Hungary may increasingly regard Transylvanian Hungarians as a political resource (see Waterbury 2010), the incentives of Romania to modify its minority policy regime toward a more pluralistic arrangement and resource allocation for Hungarian community objectives may also dwindle on the justification that those are catered for from other sources.

Kin-state policy has been a divisive issue in Hungary during the last three decades. Disagreements have been connected to rival national discourses and to the fact that the political camps did not agree on how the Hungarian political community should be redefined. We do not want to enter into details about these political struggles; suffice it to say that while right-wing parties have been interested in "virtual" national reunification, to use Csergő and Goldgeier's (2004) phrase, liberals on the left have been attracted to a rather pure form of civic nationalism, namely constitutional patriotism, modeled on German ideas.[49] The clashes connected to the so-called Status Law in 2001[50] and to the possibility of

[49]The term "constitutional patriotism" has its roots in post-World War II German political philosophy and was elaborated by authors such as Jaspers, Sternberger, and Habermas. These philosophers argued against the so-called normalization of German national identity (implying a return to its form preceding the Nazi regime). Instead of this, they fostered a new (post-national and post-ethnic) form of identity rooted in supportive relations with democratic institutions and critical publicity.

[50]The law was evaluated and criticized by the Council of Europe's Venice Commission (2001) and was cited by influential scholars of citizenship as a form of ethnic quasi-citizenship (Liebich 2009, p. 39) or even as one of the most important developments toward the re-ethnicization of the citizenship regimes in Europe (Joppke 2005, p. 245). For a collection of different perspectives, see Kántor et al. (2004).

Table 4 Applicants for simplified naturalization by first citizenship by October 2017

First citizenship	Number of applicants	% of the country's Hungarian population
Romanian	535,492	41.9
Serbian	171,063	67.6
Ukrainian	168,828	108.1
Slovak	3351	0.7
Other	24,248	–
Total	902,982	–

Source NKPI (Research Institute for Hungarian Communities Abroad)

granting external citizenship in 2004[51] are relatively well documented. The debates ended after the electoral collapse of the left-liberal block in 2010,[52] when the new parliament—controlled by a two-thirds Fidesz majority—modified the law on citizenship and made it possible for former Hungarian citizens and their descendants to obtain Hungarian citizenship without having residency in Hungary. In 2011, the electoral law was also modified and extra-territorial citizens were enfranchised for parliamentary elections.[53] The new citizenship legislation came into force in January 2011. As of 2017, the number of applicants has passed 900,000. In Romania, the proportion of applicants is close to 50% of the country's Hungarian population (see Table 4).[54]

In what follows, we briefly discuss changes to Hungary's kin-state policy strictly from the perspective of unequal accommodation. Policies

---

[51] For accounts and interpretations of this event, see Csergő and Goldgeier (2004), Saideman and Ayres (2008, pp. 120–123), and Waterbury (2010, pp. 123–128).

[52] The collapse of the left-liberal block was certainly not caused primarily by debates concerning the status of trans-border Hungarians. However, it put a definitive end to the expectations that constitutional patriotism might become a mainstream national discourse in Hungary.

[53] The Law on Citizenship was modified with a quasi-consensus, while the enfranchisement of extra-territorial citizenship was opposed by left-wing parties as they were suspicious about the attempts of right-wing parties to promote political rebalancing (Waterbury 2014). See also Kovács and Tóth (2013).

[54] The proportion of applicants among the Hungarians of Slovakia is significantly lower than in the other countries neighboring Hungary. This is due to the fact that in 2010, in response to the Hungarian "simplified naturalization" process, Slovakia abolished the possibility of dual citizenship for its citizens who voluntarily acquire foreign nationality (Bauböck 2010; Kusá 2013).

toward ethnic kin beyond the borders were not consensual in this respect either. There was general disagreement about rival national discourses. Political actors on the left argued that Hungarian minorities should be part of the political communities of the neighboring countries and not of Hungary. Consequently, they endorsed pro-integration political aspirations that extended beyond Hungary's borders. Actors on the right (while naturally accepting the international *status quo* concerning the borders) regarded the Hungarian minorities primarily as parts of the Hungarian nation, and sought institutional arrangements that could express this politically. These are the main reasons why (beyond short-term oscillations) left-wing Hungarian governments were generally supportive of the unequal accommodation model (participation in the power structures of the host-state without institutional/legal guarantees and without autonomy), while governments on the right were fairly consistent in opposing such strategies. To a great extent, this defined the different approaches to subsidy policies too.

The clearest example of Fidesz's policies toward ethnic kin beyond the border is the hostile attitude toward Slovakia's multiethnic Most–Híd party, or more precisely, Fidesz's consistent refusal to recognize the latter as a legitimate representative of Slovakia's ethnic Hungarians (despite the fact that Most–Híd is led by Hungarian elites and has enjoyed the support of over 40% of Slovakia's ethnic Hungarian voters) (Ravasz 2013; Székely 2014). The relationship between Fidesz and RMDSZ was obviously different, but tensions also became rather clear over time in this regard. We discussed earlier the initial divide within RMDSZ between the group that held office during Communist times and the group of former dissidents. The first post-Communist government of Hungary, led by the center-right Hungarian Democratic Forum (MDF), unequivocally sided with the latter faction within RMDSZ, to such an extent that Géza Domokos (president of RMDSZ and leader of the former faction) was practically unable to establish any relevant ties to the government of Hungary. We have also discussed how the assumption of a role in the governing coalition led to the polarization of conflicts within RMDSZ after 1996. Between 1998 and 2002, during its first cycle in power in Hungary, Fidesz clearly supported the opponents of the accommodating strategy (László Tőkés and the Reform Group[55]) against the central leadership of RMDSZ. The latter interpreted this as external interference, an attempt to take over the leadership of the party, to monopolize control over identity politics discourses and to bring RMDSZ into the clientelistic network of Fidesz (Waterbury 2010, p. 107).

Long-time RMDSZ president Béla Markó regarded it as especially insulting that Fidesz tried to circumvent him with regard to the subsidies meant to sustain the Hungarian institutional system in Transylvania. But between 1998 and 2002, factions opposing the accommodationist strategy still remained inside RMDSZ. As a consequence, the conflict was settled with a compromise in the context of the 2001 Status Law, and RMDSZ obtained a key role in the process of issuing Hungarian Cards.[56] The network of the so-called Status Offices in charge of this process, established through Hungary's budget, provided RMDSZ with approximately 200 job openings financed by Hungary.

The left-wing cabinets that governed Hungary between 2002 and 2010 pursued a markedly different subsidy policy. Their main objective was to dismantle the clientelistic networks set up by Fidesz beyond Hungary's borders. This was a salient issue for the center-left parties because minority political actors closely tied to Fidesz (e.g., László Tőkés in Romania, Miklós Duray in Slovakia) often formulated very sharp opinions with regard to domestic politics in Hungary. One of the tendencies of the subsidy policies of left-wing governments was pronounced centralization. On the other hand, they left the major decisions in the domain to the "legitimate representatives" of the minority communities (Waterbury 2010, pp. 118–131). By this, left-wing governments basically accepted the status quo within the political fields of the minorities, which resulted in reinforcement of the dominance of the "moderate" factions. Erika Törzsök, a defining decision-maker in the domain between 2002 and 2010, ironically but rather pertinently called

[55]The group was led by (then) young politicians socialized in Hungary who returned to Transylvania after finishing their studies.

[56]Hungarian Cards were connected to the Status Law; they took the form of official documents "proving" that the holder is a trans-border Hungarian.

the party leaders of Hungarian minorities "elected princes" (in sarcastic allusion to the prince electors of the Holy Roman Empire).

The position of RMDSZ also became very favorable with regard to resource allocation, because besides the resources extracted from Romania, it also obtained a monopoly over financial flows from Hungary. The above-mentioned status offices played a crucial role in this, as did subsidies for pupils enrolled in Hungarian-language schools (*oktatás-nevelési támogatás*). Starting in 2004, parents of Hungarian children studying in the vernacular received 20,000 HUF annually within the framework of this policy (equivalent to approximately 80 euros in 2004). According to the intergovernmental agreement concluded by Hungary and Romania, the program was administered by the Foundation for School[57] created and closely controlled by RMDSZ.

After coming back into power in 2010, Fidesz tried to vindicate its ideas about the Transylvanian Hungarian political field in a much more trenchant manner. The strategies used by Viktor Orbán and his political entourage can be classified into four (not mutually exclusive) categories, namely (1) ethnic outbidding through support for challenger ethnic parties, (2) material outbidding, (3) sponsoring factions within RMDSZ and creating a loyalty competition, and (4) establishing direct connections between Transylvanian Hungarians and Hungary.

2.6.1 Ethnic Outbidding, Material Outbidding, and a Loyalty Competition

The first strategy was ethnic outbidding. This strategy refers to sponsoring intra-ethnic competitor parties and trying to overthrow the dominant party, or at least trying to start a "spiral of radicalization" and push the dominant party to adopt more intransigent positions. As already mentioned, both the Antall government between 1990 and 1994 and the first Orbán government between 1998 and 2002 favored the "radicals" from the minority organizations. However, before 2003 RMDSZ

[57] See http://iskolaalapitvany.ro/en.

remained intact and the clashes between different factions of the Transylvanian Hungarian political class were relatively temperate. MPP was established in 2008 under the tutelage of Fidesz (then in opposition). After 2010, the subsidy system of the previous center-left governments was radically transformed and RMDSZ was almost completely squeezed out from the new structures. In 2011, the network of status offices was abolished, and the administrative apparatus for educational subsidies was transferred to the Association of Hungarian Teachers of Romania.[58] Both measures constituted important losses for RMDSZ. At the same time, a new network of offices (with a staff of approximately 150) was set up with the purpose of informing and assisting the population in the process of acquiring Hungarian citizenship. However, the new network was entrusted to EMNT which formally was an NGO, but in reality constituted one of the main pillars of RMDSZ's opposition and the sister organization of the political party EMNP (established in 2011, also under the tutelage of Fidesz). Notwithstanding these radical changes in the subsidy policy and establishment of EMNP, Fidesz was unable to significantly restructure the Transylvanian Hungarian political field. The factors conducive to the failure of outbidding were analyzed earlier. In the local elections of 2012, votes for a combined EMNP and MPP did not even equal those for MPP four years earlier. In 2012, RMDSZ passed the threshold of five percent in the parliamentary elections in spite of the fact that EMNP also fielded candidates. This was probably one of the main factors that led Fidesz to reevaluate its strategy and seek rapprochement with RMDSZ. As a result of this strategy shift, RMDSZ was invited in 2015 to participate in the naturalization process of Transylvanian Hungarians. Furthermore, RMDSZ also entered into electoral cooperation with MPP in 2016 (once again, not independent of developments in Budapest), while the other more radical party, EMNP, appears now to be gradually losing the support of the Hungarian capital. Explanations for this rapprochement are manifold, but we believe that the crucial reason was that both radical

[58]In Hungarian, Romániai Magyar Pedagógusok Szövetsége.

challenger parties failed to achieve an electoral breakthrough.[59] This also casts doubts on the capacity of the challenger parties to mobilize a sufficiently high proportion of the newly enfranchised Transylvanian Hungarian voters in Hungary's parliamentary election, prompting Fidesz to also seek RMDSZ's assistance for this purpose. Later, other factors also contributed to Fidesz's reorientation toward RMDSZ, such as Romania's increased interest in rapprochement with Hungary after a relatively tense period. Hence, RMDSZ had the potential to act as an intermediary for Romanian mainstream parties.

Since 2014, a new strategy has evolved which might be called material outbidding. As mentioned earlier, in a patronage regime an important precondition of unequal accommodation is that the resources attainable through the "host" state are superior to those attainable through the kin-state. After 2014, however, the magnitude of financial flows from Hungary directed beyond its borders increased substantially.[60] In 2015, the Hungarian government announced an economic development plan for Vojvodina (Serbia) of a magnitude of 50 billion HUF (approximately 179 million USD), followed in 2016 by a similar plan for 30 billion HUF (about 107 million USD) for Subcarpathia in Ukraine. The motivation for these plans was the precarious development situation in these regions coupled with outright neglect by their host-states. As for Transylvania, a similar plan was announced, but had not yet started at the time of writing of this chapter. However, the resources channeled to Romania have also been significantly increased.[61] For instance, in December 2017 a governmental ordinance[62] allocated

---

[59]Since 2012, the support for the two smaller parties together is approximately 15% of all votes cast by ethnic Hungarian voters.

[60]Of these four types of resources, only the last two can be measured with a satisfactory precision. Funding from the kin-state can be documented relatively well for the 1990–2012 period. See, Bárdi (2004), Bárdi and Misovicz (2010), and Papp (2010). After the 2014 shift, subsidies become less transparent. We have relied only on data about the funds allocated by the Hungarian state budget to kin communities. We thank Nándor Bárdi for providing the tables for the 2013–2016 period, which is critical for our argument.

[61]See the analysis on the topic by Zoltán Sipos (2017), an independent fact-finding journalist.

[62]Governmental Ordinance 2061/2017 (http://www.kozlonyok.hu/nkonline/index.php?menuindex=200&pageindex=kozltart&ev=2017&szam=227).

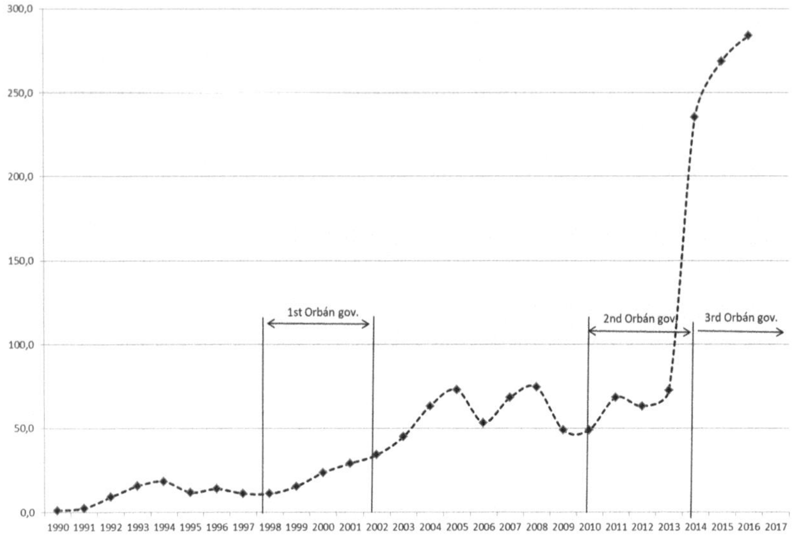

Fig. 3 The evolution of funding for ethnic kin communities from the Hungarian state budget between 1990 and 2015 (million USD) Authors' calculations (*Sources* Bárdi and Misovicz (2010); Papp (2010); http://www.bgazrt.hu/ (Accessed 12 July 2017))

more than 118 million USD to different Hungarian institutions in Transylvania, the most important beneficiary being the Transylvanian Reformed Church District. This amount was larger than the whole budget allocated for subsidies in 2015 for all the ethnic kin communities. Figure 3 summarizes the evolution of Hungarian state funding for kin communities. We do not yet have complete data for 2016 and 2017 (when the amounts grew considerably). However, the available data show that the policy of material outbidding began as early as 2014.

Following the failure of ethnic outbidding through the backing of intra-ethnic challenger parties, resources no longer seem to be deployed with the explicit intention of shifting the balance between rival minority elites or parties. However, the increased influence of kin-state actors may erode not only the model of unequal accommodation but also the dominant position and unity of RMDSZ, which by no account has a monopoly on the allocation of funds flowing from Hungary. Reconciliation between RMDSZ and Fidesz has not meant that Fidesz has reconstructed the centralized system dominated by the "elected princes" which functioned under the governments led by the Hungarian Socialist Party. As Bárdi (2017, p. 153) pointed out, the organizational structure that provides subsidies is quite complex (and in many ways confusing). The former author identified no less than thirty institutional actors involved in kin-state policy, the majority of them which also allocate subsidies. Some of these are various Hungarian government bodies (such as ministries and state secretariats); however, the Hungarian Parliament (presided over by László Kövér, who is personally involved in kin-state policy) also has its own programs and funds. Consequently, resource allocation and bargaining are quite decentralized. In this institutional structure, RMDSZ leadership is only one of the competing claimants and it is certainly not the most important one. The capacity of the resource allocation of different Transylvanian Hungarian actors depends on their personal relationships with kin-state actors.[63] One might legitimately argue that in this setting the informal-individual bargaining characteristic of the early 1990s has regained its prominence.

Increased resource allocation through informal-individual channels may also cause intra-party tensions (or even a split) in the long run. Politicians and local branches of RMDSZ or (potentially) political factions might also turn directly to kin-state actors for extra funds and the party leadership has no means of controlling such flows. This is a totally different institutional structure of bargaining in which kin-state actors can generate loyalty-based competition to secure the (ideological) compliance of Transylvanian Hungarian political actors.

2.6.2 Transylvanian Hungarian Responses to the New Citizenship Policy of Hungary

Following the adoption of new citizenship legislation in 2010, a radical shift has occurred both in Hungary's kin-state policy and the official definition of the Hungarian nation. Hungarian citizenship has

[63]It seems that the most powerful actor is Béla Kató, the bishop of the Transylvanian Reformed Church District, who has a close personal relationship with Viktor Orbán. For a general account of the system of political patronage in Hungary, see Magyar (2016).

established strong personal-bureaucratic linkages between the Hungarian state and individual members of the kin communities; moreover, it has shifted the emphasis from more conventional means of minority rights protection to the inclusion of individual members of kin communities into the Hungarian political community. This has certainly involved a paradigmatic change, and we regard it as the fourth strategy of Hungary aimed at shaping political processes among Transylvanian Hungarians.

In Transylvania, numerous actors from the minority field[64] consider the new legislation on citizenship and enfranchisement, as well as the growing kin-state activity of Hungary, to be a major challenge. Initially, the political class was divided on this issue. Some RMDSZ leaders deliberately displayed allegiance by applying for Hungarian citizenship immediately after the new legislation came into effect.[65] However, Béla Markó, by that time the president of RMDSZ, declared that he would not apply for Hungarian citizenship.[66] Later, he openly criticized the policy of the enfranchisement of trans-border Hungarians.[67] It seems obvious that most of the top leaders of RMDSZ and the members of the party's intellectual entourage were critical of the introduction of dual citizenship. However, the Transylvanian Hungarian political class (and most importantly, RMDSZ) did not formulate any coherent response to it.

The arguments of Transylvanian Hungarian elites that oppose the "transnational" (Pogonyi 2011) or "trans-sovereign" (Csergő and Goldgeier 2004) nation-building efforts of Hungary's right-wing government (including external citizenship, enfranchisement, as well the establishment of other institutional ties) may be classified into several

[64]Brubaker (1996) used the notion of minority field in a Bourdieusian sense of a social field composed of different actors struggling for definite positions and sharing a common frame of reference. In our understanding, the Transylvanian Hungarian minority field includes not only the political class but also a subelite level of ethnic activists (teachers, clerics, journalists, etc.) interested in the maintenance of minority institutions, the internal solidarity of the group and the program of ethnic parallelism.

[65]Garzó Ferenc: Kettős állampolgárság – vegyes a megítélés. *szatmar.ro*, 5 January 2011. Available at: http://www.szatmar.ro/Kettos_allampolgarsag__vegyes_a_megiteles/hirek/37445 (Accessed 18 February 2018).

[66]Markó Béla egyelőre nem igényel magyar állampolgárságot. Népszava, 4 January 2011. Available at: http://nepszava.hu/cikk/380701-marko-bela-egyelore-nem-igenyel-magyar-allampolgarsagot (Accessed 18 February 2018).

[67]Markó a magyarországi szavazati jog ellen. *szatmar.ro*, 10 June 2011. Available at: http://www.szatmar.ro/Marko_a_magyaorszagi_szavazati_jog_ellen/hirek/42622 (Accessed 18 February 2018).

categories (for an inventory of these arguments, see Waterbury 2017; Pogonyi 2017, pp. 105–111). (1) The first argument is that extra-territorial citizenship weakens the claim-making potential of Hungarian elites toward the Romanian state. Bauböck's (2007) well-known argument that there is a trade-off between autonomy and extra-territorial citizenship has been widely accepted and reproduced by Transylvanian Hungarian political elites and social scientists. At a more general level, there have been fears that if Transylvanian Hungarians rely on kin-state support and increasingly orient themselves toward politics in Hungary, they will become less mobilized and less interested in making claims toward the Romanian state through their own political parties. As a consequence, they will become increasingly dependent on kin-state support and even more marginalized in their country of residence (Bauböck 2007, p. 190). (2) The second argument focuses on migration and posits that extraterritorial citizenship eases entry to Hungary, thus accelerating the process called by Brubaker (1998) "ethnic un-mixing". (3) Third, some Transylvanian Hungarian elites also have reservations with regard to what they perceive as a general cultural and political reorientation toward Hungary. This would involve a shift from an (internally oriented) ethnic identity to a (kin-state-oriented) diaspora identity. Levente Salat has argued in a similar vein, saying that such a reorientation could lead to the transformation of the Transylvanian Hungarians into a diaspora community dominated by kin-state actors (Salat 2011).

These opposing or ambivalent views have been predominant among top RMDSZ leaders. However, since there has been widespread popular support for Hungary's new citizenship policy among Transylvanian Hungarians, political pragmatism has gained ground and RMDSZ has adopted a supportive stance on the issue. As a result, since January 2015, RMDSZ has been an official partner of the Hungarian government in the implementation of citizenship legislation. The widespread public support among Transylvanian Hungarians for dual citizenship is readily apparent in survey results. While nine percent of Transylvanian Hungarians were against the new legislation in 2012, by 2016 this number had dwindled to less than three percent.[68]

[68]Also, worth underscoring is the fact that in Slovakia Hungarian citizenship legislation is a much more divisive issue within the Hungarian community. See Ravasz (2013).

3 The Limits of Unequal Accommodation in Ethnic Claim-Making

The final part of the chapter includes two case studies, the aim of which is to illustrate the contradictions that follow from the model of unequal accommodation pursued by the Transylvanian Hungarian political class with regard to two ethno-political issues that can arguably be considered the core programmatic demands of the Hungarians in the post-Communist period: the quest for various forms of autonomy and minority language rights. We argue that in spite of the fact that both issues are prominent programmatic elements present in the platform of RMDSZ, both came to be at odds with the strategy of unequal accommodation. As in the case of autonomy almost nothing has been accomplished over the two and half decades, this has led to the gradual degradation of this issue to a mere element of electoral propaganda. With regard to language rights, the situation is more complex, and RMDSZ indeed succeeded in codifying a number of important pluralistic elements. However, when it comes to implementation, the attitude of the Hungarian political class becomes ambivalent, and quite significant tensions arise with actors who pursue other strategies, most importantly civic advocacy. We conclude the chapter with an assessment of the chances of the development of a large-scale civic minority rights advocacy movement, which could complement or even substitute the claim-making strategy based exclusively on political bargaining.

3.1 The Autonomy Movement: Valence-Based Competition Without a Real Strategy?

Autonomy is clearly the Holy Grail of Transylvanian Hungarian politics. All three currently active Hungarian political parties (RMDSZ, MPP, EMNP) define themselves as autonomist. At a rhetorical level, the competition among them mostly concerns which of them is doing the most in the struggle for autonomy. Notwithstanding this, no real progress has been registered so far in this domain, and Hungarian voters increasingly perceive the parties' autonomist manifestations as empty electoral propaganda.

The objective of self-government—even if in a less elaborate form—has been present as a core objective in the program of RMDSZ since its first congress. Between 1991 and 1995, a number of conceptions of autonomy and related bills drafted by experts of RMDSZ have attempted to translate this objective into more concrete terms. However, starting in 1996, the issue of autonomy has been increasingly pushed to the background, despite the efforts of RMDSZ's internal opposition to the contrary. This shift in the emphasis on autonomy has been the result of a changing domestic and international context. First, in 1996 the bilateral Treaty of Understanding, Cooperation and Good Neighborliness between Romania and Hungary was signed, including a—Romanian party initiated—footnote insisting that the treaty does not bind Romania to grant collective rights and autonomy to the Hungarian minority. Second, as already discussed, RMDSZ joined the Romanian governing coalition in 1996, one condition of which was the shelving of more radical ethno-political demands. Third, instead of the collective rights philosophy predicted by the adoption of Recommendation 1201 (1993), the Council of Europe eventually pursued a more low-key approach to minority protection, as materialized in the Framework Convention for the Protection of National Minorities (1995).

The issue of autonomy came to the fore once again in RMDSZ's rhetoric after the party split of 2003,[69] and since then one of the defining topics of the competition between RMDSZ and its intra-ethnic opposition has been the (mainly rhetorical) struggle for the role of "true autonomists" or "the ones who do the most for autonomy". This can be regarded as an example of *valence (or competence-based) competition*, the essence of which is that it involves some condition that is consensually regarded as good by the electorate in general; that is, parties do not formulate distinctive proposals concerning a policy area, but rather compete to portray themselves as the most credible, competent, and efficient agents for delivering results on the issue.[70] However, as discussed earlier,

[69]In 2004, the electoral slogan of RMDSZ was "Together, for autonomy!" (Együtt, az auonómiáért!).

[70]On the difference between spatial and valence competition, see Stokes (1963) and Budge and Farlie (1983). For an application to the context of the Hungarian minorities, see Székely (2014).

the return of the autonomy issue to the political agenda has resulted in the development of a dual discourse in the case of RMDSZ: while deploying a harder rhetoric toward its ethnic constituency, RMDSZ maintains its accommodative attitude toward Romanian partners and the de-ethnicized framing of community goals. Conversely, the main rhetorical element employed by the organizations ramping up in opposition to RMDSZ (the political parties MPP and EMNP, as well as the non-party organizations EMNT and SZNT) is that RMDSZ has practically defaulted on the ideal of autonomy for the sake of integration into the Romanian party cartel.

Turning now to the concrete conceptions of autonomy, between 1991 and 2014 no fewer than sixteen such documents were drafted.[71] Many of these are complex packages of bills that would institutionalize multiple types of autonomy. The drafts can be classified into three groups based on the time of their publication.[72]

The conceptions published in the first period (1991–1995) were the product of experts working within RMDSZ and illustrate conceptual disagreements about the issue that were characteristic within the organization by that time. Some of these documents should be regarded rather as political statements of purpose, while others reflect serious expertise. However, of these early proposals, only one was registered as a bill in Romania's parliament, where it was rejected without even making it to the floor.[73]

The second period of document production began after the 2003 split of RMDSZ, when the opposition organizations refurbished some of the older drafts and also commissioned new ones. In 2004, some members of RMDSZ's parliamentary group who sympathized with the opposition submitted two bills to Romania's parliament. The first was a

[71]The full text of these documents (in Hungarian), with the exception of the 2014 draft statute of RMDSZ, is available in the collection Autonomy Conceptions in Romania (Romániai autonómia-elképzelések) at: http://adatbank.transindex.ro/belso.php?alk=48&k=5. The 2014 draft of RMDSZ can be accessed at: http://rmdsz.ro/uploads/fileok/dok/A_romaniai_Szekelyfold_autonomia_statutuma.pdf.

[72]For details on the periodization, see Bakk (2004) and Bognár (2006).

[73]Bill on national minorities and autonomous communities (Törvény a nemzeti kisebbségekről és autonóm közösségekről), RMDSZ-SZKT, 1993.

statute for the territorial autonomy of Székely Land, adopted by SZNT as its official programmatic document,[74] while the second was a package of bills about personal autonomy commissioned by EMNT. The former was rejected in a plenary session of the Chamber of Deputies (only the RMDSZ parliamentary group voted for it, some members reluctantly), while the latter did not even make it through the standing bureau of the Chamber due to constitutional objections. RMDSZ responded in 2005 to these two initiatives with a draft of its own entitled *Law on the legal status of national minorities.* The adoption of this law was included into the program of the government of Călin Popescu-Tăriceanu. The bill, which came to be known simply as the "Minority Bill", was a framework law that included a general codification of minority rights and also foresaw the institutionalization of cultural autonomy on the personality principle. However, the bill has not been adopted since then, even though RMDSZ has repeatedly attempted to secure political support for it.

In the third phase, only one conception of autonomy was elaborated, entitled *Autonomy Statute of the Székely Land in Romania*, published in 2014. Beyond the fact that two elections were held in 2014 (for the European Parliament, and presidential elections), the elaboration of this document was probably also motivated by the fact that, following the events in Eastern Ukraine, the international community's (primarily the USA's) attention to the broader region seemed once again to intensify. Although the draft aimed to adapt the autonomy statue of south Tyrol to the Romanian constitutional context and its elaboration lasted for one and a half years, the final output was disappointing: the document should be regarded as a political statement of purpose intended for the internal use of the Hungarian community rather than a mature piece of expert work (Salat 2014). The draft has not yet been submitted to the parliament.

A detailed analysis of such conceptions of autonomy is outside the scope of this chapter. We limit our discussion of Transylvanian Hungarian political thinking about autonomy to a few general remarks

[74]The bill was a reworked version of an earlier draft from 1995.

(for a detailed discussion, see Bakk 2004; Bognár 2006). After two and a half decades, one can conclude that in spite of the fact that autonomy has been a core concept that structured the Transylvanian Hungarian public sphere and party competition, no progress whatsoever has been registered with regard to its legal codification. Furthermore, hardly any drafts which meet professional standards have also been politically assumed by RMDSZ (with the possible exception of the 1993 bill). Some drafts were evidently plagued by the fact that political considerations superseded professional standards—sometimes this claim has even been admitted by the drafters or commissioners. To some extent, this situation is justified by the fact that the function of conceptions of autonomy is not only to influence ethno-political processes, but also it is equally important that they should provide a vision of the future and help mobilize the affected communities. However, as Bognár has pointed out, autonomy has been present in the rhetoric of the political parties much more as a goal than as a means. Often, it has been presented as a panacea for all the problems that Hungarians face, without clarification, however, of how the envisaged future (a core ingredient of which would be autonomy) would look (Bognár 2006). Furthermore, little is said about the concrete advantages and disadvantages that could be expected from the enactment of various forms of autonomy, and invoking possible negative outcomes of such can be regarded as one of the most significant taboos in the Hungarian public sphere. Not even after twenty-five years do we have a clear picture about the economic viability of Székely Land as a potentially autonomous region. No thorough analyses or feasibility studies have been carried out in this respect; instead, what is characteristic both among supporters and opponents is the referencing of certain specific statistics that seem to justify arguments regarding the autonomy of the Székely region. It is also important to point out that Romanian partners were not invited to offer input to any of the drafts, and this is something that has been resented even by Romanian intellectuals who otherwise would not automatically reject the idea of Hungarian autonomy. In the case of the last two drafts of RMDSZ (the "Minority Bill" of 2005 and the Autonomy Statute of 2014), public debate within the Hungarian public sphere was also rather shallow.

It is not by chance that we have dedicated more attention to these two documents. As a consequence of the very fact that these drafts have been commissioned and officially adopted by the strongest Hungarian political organization, they should be regarded as the most important conceptions of autonomy currently in circulation in Romania. Were we to assess the chances of the adoption of any of the autonomy conceptions that have been elaborated in Romania since 1990, it would be obvious that these two documents should be singled out, even if the chances of the implementation of even these documents are rather low (the first and only draft so far which had a realistic chance of being adopted was the 2005 bill on the cultural autonomy of RMDSZ). As Salat and Székely have emphasized, the function of autonomy arrangements is not only to *empower* minorities through the transfer of certain competences from the level of the central government to institutions controlled by the minority; the creation of autonomous institutions also entails *recognition* of the fact that the beneficiary group constitutes a self-standing political community (Salat and Székely 2014). It seems to us that in the political thinking of RMDSZ with regard to autonomy (at least since the turn of the millennium), the latter objective has clearly become prioritized over the former. Furthermore, RMDSZ has repeatedly attempted to blur the difference between the boundaries of RMDSZ the organization and the boundaries of the Hungarian community of Transylvania. One of the specificities of the struggle of RMDSZ for autonomy—illustrated perfectly by the 2005 cultural autonomy bill—is the intention to persuade the Romanian parties to recognize such institutional designs which are much more appropriate for consolidating the position of RMDSZ within the Hungarian community than to serve as a proper framework for self-government of the Hungarians endowed with real competences (Márton and Orbán 2005). The main message of the 2014 draft statute was that, in the calculus of the main political organization of Transylvania's Hungarians, short-term political considerations have superseded the need to finally elaborate a professionally grounded conception of autonomy which could safely be adopted and presented both on the domestic and the international arena, and which could provide the Hungarian community of Transylvania a vision for the future.

3.2 Minority Language Rights Implementation: Bargaining or Advocacy?

During the past two decades, Romania has adopted several minority-friendly legislative acts concerning language use and also ratified the most important European legal documents in the domain (Salat and Novák 2015; Horváth 2002; Wolff and Cordell 2003; Ram 2009). However, deeper analysis reveals significant problems in the implementation of this relatively minority-friendly legislation. Language use is an area of huge symbolic charge as both majority and minority actors perceive it as a question of sovereignty and ownership of institutions or territory. As described earlier, many members of the majority ethnic group perceive existing linguistic rights as the illegitimate privileges of the minority group and are deeply attached to a nationalizing linguistic policy (see also Brubaker et al. 2006). Nonetheless, minority group members also perceive linguistic rights in terms of sovereignty and ownership (Csergő 2007).

Through the cases described in this section, we seek to illustrate the limits of the asymmetric bargaining model in minority rights implementation. Shortcomings regarding the implementation of minority language rights have persisted since the adoption of the legislation regulating this domain (Toró 2017a). RMDSZ, in spite of its regular participation in governing coalitions and its stable position in local councils, is unable to or uninterested in pushing the authorities to enforce legal provisions. This signals that its strategy based on asymmetric bargaining is unable to deliver when it comes to implementing the law. Relying on human rights implementation research and applying it to our cases, we also argue that advocacy-related tools might be developed in cases when political bargaining fails.

Both case studies discussed below refer to bilingual signs. The official use of minority languages is regulated in a rather straightforward way by Law 215/2001, and the implementation of minority language rights by Governmental Decision 1206/2001. The application methodology for bilingual place and institution signs is relatively well elaborated compared to that of other linguistic rights. Implementation does not require significant resources or expertise, and sanctions and deadlines are also defined. The Governmental Decision also provided a list of eligible municipalities and listed the official names in the minority languages. In other words, the only duty of the leaders of municipalities was to commission and put up signs before the deadline.

Our case studies refer to the bilingual place signs in Cluj/Kolozsvár and to schools in Târgu Mureș/Marosvásárhely. Political bargaining has fallen short in both cases and the initiative was taken over by local NGOs and civic movements. Cluj is the largest municipality in Transylvania with numerically the second-largest Hungarian community (according to the 1992 census, their proportion was 23%. The subsequent censuses in 2002 and 2011 recorded 19 and 16% ethnic Hungarians). As mentioned already, the law and the Governmental Decision regulating the use of minority languages came into force in 2001. The condition for putting up bilingual inscriptions was that the given minority's proportion should reach at least 20% in the given municipality according to the previous census. Moreover, the government's decision nominalized Cluj as being among the municipalities where bilingual signs should be put up. However, the notoriously nationalistic mayor Gheorghe Funar refused to put up bilingual signs (in 2001), arguing that the 1992 census was outdated and that since that time the proportion of Hungarians had fallen to less than 20%. The 2002 census confirmed his assumptions. However, the law regulating minority language use was changed in 2006. The new version explicitly stated that in the administrative units where the proportion of a minority was above 20% at the time of adoption of the law (2001), the provisions should be applied. Despite these positive legal developments and an arguably minority-friendly change in the composition of the local council in 2004, no settlement was reached until 2017.

Târgu Mureș/Marosvásárhely is home to the largest Hungarian community in Transylvania where, according to the 2011 census, Hungarians made up 45% of the town's population. In the town, there are thirteen primary and lower-secondary schools and eighteen upper secondary schools. All of the former are bilingual, having both Romanian and Hungarian classes or groups, while among the high schools two are exclusively Hungarian and four exclusively Romanian (the remaining twelve are also bilingual). Despite their bilingual nature and the legal provisions regarding minority language usage in public institutions subordinated to the mayor's office,[75] the linguistic landscape of these schools is mostly monolingual Romanian. As a monitoring project conducted in 2010 by a local advocacy NGO called Civic Engagement Movement (CEMO) revealed, the language of the communication between school management and pupils and their parents, circulars disseminated from other educational institutions, webpages and even signs designating classes and offices and public inscriptions on the buildings were all mostly monolingual Romanian.

3.2.1 The Bargaining Strategies of RMDSZ

The local-level political positions of RMDSZ and the strategies employed by the party concerning the two issues were rather similar. The issue of bilingual signs was on the political agenda in both cities and was used for electoral mobilization several times. RMDSZ had a relatively strong group of local councilors after each election and in both cities successfully managed to bargain their way into a coalition with the leading Romanian parties. RMDSZ also succeeded in promoting the adoption of a positive local council decision in both cases which prescribed the placement of bilingual signs. In Cluj, a decision had already been adopted in 2002 (Decision no. 99/2002), and even budgetary lines were assigned for the purpose. In Târgu Mureş, two local council decisions were adopted in 2011 following an NGO advocacy campaign (Decision no. 11/2011) and 2013 (Decision no. 30/2013). However, the mayor stalled the issue in both cases. As one of the Hungarian councilors in Târgu Mureş explained, although the decision is clear, the implementation of the decision has been left to the "good will of the mayor".[76]

[75]In Romania, public schools are subordinated to the mayor's office, thus the minority language usage on their premises is regulated both by Law No. 1/2011 on National Education and by Law No. 215/2001 on Local Public Administration.

[76]Ha lehet, akkor miért nem? Akadályozzák a kétnyelvű iskolai feliratok kifüggesztését. kozpont.ro, 11 April 2011. Available at: http://www.kozpont.ro/uncategorized/ha-lehet-akkor-miert-nem/ (Accessed 18 February 2018).

Another similarity is that RMDSZ tried to take the topic off the public agenda in both cases. In Târgu Mureş, RMDSZ politicians came out in support of the importance of multilingualism, but after on-the-spot visits in some high schools, they argued that the situation is not as bad as depicted "by others" (referring to the minority rights advocacy NGOs). Similarly, the RMDSZ vice-mayor of Cluj admitted in 2015 that the issue was not on their agenda:

> I cannot see a realistic chance for the placement of multilingual city signs by the current leadership. As long as the law does not change and does not reduce the current 20 percent threshold, I may not even see the point of investing energy in this solution. (...) Personally, I do not consider it a good idea to set advocacy goals that are predestined to fail. (...) That is why we have looked for a compromise for the time being: we have pledged to set up five-language city gates by the end of the year, in order to see for the first time for a long time the name Kolozsvár displayed at the city entrance. (Horváth 2015)

This discourse illustrates well the strategy of asymmetric bargaining and its limits. Bargaining was considered the only means of claim-making in both cases, while minority rights advocacy was excluded as an option and even deplored. In the case of Cluj, the vice-mayor argued for further modification of the national legislation, even in the case that the law already bound the mayor's office to put up the signs. In Târgu Mureş another, more precise local council decision was adopted. Meanwhile, the local RMDSZ leadership tried to avoid conflict with the mayor and looked for solutions that would diffuse community pressure. While in Cluj, the compromise took the form of the construction of city gates (which were never built), in Târgu Mureş, it took the form of downplaying the claims and pledging to monitor bilingualism and the installation of signs. In both cases, the introduction of these ideas into the public discourse served the purpose of obtaining sufficient time to continue bargaining with the executive.[77]

[77] A very similar strategy was used by RMDSZ to avoid exiting the governmental coalition in 1997. After creating an ultimatum concerning the formation of an independent Hungarian state-funded university, RMDSZ accepted a proposal for the founding of a multilingual German-Hungarian university which never came to fruition. For details, see Horváth (2002).

3.2.2 The Advocacy Strategies of Civic Actors

As already mentioned, the cases are interesting because the initiative was taken up—in both cases—by independent NGOs, namely by CEMO in Târgu Mureş and by the foundation European Committee Human Rights Hungarians Central Europe (an NGO registered in the Netherlands). Both NGOs made recourse to litigation and referred to the rule of law as part of their strategy.

In Târgu Mureş, CEMO submitted a complaint against four public schools to the National Council for Combating Discrimination (NCCD). They argued that with their monolingual practices and linguistic landscapes, the schools were discriminating against Hungarian children and parents. NCCD organized an on-the-spot visit to the thus-incriminated schools and established that discrimination had indeed occurred in both cases because of the monolingual signs outside and inside the schools and monolingual internal communication. The NCCD also clarified the responsibilities of public institutions and declared that the mayor's office was responsible for the placement of bilingual official signs, while schools were responsible for their internal communication.[78] After this success, turning to the NCCD became the central element of the strategy pursued by CEMO. After the mayor's office refused to put up signs on the façades of schools, the former organization targeted them with another complaint, demanding the maximum sanction possible under the law. This second complaint finally led to a breakthrough. The NCCD declared the practice of the mayor's office discriminative, and fined it 8000 RON (approximately 2400 USD at the time). The fine was never paid, as the mayor's office started putting up signs as the decision came into force.[79] In addition, CEMO kept putting pressure on schools concerning their internal practices and linguistic landscape by filing a second complaint against all bilingual schools in the city. Although this did not change

---

[78]See Decision no. 172/2011 of the NCCD.

[79]Diszkriminál Florea. 3szek.ro, 6 February 2014. Available at: http://www.3szek.ro/load/cikk/67520/diszkriminal_florea&cm=114627 (Accessed 18 February 2018).

monolingual practices, schools and the school inspectorate were forced to keep explaining their actions as cases of discrimination were repeatedly identified.

Turning to the NCCD has not proved to be a successful strategy in the case of Cluj. The Council did not establish the fact of discrimination, arguing that the proportion of Hungarians was below 20% and, consequently, it was at the discretion of the mayor's office to decide on the issue.[80] Therefore, the NGO took the case to court in 2014 and won the case in the first instance. The legal decision argued that it was not that the law itself is mandatory, but rather the local council decision from 2002, which has not been implemented since that time. However, the mayor's office appealed and won their lawsuit at the court of appeals. The motivation behind this decision, however, was not related to language rights, but to "the lack of active procedural quality" of the claimant (as the original plaintiff was registered in the Netherlands).[81] To continue the lawsuit, a new local NGO called the Minority Rights Association was founded in 2015, and others also joined the case. The most important actors included a grassroots advocacy movement called Musai-Muszáj,[82] and another NGO called Advocacy Group for Freedom of Identity (AGFI), which was founded by lawyers. The lawsuit lasted for two years. At first, the court decided that the claim of the Minority Rights Association was "unjustified". However, they continued with the lawsuit, the original decision was declared void, and the plaintiffs won in the new trial. The mayor's office did not appeal and had the first bilingual sign put up in May 2017. Subsequently, RMDSZ's vice-mayor promised the placement of all signs within a short timeframe.[83]

---

[80]See NCCD Decision no. 477/2011.

[81]Clujul, fără controversatele plăcuţe bilingve! Primăria a câştigat definitiv procesul. Ziua de Cluj, 6 February 2015. Available at: http://ziuadecj.realitatea.net/administratie/clujul-a-scapat-de-controversatele-placute-bilingve-primaria-a-castigat-definitiv-procesul--134976.html (Accessed 18 February 2018).

[82]Musai-Muszáj means "must" in Romanian and Hungarian.

[83]See the declaration of Emese Oláh, vice-mayor of Cluj: Oláh Emese: jövő héten kikerülnek az újabb többnyelvű kolozsvári helységnévtáblák. kronika.ro, 26 June 2017. Available at: https://kronika.ro/erdelyi-hirek/olah-emese-jovo-heten-ujabb-tobbnyelvu-kolozsvari-helysegnevtablakat-allitanak (Accessed 18 February 2018).

This, however, is yet to happen: only four of the sixteen affected place name signs had been changed by January 2018.

Just as with the case of RMDSZ, there were many similarities in the strategies employed by the NGOs of the two cities. They made reference not only to domestic legislation and also to international treaties, such as the European Charter for Regional or Minority Languages (ECRML) which was ratified by Romania in 2007. This tactic was an important novelty, as the plaintiffs tried to use the provisions of the ECRML as a resource, and to put pressure on courts to apply them. Another important comment applies to legal resources. Litigation and references to NCCD decisions were the necessary elements in the chosen advocacy strategy. However, they were not sufficient—they needed to be backed up by additional elements, such as building up public support and visibility, identifying transnational support, and applying pressure and breaking down resistance. In the following paragraphs, these strategies will be briefly discussed.

Building public support was important in both cases. CEMO had chosen to empower parents, persuading them to write petitions to relevant public institutions asking for bilingual practices.[84] Also, an open letter was sent to RMDSZ, urging the ethnic party to put the issue on its agenda,[85] and flash-mobs were organized.[86] These latter events increased the visibility of the problem, because they generated conflict between Hungarian and Romanian parents, and as a result, the director of the affected school was dismissed. Musai-Muszáj chose a different path. They started a campaign called "The spring of a thousand lawsuits", which called on private individuals to join the legal proceedings. As a result of the campaign, 371 persons joined. In 2015, the action group planned to storm a city council meeting to protest

[84]The text of the petition can be downloaded from the webpage of CEMO: http://www.cemo.ro/hu/erdekervenyesites_ketnyelvuseg_2012.html (Accessed 18 February 2018).

[85]On both the visit and the letter, see an article in the local newspaper (Villámlátogatás a Liviu Rebreanu iskolában. Népújság, 10 May 2013).

[86]Leváltják a Liviu Rebreanu iskola vezetőit. Marosvásárhelyi info, 25 June 2013. Available at: http://marosvasarhelyi.info/hirek/levaltjak-a-liviu-rebreanu-iskola-vezetoit (Accessed 18 February 2018).

against the indifference of the city leadership toward bilingualism. As there were budgetary and financing issues on the agenda, RMDSZ tried to avoid this conflictual situation, hoping for greater financial support for Hungarian NGOs. Musai-Muszáj agreed to adjourn the event, but they asked for the active involvement of RMDSZ in their lawsuit in exchange. The Hungarian vice-mayor joined in, raising both the stakes and the visibility of the issue.[87] In addition, Musai-Muszáj asked people to file official requests for bilingual signs at the mayor's office. Around 2000 requests were made, which were used to prove the existence of well-founded support.

The second additional strategy consisted of applying pressure and breaking down resistance. Both advocacy organizations constantly put pressure on RMDSZ. This was important for keeping the issue on the political agenda as RMDSZ was interested in diffusing public pressure, while their political resolution brought no results. Consequently, they had become vulnerable in terms of their accountability to the Hungarian constituency. RMDSZ was more open to working together with the civil activists in Cluj, while in Târgu Mureş, this has not happened.

Breaking the resistance of the mayors' offices was considerably more difficult. A mixture of coercion and persuasion was used in both cases. In both cases, it was a central element of the mayors' political rhetoric that their city was "a modern, multicultural city with a European mentality and a democratic framework, where many different groups live together in harmony".[88] Musai-Muszáj started mocking the mayor of Cluj on this issue. One of their high-impact actions was related to the candidacy of Cluj for the European Cultural Capital of 2021 of which multiculturalism was a central element. Musai-Muszáj exploited this occasion and sent an open letter to the selection jury. They unmasked the false multicultural discourse of the mayor and argued

[87]Horváth Anna és Vákár István is csatlakozott a Musai-muszájos Ezer per tavaszához. transindex.ro, 26 May 2015. Available at: http://itthon.transindex.ro/?cikk=25199 (Accessed 18 February 2018).

[88]The Mayor of Cluj-Napoca Highlights the City's Multicultural European Character. Interview with Emil Boc, *The European Times*, 29 June 2015. Available at: http://www.european-times.com/emil-boc-mayor-cluj-napoca-interview/ (Accessed 18 February 2018).

that with this attitude the mayor was jeopardizing claims to the title.[89] Later, when Cluj lost the race to Timişoara, the advocacy group reiterated their framing, blaming the mayor for the failure. This campaign was important in two respects: It sent a clear message to the mayor that if he continued with his discourse without erecting the bilingual signs, the organization would continue to mock him and he would ultimately lose more credibility. The campaign also illustrates the difference between the bargaining strategy of RMDSZ and the advocacy strategy of the NGOs. RMDSZ leaders were ambivalent concerning this issue. On the one hand, they were involved in the preparation of the European Cultural Capital project. On the other hand, they had a publicly disclosed coalition agreement with the National Liberal Party (PNL), the strongest party in the local council, in which the issue of bilingual signs arose. The agreement, however, stood on weak foundations, as RMDSZ recognized publicly the resentment of their partners toward bilingualism, and no deadlines were defined for its application. Therefore, RMDSZ wanted to kill two birds with one stone: They communicated that the winning of the European Cultural Capital title "would speed up this process and resolve the issue more quickly".[90] In other words, RMDSZ was looking to compromise and prioritized the title of European Cultural Capital over the bilingual signs. Compared to the mayor of Cluj, the mayor of Târgu Mureş could not be intimidated through a strategy of deconstruction of his multicultural discourse. In his case, the possibility of a significant fine was the decisive factor.

The third strategy involved raising the visibility of the issue. This approach was more salient in Cluj as Musai-Muszáj organized several high-impact campaigns that reached a large number of supporters and were framed positively, even in Romanian media. They made

[89]The whole text of the letter in Romanian can be accessed here: http://www.presalocala.com/2016/08/27/musai-muszaj-emil-boc-pune-in-pericol-succesul-proiectului-de-capitala-culturala-europeana-intra-se-vezi-de-ce/ (Accessed 18 February 2018).

[90]Csoma Botond a táblaügyről: a kulturális főváros cím felgyorsítaná a folyamatot. kronika.ro, 11 September 2016. Available at: https://kronika.ro/erdelyi-hirek/csoma-botond-a-tablaugyrol-a-kulturalis-fovaros-cim-felgyorsitana-a-folyamatot (Accessed 18 February 2018).

viral videos on social media and organized flash-mobs and communicative actions which were usually centered on the deconstruction of the mayor's multicultural discourse. One of their most important initiatives was timed to have an impact just before the final decision on the lawsuit. Live video-voting on the issue of the placement of bilingual signs was created on Facebook, which in a few hours was seen by more than 774,000 people; moreover, it was shared 6100 times and was liked by 43,000 users.[91] It was the most successful viral video created by Transylvanian Hungarians up to that point.

The last strategy of support extends beyond the two cases. Both groups (CEMO and Musai-Muszáj) tried to identify transnational contacts which would support their case. CEMO had submitted a shadow report to the ECRML, presenting their case. As this was the first ever shadow report submitted by a Hungarian NGO in Romania, the Committee of Experts during their on-the-spot visit traveled to Târgu Mureș and met with the representatives of the NGO and even the mayor of the city. The initiative may thus be considered a success. The former group succeeded in establishing such transnational links and putting pressure on the mayor's office. However, as the mayor was not concerned that the issue of multiculturalism might have a negative impact on his image, it had only limited impact. Despite this, CEMO continued its transnational work, submitting other shadow reports to the ECRML, the Framework Convention for the Protection of National Minorities and the United Nations Periodical Report (UNPR), and even went to the UN Forum on Minority Issues. Musai-Muszáj, and later AGFI, followed similar paths. They submitted shadow reports, informed foreign embassies about the legal infringement, and presented their case at the UN Forum. However, these initiatives did not pay off. The organizations were able to use them in their communicative strategies, but did not receive meaningful feedback from international organizations.

[91]https://www.facebook.com/musaimuszaj/videos/1890566064560911/ (Accessed 18 February 2018).

3.2.3 Prospects of a Large-Scale Civic Movement for Language Rights

These case studies have shown that the usual bargaining strategies of RMDSZ are of limited use when it comes to resolving the problems of the implementation of the law. NGO methods centered on legal means, and complemented with other tools might be deemed more successful. References to rule of law also have the advantage of depoliticizing the debate: instead of ethicized slogans, legal arguments are employed. Furthermore, being single-issue organizations, they were not bound by informal bargains and could openly criticize RMDSZ as well, forcing it to take action.

As already highlighted, the NGOs used advocacy strategies that are well documented in the literature on human rights treaty implementation. Simmons argues that there are three ways through which international human rights treaties influence local policymaking. First, they may alter national agendas; second, they provide legal resources for strategic litigation; and third, they may strengthen political mobilization (Simmons 2009). The latter two were important in the strategies of the aforementioned NGOs. As mentioned earlier, other analysts have argued that effective policy changes in human rights can be achieved through applying parallel pressure from "above" (by transnational actors) and "below" (by local NGOs) (Risse-Kappen et al. 1999; Keck and Sikkink 1999). Thus, norm infusion depends on the capacity of local actors to draw the attention of the international community to specific cases, and by activating a transnational advocacy network pressure is applied on the state, which is first pushed to change its discourse and then its actions. Transnational advocacy networks can help domestic NGOs to articulate their causes in a language compatible with human rights which is understood and accepted by the international community (Keck and Sikkink 1999; Merry 2006). In other words, international organizations or members of the international community will get involved only if a certain kind of discourse is employed: that of the rule of law and human rights.

The NGOs presented in the case studies tried to take into account all of these considerations: They used international treaties as a resource;

they started strategic litigation; they sought out transnational connections to put pressure on the state; and they "talked the talk" of international advocacy. These strategies, however, were only partially successful. In the remainder of this chapter, we outline several factors that hinder successful advocacy in terms of the implementation of existing legislation concerning linguistic rights.

First, existing NGOs are isolated and only locally active. The cases outlined above constitute the exception and not the rule. For a breakthrough in language rights implementation, a more consistent strategy is required with lots of NGOs following the same path.

Second, strategic litigation and reference to the rule of law was a central element in both cases. However, there are only a handful of cases currently in front of the courts or the NCCD. There is also a lack of human capacity: Few people are capable of writing good quality complaints or trial documents. Making technical or professional mistakes may damage the movement as a whole.

Third, the weakest pillar is the transnational one. Over the past twenty years, the international field of claim-making and advocacy has practically been neglected in Transylvania. Additionally, representatives of international organizations have treated RMDSZ as a political party that participates at the legislative and executive levels, and key positions in the Romanian minority protection regime have been held by ethnic Hungarians appointed by RMDSZ.[92] In many instances, the party has represented the Romanian state at international hearings. Clear examples of this perspective are the reports from the UN CCPR hearings on the Romanian state in 1999 and 2017. In both cases, in the Romanian delegation there were ethnic Hungarians who were authorized to present the situation of the implementation of minority rights in education (UN-CCPR 1999, 2017). In other words, the involvement of RMDSZ at the executive level was central evidence that minority rights issues in Romania were being resolved and solutions implemented. A related problem is that alternative reporting mechanisms for the international treaties on minority protection were not developed until recently.

[92]The key figures in the leadership of the Department for Interethnic Relations (DIR) and the NCCD have been ethnic Hungarians during the last one and a half decades.

Fourth, many actors involved in the field of language rights actually do not "talk the talk" of international human rights advocacy. RMDSZ and associated NGOs are not always interested in the legal resolution of cases or in the technicization of the discourse. Asymmetric bargaining works best when both legal insecurity and informality are high. RMDSZ also uses the issue of (unsolved) linguistic rights to sustain electoral mobilization.

To conclude, the above-mentioned cases opened the door to alternative claim-making strategies. However, the existing NGOs are far from making a breakthrough. For this, closer cooperation and a denser network would be needed. Neither is RMDSZ eager to accept that there are new actors interested in advocacy. It is highly unlikely that the party will cede this territory to NGOs who "talk the talk" of international organizations and are successfully able to find transnational partners interested in minority rights.

References

Aldrich, J. H. (1995). *Why parties? The origin and transformation of political parties in America. American politics and political economy series*. Chicago: The University of Chicago Press.

Alonso, S., & Ruiz-Rufino, R. (2007). Political representation and ethnic conflict in new democracies. *European Journal of Political Research, 46*(2), 237–267.

Bakk, M. (2000a). 1989–1999: az RMDSZ első tíz éve. In B. Bodó (Ed.), *Romániai Magyar Évkönyv*. Kolozsvár: Polis.

Bakk, M. (2000b). Modellviták – rejtett stratégiák. *Magyar Kisebbség, 6*(1), 8–12.

Bakk, M. (2004). Az autonómia-tervek két szakasza Erdélyben 1989 után. *Magyar Kisebbség, 9*(1–2), 39–60.

Bakk, M., Horváth, A., & Salat, L. (2004). Az RMDSZ 2003-ban – útkeresés integrációs határpontokban. In É. Blénesi & K. Mandel (Eds.), *Kisebbségek és kormánypolitika Közép-Európában, 2002–2004*. Budapest: Gondolat–MTA Etnikai-Nemzeti Kisebbségkutató Intézet.

Bárdi, N. (2004). *Tény és való. A budapesti kormányzatok és a határon túli magyarság kapcsolattörténete. Problémakatalógus*. Pozsony: Kalligram.

Bárdi, N. (2017). Álságos állítások a magyar etnopolitikában. A külhoni magyarok és a budapesti kormányzatok magyarságpolitikája. In A. Jakab & L. Urván (Eds.), *Hegymenet. Társadalmi és politikai kihívások Magyarországon* (pp. 130–155). Budapest: Osiris.
Bárdi, N., & Misovicz, T. (2010). A kisebbségi magyar közösségek támogatásának politikája. In B. Bitskey (Ed.), *Határon túli magyarság a 21. Században* (pp. 66–76). Budapest: Köztársasági Elnöki Hivatal.
Bauböck, R. (2007). The trade-off between transnational citizenship and political autonomy. In T. Faist & P. Kivisto (Eds.), *Dual citizenship in global perspective: From unitary to multiple citizenship* (pp. 69–91). Basingstoke and New York: Palgrave Macmillan.
Bauböck, R. (2010). *Dual citizenship for transborder minorities? How to respond to the Hungarian-Slovak tit-for-tat?* (EUI Working Papers No. 75).
Birnir, J. K. (2007). *Ethnicity and electoral politics.* Cambridge and New York: Cambridge University Press.
Biró, Z. A. (1998a). Intézményesedési folyamatok a romániai magyarság körében. In Z. A. Biró (Ed.), *Stratégia vagy kényszerpályák? Tanulmányok a romániai magyar társadalomról* (pp. 16–47). Csíkszereda: Pro-Print.
Biró, Z. A. (1998b). *Stratégia vagy kényszerpályák? Tanulmányok a romániai magyar társadalomról.* Csíkszereda: Pro-Print.
Bíró, A., & Pallai, K. (2011). *Public financing of national minority organisations: Policy paradigms, policy regimes and good practice.* Study prepared for the committee of experts on issues relating to the protection of national minorities. Strasbourg: Council of Europe.
Bognár, Z. (2006). Romániai magyar autonómiakoncepciók. Az 1989 és 2006 között kidolgozott törvénytervezetek. In M. Ludassy, Z. Bognár, G. Egry, L. Salat, & F. Fejtő (Eds.), *Autonómia, liberalizmus, szociáldemokrácia. Fejtő Ferenc, Salat Levente, Ludassy Mária, Egry Gábor és Bognár Zoltán írásai* (pp. 85–117). Budapest: Európai Összehasonlító Kisebbségkutatások Közalapítvány.
Bourdieu, P. (1991). *Language and symbolic power.* Cambridge, MA: Harvard University Press.
Bourdieu, P. (1993a). *The field of cultural production: Essays on art and literature.* New York: Columbia University Press.
Bourdieu, P. (1993b). *Sociology in question: Theory, culture & society.* London and Thousand Oaks, CA: Sage.
Bozóki, A. (2002). *The roundtable talks of 1989. The genesis of Hungarian democracy: Analysis and documents.* Budapest: Central European University Press.

Brubaker, R. (1995). National minorities, nationalizing states, and external national homelands in the new Europe. *Daedalus, 124*(2), 107–132.
Brubaker, R. (1996). *Nationalism reframed nationhood and the national question in the New Europe*. Cambridge and New York: Cambridge University Press.
Brubaker, R. (1998). Migrations of ethnic unmixing in the "New Europe". *International Migration Review, 32*(4), 1047–1065.
Brubaker, R. (2000). Accidental diasporas and external "homelands" in central and eastern Europe: Past and present. *IHS Political Science Series*, 71, 1–19.
Brubaker, R. (2004). *Ethnicity without groups*. Cambridge, MA: Harvard University Press.
Brubaker, R. (2005). The 'diaspora' diaspora. *Ethnic and Racial Studies, 28*(1), 1–19.
Brubaker, R. (2009). National homogenization and ethnic reproduction on the European periphery. In M. Barbagli & H. Ferguson (Eds.), *La teoria sociologica e lo stato moderno: saggi in onore di Gianfranco Poggi* (pp. 201–221). Bologna: Il mulino.
Brubaker, R. (2011). Nationalizing states revisited: Projects and processes of nationalization in post-Soviet states. *Ethnic and Racial Studies, 34*(11), 1785–1814.
Brubaker, R., Feischmidt, M., Fox, J., & Grancea, L. (2006). *Nationalist politics and everyday ethnicity in a Transylvanian town*. Princeton: Princeton University Press.
Budge, I., & Farlie, D. (1983). Party competition: Selective emphasis or direct confrontation? In H. Daalder & P. Mair (Eds.), *Western European party systems: Continuity & change* (pp. 267–305). Beverly Hills, CA: Sage.
Cederman, L.-E., Wimmer, A., & Min, B. (2009). Why do ethnic groups rebel? New data and analysis. *World Politics, 62*(1), 87–119.
Cercel, C. (2017). Postwar (west) German-Romanian relations: Expanding Brubaker's analytic triad. *Nationalism and Ethnic Politics, 23*(3), 297–317.
Chandra, K. (2004). *Why ethnic parties succeed: Patronage and ethnic head counts in India. Cambridge studies in comparative politics*. Cambridge, UK; New York: Cambridge University Press.
Chandra, K. (2005). Ethnic parties and democratic stability. *Perspectives on Politics, 3*(2), 235–252.
Chandra, K. (2012). Introduction. In K. Chandra (Ed.), *Constructivist theories of ethnic politics* (pp. 1–50). New York: Oxford University Press.
Choudhry, S. (2008). Bridging comparative politics and comparative constitutional law: Constitutional design in divided societies. In S. Choudhry (Ed.),

Constitutional design for divided societies: Integration or accommodation? Oxford (pp. 3–40). New York: Oxford University Press.

Csergő, Z. (2007). *Talk of the nation: Language and conflict in Romania and Slovakia*. Ithaca: Cornell University Press.

Csergő, Z. (2013). Kosovo and the framing of non-secessionist self-government claims in Romania. *Europe-Asia Studies, 65*(5), 889–911.

Csergő, Z., & Goldgeier, J. M. (2004). Nationalist strategies and European integration. *Perspectives on Politics, 2*(1), 21–37.

Csergő, Z., & Goldgeier, J. M. (2006). Virtual nationalism in comparative context: How unique is the Hungarian approach? In I. Osamu (Ed.), *Beyond sovereignty: From status law to transnational citizenship?* (pp. 281–302). Sapporo: Slavic Research Center, Hokkaido University.

Csergő, Z., & Regelmann, A.-C. (2017). Europeanization and collective rationality in minority voting. *Problems of Post-Communism, 64*(5), 291–310.

Csigó, P. (2016). '89 mint társadalmi csapda. In G. Földes & A. Antal (Eds.), *Holtpont. Társadalomkritikai tanulmányok Magyarország elmúlt 25 évéről* (pp. 106–145). Budapest: Napvilág.

Domokos, G. (1991, February 12). Az irreális azonnaliság nem lehet kenyerünk. Válasz Eva Maria Barkinak. *Romániai Magyar Szó.*

Domokos, G. (1996). *Esély I.* Csíkszereda: Pallas-Akadémia.

Fearon, J. D. (1999). *Why ethnic politics and 'pork' tend to go together* (Working Paper). Stanford, CA: Stanford University.

Goodman, R., & Jinks, D. (2004). How to influence states: Socialization and international human rights law. *Duke Law Journal, 54*(3), 621–703.

Gorenburg, D. P. (2003). *Minority ethnic mobilization in the Russian Federation.* Cambridge and New York: Cambridge University Press.

Hall, P. A., & Taylor, R. C. R. (1996). Political science and the three new institutionalisms. *Political Studies, 44*(5), 936–957.

Horowitz, D. L. (1985). *Ethnic groups in conflict.* Berkeley: University of California Press.

Horowitz, D. L. (1991). *A democratic South Africa?: Constitutional engineering in a divided society perspectives on southern Africa.* Berkeley: University of California Press.

Horváth, A. (2015). Inkább gazda volnék, mint politikus. In J. Szántai (Ed.). *foter.ro.*

Horváth, I. (2002). *Facilitating conflict transformation: Implementation of the recommendations of the OSCE high commissioner on national minorities to Romania, 1993–2001* (Working Paper). Hamburg: CORE.
Horváth, I., & Lazăr, M. (2001). Dinamica relațiilor interetnice din ultimul deceniu. *Altera, 16,* 120–136.
Horváth, I., & Scacco, A. (2001). From the unitary to the pluralistic: Fine-tuning minority policy in Romania. In A. Bíró & P. Kovács (Eds.), *Diversity in action: Local public management of multiethnic communities in central and eastern Europe* (pp. 243–271). Budapest: OSI.
Järve, P. (2000). *Ethnic democracy and Estonia: Application of Smooha's Model* (ECMI Working Papers 7).
Jenkins, R. (2008). *Rethinking ethnicity* (2nd ed.). Thousand Oaks, CA: Sage.
Jenne, E. K. (2007). *Ethnic bargaining: The paradox of minority empowerment.* Ithaca, NY: Cornell University Press.
Joppke, C. (2005). *Selecting by origin: Ethnic migration and liberal state.* Cambridge, MA: Harvard University Press.
Kántor, Z. (2000). Kisebbségi nemzetépítés. A romániai magyarság mint nemzetépítő kisebbség. *Regio, 11*(3), 219–241.
Kántor, Z. (2014). *A nemzet intézményesülése a rendszerváltás utáni Magyarországon* (p. 298). Budapest: Osiris.
Kántor, Z., Majtényi, B., Ieda, O., Vizi, B., & Halász, I. (Eds.). (2004). *Beyond sovereignty: From status law to transnational citizenship?* Sappuro: 21st century COE program Slavic Eurasian studies.
Keck, M. E., & Sikkink, K. (1999). Transnational advocacy networks in international and regional politics. *International Social Science Journal, 51*(159), 89–101.
Kiss, T. (2015). Increasing marginality, ethnic parallelism and asymmetric accommodation. Social and political processes concerning the Hungarian community of Transylvania. *Minority Studies, 18,* 33–69.
Kiss, T. (2017). Beyond the ethnic vote: Shifting determinants of the electoral behavior of Transylvanian Hungarians. *Problems of Post-Communism,* 1–17. https://doi.org/10.1080/10758216.2017.1336422.
Kiss, T., & Székely, I. G. (2016). Shifting linkages in ethnic mobilization: The case of RMDSZ and the Hungarians in Transylvania. *Nationalities Papers, 44*(4), 591–610.
Kiss, T., Székely, I. G., & Barna, G. (2017). Factors affecting turnout among ethnic minority voters: The case of Hungarians in Transylvania. *Intersections-East European Journal of Society and Politics, 3*(4), 87–119.

Kitschelt, H. (2001). Divergent paths of postcommunist democracies. In L. J. Diamond & R. Gunther (Eds.), *Political parties and democracy* (pp. 299–326). Baltimore, MD: Johns Hopkins University Press.
Kopecký, P., & Scherlis, G. (2008). Party patronage in contemporary Europe. *European Review, 16*(3), 355–371.
Kovács, M., & Tóth, J. (2013). *EUDO citizenship observatory country report: Hungary*. Florence: EUDO.
Kusá, D. (2013). *EUDO citizenship observatory country report: Slovakia*. Florence: EUDO.
Kymlicka, W. (2007). *Multicultural odysseys: Navigating the new international politics of diversity*. Oxford and New York: Oxford University Press.
Kymlicka, W. (2011). Beyond the indigenous/minority dichotomy? In S. Allen & A. Xanthaki (Eds.), *Reflections on the UN declaration on the rights of indigenous peoples* (pp. 183–208). Oxford and Portland, OR: Hart Publishing.
Laitin, D. D., & Van der Veen, M. A. (2012). Ethnicity and pork: A virtual test of causal mechanisms. In K. Chandra (Ed.), *Constructivist theories of ethnic politics* (pp. 341–358). New York: Oxford University Press.
László, M., & Novák, C. Z. (2012). *A szabadság terhe. Marosvásárhely, 1990. március 16–21*. Csíkszereda: Pro-Print.
Liebich, A. (2009). Altneul€ander or the vicissitudes of citizenship in the New EU states. In R. Bauböck & B. Perchinig (Eds.), *Citizenship policies in the New Europe* (Expanded and updated ed., pp. 21–42). Amsterdam: Amsterdam University Press.
Lijphart, A. (1977). *Democracy in plural societies: A comparative exploration*. New Haven: Yale University Press.
Magyar, B. L. (2016). *Post-communist mafia state: The case of Hungary*. Budapest: Central European University Press, in association with Noran Libro.
Markó, B. (2008). Egy elmaradt egyezség története. *Élet és Irodalom* (no. 38).
Markó, B. (2009). Kormányból ellenzékbe. A romániai magyar politika tizenkét éve. *Élet és irodalom* (no. 3).
Márton, J., & Orbán, B. (2005). Elemzés a 2005-ös kisebbségi törvénytervezetről. *Magyar Kisebbség, 9*(1–2), 5–38.
McGarry, J., O'Leary, B., & Simeon, R. (2008). Integration or accommodation? In S. Choudhry (Ed.), *Constitutional design for divided societies: Integration or accommodation?* (pp. 41–88). Oxford and New York: Oxford University Press.
Medianu, N. (2002). Analysing political exchanges between minority and majority leaders in Romania. *Global Review of Ethnopolitics, 1*(4), 28–41.

Melvin, N. (2000). Post-imperial ethnocracy and the russophone minorities of Estonia and Latvia. In J. Stein (Ed.), *The policies of national minority participation post-communist Europe: State-building, democracy and ethnic mobilisation* (pp. 129–166). New York: East-West Institute.

Merry, S. E. (2006). *Human rights and gender violence: Translating international law into local justice. Chicago series in law and society*. Chicago: University of Chicago Press.

Mitchell, P., Evans, G., & O'Leary, B. (2009). Extremist outbidding in ethnic party systems is not inevitable: Tribune parties in Northern Ireland. *Political Studies, 57*(2), 397–421.

Nastasă, L., & Salat, L. (Eds.). (2000). *Relații interetnice în România postcomunistă*. Cluj: Fundația CRDE.

OSCE-HCNM. (1999). *The Lund Recommendations on the effective participation of national minorities in public life & explanatory note*. OSCE High Commissioner on National Minorities.

OSCE-HCNM. (2012). *Ljubljana guidelines of integrating diverse societies*. OSCE High Commissioner on National Minorities.

Papp, A. Z. (2010). Határon túli magyar oktatási támogatások és hasznosulásuk 2006–2010 között. *Educatio, 11*(1), 88–110.

Pettai, V. (2007). Explaining ethnic politics in the Baltic States: Reviewing the triadic nexus model. *Journal of Baltic Studies, 37*(1), 124–136.

Pierson, P. (2000). Increasing returns, path dependence, and the study of politics. *American Political Science Review, 94*(2), 251–267.

Pogonyi, S. (2011). Dual citizenship and sovereignty. *Nationalities Papers, 39*(5), 685–704.

Pogonyi, S. (2017). *Extra-territorial ethnic politics, discourses and identities in Hungary*. New York, Berlin, and Heidelberg: Springer.

Posner, D. N. (2005). *Institutions and ethnic politics in Africa*. Cambridge: Cambridge University Press, p. 337.

Rabushka, A., & Shepsle, K. A. (1972). *Politics in plural societies: A theory of democratic instability. Merrill political science series*. Columbus, OH: Merrill.

Ram, M. H. (2009). Romania: From laggard to leader? In B. Rechel (Ed.), *Minority rights in central and eastern Europe* (pp. 180–194). London and New York: Routledge.

Ravasz, Á. (2013). Szlovákiai magyarok mint választók, 2009–2013. *Magyar Kisebbség, 18*(2), 42–68.

Rechel, B. (2009). Introduction. In B. Rechel (Ed.), *Minority rights in central and eastern Europe* (pp. 3–16). London and New York: Routledge.

Risse, T. (1999). International norms and domestic change: Arguing and communicative behavior in the human rights area. *Politics & Society, 27*(4), 529–559.

Risse-Kappen, T., Ropp, S. C., & Sikkink, K. (1999). *The power of human rights: International norms and domestic change. Cambridge studies in international relations.* New York: Cambridge University Press.

RMDSZ. (2016). Benkő Erika az ENSZ Ember Jogi Tanácsának Fórumán: a magyar közösség folyamatosan támadásoknak van kitéve.

RMDSZ. (2017). ÁLLÁSPONT - a magyar nyelv használata az egészségügyben és a szociális szolgáltatásokat nyújtó intézményekben.

Saideman, S. M., & Ayres, R. W. (2008). *For kin or country: Xenophobia, nationalism, and war.* New York: Columbia University Press.

Salat, L. (2003). Kisebbségi magyar jövőképek esélyei és buktatói Erdélyben. *Kisebbségkutatás* (3).

Salat, L. (2011). A politikai közösség kérdése a többség–kisebbség viszonyának a nézőpontjából. *Magyar Kisebbség, XVI*(3–4), 159–190.

Salat, L. (2014). Az RMDSZ tervezete az autonómia látszatát próbálja kelteni. In M. Kertész (Ed.), *transindex.ro.*

Salat, L., & Novák, C. Z. (2015). Ethnicity, nationalism, and the minority regime. In L. Stan & D. Vancea (Eds.), *Post-communist Romania at twenty-five: Linking past, present, and future* (pp. 63–86). Lanham: Lexington Books.

Salat, L., & Székely, I. G. (2014). Conclusions. In L. Salat, S. Constantin, A. G. Osipov, & I. N. G. Székely (Eds.), *Autonomy arrangements around the world: A collection of well and lesser known cases* (pp. 443–478). Cluj: Romanian Institute for Research of National Minorities.

Simmons, B. A. (2009). *Mobilizing for human rights: International law in domestic politics.* Cambridge and New York: Cambridge University Press.

Sipos, Z. (2017). Határon túli támogatások 2: Az állandó tételek és a legjobb barátok. *Átlátszó Erdély*, 20 March. Avaialble at: https://erdely.atlatszo.hu/2017/03/20/hataron-tuli-tamogatasok-2-az-allando-tetelek-es-a-legjobb-baratok/ (Accessed 18 February 2018).

Smith, D. J. (2002). Framing the national question in central and eastern Europe: A quadratic nexus? *Global Review of Ethnopolitics, 2*(1), 3–16.

Smooha, S. (2001). *The model of ethnic democracy* (ECMI Working Papers 13).

Stokes, D. E. (1963). Spatial models of party competition. *American Political Science Review, 57*(2), 368–377.

Stroschein, S. (2011). Demography in ethnic party fragmentation: Hungarian local voting in Romania. *Party Politics, 17*(2), 189–204.

Stroschein, S. (2012). *Ethnic struggle, coexistence, and democratization in eastern Europe. Cambridge studies in contentious politics*. Cambridge and New York: Cambridge University Press.

Szabó, T. (2017). Semmi sem garantálja a magyar nyelvű ellátást a kórházakban. *foter.ro*, 18 April. Avaialble at: http://foter.ro/cikk/20170418_semmi_sem_garantalja_a_magyar_nyelvu_ellatast_a_korhazakban?utm_source=foter_ro&utm_medium=link&utm_campaign=foter_ro_201712.

Székely, I. G. (2011). *Democrație consociaționistă sau împărțirea puterii în societăți multietnice. Cadru teoretic și patru studii de caz*. Cluj: Institutul pentru Studierea Problemelor Minorităților Naționale and Kriterion.

Székely, I. G. (2014). *Dynamics of party politics, electoral competition and cooperation within the Hungarian minorities of Romania, Serbia and Slovakia*. PhD thesis, Central European University, Budapest.

Székely, I. G., & Horváth, I. (2014). Diversity recognition and minority representation in central and southeast Europe: A comparative analysis. *Nationalities Papers, 42*(3), 426–448.

Szilágyi, N. S. (1991). Mi lesz veled, RMDSZ? *Korunk, 2*(2), 159–166.

Thelen, K. (1999). Historical institutionalism in comparative politics. *Annual Review of Political Science, 2*(1), 369–404.

Tőkés, G. (1999). A szétszedett végrehajtás. Az RMDSZ Ügyvezető Elnökségének szervezetei elemzése. *WEB, 4–5*, 52–63.

Toró, T. (2013). *A romániai magyar nyilvánosság alakulásának diskurzusa politikai filozófiai megközelítésben*. Ph.D., Babeș-Bolyai Tudományegyetem, Kolozsvár.

Toró, T. (2016). Hungarian minority politics in post-socialist Romania: Interests, strategies, and discourses. *Acta Universitatis Sapientiae, European and Regional Studies, 10*(1), 79–106.

Toró, T. (2017a). Detached implementation. Discourse and practice in minority language usage in Romania. Manuscript.

Toró, T. (2017b). Ethnicization or de-ethnicization? Hungarian political representation in the Romanian parliament. *Nationalities Papers, 46*(2), 219–236.

Tsebelis, G. (1990). *Nested games: Rational choice in comparative politics. California series on social choice and political economy*. Berkeley: University of California Press.

UN-CCPR. (1999). *Summary record of the 1768th meeting: Romania*. 1 November 1999: International Covenant on Civil and Political RightsCCPR/C/SR.1768.

UN-CCPR. (2017). *Summary record of the 3428th meeting. Consideration of reports submitted by Romania*: International Covenant on Civil and Political RightsCCPR/C/SR.3428.

Vasi, I. B. (2004). The fist of the working class: The social movements of Jiu Valley miners in post-socialist Romania. *East European Politics and Societies, 18*(1), 132–157.

Veres, V. (2008). *Analiza comparată a identității minorităților maghiare din Bazinul Carpatic. A Kárpát-medencei magyarok nemzeti identitásának összehasonlító elemzése* (ISPMN Working papers 44).

Vermeersch, P. (2011). *Theories of ethnic mobilization: Overview and recent trends* (RPD Working Paper 3).

Volintiru, C. (2012). *Institutional distortions, clientelism and corruption: Evidence from Romania* (CCREI Working Papers 1).

Waterbury, M. A. (2010). *Between state and nation: Diaspora politics and kin-state nationalism in Hungary* (1st ed.). New York: Palgrave Macmillan.

Waterbury, M. A. (2014). Making citizens beyond the borders. *Problems of Post-Communism, 61*(4), 36–49.

Waterbury, M. A. (2017). National minorities in an era of externalization: Kin-state citizenship, European integration, and ethnic Hungarian minority politics. *Problems of Post-Communism, 64*(5), 228–241.

Wimmer, A. (2002). *Nationalist exclusion and ethnic conflict: Shadows of modernity.* Cambridge and New York: Cambridge University Press.

Wolczuk, K. (2010). History, Europe and the "national idea": The "official" narrative of national identity in Ukraine. *Nationalities Papers, 28*(4), 671–694.

Wolff, S., & Cordell, K. (2003). Ethnic Germans as a language minority in central and eastern Europe: Legislative and policy frameworks in Poland, Hungary and Romania. In G. Hogan-Brun & S. Wolff (Eds.), *Minority languages in Europe: Frameworks, status, prospects* (pp. 99–119). Basingstoke: Palgrave Macmillan.

4

Language Use, Language Policy, and Language Rights

István Horváth and Tibor Toró

This chapter discusses the most important characteristics of the Hungarian linguistic community, their linguistic behavior and attitudes, and the subsequent language policies in force in Romania that shape everyday language use in both the private and public domains.

By language policy, we mean a complex set of political, institutional, demographic, and social factors that influence the general communicational patterns of individuals. According to Spolsky (2004), the language policy of a speech community consists of three interrelated elements: language practices, language ideologies, and language management. The first describes the habitual patterns characteristic of a group with regard to selecting between different languages; the second

I. Horváth (✉)
Romanian Institute for Research on National Minorities, Cluj-Napoca, Romania

T. Toró
International Relations and European Studies Department, Sapientia Hungarian University of Transylvania, Cluj-Napoca, Romania
e-mail: torotibor@sapientia.ro

T. Kiss et al. (eds.), *Unequal Accommodation of Minority Rights*, Palgrave Politics of Identity and Citizenship Series,
https://doi.org/10.1007/978-3-319-78893-7_4

describes the beliefs that surround language and language use; and the last comprises efforts to modify or influence language practices through planning, regulation, or management of language use, mostly by government interventions based on formal instruments. Similar analytical guidelines are proposed by Kaplan and Baldauf (1997), who argue that language policy (and planning) should be analyzed in parallel on two levels: the macro-level, where measures of intervention and regulation are formulated, mostly by governmental agencies and actors, and the micro-level, where the policies are actually implemented and attitudes toward these are formed.

An appealing methodology for the study of the implementation of language policies is offered by Grin (2003), who proposes three levels of analysis. First, one should look at the *capacity* to speak the language. This is mostly guaranteed by the educational system which is responsible for the reproduction of a certain number of speakers on a given territory. Second, one should focus on the *opportunity* to speak the language. This is linked to the language-related policies which provide opportunities for minorities to use their own language. The third element is *desire/willingness*, which is related to the language practices and attitudes of minority members. Grin argues that one can speak about fully fledged language policies only if all three elements are in place.

In this chapter, we follow this framework of analysis, with the qualification that only the first two elements will be assessed thoroughly, while the desire and willingness to use the language are discussed only in an illustrative manner in a section about language rights implementation. Following this framework of analysis, the chapter is divided in the following way: First, we describe the Hungarian speakers of Transylvania, providing data about their numbers and geographic distribution, assessing the linguistic skills of ethnic Hungarians, and paying special attention to bilingualism.[1] Then, we shift our focus to opportunity, analyzing the official language policies of Romania in several key areas. We discuss

[1]Note that, despite the paramount importance of the educational system in language reproduction, we do not deal with this topic in this chapter as Hungarian-language education in Romania is discussed in great detail in Chapter 6 in this volume.

not only the status of the Hungarian language, but try to also shed light on the dominant language ideologies characteristic of the country. The third part summarizes the most important findings of research about the implementation of language policies in Romania and patterns of language use among Transylvanian Hungarians in various domains of everyday life.

1 The Hungarian Linguistic Community in Romania

Despite the various methodological problems that plague the recording of identity-related data (DeVries 1985; Skutnabb-Kangas 1997), the census remains the most comprehensive systematic data source about the linguistic situation of ethnic communities. In Romania, every census held since 1930 has contained items about respondents' mother tongue and nationality (ethnicity). However, census questions regarding language were limited to ask for the mother tongue of respondents; in none of the censuses were there included any questions about knowledge of other languages, the linguistic behavior of multilingual people, or about other dimensions of linguistic identity such as language use within different domains or the relationship between ethnic origin and linguistic identification. Mother tongue, as registered in the census, is formally defined as the language first acquired in early childhood.

As shown in Table 1, before 1918 the number and percentage of native Hungarian speakers in Transylvania were gradually increasing. This can be explained mostly by the assimilationist policies of the Hungarian state at the time. After 1918, however, their number decreased drastically as a consequence of migration on the one hand and of the new census methodology used by the Romanian state on the other hand.[2] Between World War II and 1990, the Hungarian-speaking community grew in absolute number but decreased in proportion. In

[2]For a detailed account of census methodology, see Chapter 10 in this volume.

Table 1 Native speakers of Hungarian in Romania and Transylvania (1869–2011)

	Romania		Transylvania	
	N	%	*N*	%
1869			1,052,300	24.99
1880			1,007,425	25.10
1890			1,198,147	27.18
1900			1,433,252	29.56
1910			1,653,943	31.64
1930	1,554,525	10.89	1,480,712	26.69
1948	1,499,851	9.45	1,481,903	25.72
1956	1,653,700	9.46	1,616,199	25.93
1966	1,651,873	8.65	1,625,702	24.13
1977	1,750,000	8.12	NA	NA
1992	1,639,135	7.19	1,630,584	21.11
2002	1,443,970	6.66	1,429,473	19.79
2011	1,259,914	6.26	1,248,623	18.39

Source Authors' own calculations based on Varga (1998) and census data

the post-socialist period, the decline has been rather significant with regard to both indicators.[3]

As discussed in detail in Chapter 10 on demographic dynamics, ethnicity and mother tongue are very strongly correlated in the case of Hungarians: In 2011, 97.1% of the 1.24 million persons who identified as ethnic Hungarians also declared that Hungarian was their mother tongue. Consequently, it is precisely the exceptions that are the most interesting—the so-called partial Hungarian identities, when ethnic identity and mother tongue do not coincide.

Comparison of the last three censuses shows that both the absolute number and the proportion of native Hungarian speakers who identify with some other ethnicity than Hungarian are slowly but clearly increasing (48,845—2.92% in 1992, 53,650—4.19% in 2011), while the number and proportion of ethnic Hungarians with other

[3]In the case of the last census, the decrease can be explained partly by the fact that the original results were supplemented with data taken from the population registers, as the Statistical Office considered that due to the high number of Romanian citizens living abroad, the overall population of the country had been underestimated. The data taken from the population registers did not contain information on ethnicity or mother tongue.

mother tongues are slowly decreasing (34,669—2.07% in 1992, 21,359—1.67% in 2011). While most of the individuals in the former category come from Hungarian-speaking Roma communities (growth in absolute numbers being due to their higher fertility rates), those who declared themselves Hungarian ethnics but not Hungarian native speakers may be classified into two categories. The first category includes persons born from ethnically mixed marriages who identify as Hungarian but barely speak the language, while the second consists of individuals with Hungarian origins who identify willingly as Hungarian but do not speak the language fluently or at all. These explanations are backed up by the results of large-scale surveys: Horváth (2009) reports that 2% of those who identify as ethnic Hungarians barely speak the language. The decline in the absolute number (and share of) ethnic Hungarians who are not Hungarian native speakers is also related to the fact that in many settlements the Hungarian speech community is shrinking rather fast, and in such contexts, the exposure of individual speakers of the language to diglossia and language shift is increasing too.

As shown in Table 1, the overwhelming majority of the Hungarian-speaking population live in Transylvania (99.1% in 2011). About 10% of them live in administrative units where their proportion is below 10% (Table 2), but about half of this population live in seven larger cities where the number of Hungarian native speakers exceeds 3000 persons, so at least in theory they are able to form a speech community.[4] This means that only approximately 3.5–4% of Transylvania's Hungarians (around 50,000 people) live in settlements where they can probably use their native language only in a very limited way (in the private sphere or in media consumption).

Another important distinction comes with the 20% threshold. Theoretically, this is very important, as the law on local public administration[5] grants the right to use minority languages in relations with

[4]Being aware of the problematic and controversial nature of the concept (Patrick 2002; Morgan 2014, pp. 1–10), we use it to denote a community of a critical number of people (around 3000 persons) which has the potential to maintain mother-tongue institutions outside the private sphere (religious congregations, schools, cultural institutions, etc.).

[5]Law 215/2001.

Table 2 Hungarian speakers in Transylvania by their proportion in the administrative units (2011)

Proportion of Hungarian native speakers in administrative unit	Number of administrative units	Total number of Hungarian native speakers (No.)	Proportion of total Hungarian native speaking population (%)
No Hungarian-speaking population	110	0	0
Between 0.01–10%	661	123,893	9.93
Between 10.01–20%	87	140,295	11.25
Between 20.01–50%	121	307,825	24.68
Between 50.01–80%	76	256,175	20.54
Between 80.01–100%	126	419,069	33.60
Total	1181	1,247,257	100

Source Authors' own calculations based on census data

the public if the *proportion of members of the minority exceeds 20%* in the administrative unit. As already stressed, the official number of *Hungarian native speakers* and *ethnic Hungarians* does not fully coincide, and there are a few administrative units where the proportion of Hungarian native speakers exceeds 20% but the percentage of ethnic Hungarians remains below this threshold; in these settlements, the provisions of the law concerning language rights do not apply.

Overall, according to the results of the 2011 census, about 79% of all native speakers of Hungarian (almost 1 million people) live in administrative units where the law provides for the use of the Hungarian language. Around 70% of the latter group live in administrative units where Hungarians form a majority at the local level, and approximately one-third live in settlements where their proportion exceeds 80%. In these settlements, Hungarian is the culturally unmarked[6] and dominant public language (Table 2).

[6]We use the term in the sense Brubaker et al. (2006, pp. 211–212) use it: to describe a reference category (or reference language) that is taken for granted in the community. In contrast, "marked" describes some kind of "otherness".

According to the results of the 2011 census, 51% of Hungarian native speakers live in urban settlements, and about a quarter of a million are concentrated in the nine largest cities in Transylvania.[7] At present time, none of these cities has a Hungarian majority. This is a major change compared to the beginning of the twentieth century: In 1910 six, and in 1930 four of these cities had a Hungarian-speaking majority (Varga 1991), while by 1992 of all cities with more than 100,000 inhabitants only Târgu Mureş/Marosvásárhely had a Hungarian majority. This means that the use of Hungarian has declined in urban environments. Notwithstanding this, such cities remain important centers for maintaining certain linguistic functions and institutions (schools, culture, local media), as well as for supporting the trans-local integration of rural speech communities from the surrounding areas. Currently, the largest Transylvanian settlement where Hungarian native speakers make up the majority of the population is Sfântu Gheorghe (Sepsiszentgyörgy), with approximately 54,000 inhabitants.

2 Bilingualism and Multilingualism Among Hungarians

Censuses provide no information about patterns of language use and language skills; thus, the analysis of bilingualism and multilingualism can only be based on large-scale surveys. This line of research is important from several perspectives. First, it helps with estimating the approximate number of people with some command of Hungarian in Romania. Second, the degree of bilingualism (meaning proficiency in Romanian) of the ethnic Hungarian population can be assessed. Third, the proficiency of Hungarians in languages other than Romanian can also be evaluated.

---

[7]The administrative units with more than 100,000 inhabitants are the following: Cluj-Napoca/Kolozsvár, Timişoara/Temesvár, Braşov/Brassó, Oradea/Nagyvárad, Arad, Sibiu/Szeben, Târgu Mureş/Marosvásárhely, Baia Mare/Nagybánya, Satu Mare/Szatmárnémeti.

Early studies of bilingualism distinguished between asymmetric and balanced bilingualism (Peal and Lambert 1962), the latter category denoting equal fluency in two languages. From the perspective of language policy and planning, this concept was of special importance, as reaching a state of balanced bilingualism may have satisfied the interests of both the state and the minority group. However, later studies showed that balanced bilingualism is a mere ideal, as it can hardly be stabilized (Baetens Beardsmore 1986). In most cases, language use is clustered and different languages are used in different contexts within domains. In other words, language use in bilingual societies is always asymmetric and the choice of language depends on the subject, the situation, and the languages dominantly used by its members (Fishman 1989, 2000).

2.1 Hungarian-Language Skills Among Persons of Other Ethnicity

Although in the last census (2011) only 0.8% of Transylvania's ethnic non-Hungarian inhabitants reported that Hungarian was their mother tongue, it can be reasonably assumed that the proportion of those who can speak some Hungarian is considerably higher. Based on research by Kiss and Kapitány (2009), we can state that 3.2% of Transylvania's non-Hungarians aged 20–45 had a level of proficiency in Hungarian such that they were able to answer survey questions in Hungarian.

The acquisition of the Hungarian-language skills of non-Hungarians can be described using three patterns. First, approximately half of the former acquired Hungarian in the family live in or come from interethnic mixed marriages. Second, about a quarter are ethnic Roma who speak Hungarian in everyday life and in many cases completed Hungarian-language (elementary) education. Most individuals in this category are Hungarian native speakers. The third category (about 20%) became bilingual in their living environment: They reside in regions or larger cities where the proportion of Hungarians is higher than 20–30% of the population. The language proficiency of the members of this last category is on average lower than that of persons belonging to the other two categories.

These findings reinforce our thesis about the asymmetric character of bilingualism in Romania, as the overwhelming proportion of ethnic Romanians are monolingual. Consequently, communication in Hungarian is limited mostly to intra-community interactions, as communicational situations that involve both majority and minority members (of the situation or domain) happen almost exclusively in Romanian.

2.2 The Romanian-Language Proficiency of Hungarians in Transylvania

As Romanian is the official and dominant language in the country, knowledge of it is of paramount importance to all citizens. Because of its legal functions and extended societal presence, most Hungarians face a variety of situations in which the usage of Romanian language is mandatory. According to the 2011 census, around two-thirds of Hungarian native speakers live in settlements where the proportion of Romanians is higher than 20%. In such settings, there are manifold everyday communicational situations (e.g., shopping, work), when (only) the Romanian language can be used. It is very important to stress that in these cases code-switching is one sided: Participants interpret Romanian as the public language and it becomes self-evident to all participants involved (including Hungarians) that they should switch to Romanian and continue conversations in this language. The explanation is twofold. On the one hand, only a few Romanians are proficient (enough) in Hungarian to use it, and on the other hand, the ideology and etiquette of language use accepted by both Hungarians and Romanians requires it.[8]

Another policy that strengthens the status of Romanian and reinforces the need to achieve proficiency in it is compulsory education

[8]It is important to point out that this situation cannot be generalized to all areas of the country. In regions where Hungarians constitute a dominant majority, in many cases Hungarian is the default language and the local Romanian population complies. However, even in those areas when ethnic Romanian communicational actors do not speak Hungarian, code-switching is typical.

in Romanian language and literature at all levels and in all types of education, including programs in minority languages. Also, Romanian is a compulsory subject in official school examinations (e.g., the National Evaluation at the end of the eighth grade and the Baccalaureate[9]). In other words, pupils studying in minority language programs are not only heavily exposed to the Romanian language within the formal framework of education, but the importance of studying the language is also continuously emphasized beyond the formal rules. Ultimately, Hungarian native speakers are expected to (at least in theory) have the opportunity to gain proficiency in Romanian both through everyday communicational situations and within the formal educational system.

Despite these possibilities, a number of studies have shown that not all Hungarians are bilingual (Horváth 2003; Horváth 2005, 2008a). The most important findings of surveys conducted about this topic can be summarized as follows[10]:

- Nearly two-thirds of Transylvania's Hungarians are highly or very highly proficient in Romanian (and about one-third consider that they speak both Hungarian and Romanian at native-speaker level);
- approximately 22–23% of Hungarians can communicate in Romanian in a satisfactory manner;
- about 12–13% of Hungarians have major difficulties speaking Romanian;
- about 4% of the total Hungarian population hardly speak the official language (more than 80% of these persons are elderly or persons with low mobility living in overwhelmingly Hungarian-inhabited small settlements).

For explaining and problematizing the (lack of) Romanian-language proficiency of Hungarians, several concurrent discourses are in circulation. On the one hand, there is the dominant discourse of the majority tending to exaggerate the lack of knowledge in Romanian of the

[9]See in detail Chapter 6 on education.

[10]The surveys measured self-reported proficiency in the language.

Hungarians, culminating in the popular urban legend that in Székely Land (a central area of Romania mostly inhabited by Hungarians) one cannot buy bread using Romanian.[11] On the other hand, Hungarians invoke the shortcomings of the educational system to explain these deficiencies. They criticize the curriculum and methodology through which the Romanian language is taught to minorities, arguing that Romanian language teaching is heavily focused on the development of literary and linguistic text analysis skills, general communicative skills that could be used in everyday life being largely ignored. A further complaint of the Hungarians concerns the lack of differentiation with regard to expectations, as at final exams the same achievements are expected from minority pupils (who speak and learn Romanian as a second language) as from native Romanian children (Szilágyi 1998). In principle, the law on education adopted in 2011[12] created the possibility for developing a parallel curriculum for children attending Hungarian-language education; however, insufficient progress has been made so far in its implementation (the law and the issue of the alternative curriculum are discussed in more detail in Chapter 6).

2.3 The Foreign (Other Than Romanian) Language Competences of Transylvanian Hungarians

According to Eurobarometer (2012) data, 54% of EU citizens were able to hold a conversation in at least one language in addition to their mother tongue, 25% in two, and 10% in three additional languages. The highest proportion of bilinguals was registered in Luxembourg (98%) and the lowest in Hungary (35%). Romania, with 48%, was located in the lower middle of the field. The most recent data that

[11]A widely mediatized recent example is the case of a vlogger who claimed that he was refused service in a supermarket in Odorheiu Secuiesc (Székelyudvarhely) after communicating in Romanian. His video (https://youtu.be/yflC_demZ_c) about the "incident" was viewed more than one million times in two months. Although eventually it turned out to be a fake, its success and agenda-setting capacity clearly showed the importance of the topic among the majority society. For more detail, see Scutaru (2017).

[12]Law 1/2011.

Table 3 Multilingualism among Transylvanian Hungarians

	Monolinguals	One additional language spoken	Two additional languages spoken	Three additional languages spoken
EU 27 (2012)	46	54	25	10
Romania (2012)	52	48	22	8
Hungarians in Transylvania (2009)	7	93	44	17
Hungary (2012)	65	35	13	4

Numbers represent percentages. *Source* Authors' own calculations based on Eurobarometer (2012) and survey data

we have about the foreign language proficiency of Transylvanian Hungarians come from 2009. According to this, 7% of the Hungarians in Transylvania are monolingual, while 93% speak at least one additional language and 44% at least two more languages (Table 3).

Unfortunately, the Eurobarometer survey does not differentiate between the minority and majority population; therefore, in the case of Transylvanian Hungarians, Romanian was probably also subsumed under the category of additional languages spoken. However, Romanian is the language of wider communication in society thus in terms of the motivation for language learning, frequency and function of usage radically differ from other second/foreign languages. Taking this into consideration, the proportion of Transylvanian Hungarians proficient in other second/foreign languages than Romanian is approximately 44%. As roughly 5% of the Romanian national sample in the Eurobarometer study consisted of ethnic Hungarians who probably declared Romanian as their second spoken language, the results for ethnic Romanians are likely to be around 44% as well. Therefore, we can conclude that the foreign language proficiency of Hungarians does not deviate from the Romanian average, and it is considerably higher than the average second language proficiency in Hungary (35%). This is a very important finding, because Transylvanian Hungarian intellectuals and elites tend to underestimate and criticize the foreign language proficiency of their community. The difference between the language proficiency of Transylvanian Hungarains and the one in Hungary can be explained by the foreign language teaching policies of the two countries, but also by the fact that Hungarians in Romania are exposed to Romanian (a language morphologically and lexically distant from Hungarian) at a relative early age, which creates a more receptive cognitive basis for acquiring a third or even fourth language (see, e.g., Cenoz 2001).

In the EU, the foreign language spoken by most people is English (38% of EU citizens speak it as a second language), followed by French (12%) and German (11%). English is most widely spoken in Romania too (31% of the population speak English), with French second (17%). In Hungary, 20% of the population speak English, while second place is occupied by German (18%). The Hungarians of Transylvania mix the patterns characteristic of Romania and Hungary: Their English-language proficiency is similar to that of Romanians, or even higher (34%), but the second most frequently spoken foreign language is not French but German (20% speak it at least on a basic level).

3 The Official Use of Hungarian, Linguistic Rights, and Their Implementation

In the past two decades, the direction of language policy in Romania has undergone a significant shift. While in the first few years after 1989 the objective was the strengthening of the state language to the detriment of minority languages (Szépe 1999), from 1997 a move toward pluralism occurred which brought about a significant expansion of minority language rights. A series of legal documents granting minority language rights in almost all relevant domains (especially education and public administration) were adopted, and Romania also ratified the European Charter for Regional or Minority Languages (ECRML) in 2008.

In order to substantiate these claims, in the following sections we analyze in detail the *opportunity* dimension (Grin 2003) of Romania's language policy. First, we compare Romania's language policy to that of the other post-Communist new member and candidate states of the EU. Then, we present the legal framework for minority language use in several domains, most importantly public administration and the judiciary. Finally, we assess the implementation of the legal provisions.

3.1 Romania's Language Policy in a Regional Comparative Perspective

To understand the peculiarities of the Romanian linguistic regime, we have chosen to compare it first to that of sixteen other post-Communist states.[13] We believe that most of these states faced similar problems and challenges regarding language and ethnicity and were exposed to similar pressures ensuing from EU conditionality, but that they responded differently, with solutions ranging from moderate/accommodative to more radical/exclusivist.

Language is central to nation-building, and thus, most states devise specific regulations to influence or shape linguistic practices within their territories that are anchored in the dominant language ideologies of the polity (Spolsky 2004; Blommaert 2006). The supreme directives are set out in constitutions which regulate the status of language(s) within the state, the nature of language rights, and the domains in which they should be applied. In addition to these, many states have adopted specific legislation on minority language rights. Therefore, we base our analysis on legal documents: constitutions, laws on minority protection and language usage, and reports submitted by states within the monitoring process of the ECRML and the Framework Convention for the Protection of National Minorities (FCNM).[14] In this section, we are only interested in the rights set out in legal documents and do not deal with their implementation, despite being aware that deficient implementation is one of the most serious problems in the region (Wolff et al. 2008).

---

[13]The chosen states are the following: Albania, Bosnia, Bulgaria, Croatia, Czech Republic, Estonia, Hungary, Kosovo, Latvia, Lithuania, Macedonia, Montenegro, Poland, Serbia, Slovakia, and Slovenia.

[14]We have relied on (mostly unofficial) English translations of relevant legal documents. ECRML and FCNM state reports were used. When the translations of relevant legal documents could not be found, we corroborated our interpretation with secondary literature.

3.1.1 Main Elements of Language Policy

Although language policies may be quite complex and any thorough comparative analysis should assess a myriad of specific details, we focus here on two main dimensions. The first refers to the existence of an official language and of further elements designed to reinforce the primacy of the official language vis-à-vis other languages. The second dimension grasps the regulations of minority language usage; regarding this, we analyze the subject of the rights that are granted, the principle on which they are granted, and the conditionality of their application, including possible restrictions. We limit the comparative analysis to minority language use in public administration, as this domain is the most conflictual and symbolically loaded, generating the strongest resistance from majorities (Csergő 2007).

1. Faingold (2004, p. 11) defines *official language* "as a language that a government uses for its day-to-day activities in the fields of legislation, judiciary, public administration, and teaching". It is not necessary for a state to have a single official language; it is at the state's discretion how many of the languages spoken within its territory are recognized (Turi 2012). The number of official languages can also be interpreted as the result of a choice between efficiency and fairness. While limiting the number of recognized languages can make the functioning of the state more efficient, recognition of minority languages can decisively affect conflict resolution (Pool 1991).

Andrássy (2011) argues that the introduction of official languages implicitly involves a hierarchization of the languages spoken in the country, as it entitles a part of the population to use their mother-tongue language in every domain, while others have to adapt to this situation. Despite this implicit differentiation, in some countries the official language enjoys additional *constitutional protection and promotion* as constitutions further specify the situations when the official language must be used and protected. In some cases, language laws even regulate the use of the official language.

To grasp the differences between states, in the following section we analyze whether any official languages are defined in the constitution, and if so, how many. Furthermore, we also look for additional provisions that contribute to the hierarchization of the languages—most importantly, for stipulations that reinforce the official language vis-à-vis other languages.

2. The analysis of the *minority language rights* granted by the constitutions or specific legislation also involves multiple aspects. First, Arzoz (2007) argues for a differentiation between language rights derived from human rights and language rights defined as specific rights granted to (the members of) a minority group. While the first category refers to the private use of the language by individuals in different domains (e.g., in the private sphere, the right to an interpreter in criminal proceedings, non-discrimination on linguistic grounds), the latter involves regulation of the use of minority languages by and in relation to public institutions. Therefore, while some aspects of language rights are generally accepted by all states which have ratified international treaties on human rights, others are left entirely to the discretion of the state. We focus only on the latter category, as we expect to find similar patterns across the states in relation to language rights derived from human rights.

A second important differentiation is based on the principle underlying language rights. The *principle of territoriality* means that language rights are applied on a specific subset of the territory of the state, while the *principle of personality* means that rights attribute a particular status to individuals or groups of individuals, regardless of where they find themselves on the territory of the country (McRae 1975; Nelde et al. 1992). While the official language(s) of states are always of a territorial nature (being binding for all those who live on the territory of the state), minority language rights can take three forms: *territorial*, *individual,* and *collective* (Nelde et al. 1992). The latter two categories represent two different variants of the personality principle, depending on who is defined as the subject of the rights.

Third, states display great variation with regard to the *conditions* under which they allow for the use of minority languages. Most often, this takes the form of thresholds expressed in absolute numbers or proportion of speakers. Some states also define additional restrictive measures to condition minority language rights.

3.1.2 The Language Policy of States: A Possible Typology

1. With regard to the choice of *official language*, two main patterns emerge among the states under analysis. The first category of states designates a single official language which is the language of the titular nation. Examples can be found in the constitutions of Albania, Bulgaria, Estonia, Hungary, Latvia, Lithuania, Poland, Romania, and Slovakia. Of these, the Estonian constitution goes even farther, as in addition to designating Estonian as the official language, it relegates the languages of minorities to the category of "foreign languages",[15] the use of which is regulated by law. This exclusionist approach clearly distinguishes Estonia from other countries in which only the language of the titular majority is official, as all of the latter tacitly acknowledge the existence of minority languages on their territory. Of all the countries analyzed, only the Czech Republic does not specify any official language, but Czech is implicitly considered to be the official language in legal regulations about citizenship, defense, and the judiciary (Zwilling 2004).

Members of the second, clear-cut group of states mention more than one official language in their constitutions. To this type belongs Kosovo, where Albanian and Serbian are recognized as official; Montenegro, where the official language is Montenegrin, but "Serbian, Bosnian, Albanian and Croatian shall also be in the official use"[16]; and Bosnia, where Bosnian, Croatian, and Serbian are recognized as official.[17]

A third, intermediate category includes states that define the titular language as official, but leave open the possibility for other languages to become official on a local or national level. Serbia, Croatia, and Slovenia grant local administrative units or municipalities the right to introduce other official languages and scripts, while the Macedonian constitution

[15]Constitution of Estonia, Art. 52.

[16]Constitution of Montenegro, Art. 13.

[17]In Bosnia, these languages are not defined on a federal level, but as both constitutive regions recognize them as official they are de facto official languages of the state.

grants the possibility for languages to become official in certain contexts if the number of speakers of the language passes a 20% threshold.[18]

With regard to the additional *protection and promotion of the official language*, two broad types emerge. Some countries (Albania, Bosnia, Croatia, the Czech Republic, Montenegro, Serbia, and Slovenia) make no additional reference to how the official language should be protected or promoted, while others have introduced additional constitutional provisions. While all the former are designed to reinforce a coded hierarchy (with a single exception), the details and nuances can be very telling.

The strongest hierarchizations can be found in Bulgaria, Estonia, Latvia, and Slovakia, where the use of the official language in some domains is presented as an "obligation",[19] or somewhat cynically, even as a "right" of every citizen.[20] Also, in some cases the constitution explicitly lists situations in which only the official language shall be used.[21] These formulations clearly reflect the strong monolingual language ideology of the state.

Simpler and somewhat softer additional measures are found in Romania and Lithuania, where the superiority of the titular language is reinforced by emphasizing its official character in various domains, such as the judiciary or education. Characteristic formulations include "proceedings shall be conducted in…",[22] "the language of instruction on all levels is…".[23] Also, in Romania, the constitutional article regulating the official language of the state is not open to amendment.[24]

---

[18]The 1991 constitution of the country stipulated exclusive Macedonian state ownership, generating interethnic conflict that brought the state to the verge of civil war. The conflict was resolved by a General Framework Agreement between Macedonians and Albanians that was adopted in 2001 (better known as the Ohrid Agreement), which made Albanians constitutive elements of the country and gave them greater representation, decentralization of state powers, and equal rights. For more on the Ohrid Agreement, see Reka (2008).

[19]Constitution of Bulgaria, Art. 36(1), Constitution of Slovakia, Art. 26(5) and 34(2).

[20]Constitution of Bulgaria, Art. 36(1), Constitution of Estonia, Art. 37 and 51, Constitution of Latvia, Art. 104.

[21]Constitution of Bulgaria, Art. 36(3).

[22]Constitution of Lithuania, Art. 117.

[23]Constitution of Romania, Art. 32(2).

[24]Ibid., Art. 152(1).

A third category of countries, including Hungary and Macedonia, promote even softer hierarchical views. The constitution of Hungary, while declaring it an obligation of the state to protect the Hungarian language,[25] in its preamble also proclaims the protection of the languages and cultures of all nationalities living in Hungary. This declaration, however, is not associated with concrete constitutional provisions similar to those referring to the titular language. Macedonia, on the other hand, codifies compulsory instruction in the Macedonian language in schools where education is carried out in the language of a nationality, but education in minority languages is not described as an exception to the rule, as it is, for instance, in Romania; instead, education in the majority and minority languages is defined as being on an equal footing.

Beyond these three hierarchical types, a fourth type is also present which could be considered a reversed hierarchy. This involves the case of Kosovo, where although both Albanian and Serbian are recognized as official languages, only Serbian receives additional constitutional protection in the domain of media access.[26]

Based on a combination of these two features of official languages (i.e., definition and promotion/protection of the official language), we classify countries into four types in the first dimension according to the existence of:

1. A constitutionally defined official language (that of the largest/titular ethnic group) and an exclusivist hierarchy between the official and minority languages;
2. a constitutionally defined official language (that of the largest/titular ethnic group) and a moderate hierarchy;
3. a constitutionally defined or implicit official language (that of the largest/titular ethnic group), but no constitutionally codified or only a mild hierarchy between languages;
4. a pluralistic language policy with or without constitutional definition of (possibly multiple) official languages.

---

[25]Constitution of Hungary, Art. H(2).

[26]Constitution of Kosovo, Art. 59(11).

2. Our second dimension of language policy refers to *minority language rights* in relation to public authorities. With regard to these, we inquired into the subject of the rights and the principles on which they are granted, and the conditionality attached to them. Very few countries do not regulate minority language rights in public administration; however, among those that do, there is great variation.

Into the category "without regulation", we classify Albania, Bulgaria, and Latvia,[27] which *do not recognize such rights* at all, rejecting such policies on constitutional foundations. Lithuania also belongs in this group, having abolished previously existing regulations on minority language rights while failing to adopt new legislation.[28] A second category of countries frames language rights as *individual* rights, codifying them for domains such as those involving the communication of members of minorities with state authorities and the translation of documents and bilingual signs. This is the case with the Czech Republic, Poland,[29] Romania, and Slovakia.[30]

The third category of states codifies language rights as *collective* rights and/or grants minority languages the opportunity to become *local official languages*. Although such rights do not differ significantly from those granted by the previous category of states, we consider that by using the term "local official language" these countries have opted to more strongly recognize minority languages. It is interesting to note that all post-Yugoslav countries (Bosnia, Croatia, Kosovo,[31] Macedonia, Montenegro, Serbia,[32] and Slovenia) are of this type. A special case of collective formulation is used in Hungarian legislation. Although

[27]On the situation in these countries, see the relevant paragraphs on the applicability of Article 10 and 11 in state reports submitted by the former to the FCNM.

[28]For more on the situation of language rights in Lithuania, see Vasilevich (2013).

[29]For more on the situation of language rights of minorities in Poland, see Baranowska (2014).

[30]For more on language rights in Slovakia, see Vass (2015).

[31]For more on the situation of language rights in Kosovo, see Romani and Fridlund (2015).

[32]We have included Serbia into this category despite the fact that it has a dual system. On the one hand, minority languages can become local official languages, while on the other hand members of the minority can also exercise their language rights in central state institutions if they reach 2% on a national level. For more on linguistic rights in Serbia, see Beretka (2016) and Szerbhorváth (2015).

minority languages are not allowed to become official languages, the subject of the rights are not the members of minority communities, but the *minority communities themselves*, whose representational bodies, minority councils, decide on the necessity of these rights. Estonia is also a rather specific case as it allows municipal administrations to introduce the minority language as an internal working language, thus making the minority language a de facto local official language.[33]

Based on this typology (related to the subject and content of language rights), we distinguish three types of states for our second dimension:

1. states without any minority language rights in public administration,
2. states that define language usage as the *individual* right of the members of minority communities, and
3. states that link the right of language usage to minority *communities*/nationalities or conditionally allow minority languages *local official status*.

Most countries define minority language rights on *the territorial principle*, limiting their effect to specific administrative units of the state, but there is great variation with regard to the *conditions* under which language rights are applicable. Some countries enumerate the territories where these rights shall apply (e.g., statutorily defined bilingual areas—Slovenia; closed list of municipalities—Kosovo), while others apply a general norm (i.e., municipalities where minorities represent a significant number or proportion—e.g., Bosnia, Croatia, Czech Republic, Estonia, Hungary, Kosovo, Macedonia, Montenegro, Poland, Romania, Serbia, Slovakia). There are also examples where no threshold or territory is specified (e.g., in the constitution of the Czech Republic, for the Slovak language), but in other cases further requirements are included (e.g., following an official request of 40% of the adult minority population in the Czech Republic for bilingual signs; registration in an official register as a municipality where bilingualism exists in Poland).

[33]See Language Act of Estonia (2011), Art. 11.

In summary, the countries can be classified using a threefold typology with regard to the conditions that are defined for language rights:

1. *High threshold*: Minorities need to form a majority or at least a very significant proportion of the local population to enjoy language rights. In Estonia, minority languages can be used only in municipalities where the proportion of speakers exceeds 50%. In Bosnia, the minorities should represent an absolute or relative majority, while in Montenegro a majority or a considerable part of the population.
2. *Medium threshold* (20–33%): In Macedonia, Poland, Romania, and Slovakia, there is a 20% threshold, while in the Czech Republic and Croatia the threshold proportion for a minority is 33%.
3. *Low threshold*: Threshold below 20% in Hungary,[34] Kosovo,[35] and Serbia,[36] or other means of defining the applicability of the law exist (e.g., closed lists of territories or municipalities in Kosovo, or statutorily defined bilingual area in Slovenia).

To conclude the comparative analysis, we classify the countries' language policies in Table 4. The rows in the table contain the four types of official language policy, while the columns three categories according to the nature of the language rights granted in public administration. We have also indicated the conditions or thresholds that apply to minority language use, as even the most pluralistic policies will be of limited use if the range of potential beneficiaries is restricted through conditions that are difficult to meet.

3.1.3 The Language Policy of Romania—An Assessment

The main purpose of this comparative analysis is to enable the positioning of Romania relative to the countries that are arguably most similar

---

[34]In Hungary, there is a 10% threshold for the translation of regulation and bilingual signs.

[35]In Kosovo, there is a 5% threshold.

[36]In Serbia, there is a 2% threshold on a national level above which the language can be used as means of communication with state authorities.

Table 4 Official language regulations and minority language rights in Central and Eastern Europe

			Subject of minority language rights in administration		
			No such rights	Right of individuals	Local official language
Institutionalization of official language	Hierarchic	Exclusivist	~~BG, LV~~	SK	**EE**
		Moderate	~~LT~~	RO	–
		No, or mild hierarchy	~~AL~~	*CZ*[a], PL[a]	*HU*
	Pluralistic/ Quasi-pluralistic		–	–	**BA**, HR, *XK*, MK, **CG**, *RS*, *SI*[b]

Notes Bold entries indicate a high threshold for the applicability of minority language rights in administration. Entries in italics indicate low and normal entries a medium threshold. Thresholds are not meaningful in the case of entries that are struck out, where no such rights are recognized

[a]In the Czech Republic and Poland, additional conditions narrow the applicability of the legislation

[b]Slovenia recognizes only Italian and Hungarian autochthonous minority communities, thereby denying rights to the significantly larger post-Yugoslav communities

to it. As can be seen, Romania is located somewhere in the middle. Although a clear hierarchy between languages is defined, with the status of Romanian also reinforced through additional constitutional provisions, the regulation of minority language use contains a number of liberal elements which grant an array of language rights to the members of minority groups, while the conditions of their applicability can be regarded as intermediate (a threshold of 20%). In this comparison, Romania emerges as being most similar to Slovakia, although in the latter country the underpinning of the official language is stronger, being classified as exclusivist in this dimension. It is also noteworthy that the other countries in which we find strong or moderate language hierarchies (Albania, Bulgaria, Latvia, and Lithuania) do not grant minority language rights at all.

On the one hand, Romania has opted for a restrictive definition of the official language similar to the approach of the Baltic states and Slovakia

("In Romania, the official language is Romanian".[37]), meaning that in all state institutions and organizations Romanian is the default language of communication and normative texts. On the other hand, there is a constitutional provision regarding the use of minority languages which is most similar in wording to the Polish and Czech case ("recognizes and guarantees the right of persons belonging to national minorities to the preservation, development and expression of their ethnic, cultural, linguistic and religious identity"[38]).

It can be concluded that clear tension exists between the two constitutional provisions: one defining the dominance of the state language and the other granting the right to persons belonging to national minorities to express their identity through the use of their mother tongue in different communicational public arenas. Romanian legislation manages the issue by creating exceptional situations for minority language use which are deduced from the right to identity. Or, as Kontra and Szilágyi (2002, p. 5) rightly formulate it: "In general rules language is always defined as Romanian, not as mother tongue. After the general regulations *special measures* are introduced, which regulate the situations where minority languages can be used".

Another specificity of Romanian legislation is that language rights are considered individual rights. Almost all the related laws underline that the beneficiaries of the rights are the *persons* belonging to national minorities. This rule prevails even in those cases when the rights that are granted cannot be exercised without the existence of a broader community.[39] For example, although language rights in administration are linked to a threshold (the de facto existence of a community), according to the letter of the law minority languages are protected as the languages spoken by the individuals who belong to the minorities. In her book on minority accommodation in Romania and Slovakia, Csergő (2007) calls this strategy language predominance, as the majority elites try to

[37]Constitution of Romania (2003), Art. 13.

[38]Constitution of Romania (2003), Art. 6.

[39]Kymlicka calls these group-differentiated rights and states that language rights in education or administration are clearly of this type (Kymlicka 1995, pp. 44–48).

integrate minority demands without challenging the primacy of the dominant language.

Generally, Romanian legislation does not differentiate between minority languages on the grounds of their historical presence, number of speakers, or territorial concentration. There is only one exception: the law through which the ECRML was ratified,[40] in which Romania differentiated between the various minority languages spoken on Romanian territory. This, however, followed from the logic of the ECRML, as countries do not have to adopt the same regulations for every language; they can personalize the "menu" with regard to the commitments they make for every language. In the case of Hungarian, Romania adopted maximum protection in almost every category.

It should be emphasized that by ratifying the ECRML Romania changed (in theory) the status of Hungarian from a language spoken by/mother tongue of the members of the Hungarian minority, to a part of the European "common heritage", as formulated in the preamble of the ECRML. However, Romania did not implement all provisions available in the ECRML. The ratification of the document merely strengthened the existing legal framework of language rights, without filling in the existing gaps.

In sum, the Hungarian language is defined in Romania as the mother tongue of persons belonging to the Hungarian minority. Therefore, it is regarded as a minority language, and the right to use it is derived from the constitutional right of persons to preserve their ethnic identity. Romanian legislation in the domain of minority rights systematically avoids formulations, whereby minority languages are defined as a collective right, as the languages of communities or regional languages.

3.2 The Policy Framework of Minority Language Use in Romania

In Romania, minority linguistic rights are not organized in a single comprehensive law on minority language use, but codified within a

---

[40] Law 282/2007.

considerable number of laws regulating various domains of public life. Taking into account the number and complexity of all legal sources, in what follows we discuss only the most important *positive* legal provisions, following a structure similar to that of the ECRML. We do not deal with language use in education, as this is discussed in Chapter 6. In each analyzed domain, we describe the regulated situations and the content of the rights and provide some clarifying remarks, where necessary.

3.2.1 Public Administration

In Romania, all language rights related to public administration are territorial rights, as they are legally binding only for those local- and county-level administrative units and deconcentrated institutions[41] where the percentage of a certain minority exceeds 20%. The only exception to this rule is the regulation concerning registry procedures, which is not linked to territory. For the sake of simplicity, in what follows we call those administrative units where the proportion of Hungarians is sufficiently high for language rights to apply *Hungarian-inhabited municipalities/administrative units* (Table 5).

As one can see, from a strictly legal point of view minority language use in administration is generally permissive. However, a closer look shows a more nuanced situation. On the one hand, detailed norms and regulations for implementation have not been adopted for all legal provisions. Some items, such as bilingual place names, the use of Hungarian names in birth certificates, and the communication of information of public interest, are indeed more or less clearly regulated, the actors responsible for implementation and related sanctions are clearly defined, and provisions are also implemented. On the other hand, in more delicate matters such as bilingual street-signs, the use of Hungarian place names in official documents, or written minority language use, even the law is sometimes unclear and the norms of implementation are completely lacking.

[41]Deconcentrated public services involve the county-level offices of the ministries and other institutions of central administration.

Table 5 Minority language rights related to public administration in Romania

Regulated situation	Legal formulation	Clarifying remarks
Registry procedures (birth certificates or other acts of civil status)	Hungarian first and last names may be recorded using Hungarian spelling. This is a personal right, not related to territory[a] If a person's name does not correspond to Hungarian spelling conventions, name change is possible through administrative procedure[b] Wedding ceremonies can also be held in Hungarian[c]	Double first names are registered in hyphenated form, which does not comply with rules of Hungarian grammar[d] Mayor's offices are not bound to hire Hungarian-speaking registrars. Therefore, the organization of Hungarian-language wedding ceremonies is contingent on the availability of such personnel
Administrative, official procedures	In Hungarian-inhabited administrative units, citizens can use Hungarian language in oral or written communication in their relationships with public administration institutions[e] These administrative units must ensure that conditions for Hungarian-language use exist (i.e., hire public servants with Hungarian-language proficiency in positions that involve direct contact with citizens)[f]	Citizens do not have to cover additional costs Authorities' responses are bilingual (Romanian and Hungarian)[g] In the case of deconcentrated institutions, the law does not specify that Hungarian can be used in oral or written communication In Hungarian-inhabited territorial-administrative units, officials speaking Hungarian must also be employed[h]

(continued)

Table 5 (continued)

Regulated situation	Legal formulation	Clarifying remarks
Local- and county-level assembly meetings	In assemblies where 1/5 of the members belong to a national minority, the language of that minority can be used at the meetings[i]	This threshold is raised to 1/3 by the rules of implementation[j] Translation into Romanian has to be undertaken by the mayor's office[k] Documents adopted at such meetings must be in Romanian[l]
Public signs and place names	Multilingual place signs must be positioned at the limits of Hungarian-inhabited administrative units[m] The name of local- and county-level public institutions and deconcentrated institutions in Hungarian-inhabited administrative units must be displayed in both Romanian and Hungarian languages[n]	The ECRML defines place names as all topographical names. Romanian legislation does not specify the meaning of the terms. Most local authorities use them to denote only the name of the municipality/locality[o]
Publicity or information of public interest	In Hungarian-inhabited settlements, information of public interest must be communicated in both Romanian and Hungarian[p] The agenda of local and county assembly meetings and normative resolutions must be translated into Hungarian[q]	Individual resolutions are translated only upon request[r]

Regulated situation	Legal formulation	Clarifying remarks
Official events organized by local public administrative authorities	In Hungarian-inhabited administrative units, both Romanian and Hungarian may be used at official events[s]	

[a]Law 119/1996, Art. 66(1)
[b]Government Ordinance 41/2003, Art. 20(1)
[c]Law 287/2009, Art. 287(3)
[d]Law 119/1996, Art. 66(2)
[e]Constitution of Romania, Art. 120(2), Law 215/2001, Art. 19 and 76(2)
[f]Law 215/2001, Art. 76(3), Law 188/1999, Art. 108
[g]Government Decision 1206/2001, Art. 2(2)
[h]Law 360/2002 (Law on the Police), Art. 79
[i]Law 215/2001, Art. 42(2) and 98
[j]Government Decision 1206/2001, Art. 3 and 6(1)
[k]Government Decision 1206/2001, Art. 6(2)
[l]Government Decision 1206/2001, Art. 6(1) and Art. 6(3)
[m]Law 215/2001, Art. 76(4)
[n]Law 215/2001, Art. 76(4)
[o]See: Paragraph 560 of the COMEX (2011)
[p]Governmental Decision 123/2002, Art. 12
[q]Law 215/2001, Art. 39(7), Art. 50 and 94(8)
[r]Law 215/2001, Art. 50
[s]Law 215/2001, Art. 9(2)

Furthermore, a clear line needs to be drawn between the applicability of minority language rights in local administration and in the deconcentrated institutions. Although in theory the law is binding for both types of institutions, in the case of the latter the regulations are limited only to the level of the most general norms. The operation of most state institutions (and their deconcentrated branches)[42] is regulated by separate laws, which have not been synchronized (sufficiently, or at all) with the provisions of the law on public administration on minority language use.

In conclusion, the legal framework of language use within both local public administration and deconcentrated institutions is theoretically permissive. However, while in the case of the former both legislation and norms of implementation are in place, for the latter these are almost completely lacking. Thus, in many cases a general permissive legal context is not backed up by a normative background (set of administrative rules) that would support its implementation.

3.2.2 The Judicial System

Another major system where minority language rights are supported by law is the judicial system. However, some argue that while language rights in administration and education are specific minority rights that assume the existence of a collectivity, minority language use in the courts is only "a well-established human right which applies to anyone facing a criminal charge against her" (Arzoz 2007, p. 5).

In Romania, minority language rights in the judicial system are codified in the constitution and three additional laws: the law on judicial organization,[43] the code of civil procedure,[44] and the code of criminal procedure.[45] It is important to stress that the provisions of these laws in

[42]For example, the law on the functioning of the police or pension funds.

[43]Law 304/2004.

[44]Law 134/2010.

[45]Law 135/2010.

this regard hardly go beyond the normative declarations formulated in the constitution and are not always in line even with the provisions of the ECRML (Table 6).

Although Romanian regulations regarding language use in the judiciary distinguish members of national minorities from persons who do not speak or understand the Romanian language (e.g., foreign citizens), the rights granted to the two categories are not very different. In both cases, the rights are applicable to all persons, indifferent of the ethnic composition of the administrative unit the court is part of, and the persons involved can only *speak* in their mother tongue in front of the court. The law clearly states that all documents, including minutes and records, must be drawn up in Romanian only. It can be concluded that these provisions do not go far beyond the formulations characteristic of general human rights.[46] Furthermore, by entrusting everything to interpreters and by restricting the written use of minority languages, these provisions fall short even of the rights codified in the Statute of Nationalities valid under the Communist regime following 1945 which granted minorities the right to use their language throughout the whole legal process.[47]

Another problem that weakens implementation is that the Hungarian linguistic infrastructure is weakly regulated. In legal documents related to the functioning of the legal system, there is only one paragraph that facilitates the employment of staff who speak minority languages. According to the regulation in force, in regions where the proportion of a minority exceeds 50%, if two applicants for a job obtain the same score the applicant who speaks the language of the minority should be awarded priority with regard to employment.[48] In practice, however, the probability of such situations occurring is very low, and thus, the practical value and effect of this measure are rather limited.

[46]See, for example, Art. 14(3)(f) of the International Covenant on Civil and Political Rights.

[47]Nationality Statute (1945), Art. 8. Available in Hungarian language at: http://www.jakabffy.ro/magyarkisebbseg/index.php?action=cimek&lapid=6&cikk=M970126.htm.

Despite the permissive legal background in Communist times, the implementation of these rights was problematic.

[48]Law 303/2004, Art. 30(6).

Table 6 Minority language rights in the judicial system in Romania

Regulated situation	Legal formulation	Clarifying remarks
Legal proceedings	Legal procedures are conducted in Romanian. Citizens belonging to national minorities are entitled to express themselves in their mother tongue before the courts. Translation is provided free of charge, with the use of an authorized interpreter or translator[a]	If all the persons involved ask to speak their mother tongue, the court session can be conducted in the requested language[b]
Criminal trials	Legal procedures are conducted in Romanian. Members of national minorities can speak their mother tongue in front of the court[c]	Plaintiffs, defendants, and witnesses have the right to an interpreter free of charge if they do not understand Romanian, cannot express themselves well, or are unable to communicate in Romanian[d] Defendants belonging to a national minority may request that the charges are translated into their mother tongue[e]
Civil trials	Legal procedures are conducted in Romanian. Members of national minorities can speak their mother tongue in front of the court, according to the law[f]	When a party or witness does not speak Romanian, a certified translator will be used. If the parties agree, the judge or the clerk can act as a translator.[g] If none of these options is available, a reliable person can be used[h]

Regulated situation	Legal formulation	Clarifying remarks
Legal documents	All documents, minutes, and records are drawn up in Romanian[i]	The recordings of debates in another language than Romanian are provided in Romanian only. The parties involved need to check if translations are in line with what they have said[j]

[a]Constitution of Romania, Art. 128 (1)–(2), Law 304/2004, Art. 14(1)–(3)
[b]Law 304/2004, Art. 14(4)
[c]Code of Criminal Procedure, Art. 12(1)–(2)
[d]Code of Criminal Procedure, Art. 12(3)
[e]Code of Criminal Procedure, Art. 289(11)
[f]Code of Civil Procedure, Art. 18(1)–(2)
[g]Code of Civil Procedure, Art. 225(1)
[h]Code of Civil Procedure, Art. 150(4)
[i]Law 304/2004, Art. 14(5)
[j]Law 304/2004, Art. 14(6)

3.2.3 Other Domains

Besides the two fields discussed above, there are also other domains of public life in which the usage of minority languages is to some extent legally regulated. Education, and mass media are two other domains of utmost importance in which there are rather broad opportunities for the usage of Hungarian. However, we do not discuss them here as this volume contains separate chapters dedicated to these topics.

One problematic field involves cinemas. Until recently, the only language in which movies could be subtitled was Romanian.[49] In this context, cinemas functioning in cities with a Hungarian-majority population had a hard time finding a way to screen movies with Hungarian subtitles, the mother tongue of most of their customers. A very recent amendment to the law on cinemas, passed in January 2018, created the legal possibility of subtitling movies simultaneously in Romanian and a minority language.[50] It is unclear, however, how this will be implemented technically and whether the solution will come at the expense of viewers' enjoyment.

With regard to economic and social life, language use regulations are embryonic: In most cases norms of implementation are missing. In economic life, the most important domain where minority languages rights should apply is taxation. Local- and county-level tax offices are deconcentrated institutions, and thus, the provisions on minority language use in administration should also apply to them. However, official documents can also only be issued in Romanian in this domain. By ratifying the ECRML, Romania also committed itself in several other fields of social and economic life (e.g., safety instructions and consumer protection). However, as concrete provisions for language rights are lacking in sectorial legislation, along with norms of implementation, these undertakings are of limited practical relevance.

[49]In Romania, foreign-produced movies are rarely dubbed; they are mostly subtitled.

[50]Law 15/2018, Art. 1(2).

In health care, patients have the right to receive information about their conditions in a language they understand.[51] Healthcare and social care institutions are obligated to hire personnel who speak the language of the minority in administrative units where the percentage of the minority exceeds 20% or their number is greater than 5,000 persons. However, Hungarian NGOs have argued that the issue of minority language use in hospitals is far from resolved with the new legislation, as institutions can comply with the law merely by employing a single person who can speak some Hungarian (Szabó 2017).[52] Furthermore, the national emergency number can be called in Hungarian.[53]

3.3 The Implementation of Minority Language Policy

So far we have seen that many aspects of the policy framework are permissive or even supportive of minority language use, as the former is defined as an institutional obligation. Of course legal framework is a tool necessary to promote a linguistic paradigm for multilingual societies, and thus, success or failure of implementation should be regarded from the point of view of ideal linguistic order envisaged to be achieved by the means of legal provisions. From this point of view, there is striking difference between the manner, how most of the minority actors and how the prevalent majority players envisage the linguistic order in the domain of governance and judiciary. While both positions are supporting linguistic diversity, there are significant differences regarding the reasonable degree of presence of minority languages in these domains. The majority tend to view linguistic rights as a set of assistive measures for those having an improper command of Romanian. Thus, minority language use in these fields is seen as an exceptional measure meant to promote fairness of administrative and judicial procedures and a non-discriminative access to public services. The prevalent minority

[51]Law 46/2003, Art. 8.

[52]Law 110/2017. Art. I(1) and II.

[53]Government Emergency Ordinance 34/2008, Art. 10(f)–(g).

representation on the rationale of minority linguistic rights is to increase the linguistic options of the ethnic Hungarians, by promoting in the envisaged domains genuine full-fledged services in minority language too. So, on the one hand, we have a vision of an occasional, exceptional, mostly assistive bilingualism and on the other hand the ideal of a symmetricity of the official and minority languages in the relevant institutional settings.

In assessing the implementation of minority language policy, we assume the minority point of view, by considering that language policies promoting the use of minority languages should aim for a fairly symmetrical usage of official and minority language in the domains subjected to regulations.

Research on the implementation of minority language rights in Romania has mostly focused on administration (mostly local administration, but a few studies have also targeted deconcentrated institutions) and education. A few local case studies have also analyzed the situation in the judiciary and media. Research on language use in economic life is presented in Chapter 9. In the following sections, we present the main conclusions of research on the implementation of minority language policies in the two most intensively studied domains: administration and the judicial system.

3.3.1 Public Administration

With regard to Hungarian-language use in local administration, in the past fifteen years two national-level surveys have been conducted (in 2008[54] and 2014[55]) which delivered rather similar results. The main findings were the following:

1. In 2008, in more than 90% of Hungarian-inhabited administrative units, bilingual place name signs have been set up, and in more than 80%, the signs on the buildings hosting mayor's offices were

[54]For details, see Horváth (2008c, 2012).

[55]For details, see Toró (2016, 2017).

also bilingual. No systematic data are available about the situation of bilingual signs on the buildings of other institutions of local public administration.

2. More than 80% of local councils declared (occasionally or regularly) using Hungarian when delivering information of public interest. The agendas of local assembly meetings are translated to Hungarian in slightly more than half of all municipalities, and local legislation is translated in around 40% of Hungarian-inhabited administrative units (municipalities where Hungarians share is above 20%).
3. More than 94% of Hungarian-inhabited administrative units have declared that the verbal communication in Hungarian in the offices of local administration is possible. This would mean that there is at least one department in each administrative unit where there is Hungarian-speaking personnel. However, on a department-by-department basis (e.g., registries, tax offices), the picture is more nuanced and fewer municipalities answer in the affirmative for the possibility of verbal use of Hungarian in any specialized office of the local administration. If summed up, the possibility of verbal of Hungarian is possible in about two-thirds of the offices of the local administration of the Hungarian-inhabited municipalities.
4. Based on the data, opportunities to submit and process written requests in Hungarian were ensured by 35.8–51.7%[56] of local administrations. The higher limit is based on self-reporting by municipalities, however the validity of these figures is questionable. The lower limit is based on a research documented by Toró (2016), in which municipalities were contacted using official letters written in Hungarian, but meaningful official answers in Hungarian were returned only by approximately one-third of the addressees.

In addition to the 323 municipalities where the proportion of Hungarians exceeds 20%, there are six counties[57] where the provisions of minority language use of the law on public administration should

[56] We have presented the results of 2008 and 2014 as an interval. Detailed comparative results can be found in Toró (2016).

[57] NUTS 3-level administrative unit in Romania.

also be applied for Hungarian language (the only entitled minority language at this level in Romania).[58] Although there is no research on minority language use at this level of public administration, it can be reasonably assumed that the aforementioned trends also prevail here. It is illustrative that two of the six county councils (Bihor and Sălaj) do not even have a Hungarian-language webpage, although the law includes a number of obligations for authorities regarding the provision of public information.[59] Furthermore, in these six counties there are in total approximately 250 deconcentrated units of central public administration, for which the legal provisions on minority language use are also legally binding. According to a study conducted in Harghita county, regarding the use of Hungarian in these institutions, the overall picture is rather diversified. More than half of the deconcentrated institutions declared that the name of the institution and other public information signs in Hungarian have been posted, and for majority (98%) Hungarian can be used in verbal communication, but only for a slight minority (17.6%) provided an opportunity for the use of the written language (Horváth et al. 2010). As Harghita county contains the highest number and proportion of ethnic Hungarians, it should be regarded as being the role model for good practice as concerns the use of Hungarian and, even with its mixed record, as a positive exception to the norm.[60]

As we have seen, minority language use provisions are comprehensively implemented in about one-third of municipalities, and in a further 35–40%, Hungarian is occasionally used in administration. Though we have no data on this, the opportunities for language usage are most probably similar at a county level for the deconcentrated

[58]The proportion of Hungarians exceeds 20% in Bihor/Bihar, Harghita/Hargita, Covasna/Kovászna, Mureș/Maros, Sălaj/Szilágy and Satu Mare/Szatmár counties.

[59]Also note that the president of Bihor County Council is a member of RMDSZ (see http://www.cjbihor.ro/). On the Sălaj County Council Web site (http://www.cjsj.ro/), automatic translation to Hungarian is offered through Google Translate (both Web sites were last accessed 31 January 2018).

[60]In Harghita/Hargita county more than 85% of the population is Hungarian, thus there are presumably more officials in public institutions with Hungarian-language fluency than in other parts of the country.

institutions of the central administration too.[61] Also, as a general rule we can establish that there is a very significant difference between the opportunities for the oral and written use of Hungarian.

In the following sections, we sketch out some possible explanations for these shortcomings: first, for the difference between oral and written language use, and second, for the low levels of implementation. For both issues, a useful analytical tool is provided by Thomas and Grindle (1990), who argue that the success or failure of a policy depends on the interplay of conflicts or challenges that arise throughout the implementation process from both the public and the bureaucratic arena, and the magnitude of resources assigned by the government to overcome these reactions. Such public and bureaucratic reactions are also present with regard to minority language use in Romania, but we argue below that these are not addressed in a satisfactory manner by state authorities.

Possible explanations for the significant gap between the opportunities for oral and written language use include the following: (1) lack of authority, (2) the linguistic deficiencies of officials, (3) concerns regarding the bureaucratic processing of documents drawn up in Hungarian, and (4) fears of conflict with the majority.

1. *Lack of authority.* Although the linguistic infrastructure for Hungarian documents exists—several Romanian–Hungarian dictionaries of administrative terms are available (e.g., Benő et al. 2004; Fazakas 2002; Mezei 2006) along with a database on the most frequently used bilingual forms[62]—no authority exists to systematize these resources, endow them with legitimacy, and encourage officials to use them in their daily routines. Without such, the deficiencies in the written use of Hungarian are reproduced even among officials with Hungarian-language proficiency.

[61]As discussed in Chapter 3, while most local administrations are politically controlled by RMDSZ in Székely Land, the same is not true of deconcentrated institutions. This is why we argue that the figures measured for local administrations may be extrapolated to the deconcentrated level only as a theoretical upper limit; the real figures are probably lower.

[62]See the "Bilingual forms" project of the Romanian Institute for Research on National Minorities (http://ispmn.gov.ro/page/formulare-).

2. *Linguistic deficiencies of officials.* The main instrument of interaction within the bureaucracy is written communication. In a bureaucratic context, oral communication is only orientative and informal. In other words, it is generally expected that administrative texts be written in precise, clear and professional, legal, and administrative terms. As officials do not receive training about how this should be done in Hungarian, these competences develop and become habitualized in Romanian even in the case of Hungarian-speaking staff. In summary, officials are not sufficiently fluent in the Hungarian administrative jargon, and thus, they tend to avoid using it in written form.

3. *Concerns regarding the bureaucratic processing of documents drawn up in Hungarian.* The routines that would regulate the evaluation and resolution of Hungarian-language documents are lacking, or at least underdeveloped. In this context, one possible explanation for the low levels of written Hungarian-language use is that officials fear that persons who do not understand Hungarian may become involved in chains of resolution, thereby jeopardizing the whole administrative process. Therefore, they do not encourage, or even dissuade, clients from submitting documents in Hungarian.

4. *Fears of conflict with the majority.* In many cases, both clients and officials want to avoid any conflict with the Romanian majority that might be caused by the use of Hungarian in their submissions. Or, being aware of the controversial and politicized status of Hungarian-language use in administration, they voluntarily forgo its use, choosing Romanian instead, which they regard as "more official" and trustworthy.

The problems discussed above represent challenges to the implementation of language use in writing. But lack of implementation is equally influenced by the systemic responses to these challenges, such as a lack of: (1) accountability and interest of the actors involved, (2) policy-based strategies and planning, (3) resources assigned to implementation, and (4) civic accountability.

1. *Lack of accountability and interest.* The implementation of minority language rights is the responsibility of several public actors. On a local

and county level, the main executive bodies are mayor's offices and the presidents of the county councils, which can be held accountable by local- and county-level assemblies. The latter do take action in exceptional cases, but success with implementation is likely only in administrative units where ethnic Hungarian councilors are in the majority. On a national level, the main actors responsible for holding accountable the institutions that should implement such rights are the central coordinating authorities and the representatives of the government in the counties (prefects). The latter even have the duty of "guarantee[ing] the application and enforcement of the Constitution, laws, ordinances and decisions of the Government".[63] However, as mentioned earlier, political will to enforce compliance with the law is apparently lacking among them, and thus, monitoring or accountability is less probable. Additionally, the record of the prefects at the county level is even more unimpressive; in many cases, they have rather limitative stances regarding the implementation of minority linguistic rights.

2. *Lack of policy-based strategies and planning*. The lack of public policy-based strategies and related planning also contributes to the ad hoc implementation. As research has shown, there are serious shortcomings in many fields with regard to both the formulation of *objectives* (i.e., definitions of the minimal targeted institutional applications of minority language rights) and assigned (normative, financial, human, and linguistic[64]) *resources*. At the level of objectives, one of the most problematic issues is the lack of consensus about the nature and content of language rights. It is not uncommon that efforts to promote or strengthen minority language rights are followed by intense public and political debate, and in many cases, individuals or organizations who oppose minority linguistic rights try to prevent such efforts through the courts.[65]

---

[63]Law 340/2004, Art. 19(1)(a).

[64]By linguistic resources we mean all multilingual material (terminology databases, related IT tools, official bilingual forms) that could facilitate the provision of multilingual services.

[65]A good example of this is the case of the Covasna County Public Library, where an opening for the position of director was attacked in court by NGOs and the prefect because fluency in Hungarian was defined as a prerequisite. See Farkas (2011).

3. *Lack of resources.* Even if the objectives are well formulated, sufficient resources are not always assigned to accomplish the goals defined by law, and even resources that do exist are not optimally utilized.[66] In many cases, assessments of the resources that are needed and available for the effective operation of multilingualism are not even undertaken. The cost of minority language usage in administration (such as bilingual signs, translators) should be supported from the budgets of the institutions required to implement it.[67] However, many local councils cannot afford this, and there are no external public financial resources upon which they could draw. As a result, many of them refrain from implementation, invoking financial constraints.

Another resource-related problem concerns the normative level: Many general legal provisions are not underpinned by concrete norms of application that define responsibilities, and most sectorial laws regulating the operation of national public administration institutions do not contain provisions related to minority language use. Furthermore, as mentioned earlier, even when norms of application do exist, systematic follow-up or accountability is hampered as the institutions that are responsible for these activities do not consider this a priority.

4. *Lack of civic accountability.* Citizens, NGOs, and political organizations engage only sporadically in strategic litigation related to the non-implementation of minority language rights.[68] This lack of mobilization can be partly explained by low levels of social awareness and knowledge about minority language rights.[69] While one cannot really

[66]For example, the *Official Gazette of Romania* translates numerous laws, governmental decisions, and ordinances into Hungarian, but the selection of the texts is often haphazard as those texts that could actually be used in public administration are rarely translated: the law on the operation of notarial offices was translated, but the norms regulating social benefits which are provided by local administrations were not (these documents include, among others, the forms that should be used and list of documents required to apply for benefits).

[67]Governmental decision 1206/2001.

[68]But see two concrete examples to the contrary in Chapter 3.

[69]A few publications (Bogdán and Mohácsek 2012; Kis and Kató 2014), lectures, and training events have been organized for high-school students by the NGO Jogaink (*Our Rights*) that tackle

expect citizens to individually commence litigation in such matters, the low level of citizen involvement is indicative of the fact that although the legal framework has undoubtedly become more pluralized and more permissive over the past two decades, dominant paradigms and ideologies have not changed in tandem.

A related problem involves the attitude of ethnic Hungarian mayors and local councils dominated by ethnic Hungarians (primarily RMDSZ) toward minority language use in administration. This issue is also relevant from the perspective of the third element of Grin's (2003) previously discussed framework of analysis, namely *desire* or *willingness* to use the minority language. Research has shown that the larger the political or demographic majority of Hungarians in a municipality, the more likely it is that Hungarian can be used both orally and in writing (Horváth 2012; Toró 2017). However, even in these cases compliance with the law is weaker than expected. As Toró (2017) shows, it is not uncommon that local ethnic Hungarian political elites have reserves in implementing or promoting comprehensively the minority linguistic rights in local administration. The various, both financial and transactional, costs associated with such measures make them rather interest consuming so even if language rights are used as the foremost issue of the minority electoral agenda, the administrative burden associated with effective promotion creates another decisional configuration for those in charge. In such a context, only some aspects of the use of Hungarian in this domain become salient (e.g., the translation of agendas or the communication of information of public interest), and thus, the implementation of policy is not a predictable outcome of successful claim-making.

3.3.2 The Judicial System

We discussed earlier how minority language use in courts is limited to oral use, and all documents must be in Romanian. Systematic data about the implementation of oral usage are unfortunately not available.

---

the issue, but these are isolated, project-based initiatives; there is no wider strategy for raising awareness and reaching out to broader segments of the Hungarian population.

As a consequence, we base our assessment only on a case study about the patterns of Hungarian-language use in the court of Miercurea Ciuc (Csíkszereda). As the town is the largest in Harghita county, where more than 80% of the population is ethnic Hungarian, we believe that the court can reasonably regarded as the one most likely to implement minority language rights. However, if major deficiencies in the application of the law are found even in this case, then we may safely generalize the situation to courts situated elsewhere in the country. The case study revealed a number of problems with regard to the use of Hungarian in the Miercurea Ciuc court. First, only a small proportion of judges and prosecutors speak Hungarian (31.6 and 14.3%, respectively), and professional interpreters are not always used.[70] Second, procedures do not allow Hungarian-speaking participants to directly interact with each other; dialogue is mediated by a judge who in most cases requires the active participation of a translator. In this way, communication becomes cumbersome and asymmetrical (Papp Kincses 2011). In summary, the study suggests that neither the linguistic resources in minority language, nor other linguistic infrastructural conditions for this are in place for the judiciary to expand minority language use. Thus, the chance that the current status quo (the marginal status of Hungarian even in administrative units with large Hungarian majorities) will change in the near future is rather low.

4 The Use of Hungarian in the Context of Bilingualism

As highlighted in the second part of this study, approximately two-thirds of Transylvania's Hungarians are bilingual (being fluent in Romanian) and a similar proportion live in settlements where they regularly need to use Romanian in everyday situations (face-to-face

[70] This is a clear decline even from the Communist era, when 80% of judges were fluent in Hungarian (Papp Kincses 2011, p. 186).

communication, work, socialization, media, etc.). Although there are several official domains where (at least in theory) the law grants the former the right to choose their vernacular language, in other contexts they can use only Romanian. Accordingly, a very complex linguistic environment exists, within which a variety of language patterns can be distinguished. In what follows, we map these patterns.

In his seminal book on language policy, Spolsky (2004, pp. 42–46) distinguishes several domains important for languages. These sociolinguistic contexts have three important dimensions: location, participants, and topic. Most often, students of sociolinguistics rely on the dichotomy between *private* and *public* domains (e.g., Fishman 2000; Ritchie and Bhatia 2004; Sachdev and Giles 2004); although this approach is appropriate for highlighting the importance of speech situations, we believe that it does not allow for sufficiently fine-grained analysis, as both domains encompass a large variety of linguistic environments with different participants, topics, and even norms of conduct. One possible refinement of the dichotomy is provided by Fishman (1972), who argues that language situations can be divided into speech domains depending on the formality of the situation. In this model, the private and the formally regulated public become two endpoints of a continuum on which several intermediate domains may also be located.

Drawing on this distinction, in this section we rely on three categories: *private*, *public,* and *institutional*, each characterized by different levels of formal regulation. The *private* category refers to communication within the family, small communities, or among friends. The *public* domain includes communication in the street, during the performance of various services (shopping, medical care, etc.), and at work. The *institutional* domain contains all settings where the language of communication is formally regulated (police, public administration, courts, education). While code-switching is regulated by legal norms in the latter, it is freely chosen by participants in the former. In the (non-institutional) public sphere, the legal codification of code-switching is only seldom characteristic. From an informal perspective, code-switching depends on the participants, the topic of discussion, and underlying social norms. As already mentioned, in Transylvania the widely accepted norm dominating both private and public discussions is that (notwithstanding the topic of discussion and the number of participants) it is "not proper" to speak Hungarian if one of the members of a group is Romanian. Furthermore, this norm is often actively defended by members of the majority, for example, by calling upon individuals who are talking to each other in Hungarian on the bus to switch languages, or by asking Hungarian-speaking customers to switch to Romanian in public institutions, where theoretically they have the right to speak in their vernacular (Kontra 1999). This type of behavior, called *language management* in the literature, involves "an effort by someone with or claiming authority to modify the language used by other speakers" (Spolsky 2004, p. 18): Its existence is very telling about both the language ideologies dominant among ethnic Romanians and the asymmetrical relationship between Romanian and Hungarian.

Research on the language use patterns of Hungarians in Romania is rich and detailed (see, for instance, Sorbán and Dobos 1997; Csepeli et al. 2002; Horváth 2005, 2008a, 2011; Dobos 2012; Sorbán 2012; Dobos and Megyeri 2014). In the following, we synthesize the main conclusions of these studies.

Within the family, 89% of Hungarians exclusively speak their mother tongue, while 11–12%[71] use both Hungarian and Romanian or only Romanian. In contrast, only approximately half speak only Hungarian with their friends, 20% casually use Romanian as well, about a quarter use both languages equally, and the remaining 5% use only Romanian. In sum, around three quarters of the adult Hungarian population mostly use Hungarian in private life, while the rest use Romanian to varying degrees, but to a significant extent. In settlements where the proportion of Hungarians does not reach 20%, the percentage of those who dominantly speak Hungarian in their private life is 56%, while in municipalities where the proportion of Hungarians is above 80% more than 95% use exclusively Hungarian (Horváth 2011, p. 123).

[71] This is roughly equivalent to the proportion of Hungarians living in ethnically mixed marriages (Gyurgyík et al. 2011, p. 91).

The dominant use of Hungarian in public domains that are not regulated by law (such as workplaces, shopping, medical care) is characteristic of approximately half of the Transylvanian Hungarians. Of the former, approximately one-third declared that they communicate exclusively in Hungarian, while the remaining 18–19% report to using Romanian occasionally. However, communicational patterns in the public sphere are influenced by the proportion of Hungarians that live in a given settlement to an even greater extent than in the case of the private domain. In municipalities where the proportion of Hungarians does not exceed 20%, Romanian is quite dominant in public communication situations and the public use of Hungarian is very rare. For example, the mother tongue is the dominant language spoken at work for only 11% of Hungarians. These figures are significantly different from the situation in dominantly Hungarian-inhabited settlements, where almost three quarters of ethnic Hungarians (73.7%) work in communities where they exclusively use Hungarian.

As already discussed, within the institutional domain a distinction should be made between institutions of central administration to include deconcentrated institutions and local public institutions. With regard to the latter, the patterns of language use in relation to mayoral offices and local authorities are regularly appraised in surveys about language use. About the former, however, we unfortunately have no comprehensive data; consequently, we only report figures about language usage involving contact with the police. Though efforts to promote minority presence in policing were made, the impact on language is rather limited (Horváth 2008b, pp. 209–210); consequently, the general pattern of the use of Hungarian in the deconcentrated institutions of public administration is probably somewhat more favorable than is suggested by the following figures strictly relevant for language use when contacting the police.

In their encounters with the police, 76.5% of Hungarians mostly or only use Romanian (57% exclusively Romanian). Put differently, the use of Hungarian with police is exceptional (11%). Moreover, this situation is not influenced by the ethnic composition of settlements, as even in settlements where the proportion of Hungarians exceeds 80%, only 20% of Hungarians report to mostly using Hungarian in their relations with the police. Also, the use of Hungarian occurs mostly in cases of low language proficiency, as only individuals who do not speak Romanian sufficiently well report to using Hungarian; this fact suggests that the former figures are not indicative of the strong implementation of language rights, even if Hungarian is used.

As for local councils, approximately half of all Hungarians mostly use their mother tongue when speaking to officials, but in writing Hungarian is used more frequently than Romanian by 23.5%. This indicates a low frequency of use, as 78.8% of Hungarians live in administrative units where the law would allow them to use their mother tongue both orally and in writing. In other words, data about language use confirm the poor implementation of minority language rights policies (Fig. 1).

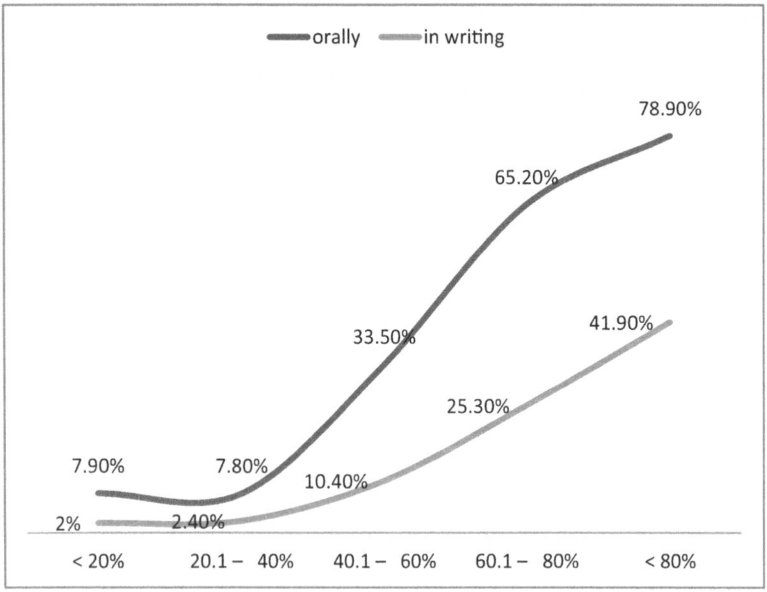

Fig. 1 Communication in Hungarian with local public institutions according to the proportion of Hungarians in the municipality (*Source* Authors' own calculations based on survey data)

5 Patterns of Language Use

From time to time, it is inevitable that members of minority groups will use a second language. The question is, however, to what extent do the former use their mother tongue in different communicational domains. To answer this question and to create a typology of the language use of Transylvanian Hungarians, we borrow from a scale developed by Silver (1975) who analyzed bilingualism among ethnic non-Russians in the Soviet Union based on census data. Focusing on the relationship between the vernacular language and Russian, his "scale of linguistic russification" contains four categories, representing different patterns of language use: parochials, unassimilated bilinguals, assimilated bilinguals, and assimilated. In Silver's conception, *parochials* were non-Russians who claimed to be monolingual in their vernacular language. *Unassimilated bilinguals* claimed their mother tongue as their first language, but stated that they spoke Russian as well. In the case of *assimilated bilinguals*, the order of language use was reversed (Russian the native/preferred language, but the language of the ethnic group was also used). In their case, bilingual language use presents clear aspects of compartmentalization of language use, first language being mostly assigned to private contexts. Those assigned to the *assimilated* category maintained their non-Russian ethnic identity, but did not speak the language, being fluent only in Russian.

This typology, although not explicitly created to appraise language use patterns, is with slight adjustments a useful tool for describing the situation of Hungarians in Romania. We consider those individuals to be parochials who use Romanian only sporadically in their everyday communication, regardless of the domain in which they communicate. Approximately one quarter of the Hungarian population belong in this category. They use Romanian to some extent in the institutional domain, although it is not the primary language even in this speech situation. A significant number of this group (around 10% of all ethnic Hungarians) may be considered pure parochials. These persons (mostly elderly or less educated individuals living in smaller Hungarian-dominated settlements) live their lives in an almost completely monolingual way.

Unassimilated bilinguals are those individuals who almost exclusively use Hungarian in their private domain, while the language of other domains is also mostly Hungarian; however, there are a significant number of other situations (work, administration, and to some extent media consumption) where code-switching takes place. Approximately 40–45% of the Transylvanian Hungarian population can be classified into this category.

The category of assimilated bilinguals comprises individuals who mostly use Hungarian in their private domains, although when communicating with their friends or consuming media they also use Romanian quite often. In the rest of the domains, although Hungarian is present the primary language is Romanian. In other words, from the perspective of language use the public and private domains are clearly separate. About 20% of Transylvanian Hungarians belong in this category.

The final category, assimilated, describes individuals who use Romanian regularly or exclusively in every domain of life. For these persons, intergenerational language change is imminent. Hungarians included in this category (whose share is about, still does not exceed 10% of the Transylvanian Hungarian population) mainly live in settlements where the proportion of Hungarians does not reach 20%.

6 Conclusions

The vast majority of Transylvania's Hungarian native speakers live in large linguistic communities that are differentiated enough to sustain the survival of the language. Most local, smaller speech communities are connected to larger cities in which numerous Hungarian-language institutions function. Almost half of the Hungarian-speaking community live in settlements where they are not only in a demographic majority, but Hungarian is also the culturally unmarked and dominant public language.

From an institutional and legal perspective, Hungarian is not an official language in Romania (even at the regional level); it merely has protected status. Despite this, there exists a complex and extensive legal framework that could reinforce the language, while many of the related policies are permissive and even supportive. However, the quality of implementation does not match that of the legislation; in many cases, the legal provisions remain only on paper, as institutional practices are not always in line with the letter of the law. In many domains—especially in deconcentrated institutions and the judiciary, but also in numerous local administrations—Hungarian-language use in practice lags behind the opportunities provided by the law: One cannot speak of the existence of a truly bilingual institutional system even in the administrative units where a large number of Hungarians live. We consider this to be a serious problem, even if in other spheres (most importantly, education and media, which are discussed in Chapters 6 and 8), the Hungarian language is strongly institutionally underpinned and widely used.

Levels of bilingualism and language use patterns are very diverse among Transylvanian Hungarians. For approximately 8–9% of Hungarian speakers, the use of the vernacular language is confined to the private sphere, and even there it is often mixed with Romanian. In the case of these individuals, an intergenerational language switch is highly probable. At the other end of the continuum, about 25% of Transylvanian Hungarians use the Romanian language relatively rarely. The rest of the Transylvanian Hungarians (approximately 65%) use Romanian on an everyday basis. In their case, a sharp distinction can be made between language use in private and in public; while the former is dominantly Hungarian, the latter is characterized by a pronounced asymmetry, which is reinforced not only by the legal/institutional framework, but also by the behavioral norms and language ideologies dominant among both Romanians and Hungarians, which are insufficiently supportive of the Hungarian language.

References

Andrássy, G. (2011). The right to use one's own language and the matter of simplicity. *Europäisches Journal für Minderheitenfragen, 4*(1), 5–19.

Arzoz, X. (2007). The nature of language rights. *Journal on Ethnopolitics and Minority Issues in Europe, 6*(2), 1–35.

Baetens Beardsmore, H. (1986). *Bilingualism: Basic principles* (2nd ed.). Boston, MA: College-Hill Press.

Baranowska, G. (2014). Legal regulations on national and ethnic minorities in Poland. *Przegląd Zachodni, 2*, 35–48.

Benő, A., Becze, O., Erdély, J., Nagy, Z., Ördög-Gyárfás, E., & Sárosi Mardírosz, K. (Eds.). (2004). *Magyar–román közigazgatási szótár*. Sepsiszentgyörgy: Anyanyelvápolók Erdélyi Szövetsége.

Beretka, K. (2016). Language rights and multilingualism in Vojvodina. *International Journal on Minority and Group Rights, 23*(4), 505–529.

Blommaert, J. (2006). Language policy and national identity. In T. Ricento (Ed.), *An introduction to language policy: Theory and method* (pp. 238–255). Malden, MA: Blackwell.

Bogdán, A., & Mohácsek, M. (2012). *Nyelvi jogok útmutató*. Cluj-Napoca: ISPMN.

Brubaker, R., Feischmidt, M., Fox, J., & Grancea, L. (2006). *Nationalist politics and everyday ethnicity in a Transylvanian town*. Princeton: Princeton University Press.

Cenoz, J. (2001). The effect of linguistic distance, L2 status and age on cross-linguistic influence in third language acquisition. In J. Cenoz, B. Hufeisen, & U. Jessner (Eds.), *Cross-linguistic influence in third language acquisition: Psycholinguistic perspectives* (pp. 8–20). Clevedon and Buffalo: Multilingual Matters.

Csepeli, G., Székely, M., & Örkény, A. (2002). *Nemzetek egymás tükrében. Interetnikus viszonyok a Kárpát-medencében*. Budapest: Balassi.

Csergő, Z. (2007). *Talk of the nation: Language and conflict in Romania and Slovakia*. Ithaca: Cornell University Press.

DeVries, J. (1985). Some methodological aspects of self-report questions on language and ethnicity. *Journal of Multilingual and Multicultural Development, 6*(5), 347–368.

Dobos, F. (2012). *Nemzeti identitás, asszimiláció és médiahasználat a határon túli magyarság körében, 1999–2011*. Budapest: Médiatudományi Intézet.

Dobos, F., & Megyeri, K. (2014). *Nemzeti identitás, asszimiláció és médiahasználat a határon túli magyarság körében 2*. Budapest: Médiatudományi Intézet.

Eurobarometer. (2012). *Special Eurobarometer 386: Europeans and their languages*. European Commission. Available at: http://ec.europa.eu/public_opinion/archives/ebs/ebs_386_en.pdf.

Faingold, E. D. (2004). Language rights and language justice in the constitutions of the world. *Language Problems and Language Planning, 28*(1), 11–24.

Farkas, R. (2011, July 5). Leváltani kényszerülnek a könyvtárigazgatót (Pert nyert a prefektúra). *Háromszék*. Available at: http://www.3szek.ro/load/cikk/40557/levaltani_kenyszerulnek_a_konyvtarigazgatot_pert_nyert_a_prefektura.

Fazakas, E. (Ed.). (2002). *Román–magyar közigazgatási szótár*. Sepsiszentgyörgy: Anyanyelvápolók Erdélyi Szövetsége.

Fishman, J. A. (1972). *The sociology of language: An interdisciplinary social science approach to language in society.* Rowley, MA: Newbury House.

Fishman, J. A. (1989). *Language and ethnicity in minority sociolinguistic perspective.* Clevedon, Avon, England, and Philadelphia: Multilingual Matters.

Fishman, J. A. (2000). Who speaks what language to whom and when? In L. Wei (Ed.), *The bilingualism reader* (pp. 82–98). London and New York: Routledge.

Grin, F. (2003). *Language policy evaluation and the European Charter for regional or minority languages.* Basingstoke, Hampshire, and New York: Palgrave Macmillan.

Gyurgyík, L., Horváth, I., & Kiss, T. (2011). Demográfiai folyamatok, etnokulturális és társadalmi reprodukció. In B. Bitskey (Ed.), *Határon túli magyarság a 21. Században* (pp. 69–119). Budapest: Köztársasági Elnöki Hivatal.

Horváth, I. (2003). Az erdélyi magyarok kétnyelvűsége: nyelvmentés és integráció között? *Erdélyi Társadalom, 1*(1), 7–24.

Horváth, I. (2005). A romániai magyarok kétnyelvűsége: nyelvismeret, nyelvhasználat, nyelvi dominancia. Regionális összehasonlító elemzések. *Erdélyi Társadalom, 3*(1), 171–200.

Horváth, I. (2008a). *Elemzések a romániai magyarok kétnyelvűségéről* (ISPMN Working Papers No. 8).

Horváth, I. (2008b). Evaluarea politicilor lingvistice din România. In L. Salat (Ed.), *Politici de integrare a minorităţilor naţionale din România. Aspecte legale şi instituţionale într-o perspectivă comparată* (pp. 203–213). Cluj-Napoca: CRDE.

Horváth, I. (2008c). A romániai nyelvpolitikák értékelése. *Magyar Kisebbség, 13*(3–4), 263–277.

Horváth, I. (2009). Nyelvi készségek, nyelvi viselkedés és etnokulturális reprodukció az erdélyi magyar népesség vonatkozásában. In Z. Spéder

(Ed.), *Párhuzamok. Anyaországi és erdélyi magyarok a századfordulón* (pp. 153–182). Budapest: KSH Népességtudományi Kutatóintézet.

Horváth, I. (2011). A romániai magyarok nyilvános nyelvhasználatának mintázatai. In I. Horváth & E. Tódor (Eds.), *Nyelvhasználat, tannyelv és két(több) nyelvű lét* (pp. 115–136). Cluj-Napoca: ISPMN.

Horváth, I. (2012). Románia: a kisebbségi nyelvi jogok és intézményes érvényesülésük. In K. Eplényi & Z. Kántor (Eds.), *Térvesztés és határtalanítás: a magyar nyelvpolitika 21. századi kihívásai* (pp. 172–198). Budapest: Nemzetpolitikai Kutatóintézet and Lucidus.

Horváth, I., Veress, I., & Vitos, K. (2010). *Közigazgatási nyelvhasználat Hargita megyében az önkormányzati és a központi kormányzat megyeszintű intézményeiben* (ISPMN Working Papers No. 27).

Kaplan, R. B., & Baldauf, R. B. (1997). *Language planning from practice to theory.* Clevedon and Philadelphia: Multilingual Matters.

Kis, J., & Kató, K. (2014). *Jogaink Romániában Magyarul.* Kolozsvár: Jogaink Egyesület.

Kiss, T., & Kapitány, B. (2009). Magyarok Erdélyben: A minta kialakítása és az adatfelvétel. In Z. Spéder (Ed.), *Párhuzamok. Anyaországi és erdélyi magyarok a századfordulón* (pp. 31–54). Budapest: KSH Népességtudományi Kutatóintézet.

Kontra, M. (1999). "Don't speak Hungarian in public!" A documentation and analysis of folk linguistic rights. In M. S. Kontra, R. Phillipson, T. Skutnabb-Kangas, & T. Várady (Eds.), *Language, a right and a resource: Approaches to linguistics human rights* (p. xi, 346p.). Budapest and New York: Central European University Press.

Kontra, M., & Szilágyi, N. S. (2002). A kisebbségeknek van anyanyelvük, de a többségnek nincs. In M. Kontra & H. Hattyár (Eds.), *Magyarok és nyelvtörvények*. Budapest: Teleki László Alapítvány.

Kymlicka, W. (1995). *Multicultural citizenship: A liberal theory of minority rights.* Oxford: Clarendon Press.

McRae, K. D. (1975). The principle of territoriality and the principle of personality in multilingual states. *International Journal of the Sociology of Language, 4*, 33–54.

Mezei, J. (Ed.). (2006). *Magyar-román-angol jogi, közgazdasági és üzleti szótár.* București: C.H. Beck.

Morgan, M. H. (2014). *Speech communities. Key topics in linguistic anthropology.* Cambridge and New York: Cambridge University Press.

Nelde, P. H., Labrie, N., & Williams, C. H. (1992). The principles of territoriality and personality in the solution of linguistic conflicts. *Journal of Multilingual and Multicultural Development, 13*(5), 387–406.

Papp Kincses, E. (2011). Kommunikációs etnográfia. Nyelvhasználat a csíkszeredai bíróságon és a Hargita megyei törvényszéken. Jogszabályok és jogérvényesítési lehetőségek. In I. Horváth & E. Tódor (Eds.), *Nyelvhasználat, tannyelv és két(több)nyelvű lét* (pp. 185–208). Cluj-Napoca: ISPMN.

Patrick, P. L. (2002). The speech community. In J. K. Chambers, P. Trudgill, & N. Schilling-Estes (Eds.), *The handbook of language variation and change* (pp. 573–597). Malden, MA: Blackwell.

Peal, E., & Lambert, W. E. (1962). The relation of bilingualism to intelligence. *Psychological Monographs: General and Applied, 76*(27), 1–23.

Pool, J. (1991). The official language problem. *The American Political Science Review, 85*(2), 495.

Reka, A. (2008). The Ohrid Agreement: The travails of inter-ethnic relations in Macedonia. *Human Rights Review, 9*(1), 55–69.

Ritchie, W. C., & Bhatia, T. K. (2004). Social and psychological factors in language mixing. In T. K. Bhatia & W. C. Ritchie (Eds.), *The handbook of bilingualism* (pp. 336–352). Malden, MA: Blackwell.

Romani, L. P., & Fridlund, H. (2015). *Monitoring and evaluation of language rights in Kosovo*. Office of the Language Commissioner—Office of the Prime Minister of the Republic of Kosovo—ECMI Kosovo. Available at: http://www.komisioneri-ks.org/repository/docs/Anglisht_Finale_160315.pdf.

Sachdev, I., & Giles, H. (2004). Bilingual accommodation. In T. K. Bhatia & W. C. Ritchie (Eds.), *The handbook of bilingualism* (pp. 353–380). Malden, MA: Blackwell.

Scutaru, C. (2017, September 1). Mici Kaufland Odorheiu Secuiesc. Adevărul a ieșit la iveală: Cum s-a făcut filmarea. *dcnews.ro*. Available at: https://www.dcnews.ro/mici-kaufland-odorheiu-secuiesc-adevarul-a-ie-it-la-iveala-cum-s-a-facut-filmarea_556542.html.

Silver, B. D. (1975). Methods of deriving data on bilingualism from the 1970 Soviet census. *Soviet Studies, 27*(4), 574–597.

Skutnabb-Kangas, T. (1997). *Nyelv, oktatás és a kisebbségek. Kisebbségi adattár.* Budapest: Teleki László Alapítvány.

Sorbán, A. (2012). *Kisebbség – társadalomszerkezet – kétnyelvűség* (ISPMN Working Papers No. 42).

Sorbán, A., & Dobos, F. (1997). Szociológiai felmérés a határon túl élő magyar közösségek körében az asszimiláció folyamatairól. *Magyar Kisebbség, 3*(3–4), 293–323.
Spolsky, B. (2004). *Language policy.* Cambridge and New York: Cambridge University Press.
Szabó, T. (2017, April 18). Semmi sem garantálja a magyar nyelvű ellátást a kórházakban. *foter.ro.* Available at: http://foter.ro/cikk/20170418_semmi_sem_garantalja_a_magyar_nyelvu_ellatast_a_korhazakban?utm_source=foter_ro&utm_medium=link&utm_campaign=foter_ro_201712.
Szépe, G. (1999). The position of Hungarians in Romania and Slovakia in 1996. *Nationalities Papers, 27*(1), 69–92.
Szerbhorváth, G. (2015). Language politics and language rights on the territory of former Yugoslavia the today's Serbia/Vojvodina. *Acta Universitatis Sapientiae, European and Regional Studies, 8*(1), 57–72.
Szilágyi, N. S. (1998). De ce nu-şi pot însuşi copiii maghiari limba română în şcoală? *Altera, 7,* 131–148.
Thomas, J. W., & Grindle, M. S. (1990). After the decision: Implementing policy reforms in developing countries. *World Development, 18*(8), 1163–1181.
Toró, T. (2016). Egy helyben topogva? Kisebbségi nyelvi jogok alakulása Romániában 2008 és 2015 között. *Magyar Kisebbség, 21*(2), pp. 18–53.
Toró, T. (2017). Detached implementation. Discourse and practice in minority language usage in Romania. Manuscript
Turi, J. G. (2012). Linguistic legislation. In Carol A. Chapelle (Ed.), *The encyclopedia of applied linguistics* (pp. 3481–3487). Wiley-Blackwell.
Varga, E. Á. (1991). Városodás, vándorlás, nemzetiség. Adatok az erdélyi városok etnikai arculatában bekövetkezett változásokról. *Regio, 2*(4), 121–141.
Varga, E. Á. (1998). *Fejezetek a jelenkori Erdély népesedéstörténetéből.* Budapest: Püski.
Vasilevich, H. (2013). *Lithuania's minority-related legislation: Is there a legal vacuum?* (ECMI Working Papers No. 70).
Vass, Á. (2015). If yes, why not? Minority language use and accommodation of minority language rights in Slovakia. *Acta Universitatis Sapientiae, European and Regional Studies, 8*(1), 43–56.

Wolff, S., Van Houten, P., Anghelea, A.-M., & Djuric, I. (2008). *Minority rights in the western Balkans*. Brussels: European Parliament. Available at: http://www.europarl.europa.eu/RegData/etudes/etudes/join/2008/385559/EXPO-DROI_ET(2008)385559_EN.pdf.

Zwilling, C. (2004). Minority protection and language policy in the Czech Republic. *Noves SL – Revista de Sociolingüística, 5*(3), 67–80.

Part II

Ethnic Parallelism: Political Program and Social Reality—Ethnically and Non-ethnically Integrated Social Fields

5

Ethnic Parallelism: Political Program and Social Reality: An Introduction

Tamás Kiss and Dénes Kiss

The notion of ethnic parallelism is well known in the literature of divided societies. In his influential study about the sources of ethnic conflict, Donald Horowitz argued that in unranked systems of ethnic groups[1] there is always a tendency to form parallel societies (1985, pp. 22–24). In this sense, ethnic groups that are in an unranked relation

[1]In case of unranked systems of groups (1) ethnicity is not associated with certain social positions and (2) ethnic groups have channels of social mobility controlled by their own elites. This is, of course, an ideal type in a Weberian sense, as ethnic stratification is never perfectly symmetrical and elites of dominant groups always control more institutional channels than elites claiming to represent minorities. However, the usefulness of this concept becomes evident if one compares the relation between Roma and non-Roma on the one hand and that between Hungarians and

T. Kiss (✉)
Romanian Institute for Research on National Minorities,
Cluj-Napoca, Romania

D. Kiss
Hungarian Department of Sociology and Social Work,
Babeș-Bolyai University, Cluj-Napoca, Romania

T. Kiss et al. (eds.), *Unequal Accommodation of Minority Rights*,
Palgrave Politics of Identity and Citizenship Series,
https://doi.org/10.1007/978-3-319-78893-7_5

with each other can be viewed as *incipient parallel societies.* Ethnic parallelism was also discussed by authors focusing on the so-called *plural societies.* The notion of plural society referred initially to colonial settings (see Furnivall 1948)—where different ethnic groups were integrated into a single administrative framework, but they often lacked even the intent to build an institutional system for underpinning a common identity.[2] Consequently, scholars who studied such formations could not employ the analytical models designed for nation-states (Jenkins 2008, p. 29). Nevertheless, the concept of plural society became used beyond colonial settings. A typology elaborated by Smith (1965) distinguishes between cultural, structural, and political pluralism. Schermerhorn (1978) added the element of "normative pluralism", implying a general ideology that maintains the desirability of preserving cultural differences among different ethnic groups. A very influential conceptualization of parallel society was offered by Lijphart (1969, 1977), who constructed a theory of *social pillars* and coined the term "pillarization" (*verzuiling*) to describe institutional processes characteristic in certain societies. In his account, pillarization described the political integration of Dutch society before the last decades of the twentieth century. According to Lijphart, deep subcultural and ideological segmentation is a prerequisite for the emergence of social pillars. The process of pillarization denotes the institutionalization of this segmentation, through which different subcultural groups acquire an institutional and organizational structure that allows their members to live most of their lives and satisfy their needs within their own institutional networks. Lijphart argued that Dutch Catholics, Liberals, and

Romanians on the other. In Romania to be Roma is a social stigma and signifies a marginal status (in spite of the fact that not all Roma are poor). Further, Roma elites control very few channels of mobility and, consequently, socially mobile Roma often depart themselves from their ascribed ethnic category. Contrary, the label of Hungarian does not mark any social status and (as we will see in this section of the volume) Hungarian elites control a wide range of institutions serving as channels of mobility.

2The British indirect rule is a well-known example. Here, the colonial administration relied on pre-existing power structures. Thus rulers, chiefs became mediators between the colonial administration and its subjects, while the population did not even interact with a unified administration.

Protestants, respectively Socialists, lived their lives encapsulated in their own institutional networks during much of the twentieth century: They studied in separate schools and universities, they participated in public life through their own parties, and they had their own newspapers, magazines, hospitals, sport, and leisure clubs. Pillarization also means that the institutions associated with a pillar form a compact organizational web. Moreover, unlike social classes, which are in ranked order, pillars integrate people vertically: Different social strata participate in the organizational system created by the pillar. Initially, this analytical framework was applied to the study of religious communities and ideological groups (such as Socialists and Liberals). Later, the literature of (deeply) divided societies extended the vocabulary of pillarization also to ethnically organized entities.

Several authors discussed whether the notion of parallel society or ethnic parallelism can be useful in understanding the case of Transylvanian Hungarians. Brubaker and his co-authors argued that the metaphor of parallelism can be misleading, because it hides the fundamentally asymmetrical relationship between the minority and majority segments of society (2006, pp. 265–301). The most important expression of asymmetry is the very fact that majority members do not have to exit their own (unmarked) world, while those belonging to the minority have to step out repeatedly from their own (ethnically marked) world and enter the wider, mainstream (in our case Romanian) society.[3] Moreover, not all minority members are equally encapsulated into the minority institutional web. Consequently, the authors propose another metaphor, namely *institutional archipelago*, as more appropriate for describing the asymmetric "parallelism" between the social organizations of the majority and the minority.

Others scholars, including Lőrincz (2008) and Culic (2016), have argued that the notion of parallel society is useful, as it is both a descriptive tool and a political project sustained by Hungarian minority elites in Transylvania. According to Lőrincz: "*the attempts to define Transylvanian Hungarians as a* [parallel] *society appeared simultaneously*

[3] We define and discuss in details the terms of marked and unmarked in Chapter 10.

with the minority status … [The parallel] *"society" is not only a descriptive tool, it is a goal, it should be created and* [elites] *should be willing to create it. Even if the existence of ethno-national minorities as a (relatively) self-sufficient society was often questioned, the aspiration toward such societal organization is an explicit or implicit part of all Transylvanian Hungarian ethno-political programs*" (2008, p. 240).[4] Culic argued in a similar vein and focused on the attempts of the Hungarian political class to create the "Hungarian Society in Transylvania" as an object of governmentality (2016, p. 194).

In our understanding, ethnic parallelism and the metaphor of parallel society have a dual character. First, the desire for institutionalized ethnic parallelism appears under the notion of Minority Society (*Kisebbségi Társadalom*). This is a central idea in the political rhetoric and self-representation of Hungarian elites. The predominant aspiration among Hungarian political elites has been to create an ethnically integrated institutional structure in which members of the community can live their lives in a "Hungarian world". According to their approach, this institutional structure is also of central importance for the ethnocultural reproduction of the Hungarian community. In the first part of this introductory chapter, we will discuss the origins and evolution of the programmatic idea of Minority Society. Second, ethnic parallelism is also useful for describing the Hungarian institutional setting, where several social fields are organized in ethnically separated structures. We agree with Brubaker et al. (2006), however, that the metaphor of parallel society is only partially adequate for describing the social organization of the Transylvanian Hungarian community. The existence of a well-structured and ethnically separated institutional system in some dimensions of social life suggests that Transylvanian Hungarians can be perceived as a distinct social segment or social pillar. In other dimensions, however, Hungarians lack separate institutional structures. Moreover, the fact that the institutional system does not cover the entire community also suggests that the Transylvanian Hungarian community cannot be perceived as a stand-alone societal segment. In the second

[4]Our own translation from Hungarian.

part of the introductory chapter, we will present a model through which the institutional structure sustaining ethnic parallelism can be captured. In the third part, we will shortly summarize our findings and introduce the chapters of this section.

1 Minority Society as a Programmatic Idea

The idea of the Minority Society traces back to the interwar period, when the Hungarian urban elites and middle classes (previously in a majority position) confronted for the first time their minority status. It appeared as a reaction to the collapse of the Hapsburg Empire and the end of Hungarian dominance in Transylvania. István Sulyok (1931), a Hungarian intellectual of the interwar era formulated the idea of the Minority Society most expressively. In his view, the Minority Society is a social totality (or a "container entity", as we would say today). Similar to the nation-state, it comprises all sorts of relations, or in Sulyok's definition, it is a social formation that "*embraces its members in every capacity, and tries to provide for all of their needs*" (Sulyok 1931, p. 174). However, there is a fundamental difference between a Minority Society and a nation-state (or a nation who owns a state[5]), namely that minorities lack state power that in the case of nation-states is the most effective means of social organization. If the state did not delegate some of its competencies to minorities in the form of territorial or personal autonomy, latter would have to face the nationalizing state power with "purely social"[6] means. Sulyok elaborated an ideology of ethno-civil society, stating that the Minority Society has to take over from the state important public functions even until the state delegates them in the frame of some sort of autonomy. "*Thus, when national dogma deprives national minorities, or more precisely minority nations, of the capacity to legally put whatever small part of state power to serve their*

[5]The question "*who owns the state*" was posed recently by Wimmer (2002).

[6]"Purely social" was used by interwar Transylvanian political thinkers with the meaning of extra-state or non-administrative power/action.

national demands, they dispose more or less freely of purely social means, a broad enough domain, which hardly can be narrowed for long by power measures" (Sulyok 1931, p. 175). Sulyok highlighted three types of institutions that should have a crucial role in integrating minority societies. The churches were the first in line, because in Transylvania religious differences reinforced the ethnic cleavage. Local social associations organized along ethnic lines represented the second pillar for Sulyok, while the third pillar was envisaged as a nationwide umbrella organization that "*provides for all spiritual, moral and material problems of our national culture*" (Sulyok 1931, p. 176). Besides, for Sulyok the main issue was the economic integration of the Minority Society, which, in his conception, could be best achieved through the cooperative movement.[7] Sulyok's ideas about the parallel Minority Society gained in value after 1990.

Some fundamental points formulated in Sulyok's text are worth emphasizing:

1. First, the Minority Society, in the sense of a parallel society or the institutionally sustained "Hungarian world", is not only a *social reality,* but also a *political program*, a desirable state, which according to the author should be pursued by the Hungarian elite. Sulyok himself had a dual stake: to understand sociologically and to realize politically the parallel society.

2. Second, following Egry (2014), we may note that the idea of the Minority Society emerging in the 1930s meant a radical change of the Transylvanian Hungarian elite's perspective, as the idea emerged from the need to adapt to the new situation brought about by the Treaty of Trianon. From a (dominant) majority perspective, ethnic encapsulation can be perceived as an anomaly, and of course, Hungarian elites in Transylvania lacked this desire before World War I. Earlier, the entire territory of Transylvania within Hungary was their taken-for-granted frame for social and political organization. Of course, this was only conceivable for these elites under Hungarian domination, and the

[7] In the interwar period, ethnically divided cooperative movements were rather strong in Transylvania. See Hunyadi (2006).

Hungarian nationalizing state had been regarded as the primary means[8] for this until 1918 (just as it became that for the Romanian elites after the Treaty of Trianon[9]).

3. Third, the relation between the Minority Society and *individual freedom* is of particular importance. The ideology of Minority Society is often criticized on the presupposition that the "*ethnic safety net*"[10] or the attachment to "*the narrowing Hungarian world*" considerably reduces individual freedom and possible alternatives for those belonging to the Hungarian community. There is, however, another interpretation of this relationship that is much closer to the standpoint of interwar intellectuals concerned with the idea of the Minority Society. According to this interpretation, members of the minority group need the Minority Society (and the autonomous institutional network sustaining it) to counterweight the *asymmetric power relations* present in the mainstream society. Due to these asymmetric power relations, someone belonging to the minority group can be free (and oneself[11]) only inside the Minority Society (their own institutionally defined world).[12]

4. Fourth, in Sulyok's view conventional minority politics and minority protection resting foremost on political and legal means and focusing on rights and interests of the community are far from adequate. They should be complemented by active *community organizing* that creates, maintains, and broadens the Minority Society and the institutional system it is based upon.

[8]Egry (2014) argues that before World War I, Hungarian elites in Transylvania (especially those who lived in regions where the majority population was ethnic Romanian) often complained that the state was not sufficiently nationalizing, meaning that it was not efficient enough in consolidating Hungarian national interests. Today, Romanian elites in Harghita/Hargita and Covasna/Kovászna counties (with a Hungarian-majority population) express similar ideas.

[9]See Livezeanu (1995).

[10]This expression (*etnikai burok* in Hungarian) was used by Zoltán Biró (1998).

[11]The fluidity, situational, and contextual character of ethnic identities is often emphasized in the literature. We agree with those authors who do not take for granted this fluidity but emphasize that it varies greatly depending on the psychological and social price of leaving one's own group or category (Jenkins 2008; Wimmer 2013).

[12]Kymlicka's theory on multicultural democracy is also relevant here. According to him, state should support minority cultures, as individuals can enjoy individual freedoms only inside their own societal culture (Kymlicka 1995).

We do not consider our task to exhaustively review the conceptual history of the Minority Society.[13] It suffices to say that the Minority Society as an intellectual construct survived unabashedly during communism in spite of radical social changes. For leftist Hungarian intellectuals "Leninist consociation" seemed plausible during the 1950s, since they envisaged that Communist modernization would bring the relaxation of ethno-national tensions. Later, after 1968, Hungarian intellectuals started to shift focus toward the establishment and development of their own parallel institutional system, paradoxically in conditions when effective institutional space of minority self-organization has been considerably shrinking.

As for the period following the collapse of the Communist regime, several authors emphasized the centrality of ethnic parallelism at a programmatic level. Bakk (2000) relied on Lijphart and argued that next to institution building, the implicit political agenda of RMDSZ was to achieve some sort of "hidden consociation".[14] Kántor (2000) talked about a process of minority nation building. His theory was based on Benedict Anderson's (2006) idea of imagined communities and focused on the mechanisms that engendered and continuously reproduced the Minority Society as a frame. It is fundamental that these mechanisms function in a field of power relations, meaning that one cannot "imagine" the Hungarian Minority Society without a political center that defines itself as Hungarian and tries to extend its discursive, political, and institutional authority on this entity.[15]

Nevertheless, from our perspective the interpretation of Biró (1998) is the most relevant. According to him, the first years after the 1989 regime collapse were the fourth period (after 1920, 1945, and 1968) characterized by a burst of ethnic institution building. He argued that the previous waves of institutionalizing ethnic parallelism were

---

[13]Bárdi's works (2006) contain detailed discussions of this issue. We thank Nándor Bárdi for pointing out the conceptual continuity that extends back to the Communist period.

[14]Obviously, full consociation is more than building parallel institutions and the political preconditions of consociation (segmental autonomy, grand coalitions, minority veto, and proportionality) are clearly missing in Romania. See Lijphart (1977).

[15]See also Culic (2016).

of central importance, because Hungarian elites perceived institution building as an "endeavor for the restoration"[16] of the Minority Society (Biró 1998, p. 30). In the eyes of these elites, the institutional web which had to be "restored" constituted the Hungarian Society in Romania itself. Biró classified the institutions in four groups: (1) non-profit organizations, fulfilling various functions (cultural, educational, social); (2) political umbrella organizations attempting to serve the whole Hungarian community and targeting leadership and administrative roles (the most important being RMDSZ); (3) institutions belonging to the state apparatus or the public institutional structure, which (in several settings) function as "Hungarian institutions" (Hungarian schools, local authorities in the Székely Land or other regions with a Hungarian majority, theaters, libraries, etc.); and (4) other institutions like Hungarian economic associations, or Hungarian events.

Biró underscored two important features of the institutional processes. First, he emphasized the objective of building up a complete organizational web, meaning "*the attempt to cover all putative or real physical, social and mental dimensions on which the Hungarian Society in Romania could operate*" (Biró 1998, p. 22). Second, he highlighted that the most important function of this institutional web was ethnic boundary maintenance.[17] This second aspect was also emphasized by Brubaker et al. (2006), who argued that Hungarian institutions create social spaces in which Hungarian becomes an "unmarked category", and in which being Hungarian is normal, natural, and taken for granted. Thus, inside these institutional spaces, individuals do not have to confront the power asymmetries existing outside the Hungarian institutions. Consequently, the institutional structure greatly relieves people from the burden of boundary production and maintenance, thus making possible the ethno-cultural reproduction of the Hungarian community.

---

[16]Many institutions were "reestablished" (or at least took the names of ones existing in the inter-war period).

[17]See also the introductory chapter of our volume for the relation between ethnic institutions and boundary maintenance.

2 Institutionally Sustained Ethnic Parallelism

The institutional system of the Transylvanian Hungarians has been the object of several empirical investigations during the last two-and-a-half decades.[18] Based on these investigations, a model of the Hungarian institutional system was also elaborated.[19] We use a revised version of this model as a conceptual tool to describe the institutional structures sustaining ethnic parallelism. The following points should be emphasized in this respect:

1. An institution can be regarded as part of the Hungarian institutional web if it operates in Hungarian language and if Hungarian is a default (unmarked) category inside its institutional spaces. This means that the institutions do not necessarily have to be "ethnic" in their purpose or goals to be labeled as Hungarian. From our perspective, a sports club operating in a predominantly Hungarian settlement is part of the Hungarian institutional net, even if its Hungarian character is not explicitly marked by the constitutive act.

2. It is worth distinguishing between several domains[20] inside the institutional web. These domains are externally defined (by us, as researchers); consequently, the institutions belonging to them do not necessary share a common frame of reference and do not necessary compete with each other for positions and resources. We propose the distinction of eight primarily ethnically organized domains, namely public administration, politics, education and research, religion, culture, mass media, sport and leisure time activities, and social care. These

---

[18]In 2003, the Hungarian Academy of Sciences carried out a wide-scale investigation aiming to create an exhaustive inventory of the Hungarian institutions (Csata et al. 2004). This investigation was repeated by the Romanian Institute for Research on National Minorities in 2009/2010 (Kiss 2010; Dániel and Kiss 2014). Several other projects focused on distinct subdomains of the institutional web (Barna 2004; Dániel 2014).

[19]See in detail in Kiss (2006). For a critical revision, see Dániel (2014).

[20]DiMaggio and Anheier (1990) used the notion of sector. We use "domain" in order to avoid confusion between domains of activity and sectors defined by ownership (public, private, nonprofit).

domains are organized primarily (although not exhaustively) through ethnically separated structures.

3. While the domains of the institutional system are externally defined, the strategies of and the relations between actors can be analyzed relying on Bourdieu's (1993) concept of social field.[21] Chapter 3 presented the minority field composed by the political class and a sub-elite level of community activists interested in the maintenance of the web of minority institutions. We also highlighted that the minority field is in an asymmetric interrelation with both the "host"-state and the kin-state. Now, we should underscore that the minority field is also constructed of different (sub)fields. The actors in such fields share a common frame of reference and compete for resources and positions with each other. In this sense, one can speak of the field of minority politics, of a Transylvanian Hungarian literary field, etc. These fields can have a certain degree of autonomy[22] vis-á-vis other fields embedded in the minority institutional system, as well as vis-á-vis the similar structures of the "host"-state and kin-state.

4. A specificity of the minority institutional system is that (compared to the majority one) it is organized more in the form of NGOs and less in the form of state-financed institutions. This does not mean that state-financed institutions would not play an important role in the minority institutional system. Some state-financed institutions are explicitly defined as Hungarian (like several schools, and theaters), while others act in several contexts as Hungarian institutions

---

[21]It should be mentioned that Dániel (2014) argued for the use of fields without any reference to (externally defined) sectors. However, he had also defined externally (and a priori) his object of research and then reified it as a field (defined by internal processes) without any convincing analysis of the internal processes. We think that it is better to maintain the conceptual distinction between our own (a priori) classification and the structures that could be found following a detailed meso-level analysis.

[22]As for the (always relative) autonomy of different fields, Bourdieu used the metaphor of "prism" and "refraction". The question is to what extent an institutional structure is able to transform external influences "*according the specific logic of the field*" (1993, p. 164).

(meaning that Hungarian becomes a default category inside their institutionally bounded spaces). The most interesting is the position of institutions sustained by local administrations. In the ethnic block area of Székely Land, many institutions sustained by the municipalities are actually by default Hungarian and play an important role in the ethno-cultural reproduction of the Hungarian community. In settlements where Hungarians are in a minority position, they may rely less on institutions run by the local government in sustaining ethnic parallelism. In areas where Hungarians live dispersed, the minority institutional system is composed mostly by NGOs and churches, which also play a key role. There are also several Hungarian institutions connected to the above-mentioned domains that operate in the form of for-profit organizations (firms). For-profit organizations forming an ethnically defined segment of the market economy (e.g., ethnic entrepreneurs) are also directly interested in the maintenance of ethnic parallelism. These businesses could be an important part of the Hungarian institutional world. For instance, in Cluj/Kolozsvár, Hungarian pubs, bars, and restaurants are crucial in sustaining a Hungarian public life. They function as important Hungarian institutions for local Hungarians, while their services are ethnically unmarked for many Romanians or foreign tourists.

5. Note that our model is not representative for several domains.[23] As mentioned earlier, an important component of the programmatic idea of the Minority Society was that all dimensions of social life should be organized in ethnically parallel structures (Sulyok 1931; Biró 1998). However, this program seems to be only partially successful. Consequently, there are several sectors in which Hungarian institutions are not dominant. Health care (in which the publicly financed structure is dominant) is not organized in ethnically parallel structures. Several physicians and private medical stations offer services in Hungarian too, and a majority of their patients are Hungarians; however, they do not constitute a network

[23]One might compare our model to the International Classification of Nonprofit Organizations (Salamon and Anheier 1996).

and there is no Hungarian hospital in Transylvania.[24] Most importantly, the *economic domain* cannot be perceived as being (primarily) ethnically organized. There are of course Hungarian entrepreneurs in Transylvania. Their networks might be ethnically segmented, and Hungarians might be overrepresented among their partners or employees. As mentioned already, some firms are connected to an ethnically defined segment of the market economy, and consequently, they are of course part of the net of Hungarian institutions. However, two important factors hinder the organization of Transylvania's economy along ethnic lines. First, there is no ethnically split labor market in the sense used by Bonacich (1972), and there are no economic sectors or niches clearly dominated by Hungarians. Second—as several investigations have shown—business is perceived by the majority of the Hungarian entrepreneurs in Transylvania as simply business, and not as "Hungarian business" (Kiss 2004; Brubaker et al. 2006). This perception has far-reaching consequences on the institutional organization of the Hungarian community. For instance, there are no Hungarian trade unions and there are only a few ethnically segmented business associations (Table 1).

In the case of public administration, it is rather difficult to delimit Hungarian institutions. Many Hungarian stakeholders (delegated by RMDSZ or by smaller ethnic parties) act in an institutional environment that can barely be considered "Hungarian". This is typical in ethnically mixed settlements where Romanian is the default language of the administration in both oral and written communication. However, even in this institutional environment, Hungarian officials (elected on the lists of or delegated by RMDSZ) often try to establish more or less formalized "Hungarian routes" of administrative procedures. For instance, in Cluj/Kolozsvár the RMDSZ vice-mayor deals with Hungarian-language schools and other minority organizations as the representative

[24]According to several media sources, the Hungarian Government aims to build one or more hospitals to serve Hungarian citizens living in Romania. See Magyar kórház épül Erdélyben? Népszava, 5 June 2015 (Accessed at: http://nepszava.hu/cikk/1059438-magyar-korhaz-epul-erdelyben). This would be, of course, an important step toward ethnic parallelism in health care.

Table 1 The sectorial structure of the Hungarian minority institutional system in Transylvania

		Institutional domains							
		Public administration	Politics	Education and research	Religious institutions	Cultural institutions	Mass media	Sport, leisure activities and recreation	Social care
Sector by ownership	Publicly financed	County councils and mayor's offices in Hungarian inhabited areas	RMDSZ	Primary and secondary education; Babeș-Bolyai and other state financed universities; RIRNM		Theatres; local- and county level libraries; museums	Hungarian redactions of public TV and radio channels	Publicly financed sport clubs	Social care organizations financed by local governments
	NGO	Developmental NGOs, regional associations	MPP, EMNP, Youth Associations of the parties (MIÉRT, etc.), Foundations of Parties (Communitas, etc.), EMNT, SZNT, minority rights advocacy NGOs	Associations supporting education; RMPSZ; Sapientia University; research institutes; scientific journals	Churches Religious movements; religious orders; missions, associations; women's associations, etc.	Dance and musical ensembles, non-profit event organizers; amateur troupes	Erdély TV; Erdély FM, religious radio stations	Amateur sport clubs, associations for leisure time activities, youth organizations (scouts, etc.)	Religious and non-religious organizations providing social services
	For profit	Consulting firms		Private schools and kindergartens, research firms	Firms run by churches	For profit editorial houses, bands, Hungarian bookshops, etc.	Print media, private radio stations	Hungarian pubs, restaurants, clubs, sport teams, etc.	For profit social care providers

of the Mayor's Office (based on informal political rules). She also has regular office hours during which Hungarians can request mediation with local authorities. In municipalities dominated by Hungarians, the "Hungarian" character of local administration is more pronounced. In Covasna/Kovászna county, for instance, the County Council and the Mayor's Office of the county seat of Sfântu Gheorghe/Sepsiszentgyörgy are represented and perceived (by both Hungarians and Romanians) as Hungarian institutions, while the Prefect's Office (directly representing the government) and some of the deconcentrated branches of different ministries are represented as Romanian institutions.[25]

As we discussed in the previous chapters of our volume, politics is obviously ethnically organized. RMDSZ is the only state-financed organization of this sector; representing the Hungarian minority in the parliament, it receives considerable public funds. The smaller ethnic parties (as they did not obtain sufficient votes in the parliamentary elections to meet the threshold of financing) do not receive such funds and they are financed practically from Hungary. EMNT and SZNT could be considered political organizations registered as associations. Party youth organizations and foundations established by the parties are also political NGOs.

The publicly financed segment of the education sector is constituted by primary and secondary schools, respectively universities, which teach entirely or partially in Hungarian language. Educational institutions teaching exclusively in Hungarian obviously belong to the Hungarian institutional system. The status of schools with parallel Hungarian and Romanian classes is not so obvious. The relation between Hungarian and Romanian lines of study is usually asymmetric, similarly to the linguistic landscape of the institutions.[26] Nevertheless, these schools can also play an important role in the reproduction of the Hungarian community, while the personnel teaching in these institutions plays an important role in minority community organizing. At the university level, there are no separate state-financed Hungarian-language

[25]On this dual power structure in the Székely Land, see Tánczos (1998).

[26]On Hungarian-language usage in the administration, see Toró (2017).

institutions; however, the Hungarian departments or study lines inside the so-called multicultural universities constitute an important part of the Hungarian educational sector. NGOs in the education sector include associations advocating for and assisting Hungarian-language education, Sapientia University (financed by the Hungarian state), NGOs engaged in scientific research, and the Association of Hungarian Teachers of Romania (RMPSZ[27]). A for-profit segment of the Hungarian education sector (private schools and kindergartens, research firms, etc.) also exists, but it is rather sparse.

The religious sector is organized as a separate societal segment, and it is clearly distinguishable from the Romanian mainstream. In Romania, ecclesiastical religiosity is very intense (in a European comparison), and churches play a relatively important role in the everyday life. In Transylvania, religious and ethnic cleavages reinforce each other. Romanians are overwhelmingly Eastern Orthodox today, and the Romanian Greek Catholic Church represents the other historical Romanian denomination. Ninety-four percent of Hungarians belong to one of the "historical Hungarian religious denominations", namely the Calvinist Reformed Church, the Roman Catholic Church, the Unitarian Church and the Evanghelic-Lutheran Church. These can be considered (more or less) as "Hungarian national churches", but some of the neo-protestant churches also have separate Hungarian congregations. Churches are partially state financed, as pastors are payed partially from state funds. They also operate their own extensive institutional system organized in the form of NGOs and for-profit institutions.

Next to education, religion and public administration, the cultural sector is the most extended (Kiss 2010; Dániel and Kiss 2014) in the Hungarian institutional web. Theaters, museums, and libraries are the publicly financed segment of the cultural domain; however, a wide range of NGOs and firms also target this area of activity. As for the mass

---

[27]In Hungarian: Romániai Magyar Pedagógusok Szövetsége. It administers the Educational Allowance provided by the Hungarian state for each family having children enrolled into the Hungarian-language educational system.

media, the for-profit segment is the most important. Newspapers and private radio stations operate in this form. Hungarian-language public broadcasting is also an important segment of the Hungarian-language media in Romania, while the sole TV station targeting national-level audience is operated by an NGO established by RMDSZ.

Leisure and sport activities and social care are also increasingly organized in ethnically parallel structures. In the case of sport, substantial state and private investments from Hungary have occurred during the last few years, strengthening the ethnically segmented character of this domain. As for professional sports, several hockey, basketball, and handball teams in Székely Land are perceived as Hungarian and provide opportunities for supporters to publicly manifest their national identity. As for the football teams, the Sepsi OSK of Sfântu-Gheorghe/Sepsiszentgyörgy represents itself as a Székely/Hungarian team, while in the case of CFR Cluj/Kolozsvár, a "pan-ethnic" Transylvanian identity (with strong Hungarian overtones) is manifested. In the social care sector, both religious and non-religious institutions are present and they operate an extended system composed of more than 200 organizations (most of them NGOs). This sector is hierarchically organized from professional and officially accredited social care providers to informal organizations.[28]

3 Summary and the Structure of the Second Part of the Book

Our introductory chapter emphasized the dual character of the concept of the Minority Society. On the one hand, it can be used in a descriptive way to analyze the institutional system underpinning ethnic parallelism and the ethno-cultural reproduction of the minority group. On the other hand, however, the performative nature of this terminology

[28]See in details Dániel (2014).

is also obvious. This duality was present already in the texts of interwar political thinkers first outlining the programmatic idea of the Minority Society. At a programmatic level, the all-embracing nature of the (envisaged) Minority Society has been stressed. At an analytical level, however, the incomplete nature of ethnic parallelism and encapsulation is also crucial. This incompleteness has important consequences, and in the next section (referring to societal macro-processes), it will be argued that it is conductive to demographic erosion and social marginalization.

The chapters of this section will discuss three sectors that are organized in ethnically parallel structures, as well as the economic sector, which for the most part is not ethnically organized, but involves a complex interrelation between economic action and ethnicity. Chapter 6 authored by Attila Papp, János Márton, Gergő Barna and István Gergő Székely focuses on Hungarian-language education. The authors argue that due to a lack of segmental autonomy and institutional planning and supervising, Hungarian-language education cannot be perceived as a coherent system or social field. This is also true in case of mass media, as Chapter 8 authored by Tamás Kiss reveals, this sector is not organized according to a coherent media policy and has highly a segmented structure. The chapter also addresses the problem of kin-state influence and asks to what extent the integration of Transylvanian Hungarians into a Budapest-centered mediascape is beneficial for the minority public sphere. Dénes Kiss offers a detailed description of the religious sector in Chapter 7. The institutions maintained by Hungarian churches are quite important in sustaining ethnic parallelism; the chapter also argues that the importance of religiosity has been increased in Romania by a process of desecularization. Last but not least, Chapter 9, authored by Zsombor Csata, discusses in detail the complex relationship between ethnicity and economic agency. Csata argues that, in spite of the fact that it is not organized primarily ethnically, the economy is not an ethnically "neutral" sector either. Further, this study also suggests that increasing territorial concentration and institutional encapsulation of the Hungarian population may result in the formation of an ethnic enclave economy. Csata highlights that this would lead also to further marginalization of the Hungarian population.

References

Anderson, B. (2006). *Imagined communities: Reflections on the origin and spread of nationalism* (rev. ed.). London and New York: Verso.

Bakk, M. (2000). Modellviták – rejtett stratégiák. *Magyar Kisebbség, 6*(1), 8–12.

Bárdi, N. (2006). Nép, nemzet, szuverenitás. *Fundamentum, 2*, 81–89.

Barna, G. (2004). Erdélyi magyar ifjúsági szervezetek szervezetszociológiai elemzése. *Erdélyi Társadalom, 2*(2), 85–112.

Biró, Z. A. (1998). Intézményesedési folyamatok a romániai magyarság körében. In Z. A. Biró (Ed.), *Stratégia vagy kényszerpályák? Tanulmányok a romániai magyar társadalomról* (pp. 16–47). Csíkszereda: Pro-Print.

Bonacich, E. (1972). A theory of ethnic antagonism: The split labor market. *American Sociological Review, 37*(5), 547–559.

Bourdieu, P. (1993). *The field of cultural production: Essays on art and literature*. New York: Columbia University Press.

Brubaker, R., Feischmidt, M., Fox, J., & Grancea, L. (2006). *Nationalist politics and everyday ethnicity in a Transylvanian town*. Princeton: Princeton University Press.

Csata, Z., Kiss, D., & Kiss, T. (2004). Az erdélyi magyar kulturális intézményrendszer. *Erdélyi Társadalom, 2*(1), 133–162.

Culic, I. (2016). Hungarian society in Romania: Political project and practical reality. In S. P. Ramet & M. Valenta (Eds.), *Ethnic minorities and politics in post-socialist southeastern Europe* (pp. 191–210). New York: Cambridge University Press.

Dániel, B. (2014). Az erdélyi magyar nonprofit hátterű szociális szféra szociológiai jellemzői. *Civil Szemle, 11*(1), 81–107.

Dániel, B., & Kiss, D. (2014). Sociological analysis of the resources of the Hungarian cultural organizations in Romania. *Civil Szemle, 11*(4), 71–106.

DiMaggio, P. J., & Anheier, H. K. (1990). The sociology of nonprofit organizations and sectors. *Annual Review of Sociology, 16*(1), 137–159.

Egry, G. (2014). Nép, nemzet, állam, társadalom: "népszolgáló" közösségkép és közösségszervezés az erdélyi magyar kisebbségi politikában. In N. Bárdi & T. G. Filep (Eds.), *A népszolgálat fogalomtörténete* (pp. 48–71). Pozsony: Kaligramm.

Furnivall, J. S. (1948). *Colonial policy and practice: A comparative study of Burma and Netherlands India. Issued in co-operation with the International*

Secretariat, Institute of Pacific Relations. Cambridge: Cambridge University Press.
Horowitz, D. L. (1985). *Ethnic groups in conflict*. Berkeley: University of California Press.
Hunyadi, A. (2006). Three paradigms of cooperative movements with nationalist taxonomy in Transylvania. In T. Lorenz (Ed.), *Cooperatives in ethnic conflicts: Eastern Europe in the 19th and early 20th century* (Vol. 15, pp. 59–102). Berlin: Berliner Wissenschafts-Verlag.
Jenkins, R. (2008). *Rethinking ethnicity* (2nd ed.). Thousand Oaks, CA: Sage.
Kántor, Z. (2000). Kisebbségi nemzetépítés. A romániai magyarság mint nemzetépítő kisebbség. *Regio, 11*(3), 219–241.
Kiss, D. (2006). Az erdélyi magyar civil szféráról. *Civil Szemle, 3*(2), 139–154.
Kiss, D. (2010). *Romániai magyar nonprofit szervezetek - 2009–2010 ISPMN* (Working Papers No. 37).
Kiss, T. (2004). Vállalkozástörténetek Erdélyben. In É. Kovács (Ed.), *A gazdasági átmenet etnikai tájképei* (pp. 23–128). Budapest: Teleki László Alapítvány.
Kymlicka, W. (1995). *Multicultural citizenship: A liberal theory of minority rights*. Oxford: Clarendon Press.
Lijphart, A. (1969). Consociational democracy. *World Politics, 21*(02), 207–225.
Lijphart, A. (1977). *Democracy in plural societies: A comparative exploration*. New Haven: Yale University Press.
Livezeanu, I. (1995). *Cultural politics in greater Romania: Regionalism, nation building & ethnic struggle, 1918–1930*. Ithaca: Cornell University Press.
Lőrincz, D. J. (2008). A kolozsvári magyarok társadalma. *Regio, 19*(2), 240–256.
Salamon, L. M., & Anheier, H. K. (1996). *The international classification of nonprofit organizations: ICNPO-Revision 1* (Working Papers of the Johns Hopkins Comparative Nonprofit Sector Project No. 19).
Schermerhorn, R. A. (1978). *Comparative ethnic relations: A framework for theory and research*. Chicago: University of Chicago Press.
Smith, M. G. (1965). *The plural society in the British West Indies*. Berkeley: University of California Press.
Sulyok, I. (1931). A kisebbségi kérdés szociológiai oldal. *Erdélyi Múzeum, 36*(4–6), 170–181.
Tánczos, V. (1998). Kettős hatalmi szerkezet a Székelyföldön. *Magyar Kisebbség, 4*(2), 339–362.

Toró, T. (2017). Detached implementation. Discourse and practice in minority language usage in Romania Manuscript.

Wimmer, A. (2002). *Nationalist exclusion and ethnic conflict: Shadows of modernity.* Cambridge, UK and New York, NY: Cambridge University Press.

Wimmer, A. (2013). *Ethnic boundary making: Institutions, power, networks. Oxford studies in culture and politics.* New York: Oxford University Press.

6

Hungarian-Language Education: Legal Framework, Institutional Structure and Assessment of School Performances

Attila Z. Papp, János Márton, István Gergő Székely and Gergő Barna

After 1989, the ideal of ethno-cultural reproduction was once again formulated as an overarching and unquestionable objective of the Transylvanian Hungarians and, in relation to this, the development

Parts of this chapter will be published as an article in a Mercator Regional Dossier (Attila Papp: Hungarians in Romania, forthcoming).

A. Z. Papp (✉)
Hungarian Academy of Sciences, Centre for Social Sciences,
Institute for Minority Studies, Budapest, Hungary
e-mail: pappz.attila@tk.mta.hu

J. Márton
Omnibus Ltd, Gheorgheni, Romania

I. G. Székely
Romanian Institute for Research on National Minorities,
Cluj-Napoca, Romania

G. Barna
Kvantum Research Ltd, Cluj-Napoca, Romania

T. Kiss et al. (eds.), *Unequal Accommodation of Minority Rights*,
Palgrave Politics of Identity and Citizenship Series,
https://doi.org/10.1007/978-3-319-78893-7_6

of a full-scale educational system in the vernacular emerged as a core ethno-political demand of the Hungarian elites. Although very significant progress was achieved in the domain in the subsequent two and a half decades, the topic (or its ramifications) is still permanently on the political agenda.

The situation of Hungarian-language education is certainly among the favorite topics of Hungarian minority politicians who constantly put forward "solutions" for the maintenance, development, and expansion of the network within the broader national educational system. Moreover, the issue of the education in the vernacular of Hungarians minorities in general and of the Transylvanian Hungarians in particular is also central to the activity of a number of public administrative bodies and institutions in Hungary. The majority of experts and social scientists also take the existence of an organic system of "minority education" for granted.

The existence of some forms of—legally supported—education for minorities is indeed a fact, as is the participation of children and youngsters belonging to the Hungarian minority in these structures. We believe that notwithstanding this fact, two fundamental questions must be raised in this respect: (1) To whom does the minority educational system belong; that is, are there clearly identifiable institutional actors that are responsible for it? (2) What is the pattern of institutionalization of education in the minority language: Is it a loose network of its own, or should we regard it as a subsystem of the Romanian education system? As long as consensual answers to these questions are lacking in Romania/Transylvania, and while the Hungarian minority has not set up appropriate institutions for the maintenance, financing, supervision, monitoring, research, and assessment of education in the vernacular, we believe that the gap between the "solutions" offered at the political level and the actual everyday processes of the educational system will remain. Hungarian minority politicians and policy-making activity in the field of education may become prisoners of thus-far dominant discourses, while the stakeholders involved in the everyday operation of the system face totally different challenges in terms of their experiences.

To respond to these questions, in this chapter we discuss in detail the legal and organizational features of education in Romania in general and of Hungarian-language education particularly and attempt an assessment of the performance of the latter.

1 The Institutional and Policy Framework of Minority Education and the Main Actors in the Hungarian Educational Network

Before starting our analysis, we believe that it is important to settle an issue closely connected to both the questions formulated above: Within the current context, who is (or could be) the actors or institutions responsible for Hungarian-language education in Romania? Under "Hungarian minority education in Romania", we understand the totality of educational and training activities carried out in the Hungarian language.[1] This does not mean, however, that all these forms of education belong to a unitary, common framework of minority education. For example, a self-supporting educational institution in rural Székely Land probably has little in common with a school situated in an ethnically mixed large city, where at most a single class is taught in Hungarian language for each grade. The legislation, national and county-level institutions in charge of the system, as well as the curricula implicitly impose some degree of homogeneity on the various institutions that teach (also) in Hungarian, but in itself this is probably not sufficient for considering the totality of these institutions a genuine subsystem. For this, it would be necessary to have institutions or organizations recognized as legitimate by all the stakeholders involved, thereby supporting, coordinating, and supervising the everyday operation of the totality of Hungarian-language educational initiatives and activities.

In the present context, multiple actors have some responsibility for education in Hungarian and for the teaching of the Hungarian

[1] We do not discuss the teaching of Hungarian language as a facultative subject. On this, see Papp and Márton (2017).

language. Of the public institutions, the Ministry of National Education[2] and the school inspectorates are the most important. Within the Ministry, there is a State Secretariat for Education in Minority Languages,[3] a Directorate-General for Minority Education,[4] subordinated to the former, and a Directorate for Minorities[5] within the Directorate-General (Gáll and Keszeg 2014). Although the role of these institutions cannot be fully differentiated, we venture to claim that the State Secretariat is responsible mainly for strategic issues (improving the quality of education in minority languages), while the Directorate deals with more practical activities, being responsible, among other things, for the concrete organization of education in minority languages, including Hungarian.

Within the Directorate for Minorities, councilors are responsible for education in each minority language. For Hungarian, there are three councilors (besides the director, who is also an ethnic Hungarian). As a matter of fact, it is this team of three—and the experts consulted by them under the conditions of law—who shape the framework for the content of Hungarian-language education, review textbooks, and participate in the elaboration and translation of official examination items and other tests. All three members of staff are practicing teachers of Hungarian language and literature—an important aspect because this is the only subject for which textbooks and examination items are indeed elaborated by teachers who belong to the minority (i.e., are not translated from Romanian language). In the opinions of some, this should be regarded as an improvement, as earlier a single person (!) used to be in charge of all Hungarian-language textbooks for all grades. However, we believe that it is still very doubtful whether a staff of three

[2]In Romanian: *Ministerul Educației Naționale*. The name of the ministry has changed a number of times over the past decades. We do deal with this issue and henceforth refer to it as the Ministry.

[3]In Romanian: *Secretar de Stat – Învățământ în Limbile Minorităților*.

[4]The name of this organizational unit has also changed several times. At the time of finalizing this manuscript, the official name in Romanian was: *Direcția Generală Învățământ în Limbile Minorităților și Relația cu Parlamentul* (relations with parliament were also under the competence of this Directorate-General).

[5]*Direcția Minorități*.

Hungarian literature teachers can provide proper professional supervision of all relevant subject matters (Gáll and Keszeg 2014).

Besides these public institutions, NGOs and political parties (primarily RMDSZ) also carry out significant activity in relation to Hungarian-language education. RMDSZ regularly organizes campaigns to facilitate the enrollment of ethnic Hungarian pupils into Hungarian-language educational institutions and, not long ago, also published a debate-starting document on the situation of minority education, which, however—to our knowledge—did not attract a significant response (Magyari 2014). The Association of Hungarian Teachers of Romania (RMPSZ)[6] was established in 1991; its most important activity has been the organization of a summer university for teachers.[7] However, this type of training is not officially recognized in Romania, and participants do not receive credit for attending such courses. Furthermore, four regional training institutes operate under the aegis of RMPSZ, as well as the Textbook Council of Transylvania[8] (a body whose main goal is to facilitate the writing of Hungarian-language textbooks and educational materials). Furthermore, RMPSZ publishes two specialized journals (*Magyar Közoktatás* and *Magiszter*), although their impact is difficult to assess. Finally, there is also a publishing house specialized in Hungarian-language textbooks.[9]

It is also important to stress that Hungarian-language education in Romania (and in the other countries neighboring Hungary) receives material support from the kin-state too. These subsidies are not very significant when compared to the resources channeled by Romania into the system of public education, but such well-targeted subsidies may be adequate for increasing innovation in the Hungarian educational subsystem. It should be highlighted that these subsidies from Hungary are channeled to Romania through NGOs (Papp 2010; Papp and Márton 2014).

---

[6]In Romanian: *Uniunea Cadrelor Didactice Maghiare din România*; in Hungarian: *Romániai Magyar Pedagógusszövetség*.

[7]The Bolyai Summer Academy, in Hungarian: *Bolyai Nyári Akadémia*.

[8]In Hungarian: *Erdélyi Tankönyvtanács*.

[9]http://rmpsz.ro/hu/h/81/magiszter; http://www.communitas.ro/interaktiv/kozoktatas/ (Last accessed: 22 January 2018); Ábel Kiadó (in Cluj), www.abelkiado.ro.

Despite the involvement of multiple actors in the organization of Hungarian-language education, we believe that the most important problem is that there is no clearly identifiable actor who is undoubtedly and authoritatively in charge of this domain. The presence of multiple actors should not be a problem in itself; the challenge comes from the absence of a body that could uniformly coordinate the entire subsystem (or the networks of minority education).[10] Of course, formally all educational institutions are subordinated to the Ministry and are financed from central and local budgets, and professional supervision is carried out by the aforementioned institutions of the Ministry and by county-level inspectorates. We believe that the existing public bodies and civil actors are carrying out tasks essential for the everyday operation of the schools, but no one is able to assume the task of elaborating strategies or development plans for the schools that teach in minority languages which would render them integrated parts of a specific subsystem. The provision of textbooks is not smooth, and the participation of minority schools in national development programs, as well as national and international evaluation programs, remains deficient; basic indicators and data about minority education are not available.[11] Although in the past few years a number of related initiatives have been started by both public and private actors,[12] we still do not have a clear picture about the internal conditions of Hungarian-language education—research projects that focus specifically on Hungarian-language minority education are typically carried out in a rushed and superficial manner, and their results are not channeled back at the level of everyday practice and development.

The education law, in force since 2011 (henceforth: EL),[13] provides for the creation of a research and innovation center in the field

[10]We are aware that both "subsystem" and "network" are problematic concepts, so we use them in the absence of a better term to refer to the totality of institutions that teach in Hungarian.

[11]It is symptomatic that no up-to-date data about the state of Hungarian-language education are available on the Web sites of either RMDSZ or RMPSZ, despite the fact that it is precisely this kind of data that would be suitable for creating—at least virtually—a Hungarian-language educational subsystem or network.

[12]http://rmpsz.ro/hu/h/32/oktatasi-intezmenyek (Last accessed: 8 December 2017).

[13]*Legea nr. 1 din 5 ianuarie 2011, Legea educației naționale, Monitorul Oficial nr. 18 din 10 ianuarie 2011.*

of education with tuition in the languages of the national minorities within the framework of the Institute of Education Sciences subordinated to the Ministry of Education. Such an institution would be of particular importance for planning in the field of Hungarian-language education; however, this structure has not been set up in the seven years since the law entered into force.[14]

2 Statistical Situation

Reliable statistical data about the evolution of the number and proportion of ethnic Hungarian pupils studying in their mother tongue, respectively, in Romanian-language educational programs are not available in a longer-term historical perspective; we are only able to document the situation starting with the 1970s. One can see in Table 1 that at the primary and lower-secondary levels most Hungarian pupils were learning in their mother tongue even in the last decades of state socialism. However, in high school, about half of the children were already enrolled into Romanian-language programs, and a deteriorating trend is also discernible in the late 1980s. The situation was most unfavorable in short-term professional education, where only a very small minority of the pupils could study in the vernacular. The most important factor

Table 1 The proportion of Hungarian pupils studying in their mother tongue (1970–2009)

	1970–1980	1985–1989	1992–2000	2005–2009
Nursery, kindergarten	76.3	76.2	87.5	83.2
Primary (1–4 grades)	86.2	82.9	85.7	85.9
Lower-secondary (5–8 grades)	79.4	78.9	–	81.5
Upper secondary: high school (9–12 grades)	55.1	49.5	70.9	74.3
Upper secondary: short-term professional (9–11 grades)	11.3	3.2	41.2	55.7

Source Authors' own calculation based on data of the Ministry of Education

[14]EL, art. 46(16).

behind the low figures characteristic of the upper secondary level was the official educational policy of the nationalizing Communist regime, which was aiming to gradually atrophy the opportunities for education in the Hungarian language. The figures referring to the post-1989 period show a significant improvement, but the drop between the lower- and upper secondary levels still remains significant, especially with regard to short-term professional education.

For the period elapsed since the regime change of 1989–1990, three important conclusions can be formulated about pupils who attend Hungarian-language schools. First, there has been a constant decline in the *number* of enrolled children. Second, the *proportion* of ethnic Hungarian children who attend school in the vernacular has constantly increased since the mid-1990s. However, and this is the third conclusion, their proportion still lags significantly behind the share of Hungarians in the population of the country.

Based on the data provided by the National Statistical Institute for the 1990–2016 period, we can establish that the number of children enrolled in pre-university education (including kindergartens and also post-high-school level) has been steadily declining in Romania: In 1990, this number was 4.87 million, dropping to 3.06 million in 2016. That is, the number has decreased by approximately one-third. The number of pupils enrolled in Hungarian-language education shows a similar trend: From 236,074 in 1990, it had dropped to 158,090 by 2016. The decrease witnessed among the Hungarians (33.03%) is smaller than that of the school-age population at the national level (37.09%), meaning that the proportion of pupils attending Hungarian-language schools has increased over the past 25 years. In 1990, their proportion was 4.84%, while the lowest number was registered in 1996 (4.59%). After that date, their proportion constantly increased (until 2013) and has stabilized at between 5.1 and 5.2% since then.[15] However, these figures indicate that the attendance of Hungarian-language schools remains lower than the proportion of ethnic Hungarians in Romania's population. While we lack precise data for

[15]Source: National Statistical Institute (Tempo online, SCL103B).

the latter indicator for 2013, according to the 2011 census 6.5% of Romania's citizens were self-declared ethnic Hungarians.[16]

In light of these negative figures, it comes as little surprise that Hungarian-language schooling has been struggling to survive in numerous settlements, primarily due to unfavorable demographic processes, despite the legal positive discrimination measures provided for pre-university education in minority languages (to be discussed later).

Between 2012 and 2015, a comprehensive survey of the Hungarian-language educational subsystem was carried out in Transylvania in the framework of a project called "Schools in danger" (Barna et al. 2016).[17] The goal of this project was to map and inventory those sites where education in the Hungarian language is likely to prove unsustainable by 2020. Locations were classified as endangered where it was assessed that in the next ten years education in Hungarian is likely to cease, or it is likely that the language of education will change in the case of a significant proportion of ethnic Hungarian children. In the first step, locations were included for analysis on the basis of demographic and educational statistics, while in a second phase extensive fieldwork was carried out in each location. The project also inventoried the number of sites where education in Hungarian completely stopped following the 2004/2005 school year (sites where after 2004/2005 at least one *simultaneous* class[18] was still running but which no longer existed at the time of data collection). Of the 290 locations included in the study, 130 were eventually classified as in danger, 10 as semi-endangered, and 44 locations were identified where education in Hungarian has stopped in the past decade (Barna et al. 2016, pp. 42–46). These figures should be correlated with the total number of schools that teach (also) in Hungarian: According to Papp and Márton (2017), in school year 2014/2015, there were 885 schools in Romania providing primary and lower-secondary education in Hungarian. Thus, the sustainability of approximately 15%

---

[16]More detailed figures about the number and proportion of ethnic Hungarian pupils studying in their mother tongue will be provided later, in each subsection dedicated to the specific levels of the educational system. Here, we only summarized the big picture.

[17]See also: www.iksolakveszelyben.ro.

[18]See the next section for the precise meaning of the term.

of the locations is doubtful, and in approximately 5% of the locations Hungarian-language education has ceased in the past decade.

3 Legal Framework

In Romania, education at all levels is regulated by Law 1 of 2011 (EL). With regard to education in minority languages, at least at the level of legal codification, the principles of both local autonomy and positive discrimination are present in the law (Veres 2012). Although the law makes it clear that every citizen has the duty to learn the official language of the state (Romanian),[19] it also recognizes the right of persons who are members of national minorities to learn in their vernacular language on every level and in every form of pre-university education. If this cannot be ensured in the settlement of their domicile, then pupils may be reimbursed for the cost of traveling to the nearest educational institution that teaches in the respective minority language, and in the case of boarding schools, the cost of accommodation in dormitories and meals will also be covered.[20] However, this provision is not consistently enforced in practice: In many cases, commuting pupils are only partially reimbursed and sometimes not at all.

For pre-university education, a per capita financing system is applied; that is, the funding of schools depends on the number of pupils that are enrolled. In the case of education in minority languages, the per capita subsidy is increased by applying a so-called corrective multiplier.[21] Positive discrimination is applied not only in this respect, but also with regard to the organizational aspects of education. Schools may be independent "legal persons" if they have at least 300 pupils.[22] However, minority education is exempted once again. On the one hand, if an institution is the only one to provide education in a specific minority language in

[19]EL, art. 10(3).

[20]EL, art. 45(1) and (7).

[21]EL, art. 45(17).

[22]EL, art. 19.

a settlement, then this institution will be granted an independent legal personality; on the other hand, in settlements that host multiple educational institutions that teach in the minority language, institutions with an independent legal personality that teach exclusively in the respective minority language may function regardless of the number of enrolled pupils.[23]

However, in practice, the principle of affirmative action is not applied fully: Surplus financing that is created by the use of the corrective multiplier cannot be regarded as positive discrimination in reality as it is only sufficient to cover the additional expenses required for teaching extra classes in the vernacular language and literature (or, from a different vantage point, for the extra classes of the official language of the state and related literature).

Positive discrimination that is prescribed with regard to the organizational dimension is sometimes simply not enforced in practice. There are multiple settlements in Transylvania (primarily towns or cities with a clear Romanian demographic majority) where efforts to establish a self-standing Hungarian-language school have been repeatedly thwarted by local governments dominated by Romanian political parties. Furthermore, even if the law was enforced, that would not mean automatically that the conditions for the smooth operation of Hungarian-language schools would be met. Most of the small Hungarian education institutions which have an independent legal personality (schools with significantly fewer than 300 pupils) are struggling with financial problems despite the increased subsidy resulting from the corrective multiplier and are only able to survive if local governments provide them with supplementary financing.[24] In the absence of such supplementary funds, the only solution is often to relinquish independent legal status.

It should be mentioned that the provisions of positive discrimination applicable to national minorities (concerning the financing and

[23]EL, art. 45(5) and (6).

[24]In settlements with Romanian-majority local councils, this may depend on political bargaining, but nor can it be taken for granted under Hungarian-majority local governments.

organization of education) can also be applied to majority (Romanian-language) schools if they operate in settlements where they are the sole educational institution (for instance, in Székely Land, where ethnic Romanian pupils are a local minority).[25]

The EL also contains some affirmative action provisions with regard to administrative and pedagogical staff of schools. National minorities are entitled to be represented on the various bodies of schools, county-level school inspectorates, and other boards in proportion to the number of classes that are taught in each language—of course, if professional requirements are also met. In institutions that also teach in a minority language, one of the deputy directors must be a person who belongs to the respective minority. Teachers who work with minority language classes or groups of pupils must prove their proficiency in the terminology of their field in the respective minority language.[26] However, teachers of Romanian language and literature are exempted from this requirement.

In the field of Hungarian-language education, practice also often deviates from legal provision with regard to these issues. In the majority of linguistically mixed educational institutions and county-level school inspectorates, the Hungarian minority remains significantly underrepresented; in the leading bodies of the institutions, the proportion of Hungarian specialists is lower than the proportion of classes or pupils learning in Hungarian would justify. There are numerous mixed-language institutions where neither the director nor their deputy is a member of the Hungarian community. Moreover, we also find schools where classes that should be instructed in Hungarian are actually taught by ethnic Romanian teachers who do not speak Hungarian—obviously, in Romanian. This occurs mainly in settlements where the proportion of Hungarians is low, and mostly affects subjects that are regarded as "less important", that is, which are not required for various graduation-related examinations (Papp and Márton 2017).

---

[25]Interestingly, the legal provisions concerning these target groups are listed together with the regulations concerning national minorities (the same art. 47 of the EL).

[26]EL, art. 45(8), (9) and (11).

Concerning the content of curricula for education in minority languages, it is a very important development that since the adoption of the new EL all subjects—including history and geography—may be taught in the minority language, but the names of settlements and other toponyms must also be learnt in the official language. Subjects which include content about the history and culture of minorities have also been introduced into pre-university education. Another novelty of the 2011 law is that Romanian language and literature should be taught at all levels of pre-university education according to special curricula and textbooks adjusted to the special linguistic characteristics of the specific minorities. If a certain minority decides not to claim their right to these special curricula, then the normal textbooks used in Romanian-language schools are used.[27] However, in practice, relatively little progress has been made with regard to the teaching of Romanian: As of the 2017/2018 school year, alternative textbooks have been finalized only for grades 1, 2, 4, and 5.[28]

The textbooks and other educational materials necessary for education in minority languages are provided by the Ministry of Education. The textbooks used in minority education may be not only original works, but also translations of Romanian books. Textbooks published in other countries may also be used, but these must be approved beforehand by the Ministry.

Although an analysis of the implementation of the EL clearly indicates that positive discrimination measures for minorities are not consistently applied, it is indisputable that the provisions concerning minorities represent obvious progress when compared to the previous education law (84/1995), as the latter contained a series of detrimental, restrictive, and discriminative regulations (for instance, the history of Romanians and the geography of Romania could only be taught in Romanian, and all pupils were required to study Romanian language and literature using the same curricula as ethnic Romanian children).

[27]EL art. 46.

[28]The alternative textbook for the 3rd grade is lagged by administrative problems related to the public procurement procedure.

Table 2 Legally defined group sizes for different levels of education

Level of education	Group size		
	Average	Minimum	Maximum
Ante-preschool (day-care nursery)	7	5	9
Preschool (kindergarten)	15	10	20
Primary	20	12	25
Lower-secondary (gymnasium or middle school)	25	12	30
High school and technological (upper secondary)	25	15	30
Post-high school	15	15	30

A very important provision concerning the organization of education in minority languages is the regulation concerning the number of pupils required to establish groups and classes (Table 2).[29]

It is important that these numbers are not specifically framed with regard to minority education. However, the law also specifies that in the case of education in minority languages, groups may also be established with fewer pupils than the required minimum, subject to special approval by the Ministry.

Given the already discussed negative demographic trends, from the perspective of Hungarian-language education the possibility of creating so-called simultaneous classes is of utmost importance. The EL does not contain regulations regarding this, but instead the rules are set out in Order No. 3062/2011 of the Ministry of Education. According to this piece of regulation, the establishment of simultaneous or merged classes is permitted in geographically or linguistically isolated settlements where the minimum required number of pupils—as set out in the law—cannot be met in primary and lower-secondary education, and the transportation of children is not feasible either. This means that two or more classes, pertaining to different years, should be merged and receive instruction simultaneously. Simultaneous classes cannot be established in upper secondary, technical, and post-high-school education, while preschool education is not mentioned in the ministerial order. In practice, however, simultaneous groups operate in a number of kindergartens too.

[29]EL, art. 63.

The total number of children in merged classes must also reach the minimum numbers detailed above. Notwithstanding this, the order allows county-level school inspectorates to approve the establishment of simultaneous classes even if the total number of children remains below the legal threshold upon the well-grounded request of the concerned educational institution. Although no minimum number of pupils has been stipulated for such cases, in practice the inspectorates condition the establishment of simultaneous groups in primary education on the enrollment of at least five children in at most four different grades (the simultaneous education of all five primary grades is not allowed, but in practice examples of this also exist). In lower-secondary education, a higher threshold is applied in practice, at least 9–10 children being required to obtain approval for merging four years into a simultaneous class.[30] Also, in bigger cities, the positive discrimination provisions of the law are not applied properly, as classes with the minimum group size are seldom approved. School inspectorates justify their decisions with the yearly directives of the Ministry, which, for budgetary reasons, set as the minimal number of required students the average number stipulated in the law.[31]

4 Education in Hungarian at the Various Levels of the Educational System

4.1 Kindergartens

The target group of early education consists of children aged 0–6. Within this, the system is divided into day-care or ante-preschool level (ages 0–3) and kindergarten or preschool level (ages 3–6). Education

[30]In the school year 2014/2015, some Hungarian-language simultaneous classes in primary education were operating with four or even three children; however, such examples should be considered sporadic. There were also some examples of simultaneous lower-secondary classes operating with fewer (6–8) pupils.

[31]See art. 3(2) of the Annex in Order 5472/2017 or 5777/2016 of the Ministry of Education. Although not clear from the text that it applies or not to minority education as well, school inspectorates tend not to make any exception regarding the issue.

in kindergartens is organized in three age groups (younger, middle, and older) and may operate according to normal, extended, or weekly schedules. The curriculum focuses on physical and cognitive development and on the screening and early correction of deficiencies in these domains.[32]

Legislation concerning ante-preschool education contains no regulation specific to minorities. However, for the kindergarten level, there is a provision that 1–2 hours should be dedicated to the learning of both the Hungarian and the Romanian language (from the total of 24–48 hours of weekly activity, depending on the type of schedule).[33]

Kindergarten education may be organized in institutions with an independent legal personality if at least 150 children are enrolled, or within the framework of other educational institutions (schools), in which case there is no requirement for the minimum number of children of preschool age, but the total number of enrolled children must be at least 300.

In the 2014/2015 school year, the total number of children enrolled in Hungarian-language kindergarten education was 34,131; more than 60% of them (21,081 children) attended simultaneous groups, and more than half of the latter (11,038 children) were in groups created through the merger of all age groups (which in practice means that all children between 2.5 and 6.5 years study together).[34]

4.2 Primary and Lower-Secondary Education

Primary education encompasses the preparatory grade, as well as grades 1–4, while lower-secondary education refers to grades 5–8. These levels of education are compulsory, and the target group is children aged 6–14. All children who reach the age of six before the beginning of the

[32]EL, art. 23, 27 and 28.

[33]*Material orientativ pentru stimularea dezvoltării copilului de la naștere la 3 ani*. Available at: http://oldsite.edu.ro/index.php/articles/c897 (Last accessed: 22 January 2018).

[34]Authors' own calculations based on reports by the Ministry of Education corrected on the basis of figures for earlier school years where data were missing.

school year must be enrolled in the preparatory grade, except for children with special educational needs.

The National Curriculum consists of compulsory and optional subjects. The former are decided by the Ministry, while regarding the latter individual schools may also offer subjects of their own to their pupils. In primary and lower-secondary education, the number of weekly compulsory class hours is 20, but in education carried out in the language of national minorities it is higher because the subjects of vernacular language and literature, as well as the history and traditions of the respective minority, must be counted in addition to this.

The curricula, pedagogical programs, textbooks, and methodological guides used in Hungarian-language education are prepared and approved by the authorized personnel of the Ministry (the State Secretariat for Education in Minority Languages and the Directorate for Minorities), but the so-called National Committee for the Hungarian Language[35] is also involved in the process. The goals and the methodology of minority education are discussed in great detail in an order of the Ministry of Education.[36]

In the school year 2014/2015, the total number of pupils enrolled in Hungarian-language primary education was 53,138, and at the lower-secondary level 41,396. The number of Hungarian-language classes or groups at the primary level was 3011, and at the middle level 2200, belonging to 885 schools in total. In 575 of these schools, there was at least one simultaneous class at either the primary or the lower-secondary level. Roughly one-fifth of all pupils in primary education attended a simultaneous class (11,010 children), while at the lower-secondary level the proportion was 7.2% (3006 children). At the primary level, 7308 children (13.75% of all pupils at this level) were enrolled in schools where primary education in Hungarian is carried out only in simultaneous classes (2700 of them in schools where all grades are merged, and 4608 in schools where there are two simultaneous classes). At the

[35] In Romanian: *Comisia Națională pentru Limba Maghiară*. Within the Directorate for Minorities, there is such a committee in charge of the subject matter of the language and literature of each minority.

[36] *Ordinul nr. 5671/2012 al Ministerul Educației, Cercetării, Tineretului și Sportului.*

lower-secondary level, the proportion was 5.3% (2203 pupils, of whom 160 attended schools where all grades were merged and 2043 institutions where two simultaneous grades operated). It is worrisome that in almost half of the schools that provide primary education in Hungarian (412 of 872; 47.2%) only simultaneous classes exist, while in the case of the lower-secondary level the same is true for 88 of the 505 schools (17.4%) that provide education in Hungarian.

4.3 Upper Secondary Education

In Romania, upper secondary education (ISCED Level 3 OECD classification) is of two main types: the so-called high school (also known as lyceum) education and professional (or short-term technological) education. The duration of the former is four or five years, and of the latter at least three years.[37] High school education comprises the following three broader domains: (1) theoretical programs, with humanity- and science-related qualifications; (2) technological programs with training in the technical, services, natural resources, and environmental protection domains; and (3) vocational programs, comprising the military, theological, sports, artistic, and pedagogical qualifications. The teaching in these programs is usually carried out in a daytime system; opportunities for other formats (e.g., evening classes, part-time) are rather limited. According to the EL, grades 9 and 10 are compulsory.

Technological or vocational training may be organized in high schools with a specific profile by a decision of the county-level school inspectorates, or at the request of companies or the National Employment Agency.[38] Pupils participating in the latter programs may undertake their traineeships either at the schools or—on a contractual basis—at companies.

Graduating from high school involves passing a school-leaving examination (Baccalaureate) consisting of both oral and written tests. Pupils

[37] EL, art. 31(3).

[38] EL, art. 31(7) and 32(2).

studying in Hungarian-language schools must also take oral and written tests in Hungarian language and literature, in addition to the examinations that are compulsory for all graduates (see Section 5.1). Those who successfully pass the examination receive a high-school-leaving certificate which makes them eligible to apply to institutions of higher education. Besides the leaving examination, high school students may also take an examination to obtain a professional qualification whereby they receive a certificate confirming their profession in accordance with the National Qualifications Framework.[39]

The so-called post-high-school (or post-lyceum) level of education can be considered a sort of middle ground between high school and higher education. It consists of professional and technical training; graduates of such programs obtain professional qualifications at the tertiary level. The duration of studies ranges from one to three years, and participants may also obtain a partial subsidy from the state for this period.[40] Enrollment in post-high-school education is not conditional on obtaining a high-school-leaving certificate.

In the school year 2014/2015, 33,957 pupils were enrolled in Hungarian-language upper secondary education. Almost 90% of them were studying in high school programs (30,109), while in short-term professional education there were only 3848 pupils. Almost half of those enrolled in lyceums were participating in theoretical programs, approximately 40% in technological programs and the remaining 13.7% in vocational training. Only 715 students were enrolled in Hungarian-language post-high-school education, and in this respect, the decrease is clear: In 2002, their number was 2001, and in 2011, it was 1382.[41]

4.4 Short-Term Professional or Technological Education

This form of education, a subdomain of upper secondary education, trains students to become skilled workers. Instruction may be

[39] EL, art. 77.

[40] EL, art. 44

[41] The source for 2002 and 2011 is the census.

organized either in independent professional schools or within high schools (lyceums). According to the original form of the EL, the duration of the training of skilled workers ranges from six months to two years; however, in 2014, the upper limit was modified to three years. As a consequence of these amendments to the EL, short-term professional training has been placed on new foundations starting with the school year 2014/2015. Its organization and operation are regulated by a methodological guide adopted as an appendix to an Order of the Minister of Education.[42]

Professional training must be organized through daytime courses with a normal program. Participants may receive so-called professional scholarships. It is exclusively those educational institutions that may offer such programs which conclude contracts with economic actors or public institutions and are thereby able to supply the technical and human resources necessary for carrying out the practical component of such education.

The methodology also allows for the organization of professional education in the languages of national minorities. In spite of this, Hungarian-language professional education is rather underdeveloped, even though—starting with school year 2014/2015—some improvements have occurred in this respect compared to previous years. The vast majority of high schools where teaching goes on (also) in Hungarian still have a strong preference for theoretical or long-term (4-year) technological programs. In the aforementioned school year, 3848 pupils were enrolled in Hungarian-language short-term professional education. More than three quarters (77.4%) were studying in settlements with a Hungarian demographic majority, and only 867 were attending schools located in settlements where Hungarians are a minority. The main reason for this asymmetry is the poor offering in the domain of professional education in areas where the Hungarians live dispersed (*szórvány*), which forces a significant number of ethnic Hungarian pupils to enroll in Romanian-language programs.

---

[42]*Ordin nr. 3136/2014 privind organizarea, funcţionarea, admiterea şi calendarul admiterii în învăţământul profesional de stat cu durata de 3 ani.*

The deficiencies of Hungarian-language professional education programs are to some extent compensated by the fact that the EL allows for lifelong learning programs to be offered in minority languages too. Detailed statistics about lifelong learning broken down according to language are not available, but the offerings in Hungarian are also poorer than those in Romanian in this domain (see Papp and Márton 2017 for details).

4.5 Hungarian-Language Higher Education

Romania is a signatory of the Bologna process; accordingly, higher education consists of bachelors', masters', and doctoral programs. Besides using the official language of the state, it is possible to organize programs in other international languages, as well as in the vernacular for some of the national minorities (in Hungarian and German language) in institutions specially designated by the EL (called multilingual or multicultural universities). Programs in minority languages may be organized at all three levels (bachelors', masters', and doctoral). Similarly to pre-university education, the regulation of higher education also contains a number of positive discrimination measures with regard to minority languages. The EL allows for the establishment of organizational units that operate in minority languages (faculties, educational lines, departments, and study sections) which may function in institutionalized form both at the university level and within faculties and which enjoy (university) autonomy with regard to the organization of teaching activities.[43] Financing for these programs is calculated using a higher coefficient.[44] In multilingual or multicultural institutions, at least one of the pro-rectors is appointed following the proposal of teaching staff who belong to the minority, and the same applies to at least one vice-dean in faculties that offer tuition (also) in minority languages.[45]

---

[43]EL, art. 145(1)–(3).

[44]EL, art. 135(5).

[45]EL, art. 211(2) and art. 207(5).

In the academic year 2014/2015, there were 88 accredited universities in Romania, of which 55 public and 33 private. A further ten private universities were operating with a temporary license. Public universities are financed from the state budget, but they may also charge tuition fees. Accreditation of higher-education institutions is within the competence of The Romanian Agency for Quality Assurance in Higher Education (ARACIS).[46]

Higher education in Hungarian is offered by multiple institutions. A broader spectrum of degree programs is offered by three institutions designated as multicultural by the EL: the Babeș-Bolyai University (located in Cluj but with divisions in several other cities in Transylvania), the University of Medicine and Pharmacy of Târgu Mureș, and the University of Arts of Târgu Mureș.[47] Besides these, there is one degree program offered at the University of Bucharest (Hungarology) and the University of Oradea (pedagogy of preschool and primary education). There are three private universities which operate in Hungarian: the Sapientia Hungarian University of Transylvania and the Partium Christian University (Oradea) are financed by the Hungarian government; the third is the Protestant Theological Institute of Cluj.[48] The Roman Catholic Theological Seminary of Alba Iulia also teaches in Hungarian. Hungarian-language higher-education institutions from Hungary (e.g., Budapest, Debrecen, and Tatabánya) are also present on the educational market with programs that operate in various Transylvanian cities.

Although legal arrangements concerning higher education in the vernacular are quite favorable, and since the late 1990s Hungarian-language higher education underwent a very spectacular expansion, a number of serious problems remain. First, although degree programs in Hungarian are offered in more than 125 specializations in Romania, the offer still covers only about one-third of the specializations that are available in Romanian. Furthermore, the offerings are

[46]http://www.aracis.ro/.

[47]EL, art. 363.

[48]Law 188/2017 created the conditions for financing this institute from the state budget. Formerly, it did not receive public funding.

also rather unbalanced as more than 60% of the specializations fall into the domain of social sciences. The most serious shortcomings are in the domain of engineering and agricultural sciences: The former domain accounts for less than 10% of the overall specializations available in Hungarian, and the latter for less than 1% (Szikszai 2010).

Second, the implementation of the provisions of the EL remains problematic at one of the three universities designated as multicultural, the University of Medicine and Pharmacy of Târgu Mureș, where the Hungarian departments have still not been created seven years after the EL entered into force. The main problem is that the senate of the university (in which the proportion of ethnic Romanians is approximately 75%) refused the creation of the Hungarian departments and voted for the establishment of five ethnically mixed departments in General Medicine.

In March 2012, the Government of Romania attempted to create a new trilingual Romanian-Hungarian-English Faculty of Medicine and Pharmacy through governmental decree. The decision, however, was not in concordance with the provisions of the EL. Being issued in a delicate political context, the action led to the dismissal of the cabinet of M. R. Ungureanu, as the opposition immediately filed a motion of no-confidence. Furthermore, the decision was also attacked in court and repealed.

Neither legal nor political attempts to find a solution have led to any results so far. The leadership of the university justifies its refusal by referring to university autonomy in the matter. However, this argument is not valid as the EL clearly stipulates that university autonomy cannot contradict the law.[49] The Ministry has not used its full powers either to secure a solution, because on the basis of the EL[50] it could have initiated the reorganization or even the dissolution of the entire university (this right of the Ministry was revoked later[51]). Finally, it should be mentioned that the university leadership has not even refrained from

---

[49]EL, art. 123(3).

[50]EL, art. 125(1).

[51]Governmental Emergency Ordinance 117/2013.

making attempts to intimidate and punish ethnic Hungarian faculty members who openly criticized the hostile attitude of the leadership (for a detailed account, see Toró 2016).[52]

Third, the EL also provides for the establishment of centers for continuous education in the language of the national minorities[53] which would be in charge of the continuous training of pedagogues who teach in minority languages. While such a structure has been created for the German language, it has not yet been set up for the Hungarian language. Although this is not a minority-specific issue, the training of teachers for pre-university education deserves a brief discussion, because it is in this context that the absence of such a center of continuous training for Hungarian-language staff should be assessed.

Currently, the Babeș-Bolyai University of Cluj is the sole center of teacher training for the Hungarian community, where degree programs are offered in a variety of specialization combinations. The curricula of these programs contain modules pertaining to both the subject matter of the specialization and to pedagogical training. Since 1990, the balance has increasingly shifted toward more scientific content, while the pedagogical modules have been neglected. Currently, the teacher-training module is only a supplement to a curriculum heavily focused on subject matters pertaining to the respective science. In practice, this means that all graduates are entitled to apply for teaching positions, if they complete the so-called pedagogical module (Szikszai 2010, pp. 80–82; Péntek 2004). It is against this background that we believe that there would be great need for centrally coordinated post-university training programs for the Hungarian pedagogical staff.

Educational statistics, published yearly, do not contain information about the precise number of ethnic Hungarian students enrolled

---

[52]In April 2018, the senate of the University of Medicine and Pharmacy voted for the unification of the University with the other institution of higher education of Târgu Mureș, Petru Maior University, which offers tuition only in Romanian language. The Hungarian members of the senate walked out in protest against the decision, RMDSZ also condemned it, calling upon the Hungarian stakeholders to attack the decison in court, while a number of advocacy NGOs announced public protests.

[53]EL, art. 99.

Table 3 Ethnic Hungarian students enrolled in higher education at the time of the 1992, 2002, and 2011 censuses

	1992	2002		2011	
	Students	Students	%	Students	%
University	**12,842**	**27,522**		**31,730**	
In Hungarian	n.a.	9268	33.7	12,195	38.4
In Romanian	n.a.	18,254	66.3	19,535	61.6

Source Veres (2015, pp. 88–98)

in higher education in Romania.[54] According to official figures, in 2016 the total number of students enrolled in universities in Romania was 405,638. Numbers have steadily decreased since 2007, when the highest number of students were registered (907,353 students).[55] At the end of academic year 2009/2010, the number of students enrolled on Hungarian-language degree programs was estimated to be 12,000, amounting to approximately 1.5% of all students in Romania (in this academic year, the official number of enrolled students was 775,319). The number of ethnic Hungarian students enrolled in Romanian-language degree programs is higher than that of their co-ethnics who study in their mother tongue. According to the best existing estimates, in 2010 approximately one-third of all ethnic Hungarian high school graduates and about half of the Hungarian young people who graduated from Hungarian-language high schools continued their studies in their mother tongue (Szikszai 2010, pp. 67–68; Márton 2012, pp. 101–102).

These estimates are reinforced by data from the last three censuses (1992, 2002, and 2011), the only data source where the number of enrolled students is recorded according to both educational levels and nationality; by corroborating these figures with the data published by the Ministry, we were able to obtain a relatively clear picture of the situation, at least for these three years. As Table 3 shows, the number of ethnic Hungarian students has tripled between 1992 and 2011, and the most recent data available show that 38.4% of them studied in the vernacular at university.

[54]This does not mean that such data do not exist; only that they are not retrievable from publicly available sources about educational statistics.

[55]Source: National Statistical Institute (Tempo online, SCL103L).

5 Assessing the Performance of Hungarian-Language Education

Having described its legal and organizational features, in the last section of this chapter we try to assess the efficiency of Hungarian-language pre-university education relative to education in the official language of the state. This question is very relevant because any performance gaps confront ethnic Hungarian parents with a choice that we may call the *dilemma of the minority parent.* The dilemma arises if parents (or children) who belong to the minority perceive that education in the official language offers better chances of social mobility than education in the vernacular, but from the perspective of intergenerational ethno-cultural reproduction (as opposed to cultural and linguistic assimilation) they would still prefer the latter (Kiss 2017; see also Csata 2014). Such a dilemma does not exist if the minority school system is (also) associated with higher mobility opportunities,[56] or if minority members do not have a preference for ethno-cultural reproduction.

We discuss two related aspects of this phenomenon. The first question is whether there is sufficient "objective" evidence to support the dilemma of minority parents, i.e., whether Hungarian-language schools do indeed lag behind majority-language schools in terms of performance. To do this, we will compare the performance of pupils attending Hungarian- and Romanian-language schools, drawing first on data from official examinations and then on competence assessment research. A second, related question refers to the performance of ethnic Hungarian children who attend Romanian-language schools, for which we rely mostly on competence tests, though some limited comparisons can also be carried out on the results of graduation examinations taken at the lower-secondary school level.

Before proceeding, we would like to emphasize that the vast majority of pupils enrolled in Hungarian-language schools are of Hungarian

[56] In Romania, this is the case with German-language schools, which are attended mostly by ethnic Romanian pupils, the number of ethnic German children being very low.

mother tongue.[57] Those few pupils at Hungarian-language schools who speak a different language at home are mostly children from mixed, Romanian–Hungarian marriages.

5.1 Performance as Reflected in Official Examinations Results

First, we approach the issue of relative performance by relying on official indicators intrinsic to the system: the results of graduation examinations that are taken at the end of lower-secondary school called the National Evaluation and of the high-school-leaving examination (Baccalaureate). Both examinations have become the subject of much public debate in Romania in recent years, especially after classrooms were fitted with security cameras to prevent and screen fraud committed by students or supervisors (starting in 2011 for the high-school-leaving examination and in 2012 for the National Evaluation) which brought about a rather spectacular decline in pass rates.

The current National Evaluation system has been applied since 2010. All students have to take written examinations in Romanian language and literature and mathematics. Students of minority language schools in addition are required to take an examination in minority (mother-tongue) language and literature. Participation in the National Evaluation system is not compulsory, but the results obtained therein define the range or type of upper secondary schools at which students can continue their studies; good results in the National Evaluation are required to continue studying at prestigious schools.

Taking a high-school-leaving graduation is obviously not compulsory (and it is even possible to enroll in post-high-school education without it), but successfully passing the Baccalaureate is a requirement for entering higher education, and it is also an important asset on the labor market.

---

[57] This may refer not only to ethnic Hungarians, but also to Hungarian-speaking Roma or to Sathmar Swabs who assimilated into the Hungarian linguistic community around the end of the nineteenth century.

The current system of examinations—applied since 2010—consists of oral examinations in Romanian language and literature and a foreign language, and for students of minority language education the language and literature of the minority. Students also have to take a practical examination in digital skills and competences. Written examinations must be taken in Romanian language and literature, one compulsory subject and an elective subject—both of the latter selected according to the profile of the high school, and for students of minority language programs the language and literature of the respective minority. Examination GPA is computed as the average of the three written examinations (four written examinations for minority students). While for the individual subjects the pass grade is 5, successful graduation requires an average of at least 6. There are two periods of graduation examinations each year: one in June-July and one in August-September. The results that are analyzed here refer only to the summer session.

In the official statistics, the pass rates at both the National Evaluation and the Baccalaureate are computed as the ratio of students obtaining a passing GPA to students taking the examination. However, not all eligible students register for the examinations, and of those who do, not all actually show up on examination day. That is, students who do not register or show up are not taken into account in the pass rate. Consequently, we consider that an assessment of educational performance would be more valid if pass rates were compared to the total number of students that graduate in the respective year, instead of those who do indeed start the examination.

The real proportion of eligible eighth graders who passed the National Evaluation between 2012 and 2016 fluctuated between 58 and 67%, a proportion significantly lower than the 65–77% recorded in the official statistics (see Table 4). This is due to the fact that approximately 15–20% of eighth graders do not participate in the examination. It is also important to note that the pass rate has not improved over the years; rather, we can speak about a fluctuating, or alternatively, stagnating trend.

The results of students learning in Hungarian remained under the national average in all five analyzed years, the pass rate ranging from 54 to 63%, as compared to the national rates of 58 to 67%. It is also

Table 4 Pass rates at the National Evaluation (2012–2016)

Year	Romania			Students in Hungarian educational programs			Proportion of students in Hungarian programs	
	Students enrolled in 8th grade	Students passing	Pass rate (%)	Students enrolled in 8th grade	Students passing	Pass rate (%)	In 8th grade population	Among passing students
2012	190,535	110,258	57.9	9990	5686	56.9	5.2	5.2
2013	190,787	123,194	64.6	9770	6162	63.1	5.1	5.0
2014	191,839	113,721	59.3	9832	5376	54.7	5.1	4.7
2015	187,628	125,852	67.1	10,078	6238	61.9	5.4	5.0
2016	187,088	111,327	59.5	10,040	5450	54.3	5.4	4.9

Source Authors' own calculation based on data published by the Ministry of Education

apparent that the gap between Hungarian-language schools and the national average widened: While the success rate was very similar in 2012 and 2013, in 2015 and 2016 Hungarians were already lagging behind by more than 5 percentage points.

There are significant regional differences concerning the performance of graduates of Hungarian-language classes. The best results are recorded in the regions where the proportion of Hungarians is low (*szórvány*) (pass rate of 79%), while the gap is considerable in Székely Land (69%) and even more so in the counties of Partium. Conversely, Cluj/Kolozs county had outstanding results throughout the period.

One of the most important factors that influences the success rate is size of settlement. This is true both at national level and with regard to students learning in Hungarian: In smaller rural settlements, the language of education does not make a significant difference, but its importance continuously increases as we move toward the big cities (Fig. 1).

Throughout the years, the scores of ethnic Hungarian pupils in Romanian language and literature have been significantly weaker than

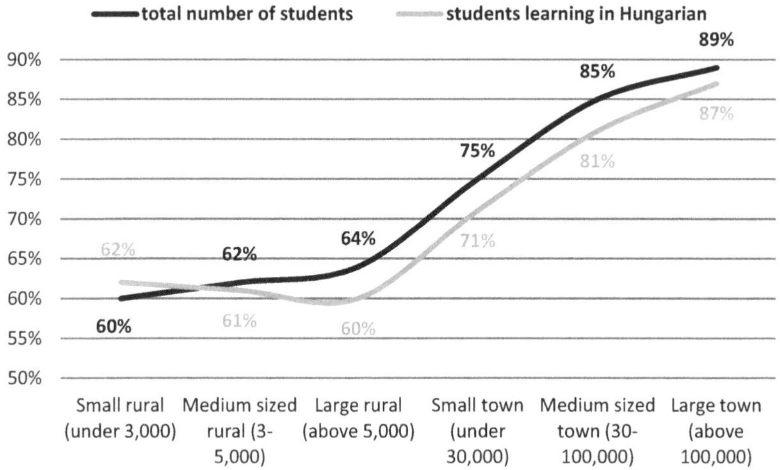

Fig. 1 Pass rates at the National Evaluation by size of settlement and language of education (*Source* Authors' own calculation based on data published by the Ministry of Education)

Table 5 Average GPA at the National Evaluation by language of education (2014)

Language of education	Number of pupils	Romanian language and literature	Mathematics	Mother tongue
Hungarian	5586	5.13	6.42	7.42
Romanian	32,588	6.55	6.71	

Source Authors' own calculation based on data from admitere.edu.ro

those of their ethnic Romanian peers, but they also usually lag behind (in a statistically significant manner) with regard to mathematics, even if to a lesser extent. Table 5 presents data from 2014.[58]

A direct assessment of the performance of ethnic Hungarian pupils who studied in Romanian-language schools is impossible because the ethnicity of pupils is not recorded in the databases of official examinations. However, it is possible to compare the performance of eighth graders that graduate from Hungarian-language programs according to the language in which they continue their education.

Based on the 2014 data, one can conclude that the performance of students who continue their studies in Romanian lags significantly behind that of their peers who continue their studies in the vernacular. In 2014, this was true with regard to all three subject matters in which students were tested (see Fig. 2). Those who enrolled in Romanian-language upper secondary education obtained significantly lower scores in both mathematics (1.25 points lower on a scale of 1–10) and Hungarian language and literature (1.22 points lower). Furthermore, and somewhat paradoxically, their grades were lower also for Romanian language and literature. These findings predict that the educational performance of ethnic Hungarian pupils who continue their studies in Romanian language will be poorer, and their chances on the labor market will probably be negatively affected too. We would also like to emphasize that these findings are in line with the results of PISA and other competence tests, to which we will turn in the next section.

Turning to high-school-leaving examinations, the official pass rate ranged between 55 and 76% nationally and between 47 and 69% in the

[58]For a quick analysis of the 2015 results, with similar findings as for 2014, see Barna (2015).

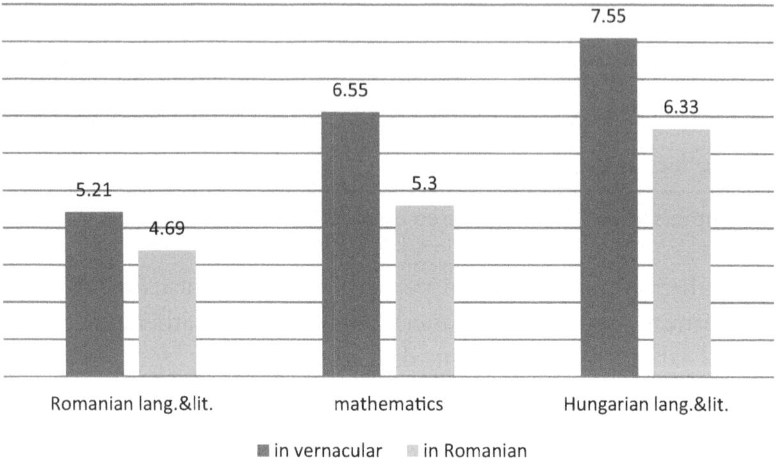

Fig. 2 National Evaluation exam scores of ethnic Hungarian pupils by the language of upper secondary education chosen (2014) (*Source* Authors' own calculations based on data from admitere.edu.ro)

case of students studying in Hungarian. However, use of the alternative methodology which relates the number of those who passed to the total number of students graduating in that particular year yields significantly lower success rates, as shown in Table 6.

It turns out from the data that the proportion of high-school graduates registering for the Baccalaureate is higher among students who attended Hungarian-language programs, and the proportion of those who actually take the examination relative to the number of those who registered is also higher. Consequently, the gap between students who graduate from Hungarian-language programs and the national average is actually smaller than that suggested by the official data. However, except for 2016, the success rate of graduates of Hungarian-language programs remained below the national average by 1–3 percentage points. Perhaps a more realistic interpretation of the data is that the performance of Hungarians is not necessarily worse than that of the Romanians, but it is at least as poor as the national average.

Regional differences among graduates of Hungarian-language schools are also significant with regard to the high-school-leaving examinations

Table 6 Results and pass rates of high-school-leaving examinations (2012–2016)

Romania					
Year	Proportion of high-school graduates registered for examination (%)	Number of students registered (full-time students)	High-school graduates (estimated number)	Number of students who passed examination (full-time students)	Proportion of high-school graduates successfully passing (%)
2012	80	138,299	172,874	74,139	43
2013	71	137,085	193,077	86,098	45
2014	73	123,039	168,547	84,049	50
2015	77	141,121	183,560	101,655	55
2016	71	113,127	158,819	82,791	52
Students attending educational programs in the Hungarian language					
Year	Proportion of high-school graduates registered for examination (%)	Number of students registered (full-time students)	High-school graduates (estimated number)	Students passing the examination (full-time students, respective year)	Proportion of high-school graduates successfully passing (%)
2012	87	6468	7434	2946	40
2013	78	6437	8236	3451	42
2014	79	5697	7175	3539	49
2015	81	6377	7893	4221	53
2016	82	5442	6650	3625	55

Source Authors' own calculation based on data published by the Ministry of Education

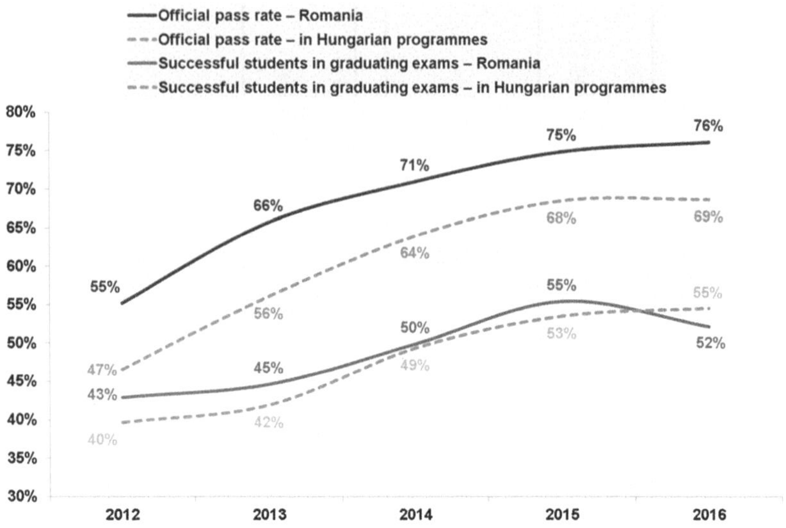

Fig. 3 High-school-leaving examinations: official pass rates and the rate of success compared to the number of high-school graduates, Romania and Hungarian-language programs (2012–2016) (*Source* Authors' own calculation based on data published by the Ministry of Education)

(Fig. 3). Students living in Central Transylvania (especially Cluj/Kolozs, but also Mureș/Maros counties) performed relatively better in the analyzed years than those from other regions. The counties with low proportions of Hungarians (*szórvány*) follow closely, followed by the Partium region. The poorest scores were recorded in the Székely Land (the average pass rate is 50% in Harghita/Hargita county over the five analyzed years, and 54% in Covasna/Kovászna).

The size of the settlement has a huge impact at the Baccalaureate too, both at the national level and among students who study in Hungarian. The lowest pass rates are recorded in rural high schools; furthermore, the Hungarians lag most significantly behind the national average in this category of schools: While the average pass rate for rural Romania was 40% in the analyzed years, for Hungarian-language programs operating in villages it was only 28%. It should be noted that the majority of graduates who registered for the examination within this category came from technological programs (62% at a national

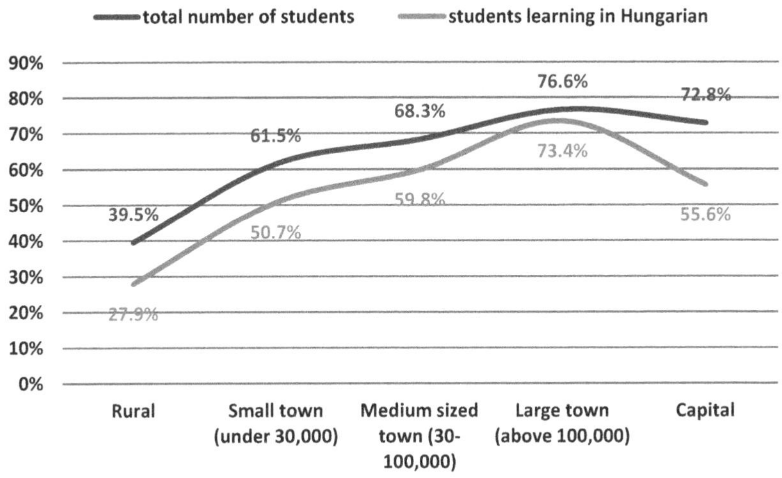

Fig. 4 High-school-leaving examination pass rates by settlement size and language of education (*Source* Authors' own calculation based on data published by the Ministry of Education)

level). The rate of success increases with the size of settlement for students learning both in Romanian and Hungarian, but the latter perform worse in all settlement types (Fig. 4).

The gap according to language is particularly large for technological schools (success rate at the national level is 42% on average for the analyzed period, while for Hungarian-language programs it is only 26%). This also helps explain to some extent the poor results registered in the Hungarian schools of the compact Hungarian-majority regions. For instance, in Harghita/Hargita county, the majority of students had received technological education over the studied period. In contrast, the pass rate of students who studied at schools with a theoretical profile is outstanding in Harghita/Hargita county (81%).

The pass rates and GPA of students from Hungarian-language programs are most significantly affected by the examination in Romanian language and literature. Very many graduates fail the Baccalaureate because they fail the Romanian examination (e.g., in 2013 over one-third of all students from Hungarian programs who failed did so for this reason). Moreover, the pass rate for the Romanian examination increases as the proportion of Hungarians in the settlement area of the school decreases, which highlights the issue of low Romanian proficiency, especially in the compact Hungarian-majority areas, most importantly in the Székely Land (for details, see Toró 2013).

5.2 Competence Evaluations

After an analysis of the pass rates and average GPAs obtained at graduation exams, we now turn to data from competence tests, more precisely the results PISA studies,[59] which assess the knowledge of students aged 15 in the domains of reading, mathematics, and science.[60] In order to grasp the relative performance of Hungarian-language schools as compared to the national average, we use data from the last four waves of PISA measurements, carried out in 2006, 2009, 2012, and 2015.

Before discussing the results, we would like to emphasize two things. First, Romania's scores have regularly been rather weak in European comparison, a problem that would deserve detailed analysis on its own, but which is beyond the scope of this chapter. Second, rather few students that attended Hungarian-language programs were included in all PISA waves (see Table 7). The number of Hungarians enrolled in Romanian-language education was even lower. This means that the uncertainty about all estimates concerning ethnic Hungarian pupils is considerably higher than for ethnic Romanians. Consequently, the results presented below should be interpreted cautiously. Furthermore, this methodological issue reduces to a great extent the possibility of policy-oriented research and planning for minority language education.[61]

[59]PISA: Program for International Student Assessment. https://www.oecd.org/pisa.

[60]Due to space considerations, we cannot discuss other competence measurements. The results of the Trends in International Mathematics and Science Study (TIMSS) and the Progress in International Reading Literacy Study (PIRLS) measurements are mostly in line with the conclusions of PISA studies. On the TIMSS results of Transylvanian Hungarian pupils, see Csata (2014), for PIRLS, see Papp and Márton (2017).

[61]For details about the sampling, see Kiss (2017). On the methodological issues of applying PISA scores to assess the performance of pupils who belong to ethnic or linguistic minorities, see also Papp (2015).

Table 7 Results of PISA competency evaluations by language of education and language spoken at home (2006–2015)

		2006	2009	2012	2015
N	Romanians	4838	4423	4693	4343
	Hungarians—in vernacular	146	222	222	396
	Hungarians—in Romanian	133	102	43	38
PV mathematics	Romanians	416	424	445	445
	Hungarians—in vernacular	427	492	445	439
	Hungarians—in Romanian	390	387	404	426
PV reading	Romanians	392	423	438	433
	Hungarians—in vernacular	406	504	456	445
	Hungarians—in Romanian	345	359	369	418
PV science	Romanians	416	425	438	432
	Hungarians—in vernacular	440	515	466	472
	Hungarians—in Romanian	391	381	389	414

Source Authors' computations based on PISA data

For the purposes of the analysis, students were classified into three categories based on the language of testing and a variable from the individual questionnaire which refers to the language used in the family. The average plausible values[62] recorded in the four waves of PISA testing are presented in Table 7, broken down according to the three groups of interest: ethnic Romanians (more precisely, children who attend Romanian-language programs and speak Romanian with their families), ethnic Hungarians (attending Hungarian-language programs and speaking Hungarian at home), and ethnic Hungarians in Romanian education (also Hungarian-speaking at home but have completed the related tests in Romanian). Table 7 presents the results for all three tested domains: mathematics, reading, and science for all three groups.

The figures show that, in general, ethnic Hungarian pupils studying in the vernacular do not perform worse than their ethnic Romanian peers; moreover, in 2009, their scores were even significantly higher on average. In the last two waves, the gap closed, that is, Romanian-language schools improved while Hungarian-language schools stagnated. In 2015, the Hungarian schools scored significantly better only

[62]In PISA methodology, indicators of individual student performance are called plausible values.

in the domain of science, while in the case of reading and mathematics the difference was not significant.

Turning to the second question, the results unequivocally show that ethnic Hungarian children studying in Romanian-language schools lag significantly behind their co-ethnics who attend school in the vernacular (and also behind ethnic Romanian pupils). The gap (although of varying magnitude) persisted across all waves and for all three domains of testing. This signals that studying in the vernacular usually also means studying more efficiently and thus also confers benefits from the perspective of future prospects on the labor market.

To summarize this section, the results of competence tests show that ethnic Hungarian students attending school in the vernacular perform unequivocally better than their co-ethnics enrolled in majority-language programs, and in some cases, they also outperform ethnic Romanian students. These findings provide some grounds for optimism, as they seem to undermine the "objective" grounds of the dilemma of the minority parent.

However, a comparison of the official indicators of educational performance (National Evaluation and Baccalaureate scores) with the results of the international competence tests reveals an interesting contradiction. While the latter measure either no significant differences, or sometimes even better performances for students enrolled in Hungarian-language education, in official examinations students who have studied in Hungarian regularly obtain weaker results, even if the real gap may be less in the case of the high-school-leaving examination than what is reflected in official results (as shown above).

When trying to explain this apparent contradiction, one should be aware that some issues may arise with regard to the external validity of the findings about competence testing, as the margins of error are too high due to the relatively small number of ethnic Hungarian pupils included in the samples.[63] Also, it should be noted that the two types of data result from very different methodologies. Still, the lack of

[63]The sampling methodology in the case of PIRLS and TIMSS is similar to that of PISA as concerns the number of ethnic minority students that are included. See Csata (2014) for details.

concordance that is apparent at the general level between the two types of performance evaluation calls for an explanation. Moreover, the contradiction is also present if we restrict the scrutiny to the domain in which a comparison is most meaningful, namely mathematics: Students of Hungarian-language programs regularly obtain slightly worse results in mathematics at the National Evaluation, but not in PISA tests.

We believe that some sort of reverse causality may also be involved in the apparently better performance of students of Hungarian-language schools in competence testing, which is related to the structure of the Hungarian-language educational system. One possible alternative explanation for the better performance of pupils who attend Hungarian schools and for the weaker results of those who do not study in the vernacular is that ethnic Hungarian children with weaker abilities are more likely to continue their studies at the upper secondary level in Romanian-language schools, as described in the previous section of this chapter. To some extent, this is caused by the asymmetries inherent in the educational system, i.e., the poor educational offerings in the vernacular in areas where the proportion of Hungarians in the population is small. Thus, pupils who do not aspire to continue at high schools with theoretical program must opt for technological education in the Romanian language.

Papp (2013, 2014) and Csata (2014) argue that Hungarian-speaking parents with lower levels of education are more likely to send their children to Romanian-language schools. According to Papp, an "assimilation spiral" is created: Children attending non-mother-tongue education will have lower competences; thus, there is a chance that they will achieve lower socioeconomic status, and families with such backgrounds are less conscious in choosing mother-tongue education; thus, the choice favoring Romanian-language education is reproduced (Papp 2013, pp. 105–106). Csata also found that Hungarian-speaking parents with lower levels of education are more likely to send their children to Romanian-language schools (at the lower-secondary level), but highlighted as a possible explanation for this the behavior of Hungarian-speaking Roma (Csata 2014, p. 144).

However, other evidence nuances this explanation. In families of mixed ethnic background, the likelihood that children will be declared as being of Romanian ethnicity increases with the socioeconomic situation of the family, being higher among middle-class (or better situated) families (see Chapter 10 of this volume on this matter). This also means that the children of better situated mixed families are more likely to choose Romanian-language upper secondary schools (while the families still speaking at least some Hungarian at home); consequently, as the socioeconomic situation of the family improves, the likelihood that their children continue studying in Romanian-language theoretical upper secondary programs also increases. Also, based on PISA data, Kiss (2017) concludes that the socioeconomic background of ethnic Hungarian children enrolled in Romanian-language programs is better. These findings seem to be at odds with the hypothesis that the academic lag of ethnic Hungarian children who study in Romanian may be attributed to the weaker abilities of pupils who are forced by structural factors to continue in Romanian-language professional schools due to the lack of Hungarian-language options. Further research is definitely required to clarify these phenomena.

There are also some structural factors that must be taken into account when discussing the weaker results of students enrolled in Hungarian-language programs at official examination sessions, relative to their ethnic Romanian peers. First, Hungarian students are overrepresented in rural areas and in small towns, and, as explained previously, the type of settlement influences success at examinations to a great extent. Second, the structure of the Hungarian educational subsystem is different from that of the Romanian-language system with regard to the proportion of the type and profile of programs that exist. As already noted, problems are most evident in the case of technological programs.

Third, children who study in Hungarian must take an additional mandatory examination at the National Evaluation and two additional examinations at the high-school-leaving examination, as compared to their ethnic Romanian peers. This involves the examination in Romanian language and literature, which for the ethnic Romanians is the vernacular, but for Hungarians basically represents another foreign language. Even more significant than the extra workload required by an additional examination is the fact that Hungarian students living in

Hungarian-majority areas have rather low proficiency in the Romanian language. This is why results in this subject matter are the weakest in the Székely Land and in parts of the Partium region, where many students live in an almost entirely Hungarian-language social environment. According to the policy-makers of RMDSZ, pupils who are enrolled in the 5th grade in school year 2017/2018 should already take the Romanian examination at the National Evaluation according to an alternative curriculum (i.e., as a foreign language).

6 Conclusions: Processes and Trends in Hungarian-Language Education

The purpose of this study was to provide an overview of the legal framework of Hungarian-language education in Romania, to evaluate the processes internal to this domain and to identify the most important weaknesses of the system.

In summary, the legal framework is in principle favorable; it allows the development of education in the vernacular at all levels. However, this development is hindered by several factors: non-favorable demographic processes, the manner in which legislation and educational policies are implemented at the local-level and by county-level school inspectorates, in addition to administrative requirements and obligations. Although legislation specifies some degree of decentralization, the everyday management of education remains highly centralized in Romania.

One of the main questions formulated at the beginning of this chapter referred to the "ownership" of the schools that teach (also) in Hungarian. A proper answer to this question can only be an answer that involves deliberation at the level of the Hungarian community. In the current context, education in the vernacular is best assessed as a subdomain of the national educational system, which, however, does not have the means to determine its own institutional framework of operation, while it is not clear who the actors are and who should be in charge of its management. While RMDSZ and RMPSZ, the departments in charge of minority education at the Ministry, local governments, and school inspectorates all play some role in the process, none of them can be considered genuine masters of the domain.

In higher education, the nature of ownership is perhaps easier to specify because at this level there are only a handful of institutional actors, whose "owners" are easily determined: either the state, or private or church bodies; the latter, however, are in a dependent relationship with the kin-state. Providing an answer to the question at this level involves on the one hand an assessment of the decision-making mechanisms within Babeş-Bolyai University (and the two other smaller multicultural universities); on the other hand, however, the situation of the Hungarian-language private universities is straightforward. For instance, with regard to Sapientia University, it is often emphasized that the institution possesses all the decision-making competences that are necessary for its operation. Notwithstanding this, the answer to the question is still not unequivocal even in higher education because no procedures for interinstitutional relations are in place, despite the fact that the demographic trends call for mechanisms that would enable coordination and planning to facilitate the more efficient utilization of available resources and limit or manage the parallelisms on the supply side of the educational market.

Strategic planning is also crucial in pre-university education because the sustainability of an increasing number of schools is increasingly questionable due to negative demographic processes. Settling the question of ownership and responsibility is not important for its own sake, but because any development strategy formulated at the systemic level implies the existence and the commitment of actors in decision-making positions. In theory, it is possible under the current circumstances for certain institutions to engage in development projects, but in the absence of coordinating actors the subsystem of Hungarian-language education (if it is justified to speak about a subsystem at all) is unable to successfully engage in development projects of its own, let alone connect to the development projects of the Romanian educational system.

In addition to such actors, development requires valid and reliable data about the processes internal to the Hungarian-language education system. In the past two decades, considerable progress has been made with regard to the input side of the educational system as demographic data of good quality became available; however, documentation of internal processes and the output side are also necessary. In this chapter, we have attempted to describe some of the data sources that are available and to formulate some conclusions based on them which hopefully improve our understanding of certain aspects of the educational system (e.g., the performance of pupils and some factors that influence this). We are aware, however, that a more thorough understanding of the processes of education and any developmental interventions or policy initiatives must be grounded in much more extensive research and require significantly more data. As mentioned, the establishment of a research center for minority education would be an important step in this direction. Furthermore, we consider that larger subsamples of children who study in minority languages should be included in the future waves of competence testing.[64]

References

Barna, G. (2015, July 10). Képességvizsga – hogy teljesítettek a magyar diákok? *Maszol.ro*. Avaialble at: http://www.maszol.ro/index.php/társadalom/50121-kepessegvizsga-hogy-teljesitettek-a-magyar-diakok.

Barna, G., Kapitány, B., Kiss, T., Márton, J., & Toró, T. (2016). *Iskolák veszélyben: Tanulmányok a Székelyföldön kívüli magyar oktatás helyzetéről.* Kolozsvár: Nemzeti Kisebbségkutató Intézet.

Csata, Z. (2014). Az erdélyi magyar tanulók iskolai teljesítményének meghatározói a TIMSS-vizsgálatok alapján. *Kisebbségkutatás, 23*(4), 126–157.

Gáll, E., & Keszeg, J. (2014). A tanügyi rendszer működésének vizsgálata a magyar nyelv- és irodalomoktatás tükrében. *Magyar Kisebbség, 19*(2), 85–116.

Kiss, T. (2017). Diferențe etnolingvistice în performanța școlară. Dimensiuni neexplorate ale datelor PISA. Manuscript.

[64]Such larger samples are employed, for instance, in the case of Germans in Belgium, German speakers in South Tyrol, Swedish speakers in Finland, Basque speakers in Spain, and speakers of Gaelic in the UK. See Papp (2015) and Kiss (2017).

Magyari, T. (2014, October 13). Vitaindító a közoktatásról. *Transindex.ro*. Avaialble at: http://welemeny.transindex.ro/?cikk=24541. Accessed 2 February 2018.

Márton, J. (2012). A 2009-ben és 2010-ben érettségizett romániai magyar diákok továbbtanulása. *Educatio, 13*(1), 87–103.

Papp, A. Z. (2010). Határon túli magyar oktatási támogatások és hasznosulásuk 2006–2010 között. *Educatio, 11*(1), 88–110.

Papp, A. Z. (2013). Motivations for school choice and minority perspectives. *Minority Studies, 15*, 99–122.

Papp, A. Z. (2014). Selecting a majority-language school by Hungarian minority students, or from PISA results to discourses in the carpathian basin. *Minority Studies, 17*, 89–101.

Papp, A. Z. (2015). Hidden ethnic inequalities: A possible global educational exploration using PISA. *Ethnicity, 10*, 4–40.

Papp, A. Z., & Márton, J. (2014). Peremoktatásról varázstalanítva: A Csángó Oktatási Program értékelésének tapasztalatai. *Magyar Kisebbség, 19*(2), 7–32.

Papp, A. Z., & Márton, J. (2017). Oktatásügy. In N. Bárdi & G. Éger (Eds.), *Magyarok Romániában, 1990–2015. Tanulmányok az erdélyi magyarságról.* Budapest: Károli Gáspár Református Egyetem, pp. 341–373.

Péntek, J. (2004). A magyar közoktatás nyelvi és szakmai feltételei. In E. Bálint & J. Péntek (Eds.), *Oktatás nyelvek határán. Közelkép és helyzetkép a romániai magyar oktatásról.* Kolozsvár: Anyanyelvápolók Erdélyi Szövetsége.

Szikszai, M. (Ed.). (2010). *Az erdélyi magyar felsőoktatás helyzete és kilátásai: Támpontok egy lehetséges stratégiához.* Kolozsvár: Ábel Kiadó.

Toró, T. (2013). *Érettségi.* Kolozsvár: Mensura Transylvanica.

Toró, T. (2016). Multikulturális egyetem? A Marosvásárhelyi Orvosi és Gyógyszerészeti Egyetem (MOGYE) esete. *Magyar Kisebbség, 21*(3), 121–136.

Veres, V. (2012). Decentralizáció, minőségbiztosítás és kisebbségi oktatási jogok Romániában az új tanügyi törvényben. *Pro Minoritaté* (Tavasz), 110–121.

Veres, V. (2015). *Népességszerkezet és nemzetiség. Az erdélyi magyarok demográfiai képe a 2002. és 2011. évi romániai népszámlálások tükrében.* Kolozsvár: Kolozsvári Egyetemi Kiadó.

7
Churches and Religious Life

Dénes Kiss

Romanian society is characterized by an outstanding level of religiosity in the contemporary European context (Voicu 2007; Tomka 2005). Not only is the high level of individual religiosity characteristic, but the public presence of churches is also remarkable. As many analysts highlighted, churches (especially the Romanian Orthodox Church) are highly influential in politics, public education, social and health care (Stan and Turcescu 2005, 2007; Moise 2004; Enache et al. 2008). The influence and the presence of churches in different social domains are even more significant among Transylvanian Hungarians. In their case, the legitimacy of churches is increased by the conviction (shared also by many non-religious Transylvanian Hungarians) that they are important institutional tools of minority self-organization. This conviction lends to the Hungarian churches a further impetus to take an active role in community organizing, public education, cultural life, and social care.

D. Kiss (✉)
Hungarian Department of Sociology and Social Work, Babeş-Bolyai University, Cluj-Napoca, Romania

T. Kiss et al. (eds.), *Unequal Accommodation of Minority Rights*, Palgrave Politics of Identity and Citizenship Series,
https://doi.org/10.1007/978-3-319-78893-7_7

It would be a mistake to interpret the strong public presence of religion (especially that of the Orthodox Church's) and its infiltration into different social fields as an inherited, or a "traditional" characteristic of Romanian society. During the former regime, the activity of churches was drastically restricted. More precisely, it was constrained strictly to religious services and was pushed outside the public sphere (Gheorghe 2004). Developments into the opposite direction only occurred after the regime change. However, this latter phenomenon is not a Romanian characteristic at all, as both individual level religiosity and the public influence of churches have increased throughout Eastern Europe (Casanova 1994; Berger 1999a). The mentioned authors interpreted these processes as a trend of desecularization, or counter-secularization, meaning that religiosity regained its public relevance in societies or social fields where previously tendencies of secularization had been dominant (Berger 1999b). Desecularization has the same dimensions as secularization. It is characteristic if religious norms regained their influence in different institutions previously governed by non-religious norms and if the public influence of religion was reestablished. Cultural products (arts, literature, and philosophy) can also become more religious in their content. Last but not least, religion can (re)appear in the material culture of the society too, meaning an increase of newly built churches, the enlargement of church proprieties, and a reinforcement of the demand for religious products (Karpov 2010).

This chapter discusses the religious life and the religious institutional system of the Hungarians in Transylvania. The first section outlines the distribution of the Hungarian population by denominations and some of the main dimensions of its religiosity. The second part presents the structure of the religious institutions. It begins with the institutions connected strictly to religious practices, and then it deals with the church-founded institutions active in various social domains. The importance of this chapter is given by the fact that the process of desecularization has been remarkable in the case of the Transylvanian Hungarians too, and Hungarian churches have gained an important role in the institutional structure of the minority community.

1 Denominations and Religiosity: A Statistical Overview

According to the 2011 census, virtually all Transylvanian Hungarians (99.4%) belong to one of the Christian denominations. The vast majority (86.7%) of them are members of the Reformed or of the Roman Catholic Church, while the remaining part (13.3%) belongs to other denominations. Unitarians number 55,000, while the neo-protestant churches (Baptists, Jehovah's Witnesses, Adventists, and Pentecostals) taken together have 38,000 followers among Transylvanian Hungarians. The Orthodox Church is perceived as (and according to its self-identification it actually is) a Romanian national denomination. Nevertheless, it has 26,000 ethnically Hungarian members, while 16,000 Hungarians are Greek Catholics. Census data show that the number of those who do not belong to any denomination is extremely low in the European context (Table 1).[1] This is per se an important indicator of religiosity, showing that religious belonging is important, at least at a declarative level.

A more detailed picture of the religiosity of Transylvanian Hungarians can be obtained from surveys representative of the Hungarian population. These allow for an analytical distinction between the ritualistic, cognitive, and collective-institutional dimensions of religiosity. The first dimension refers to the frequency of performing religious practices, the second to the knowledge and beliefs concerning religious dogmas, while the third to church adherence and to the importance of the church as a religious authority. In what follows, I will present some results of a survey conducted by the Romanian Institute for Research on National Minorities[2] in 2009. The major

[1]As a comparison, in Hungary the proportion of those who do not belong to any of the denominations is of 18%.

[2]The survey Turning Points of our Life-courses, second wave, was carried out in cooperation with the Demographic Research Institute of the Hungarian Statistical Office. See http://demografia.hu/hu/tudastar/adatbazisok/22-adatbazisok/160-eletunk-fordulopontjai.

Table 1 The Hungarians in Romania by denominations (2011)

Denominations	Church members of Hungarian ethnicity	Proportion among Hungarians	Proportion of Hungarians among church members
Reformed	563,611	45.9	93.8
Roman Catholic	500,444	40.8	57.5
Unitarian	55,794	4.5	96.7
Romanian Orthodox	26,009	2.1	0.2
Greek Catholic	16,144	1.3	10.7
Evanghelic-Lutherans	12,431	1.0	61.6
Baptist	12,408	1.0	11.0
Jehovah' Witnesses	11,322	0.9	22.7
Adventist	7985	0.7	9.9
Pentecostal	6430	0.5	1.8
Other religion	8339	0.7	4.0
Does not belong to any denomination	3079	0.3	16.3
Atheist	873	0.1	4.2
Missing data	2754	0.2	0.2
Total	1,227,623	100	6.5

Source National Institute of Statistics, census data

advantage of this survey is that it was based on a careful representative sampling of 4000 Hungarian speakers throughout Transylvania and, as a consequence, in the database there are enough cases to analyze the major denominations separately.

The practical-ritualistic aspects of religiosity are most commonly measured through the frequency of church attendance and praying. Both variables indicate a high degree of religiosity among Transylvanian Hungarians: One-third of the respondents declared that they attend religious services at least once a week, and praying is a daily habit for approximately half of those interviewed. These indicators show a more intensive practical-ritualistic religiosity than what is characteristic of Hungary and similar to the figures for Romania as a whole. In Hungary, according to the 2008 wave of the European Values Study, 8.4% of the population attended religious services at least once a week and 14.8% prayed with a daily frequency. In Romania, these figures were 30.4 and

Table 2 Frequency of church attendance and praying among Transylvanian Hungarians, by denomination (2009)

	Attends religious services at least once a week[a]	Prays with a daily frequency
Roman Catholic	40.8	43.2
Reformed	27.1	51.8
Evanghelic-Lutherans	39.7	44.3
Unitarian	25.6	54.6
Neo-Protestant	80.0	86.0
Orthodox	21.7	42.0
Total	34.0	49.2

Source RIRNM survey, $N=3991$

Question wording: Apart from weddings, funerals and christenings, about how often do you attend religious services? (more than once a week; once a week; once a month; only on specific holy days; once a year; less often; never, practically never). How often do you pray to God outside religious services? (every day; more than once a week; once a week; at least once a month; several times a year; less often; never)

[a]Social desirability (i.e., the tendency to report socially desirable answers) could cause distortions in the case of church attendance. However, there is no reason to presume that these distortions are higher in case of one or another denomination

53.9%, respectively (EVS 2011). Table 2 shows significant differences of the two indicators by denomination. Roman Catholics and Lutherans attend religious services more frequently, while members of the Reformed and Unitarian Church pray more frequently. Neo-protestants perform both religious practices more frequently compared to the "historical" denominations.

The overwhelming majority of Transylvanian Hungarians (95.9%) believes in God (see Table 3) and there are no significant differences by denomination in this respect. Even if practically all Hungarians belong to Christian denominations, their representation of God is far from being uniform (see Table 4). While 80% of them believe in a personal God, 12% imagine God merely as a "life force" or "spirit". The belief in a personal God characterizes neo-protestants in a higher, and Unitarians in a lower, degree. The belief in other crucial dogmas of Christianity is less widespread but also significant: 56% believe that

Table 3 Belief in religious dogmas among Transylvanian Hungarians by denomination (2009)

	God	Life after death	Hell	Angels	Reincarnation
Roman Catholic	96.5	55.0	52.8	55.0	14.6
Reformed	96.3	55.5	47.2	50.8	15.1
Evanghelic-Lutherans	95.0	66.4	68.6	65.7	6.4
Unitarian	97.4	43.5	40.2	41.2	13.0
Neo-Protestant	96.6	78.6	69.7	84.1	15.8
Orthodox	95.8	55.9	56.1	50.5	15.1
Total	95.9	56.0	50.9	53.7	14.7

Note Proportion of affirmative answers. Question wording: Which, if any, of the following do you believe in? *Source* RIRNM, $N=4000$

Table 4 Representations of the nature of God, Transylvanian Hungarians by denomination (2009)

	There is a personal God	There is some sort of spirit or life force	I don't really know what to think	I don't really think there is any sort of spirit, God, or life force
Roman Catholic	80.4	11.9	6.2	1.2
Reformed	80.1	11.7	6.6	1.5
Evanghelic-Lutherans	87.9	7.1	2.1	2.9
Unitarian	76.0	17.7	5.7	0.5
Neo-Protestant	92.3	4.9	2.8	0
Orthodox	78.0	12.4	8.1	1.4
Total	80.3	11.6	6.2	1.5

Note Proportion of affirmative answers. Question wording: Which of these statements comes closest to your beliefs? *Source* RIRNM, $N=4000$

there is life after death and 51% that there is something like hell. As for resurrection, the two extremes are the Unitarians (only 43% of them believe in life after death) and the neo-protestants (78% of whom believe in this dogma).

Transylvanian Hungarians belong almost without exception to Christian denominations, believe in God and attend religious services, and pray incomparably more frequently than Western Europeans. However, this does not mean that they accept all religious dogmas. On

Table 5 Forms of religiosity among Transylvanian Hungarians by denomination (2009)

	I am a religious person and I follow the instructions of the church	I'm religious in my own way	I cannot decide whether I am religious	I am not religious
Roman Catholic	48.3	46.6	2.2	2.9
Reformed	37.8	54.2	3.5	4.4
Evanghelic-Lutherans	28.4	68.8	2.1	0.7
Unitarian	47.9	45.9	3.1	3.1
Neo-Protestant	73.6	22.2	2.8	1.4
Orthodox	38.9	52.1	6.2	2.8
Total	43.1	50.1	3.1	3.7

Note Proportion of affirmative answers. Question wording: Which of these statements characterizes more appropriately your belief? *Source* RIRNM, $N=4000$

the contrary, even the more crucial religious doctrines are accepted by only slightly more than a half of them. The pluralization of religious ideas and the individualization of religiosity characteristic in late modern Western civilization are important tendencies in Transylvania too. Some degree of syncretism is indicated by the fact that while almost a half of Hungarians reject the Christian doctrine of resurrection, 15% of them embrace reincarnation, which is an idea originating from the religious systems of the Far East. In other words, Transylvanian Hungarians accept the religious dogmas of their churches only more or less and they follow the instructions of these churches also only to a certain extent. To catch this tendency, we used a survey question elaborated by Miklós Tomka, who distinguished between a religiosity following the instructions of the church and a religiosity of one's own way (Tomka 1998). Based on this question (Table 5), we can characterize slightly more than a half of the Transylvanians as religious in their own way and only 43% as following the instruction of the church in this respect. Differences by denominations are also significant: The individualization of religiosity is the most widespread in the case of the Lutherans and the less frequent in case of the neo-protestants. Catholics tend to follow more faithfully the instructions of the church compared to the Calvinists.

2 The Organizational Structure of the Churches

As it was already shown, the Hungarian population in Romania is divided into numerous denominations. In some of these churches, the overwhelming majority of members are of Hungarian ethnicity, while in others, Hungarians comprise only a minority of the adherents. The Reformed and the Unitarian Churches could be considered (and represent themselves as) Hungarian national denominations. Overall, in the case of the Roman Catholic Church in Romania, 58% of the members are of Hungarian ethnic background; however, in Transylvania, this proportion reaches 78%, meaning that Hungarians form a clear majority among Transylvanian Catholics, even if the number of non-Hungarian Catholics is significant. Hungarians also form a majority (of 62%) among Evanghelic-Lutherans, another significant group of the church members being that of Slovaks.[3] Among Greek Catholics, Baptists, Adventists and Jehovah's Witnesses, Hungarians are overrepresented, while among the members of the Romanian Orthodox and the Pentecostal Churches, they are highly underrepresented. From the perspective of the ethnic organization of the different denominations, the proportion of Hungarians among church members is a key variable, because the degree of institutional autonomy that Hungarian speakers can enjoy inside these churches depends partially on this.

The Reformed, the Catholic, and the Unitarian Churches are the most numerous denominations among Hungarians, and along with the Evanghelic-Lutherans are regarded in Transylvania as the historical Hungarian denominations. In their organizational structure, one can distinguish between three levels (Table 6).[4] The lower level and the basic organizational units are the local communities (parishes, congregations); these are organized in middle-level structures (dioceses, ecclesiastical

[3]In Romania, there are two Lutheran churches. The Evanghelic-Lutheran Church is a primarily Hungarian-speaking denomination, with Slovak-speaking parishes. The Evangelical Church of Augustan Confession is German-speaking. The overwhelming majority of Transylvania's Saxons used to belong to this latter Church.

[4]In this and the next section, I relied primarily on the webpages of the churches under discussion.

Table 6 The organizational structure of the four most numerous historical Hungarian churches

	Reformed Church in Romania	Roman Catholic Church in Romania	Hungarian Unitarian Church	Evangelic-Lutheran Church in Romania
Higher level	Bishoprics or church districts	Archdioceses	Bishopric (Unitarian Church of Transylvania)	Bishopric
Middle level	Dioceses	Dioceses	Ecclesiastical district	Dioceses
Lower level	Parishes	Parishes	Local congregations	Parishes

districts), which are subordinated to higher-level structures (bishoprics, archbishoprics).

The Reformed Church has two bishoprics (or church districts) in Romania. The Transylvanian Reformed Church District covers the historical province (Principality) of Transylvania and consists of 15 dioceses. The Királyhágómellék (Piatra Craiului) Reformed Church District covers the Banat and Partium (Crișana) regions and has 9 dioceses; 61.5% of the Reformed Church members belong to the Transylvanian and 38.5 to the Királyhágómellék bishoprics. The church members living in the Old Romanian Kingdom belong to one of the five missionary parishes which are subordinated to the Diocese of Brașov/Brassó.[5] According to the 2011 census, the number of non-Hungarian church members was 37,321, of whom 19,802 were ethnic Romanians and 16,487 of Roma ethnic background. However, the majority of non-Hungarian church members speaks Hungarian and there is only one non-Hungarian-speaking parish, namely in Bucharest.

The situation of the Unitarians is specific among Transylvania's historical Hungarian churches. In 2012, the Unitarian Church of Transylvania and the Unitarian Church of Hungary merged, forming the Hungarian Unitarian Church, which has a single bishopric, located in Cluj/Kolozsvár, while the former bishopric of Budapest was transformed into the Ecclesiastical District of Hungary (*Magyarországi*

[5]These parishes are located in Bacău, Galați and Râmnicu Vâlcea and Bucharest (two parishes).

Unitárius Egyházkerület) within the unified Church. Thus, the Hungarian Unitarian Church is the only historical Hungarian denomination that organizationally bridges state borders; moreover, its leading structures are located not in Hungary but in Transylvania. The middle-level organizational units of the church are the six ecclesiastical districts, which are composed of 123 local congregations. The vast majority of the Unitarians live in the Székely Land (Harghita/Harghita, Covasna/Kovászna, and Mureș/Maros counties). As a consequence, five of the six ecclesiastical districts (*egyházkör*) are in this region, while the Unitarians living in Partium and Banat belong to the Torda-Kolozs (Turda-Cluj) district, having its seat in Cluj/Kolozsvár.

The Roman Catholic Church has six dioceses in Romania, two of them being archdioceses. The majority of ethnic Hungarian Catholics belong to the Alba Iulia/Gyulafehérvár archdiocese which does not have other dioceses in its subordination. The Dioceses of Oradea/Nagyvárad, Satu Mare/Szatmár, Timișoara/Temesvár, and Iași are subordinated to the archdiocese of Bucharest. In the dioceses of Oradea/Nagyvárad and Satu Mare/Szatmár the vast majority of the Catholics are Hungarian speakers, while the Timișoara/Temesvár diocese is ethnically mixed. The Catholics of Moldova belonging to the diocese of Iași are mostly Romanian-speakers.[6] At the local level, Hungarian- and Romanian-speaking believers belong to the same parish; however, if the community is linguistically divided, they attend separate (Romanian-, respectively Hungarian-language) masses. In several cases, the Romanian-speaking Catholics form personal parishes,[7] which are non-territorial units formed on linguistic grounds. In practice, the Romanian and Hungarian speakers form distinct communities in both cases.

The Evanghelic-Lutheran Church is the organization of non-German-speaking Lutherans and its members are mostly Hungarians and Slovaks. Organizationally it consists of three dioceses, two of them

[6]On the issue of Catholics in Moldova see Chapter 10 (*Demographic Dynamics and Ethnic Classification*) of this volume.

[7]On personal parishes see: http://resurrectioncatholic.church/personal-parish/.

being predominantly Hungarian and one is predominantly Slovak. The majority of the Hungarian Lutherans (9155 of 12,431) live in Brașov/Brassó county and (together with 797 Lutherans in Covasna/Kovászna county) belong to the Diocese of Brașov/Brassó. Cluj/Kolozsvár is the center of the other Hungarian-speaking diocese and it is also the seat of the Evanghelic-Lutherans bishop of Romania.

None of the neo-protestant churches is of Hungarian majority. In case of Jehovah's Witnesses the proportion of Hungarians is 23%, among Baptists 11%, and among Adventists 10%, while among Pentecostals less than 2%. In the case of the Baptists and Pentecostals, there are separate Hungarian unions of congregations. Thus, the Hungarian-speaking Baptist and Pentecostal congregations integrate relatively autonomously into the organizational structure of their churches (otherwise organized on territorial criteria). In the case of the Adventist Church and of the Jehovah's Witnesses territorial organization has priority and the Hungarian-speaking congregations are not organized in separate structures.

2.1 Missionary Institutions

There are several religious institutions which are external to the organizational structure of the churches, but which share their original and main scope, namely the spiritual salvation of the believers. These institutions target particular segments of the church members and usually undertake additional functions. I discuss three types of such organizations, namely women's associations, youth organizations, and religious movements.

All historical Hungarian churches have their own women's associations. The Association of Lutheran Women was founded in 1908 (Kovács 2007), the Unitarian organization in 1910,[8] the Catholic in

[8]See a short presentation on the history of the organization on the webpage of the Transylvanian Unitarian Church: http://unitarius.org/szerkezet/unitarius-nok-orszagos-szovetsege/ (Accessed on 2 February 2018).

1926 (Kuszálik 2010), while the Reformed in 1927.[9] The aim of these associations was (and is) the strengthening of religious life, providing various forms of social care, helping local religious communities, and organizing cultural events. Women's associations had been officially disbanded by the Communist authorities following 1948 and were reorganized only after 1989. These associations were established in close cooperation with the leadership of the churches, in some cases being even initiated by the religious authorities. In the case of Protestant churches, the main promoters of the women's associations are usually the wives of the pastors. This is the main reason why women's associations are more robust in the case of Protestant churches compared to the Catholics. The Catholic Church has only 33 local branches of its women's association, while more than three quarters of Unitarian and Reformed communities have their own local women's associations. However, at a closer look these differences between Catholics and Protestants are less substantive. First, one should take into consideration that in the case of the Protestant churches every creative and leisure time activity organized for women may be reported as performed by the "women's association". Second, the same activities are present also among Catholic women; however, they are performed in the framework of other organizations, such as the Altar Societies or Rosary Assemblies.

In the case of the Reformed Church, there are two youth organizations, one in each of the bishoprics. The Christian Youth Association (*Ifjúsági Keresztény Egylet* or IKE) is the youth organization of the Transylvanian bishopric, while the Királyhágómellék Reformed Youth Organization (*Királyhágómelléki Református Ifjúsági Szövetség* or KRISZ) is that of the Királyhágómellék bishopric. The Unitarian youth organization is named Dávid Ferenc Youth Association (*Országos Dávid Ferenc Ifjúsági Egylet* or ODFIE). All these youth organizations have a hierarchical structure and their territorial organization mirrors that of the churches. The Catholic youth associations are organized by dioceses. In the territory of the Alba Iulia/Gyulafehérvár archdiocese the Youth

[9] See a short presentation on the history of the organization on the webpage of the Transylvanian Reformed Bishopric: http://www.reformatus.ro/20141209noszovetseg.html (Accessed on 2 February 2018).

Archpriestship of the Archdiocese (*Főegyházmegyei Ifjúsági Főlelkészség* or FIF) coordinates the local youth organizations, also integrating other independent initiatives of the Catholic youth. In the Satu Mare/Szatmár Diocese the Szatmár County Youth Bureau (Szatmár Megyei Ifjúsági Iroda) has a similar coordinating role. The main goal of these organizations is the intensification of religious life among the youth and various tools are employed for this objective: community building, sport activities, conferences, and musical events.

There is another group of religious institutions established and run by non-mainstream church members, who are in some respect dissatisfied with the actual organization of the churches and have special religious demands. These groups usually have a movement-like organization. Some of them aspire to change the actual religious and moral order dominating the mainstream structure of the denomination they belong to. As a consequence, their relations with religious authorities is often tense or even openly conflictual. Non-mainstream movements can be found in the highest number inside the Catholic Church. On the one hand, Catholic religious orders can be classified as such, and on the other, associations of the faithful. The Catholic orders had a long history in Transylvania. They had been dismissed by the Communist authorities in 1948 and reorganized following 1989. Many of the faithful associations are connected to these orders (such as the Secular Franciscan Order or Lay Carmelites). Others are formed by clerics (Neocatechumenal Way) or by young believers (Catholic Charismatic Renewal, Net of Catholic Communities—or simply The Net, Scouts). While the Catholic religious orders have only several hundred members, several thousands of people are connected to the faithful's associations.

The CE Union is a longstanding religious movement of the Reformed Church. The movement has its origins in the USA, being connected to the Christian Endeavor Movement. The movement had taken root in Hungary during the first decade of the twentieth century, and then it appeared in Cluj/Kolozvár and spread throughout Transylvania during the interwar period. The movement was banned as a formal organization by the Communist authorities, and, as a consequence, the remaining local communities were forced to operate in illegality. The CE Union was reorganized and registered as a formal association after 1989. Both reformed pastors and lay church members are part of the movement.

While women's associations and youth organizations are controlled by the religious leadership, the position of the religious movements is different. They are based on micro-communities and on close interpersonal relations. The communities share strongly egalitarian values (between clerics and laypeople, leaders and followers, men and women, different social strata, etc.), while the organizational structure of the movements is deliberately decentralized, the local communities being organized largely autonomously (Horváth 1995). The movements have a strongly engaged membership, personal conversion, evangelization, and the emotional content of the community events playing a central role in their religiosity (Kiss 2009).

3 The Social Involvement of the Churches

In addition to organizational structures serving strictly religious purposes, church-founded institutions also have a strong influence in several other social domains. As previously mentioned, there is an overall tendency in Romania for religion to permeate other social fields too, and this is particularly strong in the case of the Hungarian community. The Hungarian churches operate a large network of educational and social care institutions; they have cultural associations; they operate printing houses in order to publish their own periodicals and book series; they have enterprises (such as restaurants, hotels) which are aimed to sustain financially their social implication. The church-run educational and social care systems are of particular importance, so in the remaining parts of this chapter, I outline some major characteristics of these systems.

3.1 Educational Institutions

The two largest denominations (Roman Catholics and Reformed) run a complex network of educational institutions, which covers the whole spectrum of public education from kindergartens to universities (see Table 7). The implication of these churches is the most significant in upper secondary education: In Transylvania, there are 23 high schools operated by these churches, the majority of them having century-long histories and functioning in buildings which had been nationalized by Communist authorities and then restituted following the change of the regime. One should also emphasize the ongoing expansion of religious education at the expanse of the secular schools. In many cases, the process of property restitution was a conflicting process. Often other (secular) educational institutions were functioning in the buildings that should have been restituted, some of them having Hungarian as their language of education. In some cases, only the newly established religious educational institution remained in the restituted building. This is the case of Reformed College in Cluj/Kolozsár and of the Gerhardinum Roman Catholic Lyceum in Timişoara/Temesvár. In other cases, the secular and the religious schools function in the same building, as in the case of Catholic Lyceums in Târgu Mureș/Marosvásárhely and Miercurea Ciuc/Csíkszereda or of the Reformed Lyceum in Târgu Mureș/Marosvásárhely. In some cases, religious background is signaled only by a sole section of theological profile in an otherwise secular institution. The majority of the religious schools perceive themselves as successors of century-long institutional structures; however, in some cases the educational institutions are completely new. According to the law, in order for an upper secondary educational institution to qualify as theological, it should have at least one class with theological profile, but alongside these classes, the institutions can offer additional specializations too (including professional education[10]). Being an educational institution with religious background has practical implications as well. These institutions receive state finances, similarly to secular ones, but they receive some degree of decisional autonomy, which is linked to the church. The most important of these is their influence on the selection of personnel. Teaching and additional staff need special permissions from the church

[10]The Hungarian-language professional training in Cluj/Kolozsvár and Oradea/Nagyvárad was reorganized in the framework of religious institutions.

Table 7 Church-run educational institutions with Hungarian-language education (2016)

	Reformed	Roman Catholic	Unitarian	Baptist	Evanghelic-Lutherans	Total/level of education
Kindergartens, primary and lower secondary schools	8	4	1	1	1	14
Higher secondary education	9	12	2	0	0	23
Post-secondary	4	1	0	0	0	5
Tertiary	3	2	1	1	1	8
Total/church	23	18	4	2	2	49

to apply for positions in these schools. This right is used in most cases to preselect the staff before the application procedure, as the permission is not issued to persons regarded as undesirable. In other words, religious educational institutions have an important advantage compared to secular institutions, which have no influence over the centralized system of employment and tenure characteristic of pre-university education in Romania.

Most elementary schools and kindergartens run by the churches institutionally belong to the high schools discusses earlier, though some of them function separately; most of the latter have been established under special circumstances. Several kindergartens are highly prestigious and target upper middle-class families with special demands. The mixed Hungarian- and English-language kindergarten in Cluj/Kolozsvár, or the music kindergarten in Oradea/Nagyvárad, can be mentioned in this respect. Some religious elementary schools and kindergartens follow alternative pedagogic methods, such as step-by-step education or the Montessori Method.

Church-operated colleges and universities are at the top of the religious educational system. The most important ones are the theological faculties responsible for training the clergy. The Protestant Theological Institute of Cluj/Kolozsvár is run jointly by the Reformed, Unitarian, and Evanghelic-Lutheran Churches, while the Catholics have their own Theological College and Seminary in Alba Iulia/Gyulafehérár. The Baptist Church also has a Hungarian language Theological Faculty, within the Emanuel University in Oradea/Nagyvárad. The training of religion teachers is, however, restricted to the two largest denominations; in the case of the Roman Catholic and the Reformed Church, it is organized within the public higher-education system, at two separate theological faculties of the Babeş-Bolyai University in Cluj/Kolozsvár. In the case of the smaller denominations, it is usually members of the clergy who carry out the religious instruction in pre-university education, as the low number of children rarely permits education in separate groups.

The low number of children is also the main reason why the smaller denominations operate only very few religious educational institutions. For instance, both the Evanghelic-Lutherans and the Baptist Church only operate a single Hungarian language kindergarten each. Of the smaller churches, the Unitarian Church is somewhat exceptional, as it operates two high schools, in Cristuru Seciuesc/Székelykeresztúr (situated in the southwestern part of Harghita/Hargita county, where Unitarian believers live in high concentration) and in Cluj/Kolozsvár, of which especially the latter has quite a high prestige, being attractive for Hungarian-speaking children of all denominations.

Next to the above-mentioned institutions there are several church-operated dormitories in the major educational centers of Transylvania, the most important being the Apafi Mihály Reformed College in Cluj/Kolozsvár and the Saint Emeric (Szent Imre) College in Târgu Mureş/Marosvásárhely. Several educational and conference centers are also part of the religious educational network.

3.2 Social Care and Social Services Provided by the Churches

As Botond Dániel highlighted, there is quite an extended network of ethnically organized social care institutions in Transylvania. In a quantitative survey conducted in 2013, Dániel identified 223 functioning organizations belonging to an ethnically defined (Hungarian) field of social care, 28.3% of these, including the most important ones, being operated by the Hungarian churches (Dániel 2014, p. 94).

The Reformed and the Roman Catholic Churches operate the most extended network of institutions providing social services.

The social and charity services provided by the Roman Catholic Church are organized in several larger organizational groups, the most important of them being the Caritas, the Charity Service of the Order of Malta, the Saint Francis Foundation in Deva/Déva, the Csibész Foundation, the Faith and Light community and the Kolping Families movement.

Caritas Internationalis is a large confederation of Roman Catholic charity and social service organizations having members in 200 countries around the world. The Romanian Caritas Confederation (*Confederația Caritas România*) is a member of Caritas Europa (residing in Brussels) and of Caritas Internationalis (residing in Vatican City). From a Hungarian perspective, Caritas Gyulafehérvár/Alba Iulia, operated by the Roman Catholic Archbishopric, is of central importance. The organization had gained the status of a public benefit organization in 2004 and became an officially authorized social care provider in 2005. It also gained the authorization to organize officially recognized trainings for social workers. Caritas has a multiple organizational structure, made up on the one hand of territorial branches and offices and on the other of programs established to cover certain domains of social care. The most important permanent programs of the charity organization are the general social program, the home care program for ill, disabled, and elderly persons, and the social reintegration program for youngsters leaving orphanages. The general social program (the so-called parish Caritas) means a permanent monitoring of the social needs of local communities. This is carried out by the county-level branches, working offices, and parish-level groups of the organization. The distribution of these local-level structures mirrors the geographic distribution of the Roman Catholic population. The network involved in the general social program is made up of three county-level branches (all of them in the Székely Land), eight working offices, and more than one hundred parish-level groups. A logistic center (in Miercurea Ciuc/Csíkszereda) having capacity to receive large aid supplies also belongs to the network. The home care program is also present in many Transylvanian localities and provides assistance for more than 6000 people. One should also emphasize that Caritas is one of the most important home care providers in Romania and a founding member of SeniorNet (the association of the home care providers in Romania). Home care services are much more widespread in Hungarian-speaking Catholic areas (most importantly in Harghita/Hargita, Mureș/Maros, and Kovászna/Covasna counties) than in other regions of Romania. The most important group of beneficiaries is that of lonely elderly people, but many ill and disabled persons also receive home care from the Caritas organizations. The program is run in close cooperation with the Ministry of Health and local governments. The "House of Hope" (*Reménység Háza*) program is present in four settlements and aims to help the social integration of orphans reaching adulthood. Next to these programs, Caritas has several periodic projects and operates four nursing homes and a daily program center for elderly people, a summer resort, and an educational center for socially disadvantaged children. The agricultural program of Caritas can be regarded as a social enterprise. It provides up-to-date expertise and machinery for people engaged in subsistence agricultural production.

The Charity Service of the Order of Malta in Romania was established in 1991 under the tutelage of the Sovereign Order of Malta and with the help of German, Austrian, and Hungarian twin-organizations. It is a non-profit organization with its own legal personality having 22 branches all around Transylvania (plus one in Bucharest) with Cluj/Kolozsvár as its headquarters. The Charity Service has 1400 volunteers, 18 local youth associations, and more than 100 periodic and permanent programs. Its most important activities are clubs for the elderly, an integration program for Roma children, and another for disabled children, while its most important occasional activity consists of distributing aid packages among socially disadvantaged families.[11]

The Saint Francis Foundation in Deva/Déva was established on local initiative and has become the best-known Catholic charity organization of Transylvania. Its most important activity consists of operating

[11]On the activity of the Charity Service of the Order of Malta, see their webpage: http://www.maltez.ro/index-hu.php.

a number of charity schools for orphans, abandoned children, and for those coming from socially disadvantaged families. The majority of its centers are run by a system of adoptive parents. The foundation also operates several dormitories, schools and more than a dozen kindergartens for its children. Additionally, it organizes after-school programs for Roma and other socially disadvantaged children.[12]

The Csibész Foundation deals with the reintegration of youngsters leaving the orphanages and takes care of orphans through a system of adoptive parents. The foundation owns more than 30 houses and has three workshops. The youngsters live in the houses of the foundation, while the workshops help them learn a profession, facilitating their integration on the labor market.[13] The "Faith and Light" groups are also connected to an international network and consist of disabled children, their relatives and persons who wish to help them. They have regular common activities each second week or at least once a month. In 2006, they were present in 11 localities. The Kolping Families movement is organized within the framework of Catholic parishes. The organization of these groups imitates that of families, meaning (among other things) that they are composed by people of different ages. They can be perceived as self-study groups and are also characterized by deep social engagement.

In case of the Reformed Church, it is much more difficult to provide a comprehensive overview of social care and charity services. The network connected to the Reformed Church is far less centralized, and many initiatives are connected to the local communities and parishes. Local congregations are legally and financially autonomous entities that have the right to establish their own foundations and associations. Consequently, the Reformed charity institutions are not connected (at least legally) to each other. Their activities are, however, similar to those of the Catholic organizations. The Reformed Church also runs charity schools, orphanages, nursing homes, provides home care

[12]On the activity of the Saint Francis Foundation, see their webpage: http://szentferencalapitvany.org/.

[13]On the activity of the Csibész Foundation, see their webpage: http://www.csibesz.ro/wordpress/hu/.

services, programs of Roma integration, organizes after-schools for disadvantaged children, and also takes care of orphans in a system of adoptive parents.

At a central level, the Diakónia Christian Foundation (*Diakónia Keresztyén Alapítvány*) should be mentioned, which was established by the Transylvanian Reformed Church District and has local branches in five Transylvanian cities, namely in Cluj/Kolozsvár, Târgu Mureș/Marosvásárhely, Sfântu Gheorghe/Sepsiszentgyörgy, Reghin/Szászrégen, and Oradea/Nagyvárad. It provides home care services, social programs for children, nursing centers, and care for addicted persons.[14] Bonus Pastor Foundation is specialized in assistance for and recovery of addicted persons. It is a founding member of the Romanian Substance Abuse and Addiction Coalition (ROSAAC).[15] The CE Union is also active in the social domain. It defines social engagement as the key domain of its activity (next to the religious mission). Its most important activities include care for the elderly (Adopt a Granny Program), large families (Family Care Program), and programs for children with tuberculosis (Hannah Project). Additionally, they run a charity school and two nursing homes.[16]

The smaller denominations also operate a number of social organizations. In the case of the Unitarian Church, the Unitarcoop Foundation should be mentioned. This organization runs the Unitarian Care Service (*Unitárius Gondozó Szolgálat*) organizing home care and daily activities for elderly people. The Christian Gipsy Mission Foundation of the Baptist Church is also remarkably active. It specializes in Roma integration and is present in more than 60 localities, especially among Hungarian-speaking Roma living next to the Hungarian border.[17]

---

[14]On the activity of the Diakónia Christian Foundation, see their webpage: http://www.diakonia.ro/index_hu.php.

[15]On the activity of the Bonus Pastor Foundation, see their webpage: http://bonuspastor.ro/rolunk/.

[16]On the activity of the CE Union, see their webpage: http://ce-union.ro/ce/index.php/hu/szolgalataink/diakonia/dorcasotthon.

[17]On the activity of the Christian Gipsy Mission Foundation, see their webpage: http://www.gipsymission.com/.

4 Conclusion

In Romania, the ethnic cleavage between Romanians and Hungarians is reinforced by the religious fault line, which further contributes to the pillar-like organization of the Hungarian community. Religious institutions have a central role in the life of Transylvanian Hungarians and in the maintenance or construction of a parallel Hungarian society. On the one hand, as the survey results pointed out, a high percentage of Hungarians are actively religious, 34% attending church, and almost half of them praying regularly. Although in the past decade this number probably dropped, it is still significant compared to both Western Europe and even other Central and Eastern European societies. On the other hand, and even more importantly from the perspective of this volume, the Hungarian churches have important non-religious institutional roles as well. Institutions supported or funded by the churches are active in the field of education and social services, and there are many NGOs closely linked to the churches. Most of these institutions have an empathically Hungarian character, and in many cases complement or even substitute state institutions in their domain of activity.

The Hungarian churches of Transylvania (the Reformed Church and the Unitarian Church in particular) take over some functions from the state and fill it with ethnic content. This role they perform in the building of a parallel Hungarian society becomes even more important in the context of the latest developments of Hungary's kin-state policies, in which the Churches have become the most important beneficiaries of the financial flows from Hungary, receiving resources of comparable magnitude to those that the Romanian state allocates for the Hungarian minority.[18] Although the consequences of these developments are yet unknown, some problems can be emphasized in the matter. First, as more and more functions and tasks are taken over from the Romanian state, Transylvanian Hungarians could become even less attached to the state they live in, and the state's interest in their accommodation could

[18]On the financial aid channeled to Transylvania by the Hungarian state (described as a strategy of material outbidding) see the relevant sections of Chapter 3 of this volume.

decrease as well. Second, by controlling significant financial resources and having a high legitimacy among the population, the churches might increasingly turn toward actively participating in the social and political affairs of the Transylvanian Hungarian community, similarly to their behavior characteristic in the interwar era.[19]

References

Berger, P. L. (Ed.). (1999a). *The desecularization of the world: Resurgent religion and world politics*. Washington, DC: Ethics and Public Policy Center; Grand Rapids, MI: W. B. Eerdmans.

Berger, P. L. (1999b). The desecularization of the world: A global overview. In P. L. Berger (Ed.), *The desecularization of the world: Resurgent religion and world politics* (pp. 1–18). Washington, DC: Ethics and Public Policy Center; Grand Rapids, MI: W. B. Eerdmans.

Casanova, J. (1994). *Public religions in the modern world*. Chicago: University of Chicago Press.

Dániel, B. (2014). Az erdélyi magyar nonprofit hátterű szociális szféra szociológiai jellemzői. *Civil Szemle, 11*(1), 81–107.

Enache, S., Andreescu, L., Ardelean, L., Cernea, R., Kacsó, J.-A., Moise, E., & Szokoly, E. (2008). *Educaţia religioasă în şcolile publice*. Târgu-Mureş: Liga Pro Europa.

EVS. (2011). European values study 2008: Integrated dataset (EVS 2008) (Version 3.0.0). Accessed 20 November 2011.

Gheorghe, M. (2004). *Religie şi schimbare socială în România*. Iași: Editura Fundaţiei Axis.

Horváth, Z. (1995). Katolikus bázisközösségi mozgalmak. In Z. Horváth (Ed.), *Hitek és emberek*. Budapest: ELTE Szociológiai-Szociálpolitikai Intézet.

Karpov, V. (2010). Desecularization: A conceptual framework. *Journal of Church and State, 52*(2), 232–270.

Kiss, D. (2009). *Revivalist movements in the Romaniai Historical Churches* (REVACERN Paper No. 78).

[19]The structure of the minority institutional system in the interwar era is discussed in Chapter 2.

Kovács, E. (2007, Január). Az Erdélyi Evangélikus Nőszövetség történetéből. *Művelődés*.

Kuszálik, P. (2010). *Erdélyi Katolikus Nőszövetség*. Magyar Katolikus Lexikon. Budapest: Szent István Társulat. Available at: http://lexikon.katolikus.hu/E/Erd%C3%A9lyi%20Katolikus%20N%C5%91sz%C3%B6vets%C3%A9g.html. Accessed 2 February 2018.

Moise, E. (2004). Church-state relation in the religious education in Romanian public schools. *Journal for the Study of Religions and Ideologies, 3*(7), 77–100.

Stan, L., & Turcescu, L. (2005). Religious education in Romania. *Communist and Post-Communist Studies, 38*(3), 381–401.

Stan, L., & Turcescu, L. (2007). *Religion and politics in post-Communist Romania. Religion and global politics series*. Oxford and New York: Oxford University Press.

Tomka, M. (1998). A vallásosság mérése. In A. Máté-Tóth & M. Jahn (Eds.), *Studia religiosa: tanulmányok András Imre 70. születésnapjára Acta Studiorum Religionis Szegedini* (pp. 18–31). Szeged: Bába és Társa Kiadó.

Tomka, M. (2005). *A legvallásosabb ország?: vallásosság Szatmárban, Erdélyben, Romániában*. PPKE: Budapest and Piliscsaba.

Voicu, M. (2007). *România religioasă: pe valul european sau în urma lui?* Iași: Institutul European.

8

Media Consumption and the Hungarian-Language Media in Transylvania

Tamás Kiss

This chapter discusses the institutional structure of the Hungarian-language media in Romania and its impact on the media-consumption patterns of Transylvanian Hungarians. The two central concepts in the literature that focus on mass media in minority languages are institutional and functional completeness. As emphasized by Moring (2007, 2013), institutional completeness (meaning that all types and genres of media are available in the minority language) is a necessary but not sufficient condition of functional completeness (which means that a wide range of minority language channels is used regularly by members of the community and that the mother tongue dominates their media consumption). By contrast, if some types and genres of media are not covered by minority language providers, the bilingual minority audience would inevitably shift toward majority-language products.

T. Kiss (✉)
Romanian Institute for Research on National Minorities,
Cluj-Napoca, Romania

T. Kiss et al. (eds.), *Unequal Accommodation of Minority Rights*,
Palgrave Politics of Identity and Citizenship Series,
https://doi.org/10.1007/978-3-319-78893-7_8

One of the main arguments of this chapter is that the media-consumption patterns of Transylvanian Hungarians are unusual. The community under discussion is one of Europe's largest ethnic or national minorities, which, at least theoretically, could support a complex and complete media structure. But the system of Hungarian-language media produced in Transylvania is far from institutional—and thus functional—completeness. According to Morning's thesis, this situation should have produced a shift toward Romanian-language media organs. However, this has not happened in Transylvania. On the contrary, the Hungarian language has become dominant in the media consumption of Transylvanian Hungarians during the last two decades, but this is due to their incorporation in a Budapest-centered transnational Hungarian-language media-space. In other words, the incomplete structure of the minority media did not lead to a shift toward majority-language products, but to increased consumption of media content produced in Hungary.

This chapter not only provides a description of the minority media system and of media-consumption patterns, but also attempts to analyze the consequences of the above-mentioned shift, making use of several conceptual and normative models. The first section presents these theoretical frameworks. This is followed by a discussion of some general features affecting the institutional structure of the Hungarian-language media in Transylvania. The third part provides a mapping of the institutional actors and presents survey data about the media consumption of the Transylvanian Hungarian public. The fourth part contains some concluding remarks, focusing on the possible consequences of institutional incompleteness and the growing predominance of broadcasters from Hungary.

1 Complementary Normative and Analytical Frameworks

There are several normative and analytical frameworks in which the issues of minority (language) media are usually discussed, or can be discussed. In this chapter, we rely on three alternative frameworks: namely on the models of *language preservation*, of *media pluralism*, and on an argument about *competing nation-building projects*. Minority media is often discussed in the first two frameworks, while the third framework is closely connected with the topic of this section of the present volume—namely institutionally sustained ethnic parallelism. In my opinion, these frameworks are complementary and non-exclusive. Nevertheless, they focus on different functions of the minority language media. In the language preservation paradigm, sociolinguistic functions and language policies are at the forefront. The media pluralism approach focuses on how minorities participate and are represented in the public sphere, which is considered essential from the perspective of both social inclusion and functioning democracies. Finally, the framework of competing nation-building projects deals with the effects of media on national identity, political mobilization, and ethnic boundary maintenance. It is also important that the dominance of the broadcasters based in Hungary can be evaluated differently from the perspective of these three theoretical approaches.

Minority media is most frequently discussed within the framework of *language preservation*. The rise of this paradigm as both an analytical and normative framework is not accidental: It is connected to the transnational and especially European-level institutionalization of minority language preservation efforts. The most important instruments are the 1992 European Charter for Regional or Minority Languages and the 1995 Framework Convention for the Protection of National Minorities. The Charter's Article 11 explicitly refers to electronic media and written press in minority languages as important tools of language preservation.[1] Joshua Fishman (1991, 2001) and the ethno-linguistic vitality approach (Giles et al. 1977; Yagmur and Ehala 2011) represent the most important intellectual roots of this perspective. Authors associated with the language preservation paradigm emphasize the deeply asymmetric character of language regimes (Cormack 1998, 2007). Due to these asymmetries, minority languages become vulnerable and endangered and there exists a permanent threat that they will be overwhelmed by

[1]Reports, shadow reports, and other documents are produced within the monitoring mechanism of the Charter. This clearly increases the visibility and influence of the language preservation discourse in the field of minority media. The Mercator Research Center should also be mentioned in this context. See https://www.mercator-research.eu/en/.

the majority language.[2] Consequently, special policies are needed to counterbalance these tendencies and to increase the vitality of minority linguistic communities. Mass media is one of the most important domains of language preservation policies, as media consumption is an important everyday activity which affects daily language use and is also an important tool of language normalization and standardization. It is a widespread presupposition that (at least autochthonous) minorities are largely bilingual and they use majority-language media too. Under these circumstances, policies concerning minority media are aimed at counterbalancing the predominance of majority-language media. One should also highlight that, from the perspective of language preservation, the language used in media takes prominence, while it is of secondary importance whether the media content is produced by the minority community itself or transmitted from the kin-state.[3]

Minority media is also often discussed in the framework of *media pluralism*, another robust analytical and normative framework connected to EU-level institutions, such as the Media Pluralism Monitor.[4] Researchers connected to this framework focus on the media access and representation of minority groups. As Klimkiewicz has highlighted, three indicators are of primal importance here (2015, p. 84): (1) the fair and adequate representation of minorities (meaning their language, lifestyle, etc.) in the mainstream media; (2) the access of minority group members to media services, including media production; and (3) the existence of minority (language) media structures. In this framework, the notion of the public sphere is of primary importance. Without entering into further detail and debate, the public sphere can be defined operationally as a social field in which actors communicate, discuss, and reconcile different interpretations concerning issues of public interest.

[2]Under the circumstances of globalization, this issue also arises at the transnational level due to the predominance of English, so that even some languages with official status could become overwhelmed and thus endangered (Moring 2013).

[3]For a comparative analysis concerning Transylvanian Hungarians, see Vincze (2013). This author makes no difference between media content produced in the kin-state and by minority actors.

[4]MPM is a project founded by the EU. It assesses the risks to media pluralism in the member states. See Valcke et al. (2015) for a general presentation.

Mass media is obviously the most important institution of the public sphere, as it provides the information which is the basis of public discussion. Cormack has highlighted that public spheres can be defined as "speech communities", and, as a consequence, bilingual minority members may participate simultaneously in both majority-language and minority language public spheres (1998, p. 43). Therefore, indicators of media pluralism refer to both majority- and minority language public spheres. In an optimal situation, minority group members should be able to manage the image of their community in the mainstream (majority language) media and should have their own media system (in their vernacular) which functions as an arena for internal public debate.

This duality of the majority (or mainstream) and minority public spheres is reflected by two partially overlapping typologies of policies concerning media pluralism and minority media, as elaborated by Beata Klimkiewicz (2003, 2015). In her most recent typology, Klimkiewicz distinguished between external and internal media pluralism on the one hand and proportional and open representation of cultural diversity on the other (2015, pp. 100–102). The external approach to media pluralism tries to establish an institutional system that underpins a parallel minority public sphere while the internal approach focuses on access to and adequate representation in mainstream media of minorities. The proportional approach of cultural diversity allocates time and space in public media to different groups according to their proportion in the overall population, while the open approach tries to represent different cultural preferences equally. This fourfold typology overlaps partially with an earlier classification of Klimkiewicz (2003, pp. 173–176), in which she differentiated between four types of media policies, namely: (1) the autonomous media system model; (2) the minority protection model; (3) the anti-discrimination model; and (4) the assimilationist model. In the *autonomous model*, the emphasis is on the existence of a separate minority media system. This system is not part of the public broadcasting system and is not financed directly by central governmental structures of the minorities' host state, but is sustained by private economic actors or by organs of self-government. This latter situation is possible if territorial or non-territorial forms of autonomy exist. In the autonomous model, media content is produced by minority elites, who also dominate minority media institutions. In the *minority protection* model, the minority media is part of the public broadcasting system. Time and space for minority language broadcasting can be allocated proportionally (meaning several hours of minority language TV and radio programs per week), and it is also possible that a wider range of minority language electronic media and written press is sustained by the central government. Media content is produced by journalists belonging to the minority community; however, these structures do not have financial autonomy vis-á-vis state structures, and minority elites do not have institutional dominance. The *anti-discrimination* model focuses on the media representation and access of minorities in the mainstream media. The first stake involves the politically correct and adequate presentation of the minority group, which is often monitored by specialized authorities. It is also an important question whether minority journalists have access to media production and whether minority group members can manage the image of their own community. Consequently, an important tool of anti-discrimination policy is financing minority broadcasting offices which produce media content in the language of the majority. Lastly, in the *assimilationist model*, the emphasis is once again on access to the mainstream media; however, minorities are not regarded as a visible category who are deemed capable of managing their own image.

One should emphasize that the massive presence of satellite channels and of media produced by kin-state actors raises important questions concerning media pluralism. It is often argued (mostly concerning immigrant communities) that intensive consumption of "home-state" media products can be a barrier to social integration and participation in the (mainstream) public sphere of the "host" country. Another striking question is, whether minority communities (or minority elites) are capable of managing their own image in the kin-state media?

The third framework is that of *nation building*. Scholars of nationalism have emphasized that mass media and nationalism are intertwined phenomena: Mass media was created in the framework of nation-states and played an essential role in consolidating "imagined communities", i.e., creating a sense of simultaneity beyond local communities and micro-milieus (Anderson 2006). In Chapter 3, which focuses on the political organization and mobilization of the Hungarian minority, we have relied on the triadic nexus model of Brubaker (1996) and argued that minority populations are in general exposed to the competing nationalizing projects of different actors which try to extend their influence over these entities and which compete for their loyalty. The nationalizing state tries to institutionalize its vision of an ethnic or national minority which should be accommodated or integrated. Minority elites try to establish and maintain a solidary and politically mobilized community, or to push for an institutionally sustained ethnic parallelism. The kin-state tries to institutionalize its claim that the minority group belongs to the transnation which should be virtually unified across state borders. In the institutionalization of these claims, mass media is of central importance. Patterns of media consumption among national minorities determine what kind of "imagined community" is plausible. The institutional structure of the mass media also affects directly the political mobilization capacity of different actors.

2 General Features That Affect the Hungarian-Language Media System in Transylvania

Scholars of minority language media emphasize that the size and the structure of the minority matter (de Swaan 1991; Cormack 1998). Transylvanian Hungarians are one of the largest minority communities in Europe: Their number exceeds that of the titular groups in Estonia and Latvia and comes close to that of Slovenes. Furthermore, they are not an assimilated minority community whose ethnic differences are expressed only symbolically on festive occasions, but their ethnic and linguistic boundaries are consistently salient in a broad array of contexts ranging from everyday interactions to the marriage market, choices concerning education and political options.[5] Also, Hungarians and Romanians are components of an unranked system of groups,[6] meaning

[5]For symbolic ethnicity, see Gans (1979). For an interpretation of assimilation as ethnic boundary blurring, see Alba and Nee (2003).

[6]For the distinction between ranked and unranked systems of groups, see Horowitz (1985, pp. 21–36).

that Hungarians are present in each social stratum and that Hungarian elites still successfully control numerous institutional channels of social mobility. This also means that Transylvanian Hungarians have their own elites who are interested in community organizing and aware of the role played by mass media in this process. Finally, Transylvanian Hungarians are a politically organized and mobilized minority community with a political class engaged in a process of bargaining with majority political actors. Based on these features, one would expect, at least in theory, the existence of an autonomous and institutionally complete system of Hungarian-language media in Transylvania.

However, the Hungarian-language media in Romania is far from being either instructionally complete or autonomous. To cite the sociologist and media researcher Tivadar Magyari, "*Hungarian-language media in Romania is too complex and too wide-ranging to be considered a typical minority media system, but it is too 'minoritarian' to be considered a fully-fledged system*" (2003, p. 113). There are several factors hindering institutional completeness. First, as Magyari emphasized, Hungarians in Transylvania are not geographically concentrated but territorially dispersed over a large area of more than 100,000 km^2. Regional differences are also considerable: In the Székely Land, they constitute the majority; however, only less than 40% of the total Hungarian population is concentrated in this area. Outside the Székely Land, Hungarians are mostly a minority locally, and this is even more accentuated in the large and economically prosperous urban centers. Consequently, media marketing professionals do not consider Transylvanian Hungarians a distinct segment, and this significantly reduced the chances of Hungarian-language advertising.[7] Second, the Romanian administrative structure is highly centralized, and no regional bodies or institutions of minority segmental autonomy exist which could support an

[7]One should emphasize that segments for media marketing are obviously socially constructed, and in this process, not only "objective characteristics" (such as territorial dispersion or concentration) but also perceptions matter. From this perspective, the problem is that the perception that ethnic parallelism does not work in the economic sphere is widely shared.

autonomous media system.[8] One could argue that the state does allocate financing directly to the minority organizations, among them RMDSZ, and that that some funds are actually channeled toward minority language media (Mohácsek 2009). However, these funds are far from sufficient for financing a complete media system. Third, the Romanian policies concerning minority language media are closer to what Klimkiewicz (2003) called the minority protection model than to supporting an autonomous Hungarian-language media system. The most important consequence is that there is no public Hungarian-language TV station which can be received across the entire territory of Transylvania. Furthermore, Romanian public TV allocates insufficient time to Hungarian-language broadcasting. On the nationwide public networks, the proportion of Hungarian-language programs is less than 1%. In 2007, a foundation specially set up for this purpose by RMDSZ started to create the channel *Erdély TV* (Transylvania TV), with the intention of later providing 24/7 programming in Hungarian language that could be received over the entire territory of Transylvania.[9] However, this project lacks substantial and sustainable financing, and the programs still cannot be received in the majority of Hungarian-language households. Fourth, some characteristics of Hungarian journalism also hinder institutional completeness. Papp (2005) emphasized that elitism and contempt for certain popular genres are widespread among Transylvanian Hungarian journalists. Hungarian-language media is an intellectualized field which is reluctant to address the experiences of lower social strata, largely lacks a business orientation, and is focused mostly on highbrow culture and politics. These characteristics, however, explain only partially the general lack of popular genres (entertainment, tabloids, etc.) in the Hungarian-language media. The lack of adequate financial support is far more significant in this respect.

---

[8]As Cormack (1998, p. 41) highlighted, the weakness of central government and the strength of relevant regional bodies is constitutive, as "governments are not likely to give anything to a minority". Klimkiewicz (2003) also argued that autonomous regional bodies are the most important financers of autonomous media systems (where they exist).

[9]The Janovics Jenő Foundation, created in 2004. Erdély means Transylvania in Hungarian.

3 Institutional Structure and Media Consumption

In the empirical part of this chapter, we rely on two types of sources. First, an exhaustive survey that targeted Hungarian-language media institutions was carried out by the Media Institute of the Hungarian National Media and Info-communication Authority in 2010 (Apró 2012).[10] Based on this source, we describe the actors in the Hungarian-language media market in Transylvania. Second, several surveys representative for Transylvanian Hungarians were carried out between 1997 and 2015. The most important of these was a survey carried out in October 2015 by the Romanian Institute for Research on National Minorities, which focused exclusively on patterns of media consumption among Transylvanian Hungarians.[11]

The institutional survey identified a total number of 117 media organs in 2010 (see Table 1), 84% of which responded to the questionnaire. The number of print media outlets (editorial offices of newspapers and periodicals) was 58, and an additional 54 electronic media outlets and five Hungarian-language Web portals were counted in Transylvania. Their regional distribution followed to a great extent the demographic distribution of the Transylvanian Hungarian population, with the notable difference that Cluj/Kolozsvár was highly overrepresented: One-third of the editorial offices were located in this town (where only about 4% of the Transylvanian Hungarian population resides).

In what follows, we discuss print media, radio and television stations, and then Web portals in separate subsections. Alongside the institutional actors, we also provide a description of the general patterns of consumption for each media type.

[10] The survey was repeated in 2016; however, the results of this second wave have not been published yet. Consequently, we must rely on the earlier wave, pointing out, where necessary, the changes that have occurred in the institutional structure of the Hungarian-language media since 2010.

[11] See Kiss et al. (2016). The sample size of the survey was 1600.

Table 1 Hungarian-language media in Transylvania (2010)

Print media	Daily newspapers	15
	Weekly publications	13
	Monthly publications	20
	Religious periodicals	10
	Print media total	**58**
Electronic media	Radio stations	23
	TV stations	15
	TV broadcasting production offices	16
	Electronic media total	**54**
Web portals		5
Total		**117**

Source Media Institute of the Hungarian National Media and Info-communication Authority

3.1 Print Media

County-level newspapers are the most important outlets of the print media market. In 2010, there were two national-level Hungarian langue dailies,[12] alongside 13 county or micro-regional-level ones. Table 2 synthesizes the circulation figures of these newspapers.[13]

The circulation figures for the national-level newspapers were already rather low in 2010 and have probably decreased further since then.[14] One of the reasons is that these newspapers lacked a functioning supply chain and were sold only in some major urban centers. In contrast, county-level newspapers had solid market positions. In each of the counties where a large Hungarian community existed, there were one or two

[12]Since 2012, there has only been one Hungarian-language daily newspaper targeting Transylvania as a whole, as Új Magyar Szó was discontinued in print form, being transformed into a Web portal.

[13]One should emphasize that it is not an easy task to determine the real circulation figures. The majority of the Hungarian-language media organs do not take part in the process of monitoring carried out by BRAT (the Romanian Joint Industry Committee for Print and Internet). In 2010, only 4 of the 15 newspapers had taken part in the monitoring process, while in 2017 only 2 of the 14. In 2010, three of the newspapers did not respond to questions concerning circulation figures either. In the case of others, the reported figures are obviously exaggerated.

[14]According to information we received from personal discussions with journalists, the figure for Krónika from 2010 is no longer valid for 2017.

Table 2 Circulation figures for daily newspapers (2010)

		Regional target (country, region)	BRAT registration	Survey results		
				Subscribers	Free sales	Total
National-level newspapers	Krónika	Transylvania	–	5800	2300	8100
	Új Magyar Szó	Transylvania	–	4000	1000	5000
Local-/county-level newspapers	Háromszék	Covasna/Kovászna	–	12,000	1000	13,000
	Csíki Hírlap	Ciuc/Csík micro-region[a]	9600	10,000	1000	11,000
	Bihari Napló	Bihor/Bihar	12,400	9000	2000	11,000
	Székely Hírmondó	Covasna/Kovászna	–	8425	1700	10,125
	Szatmári Friss Újság	Satu Mare/Szatmár	7850	7500	820	8320
	Hargita Népe	Harghita/Hargita	7900	7600	600	8200
	Nyugati Jelen	Arad, Timiș/Temes, Hunedoara/Hunyad	–	6512	230	6742
	Szabadság	Cluj/Kolozs	–	4500	1500	6000
	Szatmári Magyar Hírlap	Satu Mare/Szatmár	–	4000	500	4500
	Reggeli Újság	Bihor/Bihar	–	2000	1000	3000
	Népújság	Mureș/Maros	–	–	–	–
	Vásárhelyi Hírlap	Mureș/Maros	–	–	–	–
	Udvarhelyi Híradó	Odorhei/Udvarhely micro-region[a]	–	–	–	–

Source Media Institute of the Hungarian National Media and Info-communication Authority
[a]Located in Harghita/Hargita county

daily newspapers with relatively high circulation figures. Our 2015 survey confirmed this tendency. Results show that 45% of adult Hungarians reported to reading at least one print media product once a week. Eighty-nine percent of those who read newspapers could mention (to an open-ended question) one of the local or regional Hungarian-language dailies or weeklies.[15] Romanian-language local newspapers were mentioned by 9% of respondents while only a few respondents mentioned national-level newspapers either in Hungarian (5%) or Romanian (3%) language. About 7% claimed to have read print media products from Hungary, the vast majority of these being magazines and tabloids, not dailies. To summarize: the print media consumption of Transylvanian Hungarians is largely dominated by the reading of local Hungarian-language newspapers, especially in the ethnic block area of Székely Land and in other counties where Hungarians are more concentrated. Romanian-language newspapers played a more significant role among Hungarians living in dispersed communities. One should also emphasize the aging of the readers of the Hungarian-language written press. As already highlighted by Magyari, the use of print media was characteristic of middle-aged people during the late 1990s (2003, pp. 116–117). In 2015, it was mostly pensioners who regularly read newspapers in print format (Kiss et al. 2016).

Arguably, the solid position of local newspapers and the weakness of national-(Transylvanian) level ones are (at least partly) a historical legacy. Transylvania used to be a peripheral region within Hungary before the Treaty of Trianon, and its town centers were dominated by local newspapers, not by the media produced in Budapest (Fleisz 2005). After the region came under Romanian authority, the significance of these local newspapers increased even further. In the interwar period, there were daily or weekly newspapers in the majority of towns inhabited by Hungarians. Cluj/Kolozsvár was the most important center of the Hungarian-language media during this period, followed closely by the major urban centers close to the Hungarian border: namely Oradea/

[15]In some counties where the number of Hungarians is lower (such as Braşov/Brassó, Timiş/Temes, Sălaj/Szilágy, and Maramureş/Máramaros), Hungarian-language newspapers are weeklies, not dailies.

Nagyvárad, Arad, and Timişoara/Temesvár (Magyari 2017). During state socialism, the daily newspapers operated by the county committees of the Romanian Communist Party were by far the most important Hungarian-language media organs. In the 1980s, nine county-level and one national-level Hungarian-language daily newspaper existed.[16] This institutional structure was also constitutive for the post-Communist period. Following the collapse of the Ceauşescu regime, the titles of these newspapers were changed, but the same editorial office continued to edit them, and they also succeeded in maintaining their audience. Meanwhile, the structure of ownership changed. The majority of newspapers were privatized by editorial staff right after the regime change; others were moved under the financial umbrella of county councils. Today, only one newspaper is run by the county councils (*Hargita Népe*) and two by foundations managed by editorial staff (*Szabadság* in Cluj/Kolozsvár and *Háromszék* in Covasna/Kovászna county). A relatively new phenomenon is the concentration of ownership in the hands of economic actors connected to Viktor Orbán's right-wing Fidesz in the kin-state. The most important actor is the Foundation without Borders for the Hungarian-language Media (*Határok Nélkül a Magyar Sajtóért Alapítvány*) which owns four local daily newspapers[17] and the most important Web portal in Székely Land (szekelyhon.ro), in addition to the only surviving national-level newspaper (*Krónika*). Another actor is Inform Media, a company owned until August 2017 by Austrian investors, when it was bought by an entrepreneur associated with Fidesz (Szémann and Földi 2017). Besides several Romanian-language newspapers, Inform Media also owns the two most important Hungarian-language daily newspapers in the Crişana/Partium region (*Szatmári Friss Újság* and *Bihari Napló*).

[16]Hungarian-language newspapers existed in Arad, Bihor/Bihar, Braşov/Brassó, Cluj/Kolozs, Covasna/Kovászna, Harghita/Hargita, Mureş/Maros, Satu Mare/Szatmár and Temes/Timiş counties (Apró 2012).

[17]Udvarhelyi Híradó, Csíki Hírlap, Vásárhelyi Hírlap, and Gyergyói Hírlap (established in 2014).

3.2 Radio Stations

The media survey of 2010 identified 23 radio stations that broadcast programs in the Hungarian language. According to their area of coverage, we can distinguish between micro-regional, county-level, macro-regional, and national broadcasters, while according to type/ownership the radio stations can be public, commercial, or religious.

Most Hungarian-language private stations are limited to micro-regions, typically one town and its surrounding area. There are two county-level broadcasters (in Covasna/Kovászna and Bihor/Bihar counties) and two private radio stations, targeting larger areas. In this latter category belongs City Radio, which covers the counties of Satu Mare/Szatmár, Sălaj/Szilágy and Maramureș/Máramaros, and Erdély FM, which has frequencies in the centers of Mureș/Maros and Harghita/Hargita counties. Another important cluster is that of public broadcasters, meaning the regional studios of Romanian Radio, in addition to the Hungarian-language program of the central studio which is broadcast nationwide. The third cluster consists of two religious stations, Agnus Radio of the Reformed Church and the Maria Radio of the Roman Catholic Church.

The developmental pathway of Hungarian-language radio broadcasting differs significantly from that of print media. The first Hungarian-language radio programs in Romania were aired in Bucharest in 1945, while the regional studios in Cluj/Kolozsvár and Târgu Mureș/Marosvásárhely were established in the 1950s. However, all the regional studios were abolished in 1985, and no Hungarian-language broadcasting existed at the time of regime change. Nevertheless, members of the former editorial staffs played a key role when Hungarian-language public broadcasting restarted in 1990. The regional studios of Romanian Public Radio in Cluj/Kolozsvár, Târgu Mureș/Marosvásárhely, and Timișoara/Temesvár have remained an important pillar of the Hungarian-language media until today. The former two broadcast Hungarian-language programs 24/7 since 2015, while the Timișoara/Temesvár studio airs Hungarian-language programs several hours a week. According to our 2015 survey, 48% of radio listeners (64% of the adult Hungarian population) listened to

Hungarian-language public programs. The Târgu Mureș/Marosvásárhely regional station was the most frequently mentioned broadcaster: 27% of Transylvanian Hungarians reported that they listened to it regularly.

The majority of the Hungarian-language private stations were established after 2004. The 504/2002 Audio-Visual Law made possible broadcasting exclusively in minority languages. Following 2004, as a consequence of its governmental participation, RMDSZ succeeded in allocating a number of local frequencies to entrepreneurs who belong to the clientele of the party. However, due to the decentralized structure of RMDSZ, the fact that these frequencies were distributed to local elites proved to be a barrier to the development of an integrated institutional system and program structure. The (top-level) leadership of RMDSZ was planning to establish such an integrated structure through the creation of Erdély FM, which initially (in 2007) was envisaged as a production office that would produce blocks of news and other program panels which could be transmitted through local frequencies.[18] However, the relationship between Erdély FM (connected to top-level RMDSZ leadership) and the owners of the local frequencies and radio stations (connected to local political elites) quickly deteriorated, not least due to the desire of the Erdély FM editorial staff to acquire its own local frequencies.[19] This latter goal did not come to fruition, however. Today, Erdély FM can be received only in Târgu Mureș/Marosvásárhely and its surroundings, as well as some towns in parts of Harghita/Hargita county. Its audience was rather small, according to our 2015 survey.

In spite of failures to establish an integrated structure, the local private radio stations established after 2004 have considerably altered the patterns of media consumption among Transylvanian Hungarians. Taken together, Hungarian-language commercial radio stations have a quite large audience. As presented in Fig. 1, in 2007, 44% of survey respondents who declared themselves radio listeners mentioned them, while by 2015 their number has risen to 56%.

---

[18]See http://www.erdelyfm.ro/?belso=rolunk. We also rely here on informal interviews conducted with RMDSZ stakeholders, as well as journalists and radio station owners.

[19]Only two of the local stations with a sizeable audience maintained a partnership with Erdély FM until 2016.

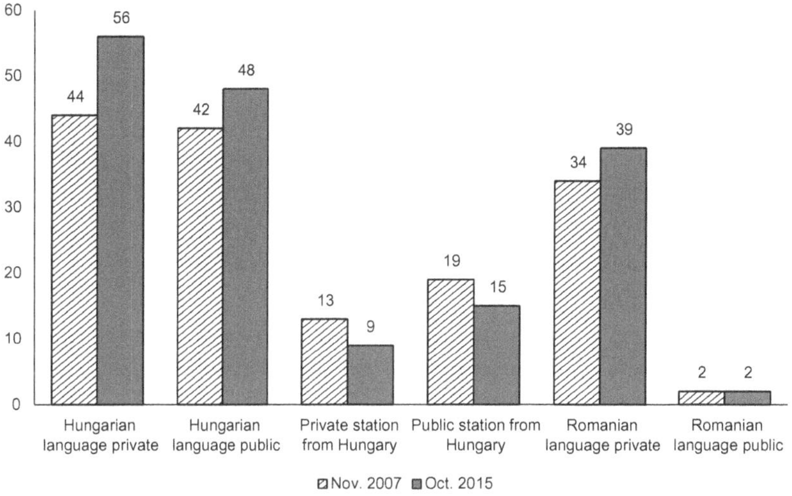

Fig. 1 Audience of different types of radio stations (2007 and 2015). Figures represent percentages among respondents who reported that they listened to the radio (*Source* Romanian Institute for Research on National Minorities 2015 and TransObjective Consulting 2007)

Survey data also show that Romanian-language commercial channels (especially the nationwide stations Europa FM, Pro FM, and Kiss FM) also have a significant and growing audience. Public stations from Hungary (especially Kossuth Radio) had their listeners too; however, their significance decreased between 2007 and 2015.

3.3 TV Stations

In spite of the different historical pathways, there are some obvious similarities in the structure of Hungarian-language radio broadcasting and the written press. Both markets are dominated by Hungarian-language media produced in Transylvania, and nationwide organs covering the entire community are obviously of secondary importance as compared to local-level media. However, television broadcasting is costlier and requires more capital. Consequently, local Hungarian-language producers are less able to dominate this market.

Time budget surveys highlight the importance of television when compared to other types of mass media. According to a survey from 2011,[20] the average time spent in front of the television by Transylvanian Hungarian adults was three hours per day (62.5% of their leisure time). These figures are similar for Romania as a whole and can be considered rather high in cross-national comparison. From the perspective of time budgets, the consumption of other types of media is far less relevant. A 2001 survey asked respondents in general about reading, including print and online media, books, and other written content. The average time spent reading was 45 minutes per day, which was nearly double compared the Romanian average, although not unusually high in cross-national comparison. Listening to the radio was subsumed under the category of "other leisure time activities".[21] Another survey, carried out in 2013,[22] inquired about the time spent watching individual channels. Results show that Transylvanian Hungarians spent on average 100 minutes per day watching (satellite) channels from Hungary—more than double the time spent watching Romanian-language channels (46 minutes per day). Time spent watching Hungarian-language programs produced in Romania (Erdély TV and the Hungarian-language programs of the Romanian Television) was even less, at 10 minutes per day.

These results clearly highlight the dominance of channels transmitted from Hungary. The question is, to when can their dominance be dated? In the counties next to the Hungarian border (where some 20% of the Hungarian population live), Hungarian channels dominated as early as the 1980s. Moreover, their dominance was even more pronounced during this period, as Romanian public TV broadcasted for only a few hours per day, and its programs mainly involved

[20]The survey was carried out by the Center for Research and Consultancy in Culture (Bucharest) and the Romanian Institute for Research on National Minorities using a nationwide sample of 3500 and on an additional Transylvanian Hungarian sample of 1200 respondents.

[21]One should highlight that listening to the radio usually occurs simultaneously with other activities (driving, working, cooking, etc.).

[22]The survey was carried out by the Romanian Institute for Research on National Minorities using a 1200 sample representative for Transylvanian Hungarians.

propagandistic reporting about the achievements of the Ceaușescu regime.[23] The first Hungarian-language broadcaster to reach the whole territory of Transylvania was Duna TV, a publicly financed satellite channel designed by the Hungarian government specially to transmit programs to cross-border minority communities. Except for the border region, this was the only available Hungarian-language channel during the 1990s.

Unfortunately, the patterns of media consumption cannot be reconstructed for the entire period that has elapsed since the regime change due to a lack of survey data. The earliest available data come from a survey carried out in 1999,[24] which asked respondents about the frequency of watching individual channels, among them both Hungarian- and Romanian-language ones. Duna TV was the most frequently watched channel, followed closely by PRO TV, the first and most important Romanian commercial broadcaster. The Romanian public channel (RTV), including its Hungarian-language programs, was also widely watched. By this time, the Hungarian commercial and public channels could only be received in the area close to the Hungarian border; in this region, the positions of both Duna TV and the Romanian-language channels were far weaker. In the ethnic block area of Székely Land, Duna TV was the most popular channel; however, Pro TV was also widely watched, especially by younger generations. Romanian-language channels were obviously dominant outside the Székely Land and the border region.

Eight years later (in 2007), we find markedly different patterns.[25] The dominance of Hungarian channels, especially the commercial ones, was already evident in the Székely Land. Duna TV remained the most frequently watched channel, but it was closely followed by the

[23]In this area where Hungarian TV programs could be received, it was not only Hungarians but also Romanians who regularly tuned in during the 1980s.

[24]Unpublished survey data. The survey was conducted by the Research Center on Interethnic Relations (CCRIT) using a sample of 1178 respondents, representative for Transylvanian Hungarians.

[25]Unpublished survey data; survey conducted by TransObjective Consulting using a sample of 1200 respondents, representative for Transylvanian Hungarians.

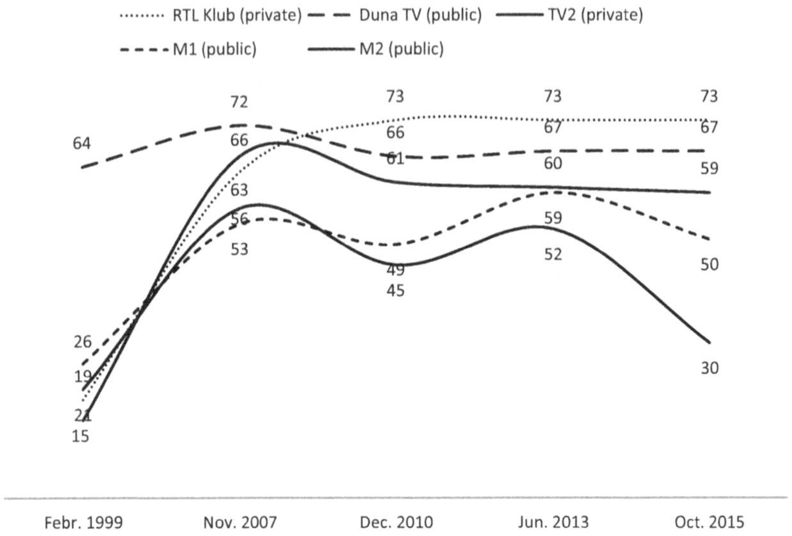

Fig. 2 Audience of TV channels transmitted from Hungary (1999–2015). Figures represent percentages of respondents who mentioned the respective TV channels (*Source* Kvantum Research 2010; TransObjective Consulting 2007; Romanian Institute for Research on National Minorities 2013, 2015)

two Hungarian commercial channels which became widely available across Transylvania. As shown in Fig. 2, the dominance of the commercial channels has increased following 2007. A possible explanation to the drop in the audience of Hungarian public channels in 2015 is linked to the restructuring in the domain. Duna TV became a regular public channel and is no longer tailored to a transborder audience. M1 became a news channel which often acts as a mouthpiece for the Orbán government, while M2 was transformed into a channel for children and youth.

Pro TV has remained the most popular among the Romanian-language channels; however, the size of its audience has fallen below that of the Hungarian-language channels (see Fig. 3). One should also emphasize that Romanian-language broadcasters have clearly lost ground among Transylvanian Hungarians during the last two decades.

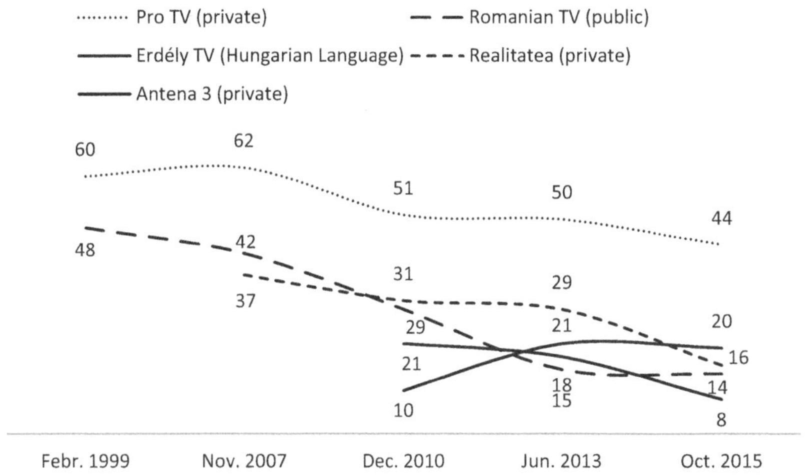

Fig. 3 Audience of TV channels transmitted from Romania (1999–2015). Figures represent percentages of respondents who mentioned the respective TV channels (*Source* TransObjective Consulting 2007; Kvantum Research 2010; Romanian Institute for Research on National Minorities 2013, 2015)

3.4 Web Portals

As some authors have emphasized, the spread of the internet brought both challenges and new opportunities for the minority media (Moring, 2013). According to a 2015 survey, 58% of adult Transylvanian Hungarians were Internet users. The most widespread way of utilizing the Internet was social media and networking. Seventy-six percent of Internet users and forty-nine percent of the total Transylvanian Hungarian adult population had a Facebook account, meaning that social media has become one of the most important media platforms.

Meanwhile, even in 2015, only 25% of users were consuming media in a more restricted sense on the Internet, meaning reading newspapers and articles on Web portals, watching TV programs, and searching for news online. Table 3 shows data about the proportion of Internet users who read Transylvanian Hungarian-language Web portals. One should emphasize that the audience of these media organs is rather thin.

Table 3 The audience of Transylvanian Hungarian-language web portals (proportion of internet users)[a]

	Daily	Weekly	Less frequently	Never ↑
szekelyhon.ro	11.4	13.5	9.1	66.0
maszol.ro	6.5	12.0	9.7	71.8
transindex.ro	6.5	11.1	10.5	72.0
erdely.ma	3.3	8.6	11.6	76.5
foter.ro	1.5	3.8	7.2	87.6

Source RIRNM survey
[a]The audience is similar to the figures published by the leading Web-auditing and ranking site in Romania, trafic.ro

The most widely visited Web portal (szekelyhon.ro) is a regional one, targeting the ethnic block area of Székely Land. Web portals with nationwide targets are visited with daily frequency by only 3–4% of adult Hungarians.

4 Conclusions

Having described the institutional structure of the Hungarian media in Transylvania and analyzed the related consumption patterns, at the end of this chapter we turn back to the analytical and normative frameworks of minority media research outlined at the beginning of the chapter, trying to evaluate the situation of the Hungarian-language media in Transylvania with a special focus on the increasing dominance of kin-state actors.

Our first framework was that of language preservation. From this perspective, minority language use in media consumption is of primary importance, regardless of whether programs are produced and broadcast by members of the minority or individuals from abroad (the kin-state). In this respect, it is of primary importance that the Hungarian language has gained ground in the media consumption of Transylvanian Hungarians. Survey data about the language of media consumption collected between 1997 and 2015[26] show that Romanian-language media

[26]The 1997 survey was carried out by the ELTE-UNESCO Minority Studies Department (1200 respondents); the 2004 one by CCRIT (1100 respondents). The 2011 (CCCDC-RIRNM) and 2015 (RIRNM) surveys have already been mentioned.

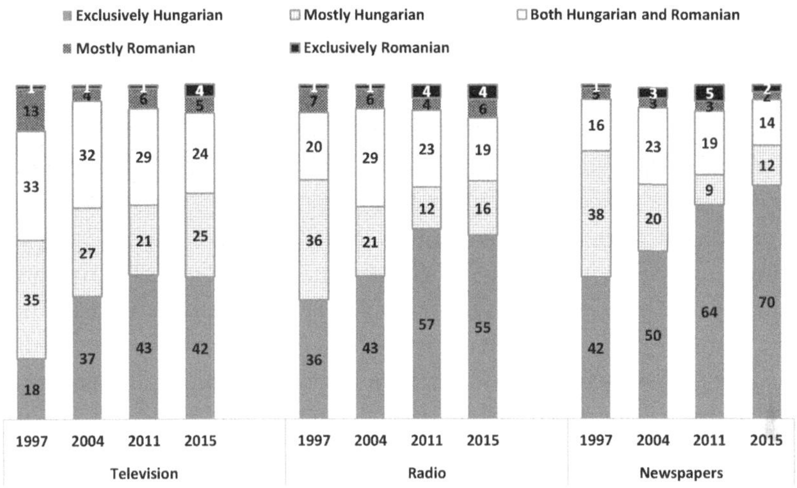

Fig. 4 Language use in media consumption (1997–2015). Numbers represent percentages (*Source* ELTE-UNSECO Minority Studies 1997; CCRIT 2004; RIRNM 2011, 2015)

dominates the consumption of only a very narrow segment of the Hungarian population: 9% in the case of television, 10% in the case of radio, and 4% in the case of newspapers[27] The proportion of those using exclusively and mostly Hungarian-language media has clearly increased over time (Fig. 4).

From the perspective of the media pluralism model, the picture is more equivocal. First, Hungarian elites have placed less emphasis in the past two decades on promoting internal media pluralism and on a non-discrimination approach. As a consequence, they lack the capacity to influence, let alone manage, the image of the community in the Romanian-language media. There are no production offices or media outlets (financed either by the Romanian state or by Hungarian organizations) where Hungarians could produce Romanian-language content for mainstream media. In one of the few investigations to focus on the presentation of Hungarians in the Romanian media, Salat et al.

[27]Languages other than Hungarian and Romanian could also be mentioned, although the proportion of respondents who mentioned any other language did not in any case reach 1%, so these responses were treated as missing values when the figure was created.

(2014) found that negative framing (involving the perception of the Hungarians as a threat, a security dilemma, invoking discrimination by the Romanian majority, or criticism of power-sharing) was dominant. In the last few years, the situation has probably worsened as several hysteria-stoking campaigns against the Hungarian community have been run in the Romanian mass media.

Second, the capacity of the Transylvanian Hungarian elites to manage the image of their community is also questionable with regard to the mainstream media produced in Hungary (which is consumed by Transylvanian Hungarians to a much greater extent than Romanian language media). Feischmidt (2005) has argued that the representation of Transylvanian Hungarians in Hungary is clearly Orientalizing. In this frame, Transylvania is portrayed as a combination of backwardness and authentic Hungarian identity; however, these elements have little to do with the everyday experiences and self-representation of those living in the region. Yet, it would be a mistake to see Transylvanian Hungarians as passive objects of "kin-state colonization". In fact, Transylvanian Hungarian journalists partially produce these representations. In 2010, there existed 18 production offices with 85 employees working mostly for broadcasters in Hungary.

Third, from the perspective of the political pluralism of the minority media, the changing structure of ownership and financing could be considered a problem. While Transylvanian Hungarians watch Hungarian satellite channels, an increasing proportion of the domestic media is indirectly owned by right-wing kin-state political actors. The remaining part of the Hungarian-language media is directly or indirectly dominated by RMDSZ, but this is also increasingly dependent on financing from Hungary.

The framework of competing or clashing nation-building projects is also relevant when evaluating the situation of the Hungarian-language media and media consumption among Transylvanian Hungarians. From the Romanian perspective, this does not seem to involve a success story. The proportion of Transylvanian Hungarians who do not use Romanian-language media at all has increased over time, and these people can barely be considered participants in the Romanian mainstream public sphere. From the perspective of the kin-state, the evaluation is different. Media consumption and the integration of Transylvanian Hungarians into the transnational Hungarian-language media-space is one of the most important institutional tools for the virtual unification of Hungarians distributed across borders.

From the perspective of the minority elites engaged in the project of ethnic parallelism, the picture is more ambivalent. The increasing dominance of the Hungarian language may contribute to the maintenance of ethnic boundaries vis-á-vis the majority. However, the fragmented nature of the institutional system (especially the weakness of media outlets that cover the entire territory of Transylvania) and the dominance of kin-state actors can be considered major challenges. First, due to the strong regional fragmentation, it is partially misleading to talk about a Hungarian-language public sphere in Transylvania. Patterns of media consumption and, moreover, the institutional structure of the written press and radio stations sustain mainly smaller local or regional public spheres. This is partially the consequence of the pattern of settlement of the community, which is dispersed over an extensive geographical area. However, it is also a consequence of the failure of the institutional efforts of the political class and community organizers to build an integrated media structure. Elements of this failure include the inability to sustain a nationwide newspaper, to build an integrated program structure for local commercial radio stations, and to make Erdély TV financially sustainable. Second, the fragmentation of the media structure is also due to the divergence between policy projects that focus on the minority language media. The Hungarian elites mostly imagined an autonomous media system, and some elements of this system have indeed come into existence. However, an institutionally complete autonomous media system is presently financially unsustainable. Moreover, an important pillar of the Hungarian-language media is organized mostly according to the logic of the minority protection model and is not integrated into an (incomplete) autonomous structure. The consequence of this fragmentation and incompleteness is the shift in public preferences toward media channels from Hungary, which in the long run could reduce the influence and mobilization capacities of the Transylvanian Hungarian elites.

References

Alba, R. D., & Nee, V. (2003). *Remaking the American mainstream: Assimilation and contemporary immigration*. Cambridge, MA: Harvard University Press.

Anderson, B. (2006). *Imagined communities: Reflections on the origin and spread of nationalism* (Rev. ed.). London and New York: Verso.

Apró, I. (Ed.). (2012). *Határon túli magyar nyelvű médiumok 2010/2011*. Budapest: Médiatudományi Intézet.

Brubaker, R. (1996). *Nationalism reframed nationhood and the national question in the New Europe*. Cambridge and New York: Cambridge University Press.

Cormack, M. J. (1998). Minority language media in western Europe. *European Journal of Communication, 13*(1), 33–52.

Cormack, M. J. (2007). The media and language maintenance. In M. J. Cormack & N. Hourigan (Eds.), *Minority language media: Concepts, critiques and case studies* (pp. 52–69). Clevedon and Buffalo: Multilingual Matters.

de Swaan, A. (1991). Notes on the emerging global language system: Regional, national and supranational. *Media, Culture and Society, 13*(3), 309–323.

Feischmidt, M. (2005). A magyar nacionalizmus autenticitás-diskurzusainak szimbolikus térfoglalása Erdélyben. In M. Feischmidt (Ed.), *Erdély-(de) konstrukciók* (pp. 7–32). Budapest and Pécs: Néprajzi Múzeum, PTE Kommunikáció and és Médiatudományok Tanszék.

Fishman, J. A. (1991) *Reversing language shift: Theoretical and empirical foundations of assistance to threatened languages*. Clevedon and Philadelphia: Multilingual Matters.

Fishman, J. A. (2001). From theory to practice (and vice versa): Review, reconsideration and reiteration. In J. A. Fishman (Ed.), *Can threatened languages be saved?: Reversing language shift, revisited: A 21st century perspective* (pp. 451–483). Clevedon and Buffalo: Multilingual Matters.

Fleisz, J. (2005). *Az erdélyi magyar sajtó története 1890–1940* (p. 288). Pécs: Pannónia.

Gans, H. J. (1979). Symbolic ethnicity: The future of ethnic groups and cultures in America*. *Ethnic and Racial Studies, 2*(1), 1–20.

Giles, H., Bourhis, R. Y., & Taylor, D. M. (1977). Toward a theory of language in ethnic group relations. In H. Giles (Ed.), *Language, ethnicity, and intergroup relations* (pp. 307–348). London and New York: Academic Press.

Horowitz, D. L. (1985). *Ethnic groups in conflict*. Berkeley: University of California Press.

Kiss, T., Barna, G., & Duduj, S. (2016). *Médiafogyasztási szokások Erdélyben. Kutatásjelentés*. Kolozsvár: Nemzeti Kisebbségkutató Intézet.

Klimkiewicz, B. (2003). Media policy for ethnic and national minorities in Poland, the Czech Republic and Slovakia. In M. Sükösd & P. Bajomi-Lázár (Eds.), *Reinventing media: Media policy reform in east-central Europe* (pp. 155–184). Budapest and New York: Central European University Press.

Klimkiewicz, B. (2015). Cultural and geographical dimensions of media pluralism. In P. Valcke, M. Sükösd, & R. G. Picard (Eds.), *Media pluralism and diversity: Concepts, risks and global trends* (pp. 82–106). Houndmills, Basingstoke, Hampshire and New York: Palgrave Macmillan.

Magyari, T. (2003). Elemzések a romániai magyarok sajtóolvasási szokásairól. *Erdélyi Társadalom, 1*(1), 113–131.

Magyari, T. (2017). Az erdélyi magyarok nyilvánosságának általános jegyei. In N. Bárdi & G. Éger (Eds.), *Huszonöt év. Magyarok Romániában, 1990–2015. Tanulmányok az erdélyi magyarságról* (pp. 395–406). Budapest: L'Hartmattan.

Mohácsek, M. (2009). *Analiza finanțărilor alocate organizațiilor minorităților naționale* (ISPMN Working Papers No. 16).

Moring, T. (2007). Functional completeness in minority language media. In M. J. Cormack & N. Hourigan (Eds.), *Minority language media: Concepts, critiques and case studies* (pp. 17–33). Clevedon and Buffalo: Multilingual Matters.

Moring, T. (2013). Media markets and minority languages in the digital age. *Journal on Ethnopolitics and Minority Issues in Europe, 12*(4), 34–53.

Papp, A. Z. (2005). The Hungarian press system in Romania during the nineties: The World of the operators. *Regio, 8*, 141–153.

Salat, L., Andriescu, M., Gherghina, S., Jiglău, G., Székely, I. G., & Popescu-Tiganea, A. (2014). *The representation of minorities in Romania in the press*. Cluj-Napoca: College of Political, Administrative and Communication Sciences, Babeș-Bolyai University.

Szémann, T., & Földi, G. (2017, September 15). Mészáros Lőrinc és Andy Vajna lapjait olvassa az ország. *index.hu*. Available at: https://index.hu/kultur/media/2017/09/15/mediahaboru_orszagos_napilapok_meszaros_lorinc_andy_vajna/.

Valcke, P., Sükösd, M., & Picard, R. G. (2015). *Media pluralism and diversity: Concepts, risks and global trends.* Houndmills, Basingstoke, Hampshire and New York, NY: Palgrave Macmillan.

Vincze, L. (2013). *The bilingual screen: Ethnolinguistic identity and television viewing among three language minorities.* Ph.D. thesis, University of Helsinki, Helsinki.

Yagmur, K., & Ehala, M. (2011). Tradition and innovation in the ethnolinguistic vitality theory. *Journal of Multilingual and Multicultural Development, 32*(2), 101–110.

9

Economy and Ethnicity in Transylvania

Zsombor Csata

The economy in Transylvania differs from other social domains such as education, culture or mass media as it is not primarily organized into ethnically separate organizational structures. In this book, the economy is considered an ethnically non-integrated field. Romania started its transformation toward a state-controlled market capitalism after the change of regime in 1989, and (according to the mainstream neoliberal discourse) economic activity in market capitalism, by default, is not ethnically conditioned. Economic processes are controlled by the culturally and ethnically neutral principles of the market, while the individual-level decisions taken by actors are led by utilitarian considerations

Z. Csata (✉)
Institute for Minority Studies, Hungarian Academy of Sciences, Centre for Social Sciences,
Budapest, Hungary
e-mail: csata.zsombor@tk.mta.hu

Z. Csata
Department of Sociology and Social Work in Hungarian, Babeş-Bolyai University, Cluj-Napoca, Romania

T. Kiss et al. (eds.), *Unequal Accommodation of Minority Rights*,
Palgrave Politics of Identity and Citizenship Series,
https://doi.org/10.1007/978-3-319-78893-7_9

and a desire for efficiency and profit. According to this logic, the social and cultural attributes of actors are of secondary importance, the market rewards their competences and performance.

However, after (Granovetter 1985) we know that the economies of modern capitalism are not independent of social condition, and ethnicity does matter in certain economic decisions, interactions, and processes (Portes and Sensenbrenner 1993; Light and Gold 2000; Alesina and La Ferrara 2005; Eriksen 2005). Neo-institutionalist economists have a similar perspective. They regard ethnicity as a specific dimension of social coordination (Landa 1994), which gains more importance under the following institutional conditions: (1) There are substantial differences in consumer and cultural preferences across ethnic groups; (2) there are sizeable differences in the social positions of ethnic groups (i.e., ethnic inequalities are considerable); (3) institutions responsible for the enforcement of cooperation are less efficient; and (4) in line with the former, generalized trust is low.

These conditions push economic actors to rely on ethnically homogeneous relations in their everyday economic transactions. Ethnic coordination is based on "bounded solidarity", "enforceable trust" among group members, or on a common "value introjection" perceived as special and ethnically marked forms of social capital (Portes 1998). Their institutionalization may reduce the level of uncertainty and the transaction costs of economic cooperation, granting a competitive advantage over those actors who are not ethnically integrated (Granovetter 1995). Economic transactions can be made smoother when participants have a common ethnic background. A common identity usually relies on shared representations, similar values and preferences, and may facilitate consensus in decision-making situations. Coordination will be also smoother if actors speak the same language, as sharing a common tongue may reduce misunderstandings and the costs of communication are also lower.

Nevertheless, if the above-mentioned conditions were different, cooperation along ethnic lines would not be efficient and would involve considerable alternative cost. In homogeneous and closed systems of communication, information is often redundant, and members of such networks may easily miss good market opportunities. Under these circumstances, ethnically segregated parts of the economy could fall behind the better-performing "mainstream" segments. The lack of diversity might also be detrimental to business, as homogeneous working groups have been proved to be less creative (Page 2007) and to have a lower level of adaptive capacity (Ottaviano and Peri 2006).

The literature on ethnic economy defines dense relations within one's own group as bonding social capital (Putnam 2007). Such bonds may rely on common traditions, customs, culture, or, sometimes, on the collective perception of an external threat. Bonding capital increases in-group solidarity and trust. In contrast, "bridging" capital involves ties with individuals from outside the community and is responsible for the integration of the minority community into wider society. According to Granovetter (1995), neither a very high, nor a very low level of internal solidarity is desirable for the economic development of a minority group. Success is more likely if a smooth balance exists between coupling to—and decoupling from the network structures and normative value-systems of the dominant society. Hartford (2016, pp. 38–39)—and in an earlier context, Aldrich and Waldinger (1990)—called these resources "opportunity structures" and argued that it depends on the context whether bonding or bridging ties are more useful; however, most tasks require a combination.

In the case of Transylvanian Hungarians, strong institutional relations with Hungary could also extend their "opportunity structures". Kin-state actors are interested in building and extending their market and influence using ethnic-based economic relations outside Hungary. So the in-between position of Transylvanian Hungarians (living in Romania but belonging to the culturally—and through dual citizenship even to the politically defined Hungarian nation) also provides them with a good networking position to build and sustain fruitful economic relations across two different cultures. Minority Hungarians can easily become bridges or brokers, a role that brings them a series of advantages. They can cultivate various and economically efficient weak ties (Granovetter 1973) that facilitate their access to information and economic opportunities. Staying in a "structural hole" (Burt 1992), minority Hungarians can also be mediators, performing integrative roles by accessing resources from both sides. They can also contribute to the economic exchange between ethnically homogeneous regions and states (Alesina and La Ferrara 2005). Romania's accession to the EU gave a tremendous boost to this potential by reducing the transaction- and logistics-related costs of trade and cross-border economic cooperation in general.

Strategic documents concerning the development of the Transylvanian Hungarian society envisioned different economic roles for the community.[1] Some accounts propose the establishment of a parallel, ethnically separated enclave economy which may serve as the base for future minority autonomy. Others would like to see Hungarian minority communities as brokers or bridges which link economic networks disjointed by cultures and state borders (Papp and Márton 2011). Apart from these role-expectations, several investigations have found that ethnicity does not play a central role in the self-representation of economic actors. This was emphasized by Kiss (2004) who analyzed narrative biographic interviews of Transylvanian Hungarian entrepreneurs. He found that ethnic affiliation is not considered a key factor in their narratives of becoming entrepreneurs and even if it is present, is considered mostly only as symbolic capital used in individual career-making. Statistical analyses have found only a loose connection between the proportion of Hungarians, entrepreneurial activity and economic well-being and only in a few micro-regions in Transylvania (Csata 2012, 2015). Szabó in his locally focused ethnography concluded that "in present-day Transylvanian villages we can talk about the ethnic determination of the economy only with reservation", and that "belonging to an ethnic community might be an organizing element of the economy,

[1] See the strategies promoted by the Hungarian Government: Wekerle Plan (*Wekerle Terv*), the chapter of the Széchenyi Plan concerning the Economic Development of the Carpathian Basin (*Széchenyi terv—Kárpát-medencei térség Gazdaságfejlesztési Övezet alprogram*), the chapters of the Book of Reforms (*Nagy Reformkönyv*) and those from External Economic Strategy (*Külgazdasági Stratégia*), as well as the Mikó Imre Plan (*Mikó Imre terv*) designed for Transylvania, in addition to the relevant passages of the National Cooperation System (*Nemzeti Együttműködés Rendszere*).

but not solely, not primarily and not exclusively" (Szabó 2010, p. 7). Nevertheless, the same author underscores in his more recent analysis (Szabó 2015) that ethnicity may shape economic structures and patterns of consumption. This happens in those local environments where ethno-political rivalry is strong and concurrent projects of ethnic community building are present.

One should also emphasize that important changes have occurred during the past decade. A series of business initiatives were established which explicitly target consumers who belong to the Hungarian minority. These enterprises strongly appeal to ethnic solidarity of the Hungarians and build up their business narratives using ethnic markers. Their employment strategies and business networks are also ethnically selective (Gáll 2011). Additionally, EU accession brought important legislative changes. More relaxed state control of the economy and market deregulation have created better conditions for the construction of ethnically defined market segments, for the commodification of ethnic products, and for cooperation along ethnic ties.

1 Research Questions

The analysts highlighted above tend to agree that ethnicity can be perceived as a resource incorporated into different forms of social capital.[2] Ethnicity as social capital might take different forms—the bridging and bonding aspects have already been mentioned. The distinction between cognitive and structural dimensions (e.g., attitudes and values vs. network composition) will be further elaborated. Importantly, ethnicity as social capital (in all its forms) may determine directly one's social position, labor market opportunities, and performance. Next to this relationship, language knowledge should also be taken into account. Language and ethnicity in Transylvania are closely interlinked

[2]For a review of the relevant literature, see Csata (2015).

(the overwhelming majority of Hungarians are native speakers of Hungarian), and knowledge of the Romanian language can be considered a human resource and also an important determinant of labor market opportunities and performance.

Tamás Kiss, in the chapter focusing on ethnic stratification systems, has highlighted the ongoing process of socioeconomic marginalization of the Hungarian community.[3] This is related (among other ways) to the regionally diverging prospects of the ethno-cultural and demographic reproduction of the Hungarian population, namely to the increasing territorial concentration of Hungarians in ethnic block areas (primarily Székely Land, but also in some micro-regions next to the Hungarian border). These Hungarian-majority areas are peripheral in economic terms: they are less urbanized, have worse infrastructure, and are less developed in many other respects. This chapter does not deal with these macro-level processes[4] that are conducive to marginalization.

Instead, I focus on the micro-level economic consequences of territorial concentration. My main argument is that this process affects the distribution and reproduction of different types of social capital connected to ethnicity. First, the density of network ties connecting ethnic Romanians and Hungarians in Transylvania will most probably decrease, while the density of ethnically homogeneous ties will grow. As Putnam (2000) would put it, this also means that the bonding capital will gain ground at the expense of bridging capital. Second, the Romanian-language knowledge of the Hungarians will also decrease due to their lower exposure to ethnically mixed interactions. This will lead to further economic marginalization through affecting negatively the labor market prospects of the Hungarians. Third, the possibility and profitability of creating ethnically (or ethno-territorially) defined market segments will also increase. Ethnically differentiated marketing and advertising will become more cost-effective, and ethnic entrepreneurship may also gain ground. In the long run, these factors might increase

[3]See Chapter 11 of this volume.

[4]The operationalization and measurement of these macro-effects is beyond the scope of this paper, we do not have reliable data to capture all the relevant dimensions.

the risk of the emergence of an ethnically defined enclave economy and its isolation from the economic mainstream.

This chapter presents some evidence that the above-mentioned processes may not only happen in the distant future, but are already occurring. I document some elements of these changes by using both survey data and qualitative results. I also present models concerning the relation between the different types of social capital, on the one hand, and labor market performance, on the other. Relying on these results, I then formulate some hypotheses concerning the impact of these micro-level processes on the social positions of the Transylvanian Hungarians. The last part of the chapter deals with the different manifestations of bonding capital which serves as the glue for ethnically driven economic coordination. At the individual level, the most important manifestation of this type of capital is consumer ethnocentrism, while at an institutional level we should pay attention to ethnic enterprises.

2 Romanian-Language Knowledge as a Determinant of Labor Market Opportunities

Due to the legally restrictive measures on the official and public use of the Hungarian language between the two world wars and under socialism, the Hungarian language gradually ceased to function as a common language of communication between different nationalities. As a result, its appearance as a lingua franca is very sporadic and shows up only in the very narrow private sphere. The creation of Romanian linguistic hegemony in the public sphere has become an efficient symbolic tool of the exercise of power and authority, placing the majority and minority languages in a highly asymmetrical position.

After the change of regime in 1989, a number of legislative acts for the protection of minority languages came into effect and many concrete results were achieved, especially in education and local administration. However, the asymmetries between majority and minority languages were not eliminated. Csergő (2007) characterized the Romanian-language policy regime as language predominance. Others

Table 1 Romanian-language proficiency among Transylvanian Hungarian youth

	2008 $N=1197$	2013 $N=1224$
Mother tongue	1.3	1.6
I speak it perfectly	40.0	26.2
I speak it fluently, but with notable accent	33.4	34.6
I do not speak well but I am able to make myself understood	17.6	28.8
I understand almost everything, but I have difficulties when I try to make myself understood	6.1	7.3
I know only a few words	1.5	1.4
I do not speak Romanian at all	0.2	0.2

Source RIRNM: "Hungarian Youngsters in Romania 2008 and 2013" surveys
Figures represent percentages among ethnic Hungarians from Transylvania aged 15–29. Question wording: Which of the above statements best describes your Romanian-language knowledge?

emphasized that—beyond the seemingly positive legislative facade—neither language use in administrative settings (Toró 2017), nor the norms concerning everyday linguistic accommodation (Brubaker et al. 2006) have changed considerably. In everyday (interethnic) communication, the use of Hungarian is "marked", while Romanian remains the default tool of communication, at least in ethnically mixed areas (Brubaker et al. 2006). Members of the titular group normatively expect Hungarians to have knowledge of Romanian (Kiss 2015). In spite of the fact that many Hungarians consider the symbolic domination of the Romanian as legitimate (Horváth 2003, p. 20), this condition of asymmetric bilingualism leads to a disadvantage for minority language speakers. These disadvantages stem from the fact that learning the language of the majority involves significant expense and opportunity costs. Moreover, the majority have privileges in certain markets: Minorities are required to cover, for instance, the translation costs of formal communication (in a practically monolingual administrative system), while in oral communication (Romanian by default) they are at a considerable rhetorical disadvantage (Grin 2004, pp. 198–199; Csata 2016, p. 53).

These disadvantages are more pronounced for those who do not have the "proper" knowledge of the majority language. As illustrated in Table 1, the knowledge of the Romanian language of Hungarians is declining and represents an increasing problem, especially among younger generations.[5] The share of those who master Romanian is rapidly decreasing, and that of those who do not speak it well is growing.[6]

According to another survey conducted in 2009,[7] the income of Hungarians who spoke Romanian well was 34% higher than that of those who did not speak it well, or did not speak at all. However, this difference can partially be explained by factors that interact with the lack of Romanian-language knowledge, namely the gender, educational attainment, and residence of respondents. Table 2 summarizes the results of a linear regression analysis where the independent variable is income. The results indicate that good knowledge of Romanian has a positive effect on real income, even when the above-mentioned variables are controlled for. Moreover, a lack of Romanian-language knowledge has a pronounced negative effect on the income of less educated individuals, further worsening the position of the most disadvantaged groups.

Other investigations have also documented the impact of poor Romanian knowledge on labor market opportunities. Horváth (2008) found that there was a significant relationship between the frequency of use of Romanian and the wealth and income situation of ethnic Hungarians. He concluded that knowledge of the majority language is

[5]The "Hungarian Youngsters in Romania 2008 and 2013" surveys were conducted by the Romanian Institute for Research on National Minorities. The random sample consisted of 1197 and 1224 respondents (respectively) and was representative for Transylvanian Hungarians aged 15–29 by gender, region, residence (rural or urban), and age group.

[6]This Romanian-language competence appears especially weak if we consider the fact that an average Hungarian school pupil in Transylvania has 4–5 Romanian classes per week for 12 consecutive years. In addition—according to a recent survey—an average Hungarian high-school student spends another 3 hours per week on homework related to Romanian language and literature classes (perhaps even more in lower grades). This means that an average student who has reached the baccalaureate level has spent around 2350 hours learning Romanian in formal education. The study was conducted in 2015 by the Department of Sociology and Social Work in Hungarian at Babeş-Bolyai University, and the Max Weber Research Center. The random sample consisted of 1109 individuals and was representative for Transylvanian Hungarian upper secondary school students by region, school grade, and the profile of schools and classes.

[7]The survey was also conducted by the Romanian Institute for Research on National Minorities on a sample of 4017 respondents, representative for Hungarian speakers.

Table 2 Factors influencing income among Transylvanian Hungarians (OLS regression model)

	Transylvania	Székely Land	Outside Székely Land
Male	0.199***	0.115**	0.268***
Secondary education (compared to primary education)	0.105**	0.084*	0.119**
Tertiary education (compared to primary education)	0.300***	0.244***	0.333***
Urban residence	0.102**	0.093*	0.107**
Residence in Székely Land	−0.076**	–	–
Good Romanian-language knowledge	0.085**	0.067*	0.108**
R^2	0.169	0.091	0.215

Source RIRNM: "The Turning Points of our Life Course 2./Életünk Fordulópontjai 2". Survey (2009, $N=1651$)
Standardized regression coefficients. *$p<0.05$; **$p<0.01$; ***$p<0.001$

an important tool of social mobility among Transylvanian Hungarians. Csata et al. (2006) highlighted that Hungarian graduates of the Babeș-Bolyai University were employed in smaller proportions in the competitive business sector compared to ethnic Romanian graduates and oriented themselves toward community institutions that operate in Hungarian (e.g., educational and cultural institutions). According to Dániel, Transylvanian Hungarian youngsters (especially those living in Székely Land) do not exclude the possibility "of being employed by a dominantly Romanian company or of working with Romanian colleagues; however, they obviously prefer a Hungarian-speaking working environment where they feel themselves more comfortable" (2011, p. 196). We have good reasons to believe that many Hungarian youngsters reduce their career aspirations because they perceive their Romanian knowledge as insufficient, and that they accept lower salaries in exchange for working in a Hungarian-speaking environment. On the demand side, Geambașu (2017) met with similar argumentation among employers. Her interviewees were entrepreneurs in the software industry, many of whom reported that it was cheaper to hire Hungarian developers since they preferred earning less because it was important for them to work in a native-language environment. In the knowledge-driven sector with a high added value, a "friendly milieu" is important, and this means "among other things an ethnically homogeneous, Hungarian working team, or inversely, an ethnically heterogeneous environment would not be recognized as a 'friendly milieu' by the employees. From this perspective, the pursuit of the employers to find Hungarian software developers is an economically rational option". Further, it is also rational to rely on existing Hungarian networks to find employees.

Although a reliable quantitative study has not yet been carried out on this issue, these examples clearly show that the linguistic environment and the language skills of employees do seriously matter in the labor market, the significance of which, in my opinion, has been underestimated. Language competences determine the career orientation of individuals and the decisions of employers about the selection of new staff much more strongly than previously thought.

Chiswick and Miller identified three factors affecting the knowledge of the majority language by minority group members, namely exposure to the majority language (including media consumption), the efficiency of language instruction, and economic incentives facilitating language learning (2007, pp. 6–10). Exposure to Romanian depends on the intensity of interaction and the frequency of relations with Romanians. Consequently, in the context of territorial concentration and the institutional encapsulation of the Hungarian population, the knowledge of Romanian will further deteriorate—if the other two factors (the efficiency of Romanian-language teaching[8] and economic initiatives) do not counterbalance this tendency. Following this logic, it is also probable that the income disadvantage of Transylvanian Hungarians will continue to grow due their deteriorating Romanian-language proficiency.

[8]On the low efficiency of Romanian-language instruction and motivation for learning Romanian, see Szilágyi (1998), Tódor (2005), and Benő (2012). Regarding media exposure, it is important to note that after the turn of the millennium, the media consumption habits of Transylvanian Hungarians changed significantly. Increasing numbers joined the Hungarian media space in Hungary, while Romanian media consumption is continuously decreasing. For a detailed analysis on media consumption, see Chapter 8.

3 Forms of Social Capital as Determinants of Labor Market Performance

Ethnically mixed ties obviously facilitate the learning and efficient use of the Romanian language. However, according to the literature, connections have a direct impact on labor market opportunities and performance, independent of language proficiency.[9] This part of the chapter deals with the effects of social capital on incomes. In the conceptualization and operationalization of social capital, we rely on Lancee (2012), who conducted a similar investigation focusing on immigrant groups in Germany and the Netherlands.[10] Considering ethnicity as an individual resource, he studied the impact of ethnically homogeneous and heterogeneous ties (as social capital), and language knowledge (as human capital) on labor market performance (realized income, occupational status, and risk of unemployment). He defined bonding and bridging capitals as ethnically homogeneous, respectively, ethnically heterogeneous connections in one's personal network. Given that the ethnic minority and the majority can equally possess resources which are useful for succeeding in the labor market, the effects of bonding capital are not limited to helping individuals "get by", and bridging capital does not always help people to "get ahead", as is often assumed (Narayan 1999; Orbán and Szántó 2005). Lancee also distinguishes between the structural and cognitive dimensions of both types of capital. The former refers to ties as "wires" (with reference to range and density), the latter to "nodes", defined as "the attitudes and values such as perceptions of support, reciprocity, and trust that contribute to the exchange of resources" (Lancee 2012, p. 18).

Bonding capital means densely woven interpersonal relations and "thick trust", while bridging refers to less dense and looser ties which might emerge in "structural holes" (Burt 1992), linking the small

[9]Unfortunately, there is no survey data with which to simultaneously investigate the effects of language knowledge and social capital on labor market performance.

[10]In this respect, it is of secondary importance that Lancee investigates "new" immigrant minority groups: The conceptual and analytical framework of the research is perfectly suitable for our purposes.

Table 3 Components of (individual level) social capital of Transylvanian Hungarians

Dimension	Type of capital	Type of relation	
		Strong	Weak
Structural	Bridging	Family ties with Romanians	Extra-family ties with Romanians
	Bonding	Family ties with Hungarians	Extra-family ties with Hungarians
Cognitive	Bridging	Trust in (ethnically mixed) close interpersonal relations	Generalized trust, trust in Romanians
	Bonding	Trust in (ethnically homogeneous) close interpersonal relations	Generalized trust, trust in Hungarians

worlds of different socioeconomic categories (class, age groups, ethnic groups, etc.). Its cognitive component is the so-called thin trust which refers to a general confidence in institutions of modern society, to "organic solidarity" in a Durkheimian sense, and less to confidence in people. Table 3 presents the dimensions and types of social capital used in the analysis. We have slightly modified Lancee's original model to include a new dimension along the "strong" and "weak" ties as defined by Granovetter (1973). In a rather simplified way, I perceive family nexuses as strong ties and extra-family relations as weak ties.

As the first step, I present the changes in the volume and distribution of the above-mentioned types of social capital based on two surveys conducted in 2000 and 2012.[11] I analyze the structural dimension of social capital through a series of questions that measure the personal networks of respondents. The questions inquired whether the former can rely on others in different situations and whether there are persons with whom they socialize on different occasions. I analyze five of the

[11]The survey, entitled "Social networks in Transylvania" (Networks 2000), was conducted by the Max Weber Research Center on a sample of 925 respondents, representative for Transylvanian Hungarians (Veres 2005). The Interethnic Climate 2012 survey was conducted by the Romanian Institute for Research on National Minorities on a representative sample of 1192 Transylvanian Hungarian respondents.

Table 4 Size and composition of the personal networks of Transylvanian Hungarians (2000, 2012)

	Networks 2000 ($N=892$)		Interethnic climate 2012 ($N=1192$)	
	Mean	S.D.	Mean	S.D.
Number of ties	4.65	3.06	3.92	3.06
Family ties	1.28	1.50	1.28	1.57
Extra-family ties	3.37	2.65	2.64	2.60
Hungarian ties	3.90	3.02	3.39	2.83
Romanian ties	0.35	0.90	0.43	1.19
Family ties with Hungarians	1.10	1.43	1.19	1.51
Extra-family ties with Hungarians	2.78	2.54	2.20	2.37
Family ties with Romanians	0.04	0.26	0.06	0.38
Extra-family ties with Romanians	0.30	0.82	0.30	0.91

Source Max Weber Research Center (2000), and RIRNM (2012)

situations which were addressed in both surveys.[12] For each setting, a maximum of three people could be identified, meaning that the number of ties could vary between 0 and 15 in the case of each individual respondent. The field operators recorded (among other items) the type of relation (family member, other relative, friend, neighbor, acquaintance) and the ethnicity of the person in question. Table 4 summarizes the results by type of the relation and the ethnicity of the mentioned person.

According to the results, an average Transylvanian Hungarian could rely on 4.7 ties in 2000 and on 3.9 ties in 2012. Both surveys indicate that less than 10% of the relations are inter-ethnic, while one-fifth

[12]These are the following: We asked respondents to respond using "yes" or "no", or name up to three individuals in the following situations: *(1) "Have you been someone's guest, or has someone been your guest in the last three months?" (2) "Are there persons with whom you go out with for entertainment (to pubs, theatre, sport events, hiking,* etc.*)?" (3) "Apart from family members living in the same household with you, are there persons with whom you regularly talk about confidential issues and problems?" (4) "Let us suppose you needed money immediately. Are there any people you could borrow from?" (5) "People often need legal counselling or advice and help in official matters. Is there anyone you can rely on if you needed to?"*

Table 5 Proportion of ethnic Hungarians reporting ties with Romanian ethnics (2000, 2012)

	2000 (*N*=924)	2012 (*N*=1029)
Dispersed communities (below 20%)	38.7	37.1
Local minority (20–39.9%)	26.0	28.1
Parity (40–59.9%)	15.0	13.9
Local majority (60–89.9%)	15.2	11.9
Hungarian dominance (above 90%)	6.9	8.6
Total	18.8	17.2

Source Max Weber Research Center (2000) and RIRNM (2012)

of Hungarians reported to having ties with Romanians that they could rely on. Obviously, this proportion is higher among Hungarians living in dispersed communities (37%) and lower among those residing in ethnic block areas (9%). One-third of the nexuses are family, and two-thirds are extra-family ties. Interethnic ties are less frequent within family relations (5%) and more frequent outside the family (11%). I presumed that the proportion of intra-ethnic ties would have increased during the period between 2000 and 2012 (due to the concentration of Hungarians in ethnic block areas). However, this assumption was not confirmed by the results.[13] Only the number of Hungarian extra-family ties and the total number of ties decreased; all other indicators remained constant (Table 5).

As for the cognitive component of social capital, I could rely only on the 2012 survey. The results indicate that the level of generalized trust was rather low among Transylvanian Hungarians, and they also trusted members of the majority group significantly less.[14]

[13]It should be mentioned, however, that the samples were quite similar concerning the ethnic composition of the settlements where the respondents reside.

[14]We measured generalized trust using the following standard question: "Generally speaking, would you say that most people can be trusted, or that you can't be too careful in dealing with people?" As for trust in Romanians/Hungarians, the following question was asked: "To what extent do you trust in Romanians/Hungarians? (1) Totally; (2) Rather yes; (3) Rather no; (4) Not at all". Table 6 summarizes the proportion of affirmative answers.

Table 6 Level of trust among Transylvanian Hungarians (2012)

Generalized trust	8.1
Trust in Hungarians	79.9
Trust in Romanians	56.3

Source RIRNM

In a second step, I investigated the relation between the amount and distribution of different types of social capital and the level of income. It must be admitted that it is difficult to determine the direction of causality between these variables. Nevertheless, my hypothesis is that the more extended one's personal network and the higher the proportion of extra-family and interethnic ties, the higher the realized income and the lower the risk of poverty. I also assumed a similar relationship between the level of trust, on the one hand, and per capita income and risk of poverty, on the other. I tested these hypotheses using regression analysis. Table 7 refers to the determinants of equivalent per capita household income and contains two models, one including only the indicators of social capital, while in the second socio-demographic controls are also introduced.

According to the basic model, only extra-family ties with Hungarians (e.g., bonding-type capital) have a significant effect on the level of per capita household income, while connections with Romanians (e.g., bridging-type capital) seem to have no economic utility. It is logical to expect that the effects of social capital on income are different according to the ethnic composition of the municipality. My supposition was that extra-family ties with Romanians are associated with a higher income for those Hungarians who live in municipalities where they constitute a local minority. However, this hypothesis was not confirmed. Romanian ties matter only in the ethnically more homogeneous settlements but, surprisingly, they correlate with lower incomes. Extra-family ties with Hungarians have a more powerful effect in a minority and ethnic parity situation, while the overall explanatory power of the model is also highest in a parity setting (Table 8).

Table 7 Factors influencing the equivalent per capita income of households (OLS regression 2012)

Variable	Values	Model 1		Model 2	
		B	S.E.	*B*	S.E.
Adjusted R^2		0.036		0.327	
Constant		614.522***	33.966	971.861***	65.850
Structural social capital	Hungarian family relations	−14.918*	8.966	−11.962	7.780
	Hungarian non-family relations	33.909***	5.849	10.336*	5.755
	Romanian family relations	5.382	36.765	−12.043	31.387
	Romanian non-family relations	23.377	15.506	−17.265	14.185
Cognitive social capital	Generalized trust	27.948	50.456	−51.775	43.026
	Trust in Hungarians	44.889	31.571	55.950**	27.223
	Trust in Romanians	58.677	39.085	15.131	34.534
Age group	**20–29 years**				
	15–19 years			85.774	81.930
	30–59 years			57.728	39.385
	60+			232.341***	55.660
Gender	**Male**				
	Female			−62.225**	24.682
Marital status	**Single**				
	Married, in union			−107.257***	37.942
	Divorced, widowed			−205.215***	50.218
Educational attainment	**University**				
	Less than lower secondary			−594.543***	68.775
	Lower secondary			−553.973***	45.655
	Professional			−427.486***	41.952
	Secondary completed			−301.294***	37.292

(continued)

Table 7 (continued)

Variable	Values	Model 1		Model 2	
		B	S.E.	*B*	S.E.
Economic activity	**Employed**				
	Self-employed, entrepreneur			70.081	47.682
	Pensioner			−40.500	40.840
	Housework			−157.137***	53.536
	Student			−139.114***	63.827
	Unemployed			−303.007***	46.974
	Other inactive			−235.381***	67.669
Settlement size	**below 2000**				
	2–10,000			36.497	33.145
	10–100,000			90.827**	40.819
	above 100,000			184.888***	47.893
Region	**Székely Land**				
	Partium			−60.427	39.659
	Central Transylvania			53.645	58.000
	Southern and Northern Transylvania			46.828	53.624
% of Hungarians within the municipality	**above 90%**				
	60–89.9%			95.731***	34.362
	40–59.9%			−8.845	83.278
	20–39.9%			57.324	53.275
	below 20%			113.417*	67.214

Source RIRNM survey, 2012. The dependent variable is the income in Romanian Lei (RON)
Non-standardized regression coefficients. *$p<0.1$; **$p<0.05$; ***$p<0.01$

The cognitive aspects of social capital affect differently the per capita income of households according to the ethnic composition of the settlement. First, in ethnically polarized municipalities both generalized trust and trust in Romanians have positive effects on per capita family income. It seems that in such localities (most probably characterized by ethnic competition) having trust that extends beyond one's own ethnic group is a comparative advantage. Second, trust in Hungarians (e.g., the cognitive aspect of bonding-type capital) matters most among Hungarians who live in dispersed communities.

Table 8 Factors influencing the equivalent per capita income of households, within categories delimited by sex and percentage of Hungarians in municipalities (OLS regression 2012)

		Percentage of Hungarians within municipality				
		0–19.9	20–39.9	40–59.9	60–89.9	90–100
Structural social capital	Hungarian family relations	−0.045	−0.0038	0.038	−0.049	−0.015
	Hungarian non-family relations	0.158***	0.341***	0.265*	0.203***	0.069
	Romanian family relations	0.024	0.067	−0.095	0.084	−0.113*
	Romanian non-family relations	−0.069	−0.032	0.229	−0.064	0.074
Cognitive social capital	Generalized trust	−0.097	0.117	0.269*	0.091	0.000
	Trust in Hungarians	0.175*	−0.009	−0.398**	−0.050	0.052
	Trust in Romanians	0.060	0.151	0.417**	−0.001	0.082
R^2		0.083	0.153	0.274	0.066	0.033

Source RIRNM survey
Numbers represent standardized OLS regression coefficients. *0.05 > p > 0.01; **0.01 > p > 0.001; ***p<0.001

A model that focuses on the determinants of the risk of poverty shows similar results. It also underscores the relevance of "weak ties" with Hungarians: The risk of poverty is lower if individuals are able to mobilize extra-family but ethnically homogenous ties in different settings. The relation with generalized trust is only marginally significant (Table 9).

To sum up, ethnic homophily—with notable exceptions in parity settings—seems to bring about greater rewards for Transylvanian Hungarians. Ethnically homogeneous weak ties and trust in one's own ethnic group yield a higher per capita family income and a lower risk of poverty. Bridging capital (relations with and trust in Romanians) does not fulfill these expectations and does not help Hungarians to

Table 9 Factors influencing the risk of income poverty (binary logistic regression, 2012)

Variable	Values	*B*	S.E.	Exp(*B*)
Constant		−1.149***	0.190	0.317
Structural social capital	Hungarian family relations	0.002	0.051	1.002
	Hungarian non-family relations	−0.161***	0.039	0.851
	Romanian family relations	0.064	0.213	1.066
	Romanian non-family relations	−0.101	0.097	0.904
Cognitive social capital	Generalized trust	−0.602*	0.349	0.548
	Trust in Hungarians	−0.081	0.178	0.922
	Trust in Romanians	0.102	0.219	1.108
R^2 (Nagelkerke) = 0.036				

*$p<0.1$; ***$p<0.01$
Source RIRNM survey

"get ahead" in the labor market. It should be underscored that these results are not in line with the mainstream narrative of the literature, according to which bridging capital is a prerequisite of better labor market opportunities and social mobility. Due to their unexpected character, these results should be treated as a well-grounded hypothesis which should be validated through further in-depth investigation.[15]

[15]Both the validity and the reliability of the analysis should be increased. From the perspective of validity, the following problems may be underscored (in order of importance): (1) The 2012 survey asked only for the total income of the household, which is the result of the aggregate labor market performance of family members, while our hypotheses referred to individual labor market performance. Unfortunately, no question concerning individual income was included in the survey. (2) A more precise operationalization of the different types and dimensions of social capital is also needed. (3) I did not succeed in eliminating the problem of reverse causality, nor that of endogeneity.

As for the reliability of the surveys, the following problems should be mentioned: (1) It is a recurrent problem in the sampling of minority populations that more assimilated members of the minority groups have less chance of being included in the sample. (2) A proper investigation of the effects under discussion in several socio-demographic subcategories would require a more extended sample. For example, it is almost certain that the economic payoff of ethnically heterogeneous relationships differs in different occupational categories. (3) We did not deal with the redundancy of the relationships in these five situations—this may alter the aggregate (ethnic) heterogeneity of the connections.

4 Manifestations of Bonding Social Capital: Economic Ethnocentrism and Ethnic Entrepreneurship

Due to the limited data, I did not succeed in capturing the changes in the amount and distribution of different types of social capital. However, the hypothesis that the significance of bonding capital will increase due to the territorial concentration and institutional encapsulation of the Hungarian population remains a logical expectation and a plausible outcome of social and demographic macro-processes. On the one hand, the amount of Romanian connections an average Transylvanian Hungarian can mobilize will most probably decrease.[16] On the other hand, we have also seen that the increase in Hungarian "weak ties" may bring economic advantages.

Until now, I have discussed social capital in individual terms. However, bonding capital can also increase in-group solidarity and trust and, consequently, can lead to lower transaction costs, meaning that in intra-ethnic situations the cost of supervising economic transactions and enforcing contractual terms, etc., is less (Orbán and Szántó 2005). These savings might instead be spent on investment and other forms of development or welfare. Higher levels of trust induce lower levels of corruption and rent seeking, and lead to the more efficient management of public goods. In other words, social capital can become a collective resource.

Further, a higher frequency of ethnically homogeneous interactions is not only a cause but also a consequence of "bounded solidarity" and "enforceable trust" among members of an ethnic group (Portes 1998). This is why they tend to manage their affairs (including economic ones) among their own—they ask each other for help, do business with one another, work with each other, and buy from each other, etc. Solidarity is the normative dimension of this type of in-group cooperation which

[16] The possibility of the maintenance of personal nexuses through use of the Internet and an eventual increase in geographic mobility could counterbalance these tendencies. For instance, better infrastructure could make the maintenance of interethnic ties even across regions easier.

may be activated along shared value-introjections, collective identities, and representations. Trust can rather be perceived as a cognitive prerequisite for cooperation and as a guarantee that contractual terms will be respected.

4.1 Economic Ethnocentrism

Economic ethnocentrism is one of the visible manifestations of bonding social capital. I define all economic (consumer) predispositions and decisions involving a preference for (Transylvanian) Hungarian products and services as economic ethnocentrism, regardless of whether they are the results of profit-seeking rationality or moral considerations (Shimp 1984). The economic ethnocentrism of the Transylvanian Hungarians has been addressed through several investigations (Csata and Deák 2010; Csata 2014). The most complex operationalization of the issue was done in a survey carried out in 2008.[17] Table 10 summarizes the results of six aggregated indicators.[18]

Results indicate that economic ethnocentrism is higher among Transylvanian Hungarians than Romanians in every hypothetical situation. These differences suggest that economic ethnocentrism is not simply a general, unreflexive imprint of a more general nationalistic attitude, but somehow is related to a collective and conscious experience of

[17]The survey titled "Interethnic climate in Romania 2008" was carried out by the Romanian Institute for Research on National Minorities in cooperation with the Centre for Research on Interethnic Relations (CCRIT) on a sample of 1723 respondents, among them 607 Transylvanian Hungarians.

[18]The indicators were constructed using questions as follows: (1) "Are you willing to pay more for products made in Romania/Hungary?"; (2) "Imagine a situation when you may choose between a Romanian, a Hungarian and a Roma salesman. The quality and the price of their products are identical. Which of them would you choose?"; (3) "Imagine that you have the possibility to rent your apartment. You have the possibility to choose between a Romanian, a Hungarian and a Roma client. Which of them would you choose?"; (4) "Would you be willing to rent your apartment for a lower price in order to have a Hungarian tenant?"; (5) "Imagine that you have to sell a plot. To what extent would you be willing to sell it to a Hungarian/Romanian?"; (6) Level of agreement with the following statement: "It is obvious that Hungarian employers prefer Hungarian employees because they can trust them more". The aggregate variable takes a value of between 0 and 6, the latter indicating maximum economic ethnocentrism.

Table 10 Economic ethnocentrism among ethnic Hungarians and Romanians (2008)

	Mean	Std. dev.
Hungarians in Székely Land	2.68	1.76
Hungarians in Transylvania	2.27	1.69
Romanians in Transylvania	1.53	1.33
Romanians in Romania	1.84	1.41

Note 0 = minimum and 6 = maximum economic ethnocentrism
Source RIRNM survey, 2008. Valid $N = 587$

the minority status and as such, it is a manifestation of bonding social capital.

This is also indicated by the regression model summarized in Table 11. According to the model, the most important determinants of economic ethnocentrism among Hungarians are low trust vis-á-vis Romanians and a lack of connections with members of the majority. In line with these, economic ethnocentrism is higher among the residents of Székely Land and lower among Hungarians who live in local minority in other regions of Transylvania.

It should be mentioned that although they are referring to a variety of transaction situations and action projections all of the indicators referred to predispositions, while we know little about actual

Table 11 Factors affecting economic ethnocentrism (OLS regression 2008)

	B	S.E.	Beta
Constant	2.885	0.207	
Residence in Székely Land	0.301*	0.145	0.098
Hungarian majority	−0.097	0.179	−0.023
Parity	−0.235	0.189	−0.057
Hungarian minority	−0.462**	0.184	−0.129
Dispersed communities	0.002	0.251	0.001
Mixed marriage in the extended family	−0.337	0.252	−0.055
Romanian nexuses	−0.083***	0.025	−0.140
General trust	−0.089	0.175	−0.020
Trust in Romanians	−0.665***	0.141	−0.189
Explanatory power (R^2)	*0.125*		

*$p < 0.05$; **$p < 0.01$; ***$p < 0.001$
Source RIRNM survey, 2008, Valid $N = 587$

economic decisions. Nevertheless, our data show that there is a relatively high demand for cooperation along ethnic lines among Transylvanian Hungarians. This demand might be the root cause of ethnically defined market segments. The ethnically more sensitive strata of the Hungarian population (receptive to ethnically targeted marketing messages) may be delimitated along the above-mentioned variables.

4.2 Ethnic Entrepreneurship

The most obvious institutional manifestation of bonding social capital is ethnic entrepreneurship. In the last few years, many economic initiatives have explicitly targeted Hungarian consumers. These initiatives try to gain an economic advantage by appealing to the ethnic solidarity prevalent among members of the minority group (Gáll 2011). Some of the large multinational companies have also taken steps toward creating a marketing strategy which perceives Transylvanian Hungarians (especially those living in Székely Land) as a distinct customer segment.

Merkúr, a department store chain in Székely Land is one of the most important actors in the Hungarian ethnic economy in Romania. The firm was established in Odorheiu Secuiesc/Székelyudvarhely and presently has twelve stores in five towns in Székely Land. In Harghita/Hargita and Covansa/Kovászna counties, it is a successful competitor of the multinational companies also present in the area (Lidl, Kaufland, etc.). In 2014, it had 700 employees and a gross income of more than 50 million euros. Merkúr stores also retail the so-called Góbé products, which is a brand product of the company and embraces 350 products from 64 local producers which are sold under a common logo with a standard appearance. Góbé can also be perceived as a social brand, as it promotes the products of local producers. Merkúr advertises itself as the department store chain of Székely Land, it uses a logo and other visual elements alluding to this geographic entity and relies on stylized and conventional representations of Székely villages. Although Góbé is defined as a regional social brand, meaning that all local producers (irrespective of their ethnic background) can become suppliers, in reality has strong ethnic connotations, as the term ("góbé") is an archaic

Hungarian regionalism in Székely Land, referring to a crafty, screw-witted person you do not want to mess with—one of the characteristics of the socially constructed cultural archetype of the Szekler men. Therefore, not surprisingly, in practice all the suppliers connected to this brand are Hungarians, thus products have ethnically defined added value for consumers. This claim is also strengthened by the fact that Merkúr sells a wide range of products made in Hungary.

Igazi Csíki Sör (Real Csíki Beer) is another successful attempt to commodify Székely ethno-regional solidarity. In 2014, a small brewery was set up in Sânsimion/Csíkszentsimon, Harghita/Hargita county to produce beer under this brand name. The product's image relied strongly on symbols and narratives constructed around Székely historical and ethnographic heritage and advertising was undertaken exclusively in Hungarian. This marketing strategy proved to be relatively successful. However, the brewery became the focus of media attention due to the fact that Heineken Romania initiated a legal process against it because of the use of the trade name Igazi Csíki Sör. Heineken had previously registered the trade name Ciuc Premium for the beer they bottled in Miercurea Ciuc/Csíkszereda. According to the argumentation of the multinational company, Csíki Sör was the Hungarian translation of Ciuc Premium (or bere Ciuc).[19] However, the process proved to be profitable for the local brewery. The case was portrayed as a struggle of David against Goliath, a small local company against a heartless, profit-oriented multinational company. Following a smartly designed campaign and a badly phrased communique from Heineken (which denied the existence of Székely Land), local Hungarians began to boycott the products of the multinational company. The Hungarian government also entered the debate and threatened Heineken with a ban on its logo containing a red star[20] across the territory of Hungary. Ultimately, the process ended with a compromise: Beer produced by the local brewery is now sold under the product name Forbidden Csíki Beer (Tiltott Csíki Sör) and has maintained its popularity among Transylvanian Hungarian

[19]Actually, local Hungarians called *Ciuc Premium* "*Csíki Sör*".

[20]The red star is deemed a totalitarian symbol in Hungarian legislation.

consumers. However, an attempt by the company to enter the market in Hungary proved less successful.

The above-mentioned examples show how an economic model relying on the "bounded solidarity" and "enforceable trust" prevalent among the Hungarian population can be successful in the Székely region. The likelihood of success can be increased by combining elements of the consumer ethic (regionalism, anti-globalism, environmental consciousness, pro-organic, etc.) with ethnic markers. From this perspective, the phenomenon under investigation may also be connected to ethical consumerism (Lewis and Potter 2011). From an anthropological perspective, it is also interesting that Hungarian enterprises, ethnic brands as common contemporary symbols, and the ethnically bounded practices of economic cooperation are further amplifying solidarity among the members of the minority group. Furthermore—and this is also important from our point of view—on the ground of market deregulation, using classical instruments of consumer marketing they spontaneously contribute to the development of multilingualism in the economy. We think that without the enforcement of the laws of free competition by the European Union, this process would have encountered more obstacles from the Romanian authorities.

5 Summary and Comparative Overview

Experts and political actors tend to agree that the social positions of the Transylvanian Hungarians can be improved through investment in education and the economy. Limited decisional competences hinder the rational planning of Hungarian-language educational system[21]; however, Hungarian elites have far more influence on the evolution of the educational domain than on the economic. Economic processes are determined by spontaneous (and from the perspective of the Hungarian elites, haphazard) market mechanisms. Ethnicity is not among the most important determinants of the institutional context shaping the market

[21]See Chapter 6.

economy in Romania. Consequently, the program of ethnic parallelism is far less effective in the economic domain than it is in education, culture, or religious institutions (Kiss 2015). Nevertheless, I argue that the role of ethnicity in shaping economic processes is not insignificant and is increasing, due primarily to the territorial concentration of the Transylvanian Hungarian population.

According to the neo-institutionalist perspective, the role of ethnicity in the coordination of economic transactions depends on two broad sets of factors. (1) The first is composed of the general regulative context and the efficiency of the institutions that support the smooth working of economic interactions. The functioning of this latter set is dependent on the level of confidence vis-á-vis institutional structures, and moreover, on the level of generalized trust. (2) The second set of factors is connected to the divergence/convergence of preferences across ethnic groups. This depends on cultural differences and socioeconomic inequalities between ethnic groups. If the level of generalized trust is low and preferences are different, ethnicity will play an important role in coordinating economic interactions.

It is hard to decide and should be addressed in relative terms whether the regulatory context in Romania is efficient and democratic enough. Nevertheless, there is consensus that confidence in institutions, generalized trust, and trust between members of different ethnic groups is rather low (Csata 2011). Empirical investigations also demonstrate that ethnic inequalities (especially those concerning income) are increasing (Csata 2017b). The level of cultural differences should also be discussed in relative terms. However, in my opinion the economic significance of linguistic differences has been systematically underestimated by several analysts.[22] It is rather important that the Romanian-language

[22]See, for instance, Brubaker et al. (2006), who dedicate a separate chapter to language use in a book that focuses on interethnic relations in Cluj/Kolozsvár, but they don't discuss the economic consequences of linguistic differences. The authors mention that Romanian-language learning and language use requires an "effort" from the Hungarians, and that the shift to Romanian may cause a feeling of "discomfort". However, these remarks are not incorporated into the main narrative of the book. This is not accidental at all. If the former admitted (1) that there is a close interlink between language and ethnicity, and (2) that the Romanian-language knowledge of Hungarians cannot be taken for granted but requires significant effort and involves significant cost (which claims are objectively quantifiable) they would have to partially reconsider their thesis

knowledge of Hungarians is decreasing and this is being penalized by the labor market. Obtaining Romanian-language knowledge requires increasing effort because: (1) The efficiency of Romanian-language teaching is very low; (2) media consumption in Romanian is in decline; (3) the frequency of ethnically mixed interactions is also decreasing due to the territorial concentration and institutional encapsulation of the Hungarian population; and (4) as an aggregate effect, the motivation to learn the only official language of the state is diminishing. It seems that the threat of a decrease in income due to a lack of Romanian-language skills is not counterbalancing these tendencies. A reasonable and fair solution for eliminating such income disparities that arise from this language disadvantage could be symmetric bilingualism— a "territorially coercive linguistic regime" (Parijs 2011)—in those territories where Hungarians represent the majority. However, there is consensus among Romanian political actors that such solutions should be firmly rejected (Csata and Marácz 2016).

The process of "transnationalization" (EU accession, the opportunity to acquire Hungarian citizenship) is also an important development. Hungarian and European labor markets have become far more accessible, the transaction costs of working abroad have radically decreased, and traveling has become cheaper and faster. In contrast, the cost of Romanian-language learning and that of ethnic boundary crossing have not changed, or have even increased. Consequently, learning English instead of Romanian and working abroad have become rational options for a growing number of Hungarian youngsters, especially for those who live in Hungarian majority areas. The cost of learning English is lower due to its greater media exposure, more efficient teaching techniques and a more positive psychological disposition. Moreover, Hungarians

concerning the socially constructed character of ethnicity in Transylvania. Another possibility would be to throw away the concept of ethnicity and focus only on linguistic differences. This is the strategy of language economists who analyze the economic consequences of language differences in Quebec and Switzerland (Vaillancourt 1996; Grin et al. 1997). In Transylvania, we have seen that linguistic differences, along with other asymmetries, cause economic inequalities. Ethnic boundaries might be fluid and constructed, but linguistic ones are rigid and not negotiable. Either you know a language or not. The mother tongue(s) is a resource with palpably unequal economic consequences, regardless of what people think about one's ethnicity.

can make themselves understood using English among Romanians too. Thus, English might become a de facto *lingua franca*, even if the institutionalization of such a development is less likely. In any case, the consequences, challenges, and opportunities connected to the increasing use of English should be taken more seriously.[23]

In light of the current state of things, language-economic factors do not facilitate ethnic rapprochement and are conducive to the further deepening of an already existing ethnic parallelism. Ethnic polarization, fragmentation, and fractionalization[24] can be further enhanced by the experience that that bridging ties toward Romanians do not seem to have an economic payoff, their utility is low. According to our rather surprising results, for an average Hungarian, possessing bridging capital is not an advantage in the labor market and does not increase income. Consequently, it is not reasonable to invest in it, especially because it automatically requires further investments in learning Romanian.

As for personal relations outside the labor market, Romanian ties foster a relative recreational advantage only if similar Hungarian alternatives are not available. The poorer one's Romanian-language knowledge, the greater the feeling of discomfort caused by the use of the majority language in intimate informal settings. Even if one speaks Romanian fluently, the hegemonic institution of "linguistic bowing" (Parijs 2011) cannot easily be neglected, and the lack of "parity of esteem" reminds Hungarians that their mother tongue is considered second-rank, dysfunctional, and useless by the members of the majority group. I do not think that this kind of sensitivity characterizes all Transylvanian Hungarians and determines their disposition toward Romanians. However, I do consider that these psychological reactions to linguistic asymmetry are frequent and they are also important factors in the explanation of ethnic homophily.

In summing up the previous paragraphs, it should be emphasized that the anomalies of the regulative context of the Romanian economy

---

[23]For the economic advantages of English as a lingua franca, see Liu (2015).

[24]On the meaning of this notion, and on the relation between economy and ethnic diversity, see Csata (2017a).

(corruption, rent seeking, favoritism, etc.), the low level of generalized trust, asymmetric bilingualism, the lack of economic utility of bridging capital, and increasing territorial concentration are leading to an increase in the value of bonding relationships, ethnic fragmentation, and the consolidation of institutionally embedded ethnic parallelism. The economy still cannot be considered an ethnically organized social field; however, the relevance of ethnicity is increasing at the level of both individual economic decisions and economic institutions.

At the individual level, as we have seen, bonding capital has a higher economic utility, the level of economic ethnocentrism is rather high among Transylvanian Hungarians: almost half of them would prefer to have a Hungarian economic partner if this were possible. Ethnocentric market preferences are stronger among those living in Hungarian-majority areas in a kind of "ethnic shell", are distrustful to the Romanians, and have difficulties speaking their language. However, economic ethnocentrism does not depend on the age, gender, income, and educational attainment. It is a logical expectation that territorial concentration and lower levels of Romanian-language knowledge will lead to a further increase in ethnocentric economic dispositions.

The overall number of products that commodify ethnic solidarity and refer to the "Székely" ethnonym is increasing. The introduction and enforcement of EU trade law in Romania is also an indispensable guarantee for the undisturbed use of Hungarian language in the consumer market. As a result, not only self-government patronage units, but independent private entrepreneurs, even multinational companies started to recognize the potential benefits of marketing in Hungarian. The overall number of products that commodify ethnic solidarity and refer to the historically constructed and collectively shared meanings of the "Székely" ethnonym is increasing. Furthermore, Hungarians appreciate if they are addressed in their mother tongue (in marketing campaigns, advertisements, customer service, etc.), which makes them a less differentiated target, a much easier-to-reach, low-cost consumer segment of the market.

Nevertheless, the economic impacts of these initiatives have remained rather limited, and we can hardly say that they are significantly contributing to improving the economic situation of the Hungarian population. The significance of ethnic enterprises has been rather symbolic (at least until now): They have increased, for instance, bilingualism in the economy, making it more legitimate in the eyes of a larger public. However, under the current regulatory conditions, ethnically defined market segments are likely to grow and may also fulfill a manifest economic function: promoting the growth of Hungarian enterprises and the development of Hungarian businesses in the region.

This chapter has paid less attention to bridging social capital. However, the concerns expressed in the literature on the collective scarcity of bridging capital (Putnam 2000; Orbán and Szántó 2005) is entirely justified. Bridging capital could play a role in counterbalancing the anomalies caused by the predominance and proliferation of bonding capital, namely intolerance, exclusion on ethnic grounds, xenophobia, and aversion to cultural diversity. These phenomena can cause tension and lead to social conflict. Besides the social impacts, the lack of bridging capital may have negative economic consequences too. The most important of these is the decline of information potential: without contacts and cooperation with the members of the national majority, Hungarian entrepreneurs might miss important business opportunities and put them at comparative disadvantage vis-á-vis other economic actors. This disadvantage may only be partially offset by the strengthening governmental and business influence coming from Hungary. For instance, it is still rather difficult for Transylvanian Hungarian products and services to enter the Hungarian market. This lack of vertical economic integration might have macro-social consequences and promote the further economic marginalization of Hungarian-inhabited areas. A decline of bridging capital goes hand in hand with worsening Romanian-language skills which have already induced considerable losses in several economic domains.[25]

[25]For the problems caused by the lack of appropriate Romanian skills in the tourist industry in Covasna/Kovászna county, see Csata and Pásztor (2015).

Acknowledgments This chapter was supported by a János Bolyai Research Scholarship from the Hungarian Academy of Sciences (BO 00604/17). The author would like to thank Tibor Kuczi for his advice on the broader conceptual framework of the analysis, András Bethlendi, András Csite, Kinga Kerekes, Dénes Kiss, Gyöngyi Pásztor, and László Péter for their valuable comments and suggestions.

References

Aldrich, H. E., & Waldinger, R. (1990). Ethnicity and entrepreneurship. *Annual Review of Sociology, 16*(1), 111–135.

Alesina, A., & La Ferrara, E. (2005). Ethnic diversity and economic performance. *Journal of Economic Literature, 43*(3), 762–800.

Benő, A. (2012). Hogyan tanulják a magyar gyerekek a román nyelvet az erdélyi iskolákban? Problémák és lehetőségek. *Székelyföld, 16*(5), 54–65.

Brubaker, R., Feischmidt, M., Fox, J., & Grancea, L. (2006). *Nationalist politics and everyday ethnicity in a Transylvanian town*. Princeton: Princeton University Press.

Burt, R. S. (1992). *Structural holes: The social structure of competition*. Cambridge, MA: Harvard University Press.

Chiswick, B. R., & Miller, P. W. (2007). *The economics of language: International analyses studies in the modern world economy*. London and New York: Routledge.

Csata, Z. (2011). Confiance ou scepticisme: l'evaluation des institutions civiles et politiques en Roumanie. In D. C. Sossa (Ed.), *Nouvelles democraties et socialisation politique. Etude comparee des cas du Benin, du Bukina Faso et de la Roumanie*. Paris: L'Harmattan.

Csata, Z. (2012). The social determinants of entrepreneurial activity in rural Transylvania. *Studia Sociologia, 3*(1), 101–124.

Csata, Z. (2014). *A fogyasztói magatartás etnikai vonatkozásai a kolozsvári magyar egyetemi hallgatók körében - Kutatásjelentés*. Kolozsvár: BBTE Magyar Szociológia és Szociális Munkásképző Kar.

Csata, Z. (2015). Ethnicity and economy. A research agenda for Transylvania. *Erdélyi Társadalom, 13*(3), 31–46.

Csata, Z. (2016). Reflections on the economic aspects of multilingualism in Transylvania. *Belvedere Meridionale, 28*(2), 51–65.

Csata, Z. (2017a). Az etnikai diverzitás (polarizáció) és a jólét összefüggései Erdélyben.
Csata, Z. (2017b). Munkaerőpiaci egyenlőtlenségek Romániában, etnikai metszetbe. *Erdélyi Társadalom, 15*(1), 81–104.
Csata, Z., & Deák, A. (2010). Gazdasági etnocentrizmus, etnikai fogyasztás az erdélyi magyarok körében. *Közgazdász Fórum, 13*(4), 31–49.
Csata, Z., & Marácz, L. (2016). Prospects on Hungarian as a regional official language and Szeklerland's territorial autonomy in Romania. *International Journal on Minority and Group Rights, 23*(4), 530–559.
Csata, Z., & Pásztor, G. (2015). *Összehasonlító régiótanulmány a vidéki turizmusra és a foglalkoztatottságra vonatkozóan Bihar és Kovászna megyében.* Bukarest: OTP Consulting.
Csata, Z., Dániel, B., & Pop, C. (2006). Pályakezdő fiatalok a munkaerőpiacon. *Erdélyi Társadalom, 4*(1), 7–27.
Csergő, Z. (2007). *Talk of the nation: Language and conflict in Romania and Slovakia.* Ithaca: Cornell University Press.
Dániel, B. (2011). Erdélyi magyar fiatalok jövőterveinek, munkaerő-piaci helyzetének, etnikai fogyasztásának vizsgálata. In A. Szabó, B. Bauer, & P. Pillók (Eds.), *Mozaik 2011 – Magyar fiatalok a Kárpát-medencében. Kutatási jelentés* (pp. 169–198). Szeged and Budapest: Belvedere Meridionale—Nemzeti Család- és Szociálpolitikai Intézet.
Eriksen, T. H. (2005). Economies of ethnicity. In J. G. Carrier (Ed.), *A handbook of economic anthropology* (pp. 353–369). Cheltenham and Northhampton, MA: Edward Elgar.
Gáll, Z. (2011). Fából vaskarika? Avagy: lehet-e a székely termék világmárka? *Pro Minoritate, 15*(2), 54–71.
Geambaşu, R. (2017). „A kódolás élvezete". A kolozsvári programozók.
Granovetter, M. (1973). The strength of weak ties. *American Journal of Sociology, 78*(6), 1360–1380.
Granovetter, M. (1985). Economic action and social structure: The problem of embeddedness. *American Journal of Sociology, 91*(3), 481–510.
Granovetter, M. (1995). The economic sociology of firms and entrepreneurs. In A. Portes (Ed.), *The economic sociology of immigration: Essays on networks, ethnicity, and entrepreneurship* (pp. 128–162). New York: Russell Sage Foundation.
Grin, F. (2004). On the costs of cultural diversity. In P. V. Parijs (Ed.), *Cultural diversity versus economic solidarity: Proceedings of the Seventh Francqui*

Colloquium, Brussels (1 ed., pp. 189–202). Bruxelles: De Boeck. 28 February–1 March 2003.

Grin, F., Ahmad, Z., & Sfreddo, C. (Eds.). (1997). *Langue et différentiels de statut socio-économique en Suisse*. Berne: Office fédéral de la statistique.

Hartford, T. (2016). *Messy: How to be creative and resilient in a Tidy-minded world*. Hachette: Little, Brown Book Group.

Horváth, I. (2003). Az erdélyi magyarok kétnyelvűsége: nyelvmentés és integráció között? *Erdélyi Társadalom, 1*(1), 7–24.

Horváth, I. (2008) *Elemzések a romániai magyarok kétnyelvűségéről* (ISPMN Working Papers 8).

Kiss, T. (2004). Vállalkozástörténetek Erdélyben. In É. Kovács (Ed.), *A gazdasági átmenet etnikai tájképei* (pp. 23–128). Budapest: Teleki László Alapítvány.

Kiss, T. (2015). Increasing marginality, ethnic parallelism and asymmetric accommodation. Social and political processes concerning the Hungarian Community of Transylvania. *Minority Studies, 18*, 33–69.

Lancee, B. (2012). *Immigrant performance in the labour market: Bonding and bridging social capital*. IMISCOE Research. Amsterdam: Amsterdam University Press.

Landa, J. T. (1994) *Trust, ethnicity, and identity: Beyond the new institutional economics of ethnic trading networks, contract law, and gift-exchange. Economics, cognition, and society*. Ann Arbor: University of Michigan Press.

Lewis, T., & Potter, E. (2011) *Ethical consumption: A critical introduction*. London and New York: Routledge.

Light, I. H., & Gold, S. J. (2000). *Ethnic economies*. San Diego: Academic Press.

Liu, A. H. (2015). *Standardizing diversity: The political economy of language regimes*. Philadelphia: University of Pennsylvania Press.

Narayan, D. (1999). *Bonds and bridges: Social capital and poverty*. (Policy research Working Paper). Washington, DC: World Bank, Poverty Reduction and Economic Management Network, Poverty Division.

Orbán, A., & Szántó, Z. (2005). Társadalmi tőke. *Erdélyi Társadalom, 3*(2), 55–70.

Ottaviano, G. I. P., & Peri, G. (2006). The economic value of cultural diversity: Evidence from US cities. *Journal of Economic Geography, 6*(1), 9–44.

Page, S. E. (2007). *The difference: How the power of diversity creates better groups, firms, schools, and societies*. Princeton: Princeton University Press.

Papp, A. Z., & Márton, J. (2011). Párhuzamos világok? Az erdélyi magyar gazdasági és kulturális elit szocio-demográfiai jellemzői. In I. Kovách (Ed.), *Elitek a válság korában. Magyarországi elitek, kisebbségi magyar elitek* (pp. 459–517). Budapest: MTA PTI, MTA ENKI and Argumentum.
Parijs, P. van. (2011). *Linguistic justice for Europe and for the world.* Oxford political theory. Oxford and New York: Oxford University Press.
Portes, A. (1998). Social capital: Its origins and applications in modern sociology. *Annual Review of Sociology, 24*(1), 1–24.
Portes, A., & Sensenbrenner, J. (1993). Embeddedness and immigration: Notes on the social determinants of economic action. *American Journal of Sociology, 98*(6), 1320–1350.
Putnam, R. D. (2000). *Bowling alone: The collapse and revival of American community.* New York: Simon & Schuster.
Putnam, R. D. (2007). E Pluribus Unum: Diversity and community in the twenty-first century the 2006 Johan Skytte Prize Lecture. *Scandinavian Political Studies, 30*(2), 137–174.
Shimp, T. A. (1984). Consumer ethnocentrism: The concept and a preliminary empirical test. In T. C. Kinear (Ed.), *Advances in consumer research* (pp. 285–290). Provo, UT: Association for Consumer Research.
Szabó, T. Á. (2010). Etnikai különbségtétel a paraszti gazdaságban. In M. Feischmidt (Ed.), *Etnicitás: különbségteremtő társadalom.* Gondolat—MTA Etnikai-Nemzeti Kisebbségkutató Intézet: Budapest.
Szabó, T. Á. (2015). Dairy cooperative in the making: History, ethnicity and local culture in an economic enterprise. *Erdélyi Társadalom, 13*(3), 47–65.
Szilágyi, N. S. (1998). De ce nu-şi pot însuşi copiii maghiari limba română în şcoală? *Altera, 7*, 131–148.
Tódor, E. (2005). A kódváltás és az aszimmetrikus kétnyelvűség nyelvpedagógiai összefüggései. *Magyar Pedagógia, 105*(1), 41–58.
Toró, T. (2017). Detached implementation. Discourse and practice in minority language usage in Romania. Manuscript.
Vaillancourt, F. (1996). Language and socioeconomic status in Quebec: Measurement, findings, determinants, and policy costs. *International Journal of the Sociology of Language, 121*(1), 69–92.
Veres, V. (2005). *Nemzeti identitás Erdélyben–szociológiai olvasatban: az erdélyi magyarok és románok nemzeti identitásának sajátosságai, társadalmi rétegződési perspektívában.* Budapest: Akadémiai Kiadó.

Part III

Societal and Demographic Macro-processes

10

Demographic Dynamics and Ethnic Classification: An Introduction to Societal Macro-Processes

Tamás Kiss

This chapter is an introduction to the last section of the book, which deals with societal and demographic macro-processes. The first broad part of the chapter (consisting of five subsections) provides an outline of the major demographic processes affecting Transylvanian Hungarians. This part relies mainly on census data and tries to synthesize some of the major conclusions of the ethno-demographic research focusing on Transylvanian Hungarians carried out in the last one and half decades. First, I discuss changes to the ethnic landscape in Transylvania, particularly the demographic evolution of the Hungarian community. As we will see, the number of Transylvanian Hungarians dropped significantly during the last 35 years. The next three subsections discuss factors contributing to this population decline: natural growth, migratory flows, and assimilatory processes. The fifth subsection of this part deals with

T. Kiss (✉)
Romanian Institute for Research on National Minorities,
Cluj-Napoca, Romania

T. Kiss et al. (eds.), *Unequal Accommodation of Minority Rights*,
Palgrave Politics of Identity and Citizenship Series,
https://doi.org/10.1007/978-3-319-78893-7_10

the significant regional differences in the dynamics of the demographic and ethno-cultural reproduction of the Hungarian community.

While the first broad part of the chapter is mainly a positivist quantitative analysis of demographic processes, the second part undertakes a constructivist perspective and discusses the techniques of ethnic classification on different levels. First, I discuss census classification. I rely on Wimmer (2013) and on Rallu et al. (2006) and argue that a shift from a Herderian discursive order toward an integrationist one has occurred following the collapse of state socialism, altering/questioning the existing "regime of counting". However, this shift was gradual and inconclusive. Consequently, both official and everyday ethnic classification remained attached to the Herderian paradigm, treating ethnic categories as bounded groups with mutually exclusive membership. Following these more general considerations, I discuss two groups connected to the Hungarian population in Romania, Hungarian-speaking Roma and the Csángós (Catholics of Hungarian origin) in Moldova. I will argue that in their case, standard census techniques of measuring ethno-national identity are highly problematic.

1 Demographic Processes. An Outline

1.1 The Dynamics of the Hungarian Population According to Census Data: 1910–2011

Censuses constitute the most important data sources concerning the changes in the ethnic structure of the territory under investigation. The last census carried out by the Hungarian Central Statistical Office was in 1910; thus, the results of this census can be compared to later Romanian census data (Table 1).[1]

---

[1]The methodological problems of such a comparison are multiple. In a later subsection of this chapter, I will discuss the changes of the techniques of census ethnic classification. Next to this problem, the results of both the Hungarian and Romanian censuses were contested. As for an analysis of the (defensive) reactions of the Romanian public opinion to Hungarian censuses

Census data show significant changes in the territory's ethnic structure. The proportion of the titular category has increased sharply under Romanian sovereignty. According to the last Hungarian census in 1910, Romanians comprised 54% of the population. By 2011, they constituted almost 75%. The number and proportion of Germans fell drastically during the same period: While in 1910 they made up 10% of the total population, in 2011 their proportion barely reached 0.5%. The number and proportion of Hungarians also decreased, albeit less dramatically. In 2011, about 1.2 million persons declared themselves as Hungarian, representing 19% of the total population of Transylvania.[2] The number and proportion of Roma have been rising continuously since 1966. In 1966, less than 50,000 people identified themselves as such, while in 2011, their number exceeded 270,000.

Based on demographic investigations, it is also possible to present the changes of the annual number of the Hungarian population for the 1964–2017 period (Fig. 1).[3]

between 1880 and 1910, see Botoş et al. (2016). Blomqvist discussed in detail the role of censuses in the nationalizing policies of Hungary and Romania between 1880 and 1941 (2014, pp. 75–85; 222–224; 278–280; 333–334). Brubaker et al. highlighted that struggles over census results were an immanent part of ethnic politics after the collapse of communism too (2006, pp. 151–160). Our starting point is that censuses are not simple bureaucratic exercises but are part of the political struggle over the legitimate representation of social reality (Kertzer and Arel 2002). As a consequence, one cannot omit census data but should be careful when using it in the analysis of ethno-demographic processes.

[2]From an administrative point of view, the 2011 census was quite chaotic. It was designed as a traditional census with enumerators and face-to-face interviews with paper-based questionnaires. Slightly more than 19 million persons were registered with this methodology on the entire territory of Romania. However, following the census, the government decided to supplement the census database using the population register. Due to this exercise, the population of Romania rose above 20 million, which is obviously an overestimation of the country's resident population. As the population register does not contain information about ethnic belonging, we lack this information for 1.2 million people. Similarly to the method of the National Institute of Statistics, we calculated the proportion of ethnic categories from the number of people whose ethnic identification was known. On the methodological problems of the 2011 census, see Ghețău (2013).

[3]These estimations were based on retrospective inverse projections. This method is used in historical demographic research (Lee 2004) to estimate missing data on vital statistics, and it is an inverse of demographic projections using the cohort-component method. See the detailed analysis and the methodology in Gyurgyík and Kiss (2010, pp. 66–70).

Table 1 Changes in the ethnic structure[a] of Transylvania (1910–2011)

Year	Total	Romanian		Hungarian		German[b]		Roma[c]		Other ethnic categories	
		Number	%	Number	%	Number	%	Number	%	Number	%
1910	5,259,918	2,829,389	53.8	1,661,967	31.6	565,004	10.7	60,800	1.2	142,758	2.7
1930	5,548,363	3,207,880	57.8	1,353,276	24.4	543,852	9.8	109,156	*2.0*	334,199	6.0
1941	5,912,300	3,304,400	55.9	1,743,900	29.5	535,400	9.1			328,600	5.6
1948	5,761,127	3,752,269	65.1	1,481,903	25.7	332,066	5.8			194,889	3.4
1956	6,232,312	4,051,603	65.0	1,558,631	25.0	368,255	5.9	78,362	*1.3*	175,461	2.8
1966	6,736,046	4,572,554	67.9	1,597,767	23.7	372,335	5.5	49,173	*0.7*	144,217	2.1
1977	7,500,229	5,203,846	69.4	1,691,048	22.5	347,896	4.6	123,028	*1.6*	134,411	1.8
1992	7,723,313	5,684,142	73.6	1,603,923	20.8	109,014	1.4	202,665	*2.6*	123,569	1.6
2002	7,221,733	5,393,552	74.7	1,415,718	19.6	53,077	0.7	244,475	*3.4*	114,911	1.6
2011	6,789,250	4,794,577	74.8	1,216,666	19.0	32,805	0.5	270,755	*4.2*	96,149	1.5

Source Census data (Hungarian Central Statistical Office; Romanian National Institute of Statistics)

[a]The 1910 Hungarian census used mother tongue as an indicator of ethnic belonging. Between 1930 and 1992, the Romanian censuses used nationality (*naționalitate*) as a marker of ethno-cultural belonging. Since 2002, ethnicity (*etnie*) has been used in the same sense

[b]Including Saxons (in the historical province of Transylvania) and Swabians (in Banat)

[c]The 1910 Hungarian census used the ethnonym of *cigány*, while the Romanian censuses between 1930 and 1992 that of *țigan*

Fig. 1 The annual dynamics of the Hungarian population in Romania (1964–2017) (*Source* Author's calculations; for the 1964–1992 period demographic inverse projection using 1992 census results)

One can observe that (in the context of the repressive population politics of the Ceaușescu regime[4]) the number of Hungarians increased until 1982, when according to our estimates, their number reached 1.732 million. A slow decrease already began during the mid-late 1980s, while following the regime change a more drastic drop in the number of Hungarians occurred. According to the 2011 census, there were 1.227 million Hungarians in Romania, meaning a 28% decrease compared to the early 1980s. This drastic demographic decline was caused by several factors, namely mass emigration, negative natural growth, and to a lesser degree, the assimilation process toward the majority.

[4]In 1966, a drastic ban on abortion came into force. While in other Eastern Bloc countries positive incentives were the main tools of population policy, in Romania the emphasis was on punitive measures. On this, see Kligman (1998).

1.2 The Natural Growth of the Transylvanian Hungarian Population

The natural growth of the Hungarian population is relatively well documented. The annual number of live-births can be estimated based on the age structure of the Hungarian ethnics, and additionally, the National Institute of Statistics registers the "nationality"[5] of the newborns and the deceased. According to the demographic calculations, the crude birth and death rates of the Hungarian population differ significantly from the national average, in spite of the fact that today there is no significant difference in the fertility (TFR) and mortality (life expectancy at birth) rates between the Hungarians and the national majority (Gyurgyík and Kiss 2010, pp. 70–87).

In Romania as a whole, natural growth was positive until 1992, and as a consequence, the country's population also grew up to this year. Regarding Transylvanian Hungarians, the annual number of deaths surpassed the number of births for the first time in 1983. Between 1983 and 1989, there was practically zero natural growth rate, which meant that in the context of the intensifying out-migration of Hungarians, the population numbers were already declining. Following 1989, births numbers dropped,[6] while the number of deaths increased, bringing about a drastic negative natural growth rate and an annual population loss of 6–8 per thousand caused only by this factor (Fig. 2).

During the 1980s, the total fertility rate (TFR) of Hungarian women was below the national average. However, following the regime change, the differences compared to the national average diminished. Hungarians' life expectancy at birth was also quite similar to that of the majority. In sum, one should emphasize that following the regime

[5]The parents are asked to classify their newborn by nationality (*naţionalitate*), meaning in this case ethno-national background. As mentioned already, a similar terminology was used in censuses until 2002, when it was replaced by ethnicity (*etnie*). In the vital statistics, the terminology has not been changed, leading to more and more confusion, as *naţionalitate* today can be interpreted as both ethno-national belonging and citizenship. I will discuss these aspects later.

[6]There were 22,000 Hungarian births in 1989 and only 14,000 in 1992.

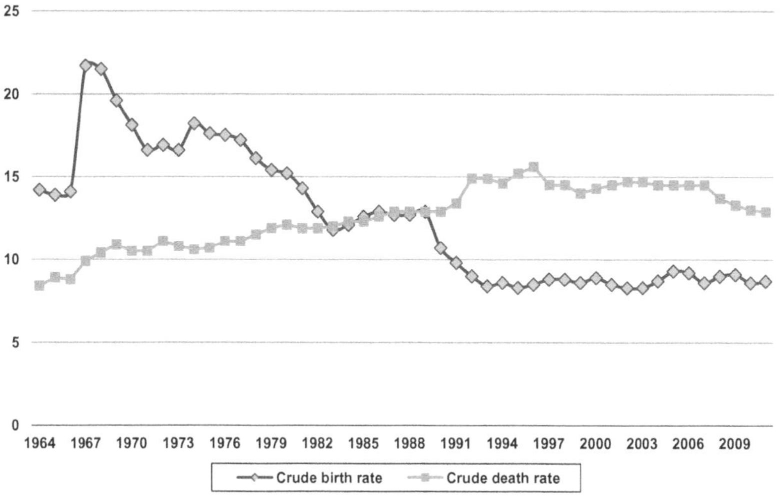

Fig. 2 Crude birth and death rates of the Hungarian population in Transylvania (1964–2011) (*Source* Author's calculations; for the 1964–1992 period demographic inverse projection using 1992 census results)

change, the negative natural growth of the Hungarian population was more drastic compared to Romania as a whole; however, this was not caused by lower fertility rates or lower life expectancy at birth, but by a less favorable age structure and an earlier process of aging caused primarily by previous migratory flows (Table 2).

Table 2 Main indicators of vital statistics: Romania and the Transylvanian Hungarian population (1992–2011)

		Total fertility rate (TFR) (children/per woman)	Life expectancy at birth (years)	Natural growth	
				Number	% (annual mean)
1992–2002	Romania	1.450	69.9	−303,838	−1.3
	Transylvanian Hungarians	1.371	69.9	−89,247	−5.8
2002–2011	Romania	1.311	72.3	−146,146	−1.9
	Transylvanian Hungarians	1.366	72.4	−66,870	−5.2

Source National Institute of Statistics; author's own calculations

1.3 Migratory Processes

Following World War II, Romania became a sending country without any significant influx of immigrants. According to the 2011 census results, the foreign-born population was below 150,000; the most numerous group within this population consisted of persons born in the Republic of Moldova, though their number did not exceed 37,000. The majority of those born abroad were the children of Romanian returnees.

On the contrary, emigration was quite significant even during state socialism. The number of emigrants officially registered between 1948 and 1989 exceeded 783,578 (Muntele 2003, p. 36). The real number of those leaving the country was certainly significantly higher than this figure.[7] One could highlight that the real goal of the former regime's migration policy was not to keep out-migration at a minimum, but to select who should be allowed to leave (Horváth and Kiss 2015, pp. 108–110). The bulk of emigrants of this period belonged to various minorities: Jews (Bines 1998; Ioanid 2005), Germans (Fassmann and Münz 1994; Münz and Ohliger 2001), and Hungarians (Horváth 2005). In the case of the Jewish and German communities, a mass exodus took place in the context of the ethnically selective emigration policy of Romania and the ethnically selective immigration policies of Western Germany and Israel.[8] According to official statistics, Hungarians were not overrepresented among emigrants until the mid-1980s. Nevertheless, the number of irregular migrants began to rise sharply starting in 1986. Initially, Hungary was mostly a transit country for refugees who tried to reach Western European destinations. However, many refugees came to a halt in Hungary. Following 1987, it had become a common practice for Hungarian authorities not to return refugees to Romania, even if the legal codification of the

[7]For a comparison between Romanian statistics concerning emigration to Germany and German statistics concerning immigration from Romania between 1975 and 1989, see Tompea and Năstuţă (2009, p. 221). For mirror statistics in Hungary for the 1981–1989 period, see Gödri (2004).

[8]Brubaker (1998) called this process migration of ethnic unmixing.

question did not occur until 1989 (see Regényi and Törzsök 1988 for details). Hungarian authorities registered 47,771 immigrants from Romania between 1986 and 1989. The outflows did not stop after the collapse of Romania's Communist regime and the proportion of ethnic Hungarians among irregular migrants reached 97% in March 1990, following the violent interethnic clashes in Târgu Mureș/Marosvásárhely[9] (Szoke 1992, p. 312). Meanwhile, the number of regular migrants also increased. As a consequence, the number of former Romanian citizens naturalized in Hungary grew from 866 in 1980 to 6499 in 1987 (Szoke 1992, p. 308). The increasing proportion of Hungarian ethnics among the total number of emigrants could be seen in the official Romanian statistics too, and if both irregular and regular forms of migration were taken into account, a huge wave of emigrants and refugees was observable. According to the estimates, the negative net migration of the Hungarian population in Transylvania was of 132,000 in the period between 1964 and 1992, while between 1987 and 1992 approximately 85,000 Hungarian ethnics left Romania (Table 3).

Table 3 The approximate number of Hungarian ethnics leaving Romania between 1964 and 2011

1964–1992	132,000
1992–2002	106,000
2002–2011	110,000
Total	348,000

Source Author's estimation based on census data and vital statistics

The collapse of the Communist regime profoundly altered the position of Romania in the European migratory system. As a consequence, the outflows have grown considerably and new forms of migration—e.g., temporary (Sandu 2006), circular (Sandu 2005), and educational migration (Brădățan and Kulcsár 2014)—have become

[9]For accounts of the Târgu Mureș/Marosvásárhely events, see Stroschein (2012, pp. 92–123), László and Novák (2012), and Cernat (2012).

widespread. However, Hungarians—due to their intensive out-migration toward Hungary[10]—have remained clearly overrepresented among those leaving the country. According to demographic estimates, the negative net migration for Romania as a whole was 825,000 between 1992 and 2002, meaning an annual migratory loss of 3.6 per thousand. In the case of the Hungarian population, the population loss caused by migratory flows can be estimated to have been 106,000, meaning an annual net migration rate of −6.6 per thousand. In other words, 13% of the migratory loss of Romania was "suffered" by the Hungarian community, comprising 7.2% of the country's population.

Following the turn of the millennium (in the pre-accession period and after the country's EU accession), the migratory regime[11] in Romania changed again drastically. While during the 1990s the Western European states had tried to limit the number of Eastern Europeans entering their labor market, the restrictions were gradually lifted before and after EU accession. Next to Poland, Romania became the major sending country of Eastern European emigrants. According the World Bank's bilateral migration matrix, more than 3.4 million Romanian citizens lived abroad in 2013. According to (preliminary[12]) census results, the migratory loss of Romania was 2.4 million between 2002 and 2011, meaning an annual net migration rate of −11.4 per thousand. In the case of the Hungarian population, the migratory loss can be estimated to be 110,000, meaning an annual net migration rate of −8.3 per thousand. In other words, in the context of the country's massive depopulation, Hungarians are no longer overrepresented.

[10]The migration of Hungarians also took various forms. Many Transylvanian Hungarians found employment in the secondary labor market of Hungary (Bodó and Bartha 1996). However, the emigration of highly skilled segments (Gödri and Tóth 2005) and the educational migration (Szentannai 2001; Horváth 2004) of the Hungarian youth has also been significant.

[11]The migratory regime is the totality of legal norms and institutions regulating the possibility of exit (in the sending country) and of the entrance and integration (in the receiving country).

[12]As mentioned already, the enumerators had registered slightly more than 19 million persons and this number was completed eventually from the population register. The migratory loss calculated based on preliminary figures is more or less in line with the mirror statistics of major receiving countries concerning immigrants from Romania.

1.4 Assimilation: Operative Definition and Processes

The notion of assimilation is a much debated issue in the literature of ethnic relations. The problem that demographers face is that in order to be able to analyze its demographic dynamics, they need a Hungarian "population" defined as a bounded entity. Further, they also need to define input and output values, which in case of a spatially defined population are the numbers of births, immigrants, deaths, and emigrants.[13] However, the Hungarian population of Transylvania is not territorially defined, but ethno-nationally or ethno-linguistically. As a consequence, demographers also have to take into account linguistic or identity shifts as input/output variables. The majority of demographic investigations used ethno-national self-identification as the criteria for delimiting the Hungarian population. As a consequence, assimilation was treated as a shift in self-identification from the minority category toward the majority.

In the following section, I discuss to what extent the shift in self-identification affected the dynamics of the Hungarian population. I also introduce the concept of assimilation as it was used in ethno-demographic research focusing on Transylvanian Hungarians. In a later part of this chapter, I will compare the techniques of classification used in censuses and in everyday practices, while in the next chapter (dealing with assimilation and boundary reinforcement) I will present a more theoretically informed and detailed analysis of ethnic boundary making and boundary crossing in Transylvania.

One should emphasize at the very beginning that compared to negative natural growth and massive emigration, assimilation has been a factor of secondary importance in what concerns the decrease in the Hungarian population. The demographic literature focusing on Transylvanian Hungarians distinguished three forms of assimilation when analyzing census data (Szilágyi 2002, 2004):

---

[13]Now, we omit the problem that the spatially bounded character of populations (societies) cannot be anymore taken for granted. In an era of transnational migration, people can be part simultaneously of more than one society. In other words, the demographic model taking migration as an output and input variable is an oversimplification. See Faist (2010).

1. The change of one's (census) self-identification, or the case in which someone who was registered as Hungarian in the previous census identifies as Romanian in the next census.
2. Difference between self-identification and pervious hetero-identification, or the case when a person becoming an adult identifies as Romanian despite being previously classified by her or his parents as Hungarian.[14]
3. The decrease in the capacity of intergenerational ethno-cultural reproduction, or the case in which Hungarian parents are unable to transmit their ethno-cultural traits (identification, language, etc.) to their children.

This typology was used as an operational definition of assimilation in investigations relying on census data. These investigations highlighted that the direction and the channels of the identity shift are relatively obvious. Changes in census self-identification are relatively rare,[15] while the decrease in capacity of intergenerational ethno-cultural reproduction is connected to ethnically mixed marriages.[16] While in the vast majority of ethnically homogenous families the identification (classification) of children is taken for granted, in ethnically mixed families parents have to choose between different alternatives of ethnic socialization. And if in a society the relation between ethnic categories is hierarchical, these choices will prioritize more prestigious categories over less prestigious ones (Laitin 1995; Finnäs and O'Leary 2003). While 12–13% of Transylvanian Hungarians were living in ethnically mixed marriages in 2011, less than one-third of the children of mixed ancestry were registered as Hungarian in censuses following the regime change.

---

[14]Wimmer (2013)—relying on Jenkins (2008)—distinguished between assimilation and reclassification. By reclassification, he meant (similarly to Szilágyi) changes in the hetero-identification of children made by parents.

[15]Of course, identification with ethnic categories in everyday settings is highly contextual in Transylvania too. See Brubaker et al. (2006, pp. 207–239). However, probably due to identity campaigns and ethno-political struggles, census identification is relatively rigid and reflected.

[16]One should emphasize that ethno-cultural reproduction and assimilation in this framework are macro-level phenomena characterizing a population and not individual biographies. See also Brubaker (2001).

These imbalances of the models of ethnic socialization in mixed families affect primarily the reproductive capacities of dispersed Hungarian communities, where the proportion of mixed marriages is higher, while the probability of identity choices leading toward the minority category is lower.[17] Next to (ethnically mixed) families, another institutional channel of assimilation is Romanian-language education. In some areas (where the proportion of Hungarians is rather low), the majority of Hungarian children (even of those growing up in homogenous families) are educated in the majority language. Under these circumstances, the intergenerational ethno-cultural reproduction in ethnically homogenous families cannot be taken for granted either.

1.5 Regional Differences of Demographic Dynamics

One should emphasize that the demographic prospects of the Hungarian community are highly diverse. As a rule, the higher the proportion of Hungarians, the better the chance of demographic and ethno-cultural reproduction of the Hungarian community in the given region. In what follows, I will analyze the difference in the demographic dynamics of the four regions defined in the introductory chapter of the volume. These regions are the ethnic block area of Székely Land, Partium, an ethnically mixed region next to Hungarian border, Central Transylvania, comprising the major towns of Cluj/Kolozsvár and Târgu Mureş/Marosvásáshely, and the rest of Transylvania, where dispersed Hungarian communities live among a large Romanian majority.

The regional differences of the demographic dynamics are synthesized in Table 4. It should be noted that in the Székely Land the population decline was slower compared to Romania as a whole, while the proportion of Hungarians in the region has not decreased at all.

[17]In Timiş/Temes, Hunediara/Hunyad, Sibiu/Szeben, and Caraş Severin/Krassó-Szörény counties, the majority of younger generation Hungarians engage in ethnically mixed marriages. In the Hungarian-majority region of Székely Land, the proportion of mixed marriages is below 5%, while the majority of children growing up in mixed marriages will have Hungarian as their first language.

Table 4 The regional dynamics of the Hungarian population (1992–2011)

Region	Hungarian population			Change in absolute numbers		Change in %	
	1992	2002	2011	1992–2002	2002–2011	1992–2002	2002–2011
Székely Land	531,568	499,219	466,086	−32,349	−33,133	−6.1	−6.6
Partium/Crișana	385,246	342,254	302,641	−42,992	−39,613	−11.2	−11.6
Central Transylvania	337,875	291,553	248,762	−46,322	−42,791	−13.7	−14.7
Dispersed Hungarian communities	349,234	282,692	207,448	−66,542	−75,244	−19.1	−26.6
Transylvania	1,603,923	1,415,718	1,224,937	−188,205	−190,781	−11.7	−13.5

Source National Institute of Statistics, census data

On the contrary, in 1992 almost 350,000 Hungarians had still lived in dispersed communities but their number has dropped to 200,000 by 2011.

2 Ethnic Categorization: Official and Everyday Practices

The study of demographic and societal macro-processes affecting Transylvanian Hungarians is impossible without analyzing census data. However, their use raises some severe methodological and epistemological problems. First, each census is *per definition* a political act (Kertzer and Arel 2002). The aim of the state administrations conducting censuses is not only to obtain information about social realities but also to form and change them (Scott 1998). As a consequence, censuses can be perceived as powerful tools of the classificatory struggles over the legitimate representation of social reality. Second, the census is the most widespread and common form of official categorization. However, official categories do not necessarily match the categories used in everyday settings. Consequently, censuses sometimes obscure rather than reveal complex social realities.

2.1 Changing Techniques of Official Classification

Census classification should be understood in its discursive and political context (Kertzer and Arel 2002). In this regard, changes to the political utilization of official categories and the broader discursive order shaping ethnic classification are of primal importance. In what follows, I will rely on two complementary conceptual frameworks. The first is that of Rallu et al. (2006) who outline a typology of the "regimes of counting". The second was outlined by Wimmer (2013) and focuses on the shift between the Herderian and integrationist discursive orders concerning ethnic relations.

"Regimes of counting" refers to official classification not only at a technical/methodological level but also includes policies aimed at managing ethno-cultural differences that lie behind the different techniques of counting. The typology distinguishes between four regimes of counting: (1) counting to dominate; (2) not counting in the name of the republican idea of national unity and integration; (3) counting or not counting in the name of multiculturalism; and (4) counting to eliminate discrimination (Rallu et al. 2006, pp. 534–536). I will use only the first two, although I recognize that the other two might become of central importance in Romania too.[18]

The first regime of counting, namely counting to dominate, is typical in colonial situations. Many authors have argued that colonial administrations classified people in distinct and well-distinguishable categories in order to administer them and to sustain the hierarchical order of ethnic or racial categories (Anderson 2006; Scott 1998). Importantly, Rallu et al. argue that Eastern European regimes of counting can also be classified as such (2006, pp. 534–535). Indeed, the very legitimacy of the state's sovereignty over a territory is based on the fact that the titular group constitutes a statistical majority. This is why there is a necessity to (re)produce this majority through statistical means. Actually, ethnic demography has been central to debates over census classification in Eastern Europe throughout the last one and a half century.

The major aspects of Romanian census classification took shape in the interwar period, the 1930 census being a constitutive act in this respect. On the one hand, the emerging census classification was in line with the tendencies in other Eastern European states (Czechoslovakia, Yugoslavia, and also the Soviet Union). On the other hand, the classification techniques of the 1930 Romanian census can be perceived as the antithesis of the previous techniques of classification employed

[18]The outlines of a regime of counting to avoid discrimination can be observed in connection with the issue of Roma integration. For instance, applicants for (nationally administered) EU funds for combating poverty and marginality are explicitly asked to annex detailed descriptions of Roma communities they would like to deal with. Local authorities can also apply for (substantial) funds following a careful mapping of Roma communities of their administrative units. See http://www.fonduri-structurale.ro/stiri/16699/pocu-ghidul-solicitantului-pentru-implementarea-strategiilor-de-dezvoltare-locala-in-comunitatile-marginalizate-publicat-spre-consultare.

by the statistical offices of the Hapsburg, Hohenzollern, and Romanov Empires.[19] In these empires, techniques of counting were quite similar to those used in the second half of the nineteenth century, ethnic classification based on mother tongue, or private language use being of central importance. Language was considered by German, Russian, Austrian, and Hungarian census takers as an "objective" indicator of a culturally defined nationality and, as such, was put in opposition with self-identification, characterized as too "subjective" to define one's real belonging (Arel 2002). The Hungarian censuses carried out between 1880 and 1910 categorized the population according to mother tongue, defined as the language best spoken by the respondent at the moment of the census. This interpretation of the national belonging was inspired by the contemporary liberal concept of the Hungarian nation, which accepted persons of allogeneic origin as members of the national community if they had been able and willing to speak Hungarian. This technique (sharply criticized by the contemporary Romanian public opinion and statisticians) obviously reflected the effects of linguistic Magyarization too.

The successor states of the Hapsburg and Romanov empires altered the classification by mother tongue and put stronger emphasis on both ethnic origin (ancestry) and self-identification.[20] The main purpose was to diminish the proportion of formerly dominant groups. In Romania, the 1930 census[21] introduced nationality (*naționalitate*) as a self-declared ethno-national belonging; however, according to the instructions for enumerators, nationality was also linked to ethnic origin (*neam*).

---

[19]There was a discontinuity compared to the censuses of the pre-World War I period in the Old Romanian Kingdom, which did not gather information about cultural belonging but asked only about the citizenship of the residents.

[20]This has happened both in the successor states of the Hapsburg monarchy (among them in Romania) and in the Soviet Union. As for the Soviet "regime of counting", see Hirsch (2004).

[21]Several authors emphasize the "objectivity" of the 1930 census, highlighting that it met international standards of the era (Varga 1999; Blomqvist 2014, p. 278). The latter may be true; however, meeting international standards does not mean that the 1930 census was independent of political considerations or that it can be interpreted without taking into account classificatory struggles.

Further, the definition of mother tongue (which was asked next to nationality) was altered, pushing classification again toward ancestral language: While in the Hungarian census "mother tongue" had been defined as the language best spoken, the 1930 Romanian definition referred to the language used in one's family during early childhood. This change in counting methodology was of paramount importance regarding the categorization of Hungarian-speaking groups of allogeneic origin, most importantly that of Magyarized Jews and Swabians. The (mostly Hungarian-speaking) Jewish population of Transylvania numbered 170,000 when the 1930 census was taken.[22]

The Romanian regime of ethnic classification can be characterized by a high level of inertia: The techniques of ethnic classification have changed little since the 1930 census. Nevertheless, one could witness a (potentially) radical but yet inconclusive change of the Romanian regime of counting in the last decade. Kukutai and Thompson (2015) argued that the politics of ethnic classification and counting are affected not only by national historical legacies but also by the international environment. In this respect, it is of central importance that Romania (among other Eastern European states) has joined the EU. As Simon (2012, 2017) argued, regimes of counting developed differently in the Western and Eastern part of Europe. On the one hand, counting by mother tongue and (culturally defined) ethno-nationality was widespread in Eastern Europe. On the other hand, Western European states (even if they practiced a detailed ethnic classification in their colonies) were reluctant to classify their metropolitan subjects by ethnicity mainly in the name of the national unity. Following World War II, ethnic classification was often associated with state-committed atrocities against minorities, especially those committed by the Nazi regime. Consequently, a regime of "not counting" in the name of integration has evolved and it is still dominant in Western Europe (even if it was questioned by those urging for counting ethnicity in order to combat

[22]On the Hungarian reception of the 1930 Romanian census, see Seres and Egry (2011). It was frequently mentioned by Hungarian commentators that in many cases census enumerators in fact hetero-identified Hungarian-speaking Jews, Swabians, Armenians, or Hungarian Greek Catholics of allegedly Ruthenian or Romanian origin.

discrimination).[23] The dominance of the integrationist framework and of the regime of "not counting" put pressure[24] on the "ethnicist" regimes of counting in Eastern Europe. This pressure (combined with the national legacies and the inertia of the statistical offices) has led to a yet inconclusive, but potentially radical, shift of the regime of counting.

In a broader sense, the Romanian regime of counting was deeply embedded in what was called by Wimmer the Herderian discursive order concerning ethnic relations (2013, pp. 16–44). According to Herder, the social world is composed of people (ethnic groups or nationalities) who are bounded groups sharing a specific cultural heritage embodied in their language, characterized by internal solidarity and a common sense of identity. This Herderian discursive order used to be in a hegemonic position until recently and had rarely been questioned by those using official statistics. It is important that Transylvanian Hungarian elites were (and are) also attached to the Herderian paradigm and used the same language of counting in their claims making. This is why they engaged in intensive identity campaigns during each census following the regime change but have not questioned the very logic and the political significance of counting (Varga 1998, pp. 220–240, for the 1992 census campaign; Brubaker et al. 2006, pp. 151–160, for the 2002 one). Nevertheless, the dominance of the Herderian paradigm has been eroded by the integrationist discourse that gained ground during the last one and a half decade.[25] According to this

[23]See on this topic Simon (2008), who analyzes the struggles over official ethnic classification in France, which is most strongly attached among the European states to the republican idea of national unity and ethnic blindness.

[24]It is better to conceptualize this pressure as indirect, as Eurostat or other EU-level institutions do not formulate direct requests to Eastern European national statistical offices to alter their techniques of ethnic counting. However, many Eastern European social scientists and statisticians have become fascinated by the integrationist ideal of not counting and many find the actual regimes of counting in Eastern Europe inadequate or immoral. They might push toward an integrationist regime of not counting, as it happened in Hungary before the 2011 census, when the Census Committee of the Hungarian Academy of Sciences formulated such a recommendation (which was ultimately rejected by the newly elected right-wing government in 2011).

[25]For a larger political significance of the integrationist discourse, see McGarry et al. (2008). Csergő and Regelmann (2017) argue that the integrationist perspective clearly gained ground in transnational structures since the late 1990s.

integrationist discursive order, the social world is no more made up by people, ethnic groups, or nationalities but is composed by an ethnically unmarked "social mainstream" on the one hand and by some ethnically marked and particular groups on the other hand. From this perspective, ethnicity is not an attribute that all people have, but it is a quality that characterizes people belonging to ethnically marked minority categories in particular situations.[26]

One can argue that today in Eastern Europe the integrationist and the Herderian discursive orders overlap. This is sometimes conducive to chaotic and in-between techniques of counting. Eastern European states are no longer unequivocally determined to count their populations ethnically or to classify people in bounded and mutually exclusive categories. This hypothesis can be underpinned by the several arguments. (1) First, in some cases even not counting was considered. In Hungary, for instance, initially there was a decision of the government to omit questions concerning ethno-cultural traits in the 2011 census. This was supported by the majority of social scientists engaged in the research of ethnicity. The questions concerning (ethno-)nationality, mother tongue, and spoken languages were reintroduced following the electoral victory of right-wing parties in 2010. In other Eastern European countries, the option of not counting was not seriously considered. However, the communication campaigns of the censuses markedly facilitated non-response to questions concerning ethnicity by stressing that answering them (contrarily to other questions) was not obligatory. The proportion of non-responses was of 14.7% in Hungary, 9% in Bulgaria, 7.1% in Slovakia, and 2.1% in Serbia. In Romania, there was a unique situation. In 2011, a traditional paper-and-pencil-based census was carried out, which counted 19 million people and registered a less than 0.3% non-response rate to the question concerning ethnicity. However, eventually data about 1.2 million persons were added to the census database

---

[26]See Fenton (2003) for an interpretation of ethnicity as an attribute only of the "non-mainstream" groups and Brubaker et al. (2006) for an attempt to adapt this framework to the study of the Hungarian–Romanian relations in Cluj/Kolozsvár.

from the population register. As the population register does not contain data concerning ethnic identification, the ethnic background of these people (6.2% of the population) is “unknown”. (2) Second, the classification of people into mutually exclusive categories also came under attack. Hungary was the first state introducing the possibility of multiple census identifications both for “nationality” and for mother tongue (Kapitány 2013). In Romania, the option of multiple identifications was considered for the first time in 2011. However, initiatives toward this direction (proposed by the Romanian Institute for Research on National Minorities and by some Roma NGOs) were rejected by the Central Census Committee of the Romanian Government.

Before discussing the match between census classification and everyday ethnic categories, I would like to emphasize that from the perspective of minority groups, the shift toward an integrationist discursive order and a statistical regime of not counting is not an unequivocally positive development. First, politically active minorities usually advocate for the official recognition of ethnic diversity. Counting is a precondition of institutionalized power-sharing and autonomy. Authors inclined toward the integrationist perspective emphasize the dangers of empowering minority elites and delimiting the ethnic groups. They tend to discuss “official ethnicity” focusing on non-democratic regimes and on violent ethnic conflicts, with perhaps the Soviet Union (Hirsch 2004) and Rwanda (Uvin 2002; Longman 2001) being the most frequently discussed cases. Nevertheless, ethnic registers exist also in other cases where power-sharing and forms of autonomy led to peaceful ethnic coexistence under the conditions of democratic regimes, such as in Slovenia, Finland, post-Milošević Serbia, or South Tyrol. Second, the asymmetry between minority and majority categories could be even more accentuated in the integrationist discursive order and in the regimes of not counting. The “ethnicist” regimes of counting were aimed at underpinning the legitimacy of state sovereignty and to reproduce the dominance of the titular majority. However, from an epistemological point of view, the majority remained only one of the ethnic groups, even if the most numerous and dominant one. In the integrationist discursive order, the very epistemological status of the majority and minority becomes different, as “majority” is redefined as an ethnically unmarked "mainstream". In this new logic of markedness,[27] the national majority loses its well-bounded contour and becomes hidden by the discursive order. However, this only means that belonging to the majority becomes even at the very conceptual level taken for granted (unmarked), while belonging to the minority becomes an unusual attachment to something defined as particular (the marked ethnicity). Third, it is also obvious that in Eastern Europe nationalizing states often use an ambivalent discourse alternating between an ethnically marked and an ethnically unmarked definition of the national majority. In previous chapters of this volume, we emphasized the duality of the Romanian minority policy regime. One may argue that the continuous back and forth between the integrationist perspective and ethnic democracy is an inherent characteristic of this regime.

2.2 Informal Classification and Identification in Everyday Settings

The next question is to what extent census classification (which remained actually connected to a Herderian definition of people) fits relevant identities and ethnic categories used in everyday settings. Generally speaking, ethnic classification happens in quite different contexts or settings. Jenkins places these contexts of classification on a continuum between formal and informal (2008, pp. 65–74). Official classification (the most obvious example being the census) takes place in the most formal setting. Informal everyday interactions are at the

[27]The notion of markedness denotes the asymmetries exiting in linguistic and cognitive structures. Most importantly, it emphasizes that the relation between categories is not symmetrical, a dominant, and a subordinated category exists. Initially, this terminology had been used in structuralist linguistics but ultimately it was borrowed by social scientists to describe the cognitive mechanisms beyond social categorization. Waugh (1982) used it to describe the relation between categories of man and woman, white and black, sighted and blind, heterosexual and homosexual, fertility and barrenness. It is also important that the relation between categories is context dependent. A category that is marked in one social context could be the unmarked one in another context. Brubaker et al. (2006) gave us examples of everyday contexts where the usually marked category of Hungarian becomes unmarked, while the usually unmarked Romanian becomes marked.

opposite end of the continuum and between these ends one can find more or less formal contexts, such as political representation (the question is whether ethnicity is politically salient), the labor market (where ethnic belonging may have severe consequences), or the marriage market. It is important to note that ethnic identification or categorization can be inconsistent among contexts and can change from one setting to another.

One can argue that in the case of Transylvanian Hungarians, census classification fits relatively well with the categories used in everyday settings and the identities of those in question. First, the two attributes used by Romanian censuses—namely self-identification with the Hungarian ethnic category and Hungarian as the mother tongue—are the major components defining membership in the Hungarian category in everyday interactions too. Furthermore, these elements, called the two major constitutive rules of identity by Abdelal et al. (2009), overlap in the case of Hungarians in the vast majority of times. According to the 2011 census results, the number of persons declaring Hungarian as their ethnicity or mother tongue was 1.24 million; 97.1% of them were classified as Hungarians in both dimensions. Second, in the majority of cases, Hungarian identification is relatively consistent across different contexts. This can be related to the psychological aspects of ethnic socialization. According to Fenton (2003, p. 88) and Jenkins (2008, p. 48), under certain social and institutional circumstances, especially when ethnic cleavages appear in well-defined forms in everyday life, people deeply internalize group membership and ethnic belonging during early childhood. In these cases, the internalization of ethnic belonging may go hand in hand with the internalization of its markers, such as language use. When this is the case, ethnicity is inscribed in the deepest layers of personal identity, like gender, for example. In such cases, ethnic identification is not independent from psychological, emotional, and cognitive constructs of personality, nor is it separate from notions of personal integrity, security, and safety. Under these circumstances, identities are less contextual and less fluid and the psychological price of leaving the group can be quite high.

Obviously, this is not to say that identification is not context dependent among Transylvanian Hungarians and that they would perceive each situation through ethnic lenses and act accordingly.[28] In a representative survey carried out in 2016, 1200 randomly selected self-identified Hungarians were asked whether there were situations in their lives in which they felt Romanian. Then, if the answer was affirmative, respondents were asked to describe the situation in an open-ended question. The first important result was that 17% responded affirmatively, while 83% declared that they never felt Romanian. The second important result refers to the contexts in which Hungarians reported having felt Romanians. People living in ethnically mixed families answered more frequently in the affirmative, showing that Hungarians consider this a setting where one can "become a Romanian". Situations abroad were also frequently mentioned. These situations can be connected to official/passport identity or to a feeling of solidarity with their fellow citizens while abroad. Some mentioned that they felt Romanian when they succeeded to behave in a relaxed manner in informal settings among Romanians. Others mentioned that they have a kind of double identity and feel as though they belong to the country. Institutional settings, such as workplaces, the (Romanian-language) school, and the army, were also mentioned (Table 5).

In sum, in the case of an average Transylvanian Hungarian (if such a person would exist), census classification matches relatively well the categories used in everyday settings, as linguistic competences and subjective self-identification are the most important constitutive rules of Hungarian identity. Further, ethnic identity is relatively consistent across different settings. Nevertheless, there are some contexts in which identification with the national majority is more likely. These are first of all in ethnically mixed families, abroad, and in institutional settings external to the parallel Hungarian pillar.

[28]See Brubaker et al. (2006, pp. 191–207) for a contrary account. For Brubaker, ethnicity (as cognition) is more a way of seeing and interpreting things and is present in situations perceived through ethnic lenses (Brubaker 2004, pp. 64–87).

3 Outlier Categories: Hungarian-Speaking Roma and Csángós in Moldova

It is also important that there are several well-distinguishable categories connected to Hungarians in Romania for which census classification is an inadequate tool of measuring identity. Historically, Hungarian-speaking Jews and other allogeneic groups could be considered as such. Today, the three most important categories for which census classifications are not adequate are ethnically mixed (Hungarian–Romanian) families, Hungarian-speaking Roma, and Csángós (Catholics of Hungarian origin) in Moldova. In what follows, I discuss the two latter categories, while ethnically mixed marriages will be discussed in a separate chapter.

3.1 Hungarian-Speaking Roma

The contested character of the Roma identity in Eastern Europe, as well as the intensive classificatory struggles to define the location and the consequences of ethnic boundaries between Roma and non-Roma, has been well explored in the literature (Emigh and Szelényi 2000; Ladányi and Szelényi 2006). The first important aspect emphasized by researchers is that in many cases external categorization as Roma does not always align with self-identification. This is why censuses and quantitative investigations have difficulties measuring and treating Roma identity as a clear-cut variable (Rughiniş, 2010, 2011). Previously, I argued that in the Transylvanian Hungarian case, attributes measured by censuses fit relatively well with the constitutive norms of Hungarian identity used in everyday settings. If someone speaks Hungarian fluently and declares himself or herself Hungarian, he or she is usually recognized as a category member. However, this is not the case for Hungarian-speaking Roma. Even if Hungarian is their sole spoken language and they declare themselves as Hungarians, Roma are barely recognized as members of the minority community. While in the maintenance of the Romanian–Hungarian boundary "groupness" and the institutions underpinning this groupness have a decisive role, for the boundaries

Table 5 Contexts in which Transylvanian Hungarians reported feeling themselves as Romanians (2016)

Contexts	Frequency	Phrasings
In an ethnically mixed family	33	"My wife is Romanian", "I became Orthodox when I got married", "My mother is Romanian"
Abroad	25	"When they looked at my passport they considered me to be Romanian", "In Germany I felt that I am like my Romanian colleagues, I felt that I am not different"
In Hungary	22	"In Hungary they regard me as a Romanian", "We are called Romanians when we enter in Hungary", "Here we are Hungarians, there we are Romanians"
Among Romanians, in informal settings	17	"When I am among Romanians I myself feel Romanian, perhaps it is easier to get on if I do so"
Dual identity, belonging to Romania	15	"We live in Romania"
Workplace	15	"Everybody is Romanian in my workplace"
In Romanian-inhabited area	11	"I worked in Bucharest", "When I was in Brașov/Brassó all my colleagues were Romanians"
School	8	"I finished my schools in Romanian. I attended a Romanian language university, I got along well with my colleagues"
Army	5	"When I was in the army they always said: 'this is not Hungary" "you live in Romania'"
During communism	3	"When Ceaușescu was alive we used to be much closer to each other"
Ceremonies, communal events	2	"I was at a football match and I sang the Romanian anthem"

Source Survey carried out by Kvantum Research (2016), N = 1200

between Roma and non-Roma social closure and exclusion are far more important. Ladányi and Szelényi (2006) argued along this line and highlighted that in the social construction of Roma ethnicity external classification is rather important. Moreover, this external classification is in many cases completely independent of linguistic skills and self-labeling. When external observers construct the category of Roma, the most important criteria are racial markers (skin color) and a way of life perceived as Roma. Ladányi and Szelényi carried out an interesting experiment (2006, p. 140). First, they asked field operators to classify the respondents of their survey as either Roma or non-Roma. Then, they asked the operators to fill in another questionnaire concerning the criteria used in the process of ethnic classification. 42% of the Romanian field operators reported that skin color was very important, while another 32% said that it was an important criterion when classifying the respondents. The ("Gypsy") way of life was very important for 47% and important for further 33%. It should be mentioned that self-identification was less important than considering racial elements and way of life; 40% mentioned that it was very important, and another 14% said that it was important, while 46% of the operators reported that self-identification of the respondents was not important at all when classifying them as either Roma or non-Roma.

The Romanian Institute for Research on National Minorities carried out an exhaustive survey of Roma communities in Romania, contacting local administrations and asking them to estimate the number of Roma living on their territory. Data concerning segregated Roma neighborhoods within the given administrative unit were also requested. According to the survey, the estimated number of those classified as Roma in Romania was of 1,215,846,[29] with an estimated 724,844 living in compact Roma neighborhoods or the so-called colonies. In these "colonies", Hungarian was one of the three most frequently used languages (alongside Romanian and Romani). Hungarian speakers are clearly overrepresented among Roma living in segregated neighborhoods: Almost 11% of them most frequently utilize Hungarian in their

[29]The response rate was 98.1% for the total number of 3284 municipalities of Romania.

daily communication (Horváth and Kiss 2017). The estimated number of all Hungarian-speaking Roma (living in segregated neighborhoods or among non-Roma) is around 110,000. The vast majority of Roma in the Székely Land, Satu Mare/Szatmár county, and northern Bihor/Bihar are Hungarian speakers.

3.2 Csángós of Moldova

The Csángós of Moldova constitute a particular population connected to but also distinguishable from Hungarians in Romania. The notion of national minority may be misleading in their case. While there is a clear sense of ethno-cultural distinctiveness vis-á-vis the dominant group among them, in the historical process of their identity formation, no national movement played any significant role (or only the national movement of the dominant majority played such a role leading to pronounced assimilation). It is also important that this minority community lacks institutional channels of social mobility controlled by their own elites.[30] Consequently, social mobility and the exit from traditional rural communities also imply assimilation into the dominant group.

In the case of the Csángós of Moldova, the most important element of ethno-cultural distinctiveness is their Roman Catholic faith in a predominantly Romanian Orthodox environment. In some of their rural communities, this is completed by the use of an archaic Hungarian dialect (strongly influenced by the Romanian language). However, in the history of the Csángós, one cannot find the phases of Eastern European national awakening described by Hroch (1985). "Indigenous" (Csángó) intellectuals have never been, for instance, preoccupied in mapping and canonizing traditional Csángó folk culture in spite of the fact that Csángós have become a powerful symbol of the authentic Hungarian folk culture among Hungarian intellectuals beginning with the last decades of the nineteenth century. This discourse and the intensive research carried out by Hungarian ethnographers were less relevant for

[30]This is one of the characteristics of ranked systems of groups described by Horowitz (1985).

the Csángó community and had little impact on their identity formation. Nevertheless, their sense of belonging was powerfully shaped by the emerging institutional infrastructure of the Romanian state. It is important to note that the "indigenous" Csángó intelligentsia, most importantly the Roman Catholic clergy of Csángó origin, successfully propagated a sense of Romanian national belonging and origin.[31]

In Moldova, there was no institutional background for a Hungarian (or at least non-Romanian) identity project. In a historical perspective, two relatively short periods can be perceived as an exception. First, following World War II, the Hungarian Popular Alliance (*Magyar Népi Szövetség*), a mass organization dominated by Communists, established Hungarian-language schools in almost one hundred Csángó villages. However, this experiment was neither long lasting nor particularly successful.[32] The second institutional experiment took place after the collapse of communism, when the Csángó Educational Program was launched. In the 2011/2012 educational year, there was facultative Hungarian-language education in 39 Csángó villages with more than 2500 children enrolled. In 21 villages, the program was part of the official educational curriculum, while in 17 locations it was organized outside of schools. According to Papp and Márton (2014), the results of the program were quite modest in terms of both increasing the Hungarian-language proficiency of children and establishing channels of educational mobility toward the Hungarian-language schools.

As for the number of Csángós, census data are of limited use. According to 2011 census results, slightly more than 181,000 Roman Catholics lived in Bacău, Iași, Neamț, and Vrancea counties. This could be considered the maximum possible number of Roman Catholics of partial Hungarian origin. However, only a minority of this group speaks the Csángó-Hungarian dialect and their vast majority can be characterized through a Romanian national identity. Vilmos Tánczos,

[31]On the problems of being simultaneously Roman Catholic and Romanian, see Diaconescu (2008).

[32]Communists tried to use the Hungarian identity project to reduce the influence of the Roman Catholic clergy. The Hungarian schools functioned between 1950 and 1955 (Nagy 2011, pp. 121–122).

a Transylvanian Hungarian ethnographer (employed as a census enumerator in one of the Csángó villages in 2011), argued that census classification was not a proper tool to reveal the distinctiveness of the Csángós vis-á-vis the Romanian majority (Tánczos 2012). In the official context of census classification, the majority of Csángós declare Romanian as their ethnicity and mother tongue. Nevertheless (ethnic or quasi-ethnic), distinctions in everyday life between Orthodox Romanians and Catholic Csángós exist. According to a study carried out between 1994 and 1996, approximately 62,000 persons spoke the Csángó-Hungarian dialect. One and a half decades later (between 2008 and 2009), this number was estimated to slightly more than 48,000, which is indicative of a rapid linguistic shift being underway (Tánczos 2010).

References

Abdelal, R., Herrera, Y. M., Johnston, A. I., & McDermott, R. (2009). *Measuring identity: A guide for social scientists*. Cambridge and New York: Cambridge University Press.

Anderson, B. (2006). *Imagined communities: Reflections on the origin and spread of nationalism* (Rev. ed.). London and New York: Verso.

Arel, D. (2002). Language categories: Backward or forward looking. In D. I. Kertzer & D. Arel (Eds.), *Census and identity: The politics of race, ethnicity, and language in national census* (pp. 92–121). Cambridge, UK and New York: Cambridge University Press.

Bines, C. (1998). *Din istoria imigrărilor în Israel*. București: Hasefer.

Blomqvist, A. (2014). *Economic nationalizing in the ethnic borderlands of Hungary and Romania: Inclusion, exclusion and annihilation in Szatmár/Satu-Mare 1867–1944*. Stockholm: Stockholm University.

Bodó, J., & Bartha, G. (1996). *Elvándorlók? Vendégmunka és életforma a Székelyföldön*. Csíkszereda: Pro-Print.

Botoş, R., Mârza, D., & Popovici, V. (2016). Censuses between population statistics and politics. The Romanian press from Hungary and the censuses between 1869 and 1910. *Romanian Journal of Population Studies, 10*(1), 5–18.

Brădăţan, C., & Kulcsár, L. J. (2014). When the educated leave the east: Romanian and Hungarian skilled immigration to the USA. *Journal of International Migration and Integration, 15*(3), 509–524.

Brubaker, R. (1998). Migrations of ethnic unmixing in the "new Europe". *International Migration Review, 32*(4), 1047.
Brubaker, R. (2001). The return of assimilation? Changing perspectives on immigration and its sequels in France, Germany, and the United States. *Ethnic and Racial Studies, 24*(4), 531–548.
Brubaker, R. (2004). *Ethnicity without groups.* Cambridge, MA: Harvard University Press.
Brubaker, R., Feischmidt, M., Fox, J., & Grancea, L. (2006). *Nationalist politics and everyday ethnicity in a Transylvanian town.* Princeton: Princeton University Press.
Cernat, V. (2012). Ethnic conflict and reconciliation in post-Communist Romania. In O. Simić, Z. Volčič, & C. R. Philpot (Eds.), *Peace psychology in the Balkans. Dealing with a violent past while building peace* (pp. 17–34). New York: Springer.
Csergő, Z., & Regelmann, A.-C. (2017). Europeanization and collective rationality in minority voting. *Problems of Post-Communism, 64*(5), 291–310.
Diaconescu, M. (2008). The identity crisis of Moldavian Catholics—Between politics and and historic myths. A case study: The myths of Romanian origin. In S. Ilyés, L. Peti, & F. Pozsony (Eds.), *Local and transnational Csángó lifeworlds* (pp. 81–93). Cluj-Napoca: Kriza János Ethnographical Society.
Emigh, R. J., & Szelényi, I. (Eds.). (2000). *Poverty, ethnicity, and gender in eastern Europe during the market transition.* Westport, CT: Praeger.
Faist, T. (2010). Diaspora and transnationalism: What kind of dance partners? In R. Bauböck & T. Faist (Eds.), *Diaspora and transnationalism: Concepts, theories and methods* (pp. 9–35). Amsterdam: Amsterdam University Press.
Fassmann, H., & Münz, R. (1994). European east-west migration, 1945–1992. *International Migration Review, 28*(3), 520.
Fenton, S. (2003). *Ethnicity. Key concepts.* Cambridge and Malden, MA: Polity Press.
Finnäs, F., & O'Leary, B. (2003). Choosing for the children: The affiliation of the children of minority-majority group intermarriages. *European Sociological Review, 19*(5), 483–499.
Gheţău, V. (2013). Recensământul şi aventure INS cu datele finale. *cursdeguvernare.ro*, 7 August. Available at: http://cursdeguvernare.ro/recensamantul-si-aventura-ins-prin-datele-finale.html.
Gödri, I. (2004). A magyarországra bevándorolt népesség jellemzői, különös tekintettel a Romániából bevándorlókra. In T. Kiss (Ed.), *Népesedési*

folyamatok az ezredfordulón Erdélyben (pp. 126–147). Kolozsvár: Kriterion and RMDSZ Ügyvezető Elnökség.

Gödri, I., & Tóth, P. P. (2005). *Bevándorlás és beilleszkedés*. Budapest: KSH Népességkutató Intézet.

Gyurgyík, L., & Kiss, T. (2010). *Párhuzamok és különbségek. A második világháború utáni erdélyi és szlovákiai magyar népességfejlődés összehasonlító elemzése*. Budapest: EÖKIK.

Hirsch, F. (2004). Towards a Soviet order of things: The 1926 census and the making of the Soviet Union. In S. Szreter, H. Sholkamy, & A. Dharmalingam (Eds.), *Categories and contexts: Anthropological and historical studies in critical demography* (pp. 126–147). Oxford: Oxford University Press.

Horowitz, D. L. (1985). *Ethnic groups in conflict*. Berkeley: University of California Press.

Horváth, I. (2004). Az erdélyi magyar fiatalok Magyarország irányú tanulási migrációja 1990–2000. *Erdélyi Társadalom, 2*(2), 59–84.

Horváth, I. (2005). *Erdély és Magyarország közötti migrációs folyamatok*. Kolozsvár: Scientia.

Horváth, I., & Kiss, T. (2015). Depopulating semi-periphery? Longer term dynamics of migration and socioeconomic development in Romania. *Demográfia English Edition, 58*(5), 91–132.

Horváth, I., & Kiss, T. (2017). Ancheta experţilor locali privind situaţia romilor pe unităţi administrativ-teritoriale. In I. Horváth (Ed.), *Raport de cercetare – SocioRoMap. O cartografiere a comunităţilor de romi din România* (pp. 9–190). Cluj-Napoca: Editura Institutului pentru Studierea Problemelor Minorităţilor Naţionale.

Hroch, M. (1985). *Social preconditions of national revival in Europe: A comparative analysis of the social composition of patriotic groups among the smaller European nations*. Cambridge and New York: Cambridge University Press.

Ioanid, R. (2005). *The ransom of the Jews: The story of the extraordinary secret bargain between Romania and Israel*. Chicago: Ivan R. Dee.

Jenkins, R. (2008). *Rethinking ethnicity* (2nd ed.). Thousand Oaks, CA: Sage.

Kapitány, B. (2013). Kárpát-medencei népszámlálási körkép. *Demográfia, 56*(1), 25–64.

Kertzer, D. I., & Arel, D. (Eds.). (2002). *Census and identity: The politics of race, ethnicity, and language in national census*. Cambridge, UK and New York: Cambridge University Press.

Kligman, G. (1998). *The politics of duplicity: Controlling reproduction in Ceausescu's Romania*. Berkeley: University of California Press.

Kukutai, T., & Thompson, V. (2015). 'Inside out': The politics of enumerating the nation by ethnicity. In P. Simon, V. Piché, & A. A. Gagnon (Eds.), *Social statistics and ethnic diversity. Cross-national perspectives in classifications and identity politics* (pp. 39–61). Cham: Springer.
Ladányi, J., & Szelényi, I. (2006). *Patterns of exclusion: Constructing Gypsy ethnicity and the making of an underclass in transitional societies of Europe*. New York: Columbia University Press.
Laitin, D. D. (1995). Marginality: A microperspective. *Rationality and Society, 7*(1), 31–57.
László, M., & Novák, C. Z. (2012). *A szabadság terhe.* Marosvásárhely, március 16–21, 1990. Csíkszereda: Pro-Print.
Lee, R. (2004). Reflections on inverse projection. Its origins, development, extensions and relation to forecast. In E. Barbi, S. Bertino, & E. Sonnino (Eds.), *Inverse projection techniques: Old and new approaches* (pp. 11–27). Berlin and New York: Springer.
Longman, T. (2001). Church politics and the genocide in Rwanda. *Journal of Religion in Africa, 31*(2), 163–186.
McGarry, J., O'Leary, B., & Simeon, R. (2008). Integration or accommodation? In S. Choudhry (Ed.), *Constitutional design for divided societies: Integration or accommodation?* (pp. 41–88). Oxford and New York: Oxford University Press.
Muntele, I. (2003). Migrations internationales dans la Roumanie moderne et contemporaine. In D. Diminescu (Ed.), *Visibles mais peu nombreux–: les circulations migratoires roumaines* (pp. 33–51). Paris: Maison des sciences de l'homme.
Münz, R., & Ohliger, R. (2001). Migrations of German people to Germany: A light on the German concept of identity. *The International Scope Review, 3*(6), 60–74.
Nagy, M. Z. (2011). *Kisebbségi érdekképviselet vagy pártpolitika? A Romániai Magyar Népi Szövetség története 1944–1953*. Pécsi Tudományegyetem: Doktori disszertáció.
Papp, A. Z., & Márton, J. (2014). Peremoktatásról varázstalanítva. A Csángó Oktatási Program értékelésének tapasztalatai. *Magyar Kisebbség, 19*(2), 7–32.
Rallu, J.-L., Piché, V., & Simon, P. (2006). Demography and ethnicity: An ambiguous relationship. In G. Caselli, J. Vallin, & G. J. Wunsch (Eds.), *Demography: Analysis and synthesis; A treatise in population studies* (pp. 531–549). Amsterdam and Boston: Elsevier.

Regényi, E., & Törzsök, E. (1988). Romániai menekültek Magyarországon 1988. In *Medvetánc. Jelentések a határokon túli magyar kisebbségek helyzetéről. Csehszlovákia, Szovjetunió, Románia, Jugoszlávia* (pp. 187–241). Budapest: Elite.

Rughiniş, C. (2010). The forest behind the bar charts: Bridging quantitative and qualitative research on Roma/Tigani in contemporary Romania. *Patterns Prejudice, 44*(4), 337–367.

Rughiniş, C. (2011). Quantitative tales of ethnic differentiation: Measuring and using Roma/Gypsy ethnicity in statistical analyses. *Ethnic and Racial Studies, 34*(4), 594–619.

Sandu, D. (2005). *Comunităţile de Romi din România. O hartă a sărăciei comunitare prin sondajul PROROMI.* Bucureşti: Banca Mondială.

Sandu, D. (2006). *Locuirea temporară în străinătate: Migraţia economică a românilor: 1990–2006.* Bucureşti: Fundaţia pentru o Societate Deschisă.

Scott, J. C. (1998). *Seeing like a state: How certain schemes to improve the human condition have failed.* New Haven: Yale University Press.

Seres, A., & Egry, G. B. (2011). *Magyar levéltári források az 1930. évi Romániai népszámlálás nemzetiségi adatsorainak értékeléséhez.* Kolozsvár: ISPMN and Kriterion.

Simon, P. (2008). The choice of ignorance: The debate on ethnic and racial statistics in France. *French Politics, Culture & Society, 26*(1), 7–31.

Simon, P. (2012). Collecting ethnic statistics in Europe: A review. *Ethnic and Racial Studies, 35*(8), 1366–1391.

Simon, P. (2017). The failure of the importation of ethno-racial statistics in Europe: Debates and controversies. *Ethnic and Racial Studies, 40*(13), 2326–2332.

Stroschein, S. (2012). *Ethnic struggle, coexistence, and democratization in eastern Europe. Cambridge studies in contentious politics.* Cambridge and New York: Cambridge University Press.

Szentannai, Á. (2001). A Magyarországon tanult fiatalok karrierkövetése. *Regio, 12*(4), 113–131.

Szilágyi, N. S. (2002). Észrevételek a romániai magyar népesség fogyásáról, különös tekintettel az asszimilációra. *Magyar Kisebbség, 7*(4), 64–96.

Szilágyi, N. S. (2004). Az asszimiláció és hatása a népesedési folyamatokra. In T. Kiss (Ed.), *Népesedési folyamatok az ezredfordulón Erdélyben* (pp. 157–235). Kolozsvár: Kriterion and RMDSZ Ügyvezető Elnökség.

Szoke, L. (1992). Hungarian perspectives on emigration and immigration in the new European architecture. *International Migration Review, 26*(2), 305–323.

Tánczos, V. (2010). A moldvai csángók magyar nyelvismerete 2008–2010-ben. *Magyar Kisebbség, 25*(3–4), 62–156.

Tánczos, V. (2012). "Hát mondja meg kend, hogy én mi vagyok!" A csángó nyelvi identitás tényezői: helyzetjelentés a 2011-es népszámlálás kapcsán. *Pro Minoritate, 16*(3), 80–112.

Tompea, A., & Năstuţă, S. (2009). Romania. In H. Fassmann, U. Reeger, & W. Sievers (Eds.), *Statistics and reality: Concepts and measurements of migration in Europe* (pp. 217–230). Amsterdam: Amsterdam University Press.

Uvin, P. (2002). On counting, categorizing, and violence in Burundi and Rwanda. In D. I. Kertzer & D. Arel (Eds.), *Census and identity: The politics of race, ethnicity, and language in national census* (pp. 148–175). Cambridge, UK and New York: Cambridge University Press.

Varga, E. Á. (1998). *Fejezetek a jelenkori Erdély népesedéstörténetéből.* Budapest: Püski.

Varga, E. Á. (1999). *Erdély etnikai és felekezeti statisztikája (1850–1992). Il Kötet.* Csíkszereda: Pro-Print.

Waugh, L. R. (1982). Marked and unmarked: A choice between unequals in semiotic structure. *Semiotica, 38*(3–4), 299–318.

Wimmer, A. (2013). *Ethnic boundary making: Institutions, power, networks. Oxford studies in culture and politics.* New York: Oxford University Press.

11

A Changing System of Ethnic Stratification: The Social Positions of Transylvanian Hungarians

Tamás Kiss

1 Introduction: The Power Asymmetries Produced by the Institutional Order of the Nation-State

The aim of this chapter is to present the positions of Transylvanian Hungarians in the Romanian and Transylvanian system of ethnic stratification. Just like in the previous chapter, the historical perspective is very important, as a synchronic inquiry tells little about the role of ethnicity in the distributive process.[1] In this respect, the historical changes

[1] The notion of a system of ethnic stratification refers to the concept of class system used by Gerhard Lenski. Lenski elaborated a multidimensional model of stratification and argued that as far as race, ethnicity, or religion plays a significant role in the distributive process, one should consider these racial, ethnic, and religious categories as classes or status groups (Lenski 1966, p. 396).

T. Kiss (✉)
Romanian Institute for Research on National Minorities, Cluj-Napoca, Romania

T. Kiss et al. (eds.), *Unequal Accommodation of Minority Rights*, Palgrave Politics of Identity and Citizenship Series, https://doi.org/10.1007/978-3-319-78893-7_11

in the positions of the different ethnic groups are even more important than present ethnic inequalities. Historical trends reveal the asymmetries produced by the institutional order of the nation-state, which should be considered the major factor shaping the system of ethnic stratification.

Wimmer (2002) emphasized that the process of modernization—which has taken place in the framework of the nation-states—created a new form of social exclusion, leading to a privileged position of titular groups. Following the creation of modern nation-states, the question of "who owned the state" (in an ethnic sense) became crucial and consecutive for the distributive process. Wimmer argued that despite the importance of these types of asymmetries produced by the institutional order of the nation-state, social scientists put little emphasis on this issue. To quote Wimmer, the issue of ethnic inequalities has become a "blind spot" of mainstream social theories (2002, p. 5).[2]

The power asymmetries produced by the nation-state are all-embracing and their consequences are manifold. Brubaker et al. used the dichotomy of marked and unmarked categories to describe asymmetries in the everyday interactions between Hungarians and Romanians in Cluj/Kolozsvár (2006, pp. 211–217). The unmarked category is the taken-for-granted one, referring to what is regarded as the usual or normal, while the marked category denotes the exceptional, something that needs explanation. In Cluj/Kolozsvár, everybody addresses a stranger in public in Romanian, because by default, the stranger is considered a Romanian. One could argue that this is a matter of probability, but in fact it is the outcome of a powerful language ideology and everyday linguistic policing (Brubaker et al. 2006, pp. 239–265). The vast majority of Romanians are convinced that Transylvanian Hungarians should be able to speak Romanian, while perceiving no obligation to learn the language of their fellow Hungarian countrymen

[2]Even a superficial review of the literature of social stratification makes this quite evident. Ethnic inequalities seem to be problematic and had a marginal position in both paradigms dominating the research on social stratification, namely structural functionalism and Marxism. This does not mean that social scientists of Marxist inclination would not theorize ethnic inequalities in relevant ways at all. See, for instance, the theory of dual labor market by Bonacich (1972).

even if they lived in a predominantly Hungarian social environment. This conviction and its everyday manifestations play a key role in the maintenance of asymmetric bilingualism. In the long run, the persistent linguistic ideology reproduced by the institutional and discursive order of the nation-state erodes local-level norms of linguistic accommodation based on more symmetric forms of bilingualism.

The most important demographic consequence of asymmetry is assimilation. As Laitin (1998) emphasized, assimilation can be perceived as a sequence of decisions which could spread out over several generations. In Transylvania, ethnic exogamy and mixed marriages play a central role in the process of assimilation. Children growing up in ethnically mixed families go through an imbalanced process of ethnic socialization. As a consequence, the acquirement of linguistic and cultural competences defining membership in the majority ethnic category is taken for granted while the acquirement of competences necessary to be recognized as Hungarian is an exception. In the Transylvanian Hungarian public discourse, there is a distinction between forced assimilation and assimilation as a "natural" process (*természetes asszimiláció*). I find the use of this dichotomy misleading, as social processes and interethnic relations are barely "natural": They are shaped by institutionalized structures and the power asymmetries inherent within them.

The system of ethnic stratification is also a consequence of these asymmetries, and it should be analyzed with an eye on historical processes. To this purpose, the first part of the chapter outlines the historical changes in ethnic stratification in Romania. First, I will discuss some aspects of the ethnic inequalities characteristic between 1880 and 1910. In this period (when Transylvania used to be part of the Hungarian Kingdom), the institutional context was the opposite of what emerged after the Treaty of Trianon. Then, I discuss the interwar period and the processes that unfolded during state socialism. These two periods stand in sharp contrast, and the changes that occurred during this latter period were very consequential for the present characteristics of the system of ethnic stratification. The second part of the chapter deals with the present ethnic inequalities, and it is based mostly on survey and census results.

2 Historical Excurse

2.1 Under Hungarian Rule

The system of ethnic stratification at the end of the nineteenth and the beginning of the twentieth centuries can be reconstructed from the Hungarian censuses carried out between 1880 and 1910, which contained (among others) questions concerning occupation, literacy, landholding, and spoken languages. As I mentioned in the previous chapter, the ethnic classification of the population relied on the mother tongue, which was considered an objective indicator of ethno-national belonging (Arel 2002).

It is important that a process of social modernization and the development of the capitalist system of production have begun during this period.[3] In Transylvania, these processes have been delayed compared to other territories of the Hapsburg Monarchy and Hungary. As a consequence, the unfavorable position of Transylvania was evident, as reflected by indicators such as the density of the railway system, the degree of urbanization, or the literacy of the population (Köpeczi et al. 1986, pp. 1508–1512). Nevertheless, the incipient process of social modernization reshaped the system of ethnic classification. One could argue that ethnic inequalities were determined by two major factors. The first one was the historical legacy, as ethnic inequalities existed even before the Austrian–Hungarian Compromise of 1867 (*Ausgleich or Kiegyezés*) and the creation of the modern (semi-independent) Hungarian state.[4] The second determinant factor was the fact that social modernization took shape within the Hungarian nationalizing state,

---

[3]World system theorists argue that Hungary (including Transylvania) became part of the emerging capitalist world system earlier, during the sixteenth or seventeenth century (Wallerstein 1974). However, I do not refer to this process but to the beginning of what is conventionally called the beginning of social modernization.

[4]One of the consequences of the Compromise was the unification of Transylvania with Hungary, which was opposed by both the Romanian and the Saxon elites (Pál 2010). Traditionally, Hungarians were highly overrepresented among the nobility and dominated the administration of the province (except for the 1850–1867 period, following the failed revolution of 1848). Saxons used to form an autonomous estate and were the dominant element of several urban centers of

which led to the improvement of the social position of the titular group and to a process of assimilation (Magyarization) in the urban centers.

One should highlight that the ethnic structure of the province was different from that of today. Although ethnic Romanians constituted a majority both in the historical province of Transylvania and in the region next to the present Hungarian border, the overall proportion of Hungarians and Germans was slightly above 40%. In the historical province of Transylvania, Hungarians formed a large ethnic block in the Székely Land and constituted the majority in several micro-regions. Romanians were the majority population in the rest of the province, living in ethnically homogenous areas (like in Hunedoara/Hunyad and Făgăraș/Fogaras) or mixed with Hungarians and Saxons. In the Eastern periphery of the Great Hungarian Plain, in northern Arad, in Bihor/Bihar and Satu-Mare/Szatmár, a more or less clear-cut delimitation between the territories inhabited by Hungarians and Romanians could be made (unlike today). In Sălaj/Szilágy, ethnically mixed territories used to be quite extensive. The German-speaking population formed two large blocks. Transylvanian Saxons were present in Southern Transylvania and in Bistrița/Beszterce, but in the former territories of the Saxon Estate there was a Romanian majority in the period under investigation. The other German block was that of Banat Swabians, who constituted a majority to the west and northwest of Timișoara/Temesvár. According to the census results, 2.6% of the population practiced Judaism in 1880 and 3.5% in 1910. However, Jews were not counted as a separate ethno-national (more precisely linguistic) group by the Hungarian authorities but were classified according to their mother tongue as either Hungarians or Germans.[5] According to the 1893 Gypsy Census in Hungary,[6] the number of Roma in the historical province of Transylvania was 105,034 or 5% of the population.

Transylvania. Romanians were highly underrepresented both among the nobility and among urban dwellers and were not considered an autonomous estate. The administrative positions of the Romanian elites were relatively strong during the period between 1850 and 1867.

[5]Yiddish, the historical language of Ashkenazi Jews, was classified as German.

[6]The census used the ethnonym of *Cigány* which can be translated as Gypsy.

The ethnic makeup of the urban centers used to be sharply different. Hungarians made up 53.8% of the urban dwellers in 1880 and 64.6% in 1910, while the proportion of Romanians was 19.7 and 17.7%, and that of Germans was 19.3 and 15.3%. The processes of both urbanization and linguistic assimilation were different in the historical province of Transylvania and in Partium and Banat. In the latter areas, the process of urbanization (the population growth of towns like Timișoara/Temesvár, Arad, Orarea/Nagyvárad, and Satu-Mare/Szatmárnémeti) had begun earlier, while the Magyarization of Germans and Jews was more intensive. As a consequence, in 1910, 37.3% of Hungarians were urban dwellers, which is in sharp contrast with the 16.6% of Germans and 3.7% of Romanians who were living in an urban environment.[7] As for the historical province of Transylvania, the German character of the major urban centers of Southern Transylvania remained more intact. The urban centers outside the traditionally Saxon area (most importantly Cluj/Kolozsvár) had a Hungarian majority in spite of the fact that their rural *hinterland* was predominantly Romanian, while the Hungarian-inhabited territorial block, the Székely Land, remained largely rural with only 7% of urban dwellers.[8]

Differences in the literacy rate and educational attainment are also talkative indicators of ethnic inequalities. The literacy rate of Romanians was (next to Rusyns) the lowest among the nationalities of Hungary. In the historical province of Transylvania, 9.9% of Romanians were able to read and write in 1880, and 27.9% in 1910. These figures were of 31.4% in 1880 and 59.5% in 1910 in the case of Hungarians, and 63.2 (1880) and 76.1% (1910) for Germans. Transylvanian Hungarians lagged behind their co-ethnics living in other territories of Hungary,[9] while Transylvanian Saxons had a higher literacy rate than

[7]One should add that these figures are in some respect misleading, as the above-mentioned urban centers had a larger area of attraction or rural *hinterland*, also comprising territories that remained part of Hungary following the Treaty of Trianon.

[8]Here, the process of urbanization began late (in the 1910s) and it was practically restricted to the town of Târgu Mureș/Marosvásárhely.

[9]44.7% of the Hungarian speakers were able to read and write in Hungary as a whole in 1880 and 67.1% in 1910.

Germans living in Hungary.[10] Statistical data show that Hungarians were increasingly overrepresented among strata with higher educational attainment. Nevertheless, according to Karády (2000), this could be interpreted also as being indicative of Magyarization. Karády argued that the educational system, especially at its higher levels, was one of the principal channels through which the process of Magyarization took place. As a consequence, the higher the educational attainment of a person of allogeneic origin, the higher the probability that he or she declared Hungarian as his or her mother tongue.

As for the occupational structure, the most important figure is related to the employment of Romanians. According to the 1910 census, 84.7% of them were employed in the agricultural sector. Per Ronnås (1984) argued that the vast majority were engaged in subsistence farming and were barely connected to the emerging capitalist system of production.[11] Consequently, Hungarians and Germans were highly overrepresented in the secondary and tertiary sectors.[12] One could also highlight the overrepresentation of Germans and Hungarian-speaking Jews in the commerce and financial sectors and the Hungarian dominance of the administration.

As mentioned already, the changes in the structure of ethnic stratification were powerfully shaped by the emerging Hungarian nation-state, which evidently privileged the titular group. However, it would be a mistake to equate the institutional orders of the nineteenth- and twentieth-century nation-states. The difference does not lie in the nationalizing intentions but in the penetrative power of state structures as organizers of everyday life. At the end of the nineteenth and

[10]In Hungary as a whole, the literacy rate among German speakers was 67 (1880) and 70.1% (1910).

[11]This statement of Ronnås should be nuanced, as some of the most disadvantaged agricultural laborers were actually enrolled in the system of capitalist production: They worked for latifundia. The proportion of this stratum of agricultural laborers lacking land proprieties was lower in the historical province of Transylvania compared to both Hungary and the old Romanian Kingdom.

[12]The proportion of those employed in the industrial sector was 21% for Hungarians and 23.4% for Germans according to the 1910 census, but only 7.6% in the case of Romanians. 14.9 of the Hungarians, 14% of the Germans, and only 3.5% of the Romanians were employed in the tertiary sector.

Table 1 Language knowledge by mother tongue (1880)

Region	Mother tongue	Spoken languages (%)			
		Romanian	Hungarian	German	Mother tongue only
Transylvania (historical province)	Romanian	–	5.2	0.8	91.8
	Hungarian	18.0	–	4.4	77.2
	German	45.0	15.8	–	38.9
Western region (Banat, Crişana/Partium)[a]	Romanian	–	6.2	1.1	93.7
	Hungarian	9.2	–	10.4	77.7
	German	15.6	17.5	–	59.1

[a]The data do not precisely cover the territories presently belonging to Romania, as they were aggregated from county-level figures
Source Ronnås (1984, p. 107)

at the beginning of the twentieth centuries, the Hungarian nation-state lacked the effective institutional capacity to reshape the social structure and the everyday lives of rural communities. A proper indicator of the lack of penetration is that in 1880 only 5.2% of Romanians and 15.8 of Germans spoke Hungarian in the historical province of Transylvania. The same figures for the western part of present-day Romania were of 6.2 and 17.5% (Table 1).

2.2 The Interwar Period

After the transfer of Transylvania to Romania, the system of ethnic stratification outlined above was perceived by the Romanian nationalizing elites as the major obstacle of the integration of the newly acquired territories into the structure of the Romanian national state. To paraphrase Per Ronnås (1984), the mostly rural Romanian community constituted a kind of underclass or a stratum below modern capitalist production. Under such circumstances, Transylvanian towns (as well as those in Bessarabia dominated by Russians and Jews) seemed to be inimical foreign enclaves that had to be conquered.

Irina Livezeanu (1995) distinguished three major focuses of the interwar Romanian nationalizing policies. The first focus was territorial, the second was on urban centers, and the third was institutional. Concerning the territorial focus, one should distinguish between the two largely Hungarian-inhabited regions of the newly acquired territories. The first large block was the Székely Land right in the center of the enlarged country, while the second was the northwestern part of Crişana or Partium, including Oradea/Nagyvárad and Satu-Mare/Szatmárnémeti. Nationalizing efforts were more concentrated over this latter territory during the interwar period, including rural colonization and more intensive Romanianization efforts in the urban centers.

In a strictly demographic sense, the nationalizing efforts focusing on urban centers could be considered partially successful. The proportion of Romanian-speakers among urban dwellers (17% in 1910) rose to 35% by 1930. Meanwhile, the proportion of Hungarian speakers (65% in 1910) dropped to 45% by 1930, the proportion of other nationalities being even lower, at 37.9%.

The education system was at the very center of nationalizing efforts focusing on institutions. Simultaneous policies concerning primary and tertiary education would have been necessary for a radical restructuring of the system of ethnic stratification. However, the Romanian state was barely successful in reorganizing primary education and, as a consequence, there were no spectacular changes in the ethnic differences of the literacy rate. The proportion of those able to read and write among Romanians was well below the proportions characteristic for the Hungarian and German communities even according to the 1956 census. This was due to the fact that in the interwar period the Romanian state could be considered rather a nation-state with a nineteenth-century structure, meaning that it lacked the institutional capacities to penetrate the local life worlds of its mostly rural subjects. This problem was raised by several groups of the Romanian intelligentsia such as the sociologists of the Bucharest School, e.g., Dimitrie Gusti, Henri Stahl, Anton Golopenţia (Muşat 2011), and by intellectuals engaged in eugenics, like Iuliu Moldovan or Petre Râmneamţu (Bucur 2002; Turda 2010).

The Romanian state proved to be more effective in restructuring tertiary education. An expansion of university-level education occurred during the interwar period. The elite positions of the enlarged national state had to be filled by the ethnically Romanian fresh graduates. The proportion of Hungarians among university students fluctuated;

however, at its highest, in the 1928/1929 academic year, it reached only 2.1% (compared to their 7.9% share in the overall population). Livezeanu also highlighted that this expansion of higher education created difficulties, because due to the low speed of the country's social modernization it was impossible for all graduates to find jobs that would have satisfied their status aspirations (1995, pp. 211–245). Due to the lack of available market sector jobs, many graduates turned toward the overloaded administrative sector.

The administrative sector and the state bureaucracy also remained the most important (or arguably the sole) tool of the Romanian nationalizing project of the interwar period. As a consequence, the system of ethnic stratification characteristic during this era can be described as having a dual structure. On the one hand, a new, ethnically Romanian middle class appeared, among which university and high-school teachers and state officials were overrepresented. This middle class was directly connected in its existence to state bureaucracy and the institutional system. However, the dominance of minorities (Hungarians, Germans, and Hungarian-speaking Jews) in the economic sphere remained nearly intact in the Transylvanian urban centers. Due to their dominant economic position, they could not be considered genuinely minorities in a sociological sense.

2.3 Under State Socialism

Hungarians became a minority group in a sociological sense (i.e., they lost their dominant position in the urban societies of Transylvania) during the state-socialist regime. This was a consequence of several social and political processes affecting the distributive system of the country. First, one should take into account the ethno-demographic processes unfolding after World War II. Second, an important process of urbanization and industrialization also took place between 1950 and 1989. Third, the role of the educational system in the distributive process clearly increased. Forth, I will also discuss some consequences of the policies concerning the territorial distribution of economic investments.

Ethno-demographic processes. I already mentioned briefly in the previous chapter that the ethnic structure of Transylvania has altered considerably after World War II. The most important factor behind this process was the ethnically selective process of emigration: First, most Jews who survived the Holocaust left the country and so did most ethnic Germans. Between 1948 and 1951, 116,500 Jews left Romania for Israel, 106,200 between 1958 and 1966, and 40,600 between 1967 and 1989 (Horváth 2005). In addition to those performing the act of Aliyah, others resettled in North America. The mostly urban Jewish population of Romania practically ceased to exist due to this mass exodus. The emigration of Germans began later. According to the 1977 census, there was a sizable German community of 358,732 in Romania, with the vast majority living in Transylvania. Based on an agreement between Romania and Western Germany, 12,000 ethnic Germans were permitted to emigrate annually between 1978 and 1989. The majority of the remaining Germans left the country right after the collapse of the Communist regime: Official statistics registered 60,000 emigrants of German ethnicity in 1990 and 15,000 in 1991.[13] As a consequence, the Transylvanian Saxon and the Banat Swabian communities lost their former weight in the ethnic structure of the province. According to the censuses, the number of German ethnics was 119,000 in 1992, 60,000 in 2002, and 36,000 in 2011. The process of aging among Germans is quite advanced, which reduces the likelihood of the generational reproduction of the community. Hungarians were also affected by the process of emigration: first right after World War II and then between 1987 and 1990. It is important that in both of these waves of refugee-seeking and emigration urban dwellers were highly overrepresented.

Another important change affecting the system of ethnic stratification was the expansion of the Roma population due to the differences in fertility rates following the end of the demographic transition in Romania (Zamfir and Zamfir 1993; Ghețău 1996; Berevoiescu 2002).

[13] One should take into account that according to the mirror statistics (e.g., referring to immigrants in Germany from Romania) the numbers are even higher (Poledna 2001; Tompea and Năstuță 2009).

As mentioned in the previous chapter, the social construction of the Roma ethnicity is different compared to that of the Hungarian or Romanian ethnicities. For the latter two, the existence of several linguistic and cultural competences plays a defining role, as well as subjective identification with the category in question. In contrast, the Roma category is constructed to a great extent by external observers, and according to research focusing on this question, racial markers and elements of the way of life perceived as Roma play a key role here (Ladányi and Szelényi 2006). This also means that there is a huge gap between the results of the census and every classification concerning the number of Roma. For instance, in the 1977 census, 227,398 people declared themselves as Gypsy,[14] while a count based on hetero-identification carried out in 1976 by the Ministry of Interior found 540,000 Gypsies (Achim 2004, p. 209). According to the 2011 census, the number of Roma was 621,573, while the SocioRoMap survey based on hetero-identification by the employees of local municipalities estimated a number of almost 1.3 million (Horváth and Kiss 2017). It is important that the position of Roma had been quite marginal in Romanian and Transylvanian society even during state socialism; however, new and extreme forms of social exclusion have since taken shape.

Urbanization was the next key factor altering the Transylvanian system of ethnic stratification. Similarly to other Eastern Bloc countries, an accelerated industrialization and urbanization process was launched in Romania beginning with the 1950s. The main source of industrial investments was the surplus redirected from the agricultural sector. As a consequence, the rural–urban differences in living standards did not diminish but actually grew during this period (Ronnås 1984, pp. 81–84). This was the main factor lying behind the attractiveness of towns and industrial employment for the peasants deprived of their land proprieties by the agricultural collectivization (Kligman and Verdery 2011). Rural–urban migration was one of the characteristic social phenomena of the era; however, the state policies behind these processes also contained elements of ethnic selectivity. Consequently,

[14]The ethnonym of *Ţigan* which can be translated as Gypsy was used until the 2002 census.

Romanians were overrepresented among internal migrants, while Hungarians and especially the Roma were severely underrepresented. Meanwhile, the ethnic selectivity of emigration decreased the weight of minority elements (Jews, Germans, and Hungarians) in urban centers. According to the 1992 census, Hungarians, who had been represented as an urban minority in the interwar period, were already underrepresented among urban dwellers. This tendency has become even more accentuated after 1989. The increasing concentration of Hungarians in rural areas (i.e., the ruralization of the Hungarian community) has obvious negative consequences on their social positions (Fig. 1).

Inequalities in educational attainment. As the state-socialist regimes radically restricted the role of the private propriety in economic production, the formal educational system gained more importance in the redistribution process. Next to the position in the redistributive state hierarchy, educational attainment has become the most important source of social inequality. During the 1950s, open class-based discrimination was applied in the Romanian educational system: Those of "bourgeois origin" were barely allowed to enroll in tertiary education.

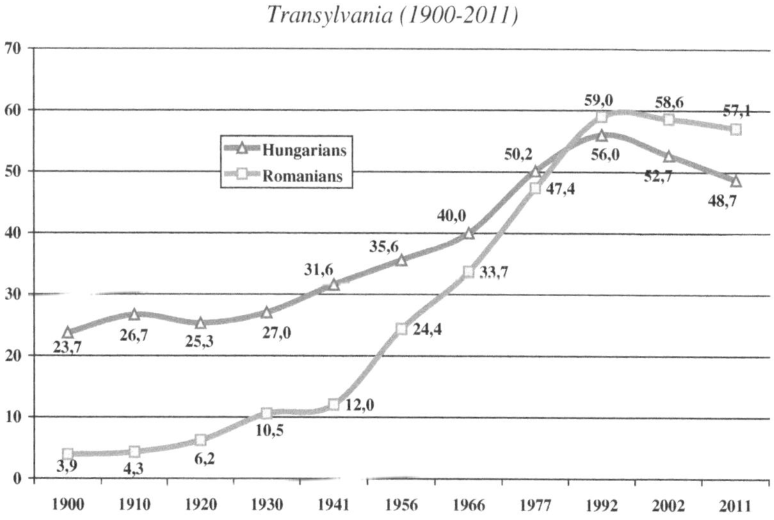

Fig. 1 The proportion of urban dwellers among Hungarians and Romanians in Transylvania (1900–2011) (*Source* Hungarian and Romanian census data)

However, this practice was abolished during the 1960s and ultimately the educational system successfully propagated a meritocratic ideology, according to which educational performance was the most important criterion of social mobility. In spite of the spread of this conviction characterizing modern societies in general, the expansion of higher education was quite slow in a comparative perspective. Moreover, during the 1980s, the absolute number of university students was stagnating, although the size of birth cohorts increased considerably following the drastic population policy measures introduced in 1966. From the perspective of the system of ethnic stratification, the most important fact is that Hungarians were significantly underrepresented among university graduates in each birth cohort (Fig. 2).

The policies concerning the territorial distribution of investments are the last factor that we take into account as affecting the system of ethnic stratification. During the first period of the state-socialist modernization (in the 1950s and 1960s), industrial development was focused

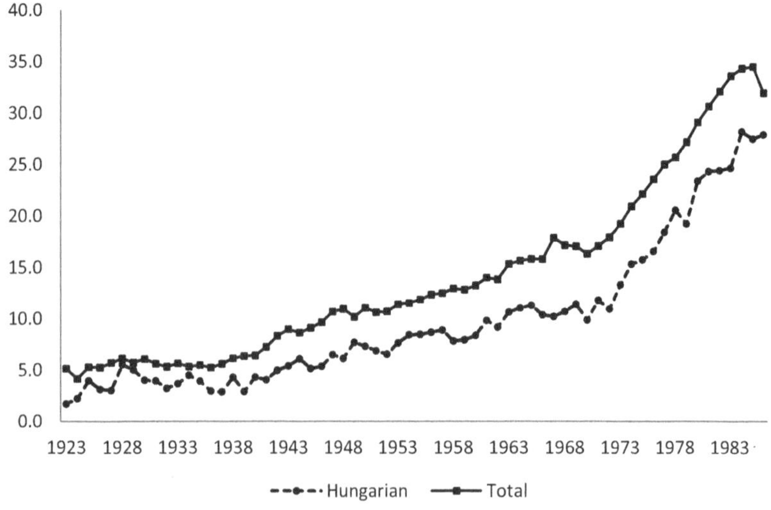

Fig. 2 The proportion of university graduates by birth cohorts among Hungarians and Romanians (2011) (*Source* IPUMS-International, 10% sample of the 2011 Romanian census—Minnesota Population Center. Integrated Public Use Microdata Series, International: Version 7.0 [2011 Romanian Census]. Minneapolis, MN: IPUMS, 2018. http://doi.org/10.18128/D020.V70)

on traditionally more industrialized regions, such as Brașov/Brassó, Timișoara/Temesvár, and Southern Transylvania in general (Hunya 1990). The regional capitals were also prioritized in the distribution of investments (Ronnås 1984, pp. 61–64). The industrialization of the overwhelmingly Hungarian Székely Land and of the Crișana/Partium region, which had a sizeable Hungarian population, began only after the territorial reorganization of the country in 1968. By and large, the regions where Hungarians constituted the majority of the population or a sizeable minority remained peripheral in the Romanian economy and this is partially a consequence of the policies concerning territorial development implemented during state socialism. It is also important that in the economically more prosperous areas the demographic erosion of the Hungarian population was much more accentuated.

3 Ethnic Inequalities: The Position of Transylvanian Hungarians in the Third Millennium

In the second part of this chapter, I focus on the present-day ethnic inequalities and social positions of the Transylvanian Hungarians. In addition to census data, I rely on a large-scale survey with a considerable Hungarian subsample carried out jointly by the Center for Research and Consultancy in Culture[15] (Bucharest) and the Romanian Institute for Research on National Minorities.[16] In what follows, I will focus on the following three dimensions: (1) educational attainment, (2) income inequalities, and (3) occupational status.

[15]In Romanian, Centrul de Cercetare și Consultanță în Domeniul Culturii (CCCDC).

[16]Next to questions concerning cultural consumption, the questionnaire contained a relatively consistent block on social stratification. The questionnaire was elaborated by a joint CCCDC-RIRNM team composed of Liviu Chelcea, Marius Lazăr, Gergő Barna, and the author of this chapter. The nationwide representative sample consisted of 3500 respondents, to which 1200 representatively selected ethnic Hungarians were added.

3.1 Inequalities of Educational Attainment

According to 2011 census data, the inequalities in educational attainment are obvious (Table 2): Hungarian university graduates are significantly underrepresented in all birth cohorts, no matter whether they graduated before or after 1989. Nevertheless, in the cohorts that enrolled into tertiary education after the regime change the proportion of graduates increased considerably among both Hungarians and the Romanian majority. In the case of the 1972 birth cohort (enrolled in 1990/1991), the proportion of graduates was 17.9 in the overall population of Romania and 10.9 among Hungarians. In the case of the 1985 cohort, the figures were 34.5 and 27.5, respectively. In other words, the expansion of tertiary education also increased the opportunities of the Hungarians to obtain a university diploma. Moreover, as between 2002 and 2007 the expansion of Hungarian-language higher education occurred faster than the national average, the expansion of tertiary education reduced ethnic inequalities in educational attainment to some extent.

In what follows, I will present a model about the influence of ascribed characteristics on the likelihood to graduate university, relying on data from the above-mentioned survey, which included questions concerning the place of birth, educational attainment of the father, gender, birth cohort, and ethnicity of the respondents. Table 2 shows the distribution of the respondents of this survey by educational attainment and compares it to 2011 census data. It is rather clear that the results of the survey are quite close to the census figures.

Table 3 shows the proportion of university graduates by the above-mentioned variables for the overall population of Romania and among Transylvanian Hungarians, as well as the results of a binomial logistic regression analysis which models the impact of these factors on the likelihood to graduate university. The comparison of the bivariate distributions highlights the categories in which Hungarians are most disadvantaged. The regression analysis reveals whether ethnic differences in the likelihood to graduate are significant even after controlling for the effect of other (possibly interfering) variables. The table displays the

Table 2 Educational attainment in Romania and among Transylvanian Hungarians and Romanians (2011)

	2011 CCCDC-RIRNM survey			2011 census		
	Transylvanian Hungarians ($N=1187$)	Transylvanian Romanians ($N=799$)	**Romania ($N=3460$)**	Transylvanian Hungarians	Transylvanian Romanians	**Romania**
Less than lower secondary	8.8	7.1	**10.5**	8.5	8.9	**10.0**
Lower secondary completed	27.9	23.6	**23.0**	31.6	27.0	**28.4**
Professional training	24.4	23.0	**21.9**	23.4	21.6	**24.4**
Upper secondary completed	27.1	27.6	**27.2**	25.9	26.0	**27.1**
University completed	11.5	18.7	**16.7**	10.6	16.5	**15.0**

Source CCCDC-RIRNM survey 2011; IPUMS-International, 10% sample of the 2011 Romanian census—Minnesota Population Center. Integrated Public Use Microdata Series, International: Version 7.0 [2011 Romanian Census]. Minneapolis, MN: IPUMS, 2018. http://doi.org/10.18128/D020.V70

Table 3 The effect of ascribed characteristics on the likelihood of graduating university in Romania (Binomial logistic regression, 2011)

Explanatory variables	Values/categories	Proportion of university graduates, Romania (%)	Proportion of university graduates, Hungarians (%)	Binomial logistic regression EXP. B
Place of birth (historical region)	Transylvania	16.7		-
	Muntenia, Dobruja	15.1		1.063
	Moldova	17.5		1.502***
	Bucharest	36.1		1.295
Place of birth (rural-urban)	Rural	10.4	7.2	
	Urban	31.3	18.6	1.686***
Ethnicity	Romanian	18.2		-
	Hungarian	11.5		0.667**
	Other	5.5		0.374**
Father's educational attainment	Less than lower secondary	2.7	1.3	
	Lower secondary	9.3	5.5	3.024***
	Secondary completed	36.7	23.2	12.909***
	University completed	82.2	80.0	92.077***
Gender	Male	17.8	13.7	
	Female	17.1	9.8	1.256**
Birth cohort (age group in 2011)	Before 1949 (62+)	6.1	3.8	
	1950-1959 (52-61)	7.1	3.8	0.852
	1960-1966 (45-51)	11.9	8.3	1.005
	1967-1973 (38-44)	20.4	13.3	1.337
	1974-1980 (31-37)	29.9	20.5	1.826***
	1981-1986 (24-30)	42.4	37.5	2.029***
R^2 (Nagelkerke) = 0.407				

*$p<0.05$; **$p<0.01$
Note The regression is based on respondents aged 24 or above
Source CCCDC-RIRNM survey 2011

odds ratios (EXP. B) and the levels of significance. The value of 0.407 of the Nagelkerke R^2 shows that the explanatory power of the model is relatively high. In other words, ascribed characteristics have a considerable effect on the chances to complete tertiary education.

The logistic regression model shows that the most important variable affecting the likelihood to graduate is family background: The children of fathers with university degrees had 92 times higher chances to obtain a university diploma compared to children of fathers with primary education. The descriptive crosstabs show that the disadvantage of Hungarians is more accentuated in the lower strata. The differences are the largest among respondents whose fathers finished only primary or lower secondary education, while in the case of respondents whose fathers graduated university the differences are negligible. The place of birth also has a significant effect, those born in urban settlements and in Moldova were more likely to graduate university. The effect of the birth cohorts is obvious and it reflects the impact of the institutional changes occurring in the educational system over time. In this respect, it is important that during communism the growth of tertiary education was quite slow in Romania in comparison with other Eastern Bloc countries and the population policy of the Ceaușescu regime also negatively affected the cohorts born between 1967 and 1973 in terms of their chances to graduate university.[17] According to the model, an improvement of the chances to graduate (compared to people born before 1949) can be seen only in the case of the two youngest cohorts (born between 1974 and 1980, respectively, between 1981 and 1986). The descriptive distributions of the data also show that in the case of the 1981–1986 cohorts the ethnic differences are already rather small. However, most importantly the regression analysis proves that ethnicity has a significant effect on the likelihood to finish university in Romania, and that Hungarians have lower chances to graduate (Table 4).

[17]As already mentioned, the restriction on abortion was introduced in 1966 and as a consequence the 1967 birth cohort was twice as large as that of the previous year. The educational infrastructure was not properly extended to face this demographic change.

Table 4 Equivalized per capita household income (2011)

	I_{equ}		Compared to Romania as a whole (%)
	RON	EURO	
Transylvanian Hungarians (*N*=1182)	718.3	171	92.4
Transylvanian Romanians (*N*=893)	834.1	199	107.3
Bucharest (*N*=339)	1259.5	300	162.0
Romania (*N*=3362)	777.5	185	100.0

Source CCCDC-RIRNM survey, January 2011

3.2 Income Inequalities

In this section, I analyze income inequalities based on the equivalized per capita income of the households[18] (I will use the expression of per capita income in this sense).

According to the results of the survey conducted in January 2011, the average per capita income in Romania was 777.5 RON (185 Euro).[19] The income of Transylvanian Hungarians was 7.6% lower than the national average and 14% lower than that of Transylvanian Romanians.

Table 5 compares the average per capita income in Romania and among Transylvanian Hungarians and summarizes the results of a linear regression analysis.[20] My main questions were whether ethnicity has a significant effect on the per capita household income and in which categories Transylvanian Hungarians are disadvantaged. The table reveals the obvious inequalities in income related to educational attainment, economic status, marital status, minors in the family, gender (women being disadvantaged[21]), and the size of the settlement. Regional disparities also exist: Those living in the Western region (Banat) earn

[18] I_{equ} = Total income of the household/$N^{0.7}$. See Kapitány and Spéder (2004, p. 15) on this issue.

[19] According to the National Institute of Statistics, the average per capita income (not the equivalized one!) of the Romanian households was of 795 RON in January 2011.

[20] *B* is the unstandardized regression coefficient. It shows the effect of a one unit change of the independent variable over the per capita income (expressed in the unit of the dependent variable, in our case the absolute amount of Romanian currency).

[21] This is due to the precarious situation of divorced and widowed women, especially those raising minor-aged children.

Table 5 Factors influencing the equivalized per capita income of the households (linear regression, 2011)

Variable	Values	I_{equ} (RON)			Linear regression
		Romania (I)	Transylvanian Hungarians (II)	II/I	B
Age group	**20-29 years**	958	843	88%	
	15-19 years	743	658	89%	137***
	30-59 years	**752**	**698**	93%	-98***
	60+	693	704	102%	8
Gender	**Male**	806	772	96%	
	Female	751	669	89%	-43***
Children under 15 years	**No**	**828**	**745**	**90%**	
	Yes	650	643	99%	-145***
Marital status	**Single**	**891**	**764**	**86%**	
	Married, in union	771	734	95%	83***
	Divorced, widowed	657	620	94%	-6
Educational attainment	**University**	**1432**	**1068**	**75%**	
	Less than lower secondary	446	566	127%	-710***
	Lower secondary	540	596	110%	-620***
	Professional	633	638	100%	-565***
	Secondary completed	832	820	99%	-430***
Economic activity	**Employed**	**1008**	**838**	**83%**	
	Pensioner	680	700	103%	-113***
	Housework	427	474	111%	-202***
	Student	841	746	89%	-172***
	Unemployed	546	479	88%	-253***
	Other inactive	725	645	89%	-121**
Settlement size	**Bucharest**	**1259**	×		
	below 1000	480	539	112%	-476***
	1000-3000	561	605	108%	-437***
	3-10.000	533	636	119%	-447***
	10-30.000	777	805	104%	-373***
	30.-100.000	888	857	97%	-306***
	above 100.000	1116	950	85%	-154***
Macro-region	**South-Muntenia and Bucharest**	**890**			
	Central	775	699	90%	61*
	Western	799	705	88%	82**
	North West	869	748	86%	53
	South-West-Oltenia	741			37
	South-East	659			-62**
	North-East	641			-60**
Ethnicity	**Romanian**	**785**			
	Hungarian	725			-57**
	Other	576			-29
Constant (aged 20-29, single, without children, university degree, employed, male, living in Bucharest) = 1695,2 RON					
R^2=0.360					

*$p<0.1$; **$p<0.05$; ***$p<0.01$

Note Decimals are not displayed for non-standardized regression coefficients

Source CCCDC-RIRNM survey, January 2011

more, while those living in the northeastern and southeastern regions (Moldova and Dobruja) earn significantly less than those living in Muntenia (including Bucharest). The explanatory power of the model (R^2) is 0.360, meaning that the basic socio-demographic variables included explaining a considerable part of the income inequalities. The regression analysis also shows that per capita income was significantly lower in Hungarian households and the difference compared to ethnic Romanians was 57 RON. However, the breakdowns of average per capita income by the independent variables reveal some even more interesting findings. Hungarians turn out to be disadvantaged (have less per capita income) compared to their Romanian counterparts if they are better educated, if they are employed, and if they live in large cities. On the contrary, the per capita income of Hungarian households is higher than that of Romanian households among lower-educated segments, among those living in villages and small towns, and among pensioners and houseworkers.

In a further step, I computed a binary variable of income poverty. Respondents were classified as poor if the equivalized per capita income of their household was less than half of the national average.[22] One should emphasize that this is a relative indicator of income poverty and, consequently, the proportion of poor does not depend on the average level of income but on the level of income inequalities. The threshold of income poverty was of 389 RON (95 Euros), meaning that those respondents were classified as poor who belonged to households with an equivalized per capita income lower than this. The level of income poverty in Romania proved to be rather high at 23.8%. This is in line with the fact that next to the Baltic States, the Romanian society is the most unequal among the EU member states (Precupețu 2013). The proportion of income poverty is lower among both Transylvanian Hungarians (16.9%) and Transylvanian Romanians (15.9%). In the capital city of Bucharest, the figure is far lower at 2.8%.

As we saw, the per capita income of Transylvanian Romanians was slightly above the national average while in case of respondents living

[22]See Kapitány and Spéder (2004, pp. 15–16) for a similar definition.

in Bucharest it was 1.6 times higher. Thus, it is not surprising that the level of income poverty is lower. However, in the case of Transylvanian Hungarians, the per capita income was lower compared to the national average and the proportion of respondents belonging to poor households was lower in spite of this circumstance. This obviously means that income inequalities are lower among Transylvanian Hungarians. Table 6 summarizes the results of a binomial logistic regression analysis concerning the factors that increase the risk of poverty.

The data show that the most important factors increasing the risk of poverty are low educational attainment, unemployment, inactivity (without pension), the presence of minors in the household, and residence in villages or small towns and in the southwestern (Oltenia), southeastern (Dobruja), and northeastern (Moldova) regions of the country. According to the results, Hungarian ethnicity is not a factor increasing the risk of poverty; on the contrary, it reduces this risk. The distribution by income quintiles also confirms that income inequalities are lower among Transylvanian Hungarians: They are underrepresented not only in the higher income strata but also among those with lower income and among those below the relative poverty line (Fig. 3).

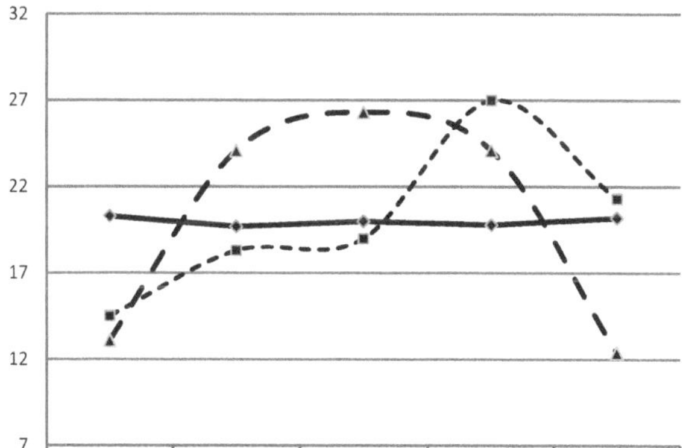

	Lower fifth	Lower middle	Middle	Higher middle	Higher fifth
Romania	20	20	20	20	20
Transylvanian Romanians	14.5	18.3	19	27	21.3
Transylvanian Hungarians	13.1	24.1	26.3	24.1	12.4

Fig. 3 Distribution by income quintiles (2011) (*Source* CCCDC-RIRNM survey, January 2011)

Table 6 Factors increasing the risk of poverty (binomial logistic regression, 2011)

Variable	Value	*Income poverty (%)*		Logistic regression
		Romania	*Transylvanian Hungarians*	EXP B
Age	**15-19 years**	24.2	10.5	
	20-29 years	17.7	15.4	1.887***
	30-59 years	27.2	20.3	2.585***
	60+	21.5	13.3	1.374
Gender	**Male**	22.9	16.0	
	Female	24.6	17.9	0.908
Children aged below 15	**No**	19.0	15.4	
	Yes	35.3	22.2	2.067***
Marital status	Single	18.0	13.8	
	Married, in union	25.0	16.8	0.796
	Divorced, widowed	26.7	21.2	1.418*
Educational attainment	**University**	**3.0**	6.7	
	Less than lower secondary	43.8	26.1	29.527***
	Lower secondary	35.6	23.0	12.853***
	Professional	30.9	18.8	8.771***
	Secondary completed	11.4	11.1	4.838***
Economic activity	**Employed**	12.3	12.4	
	Pensioner	21.4	12.9	0.896
	Housework	56.4	38.9	3.182***
	Student	15.0	7.7	2.041***
	Unemployed	39.3	41.7	2.423***
	Other inactive	33.3	28.6	2.320***
Settlement size	**Bucharest**	**2.8**		
	below 1000	42.8	36.2	16.082***
	1000-3000	34.5	21.0	11.006***
	3-10.000	39.1	20.9	11.529***
	10-30.000	16.0	9.1	6.232**
	30.-100.000	8.7	3.2	3.026***
	above 100.000	7.5	5.9	2.398***
Macro-region	Central	21.0	17.9	
	North-West	18.5	18.2	0.720***
	West	14.9	16.0	0.684***
	South-West	35.4		2.574***
	South and Bucharest	17.6		1.445***
	South-East	28.9		1.916***
	North-East	34.2		2.091***
Ethnicity	**Romanian**	23.3		
	Hungarian	16.9		**0.662***
	Other	47.6		1.299

R^2 (Nagelkerke) = 0.402
*Legend *** p<0.01; ** p<0.05, * p<0.1.*

Source CCCDC-RIRNM survey 2011

3.3 Occupational Status

In this part, I follow Chan and Goldthorpe (2004, 2010) who conceptualized social status as a hierarchy or ranked order (superiority, equality, or inferiority) based on prestige and esteem. The mentioned authors relied on Laumann and Guttman (1966) who argued that status manifests itself in social closure and distances between different groups. It can be measured through the likelihood of association in personal and informal relations between people belonging to different categories. The original research program of Chan and Goldthorpe was to find out whether social status or class position (understood in a Weberian sense as a similar position on labor market) is a stronger determinant of diverging cultural and political preferences. In what follows, I construct a status hierarchy of occupational categories; then, I will ask whether this hierarchy is similar or different in the case of Transylvanian Hungarians compared to Romania as a whole. I will also investigate in which status groups Hungarians are over- and underrepresented.

There are several reasons why status hierarchy should be considered important in Eastern Europe on the one hand, and why the status (meaning social esteem and prestige) of different occupational categories cannot be taken for granted on the other. First, one can hypothesize that in Eastern Europe (compared to Western European or North American societies) social status manifests itself more evidently in everyday interactions. Both the low- and high-status groups are more prone to express their subordinated/superior position through their gestures, postures, and language usage. Second, status hierarchy cannot be taken for granted due to radical discontinuities and ruptures in the system of stratification and in the relation between social categories. It is obvious that the distributive system in Romania has changed considerably following the collapse of the Communist regime. The most important aspect was the crisis of the working class following the process of deindustrialization (Kideckel 2008). Nevertheless, the changes affected the higher social strata too. During state socialism—as private property had been radically restricted—educational attainment and other forms of cultural capital were extremely important for achieving esteem and prestige. Analysts argued that (at least among Transylvanian Hungarians) the public intelligentsia was not only the most honored status group but also provided a role model for larger segments of professionals and graduates of tertiary and secondary education.[23] The socioeconomic transformation following the collapse of communism reduced the role of cultural capital in reproducing social prestige and questioned the honorability of some cultural practices (Zavisca 2005). The public intelligentsia and its models no longer constitute a role model for the larger society[24]; however, it is questionable whether or not a univocal new status hierarchy has emerged. The newly emerging entrepreneurial and political classes have gained more influence; however, their practices are perceived with suspicion and distance by the larger society (Sik 1994; Kiss 2004).

Chan and Goldthorpe (2004, 2010) proposed to construct the status hierarchy empirically relying on the frequency of relations between the different occupational categories. They argued that in modern societies occupation is the most important category that could be associated with social prestige and honor. The status hierarchy could be measured through the frequency or likelihood of intimate personal relations between people belonging to different occupational categories. I used the 10% IPUMS sample of the 2002 Romanian census and I focused on occupational heterogamy. In a first step, I constructed the 10% sample of those living in marriages or consensual unions. Based on this database, I obtained a cross tabulation between the occupation of the respondents and their spouses.[25] The crosstabs were analyzed according to the instructions of Laumann and Guttman (1966) and of Chan and Goldthorpe (2004), who analyzed the proportional distribution of the crosstab through multidimensional scaling and argued that one of the dimensions obtained by scaling could be interpreted as an indicator of the status hierarchy. Similarly to them, I used the scale values as indicators of the social status of given occupational categories (Table 7).

[23]Biró (1998) argued that one indicator of the high prestige of the public intelligentsia was that in 1990 they gained a central role in establishing the Hungarian ethno-national movement and quickly occupied the ranks of the newly founded ethnic party. It was a later phase when elites engaged in public administration and economic activities gained ground.

[24]Kiss (2004) emphasized the status loss of the teachers in villages. This stratum used to be the most honorable during the 1980s.

[25]This way I aggregated the occupation of husbands and wives and the resulting crosstab became symmetric by rows and columns.

I defined the occupational categories based on the three-digit ISCO88 variable used by the Romanian censuses, and I constructed 31 composite categories using ISCO occupational categories. Each of the categories contained between 0.6 and 6.8% of the Romanian employees, except for the two categories comprising agricultural laborers which contained 11.5 and 12% of the employed population. The high proportion of agricultural laborers is an element distinguishing Romania's occupational structure in a European (or even in an Eastern European) comparison.

Table 7 The hierarchy of the occupational statuses in Romania (2002)

	Composite categories using ISCO88 variables	ISCO88 codes	Scale value	Proportion among Hungarians (2002)	
				Romania	Hungarians
1 – High-status professionals	Medical and health professionals	222	1.81	0.8	0.7
	Engineers, computer engineering, natural scientists	211, 212, 213, 214, 211	1.58	2.8	1.9
	Teachers and other professionals in education	232, 233, 234, 235	1.47	2.2	2.2
	Social scientists, cultural professional, artist, clergymen	243, 245, 246, 247, 299	1.25	2.0	1.1
	Economic and legal professional	241, 246	1.15	0.8	0.3
	Public sector and general managers and administrators	111, 114, 121, 122, 123	0.98	1.9	1.5
	Managers of small firms	131	0.94	2.2	2.2
	Total			**12.6**	**9.7**
2 – Middle status: clerks, technicians and associate professionals	Buyers and sales representatives	341, 342	0.51	1.0	1.0
	Associate professionals in administration	343, 344	0.49	2.4	2.5
	Technicians, associate professionals in engineering	311, 312, 313, 314, 315	0.37	2.7	2.2
	Associate professionals in teaching		0.34	1.4	1.7
	Secretaries and clerks	411, 412, 414, 419	0.29	2.1	1.9
	Associate professionals in healthcare, nurses	321, 322, 323	0.28	1.9	1.8
	Tourism, catering, restaurants	511, 512, 514	0.27	2.7	3.6
	Police officers and armed forces	100, 345	0.24	0.6	0.6
	Customer service clerks	421, 422	0.16	1.0	1.0
	Stock and transport clerks	413	0.12	1.8	2.0
	Other technicians and clerks	243, 244, 245, 246, 247, 299	0.10	0.7	1.0
	Protective service workers	516	-0.10	1.3	0.5
	Sales workers	522	-0.13	4.0	5.0
	Total			**23.5**	**24.8**

(continued)

Table 7 (continued)

3 – Low status I.: blue-collar workers	Machinery mechanics and fitters	723, 724	-0.29	4.2	4.1
	Skilled and related manual workers in light industry	731, 732, 733, 734, 741, 742, 743, 744	-0.37	6.4	12.1
	Skilled and related manual workers in heavy industry	721, 722	-0.40	6.8	6.8
	Transport operators, car and truck drivers	831, 832, 833, 834	-0.48	4.7	4.5
	Plant and machines operators	811, 812, 813, 814, 815, 816, 817, 821, 822, 823, 824, 825, 826, 827, 828, 829	-0.49	5.5	8.6
	Personal care and other personal workers	513	-0.62	1.0	1.2
	Domestic and related helpers, cleaners, garbage collectors	911, 912, 913, 914, 915, 916	-0.65	3.6	3.8
	Skilled and related manual workers in construction, miners	711, 712, 713, 714	-0.74	3.9	5.6
	Unskilled laborers	931, 932, 933	-1.01	4.1	4.9
	Total			**40.4**	**51.7**
Low status II.: agricultural laborers	Farmers, specialized agricultural workers	611, 612, 614, 615	-2.92	11.5	6.3
	Non-specialized agricultural workers, daily laborers	613, 921	-4.13	12.0	7.5
	Total			**23.5**	**13.7**

Source Database of married couples and consensual unions created by the author based on the IPUMS-International 10% sample of the 2002 Romanian census

According to the results, some categories of highly skilled professionals can be characterized as the most prestigious ones. In a ranked order, these are: medical professionals (physicians and pharmacists); engineers (including computer engineering); teachers; cultural, social care, social science professionals, and clergymen; legal professionals and economists; public sector and general managers; and managers of small firms. The next broad category is that of clerks, technicians, and associate professionals. Sales managers and agents, lower-educated administrative professionals, technicians, teachers with secondary education, secretaries, HoReCa workers, policemen and members of the armed forces, shop salespersons and cashiers, and security agents enter in this category. The first of the lower-status composite category is that of blue-collar laborers, including different categories of industrial workers and manual laborers, respectively, truck drivers, cleaners, and domestic helpers. The second broad lower-status category is that of agricultural workers, including farmers (the majority of them being subsistence farmers) and daily laborers. According to the analysis of the occupational homogamy, agricultural laborers are largely separated from the rest of the society. It is also important that according to census data, Hungarians are under-represented among both higher strata professionals and agricultural laborers and overrepresented among blue-collar workers.

An important question was whether a separate analysis focusing on Transylvanian Hungarians would indicate a different status hierarchy. I analyzed this issue by comparing the occupational structure of the marriages and consensual unions in Romania and among Transylvanian Hungarians. Figure 4 compares the scale values used as indicators of occupational status in the case of the two populations.

The analysis yielded a number of interesting findings. First, in the case of Hungarians there is a greater distance between high-status

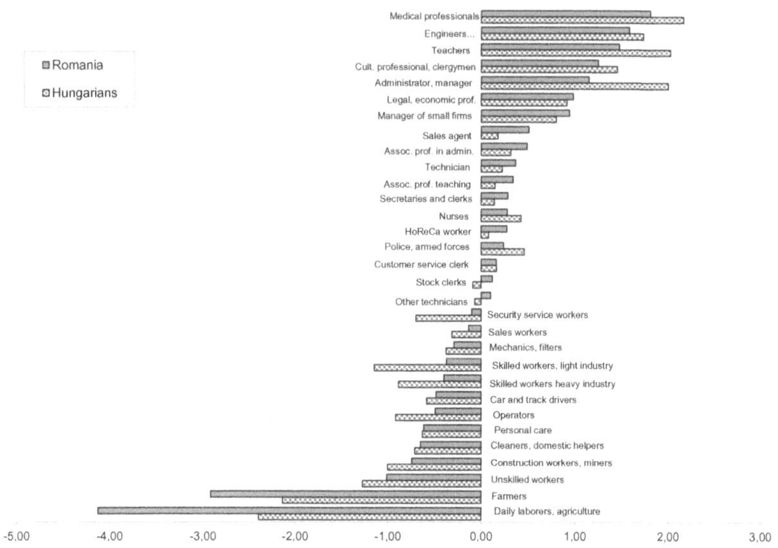

Fig. 4 The hierarchy of occupational statuses in Romania and among Transylvanian Hungarians (2002) (*Source* Database of married couples and consensual unions created by the author, based on the IPUMS-International 10% sample of the 2002 Romanian census)

professionals and middle-status clerks and technicians. The medical professionals, teachers, and public sector and general managers gained a status-index value significantly higher than the national average, and the index values are slightly higher in the case of engineers and cultural professionals too. At the same time, the status-index values of the majority of middle-status categories (sales agents, associate professionals in administration and teaching, technicians, HoReCa workers, stock clerks, security and sales workers) are lower. Second, the distance between blue-collar workers and agricultural laborers is smaller. In the case of the ethnic Hungarian subsample, all categories of blue-collar workers gained significantly lower, while the agricultural laborers significantly higher status-index values compared to the national average. In sum, the social distance between high-status professionals and the rest of the society is higher, while the social distance between the two lower-status composite categories of agricultural and blue-collar workers is lower among Transylvanian Hungarians.

Nevertheless, the prestige hierarchy of the occupational categories among Transylvanian Hungarians and in Romania is remarkably similar, the correlation between the two hierarchies being 0.917. Chan and Goldthorpe arrived to a similar conclusion after an analysis of occupational homogamy among white British and racial minority couples in the UK and of white and African American couples in the USA. Their conclusion is that even if there are significant differences in the social positions of the minority and majority, the status hierarchy existing in the larger society reproduces itself among minority populations too (2010, p. 42).

In what follows, I rely on the CCCDC-RIRNM survey from 2011 to discuss the relation between occupational statuses and educational attainment, respectively, income. It should be noted that this survey also confirmed that Hungarians were overrepresented among blue-collar workers but underrepresented among both high-status professionals and agricultural laborers (Table 8).[26]

---

[26]It should be emphasized that the CCCDC-RIRNM survey asked the question concerning occupation not only from those who were employed but (referring to the last occupation of the respondent) also from pensioners and the unemployed. For those who had never worked (15.1% of the Hungarian and 13.7% of the national sample), it is obviously impossible to define occupational status.

Table 9 investigates the effect of educational attainment (as an indicator of cultural capital) and of income on occupational status. Two aspects are worth being highlighted. First, educational attainment has an obviously stronger impact on occupational status than income. Second, the correlation between income and social status is lower among Hungarians.

It should also be emphasized that the differences in the income of the high- and low-status strata are significantly lower in case of Transylvanian Hungarians compared to the national average. The per capita income is 3.6 times higher in case of high-status professionals compared to agricultural laborers in Romania, while this ratio is only

Table 8 Distribution by occupational status composite categories, Romania and Transylvanian Hungarians and Romanians (2011)

	Transylvanian Hungarians	Transylvanian Romanians	Romania
High-status professionals	10.8	16.9	16.6
Middle-status clerks, technicians	25.2	25.0	24.7
Lower-status I: blue-collar workers	49.8	41.0	39.9
Lower-status II: agricultural laborers	14.2	17.0	18.8

Source CCCDC-RIRNM survey, January 2011

Table 9 The effect of income and educational attainment on occupational status (2011)

	Partial correlation coefficients		Linear regression coefficients		
	Income (I_{equ})	Educational attainment (years spent in education)	Income (I_{equ})	Educational attainment (years spent in education)	R^2
Romania	0.435	0.665	0.153	0.584	0.450
Hungarians 1[a]	0.272	0.536	0.124	0.501	0.301
Hungarians 2[b]	0.313	0.663	0.128	0.624	0.451

[a]Status-index calculated using the crosstabs of occupational homogamy in Romania

[b]Status-index calculated using the crosstabs of occupational homogamy among Transylvanian Hungarians

Source CCCDC-RIRNM survey (2011)

Table 10 Equivalized per capita income in Romania, among Transylvanian Hungarians and Romanians (2011)

	Transylvanian Hungarians ($N = 1004$)		Transylvanian Romanians ($N = 806$)		Romania ($N = 2922$)
	RON	% of National average	RON	% of National average	RON
High-status professionals	1069.0	74.4	1451.4	101.1	1436.0
Middle-status clerks, technicians	835.0	92.8	968.7	107.7	899.8
Lower-status I: blue-collar workers	680.9	106.4	687.2	107.4	639.9
Lower-status II: agricultural laborers	496.7	123.0	447.8	110.9	403.7

Source CCCDC-RIRNM survey, January 2011

2.2 in case of Transylvanian Hungarians. Note that while the income inequalities between these broad strata are lower, the social distances between them are higher. Based on these results, one can logically hypothesize that high-status Hungarians often perceive their position as inconsistent: They are highly honored (or pretend to be highly honored) in their own ethnic society but they earn significantly less, at least compared to their ethnic Romanian counterparts. This can be frustrating and can explain why—as we will see in the next chapter of this volume—the inclination to transgress the norms of ethnic endogamy and to choose a majority orientation for children growing up in mixed families is higher among these strata (Table 10).

4 Conclusions and Comparative Overview

Increasing marginalization is the first tendency that should be highlighted concerning the social position of Transylvanian Hungarians. Obviously, this process cannot be interpreted without taking into account the institutional and discursive order of the (Romanian) nation-state, which systematically privileges the titular ethnic category. The marginalization of Hungarians has been a long-term process: It began in the interwar period, it intensified during state socialism, and it continued after the collapse of the Communist regime. Between the two world wars, the Hungarian- and German-speaking urban middle classes of Transylvania were regarded as foreign enclaves by the Romanian political class and one of the main objectives of state policies was to alter the system of ethnic stratification considered to be unfavorable from a Romanian perspective (Livezeanu 1995). Communist authorities followed a quite similar pathway: Archive records prove the existence of an explicit state policy to alter the ethnic makeup of some major urban centers (László and Novák 2012, pp. 15–16).

However, the conclusions concerning marginalization during the post-socialist period should be formulated in a more nuanced way. Some argue that one cannot blame these processes directly on discriminative nationalizing policies. Brubaker characterized the situation of Hungarians in Romania as "nationalization without nationalism". According to him, neither the changes in the ethnic stratification system, nor the assimilation of the Hungarians into the national majority is consequences of conscious nationalizing policies (2009, pp. 211–215). However, in my opinion the conservation of a centralized state structure and an institutional and discursive order privileging the majority can only be characterized as nationalism and nationalization, even if this instructional order is taken for granted and seems to have no alternatives from the perspective of the majority. Others argue that it is self-segregation or the very project of ethnic parallelism that is conductive to marginalization. For instance, ethnic parallelism is one of the most important factors behind the insufficient knowledge of the Romanian language, which ultimately leads to a marginal position in the labor market (Csepeli et al. 2002). This is true; however, it is true only if one accepts the existing asymmetries between the Hungarian and Romanian languages and takes for granted the norms of language use according to which Romanian is the language of interethnic communication even in regions where

Hungarians constitute an overwhelming majority. By doing so, one also takes for granted that all the burdens of linguistic and cultural integration and accommodation are incumbent on the minority group (Skutnabb-Kangas 2000, p. 59).

Second, one should emphasize the relation between social marginalization and ethno-demographic trends. The ethnic blocks where Hungarians constitute a majority or at least a high proportion of the population are economically peripheral areas dominated by small towns and rural settlements. At the same time, the prospects of ethno-demographic reproduction are favorable in these areas, while quite unfavorable in economically prosperous urban centers and their metropolitan areas. The most important demographic process causing regional disparities in the demographic development of the Hungarian community is migration. Following World War I, 200 thousand Hungarians left the territories ceded by Hungary. State officials, professionals, and urban dwellers were highly overrepresented among them. The composition of later waves of emigrants and refugees has been similar. Following World War II, state officials and professionals from major urban centers were once again overrepresented among those opting for Hungary. According to a survey conducted in 1988 among Hungarian refugees who fled Romania, more than half of them came from the towns of Cluj/Kolozsvár, Oradea/Nagyvárad, and Târgu Mureș/Marosvásárhely, while those coming from rural areas and small towns were severely underrepresented (Regényi and Törzsök 1988). Surveys conducted among immigrants in Hungary in the 1990s and 2000s also confirm this tendency: 27.2% were university graduates and 60.8% completed secondary education in 2004 (Gödri and Tóth 2005, p. 50), while those coming from the ethnic block of Székely Land were underrepresented in 2001 (Gödri 2004, p. 137).

The process of assimilation is also selective from the point of view of the social status.[27] As mentioned already, demographic research

[27] This aspect will be discussed in detail in Chapter 12.

on Transylvanian Hungarians perceived assimilation mainly as an intergenerational phenomenon connected to ethnic exogamy and the unbalanced models of ethnic socialization in mixed families. We will see in the next chapter that the likelihood of exogamous marriage is higher among the better-educated strata, and that children in mixed families are most likely to be classified as Romanian if the parents were university graduates. This can be interpreted both as a consequence and as a cause of the unfavorable changes in the system of ethnic stratification. In other parts of the world, exactly the opposite situation was observed regarding some minority groups with favorable social positions. O'Leary and Finnäs examined intermarriage and identity choices for children in mixed marriages among the Swedish-speaking population of Finland and the Protestants of the Irish Republic (O'Leary and Finnäs 2002; Finnäs and O'Leary 2003). In these cases, the high-status and socially mobile individuals had a higher propensity to affirm the minority identity and, as a consequence, exogamy was less widespread in higher-status strata and children were more likely classified as belonging to the minority category in such families.

Third, in this context it is worth referring to the typology of ranked and unranked systems of ethnic groups elaborated by Horowitz (1985, pp. 22–24). These are obviously ideal types in a Weberian sense. The difference between them can be captured in two dimensions. The first dimension is that in ranked systems of groups ethnic belonging is also a marker (or a stigma) of one's social status, while in unranked systems it is not. This does not mean that ethnicity would not play a role in the distributive process for unranked systems of groups, only that there is no strict correspondence between ethnicity and social status. The second dimension refers to social mobility. In ranked systems of groups (virtually), all channels of social mobility are dominated by majority elites. As a consequence (the eventual), social mobility of minority group members will also mean assimilation toward the majority. The intergroup relation between Hungarians and Romanians is mostly an unranked one. It is obvious that in Transylvania to be Hungarian is not a social stigma and it is not interpreted in everyday situations as a marker of one's social status. As the chapters of the second part of this volume discussed, the Hungarian community has a relatively dense network of its own institutions, ranging from religious institutions to mass media and (in a certain sense) the education system. Due to this institutional network, social mobility is possible even without leaving the "Hungarian world". However, other segments—most importantly the economic sphere—are organized ethnically only to a lesser extent, and, as a consequence, channels of mobility are not controlled by the Hungarian elites. This imperfect character of ethnic encapsulation could be also perceived as a cause of the increasing marginalization of the Hungarian community, as some of its socially mobile members move toward the majority.

As a last remark, the differences compared to other Hungarian minority communities should be highlighted. It is important that in Transylvania, Hungarians are underrepresented not only among high-status and high-income strata but also among the poor. This also means that social inequalities are smaller within the Hungarian community compared to Romania as a whole. This aspect is specific compared to other Hungarian minority populations. According to studies focusing on Slovakia (Gyurgyík 2004, 2008) and Vojvodina (Badis 2008), Hungarians are overrepresented among underprivileged social strata and among the poor. This difference has its historical roots. In Slovakia and in Vojvodina, the supremacy and dominance of Hungarians had not been obvious at all, and the system of ethnic stratification changed more rapidly during the interwar period. For instance, the first Czechoslovak Republic used to be an attractive model of social modernization for many Hungarians (and it was more attractive compared to the authoritarian regime of interwar Hungary). This was not the case for Hungarians in Romania. The similarities and differences could be analyzed by a systematic comparative inquiry if the investigation was not focused primarily on the "common origin" of these communities but on the similarities and differences of the social contexts in which the ethno-cultural and social reproduction of these communities has occurred.

References

Achim, V. (2004). *The Roma in Romanian history*. Budapest and New York: Central European University Press.

Arel, D. (2002). Language categories: Backward or forward looking. In D. I. Kertzer & D. Arel (Eds.), *Census and identity: The politics of race, ethnicity, and language in national census* (pp. 92–121). Cambridge, UK and New York: Cambridge University Press.

Badis, R. (2008). A vajdasági magyar népesség társadalomszerkezete két népszámlálás tükrében. *Regio, 19*(4), 102–154.

Berevoiescu, I. (2002). O analiză demografică a populației de romi: familie și fertilitate. In C. Zamfir & M. Preda (Eds.), *Romii în România* (pp. 39–72). București: Expert.

Biró, Z. A. (1998). Intézményesedési folyamatok a romániai magyarság köré-ben. In Z. A. Biró (Ed.), *Stratégia vagy kényszerpályák? Tanulmányok a romániai magyar társadalomról* (pp. 16–47). Csíkszereda: Pro-Print.

Bonacich, E. (1972). A theory of ethnic antagonism: The split labor market. *American Sociological Review, 37*(5), 547.

Brubaker, R. (2009). National homogenization and ethnic reproduction on the European periphery. In M. Barbagli & H. Ferguson (Eds.), *La teoria sociologica e lo stato moderno: saggi in onore di Gianfranco Poggi* (pp. 201–221). Bologna: Il mulino.

Brubaker, R., Feischmidt, M., Fox, J., & Grancea, L. (2006). *Nationalist politics and everyday ethnicity in a Transylvanian town*. Princeton: Princeton University Press.

Bucur, M. (2002). *Eugenics and modernization in interwar Romania*. Pittsburgh, PA: University of Pittsburgh Press.

Chan, T. W., & Goldthorpe, J. (2004). Is there a status order in contemporary British society? Evidence from the occupational structure of friendship. *European Sociological Review, 20*(5), 383–401.

Chan, T. W., & Goldthorpe, J. (2010). *Social status and cultural consumption*. Cambridge, UK and New York: Cambridge University Press.

Csepeli, G., Székely, M., & Örkény, A. (2002). *Nemzetek egymás tükrében. Interetnikus viszonyok a Kárpát-medencében*. Budapest: Balassi.

Finnäs, F., & O'Leary, B. (2003). Choosing for the children: The affiliation of the children of minority–majority group intermarriages. *European Sociological Review, 19*(5), 483–499.

Gheţău, V. (1996). O proiectare condiţională a populaţiei României pe principale naţionalităţi (1992–2025). *Revista de Cercetări Sociale, 3*(1), 77–105.

Gödri, I. (2004). A magyarországra bevándorolt népesség jellemzői, különös tekintettel a Romániából bevándorlókra. In T. Kiss (Ed.), *Népesedési folyamatok az ezredfordulón Erdélyben* (pp. 126–147). Kolozsvár: Kriterion - RMDSZ Ügyvezető Elnökség.

Gödri, I., & Tóth, P. P. (2005). *Bevándorlás és beilleszkedés*. Budapest: KSH Népességkutató Intézet.

Gyurgyík, L. (2004). A szlovákiai magyarság társadalmi szerkezetének alakulása 1980–2001 között. *Korall, 18*, 155–176.

Gyurgyík, L. (2008). A szlovákiai magyarok társadalomszerkezete a 90-es években. *Regio, 19*(4), 77–102.

Horowitz, D. L. (1985). *Ethnic groups in conflict*. Berkeley: University of California Press.

Horváth, I. (2005). *Erdély és Magyarország közötti migrációs folyamatok*. Kolozsvár: Scientia.

Horváth, I., & Kiss, T. (2017). Ancheta experţilor locali privind situaţia romilor pe unităţi administrativ-teritoriale. In I. Horváth (Ed.), *Raport de cercetare – SocioRoMap. O cartografiere a comunităţilor de romi din România* (pp. 9–190). Cluj-Napoca: Editura Institutului pentru Studierea Problemelor Minorităţilor Naţionale.

Hunya, G. (1990). Románia területi fejlődése és gazdaságpolitikája. In G. Hunya, T. Réti, A. R. Süle, & L. Tóth (Eds.), *Románia 1944–1990. Gazdaság és politikatörténet* (pp. 159–181). Budapest: Atlantisz and Medvetánc.

Kapitány, B., & Spéder, Z. (2004). *Szegénység és depriváció. Társadalmi összefüggések nyomában*. KSH-NKI, Műhelytanulmányok, 4.

Karády, V. (2000). Magyar kultúrfölény vagy etnokrata önámítás? Mire jók a dualista kor nemzetiségi statisztikái? *Educatio, 9*(2), 239–252.

Kideckel, D. A. (2008). *Getting by in postsocialist Romania: Labor, the body, & working-class culture*. Bloomington, IN: Indiana University Press.

Kiss, D. (2004). A falusi elit átalakulása. *WEB, 12*, 9–15.

Kligman, G., & Verdery, K. (2011). *Peasants under siege: The collectivization of Romanian agriculture, 1949–1962*. Princeton, NJ: Princeton University Press.

Köpeczi, B., Miskolczy, A., & Szász, Z. (1986). *Erdély története. Harmadik kötet*. Budapest: Akadémiai Kiadó.

Ladányi, J., & Szelényi, I. (2006). *Patterns of exclusion: Constructing Gypsy ethnicity and the making of an underclass in transitional societies of Europe*. New York: Columbia University Press.

Laitin, D. D. (1998). *Identity in formation: The Russian-speaking populations in the near abroad. The Wilder House series in politics, history, and culture*. Ithaca: Cornell University Press.

László, M., & Novák, C. Z. (2012). *A szabadság terhe. Marosvásárhely, 1990, március*, 16–21. Csíkszereda: Pro-Print.

Laumann, E. O., & Guttman, L. (1966). The relative associational contiguity of occupations in an urban setting. *American Sociological Review, 31*(2), 169.

Lenski, G. E. (1966). *Power and privilege: A theory of social stratification. McGraw-Hill series in sociology*. New York: McGraw-Hill.

Livezeanu, I. (1995). *Cultural politics in greater Romania: Regionalism, nation building & ethnic struggle, 1918–1930*. Ithaca: Cornell University Press.

Mușat, R. (2011). Lamenting social change in the countryside: The publications of the Bucharest School of Sociology in the early 1930s. *ACUM, 5*(1). http://www.cooperativag.ro/lamenting-social-change-countryside-publications-bucharest-school-sociology-early-1930s/.

O'Leary, R., & Finnäs, F. (2002). Education, social integration and minority–majority group intermarriage. *Sociology, 36*(2), 235–254.

Pál, J. (2010). *Unió vagy "unificáltatás"?: Erdély uniója és a királyi biztos működése (1867–1872)*. Kolozsvár: Erdélyi Múzeum-Egyesület.

Poledna, R. (2001). *Transformări sociale la saşii ardeleni după 1945*. Cluj-Napoca: Presa Universitară Clujeană.

Precupețu, I. (2013). Inequality trends in Romania. *Calitatea Vieții, 23*(3), 249–276.

Regényi, E., & Törzsök, E. (1988). Romániai menekültek Magyarországon 1988. In *Medvetánc. Jelentések a határokon túli magyar kisebbségek helyzetéről. Csehszlovákia, Szovjetunió, Románia, Jugoszlávia* (pp. 187–241). Budapest: Elite.

Ronnås, P. (1984). *Urbanization in Romania: A geography of social and economic change since independence*. Ph.D., Stockholm School of Economics, Stockholm, Sweden.

Sik, E. (1994). Traktatus a vállalkozó szerepének de-misztifikálásáról. *Replika, 15–16*, pp. 7–12.

Skutnabb-Kangas, T. (2000). Nyelv, oktatás, kisebbségek. In K. Csernusné Otutay & É. Forintos (Eds.), *Nyelvi jogok* (pp. 41–68). Veszprém: Veszprémi Egyetemi Kiadó.

Tompea, A., & Năstuţă, S. (2009). Romania. In H. Fassmann, U. Reeger, & W. Sievers (Eds.), *Statistics and reality: Concepts and measurements of migration in Europe* (pp. 217–230). Amsterdam: Amsterdam University Press.

Turda, M. (2010). *Modernism and eugenics*. New York: Palgrave Macmillan.

Wallerstein, I. M. (1974). *The modern world-system, vol. I: Capitalist agriculture and the origins of the European world-economy in the sixteenth century. Studies in social discontinuity*. New York: Academic Press.

Wimmer, A. (2002). *Nationalist exclusion and ethnic conflict: Shadows of modernity*. Cambridge, UK and New York: Cambridge University Press.

Zamfir, C., & Zamfir, E. (Eds.). (1993). *Ţiganii între ignorare şi îngrijorare*. Bucureşti: Alternative.

Zavisca, J. (2005). The status of cultural omnivorism: A case study of reading in Russia. *Social Forces, 84*(2), 1233–1255.

12

Assimilation and Boundary Reinforcement: Ethnic Exogamy and Socialization in Ethnically Mixed Families

Tamás Kiss

Ethnic exogamy is not only an indicator of group closure and social distance, but also a factor that reduces them. This is why analysts who favor an integrationist perspective tend to celebrate ethnic exogamy[1] while those who are interested in the preservation and political activation of minority identities treat it as a factor that endangers ethnocultural reproduction.[2] Demographic research focusing on Transylvanian

[1]The often-used bridge metaphor suggests that intermarriage increases social cohesion and reduces the propensity of intergroup conflict. This integrationist perspective is dominant in the literature of intermarriage. See Kalmijn (1998), Gündüz-Hoşgör and Smits (2002), Monden and Smits (2005), Smits (2010), and Bolovan and Dumănescu (2017).

[2]This is a non-mainstream perspective in the literature about ethnic intermarriage. One must also mention sociolinguistic investigations connected to the "Ethnolinguistic Vitality" framework that seek to identify the factors "*which make a group likely to behave as a distinctive and active collective entity in intergroup situations*" (Giles et al. 1977, p. 308). See also Yagmur and Ehala (2011).

T. Kiss (✉)
Romanian Institute for Research on National Minorities,
Cluj-Napoca, Romania

T. Kiss et al. (eds.), *Unequal Accommodation of Minority Rights*,
Palgrave Politics of Identity and Citizenship Series,
https://doi.org/10.1007/978-3-319-78893-7_12

Hungarians can be characterized through this latter perspective (Varga 1998; Szilágyi 2002, 2004; Kiss 2006; Csata and Kiss 2007). As I have discussed in the second section of Chapter 8, Transylvanian Hungarian demographers have treated ethnic exogamy as a factor conducive to ethno-cultural and linguistic assimilation and defined intergenerational assimilation as the inability of parents belonging to the minority group to pass on their group identity and ethno-cultural markers to their offspring. In this respect, exogamy plays a crucial role. While in the vast majority of ethnically homogenous families, the use of Hungarian language and the Hungarian identification of children are taken for granted, in the case of mixed families ethnicity is a matter of choice. Given that the power asymmetries between the majority and minority are reproduced within ethnically mixed families, these choices are oriented primarily toward the majority group and thus erode the reproductive capacity of the minority population.

This chapter is connected to the above-mentioned demographic studies; however, it tries to go beyond them in some respects. First, the main aim of previous demographic research was to quantify the population loss caused by exogamy combined with unbalanced patterns of ethnic socialization. I will not focus on this issue but rather pay attention to the factors conducive to exogamy, among them the system of ethnic stratification and strategies of social mobility. Second, I also ask whether the model through which previous demographic research has interpreted ethnic boundary crossing is sustainable. For this, I rely on the typology of Andreas Wimmer concerning strategic moves vis-á-vis existing ethnic boundaries (2013, pp. 44–79). Two elements of this typology are important in my analysis, namely individual crossing and boundary blurring. Demographic studies about Transylvanian Hungarians have actually conceptualized assimilation as individual crossing, meaning that some individuals of (partially) minority heritage are reclassified as members of the majority group; however, the ethnic boundary between the majority and minority remains intact and its characteristics do not change during this process. Boundary blurring involves the opposite case, when due to mixed marriages the characteristics and consequences of ethnic boundaries change, and ethnic differences became less relevant in various contexts. I argue that the assumption inherent to previous demographic studies was right and that assimilatory processes in Transylvania can indeed be conceptualized rather as individual crossing than boundary blurring. However, this is not an inevitability but an effect of the boundary policing and efforts of boundary reinforcement of the Hungarian elites.

The chapter is composed of three broad sections. First, I outline some major features of the analytical framework. In the second section, I present the major data sources that enable the study of ethnic exogamy among Transylvanian Hungarians and socialization in ethnically mixed marriages, and then I discuss some aspects of the historical evolution of ethnic intermarriage in Transylvania and try to assess (through a comparison with similar minority communities) whether the proportion of exogamous marriages among Transylvanian Hungarians should be considered high or low. At the end of the second section, I present a multivariate analysis of the factors conducive to ethnic exogamy among Transylvanian Hungarians. In the third section, I examine socialization in ethnically mixed marriages and try to identify the factors shaping the identity choices of parents in mixed families concerning their children. In this section, I also use individual-level census data. The second and third sections rely on 10% samples of the 1977, 1992, 2002, and 2011 Romanian censuses available from IPUMS-International, which enable the study of these phenomena at the individual level.

1 Analytical Framework

1.1 Groupness and Closure

This chapter analyzes intermarriages in relation to ethnic boundary maintenance. Wimmer distinguished between four major characteristics of ethnic boundaries: political salience, groupness/closure, cultural differentiation, and stability (2013, pp. 81–89). Endogamy is an important indicator and a consequence of groupness/closure.

Generally speaking, closure is a characteristic of social networks and is related to access to resources which become available through different types of relations. Already Max Weber (1978) connected the formation of ethnic groups to social closure (i.e., to the pursuit of the monopolization of scarce resources of those in a dominant position for their own group). Consequently, ethnic boundaries may be associated with more or less discrimination and exclusion. However, the distinction between closure and groupness is also of central importance. Jenkins (2008) focused on ethnic identity formation and emphasized the difference between categorization and identification. By categorization he meant the situation whereby external observers (powerful others) construct ethnic categories to monopolize resources. In contrast, identification means that internal processes (e.g., the identification of specified individuals with a given category) are conducive to the same result. Jenkins also highlighted that categorization and identification interact, and socially relevant identities evolve exactly at the intersection of these processes. A strong sense of group identity can emerge among members of categories which have been externally defined, and groups glued together by a shared sense of identity can be recognized as such by external others. For Lamont et al. (2016), the power relation between groups is of central importance. To exclude and discriminate against others, a dominant position is needed, thus it is misleading to talk about exclusion and discrimination exercised by the minority[3] (if not against another, even weaker category[4]). In this framework, groupness (e.g., the establishment and reproduction of institutions underpinning group solidarity and group identity) can be an important resource when facing domination and subordination. According to Lamont et al., members of the minority may respond in a number of different ways to subordination, one of the possible responses being self-isolation. The authors conceptualize self-isolation at the individual

[3]Analysts who subscribe to (an unreflected form of) the integrationist perspective often forget to make the essential distinction between groupness and closure. For an academic article that is a telling example for treating the groupness of the minority on an equal footing with state-sponsored exclusion exercised by majority elites, see Bolovan and Eppel (2017, pp. 23–24).

[4]Those who are members of a minority category in one dimension can be members of the dominant category in another. For instance, a Transylvanian Hungarian can be majoritarian as non-Roma (i.e., against Roma) and as a Romanian citizen (against immigrants and refugees). According to surveys conducted in 2014 and 2016, Transylvanian Hungarians are even more intolerant vis-á-vis Roma and immigrants than ethnic Romanians. This, of course, has nothing to do with groupness but it does involve the exclusion of vulnerable groups.

level, namely as a self-management technique that involves less reliance on recognition by the majority and seeking support from one's own ethnic community (2016, pp. 10–11). At a collective or meso-level, groupness and the strategy of self-isolation can be conducive to the ethnic closure of personal networks and a high degree of endogamy.

One should emphasize that in the case of Transylvanian Hungarians groupness is an important factor in boundary maintenance (and is the most important factor conducive to endogamy), while the exclusion and individual-level discrimination of Hungarians do not play an important role. In contrast to Roma, for instance, the former would face few barriers should they want to assimilate into the national majority. Hungarians willing to utilize the Romanian language to enter Romanian ("mainstream") institutions and the personal networks dominated by the majority are actually recognized as (quasi) in-group members by Romanians and face relatively little individual-level discrimination.[5]

1.2 Factors Affecting Exogamy

I have discussed the distinction between groupness and closure not for its normative implications but because of its methodological consequences. When analyzing situations where exclusion and discrimination are the primary forces of boundary maintenance, theories based on identity choice are of less relevance (Wimmer 2013, p. 84). One should also highlight that causal models of exogamy pay little attention to social closure. Kalmijn (1998) and Kalmijn and Tubergen (2010), for instance, implicitly model situations where partner selection is less restricted. In these situations, the so-called third-party factors (which are closely connected to groupness), individual preferences, and

[5]Many bilingual Hungarians speak Romanian with an accent that is clearly distinguishable from that of native speakers of Romanians. However, this is of little social consequence. According to a 2008 survey conducted by the Romanian Institute for Research on National Minorities, only slightly more than 5% of Hungarians reported having experienced individual-level discrimination on the labor market or in various institutional settings.

the structural constraints of the marriage market are the broader sets of factors that influence the levels of exogamy.

Under the umbrella of "third-party" factors, analysts usually discuss the institutions and discourses which sanction (or alternatively, in many cases support[6]) ethnic exogamy. It is often emphasized that the process of social modernization weakens the influence of such discourses and institutions on individual decisions. In Transylvania, some ethnographic studies come close to this approach. According to the ethnographer Ferenc Pozsony, "sober separation" was characteristic of the religious and ethnic communities of Transylvania and "*the formation of linguistically, religiously and culturally homogenous families was preferred until the beginning of the 20th century*" (2007, p. 49). This "golden age of endogamy" was first undone by the processes of social modernization during the interwar period, and then more definitely during state socialism: The increasing trend toward exogamy is due to the fact that "*while rural communities broke up, in the context of accelerated modernization and individualization even those living in [a] rural environment take the important decisions in their live-course individually*". Tünde Turai (2003) drafted her hypothesis concerning the decline of third-party influence in more concrete terms, by referring to the parallelism between the decline of the control of parents over the production of peasant households on the one hand, and over partner selection on the other. Religious denomination also used to be an institution that fostered endogamous partner selection. Ultimately, the whole institutional system sustaining ethnic parallelism and producing ethnic boundaries may be perceived as such. Realizing this, it should be evident that there is no inevitable trend toward increasing exogamy (in parallel with the so-called process of modernization). From this perspective, trends toward endogamy depend mostly on the ability of elites (influenced

[6]The literature focuses mainly on situations where third-party factors oppose intermarriage and (similarly to the archetypical situation of Romeo and Juliet) crosscut individual preferences. Nevertheless, in some societies dominant norms and discourses facilitate intermarriage. Lamarckian eugenics and the consequent ideology of racial whitening prevalent in Brazil and other Latin American countries are examples of such discourses (Sheriff 2001; Osuji 2013). If assimilation is a collective strategy, minority institutional actors can also be supportive of exogamy.

by macro-political, structural, and demographic factors) to sustain a parallel institutional system, and moreover, on the level of encapsulation of Hungarians within this system.

The next set of factors refers to individual preferences. Many scholars have emphasized that the influence of individual preferences and (rational) choices in partner selection is gaining ground at the expense of third-party factors.[7] An important metaphor in this framework is the marriage market, with its possibilities and constraints.[8] The actors on the marriage market are single women and men looking for a spouse. Their choices are influenced by individual preferences on the one hand, and possibilities or structural constraints on the other. With regard to preferences, it is important that potential spouses are evaluated based on the resources which become available through the coupling process. These resources are diverse; however, sociological inquiries focus mostly on cultural and socioeconomic resources. Cultural resources play a key role in facilitating homogamy, as it is obvious that people (bearing in mind their own comfort) usually look for spouses with similar cultural, linguistic, and ideological preferences. However, the pursuit of social and economic resources can facilitate exogamy. In a situation where ethnicity plays a significant role in the distributive process, exogamy can be connected to strategies of social mobility and status maintenance (in the case of those belonging to the subordinated category). Intermarriage can be also regarded as a strategy for exiting the minority category/group.

Taken together, third-party factors and individual preferences are often labeled "cultural" factors and are discussed in opposition to structural ones.[9] The focus on structural constraints reveals that individual

[7]I find Thornton's (2005) concept of developmental idealism useful in this respect. The author argues that the belief that there is a causal relation between norms concerning family and reproduction on the one hand and socioeconomic development on the other has played a crucial role in the spread of modern (meaning Western) models and norms of family formation. Consequently, norms that are in opposition to the Western/modern model (among them the direct influence of third parties on partner choice) have been associated with backwardness and this perception has become an important driver of societal change.

[8]Initially, the concept was coined by Becker (1973) who adapted the model of rational choice to partner selection. Ultimately, it became an expression widely also used by analysts who do not fully accept the model proposed by Becker.

[9]See Kalmijn and Tubergen (2010).

preferences (and third-party factors) cannot fully explain the incidence of exogamy. Structural constraints can foster exogamy even in opposition to individual preferences and collective norms. Further, high rates of intermarriage are not necessary (and not exclusively) the outcome of the lack or decline of norms and preferences that foster endogamy. Blau et al. (1982) investigated heterogamy from this perspective, emphasizing that in many cases norms and preferences are not strong enough to counterbalance structural constraints. This thesis, however, is relevant due to the existing exceptions and differences in the degree of groupness. In the case when norms and preferences that support endogamy are inconsequential (i.e., the degree of groupness is zero), one may rather talk about a category created externally by analysts that employ the notion of a social group.

Structural constraints are manifold. Blau et al. (1982) emphasized the significance of group size, its proportion in the total population, and its territorial concentration. If partner selection is random, group size is the sole factor that determines the proportion of exogamous marriages. In reality, partner selection is never random, although a strong causal relation between group size and exogamy exists.[10] Further hypotheses are connected to the segmented character of marriage markets, meaning that, in reality, partner selection takes place in narrower social spaces than those of the nation-state. Logically, members of territorially concentrated groups have a higher chance of marrying endogenously. At the smaller scale, one can find local marriage markets (Kalmijn 1998, p. 403) in the form of functional spaces (such as neighborhoods, schools, workplaces, and pubs) where potential spouses can meet each other. The ethnically segmented or integrated character of such local marriage markets is, however, also a function of intuitionally sustained ethnic parallelism.

1.3 Assimilation: Individual Crossing or Boundary Blurring?

As already mentioned, demographic research focusing on Transylvanian Hungarians approached exogamy and its consequences using models of assimilation. Two problems should be discussed in this respect. First, this

[10]This is why the odds ratio (OR) indicator (to be discussed later) represents an attempt to model the tendency toward exogamy independent of group size.

research has focused on the unbalanced models of ethnic socialization in mixed families and tried to quantify the demographic consequences of this. From this perspective, assimilation is a macro-level process that affects the reproductive capacities of the minority population. However, these investigations also treated mixed marriages (implicitly or explicitly) as a cause of assimilation. This is not an entirely correct interpretation. Gordon (1964), for instance, in his classic book on assimilation, argued that mixed marriages are preceded by other factors or dimensions of assimilation, such as cultural accommodation (in language use and other cultural norms) and structural assimilation (integration into the majority institutional system and personal networks). Laitin's definition can also be employed, according to which assimilation involves a sequence of choices of minority group members through which they gradually adapt their cultural norms and enter the social circles of the majority (Laitin 1998). Obviously, mixed marriage can be a major step along this path; however, it is not a cause as such.

Second, the distinction between individual crossing and boundary blurring can be useful. Zolberg and Woon describe individual boundary crossing as the assimilation of immigrants (or minorities) which does not induce changes in the host society through adaptation of the language and the cultural norms of the majority (1999, p. 8). Conversely, boundary blurring affects the majority society too, which accepts multiple memberships and does not perceive membership in minority and majority categories as mutually exclusive. Alba and Nee (2003) and Alba (2005) focus more explicitly on the characteristics of the boundaries themselves and distinguish between "bright" and "blurred" boundaries. Alba argues that when boundaries are bright, individuals will always know on which side of the boundary they are (2005, pp. 21–25). In contrast, blurred boundaries allow for zones where multiple or ambiguous forms of identification are possible. The characteristics of the boundaries affect the form and the likelihood of assimilation. If boundaries are bright, assimilation takes the form of individual crossing; psychologically it is similar to conversion and induces a departure from the original ethnic group. In the case of blurred boundaries, the process of assimilation is less dramatic. Individuals who undergo this process are not forced to choose between minority and majority identity and can take part simultaneously in minority and majority social circles. Importantly, assimilation is not only less pleasant but also less likely across bright boundaries as the costs of assimilation are higher and benefits lower. Those trying to assimilate across bright boundaries may find themselves in a difficult situation as they simultaneously risk exclusion and discrimination by the majority and forms of excommunication by their co-ethnics. Wimmer has elaborated a quite complex typology of positional moves vis-á-vis existing boundaries (2013, pp. 49–63). In this typology, individual crossing and boundary blurring are distinct positional moves. In the case of individual crossing, individuals reposition themselves or are reclassified by others, however, without altering the very characteristics of the boundary itself. Conversely, boundary blurring touches upon the characteristics of the boundary: It de-emphasizes opposition between minority and majority and thus makes the boundary more porous and fluid.

Previous demographic studies on Transylvanian Hungarians not only examined mixed marriages in an assimilatory framework but also conceptualized assimilation as individual crossing. Using a demographic model where assimilation is an output variable and which is based on a technique of census classification that depicts ethnicity as membership in mutually exclusive categories, ethnic boundaries are actually quite bright. The main question is whether this brightness is merely an illusion induced by the model itself (involving techniques of measuring identity) or whether it reflects social reality. Mixed marriages can be regarded as a socially accepted process by which individual repositioning and especially reclassification of one's children as members of the majority become possible.[11] But whether this process can really be interpreted as (intergenerational) crossing which does not affect the boundary itself remains questionable. It may be the case instead that mixed marriages and the existence of a relatively large population with a mixed background lead to boundary blurring.[12] Despite this, I argue

[11]For a similar interpretation of mixed marriages involving Swedish speakers in Finland and Protestants in the Republic of Ireland see Finnäs and O'Leary (2003).

[12]In the context of Transylvania the question was raised by Szabolcs László (2013), relying on a different terminology, namely that of cultural hybridity borrowed from post-colonial studies—see Bhabha (1994), Hannerz (2000), and Pieterse (2001). By hybridization László meant a conceptual framework which unmakes the binary opposition between majority and minority. This, according to László, increases the possibility of a more "liberal" ethno-political discourse. In my opinion, the qualifier "integrationist" would be more appropriate for such an ethno-political discourse.

that the mixed marriages and the mixed ancestry of a significant part of the population do not lead to boundary blurring in Transylvania. The outcome of socialization in ethnically mixed families is identification with either the majority or the minority. However, I also reveal that this outcome cannot be taken for granted but is the consequence of a still dominant discursive order on the one hand, and the boundary policing practices of minority elites and minority group members on the other.

2 Intermarriage in a Historical and Comparative Perspective

2.1 Data Sources on Exogamy and Socialization in Ethnically Mixed Families

Ethnic exogamy among Transylvanian Hungarians can be analyzed on both stock and flow data. Censuses are the most important data sources for the number and proportion of those living in mixed relationships. Flow data are also available, as the "nationality" of marrying spouses is registered in an exhaustive survey of marriages carried out by the National Institute of Statistics. Earlier studies relied mostly on aggregate (county-level) data provided by the National Institute of Statistics (e.g., Horváth 2004; Kiss 2006).[13] Based on these data, researchers focused on regional differences in exogamy and examined to what extent these differences can be explained by structural factors, such as the ethnic composition of the territorial units and the territorial concentration of the Hungarian population.

In this chapter, I rely mostly on micro-level data, namely on the 10-percent samples of the 1977, 1992, 2002, and 2011 Romanian censuses provided by IPUMS-International. Based on these databases, both ethnic intermarriages and the identity choice for children born in mixed

[13] Hărăguş (2014, 2017) constitutes an exception, as she also used IPUMS-International 10% samples.

marriages can be analyzed. Through a restructuring of these data files I obtained two types of databases:

1. The 10% sample of Hungarians living in marriages (1977) and unions (1992, 2002, 2011) according to the censuses.[14] Based on this, data I present four binomial logistic regression models concerning the factors that increase the likelihood of Hungarians living in an exogamous marriage.
2. The 10% sample of minor children coming from ethnically mixed families with one Hungarian parent.[15] Based on these databases, I analyze the ethnic category chosen by the parents for children in mixed families and the mother tongue of these children. Here, I also present four binomial logistic regression models concerning factors conducive to the option of identifying as Hungarian.

Some scholars argue that flow data are more reliable than stock data (Kalmijn 1998, p. 34). First, stock data aggregate marriages from specific periods of time and, as a consequence, are less appropriate to describe longitudinal trends. Second, the ethnic identification of partners may change over time: In mixed marriages, a shift in identity of one of the parties is not only possible but likely. Third, it is also possible that the stability of mixed and homogenous marriages is not identical: There is some empirical evidence that mixed marriages are less stable than homogenous ones.[16] While being aware of these disadvantages of stock data, I also consider that the 10% IPUMS-International samples have a very important advantage, namely that they permit the analysis of intermarriages at the individual level.

---

[14] The number of cases is the following: 85,443 in 1977, 82,328 in 1992, 72,981 in 2002, and 62,167 in 2011.

[15] The number of cases is 8401 in 1977, 10,863 in 1992, 7127 in 2002, and 4450 in 2011.

[16] See Finnäs (1997) for the case of Swedish speakers of Finland, Kalmijn et al. (2005) for the Netherlands and Dribe and Lundh (2011) for Sweden. For Transylvanian Hungarians, the 2006 wave of the Turning Points of our Life-course survey can be cited. See: http://demografia.hu/hu/tudastar/adatbazisok/22-adatbazisok/160-eletunk-fordulopontjai. This survey collected data for 1326 representatively selected (first) marriages. Eight percent of the ethnically homogenous and 17.6% of the ethnically mixed marriages had ended in divorce by the date of the survey.

2.2 Intermarriage Among Transylvanian Hungarians in Historical Perspective

According to the IPUMS-International samples, the proportion of Hungarians living in mixed marriages was 9.8% in 1977, 12.9% in 1992, 13.6% in 2002, and 13.0% in 2011. The data suggest a significant increase in intermarriage during the last three decades of the twentieth century, and a slight decrease since the turn of the millennium. Census data can be compared with the flow data, which are available for 1966 and for the 1992–2015 period. In 1966, the proportion of Hungarians marrying outside their own group was 15.5%, and a considerable difference also existed between men and women, women being more inclined to exogamy. Between 1992 and 2015, the proportion of exogamous marriages was 17.9% on average (see Fig. 1). The differences between men and women practically disappeared in the 1990s but reappeared following the turn of the millennium. However, this latter trend does not indicate an increase in the number of ethnically Romanian partners but rather that Transylvanian Hungarian women are marrying foreign citizens in higher proportions.[17]

The difference in the proportions of those living in mixed marriages by age group is also illuminating (see Table 1). The following differences were statistically significant in 1977: The proportion of mixed couples was 12.9% among the 18–34 age group, 9.9% among Hungarians aged 35–54 and only 6.5% among those older than 55 years. The data suggest that there was an increase in ethnic exogamy during the state-socialist period (which began well before the 1977 census). As already mentioned, Pozsony (2007) has argued that before state-socialist modernization (which began in the 1950s) there was a "golden age" of ethnic endogamy in Transylvania; a period which can be characterized by a very low (less than 5%) proportion of ethnically heterogeneous marriages.

[17]In the case of ethnic Romanian women, the frequency of international marriages has increased even more. Many of them perceive this type of marriage as a means of social mobility. However, as Levchenko (2013) has emphasized, some of the Eastern European women engaged in international marriages become very vulnerable.

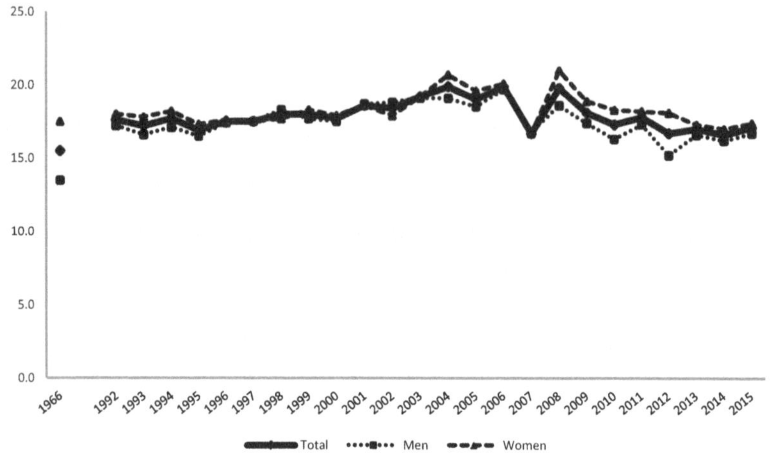

Fig. 1 Proportion of ethnically mixed marriages among Transylvanian Hungarians (flow data, 1966 and 1992–2015) (*Source* Data provided by the National Institute of Statistics)

However, Pozsony based his conclusions on an analysis of the parish registers of rural communities; consequently, his conclusions cannot be generalized. Petre Râmneamțu (1937), a well-known proponent of interwar Romanian eugenics, found a surprisingly high rate of ethnic exogamy among urban Transylvanians for the 1920–1937 period.[18] His data show that during the period 23.7% of Hungarians living in urban areas married exogamously, 62% choosing to marry Romanian and 28% German spouses. Gender differences were significant: 17.7% of Hungarian men and 28.9% of Hungarian women married "outside". These numbers are quite high in comparison with census data referring to later periods: 15% of urban dwellers with a Hungarian ethnic background were living in mixed marriages in 1977, 18% in 1992, 19% in 2002, and 17% in 2011. According to flow data, between 1992 and 2015 22.5% of marrying Hungarians living in urban environments chose a partner of a different ethnicity.

[18]See Bucur (2002) and Turda (2010) for a discussion of interwar Romanian eugenics. See also Bolovan and Dumănescu (2017) for details about intermarriage during the interwar period.

Table 1 Factors affecting the likelihood of living in a mixed union (binomial logistic regression models)

		1977* (N=85443)		1992 (N=82328)		2002 (N=72981)		2011 (N=62167)	
		%	EXP B	%	EXP B	%	EXP B	%	EXP B
Total proportion of ethnically mixed unions		*9.8*		*12.9*		*13.6*		**13.0**	
Unions with Romanian partners		*8.3*		*11.5*		*12.5*		*12.0*	
Gender	*Man*	8.9		12.4		13.9		13.1	
	Woman	10.7	1.25***	13.4	1.10***	13.3	1.07*	13.0	1.01
Age group	*18-34*	12.9		16.5		15.5		14.6	
	35-54	9.9	0.76***	14.0	0.81***	15.1	0.92***	13.6	0.84***
	55+	6.5	0.53***	8.7	0.55***	10.5	0.68***	11.8	0.67***
Region	*Székely Land*	2.0		2.4		2.6		2.7	
	Central Transylvania	7.2	2.28***	9.3	2.41***	10.8	2.86***	11.9	2.11***
	Partium/Crisana	7.5	2.65***	10.2	2.77***	10.8	2.92***	11.8	2.27***
	Dispersed communities	22.4	4.77***	27.7	5.28***	31.8	6.96***	34.6	7.62***
	Old Romanian Kingdom	65.4	9.97***	54.6	10.36***	52.0	12.04***	53.8	9.52***
Type of residence	Rural	4.7		6.6		7.6		8.0	
	Urban	14.9	1.66***	17.9	1.36***	19.1	1.43***	17.1	0.94
Weighted proportion of Hungarians (by county and type of residence)		-	0.98***	-	0.99***	-	0.99***	-	0.98***
History of internal migration	*No*	7.9		10.1		11.6		11.7	
	Yes	16.6	1.10***	16.3	1.08***	16.9	1.15***	21.6	1.22***
Educational attainment	*Primary or lower-secondary*	8.0		9.4		10.0		9.5	
	Professional	13.0	1.38***	17.3	1.49***	16.9	1.61***	13.1	1.33***
	Upper secondary finished	15.6	1.44***	16.5	1.49***	15.4	1.51***	14.5	1.46***
	University	14.8	1.33***	23.0	2.07***	23.3	2.14***	19.8	1.66***
Religion	*Reformed*			10.2		10.9			
	Roman Catholic			13.2	1.28***	13.1	1.24***		
	Greek Catholic			22.8	2.1***	26.8	2.29***		
	Unitarian			5.7	0.64***	7.1	0.77***		
	Neo-protestant			13.4	1.46***	17.4	1.78***		
	Orthodox			82.7	25.36***	77.8	17.61***		
	Evanghelic - Lutherans			16.2	0.66***	15.9	0.54***		
	Other			17.1	1.46***	18.9	1.71***		
Type of union	*Marriage*	9.8		12.8		12.8		12.4	
	Consensual union	-		15.8	1.34***	23.4	2.54***	19.9	2.11***
Nagelkerke R^2		*0.202*		*0.291*		*0.306*		*0.227*	

Source IPUMS-International 10% sample of the Romanian censuses (Minnesota Population Center. Integrated Public Use Microdata Series, International: Version 7.0 [1977, 1992, 2002 and 2011 Romanian censuses]. Minneapolis, MN: IPUMS, 2018. http://doi.org/10.18128/D020.V70)
* p<0.1; ** p<0.05; *** p<0.01

These proportions are lower than those suggested by Râmneamţu. The difference becomes even more striking if one takes into account the change in the ethnic makeup of urban societies. Hungarians constituted a plurality of the urban population in the interwar period,[19] while their

[19]According to the data compiled by Râmneamţu, 39% of those marrying were of Hungarian background.

proportion fell drastically after World War II. To eliminate the distortion caused by the differences in the ethnic demography of urban setting, one can calculate the odds ratios (OR) for endogamy.[20] The OR for Hungarian urban dwellers living in endogamous marriages was 115.8 in 1977, while the OR for marrying endogamously was only 19.9 for the period between 1920 and 1937. This suggests a dramatic shift in marriage patterns toward ethnic endogamy.

How should these data be interpreted? Drastic socioeconomic and demographic changes should be taken into account. First, and as discussed in the previous chapter, Hungarians used to be in a dominant position in the urban societies of the interwar period. They most probably lacked the norms favoring endogamy which are prevalent today (as the consequence of intermarriage was in many cases the assimilation of the non-Hungarian spouse into the Hungarian community). Second, the post-World War II Hungarian urban population is barely identical (or contiguous) with the interwar one. The number of urban dwellers, which was 721,000 in 1930, had reached 3,558,000 by 1977, a nearly fivefold increase over a period of 57 years. Many of those who belonged to the urban middle classes emigrated were killed during the Holocaust, or were deported by the Communist authorities. Meanwhile, the number of new urban inhabitants with a rural background increased (not only of Romanian but also of Hungarian ethnicity). As for the interwar period, one can cite Gábor Egry, who argued that a common trans-ethnic culture existed among the urban middle classes of the Transylvanian towns (Egry 2015, p. 315). This claim may also be valid for the working class. Egry also argued that in these urban milieus ethnic clashes (connected to nationalizing policies) were attenuated by class-based solidarity. The high prevalence of exogamous marriages may be interpreted as indirect evidence of this hypothesis.[21]

---

[20] The odds ratio (OR) is an indicator which expresses the tendency toward endogamy compared to the hypothetical situation when ethnic preferences do not play any role in partner selection. Values of OR higher than 1 indicate that the inclination toward endogamy is higher than what it would be in the case of random partner selection, and the higher the value of OR, the greater the tendency toward endogamy. See Kalmijn (1998, p. 405).

[21] The suggestion of the existence of such a trans-ethnic middle-class culture is a quite interesting and important hypothesis due to the fact that both the nationalizing project strongly promoted by the Romanian state and the community- and social pillar-building strategies of the minority elites relied primarily on urban middle classes during the interwar period. See also Livezeanu (1995).

To sum up, one should emphasize that there is no linear tendency toward exogamy among Transylvanian Hungarians. At an overall level, the proportion of those who married non-Hungarian partners certainly increased during state socialism. However, the "golden age of endogamy" existed only in (some of the) rural communities, while in urban environments exogamy was more prevalent in the interwar period than after World War II. Nor did exogamy increase during the post-Communist period.[22]

2.3 Intermarriage in a Comparative Perspective

The next question is whether exogamy among Transylvanian Hungarians should be regarded as high or low in a comparative perspective. Structurally similar, territorially concentrated autochthonous minority communities can be used as a reference point for such a comparison. This is not to say that I would consider that an a priori distinction should be made between "old" (autochthonous) and "new" (migrant) minorities. However, new minorities usually lack the institutional net that underpins intergenerational ethno-cultural reproduction on the one hand and face a higher level of discrimination and social closure on the other. Consequently, in their case endogamy is less the result of institutionally sustained attempts of identity reproduction and more a consequence of rejection by the majority. Besides the Transylvanian Hungarians and some other rather numerous European minorities, Table 2 also presents data about the Roma of Romania. They are also an "old" minority group; however, they are in a position similar to that of many non-European migrant groups across Western Europe or Northern America. Their level of political mobilization is rather low and groupness is less important in boundary maintenance. However, they face far more social exclusion and individual-level discrimination than Hungarians. Exogamy among them is extremely low, in spite of the

[22]Interestingly, my account contrasts with a recently published article by Hărăguş (2017) who analyzed the 1977, 1992, and 2002 IPUMS-International databases and concluded that exogamy has increased over the last few decades.

Table 2 Proportion of exogamous marriages among several autochthonous minorities in Europe

Minority group	%	OR	Period	Type of data	Proportion of group	Source
Transylvanian Hungarians[a]	13.6	200.2	2002	Stock	19.8	IPUMS-International
	17.9	138.5	1992–2015	Flow	19.8	National Institute of Statistics
Roma in Romania	6.5	8150.4	2011	Stock	3.4	IPUMS-International
	4.0	41159.3	2006–2015	Flow	3.4	National Institute of Statistics
Saxons of Transylvania[b]	14.4	907.0	1977	Stock	4.8	IPUMS-International
Swabians in the Romanian Banat[c]	22.2	122.8	1977	Stock	11.6	IPUMS-International
Hungarians in Southern Slovakia[d]	26.1	46.2	1996–2010	Flow	24.0	INFOSTAT
Hungarians in Vojvodina	28.2	50.5	2002–2009	Flow	14.3	Statistical Office of the Republic of Serbia
Russian speakers in Latvia[e]	25.0	14.2	2003	Flow	36.4	Monden and Smith (Monden and Smits 2005, p. 331)
Russian speakers in Estonia[e]	12.6	102.8	2000	Stock	29.0	Van Ham and Tammaru (2011, p. 316)
Swedish speakers in Finland[f]	38.0	–	2000–2011	Flow	12.7	Finnäs (2013, p. 39)
Irish Catholics of Ulster	7.9	229.9	2001	Stock	40.2	Northern Ireland Statistics and Research Agency

[a]Transylvania in a broader sense (16 counties)
[b]The historical province of Transylvania (9 counties)
[c]Counties of Arad, Timiș/Temes and Caraș-Severin/Krassó-Szörény
[d]16 districts (okres) including the cities of Bratislava/Pozsony and Košice/Kassa
[e]The whole country, Ukrainians and Byelorussians included
[f]The southern and Western Regions inhabited partially by Swedes (Swedish Åland, Nyland, Österbotten, Mellersta Österbotten, and Egentliga Finland)

fact that they live dispersed around the country. However, this is more a consequence of stigmatization and closure and less a consequence of institutionally reproduced group solidarity.

Another problem is that—to the best of my knowledge—there has been no systematic comparative inquiry that focused on exogamy among autochthonous minority groups in Europe, and it is difficult to access data that refer to all of them.[23]

Transylvanian Saxons and Banat Swabians are relevant reference groups, so I included 1977 census data referring to these groups. This census captured the situation before their mass exodus which took place during the 1980s and 1990s. The Saxons were quite an endogamous community before they left Transylvania. The proportion of mixed marriages among them was 14% in 1977, which is rather low, especially taking into account the fact that they constituted less than 5% of the population in the historical province of Transylvania. Banat Swabians used to be less endogamous, as shown both by the higher proportion of intermarriages and the higher value for the OR.

I also included data referring to Hungarians in Southern Slovakia and the Autonomous Province of Vojvodina in Serbia. The proportion of intermarriages is higher among both of these Hungarian minority communities than among Transylvanian Hungarians. The differences are even more significant if one looks at the OR values. One should also emphasize that in Slovakia Hungarians are geographically more concentrated than in Transylvania (and in Vojvodina): According to the 2002 census, 76% were living in settlements where they formed a majority. This factor should have facilitated endogamy; consequently, relatively high levels of exogamy indicate lower social distances between Hungarians and Slovaks compared to those between Hungarians and Romanians.

Other reference groups include Russian speakers in Estonia and Latvia, Swedish speakers in Finland and the Irish Catholics of Ulster.

---

[23]Other relevant Eastern European minorities include the Albanians in Macedonia, the Serbs in Bosnia and Kosovo, the Croats in Bosnia, the Romanians and Hungarians in Ukraine, the Turks in Bulgaria and the Poles in Lithuania. For Western Europe, Germans in South Tyrol would also be worth being included into the table.

Exogamy among Russophones in Latvia and Swedish speakers in Finland is obviously higher than among Transylvanian Hungarians. In the case of Ulster Catholics, the figures indicate a lower tendency toward exogamy. However, the difference is less striking if one takes into account the fact that Irish Catholics constitute 40% of the population of Northern Ireland. The OR values calculated for stock data concerning Ulster Catholics and Transylvanian Hungarians are close to each other (200.2 in the case of Transylvanian Hungarians, and 229.9 in the case of Irish Catholics). In the case of the Russian speakers of Estonia, the proportion of mixed marriages is slightly lower than among Transylvanian Hungarians. However, the OR value is significantly lower, indicating a higher tendency toward exogamy.

In sum, exogamy among Transylvanian Hungarians is not negligible at all, especially when comparing their situation with some stigmatized and excluded communities, such as the Roma. Nevertheless, in a comparative perspective (using as reference groups structurally similar minorities who live in unranked systems of groups[24]) these proportions cannot be considered high. Of the groups included in Table 1, only the Transylvanian Saxons and Ulster Catholics showed a higher tendency to endogamy, while all other groups were more willing to marry across ethnic boundaries.

2.4 Factors Conducive to Exogamy

In this section, I discuss the results of four logistic regression models run on the 1977, 1992, 2002, and 2011 IPUMS-International databases. Table 1 shows both the proportion of Hungarians living in mixed partnerships by different independent variables and the results of the regression models. Next to some basic socio-demographic variables I included indicators connected to the factors affecting exogamy described in the analytical framework. In this respect, however, my possibilities were limited by the indicators available from censuses. For instance,

[24]See Horowitz (1985, pp. 22–36).

Hărăguş (2014), relying on survey data, highlighted that enrollment in Romanian-language education is a decisive factor increasing the likelihood of intermarriage. However, I do not have information on the language of education of the respondents. More generally, I lack direct information concerning the level of encapsulation in the Hungarian institutional pillar of respondents, which is arguably the most important factor shaping partner selection. This is why the explanatory power (measured by Nagelkerke R^2) of the models is relatively low.

In 1977 and 1992, women lived in higher proportions in mixed marriages than men. However, differences were not significant in 2002 and 2011. Although differences by age group have decreased over time, they remain significant in all of the analyzed censuses. Younger generations are more likely to live in ethnically mixed partnerships. The effect of ethnic demography is obvious. In the ethnic block area of Székely Land less than three percent of Hungarians live in mixed families, while in the case of dispersed Hungarian communities, this proportion was 22% in 1977 and 35% in 2011. Another indicator measuring territorial concentration is the weighted proportion of Hungarians by county and type of settlement. This also has a significant effect on the likelihood of intermarriage.[25] One should highlight that Hungarians living in dispersed communities were almost eight times more likely to live in an ethnically mixed marriage than those living in the Székely Land, showing the huge impact of structural factors.[26] The probability of intermarriage is also higher among urban dwellers; however, in 2011 this effect was not significant in the regression model. Internal migration also increases the likelihood of marrying exogamously, as it may mean entrance to ethnically more homogeneous marriage markets (Fig. 2).

[25] IPUMS databases only contain information about residence at the level of county and type of settlement, thus the proportion of Hungarians in the settlements where the respondents resided cannot be determined. The weighted ratio was used as a proxy for this variable, calculated using the following formula: $Ps = \sum(p_i \times Pi)/P_{tot,}$ where p_i is the proportion of Hungarians by settlement; Pi is the number of Hungarians in the same settlement; and P_{tot} is the total number of Hungarians in the whole territory (in our case, by county and type of settlement).

[26] The impact of this factor is accentuated even more if one analyzes differences in intermarriage at aggregate level.

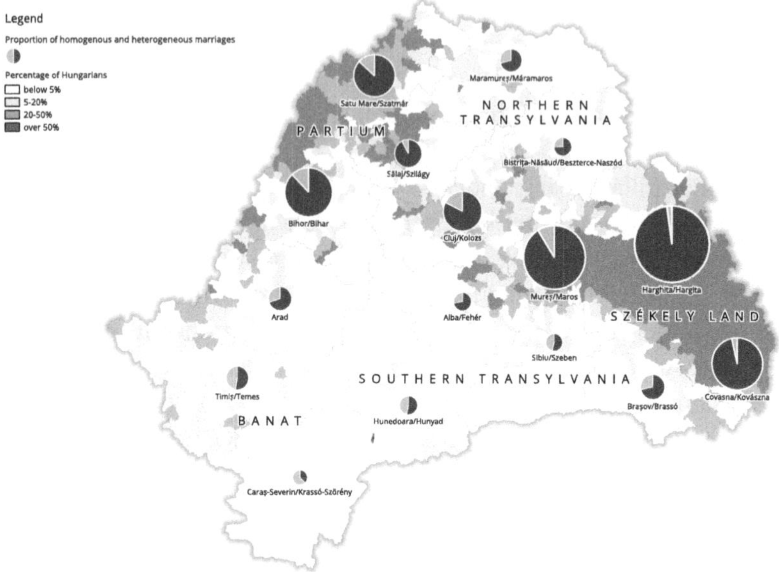

Fig. 2 Homogenous and heterogeneous marriages by counties (2011) (*Source* Map created by Samu Márton Balogh based on the IPUMS-International 10% sample of the 2011 Romanian census)

It may be related to the impact of "third-party factors" that the level of exogamy differs significantly by religion. Unfortunately, we have data about this only for the 1992 and 2002 censuses.[27] These data show that members of historical Hungarian Protestant denominations (Unitarians and adherents of the Reformed Church) are less likely to choose partners of another ethnic background. The proportions are higher among Roman Catholics, Evanghelic-Lutherans, Greek Catholics, and Neo-Protestants. The vast majority of Orthodox Hungarians were living in ethnically mixed marriages at the time of the surveys. In their case, denominational membership may be the consequence of conversion upon marrying a Romanian spouse. The proportion of mixed couples is higher among those living in consensual union compared to those

[27]The census of 1977 did not record religion, while in the 2011 IPUMS-International database all Christian denominations were lumped together.

living in marriage. This is an indirect indicator of the strength of norms opposing exogamy. Marriage is an important community event in Transylvania, often several hundred guests (relatives, friends, neighbors, etc.) being invited to weddings. Young people living in mixed relationships are obviously less inclined to organize such celebrations.

Educational attainment is an important factor in determining intermarriage. According to a hypothesis widespread in the literature, intermarriage is more likely among those with higher educational attainment. More liberal attitudes (influencing individual preferences) and a higher degree of autonomy vis-á-vis third-party factors are often highlighted as lying behind this relationship (see Goldscheider 1986). From the perspective of structural factors, it is often emphasized that taking part in formal education involves entry into an ethnically heterogeneous (local) marriage market. O'Leary and Finnäs have argued that the above-mentioned relationship cannot be taken for granted in the case of some autochthonous minorities. Some of these minorities (such the Swedish speakers of Finland and the Protestants of Ireland) used to be in a dominant position before their countries of residence gained independence and maintained a favorable position in the system of ethnic stratification even after this. In the opinion of the authors, in such cases endogamy can be a strategy of avoiding status diffusion.[28] The institutional net underpinning ethnic parallelism can also be a factor that sustains educational differences in exogamy. A further specificity of Finland and Ireland is that minority institutions are mostly designed to satisfy the needs of the upper and middle classes and thus lower-status members of the minority group are less likely to be encapsulated in this institutional system (O'Leary and Finnäs 2002).

In the case of Transylvanian Hungarians, there is a widely held opinion that assimilation and intermarriage are more likely in the case of lower strata (especially among the urban working class and among those living dispersed in Romanian-majority rural communities). This perception might be connected to the historical sense of supremacy of the Hungarian elites, according to which mixing with Romanians is

---

[28]On status diffusion, see Merton (1941).

considered to lead to loss of status. However, empirical data show that those with higher educational attainments are actually more likely to marry exogamously. In this respect, the dynamics of exogamy by educational attainment are also interesting. Among those with tertiary-level education, the year in which the maximum number lived in exogamous marriages was 1992, and in the case of university graduates 2002. This was followed by a decline in the proportion of mixed couples. These trends are most likely related to the process of the expansion of Hungarian-language higher education. A higher proportion of intermarriage among university graduates is most probably also connected to the characteristics of the system of ethnic stratification outlined in the previous chapter. Ethnically Hungarian professionals may face status inconsistency: They are well honored (or pretend to be) in their own ethnic society but they earn significantly less compared to their ethnic Romanian counterparts. This might motivate them to exit the minority category through choosing a spouse with a majority background.

3 Identity Processes in Ethnically Mixed Marriages

3.1 How to Count People of Mixed Ancestry?

I argued in Chapter 10 that census classification in Romania is still connected to a Herderian discursive order (Wimmer 2013), where membership in ethnic categories (or more precisely, groups) is universal and mutually exclusive: Everyone belongs to an ethnic group and everyone belongs to only one ethnic group. I also argued that in the case of Transylvanian Hungarians censuses are relatively good tools for assessing identities. Now I discuss the validity of census classification in the case of those growing up in ethnically mixed marriages. The question is whether in their case group membership can also be perceived as mutually exclusive.

Evidently, such data would be more valid if it were collected through census techniques that allow for multiple identification. Today, only a tiny minority of social scientists consider that classifying people in mutually exclusive categories is a correct approach to measuring identities, especially in ethnically mixed marriages. However, the validity and the legitimacy of census techniques has been taken for granted until recently. Consequently, the question is how to deal with a situation where (due to a discursive shift in the social sciences) data collected at an earlier time are no longer considered valid.

This research question is not totally novel, as it was raised by Dmitry Gorenburg (2006) in relation to the historical analysis of mixed marriages in the Soviet Union. The author emphasizes that there is a huge methodological and epistemological difference between the classification techniques of the Soviet censuses in the 1970s and 1980s on the one hand, and those used by present-day Western social sciences on the other. The Soviet system of ethnic classification was based on the assumption that each human belongs to one and only one nationality (*narodnost*). Both censuses and internal passports used this mutually exclusive definition of national membership. Gorenburg argues that using the Soviet system of ethnic classification for the analysis of mixed families is highly problematic. For the majority of people in the Soviet Union, nationality was taken for granted and assumed to be given upon birth, a phenomenon called everyday primordialism by Fearon and Laitin (2000). However, in the case of persons with mixed backgrounds or living in mixed families, identity is not taken for granted; they have to choose between different ethnically marked alternatives. This choice might be problematic for many and, according to Gorenburg's argument, the Soviet system of classification oversimplifies the results. If one classifies the offspring of ethnically mixed marriages into mutually exclusive categories, the only research question that remains is which groups can be characterized by demographic losses and which by demographic gains. From the recent perspective of Western social sciences, this approach is sustainable neither methodologically nor normatively. From a methodological perspective, the problem is that the classification of people into mutually exclusive categories is unable to capture the gradualism, contextual character, and ambivalence of ethnic identification. Consequently, it is preferable to use tools of identity measurement that make it possible to capture the intensity of attachment to different categories, or which ask about identification in an open-ended form. From a normative point of view, mutually exclusive classification forces people with a mixed background to identify themselves with categories to which they are only partially attached and also excludes them from other categories to which they are also only partially attached. Gorenburg also argues that the Soviet method of classification is not appropriate for distinguishing between different contexts of categorization. One might, for instance, simultaneously be a Russian in an urban workplace, and a Tatar in his or her ancestral village. Ethnic mixing may also create intermediate categories which do not exist in the official nomenclature. Gorenburg's example is that of *Pereverteny* of mixed Ukrainian-Russian background who speak a hybrid language, *Surzhyk.*

Gorenburg actually argues that there is a clear hierarchy between techniques of classification and that the techniques employed in Western social sciences today are clearly superior to the Soviet ones of the 1970s and 1980s. His proposal is that the Soviet mixed marriages of the 1970s and 1980s (and indeed, the whole literature that addresses this issue) should be reinterpreted by taking into account new developments in social sciences. I agree with Gorenburg only partially. The gap between the techniques of ethnic classification in Western Social sciences and Eastern European censuses concerns a matter of facts. Gorenburg's methodological proposals for using techniques that allow for the more nuanced measurement of identification are well grounded. However, I do not think that a clear hierarchy between different systems of classification (or in a broader sense, between different regimes of counting) is definable. Official classifications are always embedded in a larger discursive and institutional order, and the major task of the social scientist is to understand how the act of classification functions in that context and not to substitute techniques of classification with better ones. In the remaining parts of this chapter, I follow this latter strategy.

In our Transylvanian case, the institutional and discursive context does not support multiple forms of identification and the stabilization of mixed identities. One may therefore rely on the conceptual framework provided by Brubaker et al. (2006, pp. 311–314) and Telegdi-Csetri (2017). These authors argue that mixed marriages and socialization in ethnically mixed families can be described as a sequence of choices between ethnically marked and mutually exclusive alternatives.[29] Some choices can be perceived as junctures in one's biography. The last name that spouses adopt, the church[30] they chose for their marital ceremony, the first names of their children, the religion according to which they baptize their children, and the language in which their children will be educated all involve making choices between ethnically marked alternatives. These alternatives may be considered biographical junctures as they open some institutional alternatives while closing others. In this sense, one may speak of the path dependence of ethnically mixed relations too.[31] This means that earlier decisions (concerning the above-mentioned critical biographic junctures, for example) determine the direction of subsequent choices. This may be illustrated with the logistic regression model presented in Table 3, in which the dependent variable is the religion of the minor-age children living in ethnically mixed families with Hungarian parents, while the independent variable is the ethnic identification of the child at the census. The Nagelkerke R^2 was 0.443 for 1992 and 0.491 for 2002, indicating the very large explanatory power of this simple model (Table 3).

The model reveals how earlier choices between ethnically marked alternatives (the religion in which the child was baptized) determine their subsequent options (i.e., the ethnic category chosen for the child); 75% of children born in mixed families who were baptized as Protestants were registered as Hungarian by their parents, while in the case of children baptized as Orthodox this proportion was only six percent. The likelihood of being registered as Hungarian was 50 times higher in the case of Protestant children compared to those baptized as Orthodox. Three conclusions may be drawn from this: First, there is

[29]Laitin's (1998) model of assimilation is quite similar, and Brubaker also strongly relies on this model.

[30]As described in Chapter 7, the Orthodox and Greek Catholic Churches are considered Romanian (with the exception of Satu-Mare/Szatmár county, where there are Hungarian-speaking Greek Catholic parishes too), while the Reformed, Unitarian, Evanghelic-Lutheran, and Roman Catholic Churches are perceived as Hungarian denominations.

[31]The institutionalist framework used in this volume to analyze political processes might be useful in the study of mixed marriages too. For an interpretation of path dependence in terms of increasing returns, see Pierson (2000).

Table 3 Ethnic identification of minor children born in ethnically mixed marriages at the census by religion of the child (1992, 2002)

Religion of child	Ethnic identification at census			
	1992		2002	
	%	EXP B	%	EXP B
Orthodox	6.2		5.6	
Protestant (Reformed, Unitarian, Lutheran Evangelical)	71.4	37.6***	74.7	50.1***
Roman Catholic	53.3	17.1***	57.9	23.3***
Greek Catholic	23.8	4.7***	23.4	5.2***
Neo-protestant (Baptist, Adventist, Pentecostal, Jehovah's Witness)	23.9	7.4***	24.5	5.5
Other	33.1	7.4***	39.5	11.0***
Nagelkerke R^2	0.443		0.491	

Source IPUMS-International 10% samples of the 1992 and 2002 Romanian census (Minnesota Population Center. Integrated Public Use Microdata Series, International: Version 7.0 [1992 and 2002 Romanian censuses]. Minneapolis, MN: IPUMS, 2018. http://doi.org/10.18128/D020.V70)
***$p<0.01$

path dependence in the biographies of ethnically mixed marriages. If a family chooses the Hungarian (or the Romanian) alternative at one of the critical biographical junctures it is likely that they will consequently follow the same pathway in subsequent phases. Second, census identification is nothing else than one element in the sequence of choices between ethnically marked and mutually exclusive alternatives. In this sense, a census is not an isolated act and census classification can be interpreted only in the institutional and discursive context in which it is embedded. Census techniques may be modified, but this should be interpreted in a larger (partially politically motivated) context.[32] Third, there is an asymmetry in the path dependent character of mixed marriages too. Making a choice for a Romanian alternative makes it highly unlikely that a subsequent return to the Hungarian option will occur, while the probability of switching from a Hungarian alternative to a Romanian one is greater. According to Telegdi-Csetri (2017), in regions where Romanians are in a demographic majority, the Romanian alternative may be perceived as an unmarked one, while maintaining the

[32]In this sense, I employ the notion of regimes of counting, as used in Chapter 10.

Hungarian alternative (which is marked) requires conscious extra effort by the mixed couples.[33] This is partially due to the asymmetrical institutional and discursive order that characterizes the nation-state. However, as we will see, the boundary policing exercised by the Hungarian elites is also conducive toward this end.

3.2 Factors Affecting the Categorization of Children Born in Mixed Marriages

As already mentioned, ethnic socialization in mixed marriages is highly unbalanced. The proportion of children registered as Hungarian was 28% in 1977, 29% in 1992, 31% in 2002, and 34% in 2011. The proportion of children with Hungarian as their mother tongue was 27, 26, 28, and 33%, respectively.[34] In what follows, I outline the major socio-demographic factors affecting the classification of children living in mixed families. Table 4 presents the proportion of children registered as Hungarian with Hungarian as their mother tongue according to the variables included in the analysis, as well as the results of a logistic regression model in which Hungarian ethnicity is the dependent variable. The value of Nagelkerke R^2 was 0.185 for 1977, 0.236 for 1992, 0.232 for 2002, and 0.102 for 2011. The following aspects are worth highlighting:

First, gender differences have changed profoundly during the last four decades. In 1977, the likelihood of being registered as Hungarian was 3.5 times higher for Hungarian fathers than Hungarian mothers. In 2011, there were no gender differences with regard to the declared ethnicity of the children. However, in the case of mother tongue declared for the child, the ethnic background of the mother mattered more in 2011; the likelihood that the mother tongue of children was declared as Hungarian was significantly higher in the case of Hungarian women living in mixed relations than in the case of Hungarian men.

[33]Of course, this varies regionally. In the ethnic block area of Székely Land the Hungarian alternative might be the unmarked one, and keeping open the Romanian alternative may require some extra effort. However, no investigation concerning mixed marriages similar to that of Telegdi-Csetri (2017) and Brubaker et al. (2006) has been conducted in the Hungarian ethnic block area.

[34]The mother tongue and registered ethnicity are the same in 90% of cases.

Table 4 Factors affecting the ethnic categorization of children living in ethnically mixed families (Binomial logistic regressions)

		1977 (N=8401)			1992 (N=10863)			2002 (N=7127)			2011 (N=4450)		
		Mother tongue	Nationality		*Mother tongue*	Nationality		*Mother tongue*	Ethnicity		*Mother tongue*	Ethnicity	
		%	%	EXP B	%	%	EXP B	%	%	EXP B	%	%	EXP B
Total		**27.4**	**28.3**		**26.4**	**29.1**		**28.0**	**30.7**		**33.4**	**33.9**	
Gender of Hungarian spouse	*Woman*	22.6	17.2		23.9	18.7		32.3	27.6		38.0	34.0	
	Man	32.7	41.1	3.47***	28.8	38.8	2.63***	25.9	33.7	1.25***	28.9	33.8	0.87
Gender of child	*Girl*	27.2	29.1		26.5	28.7		28.0	32.3		33.3	34.3	
	Boy	27.5	27.6	0.926	26.5	29.4	1.09*	30.2	29.1	0.81***	33.6	33.8	1.02
Region	*Székely Land*	47.0	42.6		50.2	49.0		57.8	54.9		65.0	55.9	
	Central Transylvania	29.4	31.2	0.84	26.1	29.5	0.61***	28.7	31.3	0.73**	34.5	36.7	0.85
	Partium/Crișana	38.3	36.7	1.09	40.0	35.7	0.69***	39.8	36.6	0.78*	43.1	39.7	1.04
	Dispersed communities	21.6	23.8	0.81	20.2	26.0	0.57***	22.3	26.4	0.81	22.9	26.1	0.68
	Old Romanian Kingdom	4.1	7.3	0.28***	6.9	8.4	0.21***	10.8	9.8	0.32***	11.8	18.2	0.40**
Weighted ratio		-	-	1.01***	-	-	1.01***	-	-	1.01***	-		1.01***
Type of settlement	*Rural*	35.9	35.4		32.7	33.6		35.5	35.0		38.9	38.7	
	Urban	24.1	25.6	1.05	24.3	27.5	1.02	25.8	29.1	1.00	30.0	30.9	1.02
Average educational attainment of spouses	*Low*	31.6	31.8		31.5	33.2		31.8	31.2		37.1	36.5	
	Medium	23.7	25.4	0.89*	24.3	28.3	0.76***	28.3	30.6	1.13	30.1	31.7	0.78***
	High	22.6	24.3	0.79**	25.3	26.7	0.87**	28.5	30.6	1.16*	36.4	35.5	1.02
Status difference (education)	*Hungarian lower*	21.0	19.5		23.2	22.1		28.8	28.9		27.9	30.1	
	Similar	30.1	32.0	1.65***	26.6	29.9	1.11	29.6	30.9	1.11	30.8	34.0	1.10
	Hungarian higher	31.1	33.6	1.69***	29.7	35.3	1.23***	28.6	32.4	1.12	38.8	38.0	1.28***
Ethnicity of non-Hungarian spouse	*Romanian*	25.4	26.9		24.2	27.9		27.4	29.6		31.1	32.5	
	Roma	54.4	39.2	1.09	45.6	29.6	0.55***	42.5	40.6	1.25	50.2	40.9	1.23
	German	35.2	34.6	2.15***	47.7	39.7	1.56**	50.6	42.7	0.83	55.3	56.6	2.10***
	Other	55.1	49.8	3.58***	53.6	52.9	2.37***	55.8	48.7	1.73***	61.9	54.0	2.65***
Religion of the Hungarian spouse	*Protestant*				33.6	35.1		35.6	37.5				
	Roman Catholic				29.1	32.8	0.85***	33.5	35.3	0.91			
	Greek Catholic				14.8	22.8	0.57**	21.3	22.0	0.81			
	Neo-protestant				19.0	23.3	0.60***	24.9	22.0	0.43***			
	Orthodox				4.1	6.4	0.18***	4.5	5.8	0.14***			
	Other				25.6	24.8	0.55**	29.7	30.6	0.81			
Religion of the non-Hungarian spouse	*Protestant*				58.7	57.8		62.5	61.9				
	Roman Catholic				49.6	49.3	0.72***	51.2	50.2	0.64***			
	Greek catholic				16.8	25.7	0.30***	22.2	21.9	0.21***			
	Neo-protestant				36.3	36.1	0.42***	50.4	45.2	0.65**			
	Orthodox				20.5	23.8	0.28***	23.9	26.4	0.31***			
	Other				37.1	39.2	0.50***	33.8	33.1	0.35***			
Type of union	*Marriage*	27.4	28.3		26.2	28.9		33.3	32.5		32.7	33.3	
	Consensual union	-	-		41.4	39.5	1.50**	38.6	30.5	1.11	37.3	37.7	1.21***
Nagelkerke R^2		*0.185*			*0.236*			*0.232*			*0,102*		

Source IPUMS-International 10% sample of the Romanian censuses (Minnesota Population Center. Integrated Public Use Microdata Series, International: Version 7.0 [1977, 1992, 2002 and 2011 Romanian censuses]. Minneapolis, MN: IPUMS, 2018. http://doi.org/10.18128/D020.V70)

* $p<0.1$; ** $p<0.05$; *** $p<0.01$

Second, regional differences are significant. In the Székely Land, a higher proportion of children growing up in mixed families were classified as Hungarian and spoke Hungarian. There was also an increase

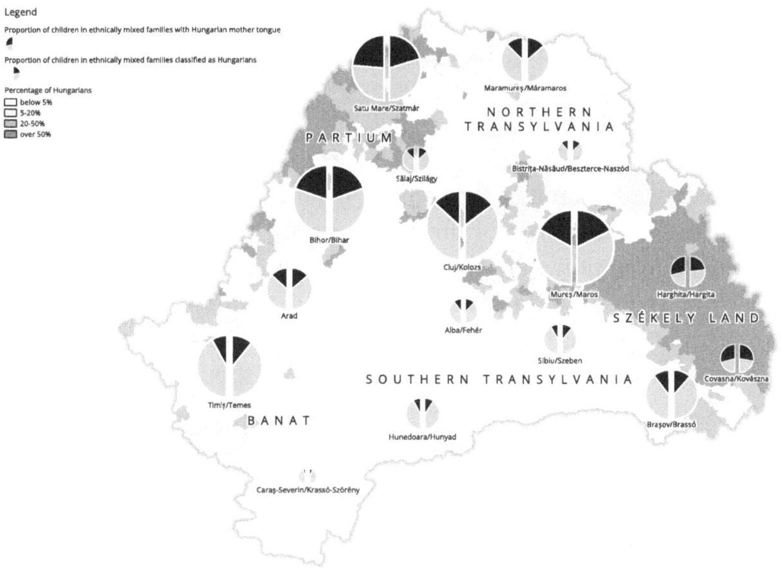

Fig. 3 Mother tongue and identity choice for children born in ethnically mixed marriages (2011) (*Source* Map created by Samu Márton Balogh based on the IPUMS-International 10% sample of the 2011 Romanian census)

over time. Consequently, the proportion of children classified as ethnic Hungarians was 56%, while of those with Hungarian mother tongue was 65% in 2011. One may conclude that in this region mixed marriages are not conducive to a demographic loss of Hungarian community, but on the contrary, they help the ethno-demographic reproduction of local Hungarian communities (Fig. 3).

Third, the level of education used to have a significant effect, but this is no longer true. In 1977 and 1992, mixed families with less well-educated parents registered their children as Hungarian in higher proportions. The education of the parents no longer had a significant effect on identity choices in 2002 and 2011. The difference in (educational) status between the Hungarian and non-Hungarian spouse maintains some explanatory power; however, its influence on identity choices has also decreased. In other words, identity options depended less on social status in 2011 than in 1977. This might be a consequence of institutionally sustained ethnic parallelism. During state socialism, social mobility (of people living in mixed families) was more likely to mean departure from the Hungarian category. Since 1989, Hungarian channels of social mobility have also been available and, consequently, the relationship disappeared.

Fourth, the religious and ethnic characteristics of the spouses matter. In the case of non-Hungarian spouses belonging to the majority (constituting the vast majority of mixed marriages) the chances of choosing the Hungarian option are lower compared to the situation with German and Roma spouses. Protestant and Roman Catholic Hungarians are more inclined toward the Hungarian option than those with other religious backgrounds. If the non-Hungarian spouse is Protestant or Roman Catholic, this effect is even more accentuated. However, in this case the nature of the causality is not entirely clear. It might be also caused by the path dependence of individual biographies (e.g., by the earlier conversion of one of the spouses).

Finally, rural–urban differences are present at the level of bivariate distributions (more children are registered as Hungarian in rural areas); however, this is a consequence of the lower proportion of Hungarians in urban areas.

3.3 Boundary Reinforcement

The last issue to be discussed is the effect of the boundary policing of Hungarian elites on boundary maintenance in general, and on ethnic socialization in mixed families in particular. As mentioned already, intermarriage and its consequences may be interpreted in the framework of an assimilation model. According to Laitin (1995, 1996), assimilation is nothing else than a sequence of changes (often spread out over several generations) which are conducive to the adaption of the cultural norms of the majority[35] and entering its social circles. One

[35]Laitin (1995, pp. 34–35) emphasizes that the cultural norms and practices of the majority are changing and, consequently, minorities are shooting at a "moving target". In the present case, the most important element of cultural adaptation is that one prefers to speak in Romanian.

might argue that in Transylvania mixed marriages play a crucial role in this process as it is practically the sole socially legitimate pathway of crossing (definitively) the boundary between minority and majority through the departure of the Hungarian spouse from the minority category and, especially, through the reclassification of children who grow up in mixed families as majority group members. According to the framework provided by Laitin, the direction of this process always operates from the subordinated toward the dominant group. The payoff for assimilation depends on multiple factors, including the economic differences between minority and majority, and the acceptance of assimilated minority group members by the majority (i.e., the level of discrimination). Another important element, however, is that of the boundary policing exercised by minority elites. In our case, such boundary policing plays a crucial role in the fact that people of mixed background are pushed toward the majority group. As already mentioned, individuals are relatively easily accepted as majority group members, while recognition as a Hungarian requires a relatively high level of cultural competences. As László Öllős (2012), a Hungarian political thinker and social scientist in Slovakia has emphasized, the Hungarian community prefers "pure" forms of national identification and rejects the "diluted" forms of Hungarianness. Consequently, those who "hesitate" or "are in the anteroom of becoming Slovaks" are denied recognition as Hungarians. This is seemingly irrational behavior, as it is conducive to the departure from the community of those who are in an ethnically mixed situation.

However, according to Laitin such forms of boundary policing and even excommunication are essential for keeping assimilation at relatively low levels. Laitin (1998, pp. 3–36, 35–38) interprets assimilation using the model of a "tipping game". The payoff of different identity choices depends on the behavior of other group members. If nobody switches, ethnic reproduction will pay off. If everybody switches, assimilation will be the rational option. According to this tipping-game model, cascades of assimilation are likely to happen if minority group members consider that identity maintenance is no longer a rational option. This may be prevented through boundary policing or, as Alba would put it, by keeping boundaries bright (2005, pp. 21–25).

As a first remark, one should emphasize that Hungarians use relatively soft tools for policing their boundaries vis-á-vis the Romanian majority. This softness becomes evident when compared with the mechanisms operating in Hungarian-Roma (and to a lesser extent,[36] in Romanian-Roma) relations. In rural areas marrying with Roma in many cases implies not only excommunication at the level of the ethnic community, but also exclusion from personal networks, including the close family. The following interview fragment describes such a case in a village inhabited by Hungarians and Hungarian-speaking Roma:

> It was a very strong family. His parents live in a pretty house in the center of the village. The young man moved to the Gypsy Colony. The children go [there] sometimes to their grandmother. One of the little girls said that they go when the old man [their grandfather] is not at home. Their grandmother gives them some milk on these occasions. She tries to help them. The [grand]father was the one who opposed [this situation] categorically [his son marrying a Roma woman]. The little girl also said that neither does Grandma like it if they go there together. Maybe by themselves... You can imagine how it is if four or five Gypsy kids appear suddenly. I can understand why they do not like it if they all go there together. (Non-Roma interviewee, interview conducted by the author in July 2015)

The forms of excommunication described in the fragment above are practically unimaginable in Hungarian–Romanian relations. Those marrying exogenously are not excluded from previously existing personal networks and are not denied recognition as social equals. Nevertheless, boundary policing and exercises that keep boundaries bright are practiced at several levels. To cite Brubaker (2004, p. 54): "*[t]he language of both politics and everyday life, to be sure, is rigorously categorical, dividing the population into mutually exclusive ethnonational categories, and making no allowance for mixed or ambiguous forms*".

At a micro-level and in everyday settings, cultural performance and Hungarian-language proficiency play a pivotal role. The following

[36]As suggested by surveys conducted by the Romanian Institute for Research on National Minorities.

phrase was formulated during the interwar period, but it is widely accepted and the considerations it encapsulates shape everyday interactions to a great extent: "*[It is n]ot that person [who] is a Hungarian [...] who has Hungarian parents, or that person [...] who claims [being in possession of] a proud consciousness, but the person who possesses the entire Hungarian culture*" (Bartha and Decsi 1938, p. 5). Thus, there exists a "Hungarian culture" that an individual can possess as an ethnic feature. We can conclude from this situation that the lack of this cultural performance marks assimilation on an individual level, while the destruction and dissolution of cultural stock marks assimilation on a community level. This idea is decisively present not only in elite discourses, but also in the cognitive structures that shape everyday interaction. Brubaker et al. (2006) emphasized that being Hungarian often appears to be an acquired status, which means that the recognition of group membership can be denied. This becomes problematic not only related to the linguistic and cultural performance of individuals with a mixed background, but also in the relations between Hungarians from different regions or belonging to different social strata. As the standards concerning linguistic and cultural performance needed for membership are not the same for each region and social strata, lower-status Hungarians, or those who come from dispersed communities, may easily find themselves disadvantaged in a more compact Hungarian cultural space.

As mentioned already, boundary reinforcement is also one of the two major dimensions of political agency exercised by Transylvanian Hungarian elites. It is a telling example that before the 2011 census the leadership of RMDSZ did not back the proposal of the Romanian Institute for Research on National Minorities to introduce an option for multiple identification. This was because they considered that the opportunity for dual identification would blur ethnic boundaries and in the long run would be conducive to a cascade of assimilation.[37] The most important tool of boundary maintenance is, however, institutionally sustained ethnic parallelism.

[37]According to an informal interview conducted by the author with an RMDSZ member of the Census Committee (Attila Markó), the then-president of RMDSZ (Béla Markó) argued personally for this decision which was also supported by other leading RMDSZ members.

At the end of this chapter, a notorious and often-cited example of boundary policing may be mentioned; a manifesto entitled "New Crying Voice for the Hungarians of Baia Mare/Nagybánya and the Bányavidék!", published on May 31, 2012, in Baia Mare/Nagybánya, a town in northwest Transylvania.[38] The Hungarian political and civic elite of the town, including leaders of RMDSZ, MPP, and EMNP, the prominent personalities involved with the Hungarian historical churches and a few important NGOs almost unanimously signed the text. A few weeks later, the local Romanian media discovered the issue and national Romanian news channels dealt with it in detail. The National Council for Combating Discrimination launched an investigation against the signatories. Moreover, following the complaint of a private person, a legal procedure was also initiated.

> All of us, the signers to this manifesto – church leaders, public and civic personalities, pedagogues responsible for Hungarians of Baia Mare/Nagybánya and its surroundings (Bányavidék) – are much concerned by the spreading of the self-abandoning attitude and public mentality [...] which threatens the existence itself of our community. The sickness – whose decade-long symptoms include the spread of mixed marriages, the rejection of education in our mother-tongue, emigration, the compliant assimilation into the majority nation, the lack of ambition and lethargy towards ourselves – has by now infected even the best of our community: it is spreading like an infectious disease among our intellectual circles.
>
> [...]
>
> YOUNG PEOPLE: seek out each other's company! Look for Hungarian friends, Hungarian partners! Yes, this means a somewhat closed and inward-looking life. But do not forget: it has been the closed nature of Transylvania's most valuable communities that has preserved them for

[38]See Új kiáltó szó a nagybányai és bányavidéki magyarságért! *Krónika*, 15 June 2012. https://kronika.ro/szempont/uj-kialto-szo-a-nagybanyai-es-banyavideki-magyarsagert/print.
For interpretations, see Culic (2016, p. 207); Bolovan and Eppel (2017, pp. 23–24).

> centuries! We give you the law as provision: exclude from yourselves everything that is foreign. Do not let an alien language, culture, or friend close to your hearts. [...] a foreign friend can easily become a foreign lover, and whoever does not declare their first love in their mother tongue [...] is much [more] likely to choose later a partner for life from other nation's children.

The manifesto also highlights that endeavors aiming at boundary strengthening are an important part of the identity politics of the Hungarian political elites. It was issued in the context of the drastic decrease of the Hungarian population of the town over the previous two decades, which also signals that institutionalized ethnic parallelism is no longer a viable option in Baia Mare/Nagybánya, which has become the home of a dispersed Hungarian community. It is obvious that the Baia Mare/Nagybánya manifesto is an uncommonly harsh representation of attempts to maintain or strengthen ethnic boundaries which reflects the desperation of the elite of a disintegrating community.[39] Knowing the context makes it easier to understand why the authors speak about "sickness", "infectious disease", the dangers threatening the existence of the community ("complicity", "lethargy", "indifference", "lack of ambition"), and why they reject everything "foreign" and find their solution in isolation; briefly, why they make use of terms which the majority would undoubtedly perceive as exclusive or chauvinistic—as many have stated when commenting on the debate over the manifesto. In Baia Mare/Nagybánya neither ethnic boundaries nor the situation of the Hungarian community are bright indeed; however, it is not obvious at all whether this manifesto contributed in any way to finding a solution, or whether it further aggravated the problem, dividing the community more deeply.

[39] The 1992 census in Baia Mare/Nagybánya counted approximately 26,000 ethnic Hungarians; by 2002 this number had decreased to 20,000, and by 2011 to 14,000. The proportion of the Hungarian population had thus decreased from 17.4 to 12.3% over a period of twenty years.

References

Alba, R. (2005). Bright vs. blurred boundaries: Second-generation assimilation and exclusion in France, Germany, and the United States. *Ethnic and Racial Studies, 28*(1), 20–49.

Alba, R. D., & Nee, V. (2003). *Remaking the American mainstream: Assimilation and contemporary immigration*. Cambridge, MA: Harvard University Press.

Bartha, A., & Decsi, S. (1938). *Az erdélyi szórványkérdés: 80 mezőségi falu alapján*: Jakabffy Elemér Alapítvány kézirat-katalógusa K43.

Becker, G. S. (1973). A theory of marriage: Part I. *Journal of Political Economy, 81*(4), 813–846.

Bhabha, H. K. (1994). *The location of culture*. London and New York: Routledge.

Blau, P. M., Blum, T. C., & Schwartz, J. E. (1982). Heterogeneity and intermarriage. *American Sociological Review, 47*(1), 45.

Bolovan, I., & Dumănescu, L. (Eds.). (2017). *Intermarriage in Transylvania, 1895–2010*. Frankfurt am Main: Peter Lang Edition.

Bolovan, I., & Eppel, M. (2017). Churches and interfaith marriages in Transylvania: From 1895 to the present. In I. Bolovan & L. Dumănescu (Eds.), *Intermarriage in Transylvania, 1895–2010* (pp. 23–47). Frankfurt am Main: Peter Lang Edition.

Brubaker, R. (2004). *Ethnicity without groups*. Cambridge, MA: Harvard University Press.

Brubaker, R., Feischmidt, M., Fox, J., & Grancea, L. (2006). *Nationalist politics and everyday ethnicity in a Transylvanian town*. Princeton: Princeton University Press.

Bucur, M. (2002). *Eugenics and modernization in interwar Romania*. Pittsburgh, PA: University of Pittsburgh Press.

Csata, I., & Kiss, T. (2007). *Népesedési perspektívák. Az erdélyi magyar népesség regionálisan tagolt népesség-előreszámítása 2022-ig és 2032-ig*. Kolozsvár: Kriterion.

Culic, I. (2016). Hungarian society in Romania: Political project and practical reality. In S. P. Ramet & M. Valenta (Eds.), *Ethnic minorities and politics in post-socialist southeastern Europe* (pp. 191–210). New York: Cambridge University Press.

Dribe, M., & Lundh, C. (2011). Cultural dissimilarity and intermarriage. A longitudinal study of immigrants in Sweden 1990–2005. *International Migration Review, 45*(2), 297–324.

Egry, G. (2015). *Etnicitás, identitás, politika: magyar kisebbségek nacionalizmus és regionalizmus között Romániában és Csehszlovákiában 1918–1944* (Első kiadás. ed.). Budapest: Napvilág.
Fearon, J. D., & Laitin, D. D. (2000). Violence and the social construction of ethnic identity. *International Organization, 54*(4), 845–877.
Finnäs, F. (1997). Social integration, heterogeneity, and divorce: The case of the Swedish-speaking population in Finland. *Acta Sociologica, 40*(3), 263–277.
Finnäs, F., & O'Leary, B. (2003). Choosing for the children: The affiliation of the children of minority-majority group intermarriages. *European Sociological Review, 19*(5), 483–499.
Finnäs, F. (2013). Finlandssvenskarna 2012. En statistisk rapport. Svenska Finlands folkting, Helsinki.
Giles, H., Bourhis, R. Y., & Taylor, D. M. (1977). Toward a theory of language in ethnic group relations. In H. Giles (Ed.), *Language, ethnicity, and intergroup relations* (pp. 307–348). London and New York: Academic Press.
Goldscheider, C. (1986). *Jewish continuity and change: Emerging patterns in America. Jewish political and social studies*. Bloomington: Indiana University Press.
Gordon, M. M. (1964). *Assimilation in American life: The role of race, religion, and national origins*. New York: Oxford University Press.
Gorenburg, D. (2006). Rethinking interethnic marriage in the Soviet Union. *Post-Soviet Affairs, 22*(2), 145–165.
Gündüz-Hoşgör, A., & Smits, J. (2002). Intermarriage between Turks and Kurds in contemporary Turkey: Inter-ethnic relations in an urbanizing environment. *European Sociological Review, 18*(4), 417–432.
Hannerz, U. (2000). *Flow, boundaries and hybrids: Keywords in transnational anthrophology* (Working Paper Series WPTC-2K-02). Stockholm: Department of Social Anthropology, Stockholm University.
Hărăguş, M. (2014). The role of education in ethnically mixed marriages. In L. Dumănescu, D. Mârza, & M. Eppel (Eds.), *Intermarriage throughout history* (pp. 389–407). Newcaslte upon Tyne: Cambridge Scholars.
Hărăguş, M. (2017). Considerations on ethnically mixed marriages in Transylvania in the last few decades. In I. Bolovan & L. Dumănescu (Eds.), *Intermarriage in Transylvania, 1895–2010* (pp. 117–125). Frankfurt am Main: Peter Lang Edition.
Horowitz, D. L. (1985). *Ethnic groups in conflict*. Berkeley: University of California Press.
Horváth, I. (2004). Az etnikailag vegyes házasságok az erdélyi magyar lakosság körében: 1992–2002. In T. Kiss (Ed.), *Népesedési folyamatok az*

ezredfordulón Erdélyben (pp. 235–257). Kolozsvár: Kriterion and RMDSZ Ügyvezető Elnökség.

Jenkins, R. (2008). *Rethinking ethnicity* (2nd ed.). Thousand Oaks, CA: Sage.

Kalmijn, M. (1998). Intermarriage and homogamy: Causes, patterns, trends. *Annual Review of Sociology, 24,* 395–421.

Kalmijn, M., de Graaf, P. M., & Janssen, J. P. G. (2005). Intermarriage and the risk of divorce in the Netherlands: The effects of differences in religion and in nationality, 1974–94. *Population Studies, 59*(1), 71–85.

Kalmijn, M., & Tubergen, F. V. (2010). A comparative perspective on intermarriage: Explaining differences among national-origin groups in the United States. *Demography, 47*(2), 459–479.

Kiss, T. (2006). Interethnic marriages and assimilation in demographic models. In B. Balogh & Z. Ilyés (Eds.), *Perspectives of diaspora existence: Hungarian diasporas in the Carpathian Basin: Historical and current contexts of a specific diaspora interpretation and its aspects of ethnic minority protection* (pp. 107–139). Budapest: Akadémiai Kiadó.

Laitin, D. D. (1995). Marginality: A microperspective. *Rationality and Society, 7*(1), 31–57.

Laitin, D. D. (1996). National revival and competitive assimilation in Estonia. *Post-Soviet Affairs, 12*(1), 25–39.

Laitin, D. D. (1998). *Identity in formation: The Russian-speaking populations in the near abroad. The Wilder House series in politics, history, and culture.* Ithaca: Cornell University Press.

Lamont, M., Silva, G. M., Welburn, J. S., Guetzkow, J., Mizrachi, N., Herzog, H., & Reis, E. (2016). *Getting respect: Responding to stigma and discrimination in the United States, Brazil, and Israel.* Princeton, NJ: Princeton University Press.

László, S. (2013). Neglected peripheries: Discovering hybridity in Transylvania. *Identities and identifications: Politicized uses of collective identities.* Paper presented at the conference Identities and Identifications Politicized Uses of Collective Identities, 18–20 April 2013, Zagreb, Croatia.

Levchenko, P. (2013). *Transnational marriages between eastern European-born wives and U.S.-born husbands.* Ph.D. Thesis, University of Minnesota, Minnesota.

Livezeanu, I. (1995). *Cultural politics in Greater Romania: Regionalism, nation building & ethnic struggle, 1918–1930.* Ithaca: Cornell University Press.

Merton, R. K. (1941). Intermarriage and the social structure. *Psychiatry, 4*(3), 361–374.

Monden, C. W. S., & Smits, J. (2005). Ethnic intermarriage in times of social change: The case of Latvia. *Demography, 42*(2), 323–345.

O'Leary, R., & Finnäs, F. (2002). Education, social integration and minority-majority group intermarriage. *Sociology, 36*(2), 235–254.

Öllős, L. (2012, June 9). Ki a magyar? *Új Szó Szalon.*

Osuji, C. (2013). Confronting whitening in an era of black consciousness: Racial ideology and black-white interracial marriages in Rio de Janeiro. *Ethnic and Racial Studies, 36*(10), 1490–1506.

Pierson, P. (2000). Increasing returns, path dependence, and the study of politics. *American Political Science Review, 94*(2), 251–267.

Pieterse, J. N. (2001). Hybridity, so what? *Theory, Culture & Society, 18*(2–3), 219–245.

Pozsony, F. (2007). Szórványok hétköznapjai. In B. Balogh, B. Bodó, & Z. Ilyés (Eds.), *Regionális identitás, közösségépítés, szórványgondozás* (pp. 49–60). Budapest: Lucius.

Râmneamțu, P. (1937). *Problema căsătoriilor mixte în orașele din Transilvania în perioada de la 1920–1937.* Buletin Eugenetic și Biopolitic.

Sheriff, R. E. (2001). *Dreaming equality: Color, race, and racism in urban Brazil.* New Brunswick, NJ: Rutgers University Press.

Smits, J. (2010). Ethnic intermarriage and social cohesion. What can we learn from Yugoslavia? *Social Indicators Research, 96*(3), 417–432.

Szilágyi, N. S. (2002). Észrevételek a romániai magyar népesség fogyásáról, különös tekintettel az asszimilációra. *Magyar Kisebbség, 7*(4), 64–96.

Szilágyi, N. S. (2004). Az asszimiláció és hatása a népesedési folyamatokra. In T. Kiss (Ed.), *Népesedési folyamatok az ezredfordulón Erdélyben* (pp. 157–235). Kolozsvár: Kriterion and RMDSZ Ügyvezető Elnökség.

Telegdi-Csetri, V. (2017). Displaying ethnicity through the practices of mixed couples from Transylvania. In I. Bolovan & L. Dumănescu (Eds.), *Intermarriage in Transylvania, 1895–2010* (pp. 193–204). Frankfurt am Main: Peter Lang Edition.

Thornton, A. (2005). *Reading History Sideways: The Fallacy and Enduring Impact of the Developmental Paradigm on Family Life.* Chicago: University of Chicago Press.

Turai, T. (2003). A családszerkezet változása a szocializmus éveiben a Szilágyságban. *Erdélyi Társadalom, 1*(1), 85–101.

Turda, M. (2010). *Modernism and eugenics.* New York: Palgrave Macmillan.

Van Ham, M., & Tammaru, T. (2011). Ethnic minority-majority unions in Estonia. *European Journal of Population, 27*(3), 313–335.

Varga, E. Á. (1998). *Fejezetek a jelenkori Erdély népesedéstörténetéből*. Budapest: Püski.

Weber, M. (1978). *Economy and society: An outline of interpretive sociology* (2 Vols., p. 1469). Berkeley: University of California Press.

Wimmer, A. (2013). *Ethnic boundary making: Institutions, power, networks. Oxford studies in culture and politics*. New York: Oxford University Press.

Yagmur, K., & Ehala, M. (2011). Tradition and innovation in the Ethnolinguistic Vitality theory. *Journal of Multilingual and Multicultural Development, 32*(2), 101–110.

Zolberg, A. R., & Woon, L. L. (1999). Why Islam is like Spanish: Cultural incorporation in Europe and the United States. *Politics & Society, 27*(1), 5–38.

Bibliography

Abdelal, R., Herrera, Y. M., Johnston, A. I., & McDermott, R. (2009). *Measuring identity: A guide for social scientists*. Cambridge and New York: Cambridge University Press.

Achim, V. (2004). *The Roma in Romanian history*. Budapest and New York: Central European University Press.

Achim, V. (2007). A második világháború alatti román lakosságcseretervekről. *Múltunk, 52*(4), 4–17.

Alba, R. (2005). Bright vs. blurred boundaries: Second-generation assimilation and exclusion in France, Germany, and the United States. *Ethnic and Racial Studies, 28*(1), 20–49.

Alba, R., & Nee, V. (2003). *Remaking the American mainstream: Assimilation and contemporary immigration*. Cambridge, MA: Harvard University Press.

Aldrich, H. E., & Waldinger, R. (1990). Ethnicity and entrepreneurship. *Annual Review of Sociology, 16*(1), 111–135.

Aldrich, J. H. (1995). *Why parties?: The origin and transformation of political parties in America. American politics and political economy series*. Chicago: The University of Chicago Press.

Alesina, A., & La Ferrara, E. (2005). Ethnic diversity and economic performance. *Journal of Economic Literature, 43*(3), 762–800.

T. Kiss et al. (eds.), *Unequal Accommodation of Minority Rights*,
Palgrave Politics of Identity and Citizenship Series,
https://doi.org/10.1007/978-3-319-78893-7

Alonso, S., & Ruiz-Rufino, R. (2007). Political representation and ethnic conflict in new democracies. *European Journal of Political Research, 46*(2), 237–267.

Anderson, B. (2006). *Imagined communities: Reflections on the origin and spread of nationalism* (rev. ed.). London and New York: Verso.

Andrássy, G. (2011). The right to use one's own language and the matter of simplicity. *Europäisches Journal für Minderheitenfragen, 4*(1), 5–19.

Andreescu, G. (2000). Continuarea participării UDMR la guvernare – prima fază a democrației consensualiste românești? *Provincia, 1*(7), 2–3.

Apró, I. (Ed.). (2012). *Határon túli magyar nyelvű médiumok 2010/2011*. Budapest: Médiatudományi Intézet.

Arel, D. (2002). Language categories: Backward or forward looking. In D. I. Kertzer & D. Arel (Eds.), *Census and identity: The politics of race, ethnicity, and language in national census* (pp. 92–121). Cambridge and New York: Cambridge University Press.

Arzoz, X. (2007). The nature of language rights. *Journal on Ethnopolitics and Minority Issues in Europe, 6*(2), 1–35.

Badis, R. (2008). A vajdasági magyar népesség társadalomszerkezete két népszámlálás tükrében. *Regio, 19*(4), 102–154.

Baetens Beardsmore, H. (1986). *Bilingualism: Basic principles* (2nd ed.). Boston, MA: College-Hill Press.

Bakk, M. (2000a). 1989–1999: az RMDSZ első tíz éve. In B. Bodó (Ed.), *Romániai Magyar Évkönyv*. Kolozsvár: Polis.

Bakk, M. (2000b). Modellviták – rejtett stratégiák. *Magyar Kisebbség, 6*(1), 8–12.

Bakk, M. (2004). Az autonómia-tervek két szakasza Erdélyben 1989 után. *Magyar Kisebbség, 9*(1–2), 39–60.

Bakk, M., Horváth, A., & Salat, L. (2004). Az RMDSZ 2003-ban – útkeresés integrációs határpontokban. In É. Blénesi & K. Mandel (Eds.), *Kisebbségek és kormánypolitika Közép-Európában, 2002–2004*. Budapest: Gondolat–MTA Etnikai-Nemzeti Kisebbségkutató Intézet.

Balić, L., & Izmirlija, M. (2013). Consociation in Bosnia and Herzegovina: Practical implementation of the theoretical principles. *South-East European Journal of Political Science, 1*(3), 121–134.

Balogh, L. B. (1999). *Dél-erdélyi magyarság 1940–1944*. Available at: http:// balogh.adatbank.transindex.ro/ (Accessed 10 March 2017).

Balogh, L. B. (2004). A dél-erdélyi magyar kisebbség helyzete (1940–1944). In Z. Körmendy (Ed.), *Korrajz 2003. A XX. Század Intézet Évkönyve* (pp. 39–53). Budapest: XX. Század Intézet.

Balogh, L. B., & Olti, A. G. (2006). A román-magyar lakosságcsere kérdése 1940–1947 között. *Kisebbségkutatás, 15*(4), 597–620.

Baranowska, G. (2014). Legal regulations on national and ethnic minorities in Poland. *Przegląd Zachodni, 2*, 35–48.

Bárdi, N. (2000). Cleavages in cross-border magyar minority politics, 1989–1998. *Regio*, 1, 3–36.

Bárdi, N. (2004). *Tény és való. A budapesti kormányzatok és a határon túli magyarság kapcsolattörténete. Problémakatalógus*. Pozsony: Kalligram.

Bárdi, N. (2005). Generation groups in the history of Hungarian minority elites. *Regio*, 1, 109–124.

Bárdi, N. (2006). Nép, nemzet, szuverenitás. *Fundamentum, 2*, 81–89.

Bárdi, N. (2013). *Otthon és haza: tanulmányok a romániai magyar kisebbség történetérol* (p. 647). Csíkszereda: Pro-Print.

Bárdi, N. (2017). Álságos állítások a magyar etnopolitikában. A külhoni magyarok és a budapesti kormányzatok magyarságpolitikája. In A. Jakab & L. Urván (Eds.), *Hegymenet. Társadalmi és politikai kihívások Magyarországon* (pp. 130–155). Budapest: Osiris.

Bárdi, N., Filep, T. G., & Lőrincz, D. J. (2015). *Népszolgálat. A közösségi elkötelezettség alakváltozatai a magyar kisebbségek történetében*. Pozsony: Kalligram.

Bárdi, N., Gidó, A., & Novák, C. Z. (2014). *Együtt és külön: az erdélyi magyarok önszerveződése (1989–1990)*. Kolozsvár: Nemzeti Kisebbségkutató Intézet.

Bárdi, N., & Misovicz, T. (2010). A kisebbségi magyar közösségek támogatásának politikája. In B. Bitskey (Ed.), *Határon túli magyarság a 21. Században* (pp. 66–76). Budapest: Köztársasági Elnöki Hivatal.

Barna, G. (2004). Erdélyi magyar ifjúsági szervezetek szervezetszociológiai elemzése. *Erdélyi Társadalom, 2*(2), 85–112.

Barna, G. (2015, July 10). Képességvizsga – hogy teljesítettek a magyar diákok? *maszol.ro*. Available at: http://www.maszol.ro/index.php/társadalom/50121-kepessegvizsga-hogy-teljesitettek-a-magyar-diakok.

Barna, G., Kapitány, B., Kiss, T., Márton, J., & Toró, T. (2016). *Iskolák veszélyben. Tanulmányok a Székelyföldön kívüli magyar oktatás helyzetéről*. Kolozsvár: Nemzeti Kisebbségkutató Intézet.

Barth, F. (1969). *Ethnic groups and boundaries: The social organization of culture difference. Scandinavian University Books*. Bergen: Universitetsforlaget; London: Allen & Unwin.

Bartha, A., & Decsi, S. (1938). *Az erdélyi szórványkérdés: 80 mezőségi falu alapján*. Jakabffy Elemér Alapítvány kézirat-katalógusa K43.

Battistella, E. L. (1996). *The logic of markedness*. New York: Oxford University Press.

Bauböck, R. (2007). The trade-off between transnational citizenship and political autonomy. In T. Faist & P. Kivisto (Eds.), *Dual citizenship in global perspective: From unitary to multiple citizenship* (pp. 69–91). Basingstoke and New York: Palgrave Macmillan.

Bauböck, R. (2010). *Dual citizenship for transborder minorities? How to respond to the Hungarian-Slovak tit-for-tat?* (EUI Working Paper No. 75).

Becker, G. S. (1973). A theory of marriage: Part I. *Journal of Political Economy, 81*(4), 813–846.

Belloni, R. (2004). Peacebuilding and consociational electoral engineering in Bosnia and Herzegovina. *International Peacekeeping, 11*(2), 334–353.

Benő, A. (2012). Hogyan tanulják a magyar gyerekek a román nyelvet az erdélyi iskolákban? Problémák és lehetőségek. *Székelyföld, 16*(5), 54–65.

Benő, A., Becze, O., Erdély, J., Nagy, Z., Ördög-Gyárfás, E., & Sárosi Mardírosz, K. (Eds.). (2004). *Magyar–román közigazgatási szótár*. Sepsiszentgyörgy: Anyanyelvápolók Erdélyi Szövetsége.

Beretka, K. (2016). Language rights and multilingualism in Vojvodina. *International Journal on Minority and Group Rights, 23*(4), 505–529.

Berevoiescu, I. (2002). O analiză demografică a populației de romi: familie și fertilitate. In C. Zamfir & M. Preda (Eds.), *Romii în România* (pp. 39–72). București: Expert.

Berger, P. L. (Ed.). (1999a). *The desecularization of the world: Resurgent religion and world politics*. Washington, DC: Ethics and Public Policy Center; Grand Rapids, MI: W. B. Eerdmans.

Berger, P. L. (1999b). The desecularization of the world: A global overview. In P. L. Berger (Ed.), *The desecularization of the world: Resurgent religion and world politics* (pp. 1–18). Washington, DC: Ethics and Public Policy Center; Grand Rapids, MI: W. B. Eerdmans.

Bhabha, H. K. (1994). *The location of culture*. London and New York: Routledge.

Bines, C. (1998). *Din istoria imigrărilor în Israel*. București: Hasefer.

Birnir, J. K. (2007). *Ethnicity and electoral politics*. Cambridge and New York: Cambridge University Press.

Bíró, A., & Pallai, K. (2011). *Public financing of national minority organisations: Policy paradigms, policy regimes and good practice.* Study prepared for the Committee of Experts on Issues Relating to the Protection of National Minorities. Strasbourg: Council of Europe.

Biró, Z. A. (1998a). Intézményesedési folyamatok a romániai magyarság körében. In Z. A. Biró (Ed.), *Stratégia vagy kényszerpályák? Tanulmányok a romániai magyar társadalomról* (pp. 16–47). Csíkszereda: Pro-Print.

Biró, Z. A. (1998b). *Stratégia vagy kényszerpályák? Tanulmányok a romániai magyar társadalomról.* Csíkszereda: Pro-Print.

Blau, P. M., Blum, T. C., & Schwartz, J. E. (1982). Heterogeneity and intermarriage. *American Sociological Review, 47*(1), 45.

Blommaert, J. (2006). Language policy and national identity. In T. Ricento (Ed.), *An introduction to language policy: Theory and method* (pp. 238–255). Malden, MA: Blackwell.

Blomqvist, A. (2014). *Economic nationalizing in the ethnic borderlands of Hungary and Romania: Inclusion, exclusion and annihilation in Szatmár/Satu-Mare 1867–1944.* Stockholm: Stockholm University.

Bochsler, D., & Szöcsik, E. (2013). Building inter-ethnic bridges or promoting ethno-territorial demarcation lines? Hungarian minority parties in competition. *Nationalities Papers, 41*(5), 761–779.

Bodó, J., & Bartha, G. (1996). *Elvándorlók? Vendégmunka és életforma a Székelyföldön.* Csíkszereda: Pro-Print.

Bogdán, A., & Mohácsek, M. (2012). *Nyelvi jogok útmutató.* Cluj-Napoca: ISPMN.

Bognár, Z. (2006). Romániai magyar autonómiakoncepciók. Az 1989 és 2006 között kidolgozott törvénytervezetek. In M. Ludassy, Z. Bognár, G. Egry, L. Salat, & F. Fejtő (Eds.), *Autonómia, liberalizmus, szociáldemokrácia. Fejtő Ferenc, Salat Levente, Ludassy Mária, Egry Gábor és Bognár Zoltán írásai* (pp. 85–117). Budapest: Európai Összehasonlító Kisebbségkutatások Közalapítvány.

Boia, L. (2015). *Cum s-a românizat România?* (p. 144). București: Humanitas.

Bolovan, I., & Dumănescu, L. A. (Eds.). (2017). *Intermarriage in Transylvania, 1895–2010.* Frankfurt am Main: Peter Lang.

Bolovan, I., & Eppel, M. (2017). Churches and interfaith marriages in Transylvania: From 1895 to the present. In I. Bolovan & L. A. Dumănescu (Eds.), *Intermarriage in Transylvania, 1895–2010* (pp. 23–47). Frankfurt am Main: Peter Lang.

Bonacich, E. (1972). A Theory of ethnic antagonism: The split labor market. *American Sociological Review, 37*(5), 547.

Botoş, R., Mârza, D., & Popovici, V. (2016). Censuses between population statistics and politics. The Romanian press from Hungary and the censuses between 1869 and 1910. *Romanian Journal of Population Studies, 10*(1), 5–18.

Bottoni, S. (2018). *Stalin's legacy in Romania. The Hungarian autonomous region, 1952–1960*. Lanham, MD: Lexington Books.

Bourdieu, P. (1985). The genesis of the concepts of habitus and field. *Sociocriticism, 2*(2), 11–24.

Bourdieu, P. (1991). *Language and symbolic power*. Cambridge, MA: Harvard University Press.

Bourdieu, P. (1993a). *The field of cultural production: Essays on art and literature*. New York: Columbia University Press.

Bourdieu, P. (1993b). *Sociology in question. Theory, culture & society*. London and Thousand Oaks, CA: Sage.

Bozóki, A. (2002). *The roundtable talks of 1989: The genesis of Hungarian democracy: Analysis and documents*. Budapest: Central European University Press.

Brădăţan, C., & Kulcsár, L. J. (2014). When the educated leave the east: Romanian and Hungarian skilled immigration to the USA. *Journal of International Migration and Integration, 15*(3), 509–524.

Brubaker, R. (1995). National minorities, nationalizing states, and external national homelands in the new Europe. *Daedalus, 124*(2), 107–132.

Brubaker, R. (1996). *Nationalism reframed nationhood and the national question in the New Europe*. Cambridge and New York: Cambridge University Press.

Brubaker, R. (1998). Migrations of ethnic unmixing in the "New Europe". *International Migration Review, 32*(4), 1047–1065.

Brubaker, R. (2000). Accidental diasporas and external "homelands" in central and eastern Europe: Past and present. *IHS Political Science Series*, 71, 1–19.

Brubaker, R. (2001). The return of assimilation? Changing perspectives on immigration and its sequels in France, Germany, and the United States. *Ethnic and Racial Studies, 24*(4), 531–548.

Brubaker, R. (2004). *Ethnicity without groups*. Cambridge, MA: Harvard University Press.

Brubaker, R. (2005). The 'diaspora' diaspora. *Ethnic and Racial Studies, 28*(1), 1–19.

Brubaker, R. (2009). National homogenization and ethnic reproduction on the European periphery. In M. Barbagli & H. Ferguson (Eds.), *La teoria sociologica e lo stato moderno: saggi in onore di Gianfranco Poggi* (pp. 201–221). Bologna: Il mulino.

Brubaker, R. (2011). Nationalizing states revisited: Projects and processes of nationalization in post-Soviet states. *Ethnic and Racial Studies, 34*(11), 1785–1814.

Brubaker, R., Feischmidt, M., Fox, J., & Grancea, L. (2006). *Nationalist politics and everyday ethnicity in a Transylvanian town*. Princeton: Princeton University Press.

Brusis, M. (2015). The European union and interethnic power-sharing arrangements in accession countries. *Journal on Ethnopolitics and Minority Issues in Europe, 14*(4), 60–78.

Bucur, M. (2002). *Eugenics and modernization in interwar Romania*. Pittsburgh, PA: University of Pittsburgh Press.

Budge, I., & Farlie, D. (1983). Party competition: Selective emphasis or direct confrontation? In H. Daalder & P. Mair (Eds.), *Western European party systems : Continuity & change* (pp. 267–305). Beverly Hills, CA: Sage.

Burt, R. S. (1992). *Structural holes: The social structure of competition*. Cambridge, MA: Harvard University Press.

Casanova, J. (1994). *Public religions in the modern world*. Chicago: University of Chicago Press.

CD. (2017). *Proiect de Lege pentru completarea Legii nr.95/2006 privind reforma în domeniul sănătății, precum și a art.41 din Legea asistenței sociale nr.292/2011*: Camera Deputațior, Parlamentul RomânieiPL-x nr. 73/2017. Available at: http://www.cdep.ro/pls/proiecte/upl_pck2015.proiect?cam=2&idp=15677.

Cederman, L.-E., Wimmer, A., & Min, B. (2009). Why do ethnic groups rebel? New data and analysis. *World Politics, 62*(1), 87–119.

Cenoz, J. (2001). The effect of linguistic distance, L2 status and age on cross-linguistic influence in third language acquisition. In J. Cenoz, B. Hufeisen, & U. Jessner (Eds.), *Cross-linguistic influence in third language acquisition: Psycholinguistic perspectives* (pp. 8–20). Clevedon and Buffalo: Multilingual Matters.

Cercel, C. (2017). Postwar (west) German-Romanian relations: Expanding Brubaker's analytic triad. *Nationalism and Ethnic Politics, 23*(3), 297–317.

Cernat, V. (2012). Ethnic conflict and reconciliation in post-communist Romania. In O. Simić, Z. Volčič, & C. R. Philpot (Eds.), *Peace psychology in the Balkans: Dealing with a violent past while building peace* (pp. 17–34). New York: Springer.

Chan, T. W., & Goldthorpe, J. (2004). Is there a status order in contemporary British society?: Evidence from the occupational structure of friendship. *European Sociological Review, 20*(5), 383–401.

Chan, T. W., & Goldthorpe, J. (2010). *Social status and cultural consumption.* Cambridge and New York: Cambridge University Press.

Chandra, K. (2004). *Why ethnic parties succeed: Patronage and ethnic head counts in India. Cambridge studies in comparative politics.* Cambridge and New York: Cambridge University Press.

Chandra, K. (2005). Ethnic parties and democratic stability. *Perspectives on Politics, 3*(2), 235–252.

Chandra, K. (2006). What is ethnic identity and does it matter? *Annual Review of Political Science, 9*(1), 397–424.

Chandra, K. (2011). What is an ethnic party? *Party Politics, 17*(2), 151–169.

Chandra, K. (2012). Introduction. In K. Chandra (Ed.), *Constructivist theories of ethnic politics* (pp. 1–50). New York: Oxford University Press.

Chiswick, B. R., & Miller, P. W. (2007). *The economics of language: International analyses. Routledge studies in the modern world economy.* London and New York: Routledge.

Choudhry, S. (2008). Bridging comparative politics and comparative constitutional law: Constitutional design in divided societies. In S. Choudhry (Ed.), *Constitutional design for divided societies: Integration or accommodation?* (pp. 3–40). Oxford and New York: Oxford University Press.

COMEX. (2011). *Evaluation report of the committee of experts on the application of the charter in Romania.* Council of Europe, European Charter for Regional or Minority Languages. Available at: https://rm.coe.int/16806db957.

Cormack, M. J. (1998). Minority language media in western Europe. *European Journal of Communication, 13*(1), 33–52.

Cormack, M. J. (2007). The media and language maintenance. In M. J. Cormack & N. Hourigan (Eds.), *Minority language media: Concepts, critiques and case studies* (pp. 52–69). Clevedon and Buffalo: Multilingual Matters.

Csata, I., & Kiss, T. (2007). *Népesedési perspektívák. Az erdélyi magyar népesség regionálisan tagolt népesség-előreszámítása 2022-ig és 2032-ig.* Kolozsvár: Kriterion.

Csata, Z. (2011). Confiance ou scepticisme: l'evaluation des institutions civiles et politiques en Roumanie. In D. C. Sossa (Ed.), *Nouvelles democraties et socialisation politique. Etude comparee des cas du Benin, du Bukina Faso et de la Roumanie.* Paris: L'Harmattan.

Csata, Z. (2012). The social determinants of entrepreneurial activity in rural Transylvania. *Studia Sociologia, 3*(1), 101–124.

Csata, Z. (2014a). Az erdélyi magyar tanulók iskolai teljesítményének meghatározói a TIMSS-vizsgálatok alapján. *Kisebbségkutatás, 23*(4), 126–157.

Csata, Z. (2014b). *A fogyasztói magatartás etnikai vonatkozásai a kolozsvári magyar egyetemi hallgatók körében – Kutatásjelentés*. Kolozsvár: BBTE Magyar Szociológia és Szociális Munkásképző Kar.

Csata, Z. (2015). Ethnicity and economy. A research agenda for Transylvania. *Erdélyi Társadalom, 13*(3), 31–46.

Csata, Z. (2016). Reflections on the economic aspects of multilingualism in Transylvania. *Belvedere Meridionale, 28*(2), 51–65.

Csata, Z. (2017a). Az etnikai diverzitás (polarizáció) és a jólét összefüggései Erdélyben.

Csata, Z. (2017b). Munkaerőpiaci egyenlőtlenségek Romániában, etnikai metszetbe. *Erdélyi Társadalom, 15*(1), 81–104.

Csata, Z., Dániel, B., & Pop, C. (2006). Pályakezdő fiatalok a munkaerőpiacon. *Erdélyi Társadalom, 4*(1), 7–27.

Csata, Z., & Deák, A. (2010). Gazdasági etnocentrizmus, etnikai fogyasztás az erdélyi magyarok körében. *Közgazdász Fórum, 13*(4), 31–49.

Csata, Z., Kiss, D., & Kiss, T. (2004). Az erdélyi magyar kulturális intézményrendszer. *Erdélyi Társadalom, 2*(1), 133–162.

Csata, Z., & Marácz, L. (2016). Prospects on Hungarian as a regional official language and Szeklerland's territorial autonomy in Romania. *International Journal on Minority and Group Rights, 23*(4), 530–559.

Csata, Z., & Pásztor, G. (2015). *Összehasonlító régiótanulmány a vidéki turizmusra és a foglalkoztatottságra vonatkozóan Bihar és Kovászna megyében*. Bukarest: OTP Consulting.

Csepeli, G., Székely, M., & Örkény, A. (2002). *Nemzetek egymás tükrében. Interetnikus viszonyok a Kárpát-medencében*. Budapest: Balassi.

Csergő, Z. (2002). Beyond ethnic division: Majority-minority debate about the postcommunist state in Romania and Slovakia. *East European Politics & Societies, 16*(1), 1–29.

Csergő, Z. (2007). *Talk of the nation: Language and conflict in Romania and Slovakia*. Ithaca: Cornell University Press.

Csergő, Z. (2013). Kosovo and the framing of non-secessionist self-government claims in Romania. *Europe-Asia Studies, 65*(5), 889–911.

Csergő, Z., & Goldgeier, J. M. (2004). Nationalist strategies and European integration. *Perspectives on Politics, 2*(1), 21–37.

Csergő, Z., & Goldgeier, J. M. (2006). Virtual nationalism in comparative context: How unique is the Hungarian approach? In I. Osamu (Ed.),

Beyond sovereignty: From status law to transnational citizenship? (pp. 281–302). Sapporo: Slavic Research Center, Hokkaido University.

Csergő, Z., & Regelmann, A.-C. (2017). Europeanization and collective rationality in minority voting. *Problems of Post-Communism, 64*(5), 291–310.

Csigó, P. (2016). '89 mint társadalmi csapda. In G. Földes & A. Antal (Eds.), *Holtpont. Társadalomkritikai tanulmányok Magyarország elmúlt 25 évéről* (pp. 106–145). Budapest: Napvilág.

Culic, I. (2016). Hungarian society in Romania: Political project and practical reality. In S. P. Ramet & M. Valenta (Eds.), *Ethnic minorities and politics in post-socialist southeastern Europe* (pp. 191–210). New York: Cambridge University Press.

Dániel, B. (2011). Erdélyi magyar fiatalok jövőterveinek, munkaerő-piaci helyzetének, etnikai fogyasztásának vizsgálata. In A. Szabó, B. Bauer, & P. Pillók (Eds.), *Mozaik 2011 – Magyar fiatalok a Kárpát-medencében. Kutatási jelentés* (pp. 169–198). Szeged and Budapest: Belvedere Meridionale and Nemzeti Család- és Szociálpolitikai Intézet.

Dániel, B. (2014). Az erdélyi magyar nonprofit hátterű szociális szféra szociológiai jellemzői. *Civil Szemle, 11*(1), 81–107.

Dániel, B., & Kiss, D. (2014). Sociological analysis of the resources of the Hungarian cultural organizations in Romania. *Civil Szemle, 11*(4), 71–106.

de Swaan, A. (1991). Notes on the emerging global language system: Regional, national and supranational. *Media, Culture & Society, 13*(3), 309–323.

de Vries, J. (1985). Some methodological aspects of self-report questions on language and ethnicity. *Journal of Multilingual and Multicultural Development, 6*(5), 347–368.

Diaconescu, M. (2008). The identity crisis of Moldavian catholics—Between politics and historic myths. A case study: The myths of Romanian origin. In S. Ilyés, L. Peti, & F. Pozsony (Eds.), *Local and transnational Csángó lifeworlds* (pp. 81–93). Cluj-Napoca: Kriza János Ethnographical Society.

Diamond, L. J. (2002). Thinking about hybrid regimes. *Journal of Democracy, 13*(2), 21–35.

DiMaggio, P. J., & Anheier, H. K. (1990). The sociology of nonprofit organizations and sectors. *Annual Review of Sociology, 16*(1), 137–159.

Dobos, F. (2012). *Nemzeti identitás, asszimiláció és médiahasználat a határon túli magyarság körében, 1999–2011*. Budapest: Médiatudományi Intézet.

Dobos, F., & Megyeri, K. (2014). *Nemzeti identitás, asszimiláció és médiahasználat a határon túli magyarság körében 2*. Budapest: Médiatudományi Intézet.

Dobre, A. M. (2003). EU conditionality building and Romanian minority rights policy: Towards the Europeanisation of the candidate countries. *Perspectives on European Politics and Society, 4*(1), 55–83.

Domokos, G. (1991, February 12). Az irreális azonnaliság nem lehet kenyerünk. Válasz Eva Maria Barkinak. *Romániai Magyar Szó.*

Domokos, G. (1996). *Esély I.* Csíkszereda: Pallas-Akadémia.

Dribe, M., & Lundh, C. (2011). Cultural dissimilarity and intermarriage. A longitudinal study of immigrants in Sweden 1990–2005. *International Migration Review, 45*(2), 297–324.

Dumbrava, C. (2016). Reproducing the nation: Reproduction, citizenship and ethno-demographic survival in post-communist Romania. *Journal of Ethnic and Migration Studies, 43*(9), 1490–1507.

Egry, G. (2008). *Az erdélyiség színeváltozása. Kísérlet az Erdélyi Párt ideológiájának és identitáspolitikájának elemzésére, 1940–1944.* Budapest: Napvilág.

Egry, G. (2014). Nép, nemzet, állam, társadalom: „népszolgáló" közösségkép és közösségszervezés az erdélyi magyar kisebbségi politikában. In N. Bárdi & T. G. Filep (Eds.), *A népszolgálat fogalomtörténete* (pp. 48–71). Pozsony: Kaligramm.

Egry, G. (2015). *Etnicitás, identitás, politika: magyar kisebbségek nacionalizmus és regionalizmus között Romániában és Csehszlovákiában 1918–1944* (Első kiadás ed.). Budapest: Napvilág.

Emigh, R. J., & Szelényi, I. (Eds.). (2000). *Poverty, ethnicity, and gender in eastern Europe during the market transition.* Westport, CT: Praeger.

Enache, S., Andreescu, L., Ardelean, L., Cernea, R., Kacsó, J.-A., Moise, E., & Szokoly, E. (2008). *Educaţia religioasă în şcolile publice.* Târgu-Mureş: Liga Pro Europa.

Eriksen, T. H. (2005). Economies of ethnicity. In J. G. Carrier (Ed.), *A handbook of economic anthropology* (pp. 353–369). Cheltenham, UK and Northhampton, MA: Edward Elgar.

Eurobarometer. (2012). *Special Eurobarometer 386: Europeans and their languages.* European Commission. Available at: http://ec.europa.eu/public_opinion/archives/ebs/ebs_386_en.pdf.

EVS. (2011). European values study 2008: Integrated dataset (EVS 2008) (Version 3.0.0) (Accessed 20 November 2011).

Faingold, E. D. (2004). Language rights and language justice in the constitutions of the world. *Language Problems and Language Planning, 28*(1), 11–24.

Faist, T. (2010). Diaspora and transnationalism: What kind of dance partners? In R. Bauböck & T. Faist (Eds.), *Diaspora and transnationalism: Concepts, theories and methods* (pp. 9–35). Amsterdam: Amsterdam University Press.

Farkas, R. (2011, July 5). Leváltani kényszerülnek a könyvtárigazgatót (Pert nyert a prefektúra). *Háromszék*. Avaialble at: http://www.3szek.ro/load/cikk/40557/levaltani_kenyszerulnek_a_konyvtarigazgatot_pert_nyert_a_prefektura.

Fassmann, H., & Münz, R. (1994). European east-west migration, 1945–1992. *International Migration Review, 28*(3), 520–538.

Fazakas, E. (Ed.). (2002). *Román–magyar közigazgatási szótár*. Sepsiszentgyörgy: Anyanyelvápolók Erdélyi Szövetsége.

Fearon, J. D. (1999). *Why ethnic politics and 'pork' tend to go together* (Working Paper). Stanford, CA: Stanford University.

Fearon, J. D., & Laitin, D. D. (2000). Violence and the social construction of ethnic identity. *International Organization, 54*(4), 845–877.

Feischmidt, M. (2005). A magyar nacionalizmus autenticitás-diskurzusainak szimbolikus térfoglalása Erdélyben. In M. Feischmidt (Ed.), *Erdély-(de) konstrukciók* (pp. 7–32). Budapest and Pécs: Néprajzi Múzeum, PTE Kommunikáció and és Médiatudományok Tanszék.

Fenton, S. (2003). *Ethnicity key concepts*. Cambridge and Malden, MA: Polity Press.

Finnäs, F. (1997). Social integration, heterogeneity, and divorce: The case of the Swedish-speaking population in Finland. *Acta Sociologica, 40*(3), 263–277.

Finnäs, F., & O'Leary, B. (2003). Choosing for the children: The affiliation of the children of minority–majority group intermarriages. *European Sociological Review, 19*(5), 483–499.

Fishman, J. A. (1972). *The sociology of language: An interdisciplinary social science approach to language in society*. Rowley, MA: Newbury House.

Fishman, J. A. (1989). *Language and ethnicity in minority sociolinguistic perspective*. Clevedon, Avon, and Philadelphia: Multilingual Matters.

Fishman, J. A. (1991). *Reversing language shift: Theoretical and empirical foundations of assistance to threatened languages*. Clevedon and Philadelphia: Multilingual Matters.

Fishman, J. A. (2000). Who speaks what language to whom and when? In L. Wei (Ed.), *The bilingualism reader* (pp. 82–98). London and New York: Routledge.

Fishman, J. A. (2001). From theory to practice (and vice versa): Review, reconsideration and reiteration. In J. A. Fishman (Ed.), *Can threatened languages be saved?: Reversing language shift, revisited: A 21st century perspective* (pp. 451–483). Clevedon and Buffalo: Multilingual Matters.

Fleisz, J. (2005). *Az erdélyi magyar sajtó története 1890–1940* (p. 288). Pécs: Pannónia.

Furnivall, J. S. (1948). *Colonial policy and practice: A comparative study of Burma and Netherlands India. Issued in co-operation with the International Secretariat, Institute of Pacific Relations*. Cambridge: Cambridge University Press.

Gáll, E., & Keszeg, J. (2014). A tanügyi rendszer működésének vizsgálata a magyar nyelv- és irodalomoktatás tükrében. *Magyar Kisebbség, 19*(2), 85–116.

Gáll, Z. (2011). Fából vaskarika? Avagy: lehet-e a székely termék világmárka? *Pro Minoritate, 15*(2), 54–71.

Gans, H. J. (1979). Symbolic ethnicity: The future of ethnic groups and cultures in America*. *Ethnic and Racial Studies, 2*(1), 1–20.

Geambaşu, R. (2017). „A kódolás élvezete". A kolozsvári programozók.

Gheorghe, M. (2004). *Religie şi schimbare socială în România*. Iași: Editura Fundaţiei Axis.

Gherghina, S., & Jiglau, G. (2011). Explaining ethnic mobilisation in post-communist countries. *Europe-Asia Studies, 63*(1), 49–76.

Gheţău, V. (1996). O proiectare condiţională a populaţiei României pe principale naţionalităţi (1992–2025). *Revista de Cercetări Sociale, 3*(1), 77–105.

Gheţău, V. (2013, Auguest 7). Recensământul și aventure INS cu datele finale. *cursdeguvernare.ro*. Avaialble at: http://cursdeguvernare.ro/recensamantul-si-aventura-ins-prin-datele-finale.html.

Giles, H., Bourhis, R. Y., & Taylor, D. M. (1977). Toward a theory of language in ethnic group relations. In H. Giles (Ed.), *Language, ethnicity, and intergroup relations* (pp. 307–348). London and New York: Academic Press.

Gödri, I. (2004). A magyarországra bevándorolt népesség jellemzői, különös tekintettel a Romániából bevándorlókra. In T. Kiss (Ed.), *Népesedési folyamatok az ezredfordulón Erdélyben* (pp. 126–147). Kolozsvár: Kriterion and RMDSZ Ügyvezető Elnökség.

Gödri, I., & Tóth, P. P. (2005). *Bevándorlás és beilleszkedés*. Budapest: KSH Népességkutató Intézet.

Goldscheider, C. (1986). *Jewish continuity and change: Emerging patterns in America. Jewish political and social studies*. Bloomington: Indiana University Press.

Goodman, R., & Jinks, D. (2004). How to influence states: Socialization and international human rights law. *Duke Law Journal, 54*(3), 621–703.

Gordon, M. M. (1964). *Assimilation in American life: The role of race, religion, and national origins*. New York: Oxford University Press.

Gorenburg, D. (2006). Rethinking interethnic marriage in the Soviet Union. *Post-Soviet Affairs, 22*(2), 145–165.

Gorenburg, D. P. (2003). *Minority ethnic mobilization in the Russian Federation.* Cambridge and New York: Cambridge University Press.

Granovetter, M. (1973). The strength of weak ties. *American Journal of Sociology, 78*(6), 1360–1380.

Granovetter, M. (1985). Economic action and social structure: The problem of embeddedness. *American Journal of Sociology, 91*(3), 481–510.

Granovetter, M. (1995). The economic sociology of firms and entrepreneurs. In A. Portes (Ed.), *The economic sociology of immigration: Essays on networks, ethnicity, and entrepreneurship* (pp. 128–162). New York: Russell Sage Foundation.

Grin, F. (2003). *Language policy evaluation and the European Charter for regional or minority languages.* Basingstoke, Hampshire and New York: Palgrave Macmillan.

Grin, F. (2004). On the costs of cultural diversity. In P. V. Parijs (Ed.), *Cultural diversity versus economic solidarity: Proceedings of the Seventh Francqui Colloquium, Brussels, 28 February–1 March 2003* (1st ed., pp. 189–202). Bruxelles: De Boeck.

Grin, F., Ahmad, Z., & Sfreddo, C. (Eds.). (1997). *Langue et différentiels de statut socio-économique en Suisse.* Berne: Office fédéral de la statistique.

Gündüz-Hoşgör, A., & Smits, J. (2002). Intermarriage between Turks and Kurds in contemporary Turkey: Inter-ethnic relations in an urbanizing environment. *European Sociological Review, 18*(4), 417–432.

György, B. (Ed.). (2003). *Iratok a Romániai Országos Magyar Párt történetéhez.* Csíkszereda and Kolozsvár: Pro-Print and Erdélyi Múzeum Egyesület.

Gyurgyík, L. (2004). A szlovákiai magyarság társadalmi szerkezetének alakulása 1980–2001 között. *Korall, 18,* 155–176.

Gyurgyík, L. (2008). A szlovákiai magyarok társadalomszerkezete a 90-es években. *Regio, 19*(4), 77–102.

Gyurgyík, L., Horváth, I., & Kiss, T. (2011). Demográfiai folyamatok, etno-kulturális és társadalmi reprodukció. In B. Bitskey (Ed.), *Határon túli magyarság a 21. Században* (pp. 69–119). Budapest: Köztársasági Elnöki Hivatal.

Gyurgyík, L., & Kiss, T. (2010). *Párhuzamok és különbségek. A második világháború utáni erdélyi és szlovákiai magyar népességfejlődés összehasonlító elemzése.* Budapest: EÖKIK.

Hall, P. A., & Taylor, R. C. R. (1996). Political science and the three new institutionalisms. *Political Studies, 44*(5), 936–957.

Hannerz, U. (2000). *Flow, boundaries and hybrids: Keywords in transnational anthropology* (Working Paper Series No. WPTC-2K-02). Stockholm: Department of Social Anthropology, Stockholm University.

Hărăguş, M. (2014). The role of education in ethnically mixed marriages. In L. A. Dumănescu, D. Mârza, & M. Eppel (Eds.), *Intermarriage throughout history* (pp. 389–407). Newcaslte upon Tyne: Cambridge Scholars.

Hărăguş, M. (2017). Considerations on ethnically mixed marriages in Transylvania in the last few decades. In I. Bolovan & L. A. Dumănescu (Eds.), *Intermarriage in Transylvania, 1895–2010* (pp. 117–125). Frankfurt am Main: Peter Lang.

Hartford, T. (2016). *Messy: How to be creative and resilient in a tidy-minded world.* London: Little, Brown Book Group.

Hirsch, F. (2004). Towards a Soviet order of things: The 1926 census and the making of the Soviet Union. In S. Szreter, H. Sholkamy, & A. Dharmalingam (Eds.), *Categories and contexts: Anthropological and historical studies in critical demography* (pp. 126–147). Oxford: Oxford University Press.

Hodžić, E., & Mraović, B. (2015). Political representation of minorities in Bosnia and Herzegovina: How reserved seats affect minority representatives' influence on decision-making and perceived substantive representation. *Ethnopolitics, 14*(4), 418–434.

Horowitz, D. L. (1985). *Ethnic groups in conflict.* Berkeley: University of California Press.

Horowitz, D. L. (1991). *A democratic South Africa?: Constitutional engineering in a divided society perspectives on southern Africa.* Berkeley: University of California Press.

Horváth, A. (2015). Inkább gazda volnék, mint politikus. In J. Szántai (Ed.). *foter.ro.*

Horváth, I. (2002). *Facilitating conflict transformation: Implementation of the recommendations of the OSCE high commissioner on national minorities to Romania, 1993–2001* (Working Paper). Hamburg: CORE.

Horváth, I. (2003). Az erdélyi magyarok kétnyelvűsége: nyelvmentés és integráció között? *Erdélyi Társadalom, 1*(1), 7–24.

Horváth, I. (2004a). Az erdélyi magyar fiatalok Magyarország irányú tanulási migrációja 1990–2000. *Erdélyi Társadalom, 2*(2), 59–84.

Horváth, I. (2004b). Az etnikailag vegyes házasságok az erdélyi magyar lakosság körében: 1992–2002. In T. Kiss (Ed.), *Népesedési folyamatok az ezredfordulón Erdélyben* (pp. 235–257) Kolozsvár: Kriterion and RMDSZ Ügyvezető Elnökség.

Horváth, I. (2005a). *Erdély és Magyarország közötti migrációs folyamatok*. Kolozsvár: Scientia.

Horváth, I. (2005b). A romániai magyarok kétnyelvűsége: nyelvismeret, nyelvhasználat, nyelvi dominancia. Regionális összehasonlító elemzések. *Erdélyi Társadalom, 3*(1), 171–200.

Horváth, I. (2008a). *Elemzések a romániai magyarok kétnyelvűségéről* (ISPMN Working Paper No. 8).

Horváth, I. (2008b). Evaluarea politicilor lingvistice din România. In L. Salat (Ed.), *Politici de integrare a minorităților naționale din România. Aspecte legale și instituționale într-o perspectivă comparată* (pp. 203–213). Cluj-Napoca: CRDE.

Horváth, I. (2008c). A romániai nyelvpolitikák értékelése. *Magyar Kisebbség, 13*(3–4), 263–277.

Horváth, I. (2009). Nyelvi készségek, nyelvi viselkedés és etnokulturális reprodukció az erdélyi magyar népesség vonatkozásában. In Z. Spéder (Ed.), *Párhuzamok. Anyaországi és erdélyi magyarok a századfordulón* (pp. 153–182). Budapest: KSH Népességtudományi Kutatóintézet.

Horváth, I. (2011). A romániai magyarok nyilvános nyelvhasználatának mintázatai. In I. Horváth & E. Tódor (Eds.), *Nyelvhasználat, tannyelv és két(több) nyelvű lét* (pp. 115–136). Cluj-Napoca: ISPMN.

Horváth, I. (2012). Románia: a kisebbségi nyelvi jogok és intézményes érvényesülésük. In K. Eplényi & Z. Kántor (Eds.), *Térvesztés és határtalanítás: a magyar nyelvpolitika 21. századi kihívásai* (pp. 172–198). Budapest: Nemzetpolitikai Kutatóintézet and Lucidus.

Horváth, I. (2013). The Romanian Roma: The dilemma of integration. In E. Dácz (Ed.), *Minderheitenfragen in Ungarn und in den Nachbarländern im 20. und 21. Jahrhundert* (pp. 305–325). Baden-Baden: Nomos.

Horváth, I., & Kiss, T. (2015). Depopulating semi-periphery? Longer term dynamics of migration and socioeconomic development in Romania. *Demográfia English Edition, 58*(5), 91–132.

Horváth, I., & Kiss, T. (2017). Ancheta experților locali privind situația romilor pe unități administrativ-teritoriale. In I. Horváth (Ed.), *Raport de cercetare – SocioRoMap. O cartografiere a comunităților de romi din România* (pp.

9–190). Cluj-Napoca: Editura Institutului pentru Studierea Problemelor Minorităţilor Naţionale.

Horváth, I., & Lazăr, M. (2001). Dinamica relațiilor interetnice din ultimul deceniu. *Altera,* 16, 120–136.

Horváth, I., & Scacco, A. (2001). From the unitary to the pluralistic: Fine-tuning minority policy in Romania. In A. Bíró & P. Kovács (Eds.), *Diversity in action: Local public management of multiethnic communities in central and eastern Europe* (pp. 243–271). Budapest: OSI.

Horváth, I., Veress, I., & Vitos, K. (2010). *Közigazgatási nyelvhasználat Hargita megyében az önkormányzati és a központi kormányzat megyeszintű intézményeiben* (ISPMN Working Paper No. 27).

Horváth, S. F. (2007). *Elutasítás és alkalmazkodás között: a romániai magyar kisebbségi elit politikai stratégiái (1931–1940).* Csíkszereda: Pro-Print.

Horváth, Z. (1995). Katolikus bázisközösségi mozgalmak. In Z. Horváth (Ed.), *Hitek és emberek.* Budapest: ELTE Szociológiai-Szociálpolitikai Intézet.

Hroch, M. (1985). *Social preconditions of national revival in Europe: A comparative analysis of the social composition of patriotic groups among the smaller European nations.* Cambridge and New York: Cambridge University Press.

Hunya, G. (1990). Románia területi fejlődése és gazdaságpolitikája. In G. Hunya, T. Réti, A. R. Süle, & L. Tóth (Eds.), *Románia 1944–1990. Gazdaság és politikatörténet* (pp. 159–181). Budapest: Atlantisz-Medvetánc.

Hunyadi, A. (2006). Three paradigms of cooperative movements with nationalist taxonomy in Transylvania. In T. Lorenz (Ed.), *Cooperatives in ethnic conflicts: Eastern Europe in the 19th and early 20th century* (Vol. 15, pp. 59–102). Berlin: Berliner Wissenschafts-Verlag.

Ioanid, R. (2005). *The ransom of the jews: The story of the extraordinary secret bargain between Romania and Israel.* Chicago: Ivan R. Dee.

Järve, P. (2000). *Ethnic democracy and Estonia: Application of Smooha's Model* (ECMI Working Paper No. 7).

Jenkins, R. (2008). *Rethinking ethnicity* (2nd ed.). Thousand Oaks, CA: Sage.

Jenne, E. K. (2007). *Ethnic bargaining: The paradox of minority empowerment.* Ithaca, NY: Cornell University Press.

Joppke, C. (2005). *Selecting by origin: Ethnic migration and liberal state.* Cambridge, MA: Harvard University Press.

Kacsó, S. (Ed.). (1937). *Erdélyi magyar évkönyv, 1937. A kisebbségi magyar polgár kézikönyve.* Brassó: Brassói Lapok.

Kalmijn, M. (1998). Intermarriage and homogamy: Causes, patterns, trends. *Annual Review of Sociology, 24*, 395–421.

Kalmijn, M., & Tubergen, F. V. (2010). A comparative perspective on intermarriage: Explaining differences among national-origin groups in the United States. *Demography, 47*(2), 459–479.

Kalmijn, M., de Graaf, P. M., & Janssen, J. P. G. (2005). Intermarriage and the risk of divorce in the Netherlands: The effects of differences in religion and in nationality, 1974–1994. *Population Studies, 59*(1), 71–85.

Kántor, Z. (2000). Kisebbségi nemzetépítés. A romániai magyarság mint nemzetépítő kisebbség. *Regio, 11*(3), 219–241.

Kántor, Z. (2001). Nationalizing minorities and homeland politics: The case of the Hungarians in Romania. In B. Trencsényi (Ed.), *Nation-building and contested identities: Romanian and Hungarian case studies* (pp. 249–274). Budapest: Regio Books; Iași: Polirom.

Kántor, Z. (2014). *A nemzet intézményesülése a rendszerváltás utáni Magyarországon* (p. 298). Budapest: Osiris.

Kántor, Z., & Bárdi, N. (2002). The Democratic Alliance of Hungarians in Romania (DAHR) in the Government of Romania from 1996 to 2000. *Regio—Minorities, Politics, Society, 2*(1), 188–226.

Kántor, Z., Majtényi, B., Ieda, O., Vizi, B., & Halász, I. (Eds.). (2004). *Beyond sovereignty: From status law to transnational citizenship?* Sappuro: 21st century COE program Slavic Eurasian studies.

Kapitány, B. (2013). Kárpát-medencei népszámlálási körkép. *Demográfia, 56*(1), 25–64.

Kapitány, B., & Spéder, Z. (2004). *Szegénység és depriváció. Társadalmi összefüggések nyomában.* KSH-NKI, Műhelytanulmányok, 4.

Kaplan, R. B., & Baldauf, R. B. (1997). *Language planning from practice to theory*. Clevedon and Philadelphia: Multilingual Matters.

Karády, V. (2000). Magyar kultúrfölény vagy etnokrata önámítás? Mire jók a dualista kor nemzetiségi statisztikái? *Educatio, 9*(2), 239–252.

Karpov, V. (2010). Desecularization: A conceptual framework. *Journal of Church and State, 52*(2), 232–270.

Kasapović, M. (2005). Bosnia and Herzegovina: Consociational or liberal democracy? *Politička misao, 17*(5), 3–30.

Keck, M. E., & Sikkink, K. (1999). Transnational advocacy networks in international and regional politics. *International Social Science Journal, 51*(159), 89–101.

Kertzer, D. I., & Arel, D. (Eds.). (2002). *Census and identity: The politics of race, ethnicity, and language in national census*. Cambridge and New York: Cambridge University Press.

Kideckel, D. A. (2008). *Getting by in postsocialist Romania : Labor, the body, & working-class culture*. Bloomington, IN: Indiana University Press.

Kiss, D. (2004). A falusi elit átalakulása. *WEB, 12*, 9–15.

Kiss, D. (2006). Az erdélyi magyar civil szféráról. *Civil Szemle, 3*(2), 139–154.

Kiss, D. (2009). *Revivalist movements in the Romaniai historical churches* (REVACERN Paper No. 78).

Kiss, D. (2010). *Romániai magyar nonprofit szervezetek – 2009–2010* (ISPMN Working Paper No. 37).

Kiss, T. (2004). Vállalkozástörténetek Erdélyben. In É. Kovács (Ed.), *A gazdasági átmenet etnikai tájképei* (pp. 23–128). Budapest: Teleki László Alapítvány.

Kiss, T. (2006). Interethnic marriages and assimilation in demographic models. In B. Z. Balogh & Z. N. Ilyés (Eds.), *Perspectives of diaspora existence: Hungarian diasporas in the Carpathian Basin: Historical and current contexts of a specific diaspora interpretation and its aspects of ethnic minority protection* (pp. 107–139). Budapest: Akadémiai Kiadó.

Kiss, T. (2015). Increasing marginality, ethnic parallelism and asymmetric accommodation. Social and political processes concerning the Hungarian community of Transylvania. *Minority Studies, 18*, 33–69.

Kiss, T. (2017a). Beyond the ethnic vote: Shifting determinants of the electoral behavior of Transylvanian Hungarians. *Problems of Post-Communism*, 1–17. https://doi.org/10.1080/10758216.2017.1336422.

Kiss, T. (2017b). Diferențe etnolingvistice în performanța școlară. Dimensiuni neexplorate ale datelor PISA. Manuscript.

Kiss, T., Barna, G., & Duduj, S. (2016). *Médiafogyasztási szokások Erdélyben. Kutatásjelentés*. Kolozsvár: Nemzeti Kisebbségkutató Intézet.

Kiss, T., & Kapitány, B. (2009). Magyarok Erdélyben: A minta kialakítása és az adatfelvétel. In Z. Spéder (Ed.), *Párhuzamok. Anyaországi és erdélyi magyarok a századfordulón* (pp. 31–54). Budapest: KSH Népességtudományi Kutatóintézet.

Kiss, J., & Kató, K. (2014). *Jogaink Romániában Magyarul*. Kolozsvár: Jogaink Egyesület.

Kiss, T., & Székely, I. G. (2016). Shifting linkages in ethnic mobilization: The case of RMDSZ and the Hungarians in Transylvania. *Nationalities Papers, 44*(4), 591–610.

Kiss, T., Székely, I. G., & Barna, G. (2017). Factors affecting turnout among ethnic minority voters: The case of Hungarians in Transylvania. *Intersections-East European Journal of Society and Politics, 3*(4), 87–119.

Kitschelt, H. (2001). Divergent paths of postcommunist democracies. In L. J. Diamond & R. Gunther (Eds.), *Political parties and democracy* (pp. 299–326). Baltimore, MD: Johns Hopkins University Press.

Kligman, G. (1998). *The politics of duplicity: Controlling reproduction in Ceausescu's Romania*. Berkeley: University of California Press.

Kligman, G., & Verdery, K. (2011). *Peasants under siege : The collectivization of Romanian agriculture, 1949–1962*. Princeton: Princeton University Press.

Klimkiewicz, B. (2003). Media policy for ethnic and national minorities in Poland, the Czech republic and Slovakia. In M. S. Sükösd & P. T. Bajomi-Lázár (Eds.), *Reinventing media: Media policy reform in east-central Europe* (pp. 155–184). Budapest and New York: Central European University Press.

Klimkiewicz, B. (2015). Cultural and geographical dimensions of media pluralism. In P. Valcke, M. S. Sükösd, & R. G. Picard (Eds.), *Media pluralism and diversity: Concepts, risks and global trends* (pp. 82–106). Houndmills, Basingstoke, Hampshire and New York: Palgrave Macmillan.

Kontra, M. (1999). "Don't speak Hungarian in public!" A documentation and analysis of folk linguistic rights. In M. S. Kontra, R. Phillipson, T. Skutnabb-Kangas, & T. Várady (Eds.), *Language, a right and a resource: Approaches to linguistics human right* (p. xi, 346 p) Budapest and New York: Central European University Press.

Kontra, M., & Szilágyi, N. S. (2002). A kisebbségeknek van anyanyelvük, de a többségnek nincs. In M. Kontra & H. Hattyár (Eds.), *Magyarok és nyelvtörvények*. Budapest: Teleki László Alapítvány.

Kopecký, P., & Scherlis, G. (2008). Party patronage in contemporary Europe. *European Review, 16*(3), 355–371.

Köpeczi, B., Miskolczy, A., & Szász, Z. (1986). *Erdély története. Harmadik kötet*. Budapest: Akadémiai Kiadó.

Kovács, E. (2007, Január). Az Erdélyi Evangélikus Nőszövetség történetéből. *Művelődés*.

Kovács, M., & Tóth, J. (2013). *EUDO citizenship observatory country report: Hungary*. Florence: EUDO.

Kukutai, T., & Thompson, V. (2015). 'Inside out': The politics of enumerating the nation by ethnicity. In P. Simon, V. Piché, & A. A. Gagnon (Eds.),

Social statistics and ethnic diversity: Cross-national perspectives in classifications and identity politics (pp. 39–61). Cham: Springer.
Kusá, D. (2013). *EUDO citizenship observatory country report: Slovakia*. Florence: EUDO.
Kuszálik, P. (2010). *Erdélyi Katolikus Nőszövetség*. Magyar Katolikus Lexikon. Budapest: Szent István Társulat. Available at: http://lexikon.katolikus.hu/E/Erd%C3%A9lyi%20Katolikus%20N%C5%91sz%C3%B6vets%C3%A9g.html (Accessed 2 February 2018).
Kymlicka, W. (1995). *Multicultural citizenship: A liberal theory of minority rights: A liberal theory of minority rights*. Oxford: Clarendon Press.
Kymlicka, W. (2007). *Multicultural odysseys: Navigating the new international politics of diversity*. Oxford and New York: Oxford University Press.
Kymlicka, W. (2011). Beyond the indigenous/minority dichotomy? In S. Allen & A. Xanthaki (Eds.), *Reflections on the UN declaration on the rights of indigenous peoples* (pp. 183–208). Oxford and Portland, OR: Hart Publishing.
Ladányi, J., & Szelényi, I. (2006). *Patterns of exclusion: Constructing Gypsy ethnicity and the making of an underclass in transitional societies of Europe*. New York: Columbia University Press.
Laitin, D. D. (1995). Marginality: A microperspective. *Rationality and Society, 7*(1), 31–57.
Laitin, D. D. (1996). National revival and competitive assimilation in Estonia. *Post-Soviet Affairs, 12*(1), 25–39.
Laitin, D. D. (1998). *Identity in formation: The Russian-speaking populations in the near abroad. The Wilder House series in politics, history, and culture*. Ithaca: Cornell University Press.
Laitin, D. D., & Van der Veen, M. A. (2012). Ethnicity and pork: A virtual test of causal mechanisms. In K. Chandra (Ed.), *Constructivist theories of ethnic politics* (pp. 341–358). New York: Oxford University Press.
Lamont, M., & Molnár, V. (2002). The study of boundaries in the social sciences. *Annual Review of Sociology, 28*(1), 167–195.
Lamont, M., Silva, G. M., Welburn, J. S., Guetzkow, J., Mizrachi, N., Herzog, H., & Reis, E. (2016). *Getting respect: Responding to stigma and discrimination in the United States, Brazil, and Israel*. Princeton: Princeton University Press.
Lancee, B. (2012). *Immigrant performance in the labour market: Bonding and bridging social capital*. IMISCOE Research. Amsterdam: Amsterdam University Press.

Landa, J. T. (1994). *Trust, ethnicity, and identity: Beyond the new institutional economics of ethnic trading networks, contract law, and gift-exchange. Economics, cognition, and society*. Ann Arbor: University of Michigan Press.

László, M., & Novák, C. Z. (2012). *A szabadság terhe. Marosvásárhely, 1990. március 16–21*. Csíkszereda: Pro-Print.

László, S. (2013, April 18–20). Neglected peripheries: Discovering hybridity in Transylvania. *Identities and identifications: Politicized uses of collective identities*. Zagreb.

Laumann, E. O., & Guttman, L. (1966). The relative associational contiguity of occupations in an urban setting. *American Sociological Review, 31*(2), 169.

Lee, R. (2004). Reflections on inverse projection: Its origins, development, extensions and relation to forecast. In E. Barbi, S. Bertino, & E. Sonnino (Eds.), *Inverse projection techniques: Old and new approaches*. Berlin and New York: Springer.

Lenski, G. E. (1966). *Power and privilege: A theory of social stratification. McGraw-Hill series in sociology*. New York: McGraw-Hill.

Levchenko, P. (2013). *Transnational marriages between eastern European-born wives and U.S.-born husbands*. Ph.D. dissertation, University of Minnesota, Minnesota.

Lewis, T., & Potter, E. (2011). *Ethical consumption: A critical introduction*. London and New York: Routledge.

Liebich, A. (2009). Altneul€ander or the vicissitudes of citizenship in the New EU states. In R. Bauböck & B. Perchinig (Eds.), *Citizenship policies in the New Europe* (Expanded and updated ed., pp. 21–42). Amsterdam: Amsterdam University Press.

Light, I. H., & Gold, S. J. (2000). *Ethnic economies*. San Diego: Academic Press.

Lijphart, A. (1969). Consociational democracy. *World Politics, 21*(2), 207–225.

Lijphart, A. (1977). *Democracy in plural societies: A comparative exploration*. New Haven: Yale University Press.

Lijphart, A. (2004). Constitutional design for divided societies. *Journal of Democracy, 15*(2), 96–109.

Liu, A. H. (2015). *Standardizing diversity: The political economy of language regimes*. Philadelphia: University of Pennsylvania Press.

Livezeanu, I. (1995). *Cultural politics in Greater Romania: Regionalism, nation building & ethnic struggle, 1918–1930*. Ithaca: Cornell University Press.

Longman, T. (2001). Church politics and the genocide in Rwanda. *Journal of Religion in Africa, 31*(2), 163–186.

Lőnhárt, T. (2008). *Uniunea Populară Maghiară în perioada instaurării regimului comunist în România*. Cluj-Napoca: Argonaut.

Lőrincz, J. D. (2004). Ambivalent discourse in eastern Europe. *Regio: A Review of Studies on Minorities, Politics, and Societies, 4*(1), 148–171.

Lőrincz, D. J. (2008). A kolozsvári magyarok társadalma. *Regio, 19*(2), 240–256.

Ludanyi, A. (1995). Programmed Amnesia and rude awakening: Hungarian minorities in international politics, 1945–1989. In I. C. Romsics (Ed.), *20th century Hungary and the great powers* (p. vii, 391 p). Boulder, CO: Social Science Monographs; Highland Lakes, NJ: Atlantic Research and Publications; New York: Distributed by Columbia University Press.

Magyar, B. (2016). *Post-communist mafia state: The case of Hungary*. Budapest: Central European University Press, in association with Noran Libro.

Magyari, T. (2003). Elemzések a romániai magyarok sajtóolvasási szokásairól. *Erdélyi Társadalom, 1*(1), 113–131.

Magyari, T. (2014, October 13). Vitaindító a közoktatásról. *transindex.ro*. Avaialble at: http://welemeny.transindex.ro/?cikk=24541 (Accessed 2 February 2018).

Magyari, T. (2017). Az erdélyi magyarok nyilvánosságának általános jegyei. In N. Bárdi & G. Éger (Eds.), *Huszonöt év. Magyarok Románában, 1990–2015. Tanulmányok az erdélyi magyarságról* (pp. 395–406). Budapest: L'Hartmattan.

Malloy, T. H., Osipov, A., & Vizi, B. (Eds.). (2015). *Managing diversity through non-territorial autonomy: Assessing advantages, deficiencies, and risks*. Oxford: Oxford University Press.

Markó, B. (2008). Egy elmaradt egyezség története. *Élet és Irodalom* (no. 38).

Markó, B. (2009). Kormányból ellenzékbe. A romániai magyar politika tizenkét éve. *Élet és irodalom* (no. 3).

Márton, J. (2012). A 2009-ben és 2010-ben érettségizett romániai magyar diákok továbbtanulása. *Educatio, 13*(1), 87–103.

Márton, J., & Orbán, B. (2005). Elemzés a 2005-ös kisebbségi törvénytervezetről. *Magyar Kisebbség, 9*(1–2), 5–38.

McGarry, J., O'Leary, B., & Simeon, R. (2008). Integration or accommodation? In S. Choudhry (Ed.), *Constitutional design for divided societies: Integration or accommodation?* (pp. 41–88). Oxford and New York: Oxford University Press.

McRae, K. D. (1975). The principle of territoriality and the principle of personality in multilingual states. *International Journal of the Sociology of Language, 1975*(4), 33–54.

Medianu, N. (2002). Analysing political exchanges between minority and majority leaders in Romania. *Global Review of Ethnopolitics, 1*(4), 28–41.

Melvin, N. (2000). Post-imperial ethnocracy and the russophone minorities of Estonia and Latvia. In J. Stein (Ed.), *The policies of national minority participation post-communist Europe: State-building, democracy and ethnic mobilisation* (pp. 129–166). New York: East-West Institute.

Merry, S. E. (2006). *Human rights and gender violence: Translating international law into local justice. Chicago series in law and society*. Chicago: University of Chicago Press.

Merton, R. K. (1941). Intermarriage and the social structure. *Psychiatry, 4*(3), 361–374.

Mezei, J. (Ed.). (2006). *Magyar-román-angol jogi, közgazdasági és üzleti szótár.* Bucureşti: C. H. Beck.

Mihailescu, M. (2008). The politics of minimal "consensus": Interethnic opposition coalitions in post-communist Romania (1990–1996) and Slovakia (1990–1998). *East European Politics & Societies, 22*(3), 553–594.

Mikó, I. (1941). *Huszonkét év: az Erdélyi Magyarság politikai története 1918. December 1-től 1940. Augusztus 30-ig.* Budapest: Studium.

Mitchell, P., Evans, G., & O'Leary, B. (2009). Extremist outbidding in ethnic party systems is not inevitable: Tribune parties in Northern Ireland. *Political Studies, 57*(2), 397–421.

Mohácsek, M. (2009). *Analiza finanțărilor alocate organizațiilor minorităților naționale* (ISPMN Working Paper No. 16).

Moise, E. (2004). Church-state relation in the religious education in Romanian public schools. *Journal for the Study of Religions and Ideologies, 3*(7), 77–100.

Monden, C. W. S., & Smits, J. (2005). Ethnic intermarriage in times of social change: The case of Latvia. *Demography, 42*(2), 323–345.

Morgan, M. H. (2014). *Speech communities. Key topics in linguistic anthropology*. Cambridge and New York: Cambridge University Press.

Moring, T. (2007). Functional completeness in minority language media. In M. J. Cormack & N. Hourigan (Eds.), *Minority language media: Concepts, critiques and case studies* (pp. 17–33). Clevedon and Buffalo: Multilingual Matters.

Moring, T. (2013). Media markets and minority languages in the digital age. *Journal on Ethnopolitics and Minority Issues in Europe, 12*(4), 34–53.

Mungiu-Pippidi, A. (1999). *Transilvania subiectivă*. București: Humanitas.

Muntele, I. (2003). Migrations internationales dans la Roumanie moderne et contemporaine. In D. Diminescu (Ed.), *Visibles mais peu nombreux...: les circulations migratoires roumaines* (pp. 33–51). Paris: Maison des sciences de l'homme.

Münz, R., & Ohliger, R. (2001). Migrations of German people to Germany: A light on the German concept of identity. *The International Scope Review, 3*(6), 60–74.

Mușat, R. (2011). Lamenting social change in the countryside: The publications of the Bucharest School of Sociology in the early 1930s. *ACUM, 5*(1), http://www.cooperativag.ro/lamenting-social-change-countryside-publications-bucharest-school-sociology-early-1930s/.

Nagy, M. Z. (2011). *Kisebbségi érdekképviselet vagy pártpolitika? A Romániai Magyar Népi Szövetség története 1944–1953*. Doktori disszertáció, Pécsi Tudományegyetem.

Nagy, M. Z., & Olti, A. G. (Eds.). (2009). *Érdekképviselet vagy pártpolitika?: iratok a Magyar Népi Szövetség történetéhez, 1944–1953*. Csíkszereda: Pro-Print.

Narayan, D. (1999). *Bonds and bridges: Social capital and poverty* (Policy Research Working Paper). Washington, DC: World Bank, Poverty Reduction and Economic Management Network, Poverty Division.

Nastasă, L., & Salat, L. (Eds.). (2000). *Relații interetnice în România postcomunistă*. Cluj-Napoca: Fundația CRDE.

Nelde, P. H., Labrie, N., & Williams, C. H. (1992). The principles of territoriality and personality in the solution of linguistic conflicts. *Journal of Multilingual and Multicultural Development, 13*(5), 387–406.

Nohlen, D., & Stöver, P. (2010). *Elections in Europe: A data handbook* (1st ed.). Baden-Baden, Germany: Nomos.

Novák, C. Z. (Ed.). (2011). *Aranykorszak?: a Ceaușescu-rendszer magyarságpolitikája I. 1965–1974*. Csíkszereda: Pro-Print.

Novák, C. Z. (Ed.). (2017). *Holtvágányon: a Ceaușescu-rendszer magyarságpolitikája II. 1974-1989*. Csíkszereda: Pro-Print.

O'Leary, R., & Finnäs, F. (2002). Education, social integration and minority-majority group intermarriage. *Sociology, 36*(2), 235–254.

Öllős, L. (2012, June 9). Ki a magyar? *Új Szó Szalon*.

Orbán, A., & Szántó, Z. (2005). Társadalmi tőke. *Erdélyi Társadalom, 3*(2), 55–70.

Orlović, S. (2015). Consociational experiments in the Western Balkans: Bosnia and Herzegovina and Macedonia. *New Balkan Politics, 17,* 29–50.

OSCE-HCNM. (1999). *The Lund Recommendations on the effective participation of national minorities in public life & explanatory note.* OSCE High Commissioner on National Minorities.

OSCE-HCNM. (2012). *Ljubljana guidelines of integrating diverse societies.* OSCE High Commissioner on National Minorities.

Osuji, C. (2013). Confronting whitening in an era of black consciousness: Racial ideology and black-white interracial marriages in Rio de Janeiro. *Ethnic and Racial Studies, 36*(10), 1490–1506.

Ottaviano, G. I. P., & Peri, G. (2006). The economic value of cultural diversity: Evidence from US cities. *Journal of Economic Geography, 6*(1), 9–44.

Page, S. E. (2007). *The difference: How the power of diversity creates better groups, firms, schools, and societies.* Princeton: Princeton University Press.

Pál, J. (2010). *Unió vagy "unificáltatás"?: Erdély uniója és a királyi biztos működése (1867–1872).* Kolozsvár: Erdélyi Múzeum-Egyesület.

Papp, A. Z. (2005). The Hungarian press system in Romania during the nineties: The world of the operators. *Regio, 8,* 141–153.

Papp, A. Z. (2010). Határon túli magyar oktatási támogatások és hasznosulásuk 2006–2010 között. *Educatio, 11*(1), 88–110.

Papp, A. Z. (2013). Motivations for school choice and minority perspectives. *Minority Studies, 15,* 99–122.

Papp, A. Z. (2014a). Kisebbségi identitáskonstrukciók a kettős állampolgárság által. *Regio, 22*(1), 118–155.

Papp, A. Z. (2014b). Selecting a majority-language school by Hungarian minority students, or from PISA results to discourses in the Carpathian Basin. *Minority Studies, 17,* 89–101.

Papp, A. Z. (2015). Hidden ethnic inequalities: A possible global educational exploration using PISA. *Ethnicity, 10,* 4–40.

Papp, A. Z., & Márton, J. (2011). Párhuzamos világok? Az erdélyi magyar gazdasági és kulturális elit szocio-demográfiai jellemzői. In I. Kovách (Ed.), *Elitek a válság korában. Magyarországi elitek, kisebbségi magyar elitek* (pp. 459–517). Budapest: MTA PTI, MTA ENKI and Argumentum.

Papp, A. Z., & Márton, J. (2014). Peremoktatásról varázstalanítva. A Csángó Oktatási Program értékelésének tapasztalatai. *Magyar Kisebbség, 19*(2), 7–32.

Papp, A. Z., & Márton, J. (2017). Oktatásügy. In N. Bárdi & G. Éger (Eds.), *Magyarok Romániában, 1990–2015. Tanulmányok az erdélyi magyarságról* (pp. 341–373). Budapest: Károli Gáspár Református Egyetem.

Papp Kincses, E. (2011). Kommunikációs etnográfia. Nyelvhasználat a csíkszeredai bíróságon és a Hargita megyei törvényszéken. Jogszabályok és jogérvényesítési lehetőségek. In I. Horváth & E. Tódor (Eds.), *Nyelvhasználat, tannyelv és két(több)nyelvű lét* (pp. 185–208). Cluj-Napoca: ISPMN.

Patrick, P. L. (2002). The speech community. In J. K. Chambers, P. Trudgill, & N. Schilling-Estes (Eds.), *The handbook of language variation and change* (pp. 573–597). Malden, MA: Blackwell.

Peal, E., & Lambert, W. E. (1962). The relation of bilingualism to intelligence. *Psychological Monographs: General and Applied, 76*(27), 1–23.

Péntek, J. (2004). A magyar közoktatás nyelvi és szakmai feltételei. In E. Bálint & J. Péntek (Eds.), *Oktatás nyelvek határán. Közelkép és helyzetkép a romániai magyar oktatásról.* Kolozsvár: Anyanyelvápolók Erdélyi Szövetsége.

Pettai, V. (2007). Explaining ethnic politics in the Baltic States: Reviewing the triadic nexus model. *Journal of Baltic Studies, 37*(1), 124–136.

Pettai, V., & Hallik, K. (2002). Understanding processes of ethnic control: Segmentation, dependency and co-optation in post-communist Estonia. *Nations and Nationalism, 8*(S4), 505–529.

Pierson, P. (2000). Increasing returns, path dependence, and the study of politics. *American Political Science Review, 94*(2), 251–267.

Pieterse, J. N. (2001). Hybridity, so what? *Theory, Culture & Society, 18*(2–3), 219–245.

Pogonyi, S. (2011). Dual citizenship and sovereignty. *Nationalities Papers, 39*(5), 685–704.

Pogonyi, S. (2017). *Extra-territorial ethnic politics, discourses and identities in Hungary*. New York, Berlin and Heidelberg: Springer.

Poledna, R. (2001). *Transformări sociale la saşii ardeleni după 1945*. Cluj-Napoca: Presa Universitară Clujeană.

Pool, J. (1991). The official language problem. *The American Political Science Review, 85*(2), 495.

Portes, A. (1998). Social capital: Its origins and applications in modern sociology. *Annual Review of Sociology, 24*(1), 1–24.

Portes, A., & Sensenbrenner, J. (1993). Embeddedness and immigration: Notes on the social determinants of economic action. *American Journal of Sociology, 98*(6), 1320–1350.

Posner, D. N. (2005). *Institutions and ethnic politics in Africa* (p. 337). Cambridge: Cambridge University Press.

Pozsony, F. (2007). Szórványok hétköznapjai. In B. Z. Balogh, B. Bodó, & Z. Ilyés (Eds.), *Regionális identitás, közösségépítés, szórványgondozás* (pp. 49–60). Budapest: Lucius.

Precupețu, I. (2013). Inequality trends in Romania. *Calitatea Vieții, 23*(3), 249–276.

Putnam, R. D. (2000). *Bowling alone: The collapse and revival of American community*. New York: Simon & Schuster.

Putnam, R. D. (2007). E Pluribus Unum: Diversity and community in the twenty-first century the 2006 Johan Skytte prize lecture. *Scandinavian Political Studies, 30*(2), 137–174.

Rabushka, A., & Shepsle, K. A. (1972). *Politics in plural societies: A theory of democratic instability. Merrill political science series*. Columbus, OH: Merrill.

Rallu, J.-L., Piché, V., & Simon, P. (2006). Demography and ethnicity: An ambiguous relationship. In G. Caselli, J. Vallin, & G. J. Wunsch (Eds.), *Demography: Analysis and synthesis. A treatise in population studies* (pp. 531–549). Amsterdam and Boston: Elsevier.

Ram, M. H. (2003). Democratization through European integration: The case of minority rights in the Czech Republic and Romania. *Studies in Comparative International Development, 38*(2), 28–56.

Ram, M. H. (2009). Romania: From laggard to leader? In B. Rechel (Ed.), *Minority rights in central and eastern Europe* (pp. 180–194). London and New York: Routledge.

Râmneamțu, P. (1937). *Problema căsătoriilor mixte în orașele din Transilvania în perioada de la 1920–1937*. Buletin Eugenetic și Biopolitic.

Ravasz, Á. (2013). Szlovákiai magyarok mint választók, 2009–2013. *Magyar Kisebbség, 18*(2), 42–68.

Rechel, B. (2009a). Introduction. In B. Rechel (Ed.), *Minority rights in central and eastern Europe* (pp. 3–16). London and New York: Routledge.

Rechel, B. (Ed.). (2009b). *Minority rights in central and eastern Europe*. London and New York: Routledge.

Regényi, E., & Törzsök, E. (1988). Romániai menekültek Magyarországon 1988. *Medvetánc. Jelentések a határokon túli magyar kisebbségek helyzetéről. Csehszlovákia, Szovjetunió, Románia, Jugoszlávia* (pp. 187–241). Budapest: ELTE.

Reka, A. (2008). The Ohrid agreement: The travails of inter-ethnic relations in Macedonia. *Human Rights Review, 9*(1), 55–69.

Risse-Kappen, T., Ropp, S. C., & Sikkink, K. (1999). *The power of human rights: International norms and domestic change. Cambridge studies in international relations*. New York: Cambridge University Press.

Risse, T. (1999). International norms and domestic change: Arguing and communicative behavior in the human rights area. *Politics & Society, 27*(4), 529–559.

Ritchie, W. C., & Bhatia, T. K. (2004). Social and psychological factors ín language mixing. In T. K. Bhatia & W. C. Ritchie (Eds.), *The handbook of bilingualism* (pp. 336–352). Malden, MA: Blackwell.

RMDSZ. (2016). Benkő Erika az ENSZ Ember Jogi Tanácsának Fórumán: a magyar közösség folyamatosan támadásoknak van kitéve.

RMDSZ. (2017). ÁLLÁSPONT - a magyar nyelv használata az egészségügyben és a szociális szolgáltatásokat nyújtó intézményekben.

Romani, L. P., & Fridlund, H. (2015). *Monitoring and evaluation of language rights in Kosovo*. Office of the Language Commissioner—Office of the Prime Minister of the Republic of Kosovo—ECMI Kosovo. Available at: http://www.komisioneri-ks.org/repository/docs/Anglisht_Finale_160315.pdf.

Ronnås, P. (1984). *Urbanization in Romania: A geography of social and economic change since independence*. Ph.D. thesis, Stockholm School of Economics, Stockholm, Sweden.

Rughiniş, C. (2010). The forest behind the bar charts: Bridging quantitative and qualitative research on Roma/Tigani in contemporary Romania. *Patterns Prejudice, 44*(4), 337–367.

Rughiniş, C. (2011). Quantitative tales of ethnic differentiation: Measuring and using Roma/Gypsy ethnicity in statistical analyses. *Ethnic and Racial Studies, 34*(4), 594–619.

Sachdev, I., & Giles, H. (2004). Bilingual accommodation. In T. K. Bhatia & W. C. Ritchie (Eds.), *The handbook of bilingualism* (pp. 353–380). Malden, MA: Blackwell.

Safran, W. (1991). Diasporas in modern societies: Myths of homeland and return. *Diaspora: A Journal of Transnational Studies, 1*(1), 83–99.

Saideman, S. M., & Ayres, R. W. (2008). *For kin or country: Xenophobia, nationalism, and war*. New York: Columbia University Press.

Salamon, L. M., & Anheier, H. K. (1996). *The international classification of nonprofit organizations: ICNPO-Revision 1* (Working Papers of the Johns Hopkins Comparative Nonprofit Sector Project No. 19).

Salat, L. (2003). Kisebbségi magyar jövőképek esélyei és buktatói Erdélyben. *Kisebbségkutatás* (3).

Salat, L. (2008). Are members of the Hungarian minority in Romania part of the Romanian political community? *Studia Politica: Romanian Political Science Review, 8*(2), 337–366.

Salat, L. (2011). A politikai közösség kérdése a többség–kisebbség viszonyának a nézőpontjából. *Magyar Kisebbség, XVI*(3–4), 159–190.

Salat, L. (2014). Az RMDSZ tervezete az autonómia látszatát próbálja kelteni. In M. Kertész (Ed.), *transindex.ro*.

Salat, L., Andriescu, M., Gherghina, S., Jiglău, G., Székely, I. G., & Popescu-Tiganea, A. (2014). *The representation of minorities in Romania in the press*. Cluj-Napoca: College of Political, Administrative and Communication Sciences, Babeş-Bolyai University.

Salat, L., Constantin, S., Osipov, A. G., & Székely, I. N. G. (2014). *Autonomy arrangements around the world: A collection of well and lesser known cases*. Cluj-Napoca: Institutul pentru Studierea Problemelor Minorităților Naționale.

Salat, L., & Novák, C. Z. (2015). Ethnicity, nationalism, and the minority regime. In L. Stan & D. Vancea (Eds.), *Post-communist Romania at twenty-five: Linking past, present, and future* (pp. 63–86). Lanham: Lexington Books.

Salat, L., & Székely, I. G. (2014). Conclusions. In L. Salat, S. Constantin, A. G. Osipov, & I. N. G. Székely (Eds.), *Autonomy arrangements around the world: A collection of well and lesser known cases* (pp. 443–478). Cluj-Napoca: Romanian Institute for Research of National Minorities.

Sandu, D. (2005). *Comunităţile de Romi din România. O hartă a sărăciei comunitare prin sondajul PROROMI*. București: Banca Mondială.

Sandu, D. (2006). *Locuirea temporară în străinătate: Migrația economică a românilor: 1990-2006*. București: Fundația pentru o Societate Deschisă.

Schermerhorn, R. A. (1978). *Comparative ethnic relations: A framework for theory and research*. Chicago: University of Chicago Press.

Scott, J. C. (1998). *Seeing like a state: How certain schemes to improve the human condition have failed*. New Haven: Yale University Press.

Scurtu, I. (Ed.). (1999). *Minoritătile naţionale din România, 1931–1938. Documente*. București: Arhivele Naţionale ale României.

Scurtu, I., & Boar, L. (Eds.). (1995). *Minorităţile naţionale din România, 1918–1925. Documente*. Bucureşti: Arhivele Statului din România.

Scutaru, C. (2017, September 1). Mici Kaufland Odorheiu Secuiesc. Adevărul a ieșit la iveală: Cum s-a făcut filmarea. *dcnews.ro*. Avaialble at: https://www.dcnews.ro/mici-kaufland-odorheiu-secuiesc-adevarul-a-ie-it-la-iveala-cum-s-a-facut-filmarea_556542.html.

Seres, A., & Egry, G. (2011). *Magyar levéltári források az 1930. évi Romániai népszámlálás nemzetiségi adatsorainak értékeléséhez*. Kolozsvár: ISPMN and Kriterion.

Sheriff, R. E. (2001). *Dreaming equality: Color, race, and racism in urban Brazil*. New Brunswick, NJ: Rutgers University Press.
Shimp, T. A. (1984). Consumer ethnocentrism: The concept and a preliminary empirical test. In T. C. Kinear (Ed.), *Advances in Consumer Research* (pp. 285–290). Provo, UT: Association for Consumer Research.
Sik, E. (1994). Traktatus a vállalkozó szerepének de-misztifikálásáról. *Replika, 15–16*, 7–12.
Silver, B. D. (1975). Methods of deriving data on bilingualism from the 1970 Soviet census. *Soviet Studies, 27*(4), 574–597.
Simmons, B. A. (2009). *Mobilizing for human rights: International law in domestic politics*. Cambridge and New York: Cambridge University Press.
Simon, P. (2008). The choice of ignorance: The debate on ethnic and racial statistics in France. *French Politics, Culture & Society, 26*(1), 7–31.
Simon, P. (2012). Collecting ethnic statistics in Europe: A review. *Ethnic and Racial Studies, 35*(8), 1366–1391.
Simon, P. (2017). The failure of the importation of ethno-racial statistics in Europe: Debates and controversies. *Ethnic and Racial Studies, 40*(13), 2326–2332.
Sipos, Z. (2017, March 20). Határon túli támogatások 2: Az állandó tételek és a legjobb barátok. *Átlátszó Erdély*. Avaialble at: https://erdely.atlatszo.hu/2017/03/20/hataron-tuli-tamogatasok-2-az-allando-tetelek-es-a-legjobb-baratok/ (Accessed 18 February 2018).
Skutnabb-Kangas, T. (1997). *Nyelv, oktatás és a kisebbségek. Kisebbségi adattár*. Budapest: Teleki László Alapítvány.
Skutnabb-Kangas, T. (2000). Nyelv, oktatás, kisebbségek. In K. Csernusné Otutay & É. Forintos (Eds.), *Nyelvi jogok* (pp. 41–68). Veszprém: Veszprémi Egyetemi Kiadó.
Smith, A. D. (1995). Gastronomy or geology? The role of nationalism in the reconstruction of nations. *Nations and Nationalism, 1*(1), 3–23.
Smith, D. J. (2002). Framing the national question in central and eastern Europe: A quadratic nexus? *Global Review of Ethnopolitics, 2*(1), 3–16.
Smith, D. J. (2013). Non-territorial autonomy and political community in contemporary central and eastern Europe. *Journal on Ethnopolitics and Minority Issues in Europe, 12*(1), 27–55.
Smith, D. J., & Cordell, K. (Eds.). (2007). *Cultural autonomy in contemporary Europe*. London and New York: Routledge.
Smith, M. G. (1965). *The plural society in the British West Indies*. Berkeley: University of California Press.

Smits, J. (2010). Ethnic intermarriage and social cohesion. What can we learn from Yugoslavia? *Social Indicators Research, 96*(3), 417–432.

Smooha, S. (2001). *The model of ethnic democracy* (ECMI Working Paper No. 13).

Sorbán, A. (2012). *Kisebbség – társadalomszerkezet – kétnyelvűség* (ISPMN Working Paper No. 42).

Sorbán, A., & Dobos, F. (1997). Szociológiai felmérés a határon túl élő magyar közösségek körében az asszimiláció folyamatairól. *Magyar Kisebbség, 3*(3–4), 293–323.

Spolsky, B. (2004). *Language policy.* Cambridge and New York: Cambridge University Press.

Stan, L., & Turcescu, L. (2005). Religious education in Romania. *Communist and Post-communist Studies, 38*(3), 381–401.

Stan, L., & Turcescu, L. (2007). *Religion and politics in post-communist Romania. Religion and global politics series.* Oxford and New York: Oxford University Press.

Stokes, D. E. (1963). Spatial models of party competition. *American Political Science Review, 57*(2), 368–377.

Stroschein, S. (2001). Measuring ethnic party success in Romania, Slovakia, and Ukraine. *Problems of Post-Communism, 48*(4), 59–69.

Stroschein, S. (2011). Demography in ethnic party fragmentation: Hungarian local voting in Romania. *Party Politics, 17*(2), 189–204.

Stroschein, S. (2012). *Ethnic struggle, coexistence, and democratization in eastern Europe. Cambridge studies in contentious politics.* Cambridge and New York: Cambridge University Press.

Sulyok, I. (1931). A kisebbségi kérdés szociológiai oldal. *Erdélyi Múzeum, 36*(4–6), 170–181.

Sulyok, I., & Fritz, L. (Eds.). (1930). *Erdélyi Magyar Évkönyv 1918–1929.* Kolozsvár: Juventus.

Szabó, T. (2017, April 18). Semmi sem garantálja a magyar nyelvű ellátást a kórházakban. *foter.ro.* Avaialble at: http://foter.ro/cikk/20170418_semmi_sem_garantalja_a_magyar_nyelvu_ellatast_a_korhazakban?utm_source=foter_ro&utm_medium=link&utm_campaign=foter_ro_201712.

Szabó, T. Á. (2010). Etnikai különbségtétel a paraszti gazdaságban. In M. Feischmidt (Ed.), *Etnicitás: különbségteremtő társadalom.* Budapest: Gondolat and MTA Etnikai-Nemzeti Kisebbségkutató Intézet.

Szabó, T. Á. (2015). Dairy cooperative in the making: History, ethnicity and local culture in an economic enterprise. *Erdélyi Társadalom, 13*(3), 47–65.

Szarka, L. (2002). Kényszerközösségek és védtelen védhatalom. A trianoni békeszerződés és a kisebbségek. In F. Glatz (Ed.), *Magyarország és a magyar kisebbségek: történeti és mai tendenciák* (pp. 17–30). Budapest: Magyar Tudományos Akadémia.

Szarka, L. (2010). Egy évszázad kisebbségben. *Korunk, 21*(4), 59–76.

Székely, I. G. (2011). *Democrație consociaționistă sau împărțirea puterii în societăți multietnice. Cadru teoretic și patru studii de caz*. Cluj-Napoca: Institutul pentru Studierea Problemelor Minorităților Naționale—Kriterion.

Székely, I. G. (2014). *Dynamics of party politics, electoral competition and cooperation within the Hungarian minorities of Romania, Serbia and Slovakia*. Ph.D. thesis, Central European University, Budapest.

Székely, I. G., & Horváth, I. (2014). Diversity recognition and minority representation in central and southeast Europe: A comparative analysis. *Nationalities Papers, 42*(3), 426–448.

Szémann, T., & Földi, G. (2017, September 15). Mészáros Lőrinc és Andy Vajna lapjait olvassa az ország. *index.hu*. Avaialble at: https://index.hu/kultur/media/2017/09/15/mediahaboru_orszagos_napilapok_meszaros_lorinc_andy_vajna/.

Szentannai, Á. (2001). A Magyarországon tanult fiatalok karrierkövetése. *Regio, 12*(4), 113–131.

Szépe, G. (1999). The position of Hungarians in Romania and Slovakia in 1996. *Nationalities Papers, 27*(1), 69–92.

Szerbhorváth, G. (2015). Language politics and language rights on the territory of former Yugoslavia the today's Serbia/Vojvodina. *Acta Universitatis Sapientiae, European and Regional Studies, 8*(1), 57–72.

Szikszai, M. (Ed.). (2010). *Az erdélyi magyar felsőoktatás helyzete és kilátásai: Támpontok egy lehetséges stratégiához*. Kolozsvár: Ábel Kiadó.

Szilágyi, N. S. (1991). Mi lesz veled, RMDSZ? *Korunk, 2*(2), 159–166.

Szilágyi, N. S. (1998). De ce nu-şi pot însuşi copiii maghiari limba română în şcoală? *Altera, 7*, 131–148.

Szilágyi, N. S. (2002). Észrevételek a romániai magyar népesség fogyásáról, különös tekintettel az asszimilációra. *Magyar Kisebbség, 7*(4), 64–96.

Szilágyi, N. S. (2004). Az asszimiláció és hatása a népesedési folyamatokra. In T. Kiss (Ed.), *Népesedési folyamatok az ezredfordulón Erdélyben* (pp. 157–235). Kolozsvár: Kriterion and RMDSZ Ügyvezető Elnökség.

Szoke, L. (1992). Hungarian perspectives on emigration and immigration in the new European architecture. *International Migration Review, 26*(2), 305–323.

Tánczos, V. (1998). Kettős hatalmi szerkezet a Székelyföldön. *Magyar Kisebbség, 4*(2), 339–362.

Tánczos, V. (2010). A moldvai csángók magyar nyelvismerete 2008–2010-ben. *Magyar Kisebbség, 25*(3–4), 62–156.

Tánczos, V. (2012). „Hát mondja meg kend, hogy én mi vagyok!" A csángó nyelvi identitás tényezői: helyzetjelentés a 2011-es népszámlálás kapcsán. *Pro Minoritate, 16*(3), 80–112.

Taylor, R. (2009). *Consociational theory: McGarry and O'Leary and the Northern Ireland conflict*. London and New York: Routledge.

Telegdi-Csetri, V. (2017). Displaying ethnicity through the practices of mixed couples from Transylvania. In I. Bolovan & L. A. Dumănescu (Eds.), *Intermarriage in Transylvania, 1895–2010* (pp. 193–204). Frankfurt am Main: Peter Lang.

Thelen, K. (1999). Historical institutionalism in comparative politics. *Annual Review of Political Science, 2*(1), 369–404.

Thomas, J. W., & Grindle, M. S. (1990). After the decision: Implementing policy reforms in developing countries. *World Development, 18*(8), 1163–1181.

Thornton, A. (2005). *Reading history sideways: The fallacy and enduring impact of the developmental paradigm on family life. Population and development*. Chicago: University of Chicago Press.

Tódor, E. (2005). A kódváltás és az aszimmetrikus kétnyelvűség nyelvpedagógiai összefüggései. *Magyar Pedagógia, 105*(1), 41–58.

Tőkés, G. (1999). 'A szétszedett végrehajtás. Az RMDSZ Ügyvezető Elnökségének szervezetei elemzése. *WEB, 4–5,* 52–63.

Tomka, M. (1998). A vallásosság mérése. In A. Máté-Tóth & M. Jahn (Eds.), *Studia religiosa: tanulmányok András Imre 70. születésnapjára Acta Studiorum Religionis Szegedini* (pp. 18–31). Szeged: Bába és Társa Kiadó.

Tomka, M. (2005). *A legvallásosabb ország?: vallásosság Szatmárban, Erdélyben, Romániában*. Budapest: Piliscsaba PPKE.

Tompea, A., & Năstuţă, S. (2009). Romania. In H. Fassmann, U. Reeger, & W. Sievers (Eds.), *Statistics and reality: Concepts and measurements of migration in Europe* (pp. 217–230). Amsterdam: Amsterdam University Press.

Toró, T. (2013a). *Érettségi 2013*. Kolozsvár: Mensura Transylvanica.

Toró, T. (2013b). *A romániai magyar nyilvánosság alakulásának diskurzusa politikai filozófiai megközelítésben*. Ph.D., Babeş-Bolyai Tudományegyetem, Kolozsvár.

Toró, T. (2016a). Egy helyben topogva? Kisebbségi nyelvi jogok alakulása Romániában 2008 és 2015 között. *Magyar Kisebbség, 21*(2), 18–53.

Toró, T. (2016b). Hungarian minority politics in post-socialist Romania: Interests, strategies, and discourses. *Acta Universitatis Sapientiae, European and Regional Studies, 10*(1), 79–106.

Toró, T. (2016c). Multikulturális egyetem? A Marosvásárhelyi Orvosi és Gyógyszerészeti Egyetem (MOGYE) esete. *Magyar Kisebbség, 21*(3), 121–136.

Toró, T. (2017a). Detached implementation. Discourse and practice in minority language usage in Romania. Manuscript

Toró, T. (2017b). Ethnicization or de-ethnicization? Hungarian political representation in the Romanian parliament. *Nationalities Papers, 46*(2), 219–236.

Tsai, K. S. (2014, August 14). *Informal institutions and historical institutionalism*. APSA 2014 annual meeting. Available at SSRN: https://ssrn.com/abstract=2454845.

Tsebelis, G. (1990). *Nested games: Rational choice in comparative politics. California series on social choice and political economy*. Berkeley: University of California Press.

Turai, T. (2003). A családszerkezet változása a szocializmus éveiben a Szilágyságban. *Erdélyi Társadalom, 1*(1), 85–101.

Turda, M. (2010). *Modernism and eugenics*. New York: Palgrave Macmillan.

Turi, J. G. (2012). Linguistic legislation. In Carol A. Chapelle (Ed.), *The encyclopedia of applied linguistics* (pp. 3480–3486). Wiley-Blackwell.

UN-CCPR. (1999). *Summary record of the 1768th meeting: Romania*. 1 November 1999: International Covenant on Civil and Political Rights CCPR/C/SR.1768.

UN-CCPR. (2017). *Summary record of the 3428th meeting. Consideration of reports submitted by Romania*: International Covenant on Civil and Political Rights CCPR/C/SR.3428.

Uvin, P. (2002). On counting, categorizing, and violence in Burundi and Rwanda. In D. I. Kertzer & D. Arel (Eds.), *Census and identity: The politics of race, ethnicity, and language in national census* (pp. 148–175). Cambridge and New York: Cambridge University Press.

Vaillancourt, F. (1996). Language and socioeconomic status in Quebec: Measurement, findings, determinants, and policy costs. *International Journal of the Sociology of Language, 121*(1), 69–92.

Valcke, P., Sükösd, M. S., & Picard, R. G. (2015). *Media pluralism and diversity: Concepts, risks and global trends*. Houndmills, Basingstoke, Hampshire and New York: Palgrave Macmillan.
Van Parijs, P. (2011). *Linguistic justice for Europe and for the world. Oxford political theory*. Oxford and New York: Oxford University Press.
Varga, E. Á. (1991). Városodás, vándorlás, nemzetiség. Adatok az erdélyi városok etnikai arculatában bekövetkezett változásokról. *Regio, 2*(4), 121–141.
Varga, E. Á. (1998). *Fejezetek a jelenkori Erdély népesedéstörténetéből*. Budapest: Püski.
Varga, E. Á. (1999). *Erdély etnikai és felekezeti statisztikája (1850–1992). II kötet*. Csíkszereda: Pro-Print.
Varshney, A. (2003). Nationalism, ethnic conflict, and rationality. *Perspective on Politics, 1*(1), 85–99.
Vasi, I. B. (2004). The fist of the working class: The social movements of Jiu Valley miners in post-socialist Romania. *East European Politics and Societies, 18*(1), 132–157.
Vasilevich, H. (2013). *Lithuania's minority-related legislation: Is there a legal vacuum?* (ECMI Working Paper No. 70).
Vass, Á. (2015). If yes, why not? Minority language use and accommodation of minority language rights in Slovakia. *Acta Universitatis Sapientiae, European and Regional Studies, 8*(1), 43–56.
Veres, V. (2005). *Nemzeti identitás Erdélyben–szociológiai olvasatban: az erdélyi magyarok és románok nemzeti identitásának sajátosságai, társadalmi rétegződési perspektívában*. Budapest: Akadémiai Kiadó.
Veres, V. (2008). *Analiza comparată a identităţii minorităţilor maghiare din Bazinul Carpatic. A Kárpát-medencei magyarok nemzeti identitásának összehasonlító elemzése* (ISPMN Working Paper No. 44).
Veres, V. (2012). Decentralizáció, minőségbiztosítás és kisebbségi oktatási jogok Romániában az új tanügyi törvényben. *Pro Minoritate* 16(1), 110–121.
Veres, V. (2014). Identity discourses on national belonging: The Hungarian minority in Romania. *Romanian Journal of Political Science, 14*(1), 61–86.
Veres, V. (2015). *Népességszerkezet és nemzetiség. Az erdélyi magyarok demográfiai képe a 2002. és 2011. évi romániai népszámlálások tükrében*. Kolozsvár: Kolozsvári Egyetemi Kiadó.
Vermeersch, P. (2011). *Theories of ethnic mobilization: Overview and recent trends* (RPD Working Paper No. 3).

Vincze, G. (1999). *Illúziók és csalódások. Fejezetek a romániai magyarság második világháború utáni történetéből*. Csíkszereda: Státus.

Vincze, G. (2003a). Bevezető. In G. Vincze (Ed.), *Történetei kényszerpályák – kisebbségi reálpolitikák II. Dokumentumok a romániai magyar kisebbség történetének tanulmányozásához 1944–1989* (pp. xv–xxviii). Csíkszereda: Pro-Print.

Vincze, G. (2003b). *Történetei kényszerpályák – kisebbségi reálpolitikák II. Dokumentumok a romániai magyar kisebbség történetének tanulmányozásához 1944–1989*. Csíkszereda: Pro-Print.

Vincze, G. (2006). Lăncrănjantól Lăncrănjanig. Fejezet a magyar–román kapcsolatok nyolcvanas évekbeli történetéből. *Magyar Kisebbség, 10*(3–4), 262–352.

Vincze, L. (2013). *The bilingual screen: Ethnolinguistic identity and television viewing among three language minorities*. Ph.D. thesis, University of Helsinki, Helsinki.

Voicu, M. (2007). *România religioasă: pe valul european sau în urma lui?* Iași: Institutul European.

Volintiru, C. (2012). *Institutional distortions, clientelism and corruption: Evidence from Romania* (CCREI Working Papers Series No. 1).

Wallerstein, I. M. (1974). *The modern world-system, vol. I: Capitalist agriculture and the origins of the European world-economy in the sixteenth century. Studies in social discontinuity*. New York: Academic Press.

Waterbury, M. A. (2010). *Between state and nation: Diaspora politics and kin-state nationalism in Hungary* (1st ed.). New York: Palgrave Macmillan.

Waterbury, M. A. (2014). Making citizens beyond the borders. *Problems of Post-Communism, 61*(4), 36–49.

Waterbury, M. A. (2017). National minorities in an era of externalization: Kin-state citizenship, European integration, and ethnic Hungarian minority politics. *Problems of Post-Communism, 64*(5), 228–241.

Waugh, L. R. (1982). Marked and unmarked: A choice between unequals in semiotic structure. *Semiotica, 38*(3–4), 299–318.

Weber, M. (1978). *Economy and society: An outline of interpretive sociology* (2 Vols., p. 1469). Berkeley: University of California Press.

Wimmer, A. (2002). *Nationalist exclusion and ethnic conflict: Shadows of modernity*. Cambridge and New York: Cambridge University Press.

Wimmer, A. (2013). *Ethnic boundary making: Institutions, power, networks. Oxford studies in culture and politics*. New York: Oxford University Press.

Wolczuk, K. (2010). History, Europe and the "national idea": The "official" narrative of national identity in Ukraine. *Nationalities Papers, 28*(4), 671–694.
Wolff, S., & Cordell, K. (2003). Ethnic Germans as a language minority in central and eastern Europe: Legislative and policy frameworks in Poland, Hungary and Romania. In G. Hogan-Brun & S. Wolff (Eds.), *Minority languages in Europe: Frameworks, status, prospects* (pp. 99–119). Basingstoke: Palgrave Macmillan.
Wolff, S., Van Houten, P., Anghelea, A.-M., & Djuric, I. (2008). *Minority rights in the Western Balkans.* Brussels. European Parliament. Available at: http://www.europarl.europa.eu/RegData/etudes/etudes/join/2008/385559/EXPO-DROI_ET(2008)385559_EN.pdf.
Yagmur, K., & Ehala, M. (2011). Tradition and innovation in the ethnolinguistic vitality theory. *Journal of Multilingual and Multicultural Development, 32*(2), 101–110.
Zamfir, C., & Zamfir, E. (Eds.). (1993). *Ţiganii între ignorare şi îngrijorare.* Bucureşti: Alternative.
Zavisca, J. (2005). The status of cultural omnivorism: A case study of reading in Russia. *Social Forces, 84*(2), 1233–1255.
Zeidler, M. (2003). A Nemzetek Szövetsége és a magyar kisebbségi petíciók. In N. Bárdi & C. Fedinec (Eds.), *Etnopolitika: A közösségi, magán- és nemzetközi érdekek viszonyrendszere Közép-Európában* (pp. 59–83). Budapest: Teleki László Alapítvány.
Zolberg, A. R., & Woon, L. L. (1999). Why Islam is like Spanish: Cultural incorporation in Europe and the United States. *Politics & Society, 27*(1), 5–38.
Zwilling, C. (2004). Minority protection and language policy in the Czech Republic. *Noves SL—Revista de Sociolingüística, 5*(3), 67–80.

Index

T. Kiss et al. (eds.), *Unequal Accommodation of Minority Rights*,
Palgrave Politics of Identity and Citizenship Series,
https://doi.org/10.1007/978-3-319-78893-7

The manufacturer's authorised representative in the EU is Springer Nature Customer Service Centre GmbH, Europaplatz 3, 69115 Heidelberg, Germany. If you have any concerns regarding our products, please contact ProductSafety@springernature.com

Printed and bound by CPI Group (UK) Ltd, Croydon, CR0 4YY

01/10/2026

02225952-0004